A SPARK
IS STRUCK!

374
67

A SPARK
IS STRUCK!

JACK HALL
AND THE ILWU
IN HAWAII

Sanford Zalburg

THE UNIVERSITY PRESS OF HAWAII
Honolulu

For Vivian Naleilehua,
    who put up with me,
and for Thurston Twigg-Smith,
    my benefactor.

If I am to be remembered for anything in these Islands, I just want to be thought of as one of the guys that struck the spark for a flame that was kept burning.

—JACK HALL, JUNE 6, 1969

CONTENTS

Part 3
THE BIG SURGE (1944–1946)

Part 4
THE SUGAR STRIKE (1946)

Part 5
FRIENDS AND FOES (1946–1947)

Part 6
REVOLUTIONARIES AND COUNTERREVOLUTIONARIES (1947–1949)

Part 7
THE LONGSHORE STRIKE (1949)

Part 8
THE TEMPER OF THE TIMES (1950–1952)

Part 9
THE SMITH ACT TRIAL (1952–1953)

Part 10
THE MIDDLE YEARS (1954–1959)

Part 11

THE MELLOWING YEARS (1960–1969)

Part 12

DOWNHILL ALL THE WAY (1969–1971)

Illustrations follow page 422.

PROLOGUE:
No Monument, No Plaque

Jack Hall didn't care what history thought of him. "I don't want to write history. I just want to make it," he told his lifetime adversary Arthur Rutledge in the days when they were on speaking terms.

Hall was not sentimental. He left no personal papers. He attached no importance to funerals or memorial services, although he himself was capable of delivering a moving eulogy.

His own ashes sat for eighteen days in a cardboard box on the dresser of his half-brother, John Junior Hall, before they were scattered on the waters off the Hilton Hawaiian Village. "You can take my ashes and flush them down the toilet; I wouldn't care," he told his brother.

Hall came to Hawaii in his twenties, a skinny seaman wearing sailor moku (blue denim) pants and a T-shirt. At one time he slept on the floor on spread newspapers or slept down at the docks; sometimes he washed his clothes and took a bath at the same time by plunging into the harbor.

He went from an ordinary seaman to the pinnacle of power. For years he and John A. Burns, the governor, were the two biggest men in the islands, and Hall was the biggest power broker. Politicians from Burns on down approached him openly or by the back door.

Hall loved politics. When he spoke of politics, "his face lighted up." To keep its gains, he said, the union had to play politics. He played it to the hilt. "We simply believe that laboring people should have their say on how our government is run and what laws our legislative bodies enact," he said. He adopted and put into force the old laboring man's battle cry: "Reward your friends and punish your enemies."

"Organized pressure of working people gave Hawaii the best labor and social legislation in the country," said Hall. He kept a hard eye on the politicians who made promises to the union in return for support. He did not threaten or pound the table. He said promises were made to be kept and if they weren't, the ILWU would get its revenge at the polls. He did not like the politically independent, whose behavior he could not predict. He could not tolerate the Tom Gills of politics.

For years Hall and Burns were close allies. Once Burns had scolded him for trying to capture the Democratic Party. "You run the union and I'll run the politics," Burns told him. Hall helped elect Burns governor in 1962 and during Burns' three terms in office the ILWU was his powerful friend—which led to the frequent accusation that Burns was in Hall's pocket.

Their paths did run parallel courses. Their goals often were the same. They had no trouble getting along. "I never had to talk too much to Jack Hall," said Burns. "We'd understand each other. . . . I never had any pressure placed on me, or anything else. . . . Jack would come to me. 'If you can do this, we'd appreciate it being done.' "

There was no *quid pro quo,* said Burns. "After all, the union is realistic. And I imagine they've had to deal. Some of the people I know they've had to deal with that way. On a straight-trade basis. But for me, the hell with it! I'm not interested in that."

Hall was regional director of the ILWU in Hawaii for twenty-five years. He developed into a skilled negotiator, a tough bargainer, a man "with an IBM machine for a brain."

The ILWU in Hawaii gave workers strength they never had before. For the first time labor confronted management on equal terms. Laboring men and women elected their own choices for office. It was a political revolution and Hall led it. The union packed power; it was united. "We have to unite regardless of race, creed or political belief," said Hall.

The man Jack Hall was a mass of contradictions: shyness and arrogance, kindness and malice. Like the five blind men touching the elephant, your opinion of him depended on where you touched him. To many he seemed abrupt and harsh. But to his daughter, Michele (Mikey), "he was a marshmallow." She meant that he bled inwardly when he had to do hard things, such as fire an incompetent. That would touch off a drinking spell.

Hall drank. He drank to relieve tension, to escape the endless burdens and problems, or because, as his wife Yoshiko said, he just liked to.

Hall often hurt the people he loved: his wife, his two children, his fellow unionists, his friends. Each man kills the thing he loves, Oscar Wilde said, and Hall did it with arrogance, with unkind words which he seldom apologized for, and with drinking.

His wife, a woman with a core of steel, said: "You know how humiliating it is to have to go look for someone who is drunk. I'd call and I hated to call but I knew he would be sick. He'd heave so much. He'd be really sick, sick, sick. And you can't get angry. So I would just start looking for him."

The search usually began with the old Ala Moana Tropics, the "ILWU Annex," as Robert McElrath, Hall's understudy and replacement as regional director, called it. Hall's great friend was named Jack Daniel and then he made the acquaintance of Jim Beam. "I've seen him drink half a glass of Jack Daniel's [whiskey] straight—before breakfast," said Dr. Willis Butler, Hall's personal physician and confidant.

Butler said Hall was amazingly well disciplined and could stop drinking if Butler ordered him to. "He was not an alcoholic," said Butler. L. Barney McNeil, a reformed alcoholic, watched Hall drinking. "Jack was what people who know drinkers call 'a heavy maintenance man.' He could stop drinking, but he would always start again and in the end it would get him," said McNeil. Once Hall was ordered to limit his drinking to "a little wine." To Hall, said McElrath, "that's two bottles."

Hall was six feet two, and he weighed 218 pounds in his well-fed years. He had a massive chest and shoulders but small feet (size 9½) for so big a man. After one vacation on the mainland, he ballooned to 260 pounds. Illness melted him down in the last years to 160 pounds.

Once when Hall was overweight, Butler told him to limit his food intake to 1300 calories a day. It seemed like a sparse diet, but Hall's sense of humor bubbled. "Not bad," he said. "Four drinks at 300 calories apiece. . . ."

In the end it all came apart: he had diabetes, prostate trouble, high blood pressure, arteriosclerosis, gout, Parkinson's disease. Yet he refused to feel sorry for himself. He kept struggling to go on working even when he lurched like a paralytic from Parkinson's and could not control his bowels. But if anyone offered an inappropriate word of commiseration, or pity, he cut them down with a withering remark. He was proud, touchy proud, and courageous.

Hall had a "quick, clean mind." He read constantly and absorbed what he read and he kept it on file in his mind. He talked like a lawyer. He wrote like an author. He was a man of extraordinary intelligence.

And yet when Dr. Morton Berk told him in the late 1940s that he was a diabetic, Hall replied: "I like to go home at night and broil a steak for dinner. And I like to have a good shot or two of bourbon before I eat. Diabetes or no diabetes, don't tell me I can't have the drinks because I'm going to anyway."

Hall shot himself daily with insulin. When he went to a Neighbor Island, he carried a thermos of insulin bottles, each equipped with a needle. He learned the technique of shooting himself with insulin by practicing on a grapefruit.

From the time he began reading Communist literature in the 1930s, Hall had a strong left-wing bent and it never wavered. He wrote the following: "Left on trip around the world westward. President Wilson, Dec. 13 [1935]. Arrived S.F. [San Francisco] March 25, 1936. . . . Officially joined the CP [Communist Party] early in 1936, presumably after March 25."

Hall never downgraded the role of the Communist Party in helping build the ILWU. However, he never did state openly that he was ever a member of the Communist Party. People who knew him in the early days in Hawaii said he was a hard-core Communist.

Jack Kimoto, who at one time headed the Communist Party of Hawaii, didn't think much of Hall as a Communist. He said Hall can be regarded as a labor leader, not a Communist Party leader. "I joined the Communist Party to get all the help I could," Hall told his half-brother, John. Hall believed no one else was effectively helping the working people in Hawaii in those days; only the Communists. And Hall was devoted to the working class. It was his life.

Hall signed the Taft-Hartley Act affidavit every year from 1950 on, which declares that the signer "is not now a member" of the Communist Party. But in his heart Hall never left the Party.

Hall was a name-dropper. He was a gourmet cook. He loved music—from jazz to Beethoven and Mozart. (His wife donated two hundred of his Fats Waller disks and other jazz records to station KQED in San Francisco after he died.) One of his favorite pieces—it would set his feet to tapping and his arms swinging—was "The Gettysburg March," the old New Orleans marching song, with George Lewis on clarinet.

Hall was odd. He could confront management across the bargaining table, but he had trouble changing a light bulb. He trained himself in accounting, but he couldn't keep a checkbook. And yet he was a mathematical wizard. Hall couldn't drive a car. Ed Berman, in the days when they were friendly, tried to teach him to drive Berman's old Hupmobile, but in vain.

Hall had extremely poor vision. With his glasses off, anything more than four inches from his eyes began to blur. And yet he had remarkable vision; "he could see a very long way down the road," said Tom Hamilton, a former University of Hawaii president. He meant Hall was astute.

Hall was a great poker player. He was a man who hated chit-chat. He was intolerant of incompetence, but he was not hard on his help. He had the gambler's instinct. If he had an intuitive feeling about something, he would act on it. He had a mischievous, often casual, attitude about things. "Thirty days in jail never hurt anybody," he used to say. He succeeded so well in Hawaii that by the late 1950s he was "bored, bored, bored," but there was no place to go.

He was not afraid of the employers. The Big Five did not scare him. Yet there he was, a man with a high school education, pitted against the Stanford and Harvard men of Merchant Street.

If you had to use just one word to describe Jack Hall, that

word would be "pragmatic." He used what he knew would work; he discarded what he knew would not. He looked things over with a cold eye.

Hall loved to deflate the pompous. He loved to tease and even torment the magisterial. He hated affectation. He had a genuineness about him that enabled him to get along with most of the hardhanded men of the ILWU who labored in the fields.

"He didn't talk . . . to make you look stupid," said Rick Labez, once his Filipino aide. "The look on his face showed he sympathized with you."

"Hall would work with people, but not be worked by them," said Louis Goldblatt, his friend and mentor. "He took his responsibilities very seriously."

Preparing for a siege at the bargaining table, he often was up until three in the morning, writing in pencil on a yellow legal tablet. Harry Bridges, the ILWU International president who hired Hall (and later regretted it), said Hall was an expert with figures.

No union is just one man or just one leader. If it is to succeed, a union has to be a disciplined army. It was the workers—chiefly Filipinos and Japanese—who made the ILWU strong. They were tough. In fact, they and the coal miners were the most militant union members in the United States.

It was not Hall who did the big organizing of the ILWU in 1944 that suddenly made the union the most powerful force in Hawaii. That credit belongs to Frank Thompson, from Sacramento, and to a host of local people on all the islands. The locals started long before Hall began his life's work.

Hall distrusted doctors, lawyers, intellectuals, and especially professors. He said liberals could be bought or swayed. He preferred a mossback whose stance he could always gauge (or to whom he could dictate) to the liberal who wavered in his allegiance. He had a slogan: "Better an avowed enemy than a double-crossing friend."

Hall was ungainly and unattractive physically, but he did appeal to women. His high cheekbones and wide, straight mouth somehow gave his face a Finnish cast. He couldn't dance or play most sports. He liked to swim and hike.

Hall was shy about exposing his feelings. He was vulnerable, but few people knew it. He kept most people at arm's length. He felt naked when he marched with thirty-eight others in the first Vietnam War protest demonstration in 1966 in Waikiki.

He could sit for hours enthralled by music. In fact, he could sit for hours wrapped in thought. It was lonely on the heights and he was a lonely man.

They were three remarkable men, Bridges, Goldblatt, and Hall. Though the ILWU was comparatively small, with never more than eighty thousand members in Hawaii and on the mainland, it had these three leaders, all of them radicals. "Enough of them at the top to give the union radical leadership," said Bob Robertson, ILWU International vice-president and director of organization.

For years Hall and Bridges were adversaries, then enemies. Hall and Goldblatt lined up against Bridges and Robertson, but somehow they kept their internal squabbles from being made public. They always presented a united front. It was marvelous acting; they could have contended for an Academy Award. "That's what you had to do," said Bridges. "All things had to be accepted in the interest of presenting a united front. . . ."

Robertson said Hall failed to develop local leadership at the top. "You can't show me one local individual in the islands that he developed into leadership of national prominence," said Robertson. He said Hall was more a political leader than a labor leader. Bridges said Hall took advantage of his political power.

Hall accused Bridges of coming to Hawaii like the conquering hero. "There would be a blare of trumpets and here would arrive Harry on a white horse. . . ." Hall claimed that Bridges often "knocked down the ducks"—that is, upset the game plan that Hall might have spent months setting up. Hall complained that no matter how hard he worked Bridges never gave him credit. Bridges laughed at Hall and his frustration.

Hall said Bridges resented the ILWU's achievements in Hawaii; that he was piqued because in Hawaii the ILWU was a bigger force politically than the ILWU on the West Coast.

Bridges called Hall "an ambitious guy—he had some pretty bourgeois ideas. He liked the good life."

"Jack didn't agree with Harry's attitude toward Hawaii," said Eddie Tangen, a lifetime friend of Hall and no great friend of Bridges:

> Jack felt the International was not playing the kind of leadership role in the labor movement it should be playing. . . . It should be doing more, not just sort of administering the day-to-day problems and that sort of thing. That it ought to be out creating again—making the labor movement the vanguard.

Hall made great friends and great enemies. He carried on long-enduring feuds: with Tom Gill and Frank Fasi, the politicians; with Ingram Stainback, the governor; with Rutledge, the labor leader. ("Lou Goldblatt makes the snowballs and Jack Hall throws them," said Rutledge.)

Even within the ILWU Hall irritated people. Some couldn't stand him because he was a *haole,* a white man from the mainland. Some were jolted by his arrogance and impatience. There was, and still is, racial antagonism among ILWU members, and there always will be: it is a human trait. Some were upset by his drinking.

At one point Hall's relations with Newton Miyagi, the Local 142 secretary-treasurer, were so strained that though their offices were just a few feet across the hall, they didn't speak to each other. "We wrote notes," said Miyagi. "To this day nobody knows. Everyone thought we were the best of friends."

As the years went by and Hall mellowed, some of his best friends turned out to be the people he confronted across the bargaining table. They found him to be a man whose word was good and who had learned their business as well as or better than they themselves. They learned to like him.

Roy Leffingwell, who sat in with employers at sugar negotiations, said: "Hall would say something at three in the morning. Never have I heard anybody question whether Hall would do what he said he'd do. In a labor leader that's an awfully fine quality. He would handle a single plantation with a telephone call. 'Okay, I'll take it.' And he would."

When Hall was convicted in the Smith Act Communist-conspiracy trial, the Big Five employers did not exult. They would rather have dealt with him than with any other labor leader. They trusted him. "From a social outcast he became in the end a statesman," said Bert Kobayashi, associate justice of the State Supreme Court.

He was an uncommon man, Jack Hall, and he helped "turn Hawaii around." He often said he wanted "to be respected, but not to be respectable." He wanted no sweet words of praise, no monument, no plaque.

Part 1
THE EARLY YEARS
(1915–1940)

CHAPTER 1
The Bitter Years

Jack Wayne Hall was born on February 28, 1915, in the town of Ashland in northern Wisconsin. An old town (9615 population), it was once a booming port on Chequamegon Bay, part of Lake Superior, that handled quarried gabbro (black granite), iron ore, and timber. There's good fishing but winters are harsh. A writer once described Ashland in these words: "From December until April, the windows in Front Street glitter with cold reflections from the frozen harbor." Though he left there as a child, Hall remembered the place all his life. He remembered his father hunting and fishing and hanging venison. He remembered the cold.

His father, a Canadian-born cleaning and dyeing plant operator named John Percival ("Percy") Hall, was of Irish and French-Canadian ancestry. His mother, Alma Swanson Hall, was born in Ashland of immigrant Swedish parents.

Hall's mother, a woman of gentle nature, shot and killed herself when she was twenty-five. Hall was then four and a half; his sister, Mildred, was two and a half. That event and Hall's unhappy relationship with his father left a mark on him all his life. For a long time he told his wife that his mother had died in the flu epidemic. Years later, he told her the truth.

When his mother took her life, the family was then living in Iwecoma, near Wakefield, in the Upper Peninsula of Michigan, forty miles from Ashland. Percy Hall was a police inspector in an iron-ore mine. He had come home from the night shift at eight in the morning and taken the two children out. They were gone about fifteen minutes. When he came home and opened the door, he could smell gunpowder. He found his wife dying.

For a time Jack and his sister were cared for by Mrs. Hall's younger sister, Aunt Lily. One winter night she and the two children were sleeping in a bedroom heated by a coal-burning stove. Percy had filled the stove with coal before he left for work. He had packed it too tightly, though, and a large piece of coal forced the stove lid up slightly.

As they slept, gas fumes seeped out. Jack and his sister were sleeping with their heads beneath the blankets. The boy smelled the fumes, woke up, and aroused his aunt. She grabbed the children and took them outside. It was ten degrees below zero and the frigid air revived them. It was a close call.

Shortly after, Percy took the children to Los Angeles where his mother lived. Percy remarried and started a new family. Jack lived part of the time with his father and stepmother, Mrs. Hazel Hall, and part of the time with his grandmother, Mrs. Martha Hall.

Percy was a handsome man who looked like Charles Boyer, the movie actor. He liked women and liquor and handled his children with an iron hand. He was not the friendly type of father who talks things over with an unruly son. He used the razor strop. He never showed emotion; a neighbor told Mrs. Hall that her husband never smiled.

"Father was stern, but that's the way they all were in those days," said Jack Hall's half-brother, John "Bobo" Hall. "He was my husband and the father of my [three] children, but I could have hit him on the head. He was very bull-headed," said Mrs. Hazel Hall. Hall told people his father was cruel to him. "He said he had a miserable youth, a terrible youth," said Edward Berman, a labor organizer who worked with Hall in the mid-1930s on the Honolulu labor newspaper, *Voice of Labor*. Berman said Hall told him his father "beat the living hell out of him, so he ran away to sea. Hall used to come clean with me. He'd tell me: 'Miserable! Son of a bitch!' He would be talking about his father."

William J. "Bill" Bailey, a union organizer who also knew Hall in the 1930s, said that when he tried to get Hall to talk about his family, "up would go the bottle to his lips."

When Hall got into the labor movement, his father wrote him

that he was against it. To him labor was a racket and his son a racketeer.[1]

Jack was a bright student at Washington Elementary School in Los Angeles and skipped four semesters. He was an average student (B minus) at Huntington Park High School in Los Angeles, which he attended from 1927 to 1931. He graduated at sixteen. He had ambitions to go to college and become a physicist, but there was no way the family could afford it.

In high school Hall was a "long drink of water" whose only extracurricular activity was swimming. He was stoop-shouldered, ungainly, and had acne. From age twelve, he wore glasses to correct acute myopia.

One day he had an argument with his stepmother. He didn't like to do chores, such as washing dishes, and he told her: "My grandmother says I don't have to mind you. You're only my stepmother." Mrs. Hall picked up an alarm clock and threw it at him. Hall ran away from home. He described what happened next: "My wonderful grandmother gave me the then princely sum of five dollars from her carefully hoarded egg money, a change of clean clothes in a pillow slip, a warm goodbye kiss, and I was on my way to destiny."

He hitchhiked up the coast to San Francisco and, after a long wait, he got his first job—as ordinary seaman aboard the old Dollar liner *President McKinley*. He was on his way to what he called "the wonderful, exciting Islands of Hawaii."

---

1. When Hall told his father shortly after Pearl Harbor Day that he was going to marry Yoshiko Ogawa, a Nisei, Percy call him "a traitor . . . a Jap lover" and vowed to come over to Hawaii, "get a gun and shoot all those Japs."

CHAPTER 2
The Green Backdrop

The newcomer never forgets his first sight of Hawaii. In 1932 Hall was seventeen, an able-bodied seaman and "occasionally carpenter's mate" aboard the liner *President Hoover,* when he saw Honolulu for the first time: "It was daybreak. Rain clouds stood over the valleys. A light cool breeze fanned those of us who stood at the rail as the ship nosed her way into the channel. I was expectant—but a little tense and excited. I had the feeling that Hawaii was different—and it was."

The mountain backdrop was green. At the pier the Royal Hawaiian Band played. Hall was struck with the beauty of the place and the feeling of "escape."

He spent a year on the *Hoover* traveling to and from the Orient. His mind was pliant as tallow and the sights of the East impressed themselves on it. He saw the dominant whites and the subordinate natives and it stirred his sense of injustice.

"The Orient had the greatest impact on me as a youth," he said. "I saw colonialism at work, and poverty. It upset me. I determined which side of the fence I was on."

By now he was strongly politically motivated and was reading left-wing literature. Sailors, as Leon Trotsky once said, are natural revolutionaries. Life at sea was hard: twenty-four men bunking and working in the forecastle. In good weather the portholes were open; in bad weather they were shut. Seamen worked six hours on, six hours off. "We never got a full night's sleep," said Hall.

On July 1, 1934, Hall's ship, the *President Garfield,* docked at Los Angeles. Big things were going on up north in San Francisco. The "Big Strike," led by Harry Bridges, was on. Hall went out to Bell Gardens to see his family for a few days. He then took the bus to San Francisco and got there "in time for all the excitement." He walked the picket line. He dodged tear gas. It was warfare and there was something exhilarating about it but it was also dangerous. He felt like the soldier who survives a battle. He found that strikers from Hawaii were among the toughest men on the waterfront when it came "to going after scabs [strikebreakers]."

On September 16, 1934, he joined the Sailors' Union of the Pacific.

In 1935 Hall came to Hawaii to stay. He still made trips aboard ship, but Hawaii was now his home port. He always remembered the day and the hour: 8 AM, October 28, 1935. The ship was the Matson liner *Mariposa.* For one thing he had had enough of cold weather that reminded him of winter in his birthplace. The ship had left New York "with gear flying, hatches open, tarps frozen still and four inches of snow on the king posts." When the ship was secured, Hall went below to the forecastle, took off his long winter underwear, and threw it out the porthole. "Never again," he said.

He had another reason for making Hawaii his home: a secret assignment. He approached it full of vigor. As he explained his role: "I had the good fortune to be one of those seamen who piled off the ships—young, eager and optimistic enough to believe that if American seamen could overcome all the obstacles that faced them in 1934, then the same job could be done for Hawaii's workers."

A man named Revels Cayton had given Hall the secret assignment. Cayton was then business agent for the CIO Marine Cooks and Stewards Union in San Francisco and, at that time, a member of the Communist Party. Cayton raised a small pot to support Hall ashore for a short time. Marine unions chipped in a few dollars; it wasn't much. "If Hall got $20 a week, he was living," said Cayton. "We needed a guy to meet the ships in Honolulu and talk to the guys." Inform them, in other words, of the issues of the day.

Forty years later Cayton still remembered the boyish Hall.

"He was just a big, lanky, awkward youngster," he recalled. "But you could tell he could carry out that kind of a job. Those were the days when labor was beginning to flex its muscles and we were looking for leaders. The whole scene was fluid and it cried out for leadership."

Maxie Weisbarth, business agent for the Sailors' Union of the Pacific (the SUP) in Hawaii, gave Hall the other part of his assignment: labor organizing. Hall drew all possible advances and clothing, deserted ship, and came ashore carrying his seabag. Weisbarth was there to meet him.

Weisbarth was only five feet eight, but with his powerful, sloping shoulders, hard, black-eyed look, and strong pugilist's face, he looked at least six feet two. "I used to fight like I was six feet two," he said. Maxie was Hawaiian-German, from Kalihi originally. At age eleven he had worked on the docks carrying lumber and at fourteen he had gone to sea. His full name was Marcus Kamakanaikaouiliokalani Weisbarth, Sr., and he was tough and smart and vocal. (He spoke Mainland English which he learned aboard ship.) Weisbarth might have become a powerful figure in the fledgling labor movement in Hawaii but he didn't want to. "I just want to be myself," he said.

He had come home at the urging of his friend, Harry Lundeberg, president of the Sailors' Union International, to open an SUP hall in Honolulu. When Hall asked Weisbarth what a man could do around town, Weisbarth said there was plenty of labor organizing to do. "You want to work for us?" "Sure," said Hall. It didn't bother Weisbarth that Hall was just twenty.

Hall wrote and distributed pamphlets and talked to seamen. It was almost impossible to talk longshoremen into joining a union. If they were seen talking to a labor organizer, they might get fired. The employers ran a paternalistic system on the waterfront. "I remember Jack Guard[1] made sure than when anybody was broke they came and got $5 and $10 to feed the family," said Hall. That tied them to the employer; they were at his service.

---

1. Manager and treasurer of McCabe, Hamilton & Renny stevedoring company.

Those were sweatshop days in Hawaii. Restaurant workers worked an average of sixty-four hours a week for thirteen cents an hour and no days off. Maids earned as little as five dollars a week. And there were men, desperate for work, who were willing to do hard labor for fifty cents a day.

The seamen were often left-wing and belonged to every political hue of the spectrum: Socialists, Communists, both Stalinist and Trotskyite, Wobblies, anarchists. Like Hall, seamen dropped off ship to do a little labor organizing. Many came, stayed a while, and departed. Most left no more trace than a wave leaves after washing up on a beach.

Weisbarth soon discovered that Hall was a radical and he didn't like it. "All you guys are hard cookies and you work for nothing," he said to Hall. "You don't want nothin'." Indeed Hall worked hard: body and soul. Weisbarth rationalized: "Did you ever see a Commie that doesn't work hard?"

He didn't trust Hall; he said Hall took advice from left-wingers at the University of Hawaii and from the "Communist cell" in Honolulu. He called Hall an opportunist and gave an illustration: suppose a desk belonged to someone else. Hall would move in, he claimed. Pretty soon, said Weisbarth, Hall would put a sign on it that said: "Jack Hall."

He accused Hall of starting whispering campaigns against people he didn't like. That riled the bellicose Weisbarth and he would confront Hall. Weisbarth was handy with his fists. "I knocked Hall down the stairway. Kicked him in the ass. 'You goddamned idiot! You belong to an outfit [and] you want to make everything move!' " He meant the Communist Party.

Longshore organizing already had started in Hilo under Harry Lehua Kamoku. Kamoku, a round-faced Hawaiian-Chinese, had been an apprentice seaman at age sixteen; had sailed for twelve years; and then had returned to Hilo to organize the waterfront. The Hilo longshoremen were the most militant union members in Hawaii. In fact, they were the ones who started the modern labor movement in Hawaii.

Kamoku was quiet and humorous, but stubborn and militant. "Harry talk union, sleep union, drink union." Sometimes he drank too much and would then become untypically unrestrained. "Madman Kamoku," they would call him then.

Eddie Paaluhi was the fifth man Kamoku had approached to join the union. Paaluhi was afraid he might be jailed if he did; but sometimes he had to work fifteen, sixteen, even as many as eighteen hours at a stretch and that made up his mind.

It was the day of the shape-up—the practice of favoritism in hiring longshoremen. "I used to come down with my lunch can and stand around Hilo docks, Pier 1," Bert Nakano recalled. "Everybody had to line up and the timekeeper would point and say, 'You, you, you.' " They were the ones who got work that day; the others were out of luck. Many days Nakano would go home with his lunch can unopened.

Harry Kamoku had a cousin, Isaac "Chicken" Kamoku, who helped him preach unionism. Isaac was "Chicken" in name only; he was in fact the muscleman of the Hilo longshoremen.[2] "I dumped scabs," he boasted. Chicken became a charter member, along with eleven others, of the Hilo Longshoremen's Association. On November 22, 1935, Harry Kamoku was elected HLA president and business agent.

James K. "Jimmie" Kealoha, a young businessman in Hilo, donated space at his Kuhio Groceteria on the Hilo waterfront for a union office. The Groceteria was a combination poolroom–store–restaurant–bar and also took in lodgers. The longshoremen gave him their business, so Kealoha closed the poolroom and fixed up space for the union office. "The bosses put the heat on and some of my business disappeared," Kealoha said.

Kealoha went along when union members tried to organize dockworkers at Mahukona and Honuapo. At Honuapo they were still "slinging sugar"—sugar went out in bags by cable to the ships. The labor organizers dove off the pier and swam half a mile out to the ship to talk to longshoremen. "It was hard work trying to organize those people," said Kealoha. "They were scared to death." The union made Kealoha an honorary mem-

---

2. Asked how he got his nickname, Chicken said: "I used to steal 'um."

ber and he sat in on their meetings. He gave credit. Members would show him their bango tags.[3] On payday he would take their money, deduct what they owed him, and give them the balance. Often there was nothing left.

"We kept struggling," said Kealoha. "I figured some day they would be in a position to help me." Someone loaned Harry Kamoku a typewriter. He didn't know how to type or spell, but he learned. Then one day a seaman dropped off a ship in Hilo and solved the office problems for both Weisbarth and Kamoku. He was Robert Bodie, a stoop-shouldered man with a cigarette always dangling from his lips and a white sailor's cap perched on his head. He may not have looked efficient (he always looked as though he needed a shave), but he knew how to run an office. Bodie flew back and forth from Hilo to Honolulu and often Kealoha put up the air fare. "He had the typewriter going all the time," said Weisbarth.

---

3. A copper plate the size of a half-dollar bearing the worker's identity number.

CHAPTER 3
The Voice of Militant Unionism

Hall arrived just in time to work on the *Voice of Labor,* a nickel tabloid that sounded a shrill call for unionism. The first issue came out November 4, 1935. At first the six-page weekly was mimeographed; later it was printed. It never sold more than about a thousand copies.

The first editor was Corby Paxton, a tall, thin Southerner who looked as though he had tuberculosis. Hall called him "an intellectual seaman." Paxton raised forty dollars to start the paper. He was the only one on the staff who was paid. He got ten dollars a week—when there was ten dollars in the till. Seamen, union members, liberal professors at the University of Hawaii, people in town who loved to see someone tweak the nose of Merchant Street—these were the readers who supported the paper.

The first issue carried a defiant message: "Hawaii has become famous the world over as a bosses' paridise *[sic]* and a workers' hell. The bosses won't like this paper, but the workers may be sure that means the paper is a good one."

Paxton told the tourists to get off the beaches and go and see workers in the pineapple canneries and on the plantations if they wanted a real look at Hawaii. "It's not all Don Blanding poetry," he wrote. He said *The Voice* was founded by a small group of workers, whom he did not name. "All of them have lived in Hawaii long enough to know that it is dangerous to think, hence none of the group use their name." Hall did not write for the first few issues. He did odd jobs, helped in the office (then located at 918 Maunakea Street), helped on the mechanical side, and some nights slept on the floor. He was in and out of town on ships, but after a while he succumbed to temptation and began to write. In 1938 he wound up as editor.

Hall never lost his enthusiasm for the printed word. "He was always reading," said Joseph "Joe Blurr" Kealalio, a longshoreman. During one stay in town Hall roomed with Paxton at Ma Luning's at 230 North Beretania Street. It was there that he began reading the Communist literature Paxton gave him.

Hall discovered a way to supplement his meager income: Take a bundle of the *Voice of Labor* and peddle the papers in the bars on Hotel Street. Many people in town now got their first sight of Jack Hall: a lanky stringbean of a youth hawking the labor paper. "I could always get a quarter or a dime or a half [dollar] and get by," said Hall.

He knew the gang—the small group of men who were trying to organize the waterfront: Weisbarth, Bodie, Harry Kealoha, Levi Kealoha, Ed Berman. In the beginning Berman was Hall's close friend and a man in whom he confided because Berman was smart. Later the two had a falling out.

Berman was also a seaman. He came to Hawaii in 1931 aboard the *Mala*. He was from South Philadelphia and was different from most seamen: he had had two years of college. To make a living he sold tailor-made suits as the representative of a New York clothing company ($28.50 to $42 for the best suit in the house). Berman was tall and thin-faced and always seemed to have a cigar going.

Young Hall left a permanent impression on Berman:

> He was a lean, lanky, half-starved kid. Hard-core. All of his energies were dedicated to organizing the working stiff. . . . He was fervent, dedicated to the principle that world revolution was coming and that he was participating in that action. He thought workers would revolt and take over and become leaders of the country. . . . All he was reading was Communist literature.

Berman had had some slight experience in the sports department of the *Philadelphia Record*. He became associate editor of *The Voice;* and when Paxton left, he became editor. Berman's interest in labor had been whetted by a Honolulu police captain named Robert Griffin. Griffin was a liberal. Berman and Hall worked hard on *The Voice*. "It was hurriedly written; had to make a deadline," said Berman. There was never any money. It was a miracle it came out, but it had an effect. "Working people read it. The agitation was not wasted. It planted roots. . . ."

The handful of staff members discussed what would go into the paper and how to write it. Sometimes Weisbarth, who knew he was dealing with a left-wing crew, listened in. He might not have been an expert on literature but he knew what the working man would read. He would look at a piece of Paxton's copy. "Naw, this is too haolefied. Those doggies just won't understand it."

It was Paxton who first put his finger on what was wrong with the labor movement in Hawaii: all of Hawaii's strikes heretofore had been nationalistic: Japanese strikes, Filipino strikes. "The future strike will be of the *working class* and not of any particular nationality," he wrote.

There was a great deal of informality at *The Voice.* One day William R. ''Bill'' Norwood, a labor reporter on the *Star-Bulletin,* dropped by. The scene stayed with him for years: ''This tall, pimply-faced, emaciated-looking fellow [Hall] was sitting at the typewriter pounding out copy. The others were yelling. He shouted at them: 'You bastards! Shut up and leave me alone.' ''

From the time Harry Bridges had led the 1934 strike on the West Coast, he was the hero of the militant union leadership in Hawaii. They pleaded with him to come over and spark the movement, but Bridges couldn't come; he had his hands full.

In June 1937, Berman wrote Bridges that from a labor standpoint Hawaii was ''in a very strategic position.'' He invited Bridges to see for himself. Berman praised the hard-bitten Weisbarth for his ''splendid leadership.'' Weisbarth, who did not suffer from false modesty, signed the letter along with Berman. ''Hawaii is a company-dominated, company-controlled oligarchy of sugar,'' Berman later wrote Bridges.

Berman wrote Matt Meehan, the ILWU's secretary-treasurer, that there were sixty-five thousand plantation workers eager to be organized. He said Antonio Fagel, a Filipino labor organizer, wanted to bring the sugar workers into an exclusively Filipino union, but that would divide ''the workers against themselves.'' What Hawaii needed was an industrial union of all workers, he said.

''The time is ripe now,'' Berman pleaded. ''Outside funds are badly needed. . . . The AFL has shown no interest.'' If Bridges sent three thousand dollars, said Berman, then the union leaders in Hawaii could launch an organizing drive and in six months prove to be ''a vital part of the West Coast labor movement.''

Meehan replied that the ILWU didn't have the money.

CHAPTER 4

On the Waterfront

Hall left on a round-the-world trip aboard the *President Wilson* in December 1935 and returned to Hawaii early in April 1936. He had joined the Communist Party; he was a militant unionist. On April 10, 1936, he got into a brawl at the docks in Honolulu, attacked a Matson guard, and was sentenced to thirty days in jail for assault and battery. He served twenty-four days at the city and county jail at Iwilei. He didn't mind jail so much; it was a chance to relax and read; but he never forgot the watery guava jelly the jail served.

In port Hall helped prepare leaflets and recorded the minutes of the Honolulu Longshoremen's Association. He did very little organizing on the waterfront. Alexander G. Budge, Castle & Cooke president, denounced the Longshoremen's Association, saying it was made up of "radical leaders and a small group of malcontents."

Hall left on the *President Taft* in May 1936 and returned in August; he made a trip to San Francisco on the *Maui* and returned in September. He sailed on the *Lurline* and came back to Hawaii on October 29, 1936, the day before the 98-day maritime strike started on the West Coast. Coming off the *Lurline* with Hall was a seaman from Memphis, Tennessee, named James Wilson Cooley. Jim Cooley was a ruddy-faced, blue-eyed Irishman, witty and talkative, with a thirst for what seamen called "tea."[1]

The *Lurline* was struck and Hall was appointed Sailors' Union delegate. Eventually twelve ships were stranded in Honolulu and 1100 seamen with time on their hands and nothing much to do

---

1. Liquor.

were roaming around. People were afraid of them; seamen and longshoremen were not beloved. *"Gorotuki"*—ruffians—some people called them. But there they were; they could not be ignored.

Stephen Alencastre, the Catholic bishop of the Honolulu Diocese, turned over the old St. Louis College on River Street to the strikers and put a roof over their heads. St. Louis College had just moved to its new home in Kaimuki. Alencastre won the gratitude of labor and the condemnation of many people. The union fed a thousand men a day at the strike relief kitchen at 475–477 North Queen Street. Some people in town were sympathetic and quietly contributed funds and foodstuffs.

Hall was chairman of the strikers' Educational Committee, and one of the committee's jobs was to seek out and "dump" strikebreakers. The police tailed Hall and it was then that he made his first painful acquaintance with a husky police sergeant named Allen Taylor. Taylor was a police "enforcer"; that is, he beat people up.

In those days there was a detective named John Anthony Burns. Jack Burns knew all about the beatings administered by policemen. They were not uncommon. Chief of Police William A. Gabrielson had a ruling: "If you did any beating, you did it privately without making any marks that left proof later on."

Although there was not yet an official Communist Party organization in Hawaii, a "seamen's faction" ran the 1936–1937 maritime strike. Among those who attended Strike Strategy Committee sessions were George Goto,[2] Ed Berman, and Levi Kealoha. Only 240 of the 600 members of the Honolulu Longshoremen's Association went out on strike. Nor did most of them stay out long; within two weeks the majority were back at work, leaving forty iron-willed longshoremen holding the bag.

As in any strike there were lighthearted moments. The striking crewmen wired union headquarters for money, but headquarters wanted them to bring the ships home so they could save support money. The seamen were in no hurry to leave Hawaii. It was a

---

2. A pseudonym. Real name: Noboru Furuya, later a Honolulu restaurant owner.

sort of madcap vacation; they were playing tourist. "Who wants to be in San Francisco in November and December?" Hall laughed.

The waterfront was a dangerous place to work and hard to organize. There was the shape-up—that unwholesome way to hire men. There was intimidation of union leaders, bribery, and attempted bribery. The men sometimes had to work until nine or ten at night without time to eat. John Rodrigues, a Hilo longshoreman, described the risk the dockworkers encountered: "We were working down in the hold, eight men, slinging loads of 21 bags of sugar to the sling, three slings at a time, and they require eight men below; 1,600 to 1,700 bags in one hour and only six men handling sugar coming down at that speed."

Alexander Chang, a member of the longshore Executive Committee, wrote Bridges that the sugar bags that came hurtling down the chutes weighed 110 pounds apiece. "Miss your foothold and drop ten feet to a lower hold and break a leg," Chang said.

Longshoreman Levi Kealoha spoke of a speedup system which had gone into effect: "If the employers found the men did not perspire, they were told to check out, and most of these men were not employed for two or three weeks."

In April 1937, the National Labor Relations Board conducted a hearing in Honolulu into the way Castle & Cooke Terminals operated. In his report, George O. Pratt, the trial examiner, wrote:

> No impartial person who observed the demeanor [of witnesses] on the stand and who heard the testimony and read the record . . . could fail to be impressed with the fact that the longshoremen in the employ of the respondent [Castle & Cooke Terminals] are afraid and have reason to be.

An employee who was fired by Castle & Cooke must "eke out a living fishing, or go as a supplicant" to seek another job, said Pratt. He described how men were hired on the Honolulu waterfront:

Every morning about 6 o'clock a large crowd gathers. . . . After the gang foreman has checked in the "basic" employees who are reporting for work, a report is made of the number of "casuals" required to fill out the gangs. Then the timekeeper or head foreman or an assistant goes to the place the crowd has congregated. They will mill around, yelling, shouting, kicking, punching, trying to attract attention. As Danny Wise [assistant personnel director for Castle & Cooke Terminals], who was in charge of this work for a time, testified: "The one who yells the loudest or pushes hardest or otherwise brings himself to my attention gets the job."

Edward J. Eagen, regional director of the NLRB's Seattle office, spent nine months in Hawaii (March to December 1937) investigating labor conditions. His report charged that the territorial government and a majority of the members of the Territorial Legislature were dominated by the Big Five. He said working people in Hawaii were "more slaves than free. . . . They have no chance to change their jobs or get away from their present environment. They speak and mumble in monotones." He said anyone engaging in union activity was "an undesirable." He called Hawaii a "picture of fascism."

To Governor Joseph B. Poindexter the Eagen Report was "too preposterous" to deserve comment. "[It] sounds like a compilation of old street rumors." Samuel Wilder King, the delegate to Congress, characterized the report as "a distortion of the true picture. Whatever defects are found in Hawaii are minor. . . . No such extremes are prevalent as pictured by Eagen." The *Honolulu Star-Bulletin* called the report "a gratuitous contribution by a Federal official who holds some sort of world's record for long-distance jumping at the wrong conclusion."

But it was true that longshoremen were afraid to join a union; they signed up one week and dropped out the next. "One week you get maybe 50 to 75 people," said a waterfront organizer named Jack Kawano. "And that's a very good week. Next week you get about 25 or 30, but about 60 or 70 get out."

There were only a few resolute waterfront leaders: Weisbarth; Harry Kamoku in Hilo; the cousins, Harry and Levi Kealoha; John Elias, Jr., a rock-hard fellow from Kauai; Fred Kamahoahoa, a Hawaiian with a little American Indian blood; Harry Montenegro, Alex Karratti, Benjamin "Benny Big Nose" Kahaawinui. Those were the people Hall knew. He didn't notice Kawano, a quiet type who didn't attract attention. "Silent Jack," they called him.

Kawano was a squat, hard-muscled man with a seventh-grade education who came from Pahoa on the Big Island. He had gone to work at age fourteen for Hakalau Plantation, had worked in Hilo as a truck driver's helper and on Lanai as a truck driver, and then had come to Honolulu to earn a living doing hard labor. He dug cesspools; he built stone walls.

Then Kawano went to work for Castle & Cooke Terminals and before long had joined the union.[3] As soon as he got into the union, Kawano became an enthusiastic member. He attended all meetings; he was in his own words "one of the crazy ones" who complained to management. "It didn't take long before the company got their eye on me and finally got me off the job," he said. "I was bringing up too many grievances."

At that point, he decided the only thing for him to do was try his hand at organizing the waterfront. "The Honolulu waterfront—if there's any man that can take credit for organizing it, I'm the man," Kawano said. "Many folks tried. That I have to agree. . . . Berman tried it. He tried very hard. Jack Hall tried. Cooley tried. Harry Kealoha—he tried. Maxie Weisbarth. . . . They all tried. The only one that came out on top . . . was me."

For seven years Kawano and Kamahoahoa worked as waterfront organizers for as little as five or ten dollars a week. Sometimes they got nothing. Kawano and his family lived in a shack at the head of Pauoa Valley. Now and then Hall slept there—on the floor. It was hard to get longshoremen to pay their

---

3. Both the Hilo and Honolulu Longshoremen's Associations were granted affiliation with the International Longshoremen's Association of America in November 1936. In October 1937, the Honolulu longshore local received an ILWU charter and was then called ILWU Local 1-37. On August 11, 1937, Bridges took the ILA Pacific Coast units out of the AFL and into the CIO. The ILA retained only the ports of Tacoma, Port Angeles, and Anacortes. The move followed a long and bitter struggle between Bridges and Joseph P. Ryan, national ILA president.

union dues. Kamahoahoa had a habit of spying on them when they went to the beer halls on payday. They'd lay their money on the table and drink up. Kamahoahoa would note who was there and then go back to the office (above the Aala Fish Market) and see how much they owed. He'd write out a paid receipt for each man, go back to the beer hall, help himself to money on the table, and hand each man his receipt and any change he had coming.

In February 1938, Kawano, as president of Local 1-37, presented his first report to Bridges. It was not a cheerful recitation. He had only forty members in good standing; the local had lost an NLRB representation election at McCabe, Hamilton & Renny. "Morale is weakening, day by day," Kawano wrote. Kawano went from house to house trying to sign up longshoremen, "but they don't seem to give a hang anymore."

In answer to his plea for help, Bridges sent back only a big aloha. He had neither the money nor the people to send to Hawaii. Bridges also made it plain that the Hawaii longshoremen could not rely on the West Coast for support. "It is an absolute mistake to plan any organizing or strike on the basis of any help that may be forthcoming from the mainland," he warned Kawano.

Berman went to see Bridges, but it was a waste of time. "All I got was a little printing done for us," Berman said. "They didn't want to bother with us. It might be an expensive route to take and no matter what they spent, [they felt] it would be a waste of money."

In May 1939 Kawano asked Bridges for a second-hand typewriter; thirty to thirty-five dollars a month to handle mass meetings, legal matters, publicity leaflets, and other expenses; and eighty dollars a month each for two organizers. He proposed himself and Kamahoahoa for the jobs. Both had been evicted from their homes because they couldn't pay the rent. They had no home address "except that of the union hall." The ILWU sent five hundred dollars.

"We earnestly beseech you, Brother Bridges, to take personal command of our forces . . . and lead the Hawaiian labor movement forward to victory," Kamahoahoa pleaded.

CHAPTER 5

Maui '37: The Last Racial Strike

Hall got some on-the-job training on Maui in April 1937. He was in Hawaii, between sea trips, from April 2 to May 2, 1937. On April 8 Weisbarth sent him and Bill Bailey to Maui to help Antonio Fagel and his Filipino labor union, called Viboro Luviminda.

Bailey was a lanky, rugged seaman, born in Hell's Kitchen in New York. He was a Communist and a member of the Marine Firemen, Oilers, Watertenders, and Wipers Union. After the 1936–1937 West Coast maritime strike, in which he took part, the Communist Party ordered him to Hawaii to "do some political work."

He came to Honolulu as a yeoman aboard the *Lurline,* invented a tale about a brother recovering from burns at Queen's Hospital, and got off the ship. He found a room on Queen Emma Street, bought some red bunting, painted the hammer and sickle on it, and fastened "the flag of the working class," as he called it, to the wall in his room.

He started calling on radical unionists and asked them to attend a meeting in his room. The meeting was held in March or early April; the date has never been fixed. Hall wasn't there. Bailey gathered about a dozen people. He pointed to the red bunting on the wall. "That's my Bible," he said. "We've got to go out and visit people and talk and talk and begin to organize the workers."

Then he signed up his guests. Each was given a small white card making him a member of "The Travelers' Club," that is, the Communist Party of America. The initiation fee was ten cents.

Not long after, Weisbarth, who usually knew what was going

on, hailed Bailey. "Hey," he shouted. "There's another Commie you should be introduced to."

"Who's that?" asked Bailey.

"Jack Hall," said Weisbarth. "He's a big Commie. Always spouting off."

So Bailey met Hall. "He was a tall, skinny kid," Bailey recalled. "We chewed the rag for a couple of minutes and I said, 'We got to do something.' " He meant go out organizing.

The opportunity soon presented itself. Fagel and his helper, Florentino "Charley" Cabe, came to Weisbarth for help. Weisbarth sent them to Bailey and Hall. "I'm organizing Maui sugar workers," said Fagel. "I understand you can help us."

"That's right up our alley," announced Bailey. He was ready to go. But not Hall. Bailey had to talk him into it. He told Hall it was his "revolutionary duty" to help organize the working class.

Hall said, "All right—if it takes only a few days." It took eight days. "He didn't like to go without a drink that long," said Bailey. "We had a heavy, demanding schedule. There was no time for hangovers."

Fagel, who was born in the Philippines, had gone to high school in California and had come to Hawaii in 1932. He had been inspired by a legendary Filipino labor leader, Pablo Manlapit. Fagel was a good speaker, but he had a fatal flaw: he insisted on a racial union. He, Manlapit, and Epifanio A. Taok revived the old Filipino Labor Union, but it was constantly under attack so he renamed the organization Vibora Luviminda to make it sound like a harmless social group.[1] For two years Vibora gathered strength in secret.

Fagel paid for the passage of Hall and Bailey (five dollars each) aboard an Inter-Island ship. They slept on deck at the stern. Bailey's wardrobe consisted of a pair of dungarees, a blue denim shirt, a pair of socks. In his pocket he carried a handkerchief, an extra pair of socks, his union book, and his seaman's papers.

A Filipino met them at dockside and drove them to Puunene.

---

1. Vibora (Viper) was the nickname of a Filipino patriot, General Artemio Ricarte. Luviminda is a coined word made up of the initial letters of the words Luzon, Visayas, and Mindanao.

At the gates of Camp 1, they talked to a crowd. Bailey, all thunder, shouted his message. "I was very bombastic." Hall spoke quietly. He was not very sure of himself and may even have been a little embarrassed. The audience had to cock an ear to hear him.

At Hall's suggestion they divided the speaking chores: Bailey did the politicizing; Hall stuck to pork chop issues—wages and working conditions. They drew good crowds: 700 at Paia, 600 at Lahaina, 100 at Haiku, 300 at Haleakala, 300 at Puukolii, 500 at Wailuku. Bailey spoke as though in a perpetual rage. "I know Harry Bridges and if you go on strike they'll support you and not a drop [sic] of sugar will leave the islands," he shouted. In a week he was hoarse.

On the night of April 22 the Filipino workers gathered near the Tanizaki store at Puunene Camp 3: "The meeting was held in the dark and had all the aspects of a council of war. A huge circle was formed, speakers standing in the center of the ring in the glare of a dozen flashlights."

At one place lunas (plantation superintendents) came to listen and they laughed at the fiery Bailey. That stung him. He had a powerful imagination and now he called it into play. He said that down in Mexico he had seen a line of men a block long hanging by their necks from trees. He said the farmers told him: "That's what happens to people that laughed at our misery for years." The lunas stopped laughing.

Hall tried to persuade Fagel to take other nationalities into his labor organization, but Fagel was stubborn. First he wanted to organize the Filipinos, then he'd think about others. Hall thought that was foolish: Fagel's organizing was haphazard; Vibora Luviminda's books were ineptly kept.

One night near the end of their mission, Hall and Bailey were tired of the chatter, tired of the grueling work, tired of Filipino food. Bailey remarked that he would like a can of pork and beans. Hall said he would like a can of beer. "We shook out our pockets and pooled our resources, which was just enough for a can of beans and a bottle of beer," Bailey recalled.

When we were safely away from our friends, the Fagels and others, and he watched me eat those beans with joy on my face, he asked me why I didn't enjoy drinking. I told him I had been through that stage—of drinking till I fell flat on my face and waking up in alleys and hallways. But now that I was committed to revolutionary activity getting gassed up or going bananas for drink did not interest me any more. Here he said clearly, "I wish I could say the same."

They stayed on Maui until April 19 and then came back to Oahu. The next day a strike broke out among Filipino sugar workers at Hawaiian Commercial & Sugar Company. It started in a small way. One morning Moses P. Claveria, a scale man, found the men standing around "sharpening their cane knives." He went to see Frank Baldwin, the plantation manager, and told him the cane cutters wanted a pay raise. The cane they were working on now was much thicker and harder to cut than the cane in the fields they had just worked. They had been getting seven cents per thirty-foot row. Now they wanted ten cents for thin cane and twelve cents for thick cane. They also wanted the company to fire four Japanese lunas who, the workers said, were cheating them.

Baldwin said he couldn't do anything about it until he talked to his assistant, John Walker. "Why not?" said the emboldened Claveria. "You are the 'father' of this company."

Claveria had the impression Baldwin thought the men were bluffing. Disgusted, he went back to them. "I said two things to them: *'Agkaykayasa tayo'* and *'Mangabak tayo.'* "[2] He and Calixto Damaso[3] assumed the leadership. They called a meeting at the water reservoir and about seven hundred attended.

Walker told the workers the employers would do something about their demands, but they had to go back to work first. Claveria replied: "We are contractors. We have to know what we are going to be paid." They marched to the plantation office and turned in their cane knives. Damaso tried to talk to Baldwin. Baldwin told him, "If you don't like it, pack your gear and get out."

The strike leaders told the single men not to work. They per-

---

2. Ilocano for "We are united. We will win."

3. He later legally changed his name to Carl Damaso and in 1964 became president of Local 142.

mitted the married men with children to cut weeds and irrigate, if they had a contract to irrigate. But no one was to cut cane.

On the third day of the strike the camp police ordered Damaso to leave. He packed his few belongings in a small suitcase and went with them. They drove him to Wailuku and dropped him off. At night Damaso sneaked back into the Puunene camp to talk to the workers.

Baldwin stood firm. He said it was a test case for the sugar industry. "They can tear down the mill, but I won't give in," he said. The Filipinos were evicted.

The Hilo longshoremen and seamen off the Inter-Island ships helped the strikers. The Filipinos were determined. "When a Filipino has his spirit aroused, he will give everything for the cause," said Fagel, the leader.

Berman, then the editor of *Voice of Labor,* asked Bailey to return to Maui. Back on Maui, Bailey tried to keep the men active so they wouldn't be demoralized. He had what he thought was a splendid idea—a parade, the first May Day parade in the islands. He thought up slogans for the marchers to carry. One was: "Mules Get an Hour for Lunch, but Workers Only Half an Hour!"

The sheriff came down and talked to him. He said the signs were inflammatory and might touch off violence. Bailey agreed that some were a bit revolutionary, so he toned them down. But not the lunch hour for mules. That one he kept.

There was something in the Maui air that sharpened Bailey's imagination. He saw some cylindrical tubes on the roof of the plantation mill that puzzled him. Could they be machine guns? He decided they were and so informed Berman. Berman brought out the print shop's biggest type and mounted this headline in *Voice of Labor:*

MAUI WORKERS FACED
WITH MACHINE-GUNS

The story carried Bailey's byline. Of course, it was incorrect. What looked to Bailey like machine guns was harmless pipe. There were, however, guns being carried. The employers had hired a hundred deputies for three dollars a day and meals. Some deputies were armed and mounted on horseback. There were also eighteen policemen.

The strike spread to the Hawaiian Agricultural Company and to Wailuku Sugar Company and at its peak 3500 men were off the job. Many workers were afraid to go on strike; about one-third of the Filipinos at HC & S did not go out.

Among them was Anastacio Manangan, president of Camp 6. That irked Fagel. He said Manangan had promised to be "a good Filipino" and not betray the camp association. A few strikers called on Manangan. He saw them coming, dropped his hoe and *kau-kau* tin, and started to run. They caught him, tied him with strips of rice bag cloth, and took him to Fagel's office. Thereupon he agreed not to break the strike and they released him. He went straight to the sheriff.

Fagel and eight others were charged with conspiracy to commit illegal imprisonment. Lawyers in Hawaii in those days seldom defended union members, but the left-wing labor leaders knew where to go for help. They asked the radical International Labor Defense organization to send a lawyer, and the man assigned was Grover C. Johnson, from San Bernardino, California.

Johnson arrived June 17. He flew to Honolulu from Oakland and then took a seaplane to Maui. Several thousand people greeted him at the airport. He was astounded. A policeman said to him: "Are you the United States Attorney?" "No," said Johnson. "I am an attorney for the International Labor Defense." That sounded official enough and when the crowd heard it, they began cheering: "Our lawyer! Our government lawyer!"

Nice, friendly place, thought Johnson. They draped leis around his neck and drove him to Wailuku courthouse where Johnson presented his license to practice and then automatically followed the *modus operandi* of any lawyer on unfamiliar grounds: he asked for a continuance.

The strike ended July 17. It had gone on for eighty-six days. The workers won a slight pay raise and recognition of the union. Brigadier General Briant H. Wells, the Sugar Planters' Association secretary-treasurer, advised the industry to settle the strike because he feared Berman was ready to file an unfair labor practices charge under the NLRB. It was the last racial strike in Hawaii and the first time the industry officially recognized strikers.

The conspiracy trial of Fagel and his fellow defendants took place in Honolulu. William B. Lymer, special prosecutor, had asked for a change of venue. He wanted to avoid the spectacle of Filipino workers being defended on Maui by an experienced lawyer from the mainland.

Eight men, including Fagel, were convicted of third degree conspiracy. A directed verdict freed the ninth defendant. All eight convicted men were offered thirteen months' probation and all but Fagel accepted. He chose to serve four months in jail and pay a one-dollar fine. He said that if he were placed on probation, it would be simple for the police to pick him up and toss him in jail.

While he was in jail Fagel received a message from the Philippines from his hero, Manlapit: "Sometimes to be in jail is just like a rest, purifying our courage to carry on in a militant spirit."

Bailey left town before the strike was over. He didn't have much choice. A Hawaiian police officer had walked alongside him one day as he took a stroll on the waterfront. He told Bailey that if he managed to get aboard the *Lurline,* which was to embark that coming Thursday,[4] then all would be well. If he didn't get aboard, he would go to jail.

Bailey talked it over with Kawano. "We haven't got a lawyer," said Kawano. "You left your mark here. Get the hell out. You're not running out on us."

So Bailey packed his gear, took down the red bunting from the wall, and left Honolulu on the *Lurline.*

---

4. May 20, 1937, according to Bailey's seaman's discharge papers.

CHAPTER **6**

Kauai: The Special Island

Kauai was the island on which Hall learned his trade. On April 22, 1937, the Port Allen longshoremen went on strike against Kauai Terminals for overtime pay for work over eight hours. They had been working ten hours at straight time[1] and William Makanui, their leader, phoned Weisbarth in Honolulu and asked for help. Hall had just come back with Bailey from Maui.

Weisbarth ordered him and George Goto to go to Kauai. "Here are the plane tickets," he said. Hall didn't ask Weisbarth what to do. Nor did he ask Goto, who was five years older than he and, although he had no labor union experience, had read a lot of Marxist literature. "Hall never asked people's advice," said Goto. "He had all kinds of confidence in himself."

They flew to Lihue. Matsuki "Mutt" Arashiro, Harry Shimonishi, and Ben Morimoto, labor men, met them at the plane and drove them to Port Allen. Next day another labor man, Ichiro Izuka, saw them at Port Allen. He recalled that Hall was wearing a white cap, a hickory shirt (white and black stripes), and blue jeans. Hall looked "long-faced" and somber. Shimonishi remembered how frail he looked: "Hall was a skinny kid. He must not have weighed 140 pounds."

Hall and Goto discussed the problem. To Hall it seemed simple. "He was pretty smart and he recommended that they go back to work," said Goto. "We told the boys to go to work, but to organize."

That was the beginning of the Port Allen Waterfront Workers' Association. Makanui became president; Shimonishi, vice-

---

1. The wage scale then was: shore longshoremen and stevedores working in the hold, thirty-five cents an hour; garagemen, thirty-two cents.

president; and Morimoto, secretary-treasurer. Hall went back to Oahu in steerage on an Inter-Island steamer. Goto stayed on Kauai for nearly a year. It was not the most pleasant of jobs; he got ulcers. Off and on, Hall himself spent the next few years on Kauai.

On August 8, 1937, the fledgling Port Allen union went on strike and demanded a closed shop. The union alleged that Kauai Terminals had hired new hands and had recruited them into a company union. The strike lasted eighty days and it signaled the beginning of Hall's education as a labor leader. First, he learned how to use a pair of chopsticks in order to survive. As he explained: "They would put five pounds of meat in fifty pounds of watercress and if you wanted any protein, you gotta move fast with those chopsticks." To the local people Hall looked half-starved. They were afraid the "wind would blow him down."

Hall soon realized that the Japanese and the Filipinos were the militants; the Hawaiians and the Portuguese were usually soft. Mel Ozaki, the union secretary, said: "The Portuguese would say: ' 'ey, no mo' bread, no mo' bacalao.'[2] But the militants never squawked."

Among the union leaders on Kauai was an organizer from New York named Ben Shear. Shear was short and swarthy and wore glasses. He was a rabble-rouser. Shimonishi and he went out on the country roads at night with a bullhorn and a gas-engine generator to furnish power for lights. "We used to talk, talk, talk, talk trying to organize the plantation people," said Shimonishi. Often they were talking only to empty cane fields.

Some of the strikers were members of the Hanapepe Congregational Church, and the pastor, the Reverend Masao Yamada, worried about them. Families were living in tents. Hanapepe was a workers' town, however, not a plantation town, and people were generous to the strikers. "We never worried about being kicked out or threatened by the higher-ups," said Yamada.

Kauai people loaned the strikers tents and trucks and the strikers had good luck soliciting food and money. "We were like

---

2. Cod.

Santa Claus with a bag over our back, picking up what we could."

As in every strike, in time a weariness set in, and finally their lack of money and lack of support beat the strikers. They accepted a seniority hiring clause and called off the strike.

Hall by now was well established as an organizer on Kauai. He worked for CIO Local 76 of the United Cannery, Agricultural, Packing, and Allied Workers (UCAPAWA). The name was long but the mainland-based union's funds were short. Hall got sixteen dollars a month, which the Port Allen longshoremen contributed. He lived on the cheap in Hanapepe at the lively Watase Hotel, a two-story, green clapboard building on the banks of the Hanapepe River. Hanapepe looked like the set for a Western movie: a long, curving, dusty main street; wooden buildings; dogs sleeping in the sun; roosters crowing. The union had an office down the street from the Watase.

Hall did a lot of talking to workers. He told them what their rights were; he told them about the gains of labor on the mainland. He always spoke straight and never talked down to them. "You have to level with people or it will catch up with you," Hall said.

Recalling those days, he commented:

> We used to have lots and lots of meetings and lots of interest and, of course, the meetings used to go on for five or six hours. I guess in those days they had to be conducted [in] three and sometimes four languages. . . . And we used to go right into the camps even though they had trespass laws and defy them to throw us out. Sometimes they would take you out, but we went back in. But they would never make any arrests. . . .

Hall lived close to the bone. He often had just two changes of clothing: blue jeans and a short-sleeve shirt that he was wearing and another pair of blue jeans and a shirt in the wash.

One of his best friends was a tough young man named Frank Silva who had started working on plantations at age fourteen. Silva was a supervisor at McBryde Sugar Company, in charge of three 15-man groups. Hall asked him to help organize. "He must have thought I was in a good position to help the union," said Silva. "Right in my hand were forty-five guys."

For a time they were inseparable. They had little money. They walked or hitchhiked. Said Silva:

> We would go to the plantations and make contact. Go where people congregate. In bars and parks. Talk up unionism. Make conversation. When we had money we would buy the beer. Then go to the plantations and the waterfront. Being a local boy, they talked to me. Hall was a likeable guy. And once he got through to them, they believed him.

There wasn't much time for play. Hall had no girl friends, said Silva.

Organizing was serious and sometimes dangerous work: Hall was a tempting target. "Workers were afraid to be seen with you," said Mutt Arashiro. "As though they thought you had cancer." Hall often dropped in for coffee at the Arashiros on Puu Street in Kalaheo and sat in the kitchen around the polished mahogany table.

One night he and Silva went to the house of Silva's uncle, August Silva, a plantation worker. They were to meet other workers and talk union. They knocked on the door. No one answered. Then Silva's aunt, Jane, came to the door. She told them Uncle August wasn't there. "That's funny," said Silva. "They were supposed to meet us here."

He and Hall sat down on the lanai. Then a voice came booming from inside the house. It was Uncle August. "Jane, did they leave yet?" he called.

Workers had been trying since October 1936 to organize McBryde, well before Hall's arrival. "We had a hard time getting the Portuguese in," said Omi Oyama, one of the organizers. "They were scared. The first Portuguese that joined the union was Frank Silva."

At Hawaiian Sugar Company (later Olokele), organizers would slip into a worker's house at night to talk to him with the kerosene lamp turned down low. "They make like dim so people cannot look at us," said Oyama. One night at Hawaiian Sugar the camp police spotted Hall and chased him. He ran across the fields and fell into a three-foot-deep cattle-guard hole, but managed to escape. It seemed odd that local people trusted the skinny *haole* kid in raggedy clothes: Who was Hall to tell them what to do? Yet they listened to him. Ben Morimoto tried to explain: "We wouldn't say to him: 'How old are you? Where did you come from?' If he had some experience with a union, that was sufficient. At least he had more knowledge than the rest of us. We trusted him and asked him what to do."

"We were all green," said Unsei Uchima, another organizer. "I didn't know what a union was. But Hall knew what he was doing."

As a militant leader, Hall attracted the attention of Charlie Fern, editor of the *Garden Island*. The CIO unionists on Kauai disliked Fern and his paper. "I would like to spit in his face," said Shimonishi. Fern called Hall the "pied piper." "When Hall came to Kauai, he was just following the Communist line," said Fern. "There's no doubt about it."

Fern said in an editorial: "Mr. Hall's mission on Kauai, we understand, was to revitalize the CIO unions on this island and to prepare them for a campaign of general hell-raising on the plantations." Hall read the *Garden Island* carefully. "Look at this!" he would guffaw. He called Fern's editorials "idi-otorials."

Hall did not win over all the union people; some disliked his harsh way. Goto said he had a "one-track mind. His own ideas had to be followed by the rest." Shimonishi said Hall was a good organizer but hotheaded. "I had arguments with him," he said. Hall brought Communist literature. "I'm a country boy," said Shimonishi. "I didn't know a damn thing about communism."

Shimonishi said Hall gathered around him people who saw things his way. "Any man that listened to him, he wanted in. Jack Hall wanted to be the general," said Shimonishi. "But as far as organization, he was in there heart and soul."

One day the Reverend Mr. Yamada ran into Hall, who was carrying a book that bore no title on the cover. "I want you to read this," Hall said and handed it to Yamada. It was Karl Marx's *Das Kapital*.

Yamada smiled. "Look here, Jack," he said. "I studied this from cover to cover in the seminary. I believe in justice. I believe in reform. . . ." Years later, Yamada pondered the meeting. "Hall was Big Brother—doing the suffering," he said.

Hall didn't worry, not even about threats to his person. He was young and healthy—if underfed—and he had a mission in life: organizing workers. When he was broke he'd collect sake bottles and sell them for a nickel each. With luck, he could get enough to buy a gallon of sake. Sometimes he and his friends would go down the street and "borrow" a chicken and invite the owner to share in chicken hekka.

There was always the comfort of drink. One night, at the Watase Hotel, Hall got annoyed at some noisy neighbors and broke down the door to the adjoining room. He was arrested, charged with malicious injury, and lodged in the county jail at Wailua. "Leave him there," Izuka told Sheriff Edwin K. Crowell. "Good lesson for him." Eventually Arashiro bailed Hall out. The case was nol-prossed in district court.

Hall's drinking upset Izuka. "We're not supposed to drink," he told Hall. "We're supposed to set an example." Hall was aware of Izuka's feelings. If Izuka suddenly appeared, Hall would sing out: "Ichi's here! Hide the stuff!"

One New Year's Eve Hall called on his friend Omi Oyama at Eleele and asked if he had any liquor. Oyama handed over a quart of Seagram's Seven Crown. The evening wore on. Then, to Oyama's amazement, he discovered that the bottle was empty. "He drank it all," Oyama said. "I used to tell him: 'Jack, don't drink so much!' 'Oh, it's nothing,' he would say."

Hall never forgot those early days on Kauai. "At 22, it's not much of a problem for a guy that came off a ship," he said. "Those were great days."

CHAPTER 7
1938: Year of Violence

In 1938, fifty people, most of them union members, were shot and wounded by the police on the Hilo waterfront. Labor called it "The Hilo Massacre."

In 1938 any militant union leader in Hawaii risked getting beaten by the police. It happened to Hall. Both the shootings in Hilo and Hall's beating took place during strikes by the CIO Inland Boatmen's Union, which Hall and his old shipmate, Jim Cooley, had played the major role in organizing.

On February 4, the IBU struck the Inter-Island Steam Navigation Company for four days to gain recognition of the union. At the time Hall was leading a double life: he alternately worked for *Voice of Labor* and also on Kauai. Going to and fro, he traveled steerage or stowed away aboard ship.

The Inter-Island ship *Hualalai* was strikebound at Pier 13 and seamen couldn't go aboard to get their things. Hall, the ship's delegate, was called. He went down to the pier where a crowd of about fifty had gathered. The mood was ugly. Police Sergeant Allen Taylor, the waterfront detective who by now knew Hall very well, saw him. "Get out of there, Jack," he ordered. Hall was a talky fellow in Taylor's opinion; he "might incite trouble." He saw Hall lift his hand, as though to take issue with his order. Thereupon Taylor seized Hall by the arm.

"You're under arrest for investigation," he said, and led him away. He clamped an armlock on Hall and steered him down the street, heading for the Bethel Street police station. Irritated by the tight hold on his elbow, Hall poked Taylor in the ribs. It gave Taylor a good excuse. In the police station he stopped the elevator between floors and thrashed Hall. The beating left a scar on the right side of Hall's mouth.

For fourteen hours Hall was held incommunicado. When he was released, police detective Jack Burns saw him, but by then Hall had washed his face and cleaned himself up. Nevertheless, said Burns, "He had a few bruises here and there."

> I remember having seen him and heard what happened from the rest of the boys. Evidently he had shot his mouth off at this lineup [at the pier] where the cops were keeping the guys from going back to the boat. . . . Hall said something about it and so he was picked out as a troublemaker and they had bounced him off to the police station and booked him and took him up in the elevator and he got a few bouncing around *[sic]* in the elevator, which was not extremely unusual.

Reporter Bill Norwood saw Hall that morning. Hall was holding his hands over his ribs. He told Norwood he had taken "quite a beating."

Hall was to have spoken on labor matters on the night of February 4 to the Honolulu Inter-Professional Association. When he failed to appear, a delegation of six, including plant pathologist Beatrice Krauss and a thin, mild-mannered labor sympathizer named John E. Reinecke, called on Chief of Police Gabrielson. Gabrielson, big and stony-faced, took their names and ordered a police stenographer to take notes.

He lectured the group and they answered him back; it was a spirited exchange. He refused to let them see Hall. He told them Hall had been arrested because the police thought "he was going to cause trouble." The police had merely taken preventive measures, he said. Gabrielson showed them the statute that gave the police the right to make a "protective arrest." Furthermore, he said, Hall resembled a man "who had been committing stick-ups." Angrily, the group left his office.

Hall swore out a warrant for the arrest of Taylor on charges of assault and battery and the use of profanity. A trial was held March 5 before District Judge Charles H. Hogg. Lawyer O. P. Soares represented Hall. Six witnesses, including Hall and

Cooley, testified that Taylor swore at Hall, grabbed him around the neck, and kneed him. Hogg acquitted Taylor "for lack of evidence."

On May 26 the IBU and ILWU longshore Local 1–37 struck Inter-Island, and on May 28 the AFL Metal Trades Council of Honolulu (MTC) joined in the strike. The issue was the closed shop—a place where only union members may work—and wages. Inter-Island employed sixty longshoremen, of whom about forty-five were Local 1–37 members. Inter-Island also employed 225 seamen, and 190 walked out. There were 275 boilermakers, carpenters, machinists, and electricians belonging to the MTC. About half walked out; the other half had been laid off.

The unions prepared for a long encounter. Kawano handled the longshoremen. Berman ran the overall strike strategy. Within twenty-four hours the unions opened a soup kitchen on Maunakea Street, set up relief and publicity committees, operated a beach patrol, and put the ladies' auxiliaries to work.

The employers began to use nonunion help and that meant trouble. On June 28 Louis E. Welch, the business manager of *Voice of Labor,* was arrested and charged with assault and battery on two taxicab drivers. He claimed they were transporting strikebreakers to pierside. He pleaded nolo contendere and was sentenced to nine months in jail.

On July 7 the police got a call from a man who said the Inter-Island ship *Waialeale* would be blown up in drydock. The police searched but found no explosives. On July 12 Charles B. Wilson, Jr., president of the AFL Honolulu Waterfront Workers Association, called Merton B. Carson, secretary of Inter-Island, and told him about a "Dynamite Plot." Carson called Gabrielson, who went to Wilson's home and found twenty-six sticks of dynamite and four dynamite caps. He arrested Wilson.

Wilson and a man named Isaac Kekipi were convicted of possession of dynamite for illegal use. Kekipi got a five-year suspended sentence. Wilson was given a five-year maximum sentence. He served six months. The striking unions were convinced the "Dynamite Plot" was a phony, designed by Wilson to embarrass them and make the public think they were ready to use violence. Berman said Wilson's Waterfront Workers "raided unions . . . recruited scabs and strikebreakers" and claimed that it was a company union "disguised as an 'AFL' union to fight the CIO and democratic unionism."

A head of steam was building. To cool it, Basil Mayo, chairman of CIO Joint Strike Committee, asked Governor Poindexter to order Inter-Island to halt all shipping until the strike was settled.

Poindexter dawdled. "Mahope Joe," politician-critic Willie Crozier dubbed him, in reference to the Hawaiian word for "afterwards" or "by-and-by." The name stuck. "All Poindexter did was to suck on a cigarette, take another spit, and say: 'I'm neutral,' " said Crozier.

On July 22 the *Waialeale,* manned by nonunion men, docked in Hilo and passengers disembarked. Captain August Hasselgren, the acting portmaster, had heard rumors that Harry Kamoku's longshoremen had vowed not to let the ship be worked. He had called the police and Deputy Sheriff Peter N. Pakele, Police Lieutenant Charles Warren, and about sixteen officers went to Pier 2. They roped off the area in front of the pier warehouse and Warren directed traffic.

Longshoremen who had been working cargo on the *Maliko* at Pier 2 and the *Makua* at Pier 3 stopped work. They pushed past Warren and began taunting the crewmen of the *Waialeale*. "Rats . . . double-crossers . . . goddamned scabs!" they shouted.

Warren threw a tear gas grenade at them. That made them angrier. Clearly, big trouble was brewing if the company sent more ships manned by strikebreakers. It seemed only prudent when Inter-Island canceled further sailings. But Hilo businessmen complained and Gordon Scruton, the Hilo Chamber of Commerce executive secretary, called a board of directors' meeting, which the police, businessmen, and Harry Kamoku attended. The businessmen said that cancellation of shipping was costing them money. They asked what the police were doing to ensure protection for Inter-Island ships.

Sheriff Henry K. Martin said preparations were being taken. "I can assure you that the next time a steamer comes here we will be fully prepared," he said. "We will have all passengers and freight unloaded under the protection of police guns."

Kamoku, in his soft-spoken way, said that nonviolence was union policy. "The strike is coming to a close and we don't want this body to interfere in our fight," he said. "We want you to keep a hands-off policy. If not, we don't know what may happen."

The businessmen pressed him for an explanation. They argued, "We businessmen cannot keep our hands off while you union men are settling your differences." Kamoku replied: "We are fighting for our living while you businessmen are thinking only of your profits."

The chamber's board of directors adopted a resolution asking Inter-Island to restore service to Hilo and, on July 28, Inter-Island announced that the *Waialeale* would sail July 31 and dock in Hilo August 1. That meant confrontation.

Portmaster Hasselgren asked for police protection for the *Waialeale*. Sheriff Martin ordered Deputy Sheriff Pakele to arrange it. Arms and ammunition were gathered. Patrolmen were sent to the National Guard firing range. There they observed the effect of buckshot and birdshot on targets. They noted the effect of buckshot ricocheted off pavement.

The plans for the police reception for the ship's arrival were published in the *Hilo Tribune-Herald*. That piece of news dismayed the union leaders. They called Scruton and asked: Are union members public enemies? Are they an "invading Japanese Army?" Why the warlike posture? They talked to Martin Pence, a lawyer, who told them they could demonstrate peacefully but that the government had the right to keep people off government property, including wharves.

On the morning of August 1, about 250 union members gathered at Silva and Kalanianaole Streets. Kamoku warned them not to use violence. They wore work clothes. No person who smelled of alcohol was permitted to join the demonstrators and no one was permitted to carry a weapon.

Sixty-nine police officers, deputies, and special police were deployed at dockside. The Hilo Fire Department sent a truck with 85-pound pressure hoses.

The police had painted a yellow line at the point where Kuhio Road joined Kalanianaole Street and a second yellow line on Kuhio Road 350 feet north of the first line. They put up a sign that read "Police Line." No one was supposed to venture past the yellow lines.

The *Waialeale* docked. The demonstrators, who included about thirty women, came singing, shouting, bantering, and headed straight for the first police line. A crowd watched. Martin and his deputies, standing behind the yellow line, raised their hands—the gesture to stop. "You have to push us aside and that will be assault and battery," Martin called out.

Some union men in the front row heard him, but those behind did not. There was too much noise. The demonstrators flowed around the small group of deputies and kept going.

When they approached the second yellow police line, the order was given to throw tear gas. The police threw thirteen grenades; the demonstrators picked up three and threw them back. People scattered. Some had a good cry from the smoke of the tear gas and then they reassembled and sat down alongside the pavement. They were still in a good mood, almost a carnival mood, laughing, whistling, singing. Women were singing "Manuela Boy."

The men taunted the crew of the *Waialeale*. "You scabs!" They spotted Lieutenant Warren and shouted insults at him. They had been furious with him ever since the affair of July 22 when he threw the tear gas.

Warren walked up to Koichi "Kai" Uratani, the demonstrator who happened to be sitting at the far end of the line along the edge of the pavement. Warren carried a riot gun (a twelve-gauge shotgun); to the barrel was fitted a seventeen-inch bayonet. "All right," he said. "You people have been yelling 'Charlie Warren!' all morning and threatening me, wanting me to shoot you people. I am here now. . . . I am only giving one warning and the next is action. Charlie Warren gives you three minutes to get back to the yellow line!"

Uratani sat motionless as though he heard nothing. "All

right, you, get out of here!'' Warren shouted. He slapped Uratani across the face with the flat of his bayonet. Uratani turned and Warren stabbed him in the shoulder. Uratani got up. He didn't seem to realize he was bleeding.

"I was so excited I don't know what I did," Warren said later. He struck David "Red" Kupukaa, the next man in line, on the side of face with the butt of his riot gun. Men began yelling; women were shrieking. People were scrambling around. Warren thought they were going for him. He said he heard Sheriff Martin give the order to fire. Warren fired his riot gun at the pavement. The buckshot ricocheted. The crowd was just twenty yards away.

Other policemen started shooting. People were screaming and running. Twenty-two shots were fired: eight rounds of buckshot; eight of birdshot; and six rounds of .45 caliber ammunition. The firing lasted one or two minutes.

Among the fifty people who were hit were two women, Mrs. Anna Kamahele and Mrs. Helen Napeahi, and a child named J. Cho. Bert Nakano was the most seriously wounded.

"When we got to the apron, the guys were singing songs," Nakano said.

I could see him [Warren] telling Kai Uratani to get up, but Uratani just sat down. But he took the bayonet and jabbed him on the shoulder. Then he went to the next guy—this was a Hawaiian boy [Kupukaa]—and he gave him a butt stroke and whacked him across the chin. As soon as the gun came down he shot him right on the ankle. . . .

They all started to fire. People started running this way and that. I got picked up by four buckshot. They spun me around and knocked the hell out of me. I got two that hit my side and one hit my artery here. I got three buckshot in one leg. One went through my thigh and two hit my artery.

Chicken Kamoku said that Harry Kamoku had told the men "to walk beautifully. 'Don't yell, don't get panicky.' " He remembered that

when we got to the police warning line, Harry said: "The hell with the yellow line. Let's go. Let's keep walking." When we passed that line they threw cans of tear gas. We kept on marching toward our goal, the Inter-Island dock. Then the fire department started spraying water and we cut the hose.

They fired buckshot at the ground and it bounced into the crowd. Some of the spectators jumped into the water.

James K. "Jimmy" Mattoon, who had helped organize the Clerks' Union in Hilo, said he had warned the demonstrators not to carry a weapon. "No club, no nothing. I said to them: 'Not even matchsticks. Empty your pockets of matchsticks.' "

Mattoon was wearing heavy logger's boots. When the firing started he

ran to the edge of the pier and was going to dive in, but I thought if I dive in with these boots on, I'll go to the bottom and that will be the end. On the edge of the pier where the fenders were, it dropped a couple of feet. I got down there and lay down, but there were a few inches of me sticking up above the pier.

"They shot us down like sheep," Kamoku told Berman.

The shooting shocked the territory. The unions held protest meetings. The Grand Jury of the Fourth Judicial Circuit conducted an investigation from September 8 to 19. No one was indicted. The grand jury report said: "A state of emergency existed on that date [August 1] and . . . said evidence is not sufficient to warrant an indictment against any person or group of persons."

The strike ended August 15. For so much effort and blood, the unions gained very little. Reinecke summarized it:

So far as attainment of expressed objectives was concerned, the strike was a total failure for the drydock workers and the longshoremen. The Inter-Island succeeded completely in preventing the establishment of a union shop in any form and the wage increase which it conceded to seamen fell far short of West Coast scales which the IBU set as standard. The ILWU gained nothing except some minor improvements in work conditions. . . .

The two strike leaders, Kawano and Berman, had a falling out they never patched up. "I argued very vehemently that we should terminate the strike," said Berman. "Kawano was arguing just as vehemently that we shouldn't."

Berman said they had to go back to work; if they kept on, he argued, they would lose everything. "I couldn't get anything for the ILWU. We got some concessions on the ships. We established collective bargaining for the first time. . . ." Kawano disagreed: "What we tried to remind them was that we were supposed to come out together and go back together."

Hall was on Kauai and in Honolulu during the Inter-Island strike. He said that whatever the strike had cost it marked a turning point:

> when the strike began, many people expected the Hawaiians in the Union to hold out about four days. "The Hawaiians," they said, "are too easy-going. All they want is a little fish and poi and their liquor." This slander has been disproved by the strike. The Hawaiians demonstrated to the world that they share the determination and stamina of workers everywhere.
>
> Particularly is this true of members of the ILWU. This small but disciplined band of workers demonstrated a militance and persistence which will stand as a model for all Hawaiian workers. And in Jack Kawano, their leader, they have produced as careful an organizer and as keen a negotiator as can be found anywhere.

CHAPTER 8
A Start in Politics

It was on Kauai that Hall learned to wield political power. On August 28, 1938, he organized the Kauai Progressive League—their object was to elect candidates who supported labor. Hall plunged happily into what De Tocqueville called "the whirlpool of politics."

"We have to play politics," he told Ben Morimoto. "Let's put out our own candidates and see what they can do."

He talked union members into running; Johnny Brun, for instance. He told Brun, "We have to have our start and make people aware of the union." He pointed to the mass of legislation on the books directed against labor: the antipicketing law; the criminal syndicalism law; the trespass law; and the law which gave the police the right to arrest, fingerprint, and take a mugshot of a person if they thought he *might* commit a crime. Hall had felt the bite of that law.

His first big political campaign was the struggle between Democrat John B. Fernandes and Republican Lindsay A. Faye for the Territorial Senate in 1938. J. B. Fernandes was an independent businessman with strong sympathy for labor. His father, Manuel B. Fernandes, Sr., had been a laborer at Pahala on the Big Island. Faye was manager of Kekaha Sugar Company.

The Progressive League had no money, but members were willing to go out and knock on doors. Fernandes was skeptical. "I bet Hall a pair of shoes I wouldn't win," he said. On the day of the general election, Fernandes cast his ballot and went home. His father was pessimistic. "How can you fight money?" he said. J. B. shrugged. He didn't know how the voting was going and there was no way to find out for a while. There was nothing he could do at the moment so he took a nap. His brother, Manuel, Jr., woke him up. "You're catching up," he said.

"How can I?" said Fernandes. "He's got 400 votes at Kekaha alone." But he *was* catching up. At McBryde he won by 650 votes—Progressive League votes. "That turned the table," he said. Fernandes won the election by 192 votes.[1]

"Faye was a good sport," Fernandes said. "He congratulated me." Faye knew who had organized the campaign against him: Hall. It seemed ironic: a popular plantation Brahman being beaten by a raggedy kid.[2]

Fernandes said Hall asked for nothing in return for his support, but during his five terms in the Senate Fernandes usually voted the union way right down the line.[3]

Fernandes was "Hall's man" in the legislature and he "shot" (introduced), as he called it, all the labor bills in the 1939 and 1941 sessions. In the 1939 session Hall drafted a "Little Wagner" bill to permit unions to organize agricultural workers. The bill didn't pass that session; in fact, it did not pass until the 1944 session.

Hall made a friend of Charlie Rice, the kingpin of Kauai politics. Rice endorsed Fernandes. Hall often visited Rice at his home on the beach at Nawaliwili: "The Great White Father," Hall called him.

In 1938 Willie Crozier came to Kauai (in steerage) to campaign for delegate to Congress. Hall and he teamed up and announced they were going to campaign at Gay and Robinson's plantation at Makaweli—trespass law or no trespass law. Sheriff Clem Crowell pleaded with Crozier. "You and I are old friends, Willie," he said. "Please don't go because I will have to put you in jail."

Crozier replied: "Now, Sheriff, I have no objection to your

---

1. 3204 to 3012.

2. Faye had noticed Hall "bumming around" in Hanapepe. "He was largely responsible for my getting licked," said Faye. "He got them to campaign against me."

3. Not always, though: during the 1949 longshore strike, Fernandes jumped the fence and voted for the Dock Seizure Bill.

jail. If you have any reason to put me in jail, do your duty by all means. I'm not discriminating against your jail.''

He and Hall went to Makaweli. They parked on the county road in front of the plantation store and Crozier turned up the loudspeaker. There was nobody in sight, but they felt that *somebody* must be listening, if only out of curiosity. For an hour and a half they harangued the cane fields and then called it quits. "They didn't put us in jail, for which we were awful *[sic]* disappointed,'' said Crozier.

That evening they had a few beers and Crozier returned to the ship for the return trip in steerage. He got there late. The gangplank was already down and the ship was starting to move off. Willie plunged into the surf, paddled out, and was hauled aboard.[4]

The Progressive League grew stronger. Hall managed to oust Elsie Wilcox from the Territorial Senate. He supported Clem Gomes against Wilcox in the Republican primary and Gomes won. Hall said that in the 1939 session he had spent as much time himself in Iolani Palace (lobbying) as had Senator Wilcox. He now sounded off in *Voice of Labor* on politicians. He described the 1939 legislative session as smelling "like mountain goats." To appraise it, he said, he had to wear "a clothespin on his nose." He lauded the prolaborites: Tom Ouye of Kauai, George H. Holt, Jr., and a rising young Republican named Hiram Leong Fong. It was the start of his lifetime friendship with Fong, a bond which often puzzled union members and liberals.

Hall said Fong was labor's only Republican friend from Oahu's "Silk Stocking" Fourth District. He called William H. "Doc" Hill of Hilo the "smartest politician" in either house. Hill introduced no labor legislation, nor did he speak in behalf of labor, said Hall. "Give Doc credit for being shrewd—but beyond that forget him as a friend of the masses of the people."

Hall's writing style already was recognizable: simple and clear so that the unsophisticated could understand what he was driv-

---

4. That was not the only dunking he took: Crozier was beaten in the primary election for delegate, 35,937 to 3379.

ing at. He rewrote the turgid press releases of the politicians he supported; he wrote the campaign speeches of Senators Gomes and Fernandes.

The *Voice of Labor* struggled to stay alive. The staff went into debt; members dug into their pockets and managed to scrape through week after week. The paper's career sounded like the Perils of Pauline. "Months have gone by when each issue of the *Voice* was another modern miracle," said Hall. "Yet in the more than three years of its existence, the *Voice* has never missed a single issue."

But by June 1939 *The Voice* was a terminal case. The staff threw a beer bust at Pier 10 as a wake. Hall was cast in gloom. The paper folded. Yet the muting of *The Voice* didn't stop him from starting another newspaper, the *Kauai Herald*. He had a target to take on: Charlie Fern, editor of the *Garden Island*.

Hall discovered there was an old linotype in Koloa where the Japanese-language *Yoen Jiho* was printed. He found a union man, Herbert Alexander, to do the backshop work. Alexander had worked in Honolulu and remembered Hall selling *Voice of Labor* on the street. Alexander inspected the linotype, found it to be in fair shape, and got ready to start. Hall paid him a dollar an hour. The cost of publication came to between thirty and thirty-five dollars an issue. Alexander paid his own transportation on the bus. He lived in Waialua Homesteads, walked three and a half miles from his home to Highway 56, then took the bus to Koloa. He got up at six and was lucky to get to work by eight thirty.

The *Kauai Herald* started publishing July 12, 1940, as a weekly. The owner and publisher (he put up $250, which he never got back) was Ichiro Izuka. Hall did most of the writing. "We quite frankly declare that we intend to be partisan," said Hall, and he was. "There is no excuse for an impartial paper. People are not impartial."

Hall sided with the workers, the small farmers, the small businessmen, and with the professionals, "when their rights and privileges are in conflict with entrenched wealth."

Sometimes Alexander stayed overnight with Hall at the Watase Hotel in Hanapepe. It was hot down there in the flats along the river, but Hall had no trouble getting to sleep. He worked hard and would have a sip or two of whiskey before he went to bed. Hall was not the best paying guest at the Watase. The landlord frequently dunned him; money was scarce as ever.

Hall wrote his friend Reinecke in Honolulu and asked him to contribute a column for the *Herald* just as he had done for *Voice of Labor* under the byline and pseudonym of "N. K. Jui." Hall told him: "We need all the rumors, news, etc., from Honolulu."

Reinecke resurrected his mythical writing friend "Jui" and posed once again as the underling Oriental put upon by the ruling-class *haole*. He had acquired some facility in the role. One day Jui-Reinecke wrote: "If we Orientals are going to meet with haoles as social equals, how are we going to do it on Oriental wages?"

Hall himself wrote passionate prose for the *Herald*, particularly on legislative affairs: "Security for tens of thousands of toil-weary, feeble widows and tattered children [was] crushed under the spike-heel of reaction during the closing hours of the twenty-first legislature [1941]."

CHAPTER 9

Young Man with a Mission

The longshoremen on Kauai were gaining experience. Shimonishi, the Port Allen union president, made it a point to meet members of the black gang (the engine room crews) on every ship. He showed them the sights and fed them chicken hekka. "And, of course, a gallon of sake," said Hall. "They are his friends for life after a little of that."

The job of organizing went on. Sometimes management was receptive: Rolland G. "Dick" Bell, manager of Kauai Pineapple Company, for example. In May 1939, UCAPAWA Local 76 organized the nonagricultural workers of Kauai Pine. The vote in the NLRB representation election was 162 to 10. "For the first time in a century of bitter opposition to labor legislation, a union has been recognized by the employers in one of Hawaii's basic industries," *Voice of Labor* said. Johnny Brun said it was easy. He was a union strawboss for the pineapple truck drivers. "We did it like that!" he said, snapping his fingers. "Dick Bell let us talk to him."

In August 1939, Hall and Koichi Imori, a fellow labor organizer, rented an old house behind the Royal Brewery on Queen Street in Honolulu. Hall called the place "The Kremlin." He slept on a couch and when he couldn't stand the bedbugs any longer, he threw the couch out.

Sometimes they used the place for beer parties and for Communist Party meetings. When bottling day came at the brewery, Hall often worked part-time. The job paid thirty or thirty-five cents an hour.

He lived hand-to-mouth: a handout here; a handout there. He bought socks at Kress's for fifteen cents a pair and wore them "till they gave up." Now and then he would get a meal at the Reineckes' on Pahoa Avenue. When Hall stayed with the Reineckes, he was a considerate guest. "He loved his whiskey," said Reinecke, "but he was never a problem drinker."

"Kay," as Hall called the handsome Imori, was a legendary lover. Hall was shy and awkward. "He just did not have the touch to get around women or even to talk to local people," said Imori. When Hall and Cooley organized the Inland Boatmen's Union, Hall took Imori along. "He had me talk to the local people because he felt he was talking over their heads," said Imori. "He just didn't relate to those guys."

Hall and Izuka were selected to attend the Communist Party Labor School in San Francisco and were aboard ship (working their way across) on September 1, 1939, the day war broke out in

Europe. On September 4, Hall watched the Labor Day parade in San Francisco. The star of the parade was Bridges, who wore a hickory shirt and Frisco jeans. "When he stood up to speak, he was cheered for five minutes," Hall said.

Hall attended a UCAPAWA Executive Board meeting on Clay Street in San Francisco and pleaded in vain with an official, Donald Henderson, to put up money for organizing in Hawaii rather than spend it on migratory workers. He also went to see Bridges to raise money—no luck there either. Bridges said he had "too many problems" at home without taking on any more in Hawaii. The Communist Party school lasted only ten days because of the outbreak of war. Hall and Izuka worked their way home aboard a ship.

The going was hard in 1940: Hall was trying to organize plantation workers, help instruct longshoremen on unionism, make political contact, and run the *Kauai Herald*. In April he presented a brief to the Agricultural Adjustment Administration on the subject of wages in the sugar industry. Hall had boned up on the topic. Reinecke, who had a Doctor of Philosophy degree, knew Hall was intelligent, but he was amazed at Hall's ability to organize and present complex material.

Hall had a fierce loyalty to old friends. In 1940, for example, McBryde Sugar Company fired Frank Silva for "insubordination." (Silva had played soccer for the Kauai Pineapple Company, which McBryde called "a rival company.") Hall jumped headfirst into the affair: he called McBryde's attitude "Hitlerlike" and wrote Alexander & Baldwin, McBryde's agency, threatening to call a strike. Reinecke and Kimoto talked him out of it. Hall raised such a commotion that Governor Poindexter felt compelled to appoint an emergency review board to investigate. "The case was built up in such a way that he [Poindexter] had no choice," Hall told Reinecke.

Taking his cue from Hall, J. B. Fernandes applied pressure. Poindexter appointed three men, Dr. L. L. Patterson, Kenichi Mukai, and Didrick Hofgaard. Hall was delighted. He knew Patterson and Mukai disliked Cecil Baldwin, McBryde's manager, so he was confident of the verdict. As Hall had predicted, the board found in favor of Silva and against McBryde, but nothing came of it. "The law had no teeth in it," Silva explained. "The board could recommend, but not mandate."

Hall never forgave McBryde for firing Silva; and he could carry a grudge for years. In February 1957, Hall phoned Dick Bell, then president of Alexander & Baldwin, and asked him to hire Silva. Bell said no; there was nothing open. Hall bristled. He told Bell he was making a bad mistake and that his refusal to correct "this long-standing injustice" might make for difficult labor relations at McBryde and complicate negotiations the next time around. Bell listened in astonishment. "What!" he exclaimed. "After twenty years?"

"Yes," Hall said curtly. "It's only seventeen years," he said. "Not twenty."

CHAPTER **10**

Ahukini: The Races Collaborate

On July 18, 1940, a strike by ILWU longshoremen broke out at Ahukini Landing.[1] Ahukini Terminal, Ltd., an American Factors subsidiary, had informed the port workers that because of the new Wage and Hour Law, they must either sign up for work in the port terminal, and thus lose their free housing, or work exclusively at Lihue Plantation and keep their housing. They could

---

1. Ahukini Landing, just north of Lihue Airport, has not been used as a port for years.

no longer work at both jobs as they had been doing. (They liked the double work opportunity; when things were slack on one job, they could go to the other.)

The majority preferred to work in the terminal, but they didn't want to lose their housing. The union proposed that if the workers took a job in the terminal and vacated their housing, they be guaranteed fifteen dollars a week for at least thirty-one weeks a year. Management refused. It did not see how it could guarantee casual labor a weekly income. Upon that rock the two sides split.

The Ahukini strike went on for 298 days, the longest strike in Hawaii history.[2] It was the first time the races cooperated in a strike and that convinced Hall the labor movement in Hawaii was bound to succeed. The Ahukini longshoremen were mainly Filipinos; the Port Allen longshoremen, Japanese. Recalling the Ahukini affair years later, Hall said not a single worker deserted the strike in Ahukini "where the principle of racial solidarity, inter-racial solidarity that made this union [the ILWU] strong, was first put into practice."

On July 29 the Matson ship *Makua* docked at Port Allen with 340 tons of Ahukini cargo which the Filipino longshoremen refused to unload. The union tagged the cargo "hot." At Port Allen the Lihue Plantation tried to unload it with some eighty-five strikebreakers, but because of the picket line the *Makua* crew wouldn't supply steam for the winches. Captain L. J. Doepfner, the port captain, ordered the cargo discharged. The eleven men working No. 4 gang refused and were fired for insubordination. The entire Port Allen membership was then locked out. "This was the first clear case of workers walking out in support of another group in the islands, even though it was made up of another race," said Hall.

Hall had no part in the walkout. He told the longshoremen they couldn't break their contract, but they didn't listen to him. As he explained it: "The decision not to handle hot cargo, which

---

2. The longshore strike of 1949 lasted 178 days; the Lanai strike of 1951 went on for 201 days.

led to the walkout, was made by the men themselves partly on trade union lines. The Communist Party had nothing to do with it.''

Hall said the Kauai branch of the Communist Party was no powerhouse; it met irregularly and "functioned weakly." Charlie Fern was convinced otherwise. The *Garden Island* attributed the strike to Communist-inspired leadership "whose main design is to create friction between employer and employee." Fern said the Port Allen longshoremen were notorious troublemakers: "It is very certain that there will be no bitter tears shed on Kauai if the union is smashed."

As the strike wore on, Fern claimed the picket line at Port Allen was a joke. "They are not halting the operation of the company. They are not stopping the shipment of sugar and pineapples from Kauai." All they were doing, he said, was forcing the cost of living up because the employers had to bring in freight by Inter-Island steamer.

The longshoremen were evicted from company housing and Hall rented the skating rink at Nawiliwili to house homeless men and their families. They slept on the floor; the Port Allen strikers and their families lived in tents pitched in the Hanapepe Valley or stayed with relatives. They planted taro; the men fished; children caught frogs. They ate fish and rice, watercress, and daikon. They had a thin time of it. The Port Allen workers assessed themselves a hundred dollars apiece to build a strike fund through *tanōmoshi,* a loan-finance idea the early Japanese immigrants brought from the old country. But as the strike went on and on, the men's spirits dropped.

"We thought the company must give in some," said Shimonishi, but management hung on. "With only Port Allen and Ahukini out, they [the company] could take it," said Shimonishi.

They wanted to win this battle. They wanted to show us that the union couldn't win. They were only taking a little loss. They could afford it.

We lived on rice. We used to get day-old bread and every morning we had coffee, bread and jelly. We used to fish. We hardly had any meat, but we managed.

Shimonishi said even Hall lost some of his confidence. "He came around only now and then. . . . Maybe he figured we couldn't win." Izuka said Hall tried to get the Honolulu longshoremen to picket but that Kawano refused. Kawano said if they joined the strike, they would be washed up. "So we asked them to cool it. Give us a chance to keep on building in Honolulu," he said. "We did not follow them."

In April 1941, Izuka attended the ILWU convention in San Francisco as the Kauai delegate and talked to Bridges and Henry Schmidt, an ILWU expert on waterfront matters. There was strong feeling among the ILWU officers in San Francisco that out in Kauai something must be wrong: the strike was going on too long. Bridges told Izuka they had made a mistake—they had fallen "into the company's trap."

It was futile to go on. Bridges said: "It was a long, hopeless strike to begin with." He had sent Clifford O'Brien, an ILWU lawyer and expert on labor negotiations, to Hawaii, and O'Brien reported directly to the International Executive Board. O'Brien told Bridges the employers would bargain but "not give up anything important." Their technique was to "kill the union with kindness."

All wars come to an end and so do all strikes. William T. Guerts, a Maritime Labor Board mediator from Washington, flew to Hawaii by Pan American Clipper and on May 11, 1941, the strike ended. O'Brien represented both locals, Ahukini and Port Allen, while Hall played the role of adviser. A new contract was signed that contained "no strike, no lockout" clauses.

Shimonishi figured that the average worker got a raise of about four cents an hour. Workers could no longer work in dual capacity; that is, both on the docks and in sugar. Izuka said sixty-five union members lost their jobs.

It was hardly a union victory and maybe even a defeat. Hall tried to put on the best face possible: "We didn't win everything we wanted," he said. "In fact, a lot of guys lost their jobs and came to Honolulu."

"In general, it was a wasted strike," Izuka said. "We got nothing; only recognition. The company was willing to sign an agreement. That's all." But a valuable precedent had been set: members of one race had proved themselves willing to endure hardship for members of another race. It signaled that henceforth they would pull together.

The organizing teams led by Hall pushed on. On November 1, 1940, the nonagricultural workers at McBryde voted 5 to 1 to have Local 76 represent them. They were the first group of Hawaii sugar workers to win employer recognition of their union. "We have won something that many have given their lives to attain," said Arashiro.

The triumph at McBryde cheered Hall. Why not take on all the sugar plantations, one at a time? He, Brun, and Arashiro worked until one and two in the morning talking to workers at Kekaha Sugar Company. Hall was exuberant. He felt confident they would win an election and it amused him to think how baffled management would be. "The company is still dizzy trying to find out how it happened so quickly."

But Faye, Kekaha's manager, was a shrewd opponent. He told his employees he didn't think it was necessary for them to join a union. "We had a company union, an association of workers," he said. "We had grievance procedures before Hall came along." UCAPAWA lost the NLRB election.

J. B. Fernandes hired Hall and Mel Ozaki of Hanapepe as his clerks for the legislative session that ran from February 19 to April 30, 1941. Hall wanted to attend the session so he could write labor legislation through his man, Fernandes. Ozaki described himself as "the front man," and he conceded that Hall did the work. "He [Hall] sat in the office and I gave him half my pay of ten dollars a day," said Ozaki. Ozaki kept five dollars and donated a dollar of that to the union.

Hall dressed so badly that Fernandes was aghast: jeans and shirt in the halls of Iolani Palace! One day Fernandes bought Hall a suit at the Hub Company. "You've got to be respectful looking," he told Hall.

Life for Hall fell into routine. Up early in the morning; home to the Reineckes late at night. Hall had met a young man named David Thompson—the son of a Salem, Oregon, doctor—who had come to Hawaii in 1939 intending to go on to India but instead decided to stay. With his curly, light-brown hair and puckish grin, Thompson looked like the All-American Boy. However, he was serious-minded; he championed liberal causes and the labor movement.

One night Thompson brought to the Reinecke home a girl named Yoshiko. She was a member of a plantation family of six sisters and a brother from Olaa on the Big Island and was working her way through the University of Hawaii. She had heard of Hall and wanted to meet him. When she and Thompson arrived, the Reineckes had already gone to bed. Hall was reading. He had taken a shower and was wearing a kimono. Thompson introduced Miss Ogawa and the rapport was immediate. All night long they sat and talked and drank tea. "Boy, I fell in love with Jack Hall the first night," said Miss Ogawa.

She didn't expect to hear from him again, but Hall called her the next day and so began their courtship. Hall never forgot the night he met Yoshiko. In 1969, on the eve of his departure from Hawaii to San Francisco and his new job as ILWU vice-president, Hall wrote the Reineckes: "I will always treasure the remembrance that I met Yoshiko in your home and married her, shy as I was, because Aiko told me she was receptive."

On June 30, 1941, the *Kauai Herald* became the *Herald* and was now published in Honolulu as a territory-wide labor paper. "A paper for people who think," said Hall. The first issue came out July 4; it cost a nickel.

"The *Herald* has axes to grind," said Hall, and he started grinding away. He liked to think that every labor organization in town—AFL, CIO, or independent—supported the paper. He wrote a column under the byline of "Publius."[3] In fact, he

---

3. The Roman praenomen that served Alexander Hamilton, John Jay, and James Madison when they wrote for *The Federalist.*

wrote everything—breaking news, speculative stories, background, features, editorials, even a three-dot column of chit-chat:

> Best coffee in town is at the Patio . . . Coolest dining room is downstairs at the Young [Hotel] . . . And we want to strike a medal for Loujo.[4] We don't know what for, but somehow we feel she deserves one.

On June 21, 1941, Hitler invaded the Soviet Union and for the Communist world the war changed overnight from an "imperialistic squabble" to an antifascist struggle. As the defense industry began to boom, workers poured into Pearl Harbor from the mainland. Hall waged a campaign in his paper to boost the defense effort. It was good Americanism and good communism at the same time. He preached for a united front against the Nazis and condemned strikes of any kind "until all established mediation and conciliation machinery has been exhausted." He said the idea of "let's take it easy and not work ourselves out of a job is nothing short of criminal at this moment in history."

He even began to feel better about employers. He said labor was now able in the islands to bargain on equal footing. "Employers in the islands," he said, "are discovering that all trade unions are not bogey-men seeking to squeeze the last possible penny out of them and drive them into bankruptcy."

Hall said sugar, pineapple, and transportation, Hawaii's basic industries, intended to get along without strife. But he retained at least a pinch of caution: "They [the employers] are, however, keeping their powder dry and storing up large quantities of it."

The *Herald,* like the *Kauai Herald* and *Voice of Labor,* had to struggle to stay alive. Hall asked for contributions from anyone, rich or poor, laborer or capitalist. He intrigued people—his intensity, his devotion to a cause—though some called him "the *pilau*[5] *haole*" because he looked so unkempt.

As the Nazi war machine bit deeper into the Soviet Union, Hall's feelings were aroused. He presented his analysis of the

---

4. Mrs. Louise Post Johansen Hollingsworth, a *Star-Bulletin* reporter.
5. Rotten.

Soviet political system: "We have not grasped one fundamental fact: RUSSIA IS A DEMOCRACY. Not our type of democracy. Some ways less democratic and some ways more democratic, but a democracy nevertheless."

Late in November 1941, Hall spoke for nearly an hour in the rain before a gathering at Aala Park. He discussed the CIO's record of achievement on Hawaii's plantations and predicted that big organizing successes were on the way. He intended to involve Roman R. Cariaga, a Filipino sociologist and author. Cariaga was to be a leader in a bold effort to organize Filipino workers.

Out in the Far Pacific, the Japanese threat to world peace had grown, but Hall, like many of the admirals and generals on Oahu, was not apprehensive. "No sense in hysterical alarm," he said in the November 24, 1941, issue of the *Herald*. At that moment the Japanese strike force had already left its fog-bound anchorage in the north of Japan for a rendezvous north of Oahu and a date thirteen days later at Pearl Harbor.

"N. K. Jui" (Reinecke) saw more clearly the shape of things to come. "Evil days are upon us," he said. "Military rule is on the way."

Part 2
THE WAR YEARS
(1941–1944)

CHAPTER 11
A Bright Sunday Morning

Early one Sunday morning Hall went to see McElrath about another in the series of crises of the *Herald*.[1] They waited for a third man—Jack Kimoto.

Kimoto had been born on Ewa Plantation; he had lived in Japan for three years as a boy, and for seven years in California as an adult. In April 1938 he came back to Hawaii. His mission was to help organize Communist Party groups.

McElrath was a small, boyish-looking seaman of strong radical bent who first came to Hawaii on the Fourth of July in 1938 as a fireman aboard the Matson vessel *Lihue*. The ship had called at Galveston, Texas, where McElrath was on the beach. The *Lihue* sailed to New York and then nonstop to Honolulu. It broke down several times on the long voyage; food ran low (except for onions); and when the *Lihue* put in at Honolulu, McElrath was glad to get off.

He explored Waikiki, lived it up until his money ran low, and topped off the last big evening with a meal of frog legs at the Waikiki Tavern. Then he took his kit to the Seamen's Institute on Halekauwila Street and looked around.

The Inter-Island strike was going on and McElrath went down to strike headquarters at Merchant and Alakea Streets. There he saw a tall, skinny fellow, "sort of bent over." It was Hall, working on *Voice of Labor*. McElrath offered to lend a hand. He had done a little writing in Seattle for the American Newspaper Guild paper published in 1936 during a newspaper strike.

---

1. O'Brien, the ILWU attorney from the West Coast, told Bridges he doubted that Hall could edit a labor paper and carry on as an effective CIO organizer at the same time.

McElrath met Berman, the man with the cigar, who was then CIO director in Hawaii, and Reinecke, who was out of a teaching job at the time and often came to the waterfront office of *The Voice.* Reinecke startled McElrath because he seemed to be more radical than the labor paper itself. "John wanted the revolution as of yesterday," said McElrath. "What Jack was trying to do was organize the workers."

McElrath stayed awhile and then shipped out. Early in 1941 Hall wrote McElrath in San Francisco and invited him to take over the editorship of the *Kauai Herald* while Hall worked at the legislature. McElrath was happy to oblige. He arrived about mid-March. The two got along well. Hall recognized that McElrath was dedicated and had brains. Hall forgave him such shortcomings as his youthful rashness.

And now he was a member of the team and concerned with Hall about how the *Herald,* the sickly descendant of the *Kauai Herald* and *Voice of Labor,* was going to survive. That Sunday morning he and Hall waited impatiently for Kimoto. Both had dates: Hall with his girl friend, Yoshiko Ogawa, and McElrath with his wife, Ah Quon, a social worker he had married in August 1941.

Kimoto finally arrived and said he had been held up. "Looks like there's some trouble over at Pearl Harbor," he said. They went outside and looked. For weeks there had been practice alerts at Pearl Harbor and antiaircraft guns had fired blank ammunition which left white bursts of smoke in the sky, looking "like bursting bales of cotton."

Something *was* going on. There were bursts of smoke in the air, but they were an ominous black. Though it must have been gunfire, they could hear no sound. They were puzzled but went back and talked some more and then called it quits for the day. Hall and McElrath got into McElrath's 1928 Model A Ford and drove off. Down the street an American Legionnaire stopped them. "Get out of town," he told them. "We don't know what the hell's going on."

McElrath dropped Hall off at Yoshiko's apartment near the Queen's Hospital and then picked his wife up. At a friend's house he heard over the radio that the Japanese had bombed Pearl Harbor.

McElrath and other seamen were immediately caught up in the war. They were issued khaki shirts and pants and GI shoes and ordered to string barbed wire for a concentration camp at Pier 2. They wondered who would occupy it. At 3 AM they found out. Trucks brought weeping Japanese men and women who were being interned.

The military government temporarily suspended publication of the *Herald*. Hall went to work as a painter at Hickam Field Hawaiian Air Depot. He knew enough about painting to hate it and was fired after an argument with a foreman. Then he worked at Hickam as a warehouseman. He also took a test for a job as a Wage and Hour Division inspector for the Territorial Department of Labor and Industrial Relations.

He was lucky he wasn't arrested. Employers in Hawaii had given Robert L. Shivers, the special agent in charge of the FBI office, a dossier on Hall "nearly a foot high" and Shivers was asked to arrest Hall "as a person dangerous to the security of the country." He did not. "In that whole voluminous file, he found nothing contrary to the best interest of the country in any of my activities, statements or associations," said Hall.

Lieutenant Colonel George W. Bicknell, in charge of internal security in the Hawaiian Department, United States Army, interceded in Hall's behalf to get him a release from his job with the military. Hall passed the labor inspector's test and got the job because L. Q. McComas, who had become the Labor Department director in 1941, liked Hall. At McComas's request, Shivers cleared Hall for loyalty for the job with the territory. Hall's appointment startled some people. "You don't ordinarily put labor agitators in jobs like that," they said.[2]

On January 12, 1942, Hall married Yoshiko Ogawa in a brief civil ceremony at the home of lawyer Arthur K. Trask on St. Louis Heights. Reinecke and Kimoto, who was then driving a cab, were the witnesses. "I invited myself to the ceremony,"

---

2. Hall started work April 1, 1942, as a CAF-1 at $317 a month.

said Reinecke. The nuptial libation was meager. Trask offered each of his guests a toast of a single drink.

The Halls moved to an apartment on South Vineyard near Queen Emma Street. About a month later they moved to 955 18th Avenue, where they lived until September 1, 1945. They had little money; Yoshiko was not working. They couldn't afford a washing machine. On Sundays Hall took the laundry in a big bag slung over his shoulder and he and Yoshiko walked nine blocks from his home to Reinecke's house on Pahoa Avenue. While Yoshiko ran the washing machine, Hall would listen to music or read.

The military lifted the ban on the *Herald* and a thin edition appeared on March 9, 1942, printed on 8½-by-11-inch paper. Hall still contributed articles, but the editor was now R. A. Bishop, a big, easygoing man who looked "like a house detective or a floor walker."

Hall wrote a signed article in the March 9 issue. He said he sympathized with Hawaii residents of Japanese descent in view of the catastrophe which had befallen them. "Yet I never kidded myself into believing that a great number of first generation Japanese—and a surprisingly large number of citizens—do not have strong emotional ties with the Shinto empire." Hall said labor must pledge for the duration of the war not to stop work even for a single day. He himself was working long hours at his job and contributed part of his pay to the paper while Bishop spent the day "raking up news and data."

Hall did not control the paper and the *Herald* soon began to publish a brand of superpatriotism written by someone who called himself "Oscar, the No-Good Haole." It was Bishop speaking to the "mama-sans."[3] He advised them to turn informer and expose people they suspected might be potential saboteurs.

Wage and Hour Division job had a drawback: Hall had to wear a jacket. He hated coats and ties. "Goddamn it," he grumbled, "I think wages and hours inspectors and Mormon missionaries are the only ones on Oahu wearing a coat and tie."

3. Mature women of Japanese descent, often a demeaning word.

Bishop changed the name of the paper to *Victory* and put out one last issue. In it he discussed Jack Hall and his job:

> It's Jack's job to snoop around, check up on little items and see that all adhere to the laws of the liberal, progressive legislation. We've known brother Jack for almost a year now and we like the old soul. He's crowded much life into his 28 years and he has learned much about the ways things are.
>
> We can say this from our intimate acquaintance with him, that if people are really on the level, Hall will shoot that way also.

Hall made a friend at the Wage and Hour Division, an accountant named Katsuto Nagaue. "Kats" liked Hall; they made a good team. "We would bend over backwards to help these guys follow the wage and hour law," said Nagaue. "The law was just passed by the 1941 Legislature. The minimum wage on Oahu was 25 cents an hour for a 48-hour work week. We were teaching these people to comply."

Nagaue often stayed with the Halls in Kaimuki. He drank with Hall and learned to respect Hall's skill as a poker player. Hall impressed him as a man who couldn't stand incompetence. Nagaue also soon realized that Hall was receptive to learning. He absorbed information like a computer. Nagaue loaned Hall books on accounting and taught him to read financial statements.

"We used to put two balance sheets together and analyze what was the difference in, say, three months' time in the two sheets. The comparative figures. This is how you get an answer on what to ask for in wage demands," said Nagaue.

Hall worked for the Wage and Hour Division for more than two years; he was in charge of the division for more than a year and advanced to the rank of chief inspector. He traveled all over the islands; he met people in key jobs; he learned to wend his way through government red tape. He learned how inept some government administrators were. He studied operations in the outports; he learned about the sugar and pineapple industries. He mastered the intricacies of the Fair Labor Standards Act "and the employer technique of ducking it." It all came in handy one day.

Hall and Nagaue were at work on Kauai one rainy day when Hall got word that his first child, Michele, was born.[4] Hall and Nagaue were staying at the old Lihue Hotel. Hall bought a box of candy and cigars at Kauai Stores and passed them around. He was jubilant.

---

4. February 1, 1943.

CHAPTER **12**

The Military Blockade

The bombs that blew up the fleet at Pearl Harbor also splintered the growing labor movement in Hawaii. Immediately, military government took over and clamped tight controls on labor.

On December 20, 1941, the military governor issued General Order No. 38 which froze wages as of December 7, 1941. On March 31, 1942, General Order No. 91 reinforced Order No. 38. The normal work schedule was set at eight hours, six days a week, with a 56-hour maximum and time and a half for work in excess of forty-four hours a week. A worker could not quit his job without a release from his employer. If he quit or failed to show up for work, he was subject to trial in a provost court. Upon conviction, he could be fined up to two hundred dollars and jailed up to two months. "Obey, or be punished."

For a while no one protested. A war had erupted; workers had a duty to perform. But after the summer of 1942 and the victory at Midway there was no need to keep labor bound so tightly. Businessmen were prospering; prices were climbing; but workers' wages were frozen. The laboring man claimed he carried an unfair share of the civilian burden.[1]

At the outbreak of war, Ingram M. Stainback, a Tennessee lawyer who had come to Hawaii in 1912, was appointed legal adviser to the military governor. Later, President Roosevelt named Stainback governor and he took office August 24, 1942. He still had his Southern accent (he retained it after living for forty-nine years in Hawaii), and some people called him a "carpetbagger."

Stainback appointed J. (for Joseph) Garner Anthony as his attorney general. Anthony, a Philadelphia lawyer, had come to Hawaii in 1928. Both he and Stainback recoiled at the power of the military. Stainback called the military governor "The Man on the White Horse." He asked Anthony to submit a report on the state of the civilian government and Anthony replied there was no such thing: on December 7, 1941, Poindexter had "virtually abdicated" his office. The two of them, Stainback and Anthony, went to Washington to talk to Secretary of Interior Harold Ickes. "The business before us is the emancipation of Hawaii," Ickes told them.

But few civilians in Hawaii were protesting; they accepted military *diktat*. Compared to the mainland, Hawaii was well off. Only liquor, gasoline, and tires were rationed: a quart of liquor a week and ten gallons of gas a month. They were living "off the fat of the land," said Anthony, and had exchanged their most precious possession—their liberties, guaranteed under the Bill of Rights—"for meat, butter, Kleenex and liquor."

The Establishment regarded Anthony with distaste. It put pressure on his law partners, the law firm of Robertson, Castle & Anthony, and threatened to take the firm's legal work away if Alexander G. M. Robertson, the senior partner, didn't "straighten out" Anthony. Anthony got some support: from Joseph R. Farrington, the delegate to Congress, and from the

---

1. Before the war broke out, unionization had been moving at a gallop. Longshoremen, brewery workers, teamsters, bartenders, hotel workers, dairy workers, taxi drivers, and metal tradesmen had signed up and a start had been made in the organization of the sugar and pineapple industries. Union membership approached the 10,000 figure on the day the bombs dropped. In the first year of the war membership fell to less than 4000.

maverick Rutledge, but he was baffled because he got so little help from labor. He said labor gave "supine acquiescence" to military control. It troubled him that the militant ILWU was silent.

But it was plain that most people agreed with Walter F. Dillingham, Hawaii's biggest industrialist, who said that the public approved of strict control of labor in wartime. Maybe a few lawyers (Anthony, Fred Patterson, Eugene Botts, Sr.) might say, "My God, we ought to maintain the rights of American citizens, and all that sort of hooey that nobody cared about." The job was to get on with the job, said Dillingham. And if that meant clamping down on labor, so be it.

Kawano, the wartime ILWU longshore leader in Honolulu, asked for a wage raise for longshoremen to meet the rising cost of living. Randolph Sevier, president of Castle & Cooke Terminals, replied that the company would be "subject to severe criticism" if it defied the military and granted a raise. The stevedores then were getting seventy-five cents an hour. The longshore wage in San Francisco at the time was $1.15.

In the early days of the war Cliff O'Brien, the ILWU lawyer Bridges sent over from San Francisco, was the CIO member of the Labor Advisory Council working with Hawaii's military government. He thought he might play a role in the war effort, but he found that the council was "a joke."

The military governor appointed Ernest C. Gray as controller of waterborne traffic. Gray not only determined priorities and ship movements but had authority over stevedoring operations. O'Brien, known for his eloquence, thought at first he could persuade Gray to be fair to the unions, but he soon wrote Harry Bridges that that hope was "rudely and quite definitely shattered." The military didn't want to hear from O'Brien or from any other union official.

On the waterfront there was a shortage of winchmen, hatch tenders, foreman checkers, riggers and jitney operators, cargo carrier and crane men. Plantation workers were pressed into service, but they remained on the plantation payrolls and were paid by the army, the navy, or the shipowners. The ILWU was not recognized as the bargaining representative for these "borrowed" workers and this arrangement worked to the advantage of the plantations.

O'Brien decided that under the military government unions would do well to hold their own "and keep locals together."

He realized there was no point in staying in Hawaii; he could do nothing for union people. He went home. Kawano kept in touch.

On Kauai in particular the union outlook was hopeless: "No leadership. Morale very low," said Kawano. The hard work of organizing at Port Allen and Ahukini had come to naught. Union men were in the minority among workers at both ports. The best the union could hope for was to extend its contracts for another year. In Hilo, Harry Kamoku, the mainstay of the longshoremen, went into the army. Kawano and other union leaders of Japanese descent found they were suspect because they were Japanese. Even though he was the local longshore president, he could not go down to the docks unless somebody called for him.

On Kauai the military paid longshoremen fifty cents an hour, the minimum laborer's wage, to build a landing strip at Barking Sands. Izuka wrote O'Brien and Howard E. Durham, special representative of the United States Department of Labor in Honolulu. For doing that, Izuka was branded "a troublemaker." In February 1942, when Izuka was working at Barking Sands, Kauai Police Chief Edwin Crowell and an FBI agent called on him. They told him they knew he had consulted with Jack Hall, O'Brien, and Kawano. Izuka knew a storm was coming.

He was summoned to Crowell's office on April 11, 1942. Bored and hungry, he waited for six hours. Finally, the three members of the Kauai Office of Civil Defense (OCD) came out.[2] Caleb Burns, the OCD chairman, beckoned toward Izuka and two aliens who also had been called. "Lock 'em up," he said.

Izuka was taken to the county jail at Wailua, held incommunicado for a week, and then brought before a civil defense hearing board. An army major questioned him; the three OCD

2. All three were sugar plantation managers: C. E. S. Burns of Lihue Sugar Company; Hector Moir of Kohala Sugar; and Lindsay Faye of Kekaha Sugar.

members sat in judgment. The major claimed that Izuka had distributed leaflets at Barking Sands advocating strikes and slowdowns.

Izuka denied it. To him the charge was ridiculous. At the time he was a staunch Communist and the Communist Party was straining every muscle to help defeat Hitler. Izuka was just following party orders: Do everything to help raise production.

He was found guilty and held in an army camp for 123 days. When he got out on August 23, 1942, he couldn't get a job. He couldn't go back to the docks because the navy wouldn't give him a pass. He came to Honolulu. Ironically, he was released into the custody of Jack Hall. He had to report to Hall regularly and Hall had to attest to his loyalty to the United States.

During his career with the Wage and Hour Division, Hall kept up his labor contacts. He was in touch with Rutledge and Kawano; they came to him for advice and he helped map out strategy for them. He wrote a statement on sugar wages which Kawano presented to an Agricultural Adjustment Administration hearing in Honolulu on September 14, 1943. He put the finishing touches to the "Kawano Plan" for better utilization of manpower on the waterfront. Hall called it the Bridges Plan with "a few local touches."[3]

Kawano presented the plan to John R. Mead, the military government's director of the Office of Labor Control. He pointed out that the antiquated system of hiring on the waterfront hobbled the war effort. Often one stevedoring company was swamped with work while another was twiddling its thumbs. Why not organize a central labor pool and transfer longshoremen as they were needed?

American Stevedores, Ltd., a longshore company set up to handle war cargo exclusively, immediately agreed. McCabe,

---

3. The Bridges Plan was the ILWU effort to speed unloading of ships. Soldiers could not do the work—they lacked the skill. Bridges suggested dispatching longshore teams to speed the critical turnaround of ships. The ILWU enthusiastically supported the National CIO promise from its affiliates to push for victory. "We are pledged that for the duration of the war there will be no strikes by any single member or local of this union," said Bridges.

Hamilton & Renny said it would consider the plan; Castle & Cooke Terminals turned it down.

Labor's cup of bitterness finally overflowed. On March 22, 1944, the AFL Teamsters Union issued a "Memorandum on Military Control," saying there was no foundation in law for the establishment of military control over labor in the territory; that the Labor Control Office was antilabor; and that the office approved the intimidation of organized labor. It cited Izuka as a case in point and accused the military of killing the labor movement on Kauai:

> We are convinced that the Office of the Military Governor is biased against unions and negligent of labor. . . . We consider the military incompetent to administer labor in Hawaii.

The memorandum may have done some good. In June 1944, a Territorial War Labor Board was set up and Rutledge was named as the board's labor representative. Rutledge was always brazen. Even during the most arrogant days of military control, he would not hold his tongue. When some bar owners ignored their contracts with his bartenders' union, he threatened to picket the most flagrant offenders. The word got to the military and a military aide called on Rutledge. "Do it [picket]," he said, "and you'll get a bayonet up your ass."

CHAPTER 13
Two Who Persisted

Things went so badly for labor unions during the first two years of the war that Arnold Wills, the head of the NLRB office in Hawaii, commented: "There isn't any [labor movement]. There's just one man running loose."

He meant Art Rutledge but he was overlooking McElrath. After Pearl Harbor McElrath shipped out until mid-1942 on the *Kilauea*. He sailed the "South Seas run" to Palmyra, Canton Island, Christmas Island. "I was on a ship, in and out, in and out, and you never knew when you were going to leave," he said.

Then McElrath got off the ship and began to work for Inter-Island in Honolulu as a machinist. Inter-Island had a contract with the AFL Metal Trades Council and John A. Owens, a roly-poly AFL organizer, announced magnanimously that labor was going to give up its holidays for the duration of the war and not collect overtime. That irked McElrath: speak for yourself, John. He told the company: "You work us holidays and you pay us overtime."

McElrath believed that the workers should forge themselves into a militant union—the only union he thought could succeed—and so he began the job. He guessed that the company would hear about it and give them a wage increase "to buy us off." It was a good prediction. The company gave them a ten-cent raise. At the next workers' meeting, McElrath said, "That's only a down payment," and they negotiated another ten-cent raise on top of that.

In February 1943, McElrath, Joe Perry, and Ernie Arena organized the Marine Engineers and Drydock Workers Association (Independent). Perry was a timekeeper in the machine shop.

Arena was a mechanic and toolkeeper. He looked like a local boy, but he was the San Francisco-born son of an Italian father and a Mexican mother.

"Bob and I decided to form an industrial union," said Arena. They talked it over with Hall at his home in Kaimuki. Arena admired Hall's lightning brain, but he was constantly amazed at Hall's mechanical ineptitude. "He couldn't drive a nail into the wall."

The drydock workers also organized the American Can Company and the shipyard division of the Hawaiian Tuna Packers. The three unions had more than five hundred members. McElrath had been deferred from military service as a person essential to the war effort. Now the job of labor leader had become so big that he couldn't handle it part-time. He took a leave of absence to work full time as the drydock workers' executive secretary. The chairman of the War Labor Board told the draft board that McElrath was "a stabilizing influence" on labor relations.

Labor organizers in those days "looked for the bulls"—the two or three key persons in a plant that the rest of the workers respected. "You'd sign them up—just like that," said McElrath. "Surprise the employers. We signed up the vast majority of the Hawaiian Pineapple [cannery] workers in 1944 in just two days."

Like many men small in stature, McElrath had drive and ambition. Like many of the early labor leaders, he was a hard drinker. He had a quick mind; he could write. He had a good feel for a word that would catch the eye and a phrase that would draw attention. He could be caustic as lime and managed to set people's teeth on edge just by the grating tone of his voice. For twelve years he had a fifteen-minute radio commentary program for the ILWU. He was assigned the radio job because there was no one else in the union, except Hall, who could handle it. McElrath expected to take abuse and he did. For many he was the man you loved to hate.

"You take on the status quo, it's going to fight back," he said. "We cost these employers hundreds of millions of dollars they wanted to keep."

Often the employers' target was McElrath, whom they called

"The Songbird of the ILWU." They were wary of him. "I always felt I had to be doubly on guard in any conversation with him," said Howard C. Babbitt, a C. Brewer & Company official. Babbitt used one word to described McElrath: abrasive. "He made the employers sore as hell," said Philip P. Maxwell, a labor negotiator for the Hawaii Employers Council.

Longshoremen who couldn't pronounce McElrath's name called him "Make[1] Rat." He didn't mind; employers called him worse names than that. Bridges didn't speak to him for a year. McElrath survived it all. He knew how to endure.

Labor had a good friend indeed in Arnold Leonard Wills, the NLRB director in Hawaii. "Len," as he liked to be called, was a gangling New Zealander who opened a one-room office in June 1938 in the Federal Building on King Street. He had only one employee (for two years it was Yoshiko Hall), but he helped labor take giant strides. He was an old-fashioned liberal—"a very moral person," McElrath described him.

Wills handled federal labor-management relations for sixteen stormy years. He helped unions obtain NLRB certification and he settled thousands of unfair labor practices cases. But just as important, he instructed unskilled labor officials how to handle themselves in their relations with employers. Wills was a Norman Thomas type of socialist who leaned so strongly toward the side of labor that he antagonized management but became a hero to the unions. He did not, of course, draw up ILWU policy. The ILWU already had an elaborate structure for setting policy. But for a time—until they came to a parting of the ways—one of his best friends was Jack Hall.

Wills said his job was to see to it that the National Labor Relations Act (signed by President Roosevelt on July 5, 1935) was used effectively. Section 7 of the act said that "Employees shall have the right to self-organization, to form, join, or assist labor organizations, to bargain collectively through representatives of their own choosing. . . ."

Wills was appalled that, as he saw it, hundreds of workers in

1. Pronounced "mah-kay." Dead, in Hawaiian.

Hawaii wanted to join a union but were afraid to. "They act . . . like scared rabbits who have just heard the sound of the hunter's gun," he said.

Wills ran a school for fledgling union leaders. Often they were young Orientals with only grade-school education and they were tongue-tied in the presence of *haole* employers. "Look, keep records," Wills said to them.

> When you talk to management about a grievance, take notes. That's how you make a case. When you come in here with a complaint, I want to know what you said; what he said. . . . Write down the minutes of what you do and how you do it. . . . Now, what else do you need to know?

He taught business agents how to make out reports, and if they couldn't do it themselves he did it for them. If management complained that he was overstepping his bounds, he responded: "Look, you have all those fancy lawyers and whatnot, and here is this little business agent over here. I'm going to help him."

When a bright young man named Thomas P. Gill came home from law school, Wills called Rutledge. "Look, you need somebody to do your book work for you. Why don't you hire Gill?" Rutledge did. It was the start of a lifetime friendship between Rutledge and Gill.

Management resented Wills, though they conceded he was doing a good job for government, "I used to get teed off at him because I felt he had a strong, anti-employer bias," said Dwight C. Steele of the Hawaii Employers Council.

Most union men loved Wills. "He was the guy that helped us organize," said Yasuki Arakaki of Olaa. "I don't think we could have done very much without him," said Kawano. "He was a great friend of labor," said Berman.[2]

Wills spoke out against the freezing of workers to their jobs

---

2. Wills didn't impress all union men. The salty ILWU organizer Frank Thompson told Wills to mind his own business. He said Wills gave "bum advice" to Arakaki on the Big Island and to Joe Kaholokula on Maui. "They have been pretty well screwed up by old man Wills," said Thompson. "And also a large part of Art Rutledge's bum ideas have been coming from him."

during the war. He had a hard word for management: "In the old days when the Boss *[sic]* was Lord of Creation, he felt secure, except when even his unorganized employees went on strike. When they organized he was fearful. When they did it boldly, he was scared to death."

Yet when Robertson, the ILWU International vice-president, declared at the top of his voice that "the boss is a bastard!" Wills heatedly rebutted him. "This is thoroughly negative, destructive and anti-social type of instruction," Wills said. "It is not founded on American trade unionism, but, on the contrary, is the thinking of the apostles of class war." Wills said the ILWU picked no quarrel with the bosses during the war. The enemies, he said, were the Nazis and the Fascists.

The friendship between Hall and Wills was wrecked on the reef of politics. At first Wills used to visit Hall at his home on 18th Avenue. They trusted each other; they traded ideas. Later the trust eroded and they stopped seeing one another.[3]

It all came about because Wills, though he was a strong liberal, was also strongly anti-Communist. He knew Hall and other ILWU leaders were members of the Communist Party. "I give you credit," he once said. "You stick your neck out for the workers." He regarded Hall with amusement. "You'll never make a good Communist, Jack," he said. "You've got a conscience."

By the late 1940s Wills had become disillusioned with Hall and with the ILWU, not only because of his dislike of the Communist Party but also because his advice to the ILWU often went unheeded. The ILWU didn't take advice from anyone. It made up its own mind. Wills accused Hall of using the plantation workers as a power base "and leading them down the primrose path."

By this time relations between the two had pretty much ruptured. Wills called the Communist Party of Hawaii "a secret, conspirational" society. He said the Party had injected itself in-

---

3. Hall wanted to hire Wills. Wills was said to have replied: "Jack, do you think I am going to spit my $13,000 salary out of this window just to take orders from you guys? If I work for the ILWU, I will give the orders."

to the Port Allen strike of 1937. Wills, the Socialist and friend of the working man, was gravely concerned about the power he thought the Communist Party was exerting over labor in Hawaii.

CHAPTER **14**

Rutledge the Irrepressible

Art Rutledge first came to Hawaii in 1934. He was tending bar in a nightclub in Seattle and there was a glorified painting of Waikiki on the wall: beach and ocean, girls and sunshine. "I was struck by all the sunshine," he said, thinking of the rain in Seattle in the fall. One night he stayed up all night listening to Hawaiian music and decided to leave town for a while.

He went to Victoria, British Columbia, boarded the *Empress of Japan,* and arrived in Honolulu on October 25, 1934, along with Babe Ruth and Lou Gehrig, who were on their way to Japan to play ball. Rutledge stayed five days.

Unfortunately, he had overlooked something—namely, that he was an alien on probation for bootlegging and that he had made "an entry without inspection," as the Immigration and Naturalization Service called it. In other words, an illegal entry.[1]

---

1. Rutledge was born Avrom Rotleider in Lublin, Poland, on January 2, 1906. He was brought to the United States as a child on September 11, 1913. He was convicted on August 16, 1930, in King County Court (Seattle) of "possession of intoxicating liquor," fined $250, and given a sixty-day suspended sentence. He was convicted of violating the National Prohibition Act (the Volstead Act) on December 21, 1932, and sentenced to twelve months and fined $500, with the sentence suspended for five years on payment of the fine. He had paid court costs and $10 on the fine when he came to Honolulu in October 1934 under an alias.

Rutledge came back once again to Hawaii before he returned in 1938 to stay permanently. He did not remember the date, but he recalled vividly the police role in the episode. The police had a bench warrant issued out of the Federal District Court in Seattle summoning Rutledge to a hearing to show cause why his suspended sentence for bootlegging should not be revoked.

"The police were a very tight corporation," Rutledge said. "There's a stranger in town. They figure, 'Who the hell are you?' They tried to get something on me. They threw my ass in jail. They began to ask questions."

In jail Rutledge screamed about his constitutional rights. He told the police he was working for Fawcett Publications and was "going to write it all up." He made waves and may even have impressed them. No one laid a hand on him. They escorted him down to the *President Hoover* and got him out of town.

The show cause hearing was held in Seattle on March 21, 1935. "There was nothing to it," said Rutledge. "I went before the judge and he said I can't leave town." The bench warrant was quashed after Rutledge agreed to pay the remainder of his fine. He paid a hundred dollars forthwith and agreed to pay the balance—and to behave.

Between 1935 and 1952, however, he was arrested twenty-three times. The immigration officials cited that fact and the bootleg charge as grounds for denying Rutledge citizenship and maybe even deporting him.[2] But the arrests were for piddling things—offenses such as blackout violations, "loitering, being told to move and not moving, and everything else under the sun," said Jack Burns, the police detective. "The police were rousting him." The arrests were the price Rutledge paid for being a forceful labor leader.

In 1938 Rutledge's period of probation ran out and he was free to return to Hawaii. He was tending bar in San Francisco and was a member of Local 41 of the bartenders' union. His commitment to the union cause had begun back in 1934 when he heard a fellow on the docks in Seattle "gesticulating and screaming" to a crowd of workers. He didn't know who the man was or

---

2. Rutledge was naturalized on September 8, 1960.

what he was saying because he was too far away to catch the words, but he liked the way the man behaved. The speaker was Harry Bridges.

In Hawaii Rutledge lived a frugal life. He shared a room with a former chief petty officer at Nuuanu Avenue and Pauahi Street for which they paid four dollars a week. Rutledge filled up on two bowls of *saimin* (noodle soup) a day at fifteen cents a bowl. He got a job as a bartender at the White Palace on Hotel Street.[3] Albert K. "Alky" Dawson, a boxer, was the bartenders' business agent. He came around to collect dues ($1.50 a month), and being a good sport he sometimes used the money to set up drinks for the house.

One day the fleet came in and the bartenders decided they wanted a raise. They went on strike. But when it came to picketing, Rutledge found he was walking the picket line by himself: "a general without an army." He needed help so he went looking for Weisbarth, the labor movement's muscleman. He walked over to the *Voice of Labor* office in the Campbell Building on King Street. There he met a tall man "smoking a big cigar" (Berman) and a taller fellow "skinny as a beanpole" (Hall). Rutledge outlined the case. The skinny fellow spoke up: "Gee, that's a perfect setup! We can take over."

The scene etched itself on Rutledge's mind. All his life he remembered his introduction to Hall: "I can hear him saying: 'We can take over!' I didn't know then what he was talking about, but the thing that stuck in my craw when I found out afterwards was what 'taking over' meant. It meant I couldn't trust him."

Of course, that was what Hall said all his life about Rutledge: that *he* couldn't trust Rutledge. "Mr. Irresponsible . . . erratic, unpredictable," he called Rutledge.

Most of the ILWU officialdom, with one curious exception, detested Rutledge. That exception was Bridges, the man Rutledge had heard haranguing a crowd in 1934. Bridges had a sneaking admiration for Rutledge. In the 1949 longshore strike Bridges asked Rutledge to walk the picket line with him and

---

3. It was then on Hotel. It later moved to Nuuanu.

Rutledge did. Predictably, it made the front page and Rutledge knew it would. He loved publicity.

"We marched up and down," said Bridges. "There was just Rutledge and me. They could have arrested us and they could have dumped us. We didn't know what was going to happen."

Bridges had a soft spot in his heart for Rutledge. He looked upon Rutledge this way:

> If we didn't have an Art Rutledge down there to make a billing *[sic]* for all of our failures, we would have to invent him. Rutledge is a tough, rough guy. He is an operator. He is a maneuverer. He's not trustworthy. But he got in there in a rough, tough time when he was needed—at my request. And you can't take that away from him. I have always got along with Rutledge.

The ILWU tried to work out a *modus vivendi* with Rutledge. "You got dibs on hotels on Oahu and leave the rest to us on the outside," Bridges said. "And Jack Hall always claimed he reached such a deal with Rutledge and Rutledge always said it was a goddamned lie and he never agreed to such a thing."

Rutledge called the ILWU "a cannibal union." Anytime they made a pact, "it's to get in bed with you," he said. He and Hall fought for years—the Hatfields and the McCoys of the labor movement, a newspaperman called them. Yet in the early days, though they were wary of each other, they were friends. Hall gave Rutledge advice. He drafted strategy for Rutledge. Rutledge helped support the *Kauai Herald* and the *Herald*. For a time he even put Hall up at his home on Kapiolani Boulevard.

The bartenders' union was floundering and the members asked Rutledge to take over. He only had a ninth-grade education, but he was a talkative fellow with a quick mind. He was also an actor: scowling one minute, laughing the next—"Edward G. Robinson in the role of labor leader."

"Look, I'll take the responsibility, but not the job," Rutledge told the bartenders. In June 1939 he became business agent of Local 5 (Hotel and Restaurant Employees and Bartenders International Union). Local 5 began organizing the Moana and Royal Hawaiian Hotels in December 1940 and the Alexander Young Hotel in February 1941. Rutledge took in dairy workers in April 1943; in September 1943 Teamster units at American Factors and Theo. H. Davies & Co. joined in. He wore two hats—hotel workers' boss and Teamster boss.

When Hall was a wage and hour inspector during the war, Rutledge made use of him. They held long sessions until midnight and one in the morning. Hall would hear him out, turn to the typewriter, and write out a position paper for Rutledge. Hall was smart, Rutledge conceded, "but he couldn't hold his liquor. He'd fall apart. . . . He was very emotional inside and soft as butter with people, but he had to create this rough, tough image on the outside."

Rutledge filled a vacuum. He built an image of a gutty, though quixotic, labor leader. In August 1943, he told the Waikiki Rotary Club that labor had started a "mild revolution" in Hawaii. A businessman cornered Rutledge after the talk. "You seem to have a chip on your shoulder," he said. Always quick on the comeback, Rutledge retorted: "If you had been through what I have in the last year or so, you wouldn't have a chip on your shoulder—you'd have a sledgehammer in both hands."

In 1943 Rutledge got a $125-a-month raise for the dairy workers at Hind-Clark Dairies and his stock jumped. "It was like a one-horse race," he said. "One horse in a race looks like a champion. I had no opposition so people were coming around."

By then he had come up with a formula for conducting labor war. As he explained:

> If you study the history of Art Rutledge, you'll find that I always had . . . short hit-and-run strikes—to consolidate the position. I'd figure out a way to get back on the job before I leave, see?

And if he lost a battle with an employer, that did not mean he had lost the war. He warned his momentarily victorious opponent:

> If you think we're going to sign a document because we're so goddamned weak and twist our arm and force us to live within conditions you impose upon us, you're crazy. The first time I think I can beat you, I'll try. Because the war isn't over.

"You see, with a company you can slow them down," said Rutledge. "The boss doesn't know what the hell happened."

It hits them two months afterward. I had nobody to back me up. I had nothing to negotiate with—except my wits, my personality and the confidence of the people to do what I asked them to do and be obnoxious to the employers. That's all I had to peddle.

For a time Rutledge's ambition soared like a bird. "I could have taken over if I had three good guys with me. But how much can one man do?"

Rutledge had the theatrical touch. In 1946 he told his Honolulu Rapid Transit bus drivers to refuse to collect fares from passengers. The HRT lost $9180 in fares and Rutledge and Henry Gonsalves, the Teamster business agent, stood trial for conspiracy. The government failed to prove criminal intent and they were acquitted. When the verdict came in after twelve hours of deliberation, Rutledge wept.

On Sunday, July 21, 1946, Rutledge met with Hall to talk over his bold plan for a "utility strike." Through the Teamster drivers, he had entry into the Mutual Telephone Company, the Honolulu Gas Company, the Hawaiian Electric Company, and, of course, the Rapid Transit. Robertson, David Thompson, and Frank Thompson, all of the ILWU, were present.

Frank Thompson listened in disbelief. Rutledge amazed him. "A first-class, double-talk" artist, Thompson called him. Thompson wrote his impressions of Rutledge: "During certain sane moments of our discussions with him, we were able to determine that he is fascinated with the idea . . . of getting control of all the utilities in Honolulu . . . in order to throw his weight around. . . ."

Thompson said Rutledge thought he could break the Employers Council, which had set up shop in Hawaii in 1943. He said Rutledge intended to call a general strike on August 1 and stay out on strike until the companies capitulated and dropped the "three clauses" which the companies insisted be part of their union contracts.[4]

The three clauses were part of labor contracts all over the

---

4. (1) No strikes, no lockouts; (2) no discrimination; and (3) the discharge clause, which enabled the employer to suspend or fire employees who refused to perform work assigned to them or refused to cross a picket line.

country. "Rutledge has no other demands other than these and it is probable that in no other place in the world would he get away with such shenanigans, except in Hawaii," said Thompson.

Thompson feared—correctly—that Rutledge had aroused people against labor. He predicted—incorrectly—Rutledge's imminent downfall.

Rutledge enjoyed being in hot water: bad guys make news; good guys seldom do.[5] We, the Women, a vocal and determined group, invited Rutledge to attend a meeting at the YWCA on Richards Street on the subject of the threatened utility strike. It was a challenge Rutledge could not refuse.

He attended and tried to speak. Two hundred women catcalled, booed, and hissed. Thelma Akana, a legislator, shook her finger in Rutledge's face. "I don't want you to say a thing," she admonished. "Are we going to or aren't we going to have a strike? I want the answer."

She almost backed Rutledge off the stage, but he stubbornly refused to answer yes or no. (He didn't know the answer himself at the moment.) Finally he said grandly, "I leave it up to you" and moved away. As he walked out, an old lady, shaking with rage, aimed a kick at his backside. "I'll bet that's the highest she had her leg in sixty years," said Rutledge.

Hal F. Hanna, a legislator from Maui, called Rutledge a disgrace to the labor movement. "He wants to paralyze the whole island," he said. In contrast, said Hanna, look at Hall and other CIO leaders. They offered "real leadership and sound reasoning. The boys of the CIO don't go off half-cocked."

That was in mid-1946. "The ILWU was respectable then," said Rutledge. "I was the only bastard running around."

---

5. Rutledge's audacity was legendary. The writer attended a meeting at the Employers Council at which both sides were to sign a hard-fought agreement. The two sides entered and sat down on opposite sides of the table. Silence reigned. Then Rutledge spoke up: "Ready for your screwing?" he said.

CHAPTER 15

Kawano Sends a Plea

In October 1943 things began to happen: Jack Owens of the AFL organized the workers at Waiakea sugar mill right under the nose of the militant Hilo ILWU longshoremen. That alarmed Bert Nakano, secretary of Longshore Local 1-36, who sent an urgent message to Kawano: "Come down here. I think we can organize the plantations."

Nakano and Kawano wrote Bridges and Goldblatt. Nakano pleaded for a qualified CIO director to come to Hawaii and work full time "if we wish to stay ahead of the AFL. The plantations are ripe."

Kawano agreed with Owens' strategy; it was exactly what he had in mind. Start with the sugar mills. Sugar was a steady industry; there was little turnover of personnel. Sugar mill workers were industrial workers and came under the National Labor Relations Act. Finally, according to Kawano, sugar mill workers, pay was "terrible"—as little as 33⅓ cents an hour.

Kawano told Goldblatt that Owens had had no trouble signing up the Waiakea mill workers. Management did not object. Owens had even had the help of the camp police. It appeared as though management was glad to assist anyone but the ILWU.

Kawano predicted a big dogfight coming up between the AFL and the CIO-ILWU. Owens' boldness flabbergasted him. The AFL didn't even have an officer on the Big Island and yet, as though thumbing their nose, they had rented a hall across from the longshoremen's office and had gone to work. Kawano had to admit Owens had got the jump on the ILWU. Waiakea, he figured, was just the start.

Kawano had no organizers to spare; his funds were limited. He decided the only hope was to make use of "the more progressive . . . faction of the AFL." He meant Rutledge. Kawano said he had "always worked closely" with Rutledge. He had no illusions about Rutledge (nor did Rutledge about Kawano), but for the moment, in this time of crisis, Rutledge might be valuable. "While he's an opportunist, he's always behaved nicely," said Kawano.

Kawano, Rutledge, and Hall got together. Hall outlined a plan. Basically, it was this: Kawano and Rutledge would go together to the Big Island and announce the formation of a "Hawaii Federation of Labor." It would be independent, neither AFL nor CIO (ILWU). Those who signed up would be channeled later into the AFL or the ILWU according to a simple formula. Everything "on wheels" would go to Rutledge and his AFL Teamsters. Everything else would go to the ILWU. Rutledge was to use his influence to swing the Waiakea mill workers around—first to the independent union, then to the ILWU.

Kawano talked not only with Hall but also with Kimoto, head of the Communist Party in Hawaii. Kawano claimed that Hall discouraged him. Kimoto, however, told Kawano to go ahead. Kawano phoned Nakano for reassurance. "This place is ripe," Nakano insisted. "Come on down and take a look."

Rutledge also felt that the plantation workers were crying out for organization, but that the ILWU International disregarded them. "Bridges didn't want them then," Rutledge said.

Rutledge and Kawano were supposed to put up some money for the organizing effort, say a thousand dollars apiece. (Rutledge never did.) The two—an ill-matched pair, one silent and one loquacious—set off on their mission on December 10, 1943. It was Rutledge who explained their mission to the press in Hilo (Hall wrote the press release): "The situation demands organization of all workers on Hawaii into a single, cohesive organization that can act with intelligence and decisiveness."

Right then the partnership came apart. Rutledge was secretary of the AFL Central Labor Council. The council read the Rutledge declaration and on December 13 Ernest Burlem, the council's acting secretary, sent Rutledge a telegram which claimed, in effect, that he was trading with the enemy—namely, the ILWU —and fired him.

Rutledge showed the telegram to Kawano. "What do I do now?" he asked. Kawano said, "Go back to Honolulu and fight." He thanked Rutledge for making a good try. Rutledge said, "Well, I did that to help you fellers *[sic]*. If you think you don't need my help anymore, it's okay with me."

He then went home to face the music, which turned out to be muted. Hall helped Rutledge prepare his defense. Throwing Rutledge out of the AFL meant losing the per capita tax assessed union members. So, after huffing and puffing for a few months, the AFL let the matter slide. It was just another in the series of crises which Rutledge seemed to thrive on. Kawano did not downgrade Rutledge's offer of help, short-lived though it was. Kawano had his own plans to do some big organizing and the trip to Hilo was just the start. "Fortunately, with the aid of Rutledge, we were able to at least chase this guy [Owens] from the Big Island," said Kawano.

By now the message was clear to the ILWU on the West Coast: Hawaii was ready for action. Lou Goldblatt had kept in touch. He sent William G. Craft, a labor organizer, to Hawaii late in 1943 to report. Craft advised the ILWU to move ahead quickly.

There was another pipeline to the ILWU. Servicemen stationed in the islands who were former redhot ILWU members had sent in their appraisals. A sergeant named Roy Gutsch, a former member of San Francisco's Local 6, told Bridges the longshoremen in Hawaii didn't have a hiring hall, a closed shop, or a six-hour day. Nor did they enjoy the uniform workloads, penalty cargoes, and standby pay that West Coast longshoremen had. Gutsch said that hundreds of longshoremen were not organized; that absenteeism was high; and that "men don't show up for work weeks at a time." He recommended that Goldblatt come down and straighten things out. "A man of Lou Goldblatt's type would settle matters in about two or three weeks," he said.

Gutsch met Hall and was not impressed. He made a snap judgment: "He hasn't the head on his shoulders that Jack Kawano has. I don't take much stock in Hall. I may be wrong."

Goldblatt told Kawano how much the ILWU International

appreciated the efforts of island labor leaders who struggled under martial law. Goldblatt said the ILWU was anxious to move ahead into the sugar mills. He said nothing about the agricultural workers; they were not covered by national law. But the ILWU's role was clear:

> We are more than ever convinced that the ILWU should drive full steam ahead on this organizational program. The other problems of labor unity, etc., will be a lot easier in solution once we have built a powerful ILWU base in the islands. Particular attention should be directed toward organization of sugar refineries, warehouses and transport groups connected with them.

Goldblatt sent charter applications and membership blanks to Hawaii. He pointed out that the ILWU had jurisdiction over warehousemen, depot employees, and pineapple and sugar workers, both "in the sheds and the refineries." He laid out the strategy: Don't worry about prewar contracts. Move ahead directly with the organization of workers and "let us handle the problem of jurisdiction." He knew that UCAPAWA—the union Hall had worked for on Kauai—was weak, and if a move to take over UCAPAWA contracts at McBryde and Kauai Pineapple Company were made tactfully, then UCAPAWA, or what remained of it, would not object.

Goldblatt already had stored up considerable knowledge about Hawaii. He was a reader: one of the rare labor leaders in those days with a college education. He had taken graduate work in economics, had registered in law school, and had given serious thought to taking a Doctor of Philosophy degree, but he had dropped out of school and gone into the labor movement. His union activity began in 1934 when he worked in a warehouse in San Francisco. In 1937 Bridges named him to head the CIO in Northern California. In 1942 he left the CIO to go back to the longshore union as a staff member. In 1943 he was elected ILWU International secretary-treasurer.

Goldblatt studied everything he could on Hawaii. He read the reports and wondered, "Why in the devil haven't we made it in Hawaii?" It hadn't been for lack of trying, though he conceded that the ILWU may have been "a trifle neglectful" of the far-off islands. But before the war there was neither the money nor the trained personnel for the job. And during the war there was martial law. Even transportation to Hawaii then was difficult: there was no travel without a military permit. Letters might be censored, so the main contact with Hawaii had to be through seamen, and often they were unreliable.

Kawano asked Goldblatt to come over and see for himself. "I'll bet if Lou came over here, he'll go back with a big story," said Kawano. But if Goldblatt couldn't come, said Kawano, then the ILWU should send a man immediately before "the reactionary AFL guys . . . start giving us more trouble." Kawano stated the job qualifications for the man he had in mind: "We want . . . a good organizer, a good negotiator, and with fairly good political background. And we want him now. Help us build a union over here."

Kawano said the ILWU had everything going for it. It could make a big pitch to the men on the plantations because the ILWU controlled the docks. The key to organizing was the waterfront: If you controlled the docks, then you had the power to organize any industry whose products passed through the docks.

On the plantations, Kawano, the quiet man, was effective. "He got hold of a few of us. We had a meeting at the Catholic gym," said Arakaki of Olaa:

> On the blackboard he explained to us the advantages of joining the ILWU over the AFI . He said: "If you get into the ILWU, you'll get support from the railroad workers [hauling sugar], the dock workers [loading sugar], and even in the refinery [at Crocket]. You will have a connecting link from the sugar producers right up to the refinery. The ILWU will organize everybody from top to bottom. We don't discriminate against any trade."

Goldblatt never had any trouble reading a clear message. The time *was* ripe. He looked around for a man to send to Hawaii to pick a regional director.

CHAPTER 16
The "Missionaries" Come to Hawaii

A group of longshoremen, many of whom knew more about shooting pool than they did about labor organizing, spark-plugged the big buildup of the ILWU in Hawaii.

One day in February 1944, Jack Kawano walked over to the pool hall on Iwilei Drive from Local 1-37's headquarters and told the pool players to put down their cues and come with him. They followed him to their meeting hall. He told them the union was gaining strength but it could all go down the drain if legislators passed bills unfavorable to labor. "You stopped a pool game to tell us that?" said Jack Osakoda, a small, blunt, young stevedore from Maui.

Kawano said the only way the union could protect its gains was to organize the plantations where the big concentrations of workers were. If the union controlled the labor vote on the Neighbor Islands and in rural Oahu, it could offset the Honolulu vote. He said the longshoremen would start an organizing drive on the plantations. "Let's do it," said Osakoda.

Kawano took the money from the longshore treasury. He asked the stevedoring companies for permission to pull some men off the waterfront on leave of absence on union business. He obtained six days' leave for eight men. He held a meeting, told them where to go, how to approach the workers, and what to say. The eight he selected, all of them from the longshore Executive Board, were Simeon Bagasol, Joe "Blurr" Kealalio, John Elias, Yoroku Fukuda, Ben Kahaawinui, William Paaoa-oa, James Tanaka, and the outspoken Osakoda. They each got ten dollars a day. Kawano named Fukuda to head the group. Fukuda was a thin-faced, bat-eared man from Maui who worked at

Castle & Cooke Terminals. "We were just a bunch of amateurs," he said.

On the day of departure, February 18, Kawano assigned Fred Kamahoahoa, the local's secretary-treasurer, to go along. Kamahoahoa was sleeping off a drunk when his secretary called him. "Hey, you're going to Hilo," she said. She helped him get dressed and called a taxi and Kamahoahoa, somewhat hung over, was driven to the pier to join the team aboard the *Hualalai*. "See that Fred doesn't drink in Hilo," she admonished. That stung him. He was now on official union business. "I couldn't drink then," he said. "I felt a responsibility."

The men shot craps to pass the time. Osakoda was seasick but recovered when the ship docked at Hilo. Nakano was there to meet them. They registered at the old Okino Hotel and Nakano took them out for a meal at the Motor Inn and left. Some of them were eating ice cream cones when they walked out.

A big marine came up to Osakoda and asked him where to get something to eat. Osakoda recommended the Motor Inn. The marine picked Osakoda up by the lapels. "You ain't kidding me?" he said. Osakoda shoved the ice cream cone in his face.

A police officer happened by and took the eight "missionaries," as some of them called themselves, into custody. "You weren't in town for four hours and here you were in the police station," said Nakano. At the police station the officers looked at the husky, six-foot marine and the 115-pound Osakoda and decided it was an uneven match and let them go.

Hall came down to the hotel and Kamahoahoa introduced him to the men. The work began next day. They rented cars and Joe Blurr borrowed one of Doc Hill's trucks. Half the team went south; the other half drove west along the Hamakua Coast. They carried 3-by-4-inch white cards that said: "This Is The Law." A message pointed out that the National Labor Relations Act gave workers the right to organize. The cards were merely "declarations of intent," the first formal step on the road to union organization.

It all went well. Workers were fed up with controls and chafing under military rule. They were hungry for better pay and better working conditions. The longshoremen found they didn't have to do a lot of persuading.

At Pahala, Blurr's team nosed around the plantation and went to the barbershop. They introduced themselves and talked about wages and fair treatment. In no time they had twenty customers. They gave each the white card. "We came back the following morning and we had about ninety-five percent of them signed up," said Joe Blurr. "It went like wildfire."

"There was no problem at all," said Elias. He was a Kauai-born Portuguese who spoke mainland English, so many people didn't know he was an islander and thought he was "foreign."

"There was no opposition," said Blurr. "We came in and went out. They didn't even know we were there by the time we left." "The people were very friendly," said Tanaka. "Everyone was more curious than aggressive."

At Laupahoehoe, Fukuda engaged the mill engineer in a little *hoomalimali*—flattery—while Osakoda slipped in. By the time the chat was over, Osakoda had gone through the mill, talked to the workers, and left the cards. "We used the decoy system," said Fukuda. Mission complete, Osakoda came out and ran into a tall *haole* wearing leggings. "He smelled 'plantation boss,' " said Osakoda.

"Just a minute," said the man, who was Robert Allen Hutchinson, one of the "Scotch Coast" plantation managers. "What are you doing in the mill?"

Osakoda decided to bluff it out. He said he was from Honolulu and just wanted to see how they made sugar; that he had got permission to go in and take a look from "a guy who works there." Hutchinson pointed out the plantation office across the street and said that's where you get permission. Sure, said Osakoda, next time he would go to the office.

"I know you guys are organizing," said Hutchinson. He had heard from the other plantations. They all were alert by this time.

The organizers called Kawano to tell him the good news. "They just breezed through—from Hilo to Kohala," Kawano told Goldblatt. Now and then, in presenting their sales talk, the long shoremen got too exuberant. At Olaa Elias flashed a bill-fold packed with twenty-dollar bills. He slapped some of the crisp banknotes on the table. "You're getting $1.30 a day," he said. "Look at what we're making!"

"We took the bait," said Yasu Arakaki, president of the Olaa "Surfriders Athletic Club." (The club had nothing to do with hanging ten on a surfboard; it was a baseball club.) Arakaki had invited the key people in other clubs in Olaa to hear the "missionaries," but he was the dominant personality and he decided to go CIO with the longshoremen.

Osakoda showed mill workers his longshore paycheck. He was getting seventy-five cents an hour—two and a half times what they were averaging. He rubbed it in a little. "Longshoremen don't need no skill," he said. "All you need is a strong back, but look at what I'm getting." He told them that with overtime he earned eighty to a hundred dollars a week. That impromptu ploy did some damage. It gave the sugar workers the impression that if you joined the ILWU, you got longshore wages. "We corrected that later on," said Hall.

The eight men returned to Honolulu and Kawano prepared Phase Two: the mission to Maui. He planned to hold up for a while on Oahu because he didn't feel the island was "ripe for organization" at the moment. First, he said, let's "show up big" on the Neighbor Islands. He had great expectations: the sugar industry had close to sixty thousand workers, including three thousand in the sugar mills. Again he picked a team and on March 8 sent them off. They included Fukuda, Bagasol, Tanaka, Osakoda, and David Kawahara. Osakoda didn't want to go to his home island, however. He was afraid he might hurt his parents. So first he went to see them and explained what he was doing there. "I'm here to get your permission," he said. He was observing the old Japanese custom of filial devotion.

The longshoremen flew to Maui and stayed at the Vineyard Hotel in Wailuku. They started at Maui Agricultural Company at Paia, where Osakoda had been born. He talked to Joe Kaholokula, a welder. "Sounds good," said Kaholokula, "but let me talk to my boss first." His boss was Sam Sniffen, manager of the plantation machine shop and Kaholokula's uncle. Sniffen encouraged the organizers. "Sooner or later the union will be in the picture," he said.

They set up a routine: Kaholokula worked part-time as an usher at the Paia Theatre. He talked to sugar mill workers at work and gave them cards; when they came to the theater at night, he would collect the cards they had signed. Fukuda would drive up in a taxi, keep the cab waiting, rush in and collect the cards, and scoot back to Wailuku. Maui Ag was easy.

At Puunene, Hawaiian Commercial & Sugar Company enforced tight security. The camp police were alert and waiting. The longshoremen worked out a plan with Frank Takahashi, an HC & S employee. It, too, made use of a taxicab. The cab would arrive at Takahashi's house promptly at 7:30 PM. He would be there with four or five others. They'd hold their session, get a briefing on how things were going, and find out who to see. The cab driver was instructed to return at 9:30. "At 9:30 on the dot he'd go cruising by." said Osakoda. "We'd open the door, run out and jump in the cab. They never caught us." Takahashi enjoyed the excitement. "We were young. It didn't matter much," he said.

HC & S was easy, too. Then they ran into their first big roadblock. It was the provost marshal of Maui, Army Major John D. Hagon. The longshoremen went to Lahaina to take on Pioneer Mill Company when word came that the military police wanted to see them at the Wailuku police station. They drove to Wailuku and were ushered into Hagon's office.

"What the hell are you doing here?" he shouted. "You want to be locked up?"

Fukuda assumed the pose of humbleness that an islander of Japanese ancestry often put on in those war days in the face of arrogant authority. It was a type of protective coloration.

"Sir," he said. "What offense have we committed?"

"You want to go into the brig? . . . Did you go down to Kahului Harbor? That's a restricted area. You know very well this is wartime. We don't mess around."

Fukuda protested that they hadn't gone into the harbor area.

Hagon was not to be placated. "You want to go into the army?" he blustered.

"Sir," said Fukuda, "if Uncle Sam wants me to go into the army, we would only be too happy to do it." Osakoda said they were on reserve because they were waterfront workers.

The major considered him for a moment and then pointed to a thick document on his desk which he pretended to be Osakoda's "file." "We don't want strangers like you on Maui," he said. Strangers? Osakoda wondered. He was a native of Maui.

Fukuda said they had their return passes and return tickets and Hagon told them to use them and go home. Fukuda called Kawano and said Hagon had threatened to jail them unless they caught the plane out. Kawano said, "Okay, pack your bags and go back."

When they got back, the union wrote Major General Robert C. Richardson, the military governor, protesting the expulsion of the organizers. Just to make sure the message got across, they sent copies to President Roosevelt, Secretary of War Stimson, Secretary of Interior Ickes, the Selective Service Board, the National Labor Relations Board, and the Office of the Military Governor's Director of Labor Control. Kamahoahoa signed the letters, but Hall wrote the statement.

Richardson replied that the military hadn't interfered with the organizers. He said that "unidentified strangers, including persons of Japanese ancestry," were on Maui and "engaged in uncertain activities in the vicinity of vital installations." He said Hagon called on them "to establish their true identity." The organizers appeared before Hagon voluntarily, he said. At no time were they placed under arrest. "Your representatives were at complete freedom to pursue their organization activities." He said Hagon told them they could leave or carry on and they chose to leave. That certainly was not Fukuda's impression.

It was one of the few unpleasant episodes in the big drive. Kawano was happy. "Send 3000 ILWU applications by air," he wired Goldblatt. "Rush applications for membership blanks," Kamahoahoa wired.

Kawano recapitulated the results: On Hawaii they had organized Pepeekeo, Hilo, Olaa, and Pauuilo sugar mills, the Hawaii Consolidated Railway, and Hawaiian Cane Products (Canec); on Maui, the Puunene, Paia, and Wailuku Sugar Company mills. "To date Local 137[1] contributed all the time, efforts, and money within our power in aiding these plantations in joining the ILWU," he said. "Our local spent over $5,000 for the campaign."

---

1. The hyphen in 1–37 had been dropped by then.

CHAPTER **17**

The "Missionary" Work Goes On

One Sunday morning in April 1944, Kawano and Fukuda, flushed with their success on Maui and Hawaii, called on Major Okada in Waipahu. "What do you think about organizing the union?" Kawano said.

Okada had spent his life at Oahu Sugar Company. As a boy he had lived in Waipahu Camp 16. When he went to Waipahu Elementary School, he worked part-time picking up cane alongside the railroad tracks. When Kawano came to call, Okada was working in the boiling house of Oahu Sugar for $1.25 a day. Yet he hesitated. A union? "That's a very good thing," he said, "but I'm not going to fuss around with a union because they're gonna break us up."

Kawano said, no, the employers wouldn't be able to smash them. What he was talking about, he said, was a big industry-wide union. And he explained to Okada: "We're gonna organize the sugar workers and the pineapple workers. We're gonna lock the ports. If they bring it [sugar] to the waterfront, we got them. If they break us down there, we block them on the mainland.''

All right, Okada said. He accepted some of the white declaration of intention cards and told Kawano and Fukuda to come back in a couple of weeks. Kawano told him to keep the visit secret. "Don't let the boss know. Just the guys in the mill."

Okada looked around for a few trusty friends to help him. He picked Tadashi "Castner" Ogawa and four others. Ogawa was a gut fighter. That's what you needed, Okada figured—a man "who no scare."

On plantations news can travel like a cane fire. George Bromley, Oahu Sugar's boiling house superintendent, called Okada and Ogawa in. "I hear you folks are organizing the union," he said.

Bromley said he wasn't against a union, but he then recited his arguments against the idea: they would have to pay dues which would go to a union headquarters on the mainland. "You'll be a rubber stamp," he said. "Some *malihinis* on the mainland will dictate to you."

The two employees didn't say much; just that they wanted to join a union. Like many Waipahu workers of that day, they were stubborn. Waipahu, it turned out, became the most militant sugar unit on Oahu.

Oahu Sugar, an American Factors plantation, was comparatively easy to organize. Management had put up a lot of *kapu* signs,[1] but it was not hard to get in. "We saw the workers at home or near the store," said Fukuda. "We signed them up—just like that!" said Okada, snapping his fingers. "At Oahu Sugar, when they found out, we had about five hundred over the majority already signed up." He said the Portuguese were the hardest to convince. They had the best jobs.

Soon the men organizing the plantations found out something: the tougher the boss, the easier it was to organize. The easier the boss, the harder it was to organize.

---

1. Taboo, off limits.

At Waialua Sugar Company on Oahu, the plantation manager, John H. Midkiff, Sr., was a friendly man. During the war he had protected the Japanese and they never forgot his kindness. Midkiff, the son of a Baptist preacher, had come to Hawaii in 1917 as wartime food administrator. He had an advantage over many plantation managers: as a boy he had worked in the summer, from dawn to dusk, sixteen hours a day, in the cornfields at Stonington in central Illinois. He knew what back-breaking work was like and sympathized with working people. "Might as well go ahead and organize," he told them.[2]

He asked only one thing of Kawano: don't start with Waialua. Tackle some other plantation on Oahu first. Midkiff advised Kawano to organize under the banner of the AFL or the CIO so that the union members would have the protection of a big national union.

Okada had a simple method of making contact with workers on other plantations. He was a baseball pitcher and he called on ballplayers he knew. At Waialua, it was Mike Nagata. Nevertheless, even though Midkiff was receptive, not all of the management personnel at Waialua were. A superintendent called the three organizers, Okada, Ogawa, and Nagata, into his office and offered each a cigar.

He said, "You know, boys, I'm not against the union but you folks are slowing down production." They listened in silence. "Same old *shibai,*" Okada thought.

Clearly they were running into trouble, so they called on Tony Rania, who worked in the laboratory. Rania wasn't much help, however. Okada said Rania was afraid. Okada then arranged to come down to camp one evening and talk to workers. But when he and Ogawa arrived, the lights were out and the doors were locked. They knocked but no one answered.

Okada had better luck with another Waialua baseball player, second baseman Ghandi Warashina. Ghandi[3] had been a schoolmate of Okada's at Mid-Pacific Institute, which Okada had at-

---

2. Waialua paid workers ten cents more an hour than did other plantations.
3. Warashina's spelling.

tended on an athletic scholarship. Warashina helped "hustle the other leaders," but it wasn't easy. "Most of them were hesitant," Warashina said. "Ten cents higher. That was a big thing in those days."

At Ewa Plantation, Okada's contact was pitcher Mike Ishikazi, a welder. Ishikazi agreed to help him. When the company heard about it and fired him, Okada informed Jack Hall. Hall told Okada to see Arnold Wills, the NLRB man. "Go ahead and organize," said Hall. "We'll see that he gets his job back." Wills went to Ewa Plantation, investigated the case, and Ishikazi was reinstated.

At Waianae, Okada called on another friend, Taro Uyehara. But there, too, workers were apprehensive. When the organizers came to call, they were "out fishing."

The war killed the CIO on Kauai: both UCAPAWA locals (McBryde and Kauai Pineapple) were "smashed by the military." At Ahukini and Port Allen, ILWU Local 1–35 was "practically demolished." The military denied it was their policy to practice union-busting, but it certainly worked out that way. Hall blamed the military commander on Kauai, Lieutenant Colonel Eugene Fitzgerald. He said Fitzgerald told workers they couldn't meet or collect union dues. The tie-up of the military and the plantation officials did the trick. Hall claimed that army intelligence authorities threatened to send elderly Japanese workers to the concentration camp if they became union members.

Takumi "Taku" Akama, a small man with a soft voice, was working for Amfac's Kauai Stores in Lihue in 1944. "I realized if we wanted to get ahead, we would have to organize," he said. He and Yoshikazu Morimoto, another Kauai Stores employee, called on the longshoremen, who gave them some of the white enlistment cards. Then they set up a meeting in a warehouse and the men opted to join the ILWU. "Without knowing what a union was, we started," said Akama. "This was before Honolulu; before they came from the other islands."

They were amateurs. "We didn't know beans about unions,"

said Morimoto. He was a salesman and now he had a real job of selling to do. He handled the west side of Kauai; Santos Barbosa, another salesman, took the east side. "It was easier for them to contact the different plantations that way," said Akama.

One day a longshoreman from Honolulu turned up. It was Elias. He came to Akama's house and said, "I heard you started a union." He asked if he could look at the white cards Akama had collected. By then Akama had about two hundred signed cards. He showed them to Elias. "Oh, that's *our* unit," said Elias. Akama was relieved. "Here, take them," he said, and from then on Elias took over responsibility.

Elias had only a fourth-grade education but he knew how to talk. "I did it almost single-handed," he said. In six days he signed up 284 employees at Lihue Plantation mill. He made headway at Koloa Plantation and at Hawaiian canneries. Elias also signed up majorities at Kekaha Sugar Company and Olokele Sugar Company.

Haruo "Dyna" Nakamoto worked for Lihue Plantation store. He sounded out the workers, but they had mixed feelings about joining a union. Many were against the idea; others figured that if you had to work long hours at short pay, you began to think "something has to be done." Such whispering began late in 1943 and slowly grew louder. By mid-1944 workers were ripe for organizing. The organizers usually went to work late in the afternoon. In those days most workers kept a garden and would spend time there after work. Between the rows of beans, tomatoes, and Chinese cabbage, Dyna called on them. "We moved, once we got started," he said.

The big selling point was the disparity between wages paid by the plantations and wages paid by the Corps of Engineers. The army was building warehouses all over the island and paid unskilled help sixty and seventy-five cents an hour and skilled help as much as $1.25 an hour. Meanwhile, on the plantations, workers were getting nineteen cents an hour plus perquisites (calculated at roughly six cents an hour). It was not hard to make the point: join the union and get better pay.

CHAPTER 18

Meehan Picks Hall

Goldblatt assigned an old pro named Matthew J. Meehan to come to Hawaii and choose a regional director. Matt Meehan was the ILWU International secretary, working out of Seattle, who had organized the ports on the Columbia River for the ILWU. He was a balding, strongly built man with mustache and rimless glasses. He had no time for nonsense.

The ILWU gave him $2250 for expenses, a munificent sum in those days. He arrived March 17, 1944, and announced he had come for an indefinite stay. He said he was setting up offices for the National Maritime Union in Hawaii. "I am here in the interests of both the NMU and the ILWU," he said. Not a word about his mission: selecting the regional director. No use telling the press what it didn't have to know.

Meehan had no sooner gotten off the ship when he saw a familiar face: a colonel on the staff of General Richardson, the military governor. He recognized the colonel as a former lawyer for Standard Oil Company. They greeted each other; the colonel asked him what he was doing in Hawaii and then bluntly told Meehan he didn't want any trouble on the plantations.

Stony-faced, Meehan told the colonel that was a matter to be settled between the union and the employers and "was of no concern to his office. I really layed *[sic]* the cards on the table." The colonel turned to an aide and said loud enough for Meehan to hear: "Lord, when the Big Five learns that Meehan is already here!"

Meehan had his expense money, but he was a frugal man and objected to paying $4.50 a day for a room. After he looked around, he decided that Honolulu was the most expensive place under the American flag. He saw servicemen paying $5 to sleep on a cot in a room with four others. They cheerfully paid $2.50 for a "four-bit meal and [they] leave a buck tip." Salaries were outrageous. "Office girls get at least $200 a month. Any white man that doesn't get at least $150 per month is nuts." Fantastic, he thought. Honolulu in wartime.

He solved the rooming problem by staying with the Reineckes on Pahoa Avenue. They always provided room (even if it was just on the floor) for visiting firemen from the unions. Reinecke found Meehan "an Irish type," pleasant enough, intelligent.

Meehan found the employers' attitude to be "business as usual." The blackout and military control hamstrung the workers and made the islands "more or less a concentration camp." In Honolulu, there were two thousand longshoremen and only six hundred were paying dues. Employers controlled the plantation workers, who couldn't leave an island without a travel permit from the military. "They are naturally scared to death, especially the Japanese," said Meehan.

One of the first labor leaders he sought out was Kawano, president of the longshore unit. Meehan told Goldblatt that Kawano was the CIO's "spearhead of the labor movement in Hawaii." He sounded as though he had a good opinion of Kawano: "I find him very capable. He is under great handicap at the present time, however, because he is of Japanese ancestry; therefore, it will be necessary to have a haole (white, to you) to front for him."

Years later, however, Meehan tempered that favorable appraisal of Kawano with another verdict. He said that when he arrived to make his survey, Kawano didn't meet him. (Kawano was on the Big Island on an organizing mission.) Meehan said he got little cooperation from Kawano. "He was seldom in his office and would be gone for days at a time without telling me where he could be located."

Moreover, Meehan complained of Kawano's work. He said longshoremen didn't hold membership meetings and that at committee meetings Kawano sat voiceless. Silent Jack. "I thought at the time that he felt he was under a handicap inasmuch as he was Japanese," said Meehan. Kawano, in turn, had the nagging feeling that Meehan looked down his nose at island people.

The two spent four days together on the Big Island. Meehan complained that Kawano didn't introduce him to a single contact nor did they even visit a single plantation. "I was convinced that Kawano was just going along for the ride," he said. He summed up his criticism: "I found Kawano lazy and indifferent and apparently getting by as a labor leader on his reputation as such, whether earned or unearned. . . ."

Meehan told Rutledge he couldn't communicate with Kawano. "He sits there like a big Buddha and he doesn't say anything." Meehan asked Rutledge who he thought should run the ILWU. Rutledge recommended Hall, though he wondered if Hall would accept the job. "He had a wife and child and this was the first time in his life that he had a steady income," said Rutledge. Rutledge said he himself wasn't interested in the ILWU job: "I just didn't want to get involved because it seemed to me, if I got involved at that time, I would get involved in one hell of a fight."

Meehan spent some time with Hall and had no trouble making up his mind. On April 21, 1944, he sent word to Goldblatt that Hall was his choice. He gave several reasons. Hall had been active in the labor movement in Hawaii for nine years. He was familiar with conditions and "has the confidence of the people." Because Hall had worked in the Wage and Hour Division, he knew the labor laws. "He knows all the angles."

Meehan said that for two years employers hadn't paid overtime for work performed on holidays. The employers told the men it was against the law to pay them overtime. "We will collect back pay for them," he predicted.

Meehan had full authority to name his man, but now he—a *haole* from the mainland—had to sell the decision to the men who counted: the Executive Board, trustees, and officers of Kawano's local. The joint Executive Board meeting was held May 12, 1944. Meehan told the members that the ILWU district office would be set up under ILWU International supervision with a $1500-a-month budget. The International would pay the salaries of an International representative and a statistician.

Kawano recommended that Hall be put on the payroll to take charge of an ILWU program to educate workers on labor organization and politics. Hall could write his own radio scripts and read them over the air. Meehan said Hall was already trying to buy radio time for an ILWU program. The program would cost two hundred dollars a month for fifteen minutes a week. Meehan recommended that Bob Robertson come to Hawaii but that, in the meantime, Hall run the district office.

Fred Kamahoahoa, longshore local secretary-treasurer, objected. "We want someone who will stay after the war," he said. "Someone who is going to be permanent." Then this exchange took place:

Meehan: That is true but what you need now is to get contracts before the war is over. I believe that Hall would be more valuable to you right now than any men the International sent down. He knows the setup and is familiar with the workers.

Kawano: I think one of the district men should come down.

Meehan: The International wants to make every local independent. We don't want to run the locals.

Kawano: But there should be someone to show the local boys the tricks.

Meehan: We want to develop local men as much as we can, but right now Hall is the man who can give you the most help.

Kawano: But I believe that there should be someone come down to start us off.

Meehan: Hall could do that with someone to dig up the statistics for him.

Kamahoahoa: I believe in having the ILWU men run the show. The ILWU has taken the lead.

Meehan: The longshoremen have and will take the initiative to lead, but we want to develop leadership. We don't want to run things forever. . . .

Meehan then pulled rank and read a letter from the International certifying that he had the right to select the name of a candidate for regional director. Kawano conceded the point.

"I cannot say as to whether it would be proper to put Hall in," Kawano said. "Personally he can do the job better than anyone here. But what the men will say I do not know. I think that if the International cannot send anyone down, this plan is the best we can get."

Then Kawano asked: "How many admit that Hall is the only man here that can do the job?"

The vote was unanimous in favor of Hall. Thereupon they voted to make Hall officer pro tem of the ILWU district office and to make John Reinecke the statistician. (Reinecke was never so informed. He was never hired by the ILWU.)

Meehan told Goldblatt that Hall "could be induced" to work for the ILWU. It took no arm-twisting. Hall was eager to take the job. He said Meehan relieved him of the "comfortable job" with the Wage and Hour Division "with a minimum of persuasion." He began work officially for the ILWU on June 1, 1944, at a salary of seventy-five dollars a week.

Part 3
THE BIG SURGE
(1944–1946)

CHAPTER 19
Hall Takes Over

Hall was off and running. He toured the Neighbor Islands for fifteen days and then wrote Goldblatt a seventeen-page, single-spaced letter on what he found. The letter was the start of their long correspondence.

To Hall the sugar plantations were a mixed lot; some unit leaders were strong and aggressive, others flaccid. All the workers were green and unfamiliar with a trade union. "It's our job to educate them," said Hall. Pahala on the Big Island was the best of the lot. At Hilo Sugar Company, a man named Antone Pacheco was talking workers into staying out of the union. At Olaa the workers wanted to know what the ILWU International in San Francisco was doing with their dues money. Hall sympathized with them. "It is true that a couple of dollars is a lot of money to workers receiving as little as those in the sugar industry," said Hall.

On Maui he liked what he saw at Hawaiian Commercial & Sugar Company. The company—the biggest plantation in Hawaii—ground 80,000 tons of sugar and cleared a million dollars a year. Of 600 workers in the HC & S bargaining unit, the ILWU had signed up 350, but at Pioneer Mill the union couldn't make any headway.

On Maui the ILWU had its most effective control of politics. Politics was catnip to Hall. He looked the prospects over: there was Harold Rice, the rancher who had left the Republican Party and joined the Democrats in 1943. Though he was hardly a liberal, he was "far to the left of the planters." The lone senator holdover was the patrician Alice Kamokila Campbell—a Democrat of Molokai "and right down the line with us when the pressure is on," said Hall.

The ILWU already had flexed its muscle. In the 1943 election it had tried to defeat Roy Vitousek, whom Hall called "the Hawaiian Sugar Planters Association braintrust and perennial speaker of the House." The union had failed by just twenty-two votes. But politicians could hardly miss the point. Most of them could count; they realized the ILWU's strength at the ballot box.

As for organizing, things were moving. On Oahu the ILWU was making a start and had agreements with independent AFL unions (Rutledge) and with the independent drydock workers (McElrath). The union was not trying to organize fieldworkers—they were excluded from the law—yet fieldworkers were crying out to be organized. Management strongly opposed the idea, said Hall, so it would take a special law to make it possible for the ILWU to bring them into the union. No use talking to the employers about it. "All the conversation with the planters is just 'waste time,' as we say down here," he told Goldblatt.

Hall added another chore to his duties: he again became an editor. The first issue of the Hawaiian edition of the *ILWU Dispatcher* came out July 3, 1944. All in all, Hall told Goldblatt, he had stepped into a big job. It was going to take a lot more than the thirty-nine hours a week he had grown accustomed to as a government bureaucrat administering wages and hours.

Goldblatt responded with his first set of instructions. It soon turned out that he was the general at headquarters and Hall was the officer in charge of troops on one of the fronts. He told Hall not to get bogged down in protracted discussions with employers but to press ahead with the organizing drive. (He already had picked the man he wanted to head organizing: Frank Thompson, who had started a local from scratch in Sacramento and built it to 1500 members.)

Goldblatt warned Hall about employer tactics: beware, he said, of the overly friendly bosses who engage in windy discussion that spins out for such a long time that it demoralizes newly formed union locals. He told Hall: "The heart of our job in the islands is organization and consolidation. We still do not represent the majority of the workers in the industry. Every effort must be made to bring about majority representation in the speediest time possible."

Make the point, he said, that if the employers were ready to drop their hostility and concede that the union had a right to live and were ready to enter into genuine collective bargaining, then the union was ready to act in good faith. More than that, the ILWU would even help the sugar industry win favorable legislation. "We are not interested in a knockdown, dragout fight with the sugar interests," said Goldblatt.

Hall handled NLRB cases, War Labor Board cases, negotiations and relations with management, public relations, and the ILWU paper. He always stood at the beck and call of union members who needed answers to questions. He faced three lawyers representing management: Montgomery Winn, C. Wendell Carlsmith, and James P. Blaisdell.

Monty Winn, a Stanford man, was the general counsel of the Hawaii Employers Council. High-strung, a workaholic, he could be charming, but he was a hard-fighter. Jim Blaisdell was imported from the mainland in January 1944 to head the Employers Council. The council was founded in 1943. The employers had realized that when civilian control returned, labor organizing would take off full speed. To prepare for it, therefore, they brought up their heavy artillery. Goldblatt and Bridges knew Blaisdell when he served as president of the Distributors Association of Northern California, a union of employers. "A very good guy to get along with," said Goldblatt.

Carlsmith was the son of a Hilo attorney and he, too, was a Stanford man. He could talk a mile a minute, had a razor-sharp mind and lots of experience in sugar. It didn't surprise him that Hall, who had only a high school education, could hold his own in verbal combat. Hall could talk and use "meaningful expression," said Carlsmith. Hall wasn't flamboyant, nor a spellbinder, "but he knew how to say things and carry his point." Carlsmith once paid Hall the supreme compliment: "In many ways he was far superior to most members of the bar."

The two teams of combatants got to know one another formally at the bargaining table and informally in bars, at Ciro's restaurant on Hotel Street and at the Waikiki Tropics. Sometimes they met at Blaisdell's home in Kahala and, inevitably, even at seven in the morning, along with the steaming pot of coffee, there would be a bottle or two of liquor. They liked to drink. It soothed the rough edges and made them friendlier. "Apparently [it's] an island infection," Goldblatt explained. "It was the way to do business," said Dwight C. Steele, who later succeeded Blaisdell as Employers Council president. "It tended to bring an amicable approach to problems, instead of getting in a fight."

Hall and Blaisdell did not hit it off well at the start. Hall sensed a certain unfriendliness. He asked Goldblatt to put pressure on the Employers Council to soften Blaisdell up. One day the two had a "hair-down" talk at a *luau.*[1] Both had soaked up drinks and Hall needled Blaisdell until he broke down and exclaimed: "For Christ sakes, let's get together." He invited Hall to his home and they drank and talked. Blaisdell discussed his friendly relationship with Goldblatt and Sam Kagel, a West Coast labor mediator. Why couldn't he come to the same sort of understanding with Hall?

Hall assured him he could, but that Blaisdell gave no indication that he "really wanted to see unions continue." Then Hall accused Blaisdell of playing second fiddle. He said Blaisdell had no real power; he was just a messenger boy for his Big Five employers.

That stung Blaisdell. He retorted that *he* determined Employer Council policy.[2]

Hall wrote Goldblatt that he thought Blaisdell had been brought over from San Francisco because of his reputation. "If his reputation doesn't help the employers, then they see no need to pay him $25,000 per annum."[3]

Goldblatt agreed with Hall that Blaisdell had little control over management's overall policymaking. He predicted that,

---

1. Hall's definition of a *luau:* "Hawaiian feast and corn-squeezing."
2. "Obviously, [I] don't believe that," Hall later told Goldblatt.
3. Randolph Crossley, who served at the time on the Employers Council board of directors, said Blaisdell's pay was $40,000 a year.

Blaisdell or no Blaisdell, the union was going to have to fight for its gains. "The island interests," said Goldblatt, "are going to give us a real run for our money. There has been no evidence of genuine friendliness or attempt to work out some basic solutions for the islands."

These impressions were reinforced by a talk Goldblatt had with Alex Budge, president of Castle & Cooke. He had told Budge it must be obvious that the ILWU had political clout. However, he said, the union was willing to cooperate with industry. Budge conceded that the union had power and was sitting pretty. But despite that, said Goldblatt, Budge was "absolutely adamant toward any proposals for immediate planning and cooperation." Of course, said Goldblatt, Budge put it more diplomatically. He told Goldblatt that as the head of Castle & Cooke, he took no direct interest in island affairs but left them to subordinates who worked with Blaisdell. "He tried to give the impression that Blaisdell had control over policy in the islands." Goldblatt said he politely told Budge he didn't believe it.

Goldblatt presented Budge with another selling point—namely, that a strong ILWU would ensure that management would not be subjected to wildcat strikes or picket lines to reinforce demands of other unions. He reminded Budge that the ILWU knew how to fight if it had to.

Nothing much came out of the chat, but it did convince Goldblatt that the ILWU was going to have to turn on "every bit of pressure possible" to gain its objectives in Hawaii. He meant pressure on government agencies, such as the NLRB and the War Labor Board.

Goldblatt predicted the employers would try to provoke a strike. Avoid it at all costs, he cautioned Hall. Look out for union members who shout: "What the hell is the union doing for us?" Warn the members against provocateurs, said Goldblatt, "so that the moment they open their traps, they will be nailed."

Hall agreed to watch out. He said he had not found "any genuine friendliness" on the part of the employers. "Under the direction of the HEC they have planned to do everything in their power to stall and break the union." He predicted a slugging match coming up. "We are in for a fight, but what the hell. We've been in plenty of fights before."

CHAPTER **20**

Thompson the Organizer

Frank Thompson came to town July 8, 1944, to do a little organizing. He phoned Marian Kelly, Hall's secretary, and she told Hall. Yoshiko Hall took Thompson to the Territorial Registration office for fingerprinting (a wartime measure) and he filled out the questionnaire demanded of all newcomers.

Thompson spent the first of many nights at Hall's home. Next morning he, Kawano, and Hall went to Waipahu and talked to 250 employees of Oahu Sugar Company. He took notes. He was always taking notes which he put in a notebook or yellow legal tablet.

"They have allready [sic] elected thier [sic] officers and will begin thier [sic] per capita tax returns commencing with the month of August," he wrote. He wasn't much on spelling, but it didn't matter. Later he had the services of a secretary and Thompson's prose came out impeccably. He had a title: ILWU International Representative. He had a mission: to organize workers. It was he who directed the big ILWU organizing drives from mid-1944 into 1946, building on the foundation laid by Yoroku Fukuda's gang of longshoremen and by the people on the Neighbor Islands and in rural Oahu who had started organizing. "I worked so hard I had no trouble sleeping," said Thompson. "Thompson came at an opportune time," said Hall.

Thompson was a blond, Nordic-looking man. He had a personal trait, not uncommon in *haoles* from the mainland, which didn't endear him to local people: he didn't take a bath or change his clothes every day. They may not have noticed in Sacramento, but they did in Hawaii.

He was five feet eleven and weighted 190, and was forceful. "Arrogant in a heavy-fashioned way," he stepped on people's toes; he cursed, he shoved things down their throat. "When I have to tell them off, I told them off," he said.

He was as necessary for the growth of the union as water is for the growth of sugar cane. "Absolutely essential," said Goldblatt who sent him over.

There had been an earlier Frank Thompson on the scene: Frank Thompson, the Matson lawyer, who died in 1943.[1] Hall quickly sorted the two out for the public's information. "He is no relation to Frank E. Thompson, corporation lawyer, who was identified with Hawaii's 'Dark Ages,' " Hall said.

The two Thompsons could not have been more dissimilar: the ILWU's Thompson was a radical labor organizer; Matson's Thompson was an ultraconservative antiunionist. The ILWU's Thompson was blunt and as diplomatic as a kick in the shins. Matson's Thompson was a skilled courtroom lawyer, witty, smooth, ruthless. But they had one trait in common: both were tough.

The ILWU's Thompson was then thirty-eight. He had been born in Minnesota and his maternal grandfather was a German Socialist from whom he had learned a few words of German (he called potatoes *kartofeln*) and the basics of socialism. He peddled papers at nine; at fourteen he was a Wobbly; and at fifteen he was working in the lumber camps of northern California. Thompson regarded most plantation managers as "Fancy Dans" with their puttees and shiny boots. He was naturally prickly and they aroused the devil in him. Once he saw a *kapu* sign posted outside a plantation. The working men with him said

---

1. By one of those quirks that history enjoys a chuckle over, the two Thompsons had exactly the same three names in the same order: Frank Edward Thompson.

that meant he couldn't go in. "That's not in English," said Thompson. "I can't read that." And in he went.

Thompson sized up Kawano and Hall as "very capable" but spread too thin. "They are covering a lot of ground." Thompson's job was organizing the outer islands. Hall's job was doing the technical work in Honolulu. He liked Hall and they became good friends. "He really puts in a day's work," Thompson wrote Goldblatt. But he also made this honest appraisal: "Hall drank too much," he said. "Otherwise, he was very pleasant to me. I got along with him very well. He was a booze drinker. I got a rash [of drinking] every so often, but he was drinking all the time."

Thompson's shrewd eye noted that all was not well on the waterfront. He told Kawano to finish the job of organizing the Honolulu waterfront "instead of running all over hell." He also pressed Bert Nakano and August Asau, the Hilo longshore leaders, to complete the organization of the Hilo waterfront. Thompson wanted the waterfronts locked up. Kawano told him there were 2400 longshoremen in Honolulu, but only 1000 were paying dues. It was fewer than that, Thompson discovered. McCabe, Renny & Hamilton had 850 employees, but only 235 were ILWU members; Castle & Cooke Terminals had 1250 employees and only 472 members.

Thompson told Kawano he wasn't going to stop riding him until the waterfront was solidly organized. "Jack Kawano is a hard worker, but he has not been able to get other people lined out on a consistent and steady program," Thompson said.

Hall also put pressure on Kawano, and Kawano started holding weekly meetings. In one week they signed up 125 members. But Thompson, the man with a single purpose in life, was not satisfied. By now he was running back and forth to the outer islands. He learned that Jack Owens, the AFL organizer, had approached the Honokaa sugar mill workers on the Big Island. Thompson talked to them and then phoned Hall and told him to file for an NLRB representation election. He was confident he could outtalk Owens, and he did.

On Maui Thompson found good leadership: Shigeo Takemoto, president of the Wailuku unit, who was an electrical engineer with a degree from Ohio State University, and Joe Kaholokula, president of the Maui Agricultural Company unit. Kaholokula was "the main plug of the whole layout," said Thompson. He meant the six units of ILWU Local 6: Maui Agricultural, Wailuku Sugar Co., Hawaiian Commercial & Sugar, East Maui Irrigation Company, American Can Company, and Maui Pineapple Company. They had a potential of 1500 nonagricultural workers and the ILWU had signed up 1000.

One day Thompson, a steak-and-potatoes man who hated rice, enjoyed a splendid meal at the Takemoto home—five kinds of fish, including *sashimi,* which Thompson, fortified by slugs of Old Taylor bourbon and Johnnie Walker scotch, gingerly sampled. He, Hall, and Kawano spent four hours at work on the feast. He began to feel better about the islands. "This Hawaiian hospitality knows no end," he said.

The ILWU men called on the Baldwins, the "rulers" of the island. Harry Baldwin, then in his seventies, ran Maui Agricultural; Frank Baldwin ran HC & S. Harry was genial and gave them an hour and a half of his time. He agreed unions were "here to stay" and said he intended to sit down and bargain with them. Maui, it was clear, was shaping up into an ILWU stronghold.

They already were signing up some nonagricultural workers, though they did not know at that point whether they might have to be dropped. "All of these local units down here[2] have a PAC [Political Action Committee] campaign in full, seeking to get everyone registered to vote," said Thompson. There was a good chance to put ILWU people in the legislature.

In his travels Thompson soon ran into McElrath, then business agent of the independent marine shipyard workers. McElrath had just organized the American Can Company in Honolulu, and after a hard month of fruitless bargaining he called Thompson and asked his advice about calling a quickie strike. This was 1944; the war was still on; and the ILWU adhered scrupulously to its no-strike pledge.

---

2. In ILWU jargon, "down here" meant Hawaii. On the mainland, the ILWU referred to Hawaii as "down there."

Thompson bawled McElrath out: "I told him he was nuts and that any action of that kind would react against the whole [labor] movement. . . . McElrath has some ability, but is somewhat irresponsible." Thompson said the contract McElrath proposed to American Can "would scare anybody to death."[3]

Thompson's method of confronting employers soon became famous. There was, for example, the William Walsh case: Walsh was general manager of the Kahului Railway Company, a narrow-gauge line that ran twenty miles east and west of Kahului. (The company also operated a fleet of passenger buses and did stevedoring work.) Walsh ran his own dispatching service and had a system that aggravated the workers: he hung brass checks on a board in front of a building. If an employee found his check turned over with the number out of sight, that meant he was not wanted for work that day—or had been fired. If he had been seen talking to a stranger, say a labor organizer, the word would get around and his brass check would be turned over permanently.

Thompson called the system "Walsh's closed shop." "We have to find some way to open it," he vowed. The opportunity came one day after Kaholokula had tried in vain for two weeks to see Walsh. Thompson took on the assignment. He called at Walsh's office. Walsh's secretary told him Walsh was too busy to see him and to come back next day. Thompson told her he intended to say there until Walsh came out. She informed Walsh and he admitted Thompson into his office.

For fifteen minutes Thompson harangued and cursed. Walsh sat close-mouthed "like a clam." He hadn't met the likes of Thompson. Finally, Thompson permitted Walsh to say something. Walsh managed to put in that he was just too busy to see Thompson and that Monty Winn, the Employers Council lawyer, had ordered him to refer all union matters to Winn.

Not legitimate union grievances! Thompson thundered. That was *union* business and they had a right to take it up with Walsh.

As they talked Kaholokula stood alongside but Walsh point-

---

3. McElrath responded: "He [Thompson] was angry because he'd settled a contract with American Can on Maui for a hell of a lot cheaper than I insisted on down here."

edly ignored him. Thompson noticed it and was disgusted. He felt Walsh was treating Kaholokula like "a dog or a child." When they left the office, Walsh offered his hand to Thompson but not to Kaholokula. Thompson fumed. The day would come, he promised, when "that old bastard would only be too glad to shake hands" with Kaholokula.

Thompson's adventures took him all over. He went to Kauai to reorganize the Port Allen workers and Hanapepe's informality delighted him. He scribbled a note to Goldblatt: "This Hanapepe is some place. You ought to be here."

One day he phoned Bridges and asked him to send someone to take charge of the ILWU's business with the War Labor Board. It was taking too much of Hall's time. He wanted Hall released to speed the organizing work. He wanted the union to become strong as quickly as possible. He did not like the rumors he heard about the employers inviting a strike to test the ILWU's strength: "Monty Winn has been boasting . . . that we are not going to get anywhere regardless of what program we have. He states that the whole thing is going to end up in a strike and that is the time they are going to beat our ears off."

From his end Goldblatt kept pounding away on the two keys to success in Hawaii: organization of sugar and the waterfront. Then the other industries, such as pineapple, would fall into their laps. The workload fell heavily on Hall and Thompson. Goldblatt often phoned with advice, consolation, and instructions. He knew how to deliver a pep talk. One phone call came at a specially opportune time. "Hall gets pretty worried about things at times and your talk gave him a new hold on things," Thompson told Goldblatt. "Hall is the only intelligent person down here in the labor movement besides Kawano, and sometimes Hall gets pretty morbid about some of the screwballs that plague him from time to time."

One day Thompson played hooky and went to a ballgame. The Seventh Air Force was playing in the Hawaiian League and they had some pretty fair ballplayers, such as Red Ruffing and Joe Gordon, formerly of the New York Yankees. Thompson sat in the bleachers and got sunburned. After the game, he decided to make a day of it and went out to Waikiki and had a swim.

Island magic was taking possession of him. He began to enjoy the food: "Plenty of steaks and no ration points," he said. The natives could produce a bottle of bourbon almost anytime. Their favorite drink *(okolehao)* had an "awful wallup." "The hospitality of these people is astounding," he said. "A tropical paradize."

CHAPTER **21**

The ILWU Gathers Strength

Under Hall's direction, the ILWU in 1944 became a strong political force in Hawaii; and as the union's strength grew, so did Hall's expectations. "We can make a real dent in sugar control of the Legislature," he predicted.

A Political Action Committee was set up. The union distributed handbills which said PAC was a boon not only to the working man but to small farmers, small businessmen, and teachers. The handbills said PAC "is not a political party nor a 'third party' nor a 'labor party.' It will support any candidate regardless of party affiliation if he is in accord with the committee's objectives."

It amused Hall to note how alarmed some of the island politicians suddenly had become. "We have a favorable press and the politicians are scared to death," he said.

Hall instructed the ILWU leadership on the Neighbor Islands to make sure they registered their people to vote. He warned: Don't make promises; don't sound off on issues. Wait until the final day for filing of nominations and then at PAC meetings the union will decide what to do.

Hall was only secondarily interested in county races. To him the key was the legislature where the laws affecting labor were written. He told the ILWU members that the union could control the 1945 legislature if the members worked together and didn't waste their time in bickering and gossip.

"Mobilize every single plantation member into a united Political Action Committee," he instructed. His main objective was to enact the "Little Wagner Act" to give the union the legal means to bring thousands of unorganized plantation fieldworkers into the ILWU. They would be the force that controlled island politics. "Labor isn't sitting on its fanny any more," said Hall.

He himself drafted a "rigorous" Little Wagner bill by lifting the best parts of legislation enacted in Wisconsin, New York, and Rhode Island.[1]

Two ILWU Neighbor Island leaders filed for the legislature: Kaholokula of Maui and Amos Ignacio of Hawaii. Kaholokula asked Hall for financial support. Hall told him that under the Smith-Connally Act, the union could not directly contribute funds to a campaign for the election of any candidate to a public office paid for in whole or in part by federal funds.

"That does not mean that the union cannot raise funds to carry on its own political campaign," said Hall. The ILWU raised money through voluntary contributions from union members and others. Hall set a goal for the 1944 Maui campaign: ten thousand dollars.

Kaholokula was nervous. He told Hall he had heard rumors that his company, Maui Agricultural, was going to fire him for political activity. "Hogwash," said Hall. "It's none of the manager's business whether you run for office or not." He told Kaholokula he was coming down to discuss the political campaign. Rent a hall and call a meeting of all Maui ILWU officers, he ordered. "Take no steps in political action until we arrive so that we can work out our strategy jointly."

Hall also went to Kauai to direct campaign work. He was up until early in the morning talking with key men, such as his old friend J. B. Fernandes. They went door to door, presenting

---

1. Final passage of the Little Wagner Act took place on May 1, 1945.

their case. Hall believed in personal contact: the handshake, the face-to-face talk.

The union's hard work paid off and the results of the primary election gratified Hall. "Between Maui and Hawaii we have really set the islands on their heads," he said. On plantation after plantation, PAC-endorsed candidates "rolled up a tremendous majority." Hall was sure the politicians got the message. "The professional politicians know that we can hold our vote together and that they must reckon with us in all future elections."

The next target was the general election. Hall told Kaholokula that there were two Maui Republicans the union wanted to remove from the legislature: Bill Engle and Henry Robinson. Hall outlined the strategy:

> The others will probably stay in line in view of the tremendous labor vote on Maui. Perhaps the wiser strategy in the General [Election] would be to concentrate in holding a vote for yourself and [Hal F.] Hanna. In this way you and Hanna can urge people to knife Engle and maybe Robinson. In this way you will not be building up other Republican candidates at your own expense.
>
> Every candidate for the Legislature—including even those you wish to dump—should be asked to make a written commitment on our program, the amendment to the wage and hour law and unemployment law which would extend coverage to agriculture. . . .

The general election resulted in an ILWU triumph. Hall exulted. Both Ignacio and Kaholokula won seats. Fifteen of the nineteen House candidates endorsed by the PAC and six of the eight candidates endorsed for the Senate were elected. Hall was amused. "The Old Guard" was now talking about cooperation and about "meeting labor half way," he said.

Of such peace efforts Hall was skeptical and he vowed to keep his guard up. "We will cooperate, of course, as long as it is not unilateral cooperation. . . . Tin pants are the uniform of the day before crawling into bed with these people."

Now that the elections were over, he warned, "the hard work begins." He told Manuel Henriques of Kauai that "promises will be cheaper than air" and cautioned Henriques, who owed his election to the ILWU, not to make commitments "until the situation has settled down." He told Henriques to come to Honolulu before February 15 (1945) and get his instructions.

Henriques replied that he would arrive on the fifteenth and stay at the Young Hotel. He told Hall he had not made any commitments to anybody, "as I already explained to you heretofore, and still am the same man as heretofore, looking to you for advice *re* matters in the House."

Hall said the ILWU would have to keep the pressure on elected politicians. The union would have to work in the legislature as hard as it had worked during the election campaign. "This means demonstrating to our enemies that we are firmly united and that the heaviest kind of pressure or persuasion will only serve to strengthen our ranks."

He told Ignacio that the ILWU would insist on both Ignacio and Kaholokula getting seats on the Finance or the Judiciary Committee—"the two most important committees in the House."[2] The Judiciary was really the big one, said Hall, because labor bills were referred to that committee.

The union could learn a lesson from the election, Hall said. "Our political strength is in direct proportion to our union strength." It was simple as counting. The more union members, the bigger the union vote and the greater the union's strength in politics.

On January 23, 1945, word came that the NLRB had sustained the ILWU's position on who was to be included in bargaining units. The NLRB ruled that fifty to sixty percent of all sugar plantation workers were subject to the National Labor Relations Act (Wagner Act). "VICTORY!" Hall proclaimed in a headline in the *Dispatcher,* and he issued an order of the day:

> Now the job is to consolidate every ILWU unit in the sugar industry to its highest possible membership. So drive ahead to get every single employee of the plantations who will be eligible to vote in the NLRB elections as a paid-up member. A paid-up member is a vote that we can count upon at the polls.

---

2. Both were named to the Judiciary Committee.

The NLRB had held hearings for twelve days in Hilo and for two days in Honolulu. Hall, Nakano, and Arakaki represented the ILWU. Carlsmith and Winn represented the sugar industry. In Washington oral arguments were presented to the board in behalf of the ILWU by Martin Raphael of the National CIO legal staff and by a bright-eyed young woman named Harriet Bouslog. She called herself the "lowest-paid lobbyist" in Washington. "Harriet Bouslog must have done a wonderful job of salesmanship," Hall said. The NLRB ruling, he claimed,

> puts all the workers in the [sugar] industry in the same boat. They live in the same house, play on the same football team, and drink out of the same bottle. It was an integrated industry and must be organized.

Organizing was now moving along smoothly with the crusty Frank Thompson running the show, but what should the union do about the sugar contract for 1945? Goldblatt discussed it with Bridges and Lloyd Fisher, the ILWU's director of research. They decided for the moment not to make waves: 1945 was not going to be a sugar year. Yes, it would be nice to get a little cash for the workers and some improvements, but that was wishful thinking; 1945 was meant for organizing and consolidating and not for a strike or even the threat of a strike. A little more cash, though, Goldblatt said almost wistfully, would help win support for the checkoff system.

The idea for a checkoff system came about as a result of some "elbow-bending" Hall did with Blaisdell and Winn in Hilo during the NLRB hearings. As so often happened during such a relaxed get-together, a hint was dropped: in this case word that the sugar industry would not be averse to putting a checkoff system in effect. "Voluntary irrevocable checkoff" meant that management took out a union member's dues from his paycheck and turned it over to the union. The employers were willing to do that because it was a "softer" method of union security than the closed shop, under which every employee was compelled to join the union. The employers reasoned that the checkoff system "provided sufficient security . . . that the ILWU chose not to battle further."

The ILWU leadership also considered the checkoff a good thing. The union didn't have to spend time collecting dues. However, some union members objected—they didn't like the idea of management taking union dues out of their pay. There was at least another disadvantage in union eyes: management knew exactly how many dues-paying members the union had.

The checkoff system[3] went into effect and the ILWU signed a sugar contract in 1945 that gave the average union member a raise of about $125 a year (seven cents an hour). There was no dispute. Goldblatt said that "the '45 contract was the first contract and there the only objective was rather a simple one: to just see if we could nail down an agreement for the industry. . . . This was just a holding operation."

Hall said under the circumstances the contract was the "best possible deal we could obtain."[4] He said the membership generally was satisfied and looked forward to consolidation and political action—the answer next time around. "Morale is high and the membership is behind us," Hall said.

The sugar industry was aware that some ILWU members were unhappy with the contract, though, and realized that the union was preparing, "at some future date, to fight for more."

In 1945 the ILWU was like a teenage boy who suddenly shoots up six inches in height in a few months. Goldblatt was concerned. He kept prodding Hall about the lack of local leadership; he called it the "most disturbing feature in the island picture":

> We will never be able to administer a union which in the foreseeable future will have a membership of thirty thousand or more over many scattered units, unless we undertake, as a major part of our work, the training of local leadership.

The same subject dominated a meeting of ILWU leaders in San Francisco. It was a touchy matter because it meant that in

---

3. It became known as "union security, Hawaiian style."
4. The two sides always remembered the informality of the signing of the 1945 memorandum of agreement. It was signed by flashlight at night on top of a garbage can in the alley back of the Waikiki Tropics.

many cases Japanese of ability would have to stand back and let other races, chiefly Filipino, take over in the name of multiracial leadership. The meeting concluded that:

> The importance of racial unity in the islands makes it imperative that steps be taken to put Filipinos, Hawaiians, Portuguese and others into prominent positions, even though in some cases they might not be as qualified or capable as the Japanese.

In 1945 Hall was thirty. He was working hard and drinking hard. He had a crushing burden and the strain was beginning to tell. He was getting tired; he could not stand mediocre people and sometimes he dealt with them brusquely. The word got back to Goldblatt. "From all reports," said Goldblatt, "Jack Hall has some real weaknesses in his work." He told Thompson to talk to Hall about it: "There is a distinct weakness in his way of working, by a failure to develop collective leadership, a tendency to monopolize all the thinking and direction of the ILWU and a general inclination to shove people when they do not move as quickly as he would like."

On a visit to Hawaii Goldblatt saw something he didn't like: drinking by Hall and other *haole* union leaders. He said no one among the ILWU International officers was a teetotaler. He, Bridges, and Robertson drank. But there was something wrong when "local boys dig up the booze but don't drink themselves." It indicated, he said, that they were trying to be hospitable but didn't really approve.

Frank Thompson realized that Hall had taken too much upon himself. He advised Hall to take a break and get off the islands for a while. He told Bridges and Goldblatt he had noted Hall's curt "one-phrase answers" to ILWU leaders who were earnestly seeking advice:

> You are going to have to convince him that these local island people are not mature enough to assimilate one-phrase answers; that in the future he must slow down and take the necessary time to be sure that our people are convinced in the matter of answers to their questions.

Kawano told Thompson he couldn't get along with Hall. He said Hall was not the kind of a man he could sit down with and have confidence in "because of Hall's attitudes." And other people in the union felt the same way, he added. Hall was very able, said Thompson, "but they don't like his general attitude and have talked to me plenty on this matter."

CHAPTER **22**
Thompson vs. Arakaki

It turned out that Paradise had problems after all, Frank Thompson found out. One was Yasuki Arakaki, the stubborn man who was president of Local 148, the Olaa sugar unit. Arakaki was a short, well-built man with heavy shoulders and a strong face. He was a rabid union man. "We were solid. We were the most advanced [local] in the union," he said. Arakaki formed opinions and they did not waver. "I am not a pendulum," he said. He didn't like Thompson and his method of operating. "He was no friend of mine."

Arakaki had grown up on the plantation and as a boy he discovered that it was a hard life built upon currying favor with the boss. "What motivated me when I grew up on a plantation company was that the perquisite system depended on how much you gave the supervisor in charge of various activities," he said. If Arakaki's father wanted to enlarge a room in the plantation house the family lived in, then he had to bribe the carpenter's boss. His family raised pigs. When they slaughtered a pig, they cut off a nice piece, wrapped it, and presented it to the superintendent on a Sunday when no one else saw them doing it.

Every worker had a garden. "We raised vegetables and we would forage around like an animal," said Arakaki. "Our parents made our school clothes once a year. When we would return from school, we were told to remove our school clothes, hang them on a nail, and return to the patched clothing." The memory of plantation life had burned itself into Arakaki's mind.

By 1945 organizing was moving fast but not fast enough for Thompson. The number of dues-paying union members climbed from 970 in January 1944 to 6610 in January 1945. By March, the ILWU had forty-six units under thirteen charters. Thompson figured the union could sign up between 18,000 and 20,000 members (all nonagricultural) in sugar, pineapple, railroads, stevedoring, and miscellaneous occupations.

Goldblatt told Thompson to push for consolidation of the units into one big local, but to be sure to let the members know why. The purpose was to gather their strength and prepare for new gains: the concept of a single unit to produce unity. Goldblatt told him to stress the development of local leadership from all races. "The locals have simply got to be trained to handle their own affairs," he said.

An unhealthy pattern had developed and Olaa was an example: Japanese held the key jobs in the mill; Filipinos worked in the fields. The Japanese supplied the leadership and often there was antagonism between the two races. Other developments also bothered Thompson. Some of the locals were building up their treasuries. That was no way to solve problems, he said. The union wasn't interested in locals with big treasuries. What the union *was* interested in was signing up everybody on the job as a member of the union. There lay the strength. Organization, consolidation, political action: those were the goals, he said. If the union had to strike, it should have one hundred percent membership to make the strike effective—"instead of some chickenshit strike fund" in locals that had only part of their membership organized.

Thompson ruthlessly pressed for consolidation.[1] Arakaki,

---

1. The Hawaii labor historian Edward Beechert said the union had to consolidate the sugar units "to prevent employer splitting tactics. Also, they had to find and train leaders, develop grievance procedures, and carry on further organizing. The goal was to merge the multiple sugar units into one consolidated local, with strong unit leadership in each company. By December 1945, they had achieved consolidation down to three locals."

who was just as determined, told him that five units of Local 142 and five of Local 143 wouldn't go along if they had to hand over their finances to one treasury under one consolidated local. Arakaki had another bone to pick: he didn't like Hall's handling of the 1945 sugar contract.

Thompson took a trip to the mainland and upon his return found out that a meeting had been held at the Young Hotel at which there was some talk about "the *haole* leadership" of the ILWU. Arakaki, Nakano, Kawano, Castner Ogawa, and Richard Shigemitsu had attended. Thompson heard a rumor that the five wanted both him and Hall "removed from the local picture."

A meeting had in fact taken place at the Young Hotel. Arakaki had questioned Hall's handling of the sugar contract, but the participants did not discuss a move "to oust any *haoles* from the ranks." Arakaki merely reflected that it would be prudent if Thompson didn't return from the mainland.

Like two fighting roosters sprung loose by their handlers, the two men flew at each other. Facing Thompson head-on, Arakaki refused to sign the 1945 sugar contract unless the majority of Big Island units first signed it. Thompson flared: "I laid down the law to this guy and told him to sign the god dam *[sic]* contract at once without any screwing around. . . . Arakaki is a little bit too cocky for his own good."

Goldblatt learned about the revolt in the canebrakes. He thought Kawano might be able to snuff it out and get some of the "hot-headed boys" back in line. If that failed, Goldblatt said, then "we will simply have to tell some of these boys who are maneuvering around and using the ILWU for personal faction fights, that we will be no party to it and will not be responsible for the mistakes."

Goldblatt himself came over to Hawaii and in his smooth way extracted some promises and pledges, but the antagonism continued. By now Thompson had discovered other adversaries, whom he considered in league with Arakaki: Nakano, who "acts very nervous toward me when I am around," and Hiroshi "Thunder" Fukuhara, the Onomea unit president with the loud voice.

Thompson decided that Fukuhara didn't level with him. He confronted Fukuhara and "really went to work on him." He had discovered a way to deal with recalcitrants: "Lay it on the line. . . . Some of these Orientals . . . can be awfully stubborn and dumb-acting," he said.

One day Arakaki called a meeting at the old Japanese language school at Olaa. Thompson was not invited but he came anyway. Arakaki told him to go away. Thompson said Arakaki acted "like Julius Caesar approaching a plebeian." Arakaki explained that it was a private meeting; Thompson wasn't wanted; and besides he intended to see Thompson the next day.

Thompson teetered on the edge of an explosion. He said he was tempted to "break every bone" in Arakaki's body and barely controlled himself. He backed Arakaki against a wall and "really told [him] off," shouting that he had come to Olaa to report to the local and nobody was going to stop him. His message completed, he pushed Arakaki aside, walked into the meeting room, and did his talking.

Saburo Fujisaki, corresponding secretary of Local 148, protested Thompson's "dictatorial and fascistic practices" and accused Thompson of undermining the ILWU on the Big Island. He said the sugar locals favored consolidation, but what alarmed them was Thompson's tactics. "He literally shoved everything down the throats of the delegates present."

Thompson had ordered that two full-time business agents be appointed at a weekly salary of sixty-five dollars and insisted that they be of different races "with the qualifications of the officers being secondary." Thereupon, with no discussion, Thompson presented his slate of officers—take it or else—for the new consolidated local: Amos Ignacio (Portuguese), president; Gus Nishihara (Japanese), first vice-president; Jacinto Conol (Filipino), second vice-president; and Henry Johnson, Jr. (Hawaiian), secretary-treasurer.

What Thompson was doing in his hard-nosed way was following orders to mix the leadership. A showdown was near. Thompson insisted that the ILWU International order Arakaki and Nakano to stay out of the affairs of other locals and not interfere with the work of consolidation. Do something about it, he told Goldblatt, "or I might as well come home." It was plain to him that Arakaki was trying to kick him out. "A couple of addle brains *[sic]* are trying a power play here," he wrote Bridges.

The next move in the accelerating contest was a letter to the International cosigned by Leoncio Velasco, Filipino secretary of Local 142, Unit 14, and Yukinori Fujioka, corresponding secretary of the local. It said Thompson was jeopardizing the ILWU's future on the Big Island, accused him of causing a split between the Filipinos and the Japanese, and called him a "Hitlerite dictator."

"We want action and not just lip service," the letter said. If Bridges didn't act, then the writers promised "to take matters in their own hands."

Arakaki then sent a telegram to the International asking for the removal of Hall and Thompson. At that point Bridges had had enough. He replied by Western Union cable on January 22, 1946:

REURTEL,[2] THOMPSON'S AND HALL'S EXECUTION INTERNATIONAL PROGRAM JUSTIFIES OUR COMPLETE CONFIDENCE. WE EXPECT AND INSIST UPON FULL COOPERATION ALL ILWU MEMBERS IN PERFORMANCE THEIR WORK. . . .

Bridges told Arakaki he had had a chance to air his grievances when Goldblatt visited the islands. He ordered Arakaki to mind his own business, stay in his own *kuleana* and cooperate with Hall and Thompson.

A copy of the telegram went to Thompson, who wrote Goldblatt that Arakaki had overplayed his hand. He told Goldblatt he had a choice: either turn the leadership over to Arakaki and Nakano on the Big Island and fragment the union, or build a collective leadership. "Please remember that there are other people on these islands besides the Japanese," he said.

Then, bluntly, the only way Thompson knew how to say anything, he said: "What you have to understand is that the dif-

---

2. "Regarding your telegram."

ferent racial groups, particularly on this Big Island, do not trust one another. . . . All racial groups, on this Big Island in particular, are continually basting *[sic]* one another." As an example, he cited the Filipino workers at Honuapo who refused to pay initiation fees to any of the three Japanese officers of the unit.

In between rounds, Thompson kept plugging away at his chief purpose in life: bringing workers into the union. He and Henry Johnson went to Hilo Sugar's Wainaku Camp 2 and signed up forty workers, all Filipinos. "They wondered why no one came out to see them," he said. Oddly, a luna collected the men so Thompson could talk to them. The Filipinos entertained them with a cockfight. Johnson bet two dollars on a cock and lost. It was a good day: a chance for Thompson to take his mind off the fight with Arakaki.

Thompson ran into Arakaki at a meeting in Waiakea town and asked him if he had got Bridges' telegram. Arakaki said yes. Then, said Thompson, what the hell was he doing over at Hilo Sugar the previous Thursday? "The trouble with this guy Arakaki is that he is so goddamned ambitious that he will do anything to be president of the 8,500 sugar workers on this island."

It wasn't going to be easy to build leadership on Hawaii, Thompson told Goldblatt. The Big Island union leaders were like a bunch of kids, but there was no one to replace them. He consoled himself in the thought that eventually they would work out their own destiny.

Organizing surely was a thankless job, Thompson mused. Every now and then, though, there were compensations, such as the day he went to Lanai with Bob Mookini of the ILWU pineapple local and Rick Labez, Hall's aide. They sailed on the *Naia* from Lahaina to Kaumalapau, the port on the south side of Lanai. It's only twenty-five miles but it took more than three hours. Thompson relaxed. "Like an excursion," he said. The sea was calm; the weather was fine. Filipinos hung their fishing lines from the stern and when they had a bite they would ring the bell in the captain's quarters and he would stop the boat and let them haul in their catch.

Thompson, Mookini, and Wallace Nishida signed up 1050 of

the 1600 workers on Lanai. While they were there, Pedro de la Cruz, a Filipino who was Kawano's brother-in-law, was elected president of the Lanai unit. De la Cruz didn't talk much, but he was shrewd and he was trusted and he meant what he said.

Thompson loved Lanai. At 1600 feet elevation the air was cool. He had a good meal: fried chicken, corn on the cob, green peas, bread and butter, fresh milk, coffee, and pumpkin pie. "Not bad *kau-kau*," said Thompson, and for a moment the restless, driving organizer was at peace with the world.

CHAPTER **23**

The Poker Player

Shortly after V-J Day[1] Hall went to attorney Richard Gladstein in San Francisco for help. Gladstein was a short, stocky man with a keen mind. Hall wanted to sue the sugar companies for violation of the Federal Fair Labor Standards Act (FLSA) for failure to pay overtime to workers during the war. He had gathered the information while working for the Wage and Hour Division. "We may not always be right in our interpretations," he said, "but this time we really have our teeth into something."

No lawyer in Honolulu was willing to take the case. In the first place it was legally shaky: the FLSA explicitly exempted agricultural workers. Moreover, local lawyers were afraid to take on the Big Five. Gladstein had no such compunction. He knew about the exemption in the act, but he also knew that in Puerto Rico a lower court had returned a decision in favor of workers in

---

1. September 2, 1945.

the sugar mills known as *centrales.* Perhaps, he thought, this could be a precedent for Hawaii's own nonagricultural sugar workers. Hall asked Gladstein to take the case on a full-contingency basis.[2] According to Goldblatt, the suit was "conceived entirely by Jack Hall."

In due course, attorney Herbert K. H. Lee filed a suit in Honolulu which sought to collect from forty-nine sugar companies and affiliates an unspecified sum. Gladstein said it took "enormous time and effort" to prepare the case. Late in 1945 Goldblatt received a telegram from the sugar companies saying they were willing to settle the case out of court. They did not name a figure. They meant to dicker.

Goldblatt went to Hawaii on December 24, 1945. He thought with luck he might get home for New Year's. (He was there until January 6, 1946.) On Christmas Day, he and Hall met with Monty Winn, representing the companies. Goldblatt boldly told Winn the union would settle for $10 million—$5 million retroactive as a lump sum payment and $5 million in the form of across-the-board wage increases. Like any good bargainer he had laid out the strategy: "It was quite apparent from the initial conversation that the employers had been expecting us to make an offer and inasmuch as we were not prepared to do so, we simply picked the highest figure we could at the moment to get the discussions going." Winn heard him out and the session was recessed.

Next day Winn came back with a counteroffer: $750,000. Goldblatt acted as though he had been insulted; he immediately broke off discussions. "No dice," he said. "It's got to be a hell of a lot more than that. We're leaving. We'll go to court and see what happens."

Goldblatt went back to his hotel room and started to pack. The phone rang. It was Hall. The employers wanted to meet again. So on December 27 Goldblatt and Hall went back to see Winn. Winn said the best the employers could offer was $1 million. Hall replied that there was a lot more coming than that.

---

2. Meaning that the Gladstein firm would pay all court costs and other expenses, repayable out of money received from the plantations. They would receive a fee of twenty percent of the amount recovered.

He and Goldblatt reported back to the union committee. A million dollars! Some of the committee members wanted to take the money and run. They figured the employers would never go any higher. Not Hall. He was one of the town's best poker players and, in essence, this was a big poker game. "Jack was of the opinion that we shouldn't settle for one million," said Goldblatt. Hall and Goldblatt argued with the committee to hold out for more and finally convinced them.

On January 3 Winn told them he would recommend a settlement for $1,500,000.[3] That was more like it, said Hall, and he and Goldblatt accepted, provided that the million and a half was "absolutely clear," with all taxes and all attorney's fees paid for by the employers.[4] The union committee was happy. It was a nice Christmas present. Hall was not happy. He thought Gladstein's fee was outrageous.[5]

At first the union members were ecstatic when the word came that they would share in the carving up of a million-dollar melon. But problems quickly arose: how much did each person get? Some workers refused to sign authorization for the suit. A few refused to accept their shares; they wanted more. There were "numerous other problems."

Goldblatt advised Hall to use the FLSA payments in conjunction with an intensive organizing drive: "A real cleanup of the industrial units," he said. The windfall was bound to have a

---

3. The exact figure: $1,501,548.02.

4. Gladstein said: "The companies directly paid $1,500,000 to us, plus a payment of an additional $300,000 to the IRS (Internal Revenue Service) representing income tax that the men would have otherwise had to pay out of their own pockets. Thus, the true settlement figure was $1,800,000. The workers received a net sum to themselves of $1,200,000. . . . I computed the 20 per cent attorney's fee of the net amount received by the men rather than the gross figure of the settlement. This resulted in a $300,000 fee rather than $360,000 as defined by our agreement.

"I turned over to Jack [Hall] $135,000 out of the fee to start a building fund for the union; a like amount was kept as my firm's fee, and $30,000 became a cost fund in part to repay what we had already spent and also to defray expenses for a test case to be taken to the U.S. Supreme Court."

5. Gladstein said: "The $135,000 that my office received for fee was actually 7½ per cent of the true total recovery of $1.8 million. My personal interest in my law partnership was at that time 16 per cent, I think; in any event, my own share of the fee was less than $25,000."

good effect, he said. It showed that the union was looking out for its people.

It had been suggested that in compiling information on how much was due each person, the union might "mark off the cards of those who might be considered ringleaders in the fight against the union." Goldblatt warned against any such temptation. He had discussed it with Bridges and Robertson. "Our general thinking," he said, "is that anybody who has money coming to him in this suit should get it." He told Hall to pay the men as quickly as possible. "It is not a good idea to have a hunk of dough like that kicking around with a lot of speculation from people as to what they have coming," he said.

Troubles grew. Hall said most workers were satisfied, but the delegates on the committee handling the distribution didn't want to take the responsibility for making decisions. Hall began to wish they hadn't collected the money. Frank Thompson felt the same way. He discovered "a hell of a lot of bickering" among Big Island union members over the money they had coming. "We should get this god damned money distributed at the earliest possible moment," he said. "I sometimes think we should have been better off if we had never gotten this FLSA money in the first place."

It took well over a year to get all the payments made. They ranged from about fifty to up to several hundred dollars. A few workers got as much as eight or nine hundred.

The union had agreed, as part of the settlement, that the employers could take a test case to a court of last resort for final determination of whom the Fair Labor Standards Act applied to. The employers looked upon this as just common sense insurance. They didn't want ever again to be in doubt.

Nine years later an FLSA test case surfaced and the ILWU got another bonus.

CHAPTER 24

The Men from the Barrios

On January 30, 1946, the *Maunawili* docked at Hilo with 1581 Filipino contract laborers who were "packed like sardines" in the hold. They were the first of six thousand postwar laborers to arrive—the last of the great mass importation of foreign fieldworkers to Hawaii. Frank Thompson, Rudy Eskovitz of the Marine Cooks and Stewards, and Rick Labez, Hall's aide, went down to dockside when the ship arrived. Hall and Kawano came next day. They were appalled.

Thompson was furious. "I have never seen a more dirtier ship and more rotten mess in my life. . . ." Hall said the union would be "raising hell" against any further importation of workers. Management bristled over the criticism. Hall predicted that the period of "sweetness and light" was over. So angry were the ILWU workers over importation of laborers that they wanted to "flex their muscles" against the Big Five. That might not be a bad idea, said Hall. It might "clear the smoke."

The issue of importation of Filipinos was handled in Washington since it required a waiver of the Tydings-McDuffie Act, permission of the War Shipping Board, and approval by the Departments of Labor and Agriculture. The sugar industry had been working for two years to arrange the move. Wendell Carlsmith said he had asked Hall to permit the import of six thousand workers. "It will mean the survival of the industry," he said. He claimed that Hall agreed.[1]

Hall prepared for indoctrinating the Filipinos by ordering each unit to act as a "godfather" for the workers. "I agreed to

---

1. Hall wrote Stainback saying the union did not object "if it can be demonstrated that such labor is required to maintain our basic economy."

put one Filipino laborer on Maui and Hawaii at our expense temporarily for the specific job of coordinating this work," he said. He also had arranged to convert the incoming workers to good union men while they were still aboard ship. The Marine Cooks and Stewards had placed a few militant crew members aboard to talk to them. By the time they arrived, they were strong for the union. The employers knew about it. They even knew how the union exerted pressure. There were ways to do it, said Slator M. Miller, the Hawaii Sugar Planters' Association (HSPA) official who organized the labor shipment in Manila. One was for crewmen to withhold fresh fruit from workers who didn't have an ILWU card.

It was not hard to get Filipinos from the villages and farms to come to Hawaii. To them, Hawaii was the "promised land." The biggest problem for the HSPA was handling the great number who wanted to come. "It was swamping us," said Miller. The HSPA bought an unused college campus in Manila as a place to process the workers. Workers signed a three-year contract and they had the right to be returned home at the end of the contract at HSPA expense. It took a year to process the six thousand. The cost of steerage passage was sixty-five dollars.

Most were Ilocanos from the three provinces of Ilocos Norte, Ilocos Sur, and Abra; a few were Tagalog-speaking Filipinos. The Ilocanos were considered the best workers—frugal, dependable. Filipinos made up the core of the plantation field hands. Tough, proud, sometimes touchy, they became fervent union men. The union gave them a sense of dignity.

Awkwardly, yet movingly, they described their dedication: Leocadio Baldovi said he was going to "bass *[sic]* his ass for our Union." He was doing organizing work among his fellow Filipinos and said: "Very soon working in this your children do not know you. But [I'm] enjoying working in this kind of job because my revenge on the Big Five is to get even with them."

Jacinto Conol, an organizer on the Big Island, said the union had enabled Filipinos "to taste the sweetness of democracy and learn that democracy is not only the road but also is the port . . . of the poor people. Brother, I am very proud to say again that I am a Filipino representing my race."

By mid-1946, the ILWU had organized eleven of the twelve pineapple plantations (all except Maui Pineapple Company) and all nine pineapple canneries. But the union had not completely organized the fieldworkers or the seasonal and intermittent labor.[2]

Early in 1946 contract negotiations started. Though the pineapple units were weak, Hall tried to get "every nickel in the poke." He predicted the industry might go for a wage increase of ten cents an hour in the basic grades. He asked for fifteen cents and the elimination of a five to ten-cent Kauai differential. At the same time the pineapple units built up pressure to take a strike vote. Hall mentioned it to Goldblatt.

Goldblatt squelched the idea and propounded the basic tenet in the ILWU's strategy of conducting economic warfare:

> Harry [Bridges] . . . pointed out that we do not give strike sanction in advance, but await breakdown of negotiations. . . . I don't know whether the people in Hawaii had in mind prior strike sanctions as a pressure move against the employers. This is not (repeat not) in line with our policy of not playing with strike sanctions. Under no circumstances would we want the employer to get the idea we turn a strike vote on and off like a water tap.

It would be unrealistic to think seriously of a pineapple strike, Goldblatt said. Organization was far from complete. Under such circumstances, taking a strike vote was a risky thing. "A light vote (in favor of a strike) or even a close vote can do great damage—a vote overriding our recommendation would be even more of a blow."

Hall knew that if the pineapple workers went on strike, the strike could not be more than thirty percent effective. The industry knew it, too. "We are not ready for a pine fight and we have to face that fact," said Hall.

An agreement was reached in June 1946. It called for a minimum ten-cent raise, retroactive for four months, and covered

---

2. Seasonals—mostly housewives and students who work during the peak summer season. Intermittents—those who work during the peak season and one or two days a week in addition.

5000 fieldworkers and 2200 cannery workers. Hall estimated the average employee would get back pay of eighty dollars. The pay raises would cost the industry $575,000. He had got all he could. "We made every pitch in the deck to squeeze a little more. . . ."

The pineapple workers ratified the contract, with the exception of some of the men on Lanai who belonged to what Hall called the "super-duper ascetic cult of Dr. Hilario Camino Moncado, the man who plays God." Hall said the next move was to complete the organization and consolidation of the pineapple bargaining units and the seasonal workers and to prepare for 1947. That year, he thought, might be a pineapple year.

Part 4
THE SUGAR STRIKE
(1946)

CHAPTER 25

The Battle Plan

Nineteen forty-six was the year of the 79-day sugar strike that tested the ILWU. It was the first territory-wide, industry-wide strike. The 1945 sugar contract expired August 31, 1946, and the union prepared for either a big gain in sugar wages or a strike. The ILWU asked for a 65-cent-an-hour minimum wage (a minimum increase of 18½ cents), a forty-hour work week, and a union shop. Hall called the demands modest. He also asked that the union have a say in the spending of what he called the employers' "$25 million housing fund." It was a figure he had come up with late one night sitting at his living room table with pencil and yellow legal tablet.

Management called the housing fund "a phantom fund"—it did not exist. It called the union's other demands excessive and said they would cost the industry over $21 million a year. It said ILWU members already were the highest-paid sugar workers in the world and that in 1945 the industry earned less than $4 million on sugar and related operations, or 2.3 percent net profit on an investment of more than $175 million.

The union warned that the sugar workers and the ILWU leadership did not embark lightly on strike action. "They know too well that strikes are not picnics; they strike only as a last resort."

Alexander G. Budge, president of Castle & Cooke, countered: "When labor asks for an increase amounting to more than 50% of the total present industry payroll, the industry has no alternative but to face the cold facts that it cannot pay the bill."

Both sides prepared to man the trenches; there was no doubt a strike was coming. The union had to show its muscle; the employers had to find out how strong that muscle was.

Hall started negotiations for the union and Dwight C. Steele, of the Employers Council, represented the sugar industry. Steele was a tall, urbane lawyer from California who had come to Hawaii earlier in the year at the invitation of Jim Blaisdell. Blaisdell had given him a good sales talk. He spoke of the joy of living in Hawaii—the good life of a well-paid business executive. "I thought this was the way to escape San Francisco—the hustle and bustle," said Steele. (He found out in his first two years in Hawaii that, thanks to the ILWU, he was so busy he seldom got home before three or four in the morning.)

Steele told Hall that management intended to end the perquisite system on the plantations and was prepared to fix the value of perquisites at fifteen cents an hour. Management would pay that much as part of wages and the employees would have to pay henceforth for housing, water, lights, and medical attention. Moreover, he said that management hoped the federal government would come to the industry's rescue by raising the price of sugar under the U.S. Sugar Act. Hall got out his pencil and yellow pad and put down some figures. "It would take about a cent per pound increase in the retail price of sugar to satisfy our demands," he calculated.

Steele asked Hall whether the ILWU would man the plantation utilities in case of a strike. Hall said yes, but they would expect to be paid regular wages. The union would assign the men to the job as part of their picket duty and their earnings "would be turned over to the strike committee."

Steele was nonplussed. "The damndest strike," he said. "We supply the housing, the utilities and the jobs for some workers to make money to feed the rest. Talk about sweetness and light! When is a strike not a strike—that is the question!"

Steele said the industry would not try to operate in the face of picket lines. He realized that the union meant business, but his employers took a while to get the point. He complained to Hall that they "do not seem to realize what they are up against in these negotiations, but they are quickly learning."

Hall looked his troops over. In May 1946, the ILWU was approaching its peak strength; membership was growing and morale was high.[1] "All our energy is going into pre-strike preparations," Hall wrote Goldblatt. A strike vote was taken

August 1: the tally was 15,406 in favor of calling a strike, 123 against. The same day the industry offered a 6½-cent wage increase. The ILWU placed ads in the papers on August 2 saying: "A Sugar Strike Looms." On August 14, Hall sent Goldblatt a cable: "SUGAR STRIKE CERTAIN SEPTEMBER ONE." Hall told Goldblatt that either he or Bridges should come over to Hawaii. Goldblatt replied that he was coming.

Strikes are battles and battles are won by careful preparation and by massing troops. In 1946 the ILWU planned to do battle. The union set up a 24-member Territorial Strike Strategy Committee (TSSC), made up of eight members from sugar units and sixteen from pineapple, longshore, and miscellaneous units. The sugar delegates had the "voice and vote"; the others had a voice but no vote. They were brought in for support.

Each plantation set up its own strike committee with both a relief and a publicity committee. All sugar workers were assigned strike duty. The ILWU estimated the strike would cost the union at least fifty thousand dollars a day.

A $15,000 fund was allocated for publicity. The ILWU purchased radio time in addition to its regular Sunday program at 6:15 PM. It started fifteen-minute programs at twenty dollars a program at 5 PM on Tuesday, Thursday, and Saturday over KGMB, KTOH, and KHBC. On September 1, the program went daily. McElrath, the union's information director, handled the radio program. Hall thought he did "a bang-up job," but said the ILWU needed another radio scriptwriter. Berman, the former CIO chief in Hawaii, was back from the mainland where he had earned a law degree. Hall asked Goldblatt: Should the ILWU hire Berman?[2]

Both sides began to beat the propaganda drums. On August

---

1. Sugar industry figures showed that at the outset of the sugar strike there were thirty-three plantations with 25,383 men and women in the bargaining units (23,913 men and 1,470 women). There were also 2598 children and 2935 adults outside the bargaining units—a grand total of 30,916 people employed in the industry.

2. Berman was never approached. Soon afterward he became a bitter opponent of Hall.

26, the industry mailed a booklet to more than sixty thousand island residents telling management's side of the story. The industry went on the air Monday through Saturday over KGMB, KTOH, and KHBC. Special announcements were made in Filipino over KGU five days a week and over KHBC six days a week. More than twenty spot announcements were broadcast on all radio stations daily.

Hall summarized the ILWU battle plan:

> All our efforts must be concentrated on strike preparations. If we win the strike we will win the political campaign. Strike committee must see to it that everyone has something to do: athletics, strike duty, meetings, etc. Must be able to account for every member at all times. Must have strike kitchen in every community to feed the bachelors. Fishing boats will give us fish at cannery prices.

Laupahoehoe workers asked Frank Thompson what they should do if the employers tried to evict them from their plantation housing. Evict 33,000 workers and their families? It seemed highly unlikely. Nevertheless, Thompson told them they would picket workers' homes just on the chance that selective eviction might be contemplated. He advised the workers to store rice and canned goods, to start planting vegetable gardens, to arrange for hunting and fishing parties. The word went out: This is the crucial test. Prepare for "a long drawn-out battle. We will win together or swing separately," said Thompson.

Fujisaki on the Big Island advised the Strike Strategy Committee to ask Ruddy Tongg, a Honolulu businessman, for permission to hunt pigs on land Tongg owned in the Volcano district. The ILWU arranged with G. A. Labrador in Honolulu to purchase at wholesale prices a thousand cases of the fish sauce known as *bagoong*. Olaa workers obtained a ten-acre plot near Volcano for a vegetable garden; they then borrowed a tractor and started planting. The Kauai relief committee polled its members and found they had food enough for a month. Ewa Plantation agreed to permit union members to raise vegetables on two acres and loaned them a tractor and a plow.

The Strike Strategy Committee sent out questionnaires to each sugar worker: What shape was he in? How big a food supply did he have? How much rice did his family use? How much canned milk, fresh milk, meat, potatoes? In what language did he want to get communications from the union—in English, Japanese, or Filipino?

On August 6 McElrath issued a call to arms. "The major task of every ILWU worker in the sugar industry is to win the strike—all other things being secondary." Hall was satisfied with all preparations, except at Local 142 on the Big Island. "Apparently [Amos] Ignacio [the local president] had the idea that the strike date is merely a threat and there is no real necessity for the organization of strike machinery." Hall sent committee members over to prod Ignacio.

Henry Schmidt, the ILWU expert on waterfront strikes, came over from San Francisco. He was impressed. "The sugar strike is one of the best planned I have ever seen," he said. "This strike can't lose." Goldblatt arrived August 26 and took over from Hall as the union's chief negotiator. He spoke to reporters: "If the industry can show that it simply cannot afford to pay what we want, we'll be willing to make counter-proposals. So far, we've seen no proof that it can't afford to pay them and still make a good profit."

At a negotiating session Goldblatt discussed the ILWU's demand for a union shop. Industry opposed it and claimed it would put workers under the complete control of the ILWU; they wouldn't be able to find work anywhere in Hawaii unless the ILWU approved. Thereupon Goldblatt proposed that the contract apply only to union members so that nonmembers wouldn't get a "free ride."

With Goldblatt's arrival the exchanges grew shriller. The ILWU brought up the subject of discrimination in housing. "People on the other side of the bargaining table have told me that Filipinos are a bunch of animals and don't need good housing," Hall said.

Steele replied that the companies were trying to eliminate discrimination. "If it would do any good, we could document these cases by the thousands," said Hall.

The last prestrike negotiating session took place on August 31. Goldblatt charged the employers with not bargaining in good faith and claimed they were trying to break the union. It was a probing attack. The battle lines already were drawn; the strike already was set. Both sides had been preparing for it "well in advance."

Robertson sent an eve-of-battle message: "Two and a half years of preparation have ended. Our cause is just. We are fighting for economic freedom and a better way of life for ourselves and our children. We will win. . . ."

Bridges and Robertson sent a night cable to Hall which said the strike "will end one hundred years of economic slavery in Hawaii. . . ."

At one minute after midnight on September 1, 1946, the sugar workers went out. It was, as they say in Hawaii, go for broke.

CHAPTER **26**

The Ricecapade

> *Empty cane cars stand idle on track sidings. Giant grabbers, their fingers empty, stand in rows in machinery yards, the red dirt caked on their sides. Irrigation flumes and channels are now dry except for stagnant pools of water.*
> —S. R. Logan (*Advertiser,* September 7, 1946)

On the second day McElrath declared that the strike was "100% effective." Most of the workers had never taken part in a strike, but they joined in eagerly. They seemed to be having fun. It was a holiday of sorts; a respite from hard work in fields and mills. To see them so carefree puzzled and even annoyed some people in management: "Their general attitude was that they were on a lark and having a good time." Fishing parties went out; hunting parties stalked wild pigs and goats in the mountains. The men manned the picket lines; served on committees; kept the utilities going.

The union expected every worker to do his duty. A battle order was issued: "A man who leaves the plantation during the strike without authorization is running out on the strike in the same way as a soldier who leaves the battlefield during the battle."

As early as midsummer Hall realized that in the union's preparations for a strike, there was one great weakness: rice. He had arranged for the purchase of 1000 cases of milk and 1000 bags of potatoes, and had tried to buy 10,000 hundred-pound bags of rice. But he was having trouble getting the rice. As word of a threatened strike went out, people began to buy rice and hoard it. Hall asked the ILWU headquarters in San Francisco to put pressure on the government to persuade California rice millers to release rice to the union or make it available to Frank Bellows, a Honolulu commission agent.

By July a black market existed in rice. Goldblatt was furious. He said the union missed a bet when it didn't move against black marketers to drive them into the open. "We ought to run down the people who are responsible and throw out some picket lines around their business places and homes," he said.

Hall grew anxious and prodded the ILWU's people on the mainland. "The rice situation is still bad and we await word from you," he wrote. Then he sent a cable: "WITHOUT RICE STRIKE PREPARATIONS SERIOUSLY WEAKENED."

He asked Harriet Bouslog, the ILWU's representative in Washington, to press the Department of Agriculture to increase Hawaii's rice quota.[1] With rice, Hall said, the strikers could hold out indefinitely. Without it, they would have to surrender. Rice was the word "uppermost in the minds of most of the membership."

Hall wrote Governor Stainback asking him to order the employers to release for sale to the workers stocks of rice at Lihue Plantation store and at McBryde Sugar Company store. When the Sugar Negotiating Committee called on Stainback, Hall

---

1. The quota for the year ending July 1, 1947, was 575,000 bags of rice.

went along. Yoshikazu Morimoto of Kauai, a committee member, acted as spokesman. "Hall was mad at Stainback at the time and didn't want to see him," said Morimoto. "Goldblatt ordered him to." They crowded into the executive chambers on the third floor of Iolani Palace. Morimoto spoke up. Stainback picked up the phone and called H. Alexander Walker of American Factors. "When we called back to Kauai, we got word that the rice was released," said Morimoto.

Robertson cabled Secretary of Interior Julius A. Krug saying the union had tried to buy ten thousand bags of rice but failed. He urged Krug to order rice allocated over and beyond the quota "to prevent starvation in the islands." That extra rice would not be sold commercially, he promised, but would go only for the relief of workers.

"Unless a large shipment of rice reaches them within the next few weeks, the strike may be lost," Robertson said. He went to the California rice millers and tried to buy rice, but they told him their brokers in Hawaii wouldn't sell rice directly to the ILWU. Robertson charged that they were "starving the workers" in an attempt to break the strike.

Strikers at Hilo Sugar, Ookala, Waiakea Mill, Honokaa, and Pauuilo were reporting shortages of rice. The Strike Strategy Committees on all the islands were reporting the same message. Some workers began eating breadfruit instead of rice. Schmidt urged Robertson to make "every effort . . . at your end to sail a relief ship as soon as possible and as frequently thereafter as possible." A relief ship *(Sea Hare)* did sail, but Schmidt claimed it brought only ten thousand cases of whiskey and eighteen thousand cases of beer. "How the heck are you going to eat whiskey?" he said.[2]

Aside from rice, Hall worried about the six thousand newly arrived Filipinos. Would they support the strike? Few had any

---

2. Schmidt was wrong. *Sea Hare*'s hatch stow documents (Matson Terminals, San Francisco, October 7, 1946) show that the ship carried 9123 cases of whiskey and 14,549 cartons of beer, but in addition it brought 3775 bags of rice and 1375 bags of potatoes.

money. "All these guys had was a buck in their pocket and a pair of jeans." Hall heard that the employers believed the Filipinos would "break ranks." "We got the word from reliable sources," said Goldblatt.[3]

But these Filipinos were hardy people. Some had fought with the Huks in the guerrilla war against the Japanese. They were strong, used to hard work, and "very dedicated." They cheerfully manned the picket lines. There were so many of them on picket duty, in fact, that word came to place at least a few non-Filipinos on every picket post.

Rick Labez, Hall's administrative assistant, worked with his countrymen. He was born in Cebu and brought to Kauai at age two. Labez was a reporter on the *Hilo Tribune-Herald* when Hall talked him into working for the union. "Rickie," he said, "you're always talking about equal treatment and justice for your people. It's not going to come any other way except through organized labor and trade unions. . . . Damn it, we might change the whole system."

Labez talked to his people; pleaded with them. He sent out a stream of messages through the union's regular communications system: "Our enemies are using the letters to the editor . . . to vilify and slander us." Deluge the editors with pro-union letters, he said, forgetting for the moment that many of the alien Filipinos could not speak or write English.

On the mainland the union's quest for rice moved ahead. Goldblatt's secretary (administrative assistant Virginia Woods) was very bright, but unacquainted with island eating habits. She researched the subject of rice and discovered that brown (unpolished) rice is more nutritious than white rice. The trouble was that nobody in Hawaii likes brown rice. They eat white rice. "Brown rice is for peasants," people said.

His work finished in Hawaii, Frank Thompson, the organizer, had gone home to Sacramento, and now Thompson, a man who hated rice, was trying to buy stocks of rice for the union. He found he could get between five and ten thousand bags im-

---

3. From the maids of the employers.

mediately. The cost delivered at dockside in Honolulu would be $11.02 per hundred-pound bag. "Keep your pants on," he told his friends in Hawaii; plenty of rice would be coming.

Virginia Woods in the San Francisco office handled the money; Thompson arranged to buy and ship the rice. Woods told Hall to cable the money for the rice—it had to be on deposit next day to guarantee delivery. It wasn't as much as they had hoped for, but it would help. By then almost every grain counted. Aboard the *Laura Drake Gill* were 4487 bags.

In due course the *Gill* arrived, the rice was delivered—and then, panic. It was brown rice and nobody wanted it. The phones from sugar units all over the islands started ringing in Hall's ears. "MISTAKE IS RAISING HELL," he cabled Robertson. He told Robertson not to ship any more brown rice and to dispose of what brown rice they had bought. Ship "only white polished rice," he pleaded. He then informed Woods that Locals 150 and 152 "do not want brown under any circumstances."

By the first of October some of the Filipino union members had to apply for welfare. David Thompson, the union's research director, told them there was "nothing shameful" about it, but the Filipinos hesitated to seek help from the government or even from their union. Often they had to have rice thrust upon them. They were proud.

Some sought outside employment during the strike and even temporarily joined the AFL. The report got around that they were abandoning the ILWU. "Spike this rumor immediately," Labez ordered. But, as was inevitable, some went hungry. Edward K. Wagner, the dog warden on the Big Island, was making his rounds at Waiakea Plantation Camp 6 toward the end of October and smelled the odor of burning hair. He asked what it was and a Filipino took him to a barbecue pit. "They were roasting three dogs," said Wagner.

CHAPTER 27

Three Bottles of Four Roses

To win the strike the union had to keep the plantations from irrigating the cane. That was the "most powerful weapon" they had. At Lihue Plantation masses of pickets stopped the supervisors from using sewer water to irrigate. At Olaa pickets marched like a phalanx. Pickets massed in depth in front of supervisors' houses at Honokaa, Honomu, and Laupahoehoe. On Oahu police received reports that Waipahu sugar workers threatened to picket small merchants if they didn't support the strike. (Hall told Okada, the Strike Strategy Committee secretary, that "we don't want violence; no picketing of stores refusing credit.")

Alex Walker, spokesman for the sugar industry, said the ILWU was exerting strong pressure on employees to join the union. "They have threatened and coerced the employees' children. . . . Wholesale intimidation is going on on virtually every plantation," he said. A management official referred to union "gangsterism." At Paia, three or four hundred Maui Agricultural Company strikers barred five strikebreakers from entering the plantation. The strikers stood shoulder to shoulder and "without using their hands, pushed the group . . . back about five feet." William Buddingh, Lihue Plantation chief engineer, said massed pickets stood "cat-calling and booing."

The employers applied for a temporary order restraining ILWU men from mass picketing and it was granted by Lihue Circuit Judge Philip L. Rice.

The union called Rice "a plantation judge" and printed a leaflet, bearing Hall's signature,[1] titled "A Lawless Judge Will Not Break the Sugar Strike." The circular said Rice had issued

---

1. Gladstein wrote it.

the injunction "after a private conference with the Lihue Plantation Company behind closed doors."

That charge aroused the Bar Association of Hawaii and it passed a resolution, prepared by Samuel P. King, condemning the ILWU circular as "a scurrilous attack on [Rice's] judicial integrity." The resolution called attention to the supposed author, Hall, who was a member of the Honolulu Police Commission, and demanded that he be fired from the commission.[2]

Gladstein was summoned to resist the injunction. He and Hall flew to Lihue and before a packed courtroom Gladstein fought but lost. The injunction stood. Hall and Goldblatt discussed the outcome. Hall didn't care much about his being a member of the Police Commission; that wasn't important. But what should they do in the face of Rice's injunction? "If we can't picket, we won't picket," they decided. "Instead, we'll have parades."

The union called a mass meeting across the street from the courthouse and, two thousand strong, they marched through town, around the homes of people alleged to be strikebreakers, and around the plantation mill. It was a show of strength and nobody in town could miss the point. Every morning union members gathered as though for army roll call. There was a head count to be sure no one was AWOL. "We had parades. . . . There was not a damned thing they could do about it," said Goldblatt.

The sugar cane started to dry up.

Back at the bargaining table negotiations turned into verbal combat. "If your intentions are not to evade the law, why do you resent the enforcement of the law [Rice's injunction]?" Blaisdell demanded. "Our men are not lawbreakers," Goldblatt retorted.

Blaisdell: Meanwhile you are trying to damage the industry by preventing irrigation.

Goldblatt: Agree to keep supervisors from irrigating and we will withdraw our picket lines.

---

2. On September 26, 1945, when Hall and Stainback were relatively at peace, Stainback had appointed Hall to the Police Commission.

Blaisdell: Are you trying to damage the industry?

Goldblatt: We're striking, picketing, and won't be used to break our own strike by irrigation.

Goldblatt spoke of the "handful of malcontents who think it is smart to ride the wagon without paying their share of the freight." He meant the sugar workers who wouldn't join the union. Blaisdell replied there were only a few of them and the union should be big enough to take it. Goldblatt responded that it wasn't the length of the thorn that hurt, but how much of it was "sticking in you."

Often after an exchange the employers' side would call for a recess to go out and talk things over. Goldblatt scoffed that they didn't have the power to bargain. They had to call their superiors: Walker, president of American Factors, "and other HSPA bigshots," he said. Constantine Samson, a cheerful fellow who was a member of the union negotiating committee, said, "Tell them we want . . . the big *uluas*." He meant the industry's power wielders.

Bargaining sessions broke off September 19. Hall said no progress had been made. "They will not yield an inch," he said.

Stanley V. White, a conciliator for the United States Department of Labor, was sent to Hawaii to mediate the strike, but he found it as hard to crack as the shell of a macadamia nut. He called a meeting in a room at the Commercial Club on Bethel Street in Honolulu and summoned Hall and Goldblatt, Steele and Blaisdell. The two sides sat stiffly on couches while White, in the center of the room, sat at a card table upon which he had placed a sacrificial offering: three bottles of Four Roses bourbon. White was nervous and didn't know how to begin. Hall spoke up gruffly: "Just one lousy dozen Roses, huh?"

That broke the ice. They started drinking and talking but got nowhere and after an hour or so they adjourned. They had made a good dent in the Four Roses and were feeling better. They went downstairs. A policeman's motorcycle was parked in shiny splendor at the curb. Hall admired it. "I used to ride those things," said White. "I'll show you how."

He climbed aboard and at that moment out walked a police officer from the nearby police station who took it all in at a glance and said, "All right, come with me." He marched them into the police station. Horrified by what had happened, White started to explain. The others, under the spell of the bourbon, pretended to be indifferent. White flashed his business card. "Is the Sergeant around? Is the Captain around? I've got to talk to him," he gabbled. Finally a police captain arrived and White told him who they were and that they were not trying to steal the motorcycle. He released them, unbooked.

When they got outside Hall turned on White in mock anger and said: "Well, you flubbed it!"

"What do you mean?" exclaimed White.

Goldblatt said he would explain: "If you had said 'Lock those pricks up,' and then gone to the newspapers and told them to start a campaign to keep us in jail until we settled the strike, you would have made headlines all over the country."

On October 16 White asked the two sides to resume regular bargaining sessions. The employers refused, saying "premature meeting would delay rather than hasten settlement." White set a meeting anyway for October 21. The employers, through a third party, relayed the information that they would not attend.

White was so angry that he committed a breach of the conciliators' code. He publicly denounced what he called the employers' "public-be-damned" attitude. That remark ended his usefulness; he was now *persona non grata* and on October 23 he was recalled to San Francisco and a cooler climate.

Steele was upset. He said White must have known the two sides were working day and night to achieve a settlement. "No one could be more fully aware of the necessity for speedy conclusion of the strike than the sugar plantations, which are losing more than $343,000 a day," he said.

Every morning the ILWU was confronted by the *Honolulu Advertiser,* a paper that treated the union with open hostility. The ILWU called the *Advertiser* a "house organ for the sugar interests" and asked its members to boycott it. The union even distributed leaflets on doorsteps and in parked cars urging the public not to buy the paper.[3] To the ILWU, the newspaper sounded anti-Semitic. It pointed to a letter, signed "Justice Be Done," in the September 30 issue: "Who are these 'Steins' and 'Golds' and 'Schmidts' that invade our home land and tell us they will not let us starve?"

Hall said the *Advertiser* whipped up the froth of red-baiting. "The latest move of the employers is to lay a foundation for the well-known 'red-scare.' " Hall focused on elements in the community who he said had made the ILWU their target: We, the Women, and the Benevolent and Protective Order of Elks, "made up of bosses who suddenly open a campaign against what they called 'un-American activities.' "[4]

The strike was the big news of the day; everything else was secondary. In Hilo, Doc Hill, the politician–business executive, offered milk to ILWU strikers' children under age three if the parents did business with him. He also offered cash and milk to the union, but he did not say how much. The Big Island Strike Strategy Committee passed a motion to accept the offer "if no strings were attached."

McElrath hired a man named Hal Lewis to work for the union as a radio scriptwriter. Lewis was broke and needed a job.[5] He worked only a short time (at fifteen dollars a day) for the union. Then he got an offer from Smith, Mansfield & Cummins, an advertising and public relations agency, and left.

In the middle of the strike the Waianae Sugar Company went out of business. Management attributed it to the cost of labor and Hall retorted that the employers' allegation was just another move to break the strike and Waianae was no loss. "We are not sorry to see Waianae go out of business," he said. "The housing is unfit for pigs. Wages are miserably low; the working condi-

---

3. Raymond Coll, Sr., the *Advertiser*'s veteran editor, called the ILWU boycott "a Communist-Fascist technique."

4. The Elks sponsored antiunion ads in the newspapers. An organization known as "12 Little Men" also campaigned against the ILWU.

5. Later, Lewis adopted the soubriquet of "J. Akuhead Pupule," or more simply "Aku," and achieved a certain fame as a radio disc jockey.

tions are lousy and Frickle *[sic]*, the manager, has no friends among the workers."[6]

Outwardly, Hall appeared confident; inwardly, he was getting desperate. The cupboard was bare and still management was hanging on. Hall cabled the ILWU International that the union was "running into desperate straits." He urged them "to act at once on our appeal for help." He wired President Truman and thirteen mainland unions. He said the Big Five "plans to starve us into submission." He asked the mainland unions to send contributions.[7]

By now the strike had reached out and touched Washington. Secretary of Labor Lewis Schwellenbach sent out a fresh team of mediators: Nathan P. Feinsinger, a University of Wisconsin law professor, and Joe Coe, a Madison, Wisconsin, lawyer. Goldblatt knew Feinsinger and said he was competent. Feinsinger went boldly into action. First he moved the bargaining from the HSPA board room to the Moana Hotel where he was staying; then he called for round-the-clock sessions. The two sides went at it day and night. Under such conditions the most valuable asset a negotiator can have is an iron bottom. Feinsinger brought about a settlement. The strike ended at 7:30 PM, November 18. These were the major points:

1. A 22-month contract with wages ranging from 70½ cents to $1.38 an hour. (The basic wage before the strike was 43½ cents plus perquisites.)

2. An end to the perquisite system.

3. A continuance of the 48-hour work week. The union lost its bid for a 40 hour week.

4. A continuance of the irrevocable checkoff system as a guarantee of union security. The union did not get a union shop.

Hall called the settlement "a tremendous victory." The employers hardly felt the union had made such startling gains, but admitted it was "a remarkable victory." "When you netted it

6. Hall meant Robert Fricke.
7. By December 6, 1946, the ILWU had received a total of $18,719.99 from twenty-two mainland unions.

out—the plusses and minuses—what the union got out of it, it got organized," said John F. Murphy, Castle & Cooke's representative on the negotiating committee.

Another management executive saw far more in it than that. Philip Brooks, the Employers Council research director, said the strike frightened the employers and

> created a general awe of the union power on the part of workers, employers and the public. For the first time in Hawaiian history the employers had been soundly and definitely thwarted. The psychological value of this display of defiance of the employers could not fail to add immensely to union power.

CHAPTER **28**

On-the-Job Training

> *It's not fair to any of the people to take snapshots of them at any period of time and say,* "This is the way it was." *Jack Hall changed all the time.*
>
> —John F. Murphy of Castle & Cooke
>
> *I didn't start as an accomplished negotiator. I had butterflies too.*
>
> —Jack Hall

Hall was learning the art of labor negotiating; Goldblatt was his teacher. An incident which took place toward the end of the sugar negotiations made it clear. It was one or two in the morning and Steele, Blaisdell, and Murphy were working with Goldblatt and Hall to iron out the seniority language in the contract.

All day long and into the night they had worked. Hall was angry; his mouth tight and hard-set, the way he looked under strain. He felt that the employers' team was stalling. In frustration, he struck the wall with his fist, as though exclaiming: "To hell with it! I'm going home."

Goldblatt turned on him and said icily: "You *read* this language, Jack. You *study* it and tell me what's wrong with it." Hall said nothing and obediently bent to the task. Murphy watched him, shocked. "It showed clearly who was running this thing," he said. "If anyone said that to me [in that way] that would be the end of it. I feel he put him down something awful."

Hall was still a novice then. When Goldblatt felt the need to do so, he would "ruthlessly shove him aside." ILWU leadership was merciless, said Murphy. "They operated Hawaii the way the Romans operated England. They put a fellow in charge and expected him to solve the troubles and difficulties." He continued:

> On many occasions Goldblatt came in when the negotiations had been going on and Hall had been running them and they displaced him. In fact, Goldblatt was, by reason of experience, the better negotiator than Hall. When Goldblatt decided that the time had come to settle, he was ingenious in finding solutions to the small problems that can stick in our throat. Clever! That was the word for Goldblatt.

Howard Babbitt, Brewer's representative on the sugar industry's negotiating committee, was not impressed with Hall during the 1946 negotiations. "He definitely was second echelon to Goldblatt, under Bridges," said Babbitt.

> But he certainly was an apt student and he rapidly caught on to the technique of negotiations and to the various parts of it, like the job classification system, the mechanics of a pension plan, life insurance, and the costs of plantation operations. To get into sugar negotiations, he had to do a tremendous amount of work.

The employers' negotiating team operated by consensus. Management set up a committee with each of the Big Five represented and tried to come to agreement on a wage offer and a policy. "We tried to hammer out decisions that would run along a unanimous basis," said Steele. But trying to get five diverse agencies to work in harmony was hard. All plantations are different. Wet versus dry: irrigated versus nonirrigated. Each plantation has its own long-range and short-range objectives; each has a different method of operation and a different philosophy.

During the 1946 strike the Hamakua Coast plantations were in good shape because they were getting plenty of rain. But the irrigated plantations, deprived of water, began to suffer. "That intensified the feeling of the two groups within the sugar industry itself and the longer the strike went on, the more that went on," said Philip Maxwell of the Employers Council.

Often the union was able to steal the employers' signals. Suppose management decided to authorize its negotiators to offer an eight-cent wage raise. At the bargaining table Steele might open with, say, a four-cent offer. The union spokesman would scoff. "We know you got eight cents in your pocket," he would say.[1] Both sides tried to ferret out the other's trade secrets and often succeeded. Moreover, during the negotiations there were a lot of "nonverbal communications" and a "lot of hints" dropped. Anyone with a sharp ear (and Hall could hear very well) could pick up things.

The men who faced Hall across the bargaining table in those early days of big labor negotiations remembered him as a revolutionist. "I think he thought he might even convert me," said Steele. "And he might have." Steele was impressed with Hall's capacity for hard work and his attention to detail: "He was the first union negotiator I've run across who, at the conclusion of a negotiation, when the contract was drafted for signature, took the time in the meeting to read the contract, word for word, to make sure it was accurate."

Hall grew, said Steele. He became more confident and more powerful, and as the union became more secure there was "less speech-making and sword-rattling and more businesslike negotiations."

---

1. Steele could never understand how the union often was privy to management secrets. McElrath offered an explanation: he said that sometimes the union was tipped off by second-echelon members of management who for some reason or other were irked with their bosses.

Both sides took credit in 1946 for the elimination of the plantation perquisite system. Management claimed it was determined from the start to get rid of the system, but argued that the union was hesitant until the deed was done and then took credit for it.

The sugar industry had decided by mid-1945 that the perquisite system had to go for two reasons: to clear up the problem of overtime under the Fair Labor Standards Act and to prevent the union from using the subject of perquisites, such as housing, to drive a hard bargain. Budge, the Castle & Cooke president, told the employers' negotiating team that they had to "clean up" (read, "get rid of") the perquisite system. He said it was a hangover from the old days.

Philip Brooks, a member of the management team at the negotiations, said that, throughout the sessions,

> Goldblatt had reminded the employers that it was they who had proposed conversion [of perquisites], not the union. He had even suggested delaying or omitting the conversion and giving straight increases with the perquisites continuing in effect as in the past, but in his speech [after the strike was settled] he hailed the perquisite conversion as a great victory for the union.

Indeed, after the settlement was announced, Goldblatt contended that getting rid of perquisites was a prime union objective. Over the radio he said:

> Just as long as perquisites continue to exist, so will favoritism be a powerful weapon in the hands of the employers. Just so long as the perquisite system is used on the plantations, just that long will it be impossible to bring about American standards.

Recalling the 1946 negotiations, Goldblatt said: "One of the things we *had* to get rid of was the perquisite system." It incensed Goldblatt to hear workers talk about "free" housing, "free" water, "free" medical care. "Free?" he would exclaim. "What do you mean 'free'? You're getting paid twenty-four cents an hour."

Goldblatt said the ILWU won the 1946 strike because it had set up the machinery with which to battle the employers. The union knew it could not win in Hawaii until the "heart of economic power'' had been won: namely, the sugar industry. Said Goldblatt:

> We had a new type of organization that helped make this the first successful strike against the Big Five. We had an industrial organization, from top to bottom, clear through from the workers in the fields to the dock workers and longshoremen, and we added one thing—a direct line to the maritime workers, through the ILWU.

Once the strike was won, Hall issued a confidential memorandum to all sugar units and locals urging them to "minimize job action." He meant not to act cocky and tough but to take part willingly in a cooling-off period. That did not mean, he said, that the union "should drop its beefs." He explained: "This period of playing down job action is important in order to build our record with the public and center attention on our fight at Lahaina with Pioneer Mill manager John Moir."

By November 27 all the sugar workers, except at Pioneer Mill, were back on the job. Moir, "a hardheaded Scotchman," insisted on his right to fire eleven employees who, among other things, had beaten three supervisors.

CHAPTER 29
The Unpleasantness
at Pioneer Mill

The Pioneer Mill prolongation of the 1946 sugar strike lasted forty-four days and didn't do Harry Bridges' ulcers any good. Bridges was in Hawaii at the time and he tried, with Hall, to find a solution. The Pioneer Mill strike involved 1067 workers, many of them Filipinos. When Moir fired the eleven employees on November 19, the other union members walked off the job and voted to continue the sugar strike. Hall said Moir's action violated the memorandum of agreement that ended the strike.

Moir[1] was a man who believed a plantation manager's job was to manage. Over the years he had earned a reputation for being tough but fair. He knew sugar, the ILWU conceded, "from top to bottom." He had grown up on a plantation and for a time he was the only *haole* boy at Papaikou on Hawaii. His first job on a plantation was shoveling manure. He had had eleven and a half years of experience as manager of the old Koloa Sugar Company on Kauai and by 1946 had been at Pioneer Mill for thirteen years.[2]

"When the strike was settled," said Moir, "they neglected to tell the union that certain guys were going to be fired for beating up on the supervisors. They made a settlement. When our guys came back to work, I called in half a dozen of the worst guys and talked to them."

The altercation had come about over irrigating. Mac Masato Yamauchi, the unit's Strike Strategy Committee chairman, had ordered the men to stop any attempt by management to irrigate.

---

1. Pronounced "Moyer."
2. Moir spent almost twenty years at Pioneer Mill.

On November 6, union members attacked Harlow Wright, the industrial relations manager, M. H. Nelson, the chief mill engineer, and James Backlund, the steam plant engineer. They beat Wright and broke his glasses and knocked Nelson and Backlund into an irrigation ditch. "He water; he get hurt," said one man.

Goldblatt told Hall the ILWU wanted reinstatement of the men without discrimination against them of any kind. He said the union would give the company "a face-saver"—namely, that the reinstatement would be probationary, depending on the outcome of the cases in court. Goldblatt said the ILWU must establish two principles. First, that disciplinary action against a union member must be held in abeyance until the court decided his case. Second, that if the union member was found guilty of violating the law, once he paid the penalty then he must not lose his job. That would be double jeopardy.

Hall tried to invoke the Goldblatt Formula to end the strike. He offered to send the men back to work, pending the outcome of the case, but management refused. Hall said three of the eleven were charged with "unlawful assembly," a statute passed in 1869 by the Kingdom of Hawaii and, according to Hall, "invoked only once in seventy-seven years."

After "dickering back and forth for three days," the two sides met in Moir's office. There was a full array: Bridges and Hall; Moir and Peter Faye, the HSPA president; and the conciliators, Feinsinger and Roe. Bridges put a brown paper bag on the table containing a half-pint carton of half-milk, half-cream. He puffed on a cigarette and at intervals took a swig from the carton. His ulcer was biting.

Hall noticed a disassembled recording machine in the room. He got upset because he thought Moir was taping their conversation. "They thought I was crooking," said Moir. He and Hall had known each other from the time Hall "jumped ship at Port Allen," but at the bargaining table, with a stubborn issue to be solved, Moir was all business. Moir told Bridges he'd better get his men back to work; they were tired of eating cabbage soup.

The problem was the court cases. Feinsinger said that on the mainland, under similar circumstances, employers thought nothing of getting a settlement arranged with a judge ahead of time. Moir said he was astounded to hear that; that was not the way *he* operated. As for going down to see the judge, Moir said, that was out. Definitely. He was not going to do it. Let the law take its course. As he spoke, Faye kicked Moir in the shins under the table.

At that moment the phone rang. Someone wanted to talk to Feinsinger. He got on the line and suddenly his face brightened. "Okay, they're going back to work," he said with a smile. He had hardly put down the phone when it rang again. Feinsinger picked it up. It was Yamauchi, the Strike Strategy Committee chairman, on the line and he was angry. "Who told you we're going back to work?" he demanded. "We haven't even had a meeting."

Feinsinger argued with him for a while and then "laid it down" to him. "You're going back to work!" he ordered and hung up. "That was that," said Moir. The men went back to work on January 2, 1947.

Twenty-one union members were charged with felonies that included unlawful assembly, riot, third-degree conspiracy, and assault and battery. They pleaded nolo contendere. Harriet Bouslog handled the defense and pleaded for leniency and cited mitigating circumstances. Emotions run high during a strike, she said. "It is the opinion of the counsel that considering the number of people involved of the rank and file, it was a peaceful strike."

Circuit Judge Cable Wirtz fined Yamauchi $600 and gave him a suspended sentence. The other defendants were found guilty of taking the law in their own hands and were fined amounts that ranged from $200 to $25. No one went to jail. It cost the union more than $50,000 for the Pioneer Mill strike, which the unit repaid. All the discharged union members went back to work. "That burned me up," the iron-clad Moir said. "They made me take them back."[3]

---

3. Clark Kerr of the University of California at Berkeley arbitrated the case. He held that the workers' discharge was unwarranted and ordered them reinstated.

Part 5
FRIENDS AND FOES
(1946–1947)

CHAPTER 30
Farrington and the 1946 Election

In 1946 Hall supported Delegate Farrington for reelection to Congress, and that support may have cost Farrington several *haole* friends. One of them, realtor Lindsley Austin, was so incensed that upon meeting Farrington at a polling place on election day, he tried to hit him. "You *Communist!*" Austin shouted.

Joseph R. Farrington, the conservative Republican son of Governor Wallace Rider Farrington, had created instant enemies merely by accepting Hall's support. But Hall's support for Farrington also puzzled a number of ILWU members. Farrington was the owner and publisher of the afternoon *Star-Bulletin,* whose editorial page often castigated the union.[1]

Farrington was first elected in 1942. He once warned the big employers that their indiscriminate loathing of unions would backfire. "Now look here," he told them, "if you don't let a good union in, some day a militant one will come along." And it had come to pass: the ILWU came along. Farrington conceded that the ILWU got plantation workers higher pay and better working conditions "they wouldn't have gotten otherwise." In 1938, when he was a territorial senator, he told a gathering in Miller's Gymnasium[2] that the only way labor was going to get anywhere in Hawaii was to play politics. In the audience were Hall, Kawano, and Willie Crozier. He didn't have to tell them. They knew it already.

---

1. Thirty years later former members of the union still couldn't understand the ILWU's support for Farrington.

2. On the third floor of the Arcade Building at Merchant and King Streets in Honolulu.

For Farrington there was one great mission in life: statehood. From Washington he had a pipeline to Hawaii through his friend and confidant, Riley H. Allen, editor of the *Star-Bulletin*. Allen was one of Hawaii's most industrious letter writers and kept a steady correspondence with Farrington. He was informer, adviser, instructor, and teller of tales. He came to the office every weekday, Sundays, and holidays. He was there on Sunday, December 7, 1941, and directed his news staff on the biggest story of the century in Hawaii.

Allen loved politics and he watched the 1946 election with rabid interest. In mid-July Governor Stainback tapped William Borthwick, the tax commissioner, to run against Farrington. Allen figured the Democrats had no one else "willing to make a fight of it" and was not inclined to take Borthwick's candidacy very seriously. "I would not feel that Bill is a formidable candidate," he said. But, as was his custom, he instructed his political writers[3] to give Borthwick "courteous and objective treatment." He told them:

> We must make every effort to see that he has no excuse for claiming that he is getting an unfair deal from "Joe Farrington's" paper. On the other hand, there is certainly no need for us to get unduly excited about the sort of competition he is going to give.

In due course, the ILWU's Political Action Committee endorsed Farrington. Although Hall was not an officer of the committee, his influence was decisive. At once a rumor was born and took wing—namely, that Farrington had "made a deal" with Hall: that Hall would support Farrington if the *Star-Bulletin* played the news "straight" during the sugar strike and didn't badger the union. "Balderdash," said Allen when he heard about it.

Hall said he supported Farrington because Farrington had been a good delegate and because he was for statehood. "We ache for statehood," Hall said. He did not think Borthwick believed in statehood. In any case, a delegate to Congress was simply an onlooker; he had no vote, no real power, though

---

3. Millard Purdy and Adam A. "Bud" Smyser.

often, through the force of his personality (or the size of his bankroll), he might make an impact. Hall thought Farrington had accomplished at least that. Moreover, he could talk to Farrington and Farrington would listen. He might not do what Hall wanted, but he would listen to him.

McElrath, Bob Mookini (of the pineapple local), and Marshall McEuen,[4] the ILWU's director of education, interviewed Farrington. He told them that his whole program was going to be statehood for Hawaii. "Nothing else. If you endorse me on that basis, I'd appreciate it," he said. On that basis, the Political Action Committee did. "We saw no reason for a change," said McElrath.

So the PAC commitment was made and the weapons were loaded. Ed Berman, the former labor leader, helped Borthwick. He and Hall were now at odds. Borthwick opened fire. He said Farrington was "romancing now with the PAC and any other group he thinks will support him." Borthwick said Hall had told him in 1944 that the ILWU was going to back Farrington. "Joe sold out his conscience and his editorial page," said Borthwick. "I looked Jack Hall in the eye, or as near as you can because Hall won't look you in the eye, and he told me he was committed to Farrington."

Berman said Farrington wanted "a nice, on-the-platter bunch of votes from the ILWU and he got them." Other people sounded off, among them Lorrin P. Thurston, publisher of the *Advertiser*. It rankled him that the *Star-Bulletin* did not condemn the ILWU. Over the radio, Ray Coll, Sr., the *Advertiser*'s editor, asked why the *Star-Bulletin* wasn't lashing out against the ILWU. Said Coll:

Fires are being kindled to singe capitalism in these islands and eventually destroy it. Neither Delegate Farrington nor Citizen Farrington's investments will be safe if the flames are permitted to spread. . . .

4. McEuen, a *Star-Bulletin* linotype operator, held strong Christian Socialist opinions. In December 1946 he was elected a director of the PAC. In November 1947 he began an education program for the ILWU to develop union leadership at the grass roots.

On November 4, the day before the general election, the *Advertiser* ran an eight-column headline over a photostatic copy of a report submitted by McEuen, director of the PAC. McEuen's report, "Director's Report September 29 to October 12," contained this paragraph:

> If we [the PAC] endorsed Mr. Borthwick for Delegate, we would have had the *Advertiser* cutting our throats and the *Star-Bulletin* neutral or against us. I am sure that all of our people have noticed that the *Star-Bulletin* gave the PAC every possible break in the news columns. They have been thoroughly friendly to us.

Berman flared; he said McEuen's report proved that "a deal" had been made. "Just re-read those words about the *Star-Bulletin* being neutral or against us."

Every morning the *Advertiser* greeted the Farringtons at breakfast and Betty Farrington, the candidate's wife, lost her appetite. "Joe had become the evil one," said Mrs. Farrington. The Farringtons protested, but in vain. "The bombardment kept on. Our friends deserted us." It was all nonsense, said Mrs. Farrington. All the *Star-Bulletin* was doing was simply trying to present impartial news coverage. "There was no question about slanting our columns," she said. "It didn't mean we would support them [the ILWU] in any way. It was merely fair news coverage. Joe never had a deal with them in his life."

Mrs. Farrington invited Marian Martin, head of the Women's Division of the Republican National Party, to Hawaii and arranged a luncheon for her. Only five friends showed up. Said Mrs. Farrington:

> That's how bad it was. They just wouldn't speak to us. And Joe resorted finally to even putting a paid ad in the paper to say that they [the ILWU] endorsed him, but he didn't endorse them. And that he naturally accepted any vote, but that he had no deal whatever.

On election day Farrington was grateful that the ILWU had stationed some of its own stalwarts near the precincts. He felt they kept him from being assaulted by irate Republicans. At the polling places Farrington had to fend off people who kept asking him why he had accepted ILWU support. He told them: "I don't understand what you're talking about. A bank takes money from a depositor and I take a vote from a voter."

Some ILWU leaders from Maui and Kauai came to Oahu and asked Kimoto why the union supported a Republican rather than a Democrat. Kimoto said he didn't know. He said the party (the Communist Party) didn't make the decision. It had to be Hall, he said. The Neighbor Island ILWU men went home troubled. They resented the way the endorsement had been handled; it even appeared they might support Borthwick and not Farrington. Kimoto flew over to Kauai and told them: first things first. He said the most important thing was to win the sugar strike and not let politics divide them at such a crucial time. The ILWU had made a public commitment to Farrington; so be it. He himself was not convinced there was good reason for that commitment, but unity—like a cool head—was the main thing.

In 1946 Doc Hill was running for reelection to the Territorial Senate. At the time he was antiunion, so the ILWU tried to defeat him. But Hill was determined; he had money, power, prestige—and ran his side of the Big Island like a private fief. To him politics was a game, albeit "a different type of game," and he soon mastered "the weapons."

In 1946 he spent a lot of money getting reelected.[5] He liked to spend a lot during a campaign. He didn't wait until just before an election to hit the campaign trail; he campaigned all year round. He was more than just an entrepreneur. He was sort of a "father confessor" and one-man "charity thing" on his island. "Everybody came to me with their troubles," he said. Suppose a mortgage payment was due on a car and the debtor didn't have the money. Hill would loan him the money. Doc expected a *quid pro quo*. Remember me on election day, he would tell the beneficiary. "Get out [and vote] and have your friends give me a vote," he said.

Hill believed he knew more ILWU leaders on the Big Island

---

5. Eighty thousand dollars, McElrath said.

than Hall did, especially in the Hilo precincts. Nor did he ignore the plantation vote. He went around to the camps and talked to ILWU leaders. He explained his technique:

> Two or three of the ILWU leaders . . . liked to fish. So I went down one day and made arrangements ahead of time. On Saturday morning, I got in my boat and we sailed all the way and came in here [Keauhou, Hill's home]. Saturday night we tied up and I brought 'um over here for dinner and sleep, and Jesus Christ, they wrote me they felt like a king sleeping in my bed and the food—they've never seen anything like it. . . . I don't care what you would tell any of these guys about me—they'd get the votes. . . .

In mid-1946 Frank Thompson and Bob Robertson called on Hill to discuss the union's case for a new sugar contract. After hearing them out, Hill told them he'd like ILWU support in the upcoming election. Robertson replied that the ILWU wasn't about to endorse him unless the union had "his written resignation beforehand—with the date left blank."

That piece of information rocked Hill, but he did not lose his composure. He invited the two hard-bitten labor leaders to have dinner with him the next week. "What a character," Thompson remarked.

Hill didn't worry about the outcome of the election. He was confident he would win—with or without the ILWU's blessing. Over the years the union had "passively" endorsed him on occasion, but it never went out and worked for him. He didn't care. Certain strong politicians, like Hill, could win without the union. The voting pattern already had been set: the ILWU was strong in the Neighbor Island areas where there was a homogeneous "working class electorate." But in Honolulu it was a tough go for the union and it had to have allies.

In 1946 the precinct work by the ILWU in Honolulu did not go well; the rank and file who had to do the canvassing were not attending club meetings. "Too few people are trying to do too much work," said David Thompson.

The election results bore him out. In the territory-wide election, Farrington won in a good race.[6] But in Honolulu, where the ILWU supported Democrat John H. Wilson against Republican Herbert M. "Montie" Richards for mayor, Wilson won in a squeaker by just sixteen votes. Twenty of the thirty-four territory-wide candidates endorsed by the PAC were elected. But in the race for the Honolulu Board of Supervisors only three of the six candidates endorsed by the PAC won.[7]

6. Farrington, 45,765; Borthwick, 37,209.
7. John M. Asing, Noble K. Kauhane, and Richard M. Kageyama.

CHAPTER **31**

The Pineapple Strike of 1947

They were going to strike us. Come hell or high water, they were going to strike.
> —C. C. Cadagan, a vice-president
> of Hawaiian Pineapple Company

We walked into the trap because we were kidding ourselves about our own strength.
> —ILWU pamphlet

On January 27, 1947, Hall telephoned Goldblatt to discuss the pineapple negotiations which were under way. Hall said the employers had made an offer of an eight-cent-an-hour pay raise. They "made a big song-and-dance on the poverty-stricken situation of the industry," he said. Hall predicted (incorrectly) that the industry would "go over the heads of the union leaders" with a fifteen-cent offer to the membership.

The conversation continued:

Goldblatt:	Where did you get the impression of a 15-cent offer?
Hall:	In an off-the-record conversation with Steele. . . . We go into negotiations tomorrow and tell them we are prepared to reduce our demand to 20 cents.
Goldblatt:	Make it 25 cents in keeping with CIO.
Hall:	Okay. We can do that. The employers are getting tough now.
Goldblatt:	Really getting tough, how?
Hall:	Red-baiting with increased intensity.
Goldblatt:	How far are they getting with the membership?
Hall:	The membership is boiling mad and we are tightening them up. . . .
Goldblatt:	We better watch a couple of things. . . . Number 1, watch out on termination. Insist that the contract be wound up by termination. . . . If they don't terminate, they may go along with all provisions except checkoff. The way to handle that is to get the jump on them. Around Wednesday throw out the proposal of mutual agreement [that is, continue negotiating with the old contract still in effect] or extend the contract for another 30 or 60 days. Tell them we want to make a genuine effort to settle by collective bargaining. Offers made by the employers so far have been impossible. . . .
Hall:	We will ask for retroactive pay. . . .
Goldblatt:	Get the extension first—argue for retroactivity later. . . .
Hall:	. . . Hawaiian Pine is carrying the brunt. . . .
Goldblatt:	Have you talked to Libby?
Hall:	They are pretty soft but they feel they must go along with Hawaiian Pine. . . .
Goldblatt:	Let them release some of their profit figures. First get the contract extension. Their reaction will give

you an indication pretty quickly on what the employers figure on doing. Let's not be overconfident on this. Explain to the membership that they may be in for a tough one. . . . Tell the membership point-blank the reason for this insulting offer. And it is insulting, with the longshore getting 30 [cents an hour raise] and the sugar workers 25. God knows, pineapple is a thousand times better able to pay than sugar. They are throwing this offer out because they think the pineapple workers are soft. . . .

Hall: We are driving through with consolidation of the pine workers into a single local.

Goldblatt: Figure on the worst in this case. You may have a lockout[1] on your hands February 1. . . . How much would it cost them if they lost the entire crop?

Hall: About $15 million.

Goldblatt: Could they stand it?

Hall: I don't think so. I think they would go broke. They might, though.

Goldblatt: They may have a tax rebate coming to them. In that case they could lose the entire crop and still make a profit. Tell the pine workers it's a tough struggle ahead. . . . Throw in the whole 90 days.

Hall: We can't strike for 90 days.

Goldblatt: They [the employers] aren't that dumb. Throw in 30 or 60 days extension. Chuck it in there. See that collective bargaining sessions are conducted in a good atmosphere. Don't give them anything to hang their hats on. . . . Don't go for more than a 30-day postponement. . . .

---

1. Closing of a factory or an industry by an employer to force the employees to agree to the employer's terms.

That conversation set the tone for confrontation. Goldblatt had sensed soon after the sugar strike ended that there was trouble ahead. He figured that the employers had been caught off balance during the sugar strike. The ILWU had won a battle in sugar, but not the war. The employers, said Goldblatt, "are not going to take the licking they took . . . and quietly creep away into the night to lick their wounds. They are bound to counterattack."

There's a natural letdown after battle: an urge to take it easy and savor the victory. Goldblatt looked around and he didn't like what he saw:

> The guys are not driving through with the right kind of consolidation. . . . They are letting petty beefs and small grievances override and overshadow the tremendous victories they have won. They want the world with a ring in it, and they are amazed to find—just because they have licked the employer once—that they come back fighting.

Hall agreed that the union seemed to be in the doldrums after the sugar victory. He called it a "setback" period and explained: "The guys aren't interested in the union. They want to take a rest."

Both knew that the pineapple workers would expect their share of the pie. Sugar and longshore had done well; now it was their turn. But pineapple was different: sugar and longshore were strong; pineapple was weak. In pineapple there are regular workers, seasonal workers, and intermittent workers—and at that point the ILWU had not completed organizing even the regulars. Less than thirty-five percent of the intermittent force that worked during the peak season was organized. The seasonals were chiefly housewives and students who looked forward to the summer season to earn some money. They had no strong bond of loyalty to the union.

On December 13, 1946, Hall gave notice that the union wanted to negotiate a new contract and he asked for a 35-cent raise. On January 25 the employers offered eight cents. Hall relayed the information to San Francisco. It was then that Goldblatt read their message: the employers had decided that the pineapple workers weren't in shape to fight. Management was cocky, he said. They had tossed out the offer merely as a challenge; or perhaps to provoke the union into premature action, such as taking a strike vote. Let's adopt a different strategy from the sugar strike, said Goldblatt. Let's mix our pitches. He told Hall to get a mutual extension of the old contract (it ran out on February 1) and call for arbitration of wages and other issues.

"I have in mind," he said, "moving deliberately to answer arguments made by the employers during the course of the sugar strike, such as the one that they are forced to negotiate 'with a gun at their head'—[because of] a strike vote."

Push "like blazes" for consolidation, he urged Hall. "Tighten the ranks before the hardening process sets in where a small minority gets the fixed idea that they can stay out of the union and still get all the benefits of union organization." He predicted the ILWU could easily lose a pineapple strike: "If the rank and file is ready to go, we can make the grade. If they are not, we'll just have to take what the company offers. It's just that cold, and no high-powered brain-busting or maneuvering at this end will do any good."

Hall followed instructions. At the negotiating table he acted in "a conciliatory but tough" manner. He gauged the employer's attitude and decided they were "looking for a weak spot to drive in a wedge and split us." This incensed the pineapple workers, said Hall.

On February 15 management offered a ten-cent raise on classification with a five-cent minimum. The union rejected the offer, calling it a "nickel offer." (Hall referred to it as the "Woolworth" offer, alluding to the five-and-ten-cent store.) "Five copper pennies an hour wage increase! That's the miserable few crumbs the pineapple industry arrogantly brushes from its abundant table. . . ."

The employers reacted. They said eighty-five percent of the pineapple workers would get ten cents; only fifteen percent would get less. Ben Butler of Libby, McNeill & Libby charged that the ILWU had "deliberately misrepresented" the industry offer. Cadagan of Hawaiian Pineapple said: "I take violent issue with these tactics which have done much to magnify the differences we now face."

Another test of strength was coming up. As McElrath saw it:

> The Big Five has not tossed in the sponge since the beating we gave them in the sugar strike, but on the contrary bandaged their wounds and apparently are out to take us on in another round. It looks like the showdown will come in pineapple in a very short time.

Management was confident and held firm; it felt this time it had the best hand. In its view, the question was simply this: "Is there a point beyond which management must resist union demands or face economic ruin? Hawaii's highly competitive pineapple industry felt it had reached that point. . . ."

Reading Hall's reports, Goldblatt grew increasingly alarmed. "I don't want to sound like Cassandra," he said, as he warned Hall to look out for provocation and an attempted lockout.

At a bargaining session Hall tried a new tactic: he sprang W. K. Bassett on the astonished industry. Bassett, administrative assistant to Mayor Wilson, was a talkative little man who wore what Riley Allen called a goatee. Hall called him "a very good guy." He designated Bassett as a union representative whose job it was to sit and listen and then report to the public.

The employers "hit the ceiling." How could outsiders contribute to solving the impasse? asked Steele. He discounted Hall's contention that Bassett would not grandstand for the audience. Bassett speechless? That was hard to imagine.

Goldblatt told Hall to concentrate on management's attempt to cut wages and break down union security rights. He said to tell the pineapple workers: "If they get away with their plans in pineapple, they will drive all workers back to the days when they paid them a buck a day and told them to like it or lump it."

He instructed Hall to send Bridges a cable saying that negotiations appeared to have failed and that the employers were resolved to force their offer "down our throats" even if it meant the shutdown of the industry. Point out, he said, that there had been only a ten-cent raise in wages in the industry since 1943 and that the cost of living had soared.[2] Hammer away at the public. The employers were "driving and driving hard," said Goldblatt. A strike was the weapon of last resort, but industry seemed to welcome it:

> There is every likelihood that they may be willing to go whole hog and run the risk of losing the season in order to break the union. No strike vote should be taken under any illusions that they're going to win hands-down victory by having these employers against the season. The workers must be told point-blank at the right time that if these demands are rejected and no satisfactory proposal is forthcoming, we might well be headed for the type of strike where the employers will risk tremendous losses in their efforts to crack us. . . .

Hall assessed the union's strength. At Libby on Oahu and Molokai, the union was relatively strong, but on Maui it was dangerously weak. There the rank and file, particularly the Filipinos, were critical of unit leadership. At California Packers on Oahu, the union was in good shape, but it had been "touch and go" for a while because of the defeatist attitude of the unit leadership. Hawaiian Pine union membership on Lanai and Oahu was sound and united. The union was well off at Maui Pine, Baldwin Packers, and Hawaiian Canneries, but Kauai Pine members seemed reluctant to move.

The time was ripe to consider the big question: *When* would it be best to strike? Hall weighed it carefully:

> The season looks like it will get into full swing a little later than usual, probably toward the end of June. From a strategic point of view it might be better anyway to set a date for intention to strike a couple of weeks after the season commences. That would force the industry's hand on the employment of seasonal workers. They would have to commence hiring and get into operation. This would put them over a barrel because it would give us a chance to reach the seasonal workers on the job, convince them of the issues and make more certain their support in the event we are unable to avoid a defensive strike.

---

2. Minimum wages in pineapple then were seventy cents an hour for women and eighty cents for men.

"It is clear from the sessions and the off-the-record talk with Blaisdell and Steele that the industry wants a strike and has no intention of budging on the wage position," said Hall.

On May 17 the ILWU Pineapple Negotiating Committee authorized a strike vote and a five-dollar assessment of union members.

In Washington, Delegate Farrington predicted that a pineapple strike would have "unfavorable repercussions." He said it would give Congress additional cause to place restrictions on unions. Hall told Yoshikazu Morimoto, secretary-treasurer of Local 149 at Lihue, that the outlook was grim. Goldblatt announced he was coming with a peace plan. He presented it in person June 3. It called for resumption of bargaining and suggested that at the end of two weeks all points in agreement would be reduced to writing and all unresolved issues would go to binding arbitration. In the employers' view it was warmed-over hash; Randolph Crossley called it "disappointing."

At the negotiation session on June 9, Goldblatt repeated an ILWU demand for a guaranteed work week. Steele replied that was impossible because of uncertainties of weather and the difference in crop yields. On June 11 Goldblatt charged that the industry planned a lockout. Steele rejected the charge. A lockout at the peak of the season when losses would be greatest? That made no sense, he said.

Goldblatt flew home June 22. On June 25 Bob Robertson came to Hawaii. To the industry he was bad news. Robertson, a big man with a hard look and a voice that sounded like coal coming down a chute, had the reputation of being a union hatchetman. "We understand his function is not to negotiate," said Steele.

On July 7 Bridges came for a "look-see," as he called it. Schmidt, the ILWU expert on stevedoring, had been in Hawaii since February. The ILWU had deployed its first team.

Hawaii's residents, with the trauma of the sugar strike fresh in their minds, watched nervously as another big strike in a basic industry appeared certain. Herbert Tanigawa, president of the McKinley High School student body, presented Governor Stainback with a petition, pleading with him to do what he could to stave off the strike. School principals appealed to both sides to avoid a strike that would bring "a major dislocation to our economic life."

Goldblatt told Bridges the union should be able to get a combination of a ten-cent across-the-board wage increase plus classification adjustment. "If they fail to come that far, then it is clear they are determined on a showdown," he said. On the other hand, if the ILWU accepted the classification adjustment with a five-cent minimum increase—or accepted ten cents without classification adjustment—such a move "will inevitably split the union."

Temperatures were rising. The administration in Washington cabled Bridges and the industry that mediator Feinsinger was coming. A pineapple strike would mean the loss of a major portion of the world's pineapple crop, the message said.

CHAPTER **32**
Five Exhausting Days

Feinsinger checked into the Moana Hotel and prepared to act as "honest broker" and bring the two sides together. He was forceful and businesslike with "all kinds of tricks in his bag" and enormous self-assurance. He felt he had the confidence of both sides but he had no idea he was getting into one of the toughest cases he had ever handled.

On July 8 Bridges dropped the union's wage demand from 23½ to 15 cents and told Feinsinger that although the ILWU strike machinery was set up and ready to be put to use, the union hoped to come to agreement without a strike. At an off-the-record session, the union hinted that if the industry offered classification changes along with a ten-cent raise across the board, plus retroactivity, then it was likely the union would come to terms. It seemed as though a settlement was imminent.

The two sides settled the wage issue and classification adjustment and decided to drop the five-cent Kauai differential. All that was left was the termination date for the new contract. They had narrowed the gap to a difference between them of just four months and on the night of July 10 they were working late, trying to meet a midnight deadline.

They didn't make it. At 2 AM they took a break. The employers' team was to confer with its side and return at 4 AM. During negotiations they had heard disturbing rumors that a strike had already been called, but they ignored the report and went on working. While their discussions were going on, McElrath announced over the radio that the strike was to begin at five minutes after midnight. "I was directed to go on the air at midnight and say the strike was on," McElrath said.

The employers confirmed the news during the break. "We got the word they had walked out at Dole," said Randolph Crossley, chairman of the Pineapple Industry Negotiating Committee. "I told Hall and Bridges to shove it and we walked out."

At 4 AM, as scheduled, the management team returned to the Moana Hotel but only to declare a recess. At 11 AM they handed the ILWU a document which said they were withdrawing their offers to date. They claimed they had been double-crossed. The union had called a strike without warning while they were in the middle of negotiations. "The ILWU recklessly plunged into its strike," said Crossley. He maintained that during the midnight session the union had assured management that no strike had been called. Later, according to Crossley, Bridges told him: "We couldn't hold the members." Crossley continued: " 'Well,' I said, 'if you get them back in the morning, let us know.' Next morning they showed up and said they couldn't get their people back to work so the strike was on."

Crossley told Bridges the ILWU couldn't win. His own small

operation (six hundred employees at Hawaiian Fruit Packers at Kapaa, Kauai) was unorganized. "Bridges believed me," Crossley said; "Hall didn't."

Feinsinger was dismayed. He said the gun had gone off "before it was timed to go off." He had assured everyone there would be no strike and now he couldn't deliver. He had assumed it was all over but the signing and now the industry was "in the throes of a serious strike, vitally affecting the economy of the islands and the welfare of its inhabitants." Goodwill had fled; two bitter adversaries faced each other. "Nevertheless," said Feinsinger, "this dispute will be settled sooner or later. Time will aggravate rather than heal the present breach. . . . As far as the public is concerned, no labor dispute involving the interruption of production is ever 'won' or 'lost.' Whatever the outcome, the public loses."

Robertson cabled Goldblatt from Honolulu on the morning the strike broke out and told him the industry was shut down. "ALL FIELDS TIGHT AND CANNERIES 95 TO 100 PER CENT SOLID STOP THIS IS A SHUTDOWN WITH EMPHASIS."

Robertson was wrong. The strike (or lockout, as the union called it) never was "solid." It was a lost cause from the beginning because unorganized workers went through the picket lines. When picket lines are breached, a strike fails.

The strike did best on the Neighbor Islands. On the first day, six of the ten Neighbor Island plantations and four of the six Neighbor Island canneries were shut down. On Oahu the three canneries carried on limited operations: at Hapco, 500 workers out of the 4000-member work force operated five of the forty-six work lines; at Libby, 250 out of 850 workers operated six out of fourteen work lines; and at Calpac, 110 workers kept six out of twenty-four lines operating.[1]

Cadagan said the only place where the union was able "to lock up tight" was Lanai. "We didn't get a hell of a lot of pro-

---

1. In 1947 the pineapple industry employed 8691 regular workers and 10,000 to 12,000 seasonals during the peak of the season in July.

duction [at the canneries], but we made out like we did. We turned on the Ginaca [pineapple-coring machines] and it sounded like we were going at full blast—to fool them.''

By July 15, the fifth day of the strike, most canneries were operating. The strike was lost and Bridges knew it. ''This is not shaping up right,'' he told Schmidt. ''I'm going to tell these people they're going to have to go back to work and try it some other time.'' From the time he had arrived in Hawaii on July 7, Bridges had felt uneasy. The sharp instinct honed over the years in labor-management struggles told him something was wrong. ''I just couldn't put my finger on it,'' he said.

We were in negotiations. We were working there in the Moana Hotel. Steele was there and we were working toward the deadline at midnight. And, of course, Steele and the employers had it all lined up, ready to go. . . . They had all the restraining orders . . . and the subpoenas. . . . I kind of smelled a rat. . . .

The union ''walked into a trap,'' said Bridges. ''I was the one that took the lead, saying that we had to knock off the strike. We were locked out and [had to] get back to work. I think we were licked right then and there.'' In cold anger he told Steele at an off-the-record meeting at Hall's house, ''Look, Dwight, I'm warning you right now. Don't punish these workers because of our mistake. . . .'' He didn't blame Hall. ''I was there on the scene,'' said Bridges. ''I couldn't run around saying it was Hall's responsibility or anyone else's . . . but we walked into a beautiful trap.''

Bridges told Feinsinger the union was willing to call the strike off and resume bargaining, with the terms of the old agreement to remain in force in the interim. He also promised ''no monkeyshines.'' Feinsinger, with the union's backing, urged the industry to go back into bargaining sessions, even though management considered such talk largely ''window dressing.''

The call for a strike had come chiefly from the Neighbor Islands. Hall could guide; he could coax; he could argue. But he could not dictate. The ILWU's structure gave each unit great latitude in making decisions. Bridges, Goldblatt, and Robertson said the strike couldn't win, but the pineapple workers went out anyway. Yoshikazu Morimoto of Local 149, Lihue, explained: "We put pressure on the Honolulu group—Maui and Kauai, that is. They [Honolulu] didn't want to go out but they did because we took a militant position. We were headstrong because of the [success of] the 1946 strike."[2]

"At the moment we thought [the strike] was a good idea," said Toyomasa Oshiro, then secretary-treasurer of the ILWU Pineapple Negotiating Committee. "We were inexperienced. We thought it was the best time to call a strike—at the peak of the season."

"The union made a mistake," said McElrath.

The strike lasted only five days but it was unruly. Pickets massed; threats were shouted; and some people were beaten. On July 11 six hundred pickets on Kauai held up three pineapple trucks. The drivers had to abandon the vehicles and let the load of pineapples sit there. On July 12 strikers on Lanai prevented company officials from moving vehicles. On July 14, at Lanai's port of Kaumalapau, some three hundred pineapple workers crossed a white *kapu* line on the road to Hapco's south boundary. When Anthony "Sonny" Fernandez started to operate the crane to lift bins of pineapples into a barge that had docked, striking workers chased him out of the cab. He jumped into the water and started swimming and they pelted him with pineapples. On July 15 workers on Lanai beat two truck drivers.

Pineapple industry executives visited Oren E. Long, the acting governor, at Iolani Palace on July 14 and left him a letter which said: "Men have been beaten. . . . Missiles have been thrown into windows of private homes. Wives and children have been threatened. . . . Masses of illegal pickets have blocked public highways and private roads and plants."

The union went back to work on July 16. The ILWU called it

2. The ILWU called in leaders from all locals to sit with the Pineapple Strike Committee. They were asked whether they would mount a general strike against Big Five operations to save the union in pineapple. They were told: "The employers are united. If they can do this to pine workers, they can do it to you, too." The local leaders replied: "We understand that but our members don't. They won't strike for pineapple."

a victory. "Lockout Won!" a union leaflet said. Feinsinger called for "an atmosphere of calm" and for renewed negotiations. "Mistakes were made by all concerned, including myself, but that is past now," he said, diplomatically. Hall confessed he was relieved that the men were back at work and negotiations had resumed. "Lucky to get out in one piece," he said.

Allen and Farrington worried about how the strike would affect statehood. Allen saw the brief strike as a "serious setback" for the ILWU, but found there was something to be thankful for: "The net result of the sudden ending of the pineapple strike will discourage not only CIO but AFL leaders from pulling 'quickies,' which is one of Art Rutledge's favorite tactics."

The man who felt the most profound relief was Feinsinger. He was afraid that if the strike were not settled quickly, it would go on for months and drag sugar and longshore along with it.

At the reconvened negotiating sessions Bridges was truculent. "There was little talk of wages, but much threat of ILWU action in the future," a management observer said. It took twenty-one days to hammer out the agreement. Cadagan sat through it all:

> We went round and round trying to tie down the contract. We went day and night. They ran in relays. They were trying to wear us down. Goldblatt would take over from Bridges. . . . If there are two experts on going round and round without saying anything, it's Goldblatt and Bridges.

At the July 18 session Bridges spoke of publishing a union newsletter on the progress of negotiations. Steele said management reserved the right to correct anything it felt was incorrect. Bridges said it would not be wise for the employers to talk to their employees. "We'll do the talking," he said. "I want to tell you that we intend to use these negotiations in every way we can to build up the union and to get the non-union people into the union."

In spite of hard talk a settlement was reached. They agreed on a ten-cent wage raise, on classification changes for merit, on dropping the five-cent Kauai wage differential, and on July 16 as the retroactive date of the contract. There was one more troublesome point and Feinsinger tiptoed around it. Steele said the industry wanted protection against wildcat strikes. As a last resort, he said the industry wanted the right to invoke the Taft-Hartley law. "We must have protection."

Taft-Hartley was an offensive word to the ILWU. "The employers' Taft-Hartley law is too dangerous for us to fool around with," said Bridges. "We are not going to take any chances with your judges in Hawaii. They all belong to the bosses."

Feinsinger then reached "into his bag" for a solution. He offered the two sides a choice: Plan A or Plan B. Plan A suggested that the ILWU International not sign the agreement and thus not be liable for suit under Taft-Hartley. Both sides turned down that proposal. They agreed to accept Plan B, which said that the ILWU International would not be held responsible for acts of individuals or groups of workers who took action not authorized by the union (that is, a wildcat strike).

The memorandum of agreement was signed August 9. For the union the "debacle" was over.

Randolph Crossley went to San Francisco shortly after the strike ended and talked to Bridges. Bridges still smarted over the licking the union had taken in Hawaii. He warned the industry not to try to take advantage of the weakness of the ILWU pineapple local and not to insist on bargaining, company by company, or even plantation by plantation, instead of on an industry-wide basis. He knew the idea was tempting, but he warned the industry to resist it. Crossley carried the message home. "One impression is indelible," Crossley said:

> If anyone has in mind that he can negotiate separately on the company level, he had better get it out of his head. Bridges said he was going to sit in personally on all final decisions in Hawaii. He indicated to me he would never allow his union to get in the position it was in this time. . . . Bridges told us everything he plans to do in the future. . . . We are just damn fools if we do not pay attention to what Bridges says. . . .

There was another warning sign: the militancy of the Lanai pineapple workers. "They were a bunch of real wildcats," said Cadagan. Nine hundred tough men. Hall had sent Kenji

"Sleepy" Omuro, president of the Olaa local, over to Lanai during the strike. A single incident convinced Omuro of the Lanai workers' solidarity.

Six union men had been arrested and charged with inciting to riot. Unless they raised six thousand dollars in bail money within thirty minutes, they would be taken to Maui to appear before a circuit court judge. It was late in the day; banks were closed. Yet within fifteen minutes the union had raised the money. One man put up a personal note for three thousand dollars. "They dug in their pockets and raised the sum in record time to meet the challenge of the bosses and the police," said Omuro. "It is my feeling that with a little outside help now and then, the unit on Lanai may develop into a real tough union."

Four years later his words sprang to life.

CHAPTER **33**
Bouslog & Symonds

Labor battles are fought not only on the picket line but on a second front as well: in the courtroom. As an aftermath of the 1946 and 1947 strikes, several hundred ILWU members faced charges ranging from simple assault and battery to illegal assembly and riot—felonies that carried maximum twenty-year prison sentences.

The union needed lawyers in a hurry and couldn't find anyone in Hawaii willing to represent ILWU workers. In San Francisco there was Gladstein and his firm, but he had his hands full. He couldn't hop over to Hawaii all the time; it was a twelve to fourteen-hour plane ride. Bridges cast a sharp blue eye on Harriet Bouslog, the ILWU representative in Washington. He liked her. He thought she was able and courageous.

Moreover, Harriet Bouslog knew Hawaii. She had come to the islands in August 1938 as the wife of Charles Bouslog, an English instructor at the University of Hawaii. Herself the daughter of a history teacher, Mrs. Bouslog was born in Florida as Harriet Williams. She had been reared according to a strict Christian ethic; both parents regarded education "as the most important thing there was." She had earned her law degree at Indiana University.

Harriet Bouslog was obstinate, hardworking, talkative, and emotional. With her good figure, hazel eyes, and glossy black hair, often adorned with a big red hibiscus, she "was quite a chick," as plantation manager Jack Moir said. She went to work in the law offices of the Big Five firm of Stanley, Vitousek, Pratt & Winn. While working for them, she studied for the bar examination. She passed the bar and was notified on December 11, 1941, four days after Pearl Harbor Day.

Harriet Bouslog said Hawaii radicalized her. She saw the hierarchy of *haole* ruling class and non-*haole* subordinates. She noted the discrepancies in the wage system and the sharply delineated class system. She remembered going home from a party at three in the morning and watching the women who were going to work at that hour. She felt that for the privileged it was a good life; for the underprivileged it was hard. "I decided that there was something about the oppression of people here that turned me from what you might call 'parlor liberal' to radicalism."

The war broke out and Harriet Bouslog was determined not to live under the military rule which controlled the courts. She went to Washington in August 1942, and through a letter of recommendation from Cliff O'Brien, the ILWU lawyer-adviser, to Wayne Morse, the Oregon congressman, she got a job in the general counsel's office of the War Labor Board. Later Bjorne Halling, the ILWU representative in Washington, recommended her as his replacement. He told Bridges she was smart and pro-labor. Bridges hired her at seventy-five dollars a week. (She was earning ninety dollars a week when she left Washington.) The job was challenging and Washington was the most exciting place in the country to be. Harriet Bouslog loved it. Then, in the fall of 1946, Bridges called and told her to come to Hawaii and handle the load of ILWU cases.

"But Harry," she protested, "I'm learning things here. I'm not ready yet. I haven't learned all I can."

"You have to go," said Bridges. "There's no other [ILWU] lawyer there. We've got four hundred criminal cases—and there's no lawyer we can trust."

"Harry, I've never tried a criminal case in my life."

"It's okay," said Bridges. "You're not afraid and you won't sell out."

He had the last word. She came reluctantly back to Hawaii in October 1946. Hall, who knew her, had sent her an SOS: "COME URGENTLY." Bridges had great confidence in her, almost to the point of arrogance. He introduced her to some of the ILWU defendants. They looked at the bright-eyed woman and were not impressed. A *wahine* lawyer?

"Here's our attorney," said Bridges. "Nobody's going to jail. Never fear."

Harriet Bouslog pleaded with him not to say such things. "You're only making it more difficult," she said. She was sure his cockiness would only serve to irritate the employers and they would put pressure on "to make liars out of Harry."

"I was frightened to death because I wanted to be adequate," she said. "Because I was a crusader and I believed in my cause."

It was obvious she was going to need help, and in San Francisco Gladstein looked around for a helpmate and came up with Myer Symonds. Symonds was born in Sydney, Australia, and was brought to the United States in 1920 at age eleven. He had gone to school in Vallejo, California, where his father ran a dry goods store. He had a degree from the University of California at Berkeley and a law degree from Hastings Law School. He was practicing bankruptcy law before the war. From 1942 to 1944 he worked for the Office of Price Administration (OPA) and became Western Division litigations attorney.

In 1944, at age thirty-five, he was inducted into the army and served in combat in Germany with the 29th Infantry Division. He got out of the army in February 1946 and, no longer charmed with bankruptcy law, went to work for Gladstein's firm. Symonds agreed to go to Hawaii, but there was a problem. He would have to take the bar examination to practice in Hawaii and until he passed the bar, he was of limited use since he could not appear in court and had to function, more or less, "as a kind of law clerk."

That dismayed Bridges not a whit and he gave Symonds the same jaunty blessing he had given Harriet Bouslog. Symonds reacted to it in the same way. It embarrassed him. "Sy," said Bridges, "I've been traveling to all the islands and telling everybody, 'Don't worry. No one's going to jail.' So don't go out there and make a liar out of me."

Symonds arrived December 6, 1946. He was tall, good-looking, lucid. Like Bouslog, he was of a radical bent and a tireless talker. He had a habit, though, which grated on Harriet Bouslog from the beginning. He liked to tell dirty jokes. In fact, he seemed to have one of the biggest repertoires in town and made it a point to tell a friend (or a foe) a spicy story. There usually was no escape.

Symonds and Bouslog decided she would take all the civil matters and injunction cases and handle the work in court. He would work on criminal matters in the office and "do all the negotiating with the prosecutor, and that sort of thing." They had an understanding: he would study for two hours every morning preparing for the bar exam. "I hadn't taken the bar for many years and I was just a bankruptcy lawyer."

At first the two were paid by the Gladstein firm and received a small retainer from the ILWU.[1] After a few years, however, it became obvious it was awkward for them to be part of a mainland law firm, so they terminated their relationship and repaid the Gladstein firm. Both law firms served the ILWU: Bouslog & Symonds in Hawaii; Gladstein on the West Coast.

Harriet Bouslog faced the multitude of court cases arising out of the two strikes and tried not to panic. She rented an office in the old Terminal Building at Pier 11 alongside the ILWU of-

---

1. Symonds produced balance sheets which show that in 1947 he drew $6500 and Bouslog $5900.

fices. The Bouslog office was in a corner and opened onto the roof. All she had to do when she wanted to confer with Hall was to step out onto the roof and into the window of Hall's office. "We were very close," she said. "We saw each other. We had lunch together. We went in and out of each other's windows." She had a secretary, a bright, Philippines-born girl named Priscilla Yadao, the daughter of the Reverend Emilio Yadao.[2]

George R. Andersen of the Gladstein firm talked to Harriet Bouslog about how to handle the accumulated cases involving the ILWU defendants. They hoped to work out a deal: suspended sentences or fines for the men adjudged guilty. They reasoned that after a strike was over and the hard feelings had eased, a spirit of live-and-let-live would be born. On that happy note, Andersen departed. Soon after, Bouslog informed him that he had been overly optimistic:

> You may recall that at the time you left we had 133 defendants in criminal cases ranging from 20-year felonies to A and B [assault and battery]. You expressed hope the criminal cases growing out of the strike may blow over, but I am afraid it is not in the cards. . . .
>
> Since you left I have been working at a pace which is impossible to keep up, and even so am considerably concerned about the ability for anyone, even more experienced than I, to gather the facts and examine the law and prepare for these cases.

She worked eighteen hours a day. "I didn't drink. I was scared to death." She was trying to gain time and she used the unprepared lawyer's gambit: pleas for continuance. But C. Nils Tavares, the territorial attorney general, was under instructions from Governor Stainback to push the cases to trial. Her work continued to mount. One day she had to be in courtrooms on three islands. She chartered a small plane and managed it.

The Pioneer Mill cases came first. She thought she had an agreement to get a short, suspended sentence for the ringleader in the strike, Mac Yamauchi, chairman of the Strike Strategy

---

2. Later both father and daughter worked for the ILWU: she as librarian, he as director of Filipino public relations.

Committee. But in court it sounded to her as though Circuit Judge Cable Wirtz gave Yamauchi three-year consecutive suspended sentences on two charges: a total of six years of suspended sentences. She thought she had lost; she began to cry, out of frustration and disappointment. But it turned out she had misheard him; Wirtz's sentences were concurrent, not consecutive.

From Honolulu, Symonds watched apprehensively; he knew she was an amateur. "Sy thought I was doing miserably because I told him I didn't know how to try cases," said Bouslog.

Tavares flew to Maui to handle the cases to be presented to the grand jury. Indictments were returned against seventy-nine ILWU members on charges of unlawful assembly. Bouslog was dismayed and accused Tavares of being antilabor. He denied it. "I don't see why you think I'm antilabor," he said. "My father was a plantation worker."

Thirty-nine ILWU members at Paia were charged with unlawful assembly. Bouslog went to Wendell Crockett, the deputy county attorney. "This injunction is against the provisions of the National Labor Relations Act," she said. "The National Labor Relations Act was written in Moscow," Crockett replied.

The charges arose out of the mass picketing at Maui Agricultural Company during the sugar strike. Some men working for management had tried to bull their way through the picket line. The pickets, led by Joe Kaholokula, stood shoulder to shoulder. "It was sheerly a matter of provocation," said Bouslog. "There were no blows. There was a pushing of bodies. It was just like trying to push through a solid wall."

Bouslog began her attack on the unlawful assembly and riot act statute[3] by alleging that the composition of the Maui grand jury violated the constitutional rights of the workers. She said the jury was made up of a few workers and many representatives of the employer's class. The case was heard by Circuit Judge Albert M. Cristy in mid-September, 1947. Cristy ruled against her. Bouslog appealed to the Territorial Supreme Court, which

---

3. Revised Laws of Hawaii 1945, chap. 277, secs. 11570–11587.

sustained Cristy. She then appealed to the Federal District Court of Hawaii and the case was heard *en banc*.[4]

During the trial before Cristy, Hall had testified that the unlawful assembly act had forced the ILWU to terminate the 1947 pineapple strike. He said that during the 1946 sugar strike the threat of a twenty-year sentence hanging over their heads "had struck . . . terror into the workers."

In their written opinion, the *en banc* judges commented:

> The labor movement is an unpopular one in the Hawaiian Islands and these gentlemen [the Territorial Attorney General and the Maui Prosecuting Attorney] do no more than reflect the mores of their time and their locality. . . . The record seems to indicate beyond peradventure, however, that the unlawful assembly and riot act has been employed as a club to beat labor and the conspiracy statute is an apt instrument to the same end.

The court said that eighty-four percent of the people selected for grand jury duty on Maui in 1947 came from the ranks of employer-entrepreneurs and their salaried employees. The court quoted the testimony of Augustine Pombo, one of the Maui grand jury commissioners, who was asked during the trial why there had never been a Filipino on the grand jury. He replied: "We just have a lot of other men a lot better."

This exchange then took place:

Cristy: Did you pick them because they were haoles?

Pombo: No. I pick them because I want to give them something to do—if they want a chance to run the country—. . . . The majority—lots of these—the Baldwins—they own the place. . . . And if they want to run politics, just as well give them something to do in courts.

The three-judge court concluded that the 1947 Maui County grand jury was illegally constituted and that the assembly and

---

4. By three judges "sitting as a court": Delbert E. Metzger and mainland federal judges John Biggs, Jr., and George B. Harris.

riot act and the conspiracy statutes of the territory were void and unconstitutional.

The ruling cheered Bouslog. "That marvelous Judge Metzger," she said. That was not the end of the case, however. The territory appealed to the Ninth Circuit Court of Appeals in San Francisco and the Ninth Circuit reversed the ruling. A petition for a rehearing before the Ninth Circuit was denied and an appeal for certiorari to the United States Supreme Court also was denied. Harriet Bouslog had lost, but in the end she won. The next grand jury on Maui was more representative of the racial spectrum that is Hawaii; and so were future petit and grand juries on all the islands.

Harriet Bouslog harassed judges and lawyers. She talked without pause in court; she appeared to be tireless. She sued Judge Wirtz under the Norris-LaGuardia Act, alleging that his injunctions against the union were illegal. She sued Circuit Judges Philip Rice of Kauai and Willson C. Moore of Honolulu, alleging they had violated the rights of labor.

"By the time I got through, I had sued judges on practically every island," she said. "Through sheer gall and persistence and the use of civil rights suits . . . I kept the cases from going to trial until, finally, when the cases were to be tried or disposed of, the atmosphere had changed so that neither the employer nor the court wished to disturb the harmony."

The employers began to see that nothing was to be gained by drawn-out court battles against the union. "They began to be afraid because I was taking them to court," said Bouslog. They looked for a *modus vivendi,* a way of getting along with the union.

At first Bouslog & Symonds had few clients except the ILWU; that kept them busy enough. But after a while they became known as fighting lawyers willing to take on unpopular causes. Bridges sometimes got annoyed with Bouslog: "Harriet used to seize upon these 'cause' cases. I used to be as irritated as hell with her, but the things she took on were proven right and she proved us wrong every time."

From 1946 through the Smith Act trial (1952–1953), "I worked my silly head off," said Bouslog.

> I didn't look up, right or left. I did all the research for all the other people on the Smith Act case. I worked for two years on the Majors and Palakiko case. I worked with the Damon Tract people. I followed them through three or four transportations—out to Pupukea. . . . I never lost a client. Sometimes I wish I had.

Jack Hall seldom praised lawyers. Symonds he merely tolerated. And in latter years, when Harriet Bouslog prospered, he disliked her. She had recognized early on that Hall was a natural labor leader. In 1945 when the ILWU was considering whom it should appoint as regional director, she recommended Hall. "There is no question in my mind," she told Bridges. "Jack is the one."

Symonds said that Hall was an independent person. "The word 'lawyer' didn't frighten him and he didn't think he had to hero-worship anyone and he didn't have to play second fiddle to anyone," said Symonds.

> He made that clear in all his relations with any lawyers. The lawyers were a necessary evil for the labor movement. [He felt] the union will do what it thinks is best for the union and let the lawyers find some way to get them out.
>
> Jack's philosophy was that the law was written by legislators, who were anti-union, and so what could you expect in the courts but anti-union decisions? And if the unions were to obey the courts, unions would be ineffective because they wouldn't be able to do what was needed to be done to get the job done. The only reason they needed lawyers around was to find some way to get them out of the mess; and if they couldn't, then the guys went to jail.

There is an addendum to the Bouslog & Symonds story: though Harriet Bouslog and Myer Symonds worked together in partnership for more than thirty years, they couldn't stand each other. Like an unhappy marriage that survives because of children, they stayed together because of a client: the ILWU. As the childless Harriet Bouslog said, her clients were her "children."

CHAPTER 34
Stainback's Crusade

In 1947, at the bidding of the army, Governor Stainback embarked on a "crusade against communism." This touched off a red-baiting campaign that racked Hawaii for years. Stainback's chief target was Jack Hall and the ILWU.

It started one day in March 1947 when General John E. Hull, commanding general of the United States Army, Pacific, and his intelligence officer called on Stainback at Iolani Palace. They told him that Communists had been active in the territory for at least ten years and they presented him with a list of more than a hundred "well-known Communists, card-carrying Communists." Hall's name was on the list. Stainback said he was shocked. "Strange as it may seem, I had never heard of Communists in Hawaii," he said.

Hull also gave Stainback a typescript, written by Reinecke, titled, "What Must We Do?"[1] Reinecke had composed it in late 1933 or early 1934 when he was a teacher at Honokaa. The paper discussed propaganda, how to advance civic and social causes, and how to combat militarism. Reinecke confessed that it was rather juvenile. For example, the sixth paragraph said:

> First attack ROTC in the high schools, then in the University. Attack kowtowing to military in the local press and public affairs. Weaken the National Guard unit as much as possible and propagandize and make them sympathetic to unions. Attack militarization of Boy Scouts.

---

1. Reinecke borrowed from the title of Lenin's famous work "What Is to Be Done?", published in 1902.

"It was a silly piece of writing, immature even for a thirty-year old," Reinecke conceded. "I ended up wishing I had never written that thing."

Stainback, however, took alarm. He regarded the tract as a recipe for revolution. He asked Hull what he should do. "Well, make a speech," said Hull. Stainback promised to start "a one-man crusade," and a month later, on Army Day, he spoke to the reactivated 442nd Regiment. "We are not free from the danger of a Cold War," he exclaimed, and warned the soldiers to be ever alert; there were enemies within the gates. That was the first speech. By Armistice Day, November 11, 1947, he was in full voice. He promised a "Red probe" and warned that the Communists looked on Hawaii "as the most fruitful field for communism in the United States." For two years he lighted fires.

Ingram Stainback was a native of Somerville, Fayette County, Tennessee. He had graduated with honors from Princeton and from the University of Chicago; had a law degree from Chicago; and came to Hawaii in 1912. He had served as territorial attorney general, as United States Attorney in Hawaii, and as Federal District Court judge in Hawaii. On August 24, 1942, he was sworn in as governor to replace vacillating "Mahope Joe," Governor Poindexter.

What surprised many people was Stainback's assertion that he had never heard of Communists in Hawaii before General Hull brought him the news. That seemed hard to believe. "How could you have been fooled, having lived there so many years as you had?" asked Senator Arthur V. Watkins of Utah at a statehood hearing in 1953. Stainback replied, "We didn't know anything about the Communists and nobody that I knew ever guessed it."

Watkins wanted to know why Stainback had appointed Jack Hall to the Honolulu Police Commission in 1945. Stainback said Hall had been recommended to him by Marshall McEuen, of the Democratic Party, and that he had routinely followed the recommendation. "I had not the slightest notion that [Hall] was a Communist," said Stainback.

That did not satisfy Watkins:

Watkins:	He [Hall] was a union man then [in 1945] and they [the ILWU] were about as radical then as they are now. . . .
Stainback:	There was a union. It was part of the CIO organization and as far as I know it was nothing except they were following union tactics, and I knew nothing of any so-called communism.
Watkins:	You did not see anything wrong until 1947?
Stainback:	Not the slightest. I do not think anybody else did, as far as I know. They never told me about it.

Stainback owed his job as governor to a recommendation made in his behalf just before Pearl Harbor Day by Norman M. Littrell, the United States assistant attorney general, to Marvin H. McIntyre, personal secretary to President Roosevelt. The Roosevelt administration was looking for someone to replace Poindexter. Littrell wrote McIntyre:

> Stainback may not be brilliant or fast in his processes, but he is able, fearless, unshakable. . . . A good, tough lawyer faithful to the Democratic ideal, and to the President, is what the country needs in Hawaii. Stainback appears to fill the equation.

McIntyre sent Littrell's recommendation to Secretary of Interior Harold Ickes, who did not share Littrell's enthusiasm for Stainback but admitted it was hard to find a suitable appointee since that person had to be restricted to a "resident Democrat."

At that point, according to Ickes, Roosevelt thought about suggesting that the Organic Act be amended so that a mainlander could be appointed governor of Hawaii, "but this did not seem politic at the time. . . ." When war broke out, Roosevelt insisted on a replacement for Poindexter and Stainback was chosen. With unionism throttled, it did not matter to labor leaders who the governor was—there was the military (which Stainback himself didn't like) to contend with. But with the end of the war and the sudden march of unionism, it mattered enormously. As Stainback's first four-year term came near to an end, Hall considered whether or not to support him for a second term. He didn't like Stainback but he was afraid of getting someone worse. In 1946 Stainback's anticommunism crusade had not begun.

"We recognize all of the weaknesses in Stainback, but it appears that he is the lesser of many evils as far as we are concerned," said Hall. Oddly, Stainback had come to Hall and asked him for the ILWU's support in getting reappointed. It was the request of a politician for a favor and it carried with it, in Hall's mind, the implicit promise that the favor would be returned: the *quid pro quo* of politics. "Our endorsement [of Stainback] at this time . . . will place us in a rather enviable position," said Hall.

So in May 1946, Hall wrote Secretary of Interior Julius A. Krug, saying that "in behalf of the 33,000 members" of the ILWU in Hawaii, "in our considered opinion Governor Stainback has creditably handled the executive office during a difficult and trying period."

Allen and Farrington judged Stainback chiefly on how he stood on statehood. They were inclined to believe he gave it only lukewarm support. Nevertheless, in March 1946, Farrington informed the Department of Interior that Stainback's appointment was "in the best interests of the territory." He said the only alternative was Garner Anthony. He thought Anthony would "make a great governor," but to replace Stainback at that moment would be a mistake "in view of his fine record on basic issues of Hawaii's future."

CHAPTER 35

The Burns Connection

It didn't surprise Jack Burns that many ILWU leaders were members of the Communist Party. Nor did he, as a Honolulu police detective privy to the dossiers of many people, have any doubts that Hall was a Party member.

Burns worked in police intelligence before and during World War II. He swapped information with the FBI, the Office of Naval Intelligence (ONI), and with G-2, army intelligence. One of his sources of information about the Communist Party in Hawaii was his mother, Mrs. Anne Burns, who worked in General Delivery at the downtown Honolulu Post Office. Often letters came from the Communist Party of the United States of America, through General Delivery, addressed to Hawaii residents. She made it a point to alert her son about those letters.

Burns was a simple man. A practicing Catholic, he had been influenced in life by two papal encyclicals, *Rerum Novarum* and *Quadragesimo Anno.*[1] Both spoke of mankind's deep social problems and how to treat them; both were friendly to labor. Burns had grown up in Hawaii; he was sympathetic to social change. Burns believed that radical labor in Hawaii used Communist Party techniques. "They used the Communist Party cell formation to organize and develop a labor union," he said.[2] "I mean they had a regular layout. . . . They tell you how to orga-

---

1. Pope Leo XIII delivered his encyclical, *Rerum Novarum,* on "The Condition of Labor," in 1891. Pope Pius XI wrote *Quadragesimo Anno* on "The Reconstruction of the Social Order" in 1931.

2. Burns exaggerated the role of the Communist Party in organizing labor in Hawaii. He underestimated the ability of local labor leaders who were the backbone of *all* the organizing done in Hawaii.

nize and how they transferred between cells without identification and everything else. It was most useful out here to labor."

Burns asked: Where else could radical labor in the 1930s and 1940s turn for help except the Communist Party? The Establishment—the police, the courts, big business, the press—was hostile. "Who else is going to help them?"

It was crucial in the war years that the waterfront run efficiently, and Burns learned who knew the waterfront. In November 1941, he suggested to Colonel Kendall J. Fielder, chief intelligence officer for the army in Hawaii, that he make use of Kawano, the ILWU longshore leader, as a source of waterfront information. Fielder did so, said Burns. Burns said Hall also supplied information to Colonel George W. Bicknell, head of military intelligence, and to Robert L. Shivers, special agent in charge of the FBI in Hawaii, "on what was good and bad on the waterfront." Hall's political feeling didn't matter because, as Burns said: "Jack [Hall] could provide them with the best information on the waterfront. Hall—he might be interested in some radical causes and he might be a member of the CPA.[3] At the time, to my memory, he was . . . according to the records we had."

Burns met Hall formally in 1942 when Hall was working for the Territorial Department of Labor. He remembered Hall from that day in February 1938 when he saw him at the police station after Hall had been beaten by Sergeant Taylor. Burns had read Hall's dossier, which the military had on file. "We had a file on almost everybody around here who had done anything," said Burns. "Every one of your so-called radicals." The purpose of the personnel file was simple: to pick up, if need be, anyone the military thought might be "unfriendly to the United States."

As for Hall, he had taken note of Burns as a "good cop" and early in 1946, when Hall was on the Police Commission, he asked Burns if he was interested in applying for the job of chief of police. Hall was determined to get rid of Police Chief Gabriel-

---

3. Not Certified Public Accountant, but Communist Party of America.

son, whom he blamed for the police department's strong anti-union activity. Hall also blamed Gabrielson for the beating he got in 1938.

Burns told Hall, no, thanks, he wasn't interested in the chief's job. By then it was too late; he had something else in mind: politics. "I told him what I was trying to do. Whatever time I had extra from trying to make a living [I was using] to create a Democratic Party in Hawaii. The needs, to me, were apparent," said Burns.

Burns never forgot Hall's confidence in him. It made a lasting impression and laid the foundation for the close connection between the two.

In the early days Hall listened to Communist Party members in Hawaii. He used anybody who could contribute to the cause of militant unionism. If the Communist Party could help, well and good. "Labor," he said, "has [accepted] and will continue to accept constructive support and advice from *any* individual, group or party that is aiding in improving wages, working conditions, and the general well-being of the people." But Hall set his own course. He never lacked self-confidence. He believed he knew what was best.

Hall was never a *good* Communist, according to Jack Kimoto, who headed the Communist Party. Hall admitted it. "I'm supposed to have been a Marxist," Hall said. "I always felt closer emotionally to the Wobblies,[4] except for their denial of the importance of political action." Hall was, "first, last and always, a trade union man."

For a time, according to Kimoto, he and other members of the Communist Party, such as Eileen and Charles Fujimoto, and Reinecke, offered advice to Hall. Reinecke was presumed to be experienced in all kinds of left-wing activity,[5] but he was a gentle

---

4. The Industrial Workers of the World (IWW), those itinerant, irreverent radical unionists of the early 1900s.

5. Reinecke's experience, in reality, was limited to one year in an academic Communist Party in New Haven, Connecticut, and the isolated, union-oriented Party in Hawaii.

soul and not given to bold action. The others? What would they know about running a union?

Whatever Hall's feelings were, said Kimoto, he could not be regarded as a Communist leader, but as a labor leader. He was not the type who read and applied doctrinaire Communist theory; he was not the type to educate the masses.

The Communist Party of Hawaii did not take orders from afar, said Kimoto. The members in Hawaii made up their own minds on local policy. It was not Party rhetoric that swayed them; it was common sense. It gave Kimoto and the other Party members a laugh when they read about how they were being bought "by Moscow gold." What advice and instructions the Communist Party did give in the early days came from California and was delivered orally by seamen-couriers, said Kimoto. The messages were verbal; Kimoto said they were delivered to Hall, not to him. Party meetings were held in Kimoto's home or in the homes of other members. Sometimes a few members held a session in a parked car. In time Hall began to resent Party "intrusion" into union affairs and stopped attending Party meetings, said Kimoto.

Labor would have been organized in Hawaii, Communist Party or no Communist Party, Jack Hall or no Jack Hall. The time was ripe for it, said Kimoto. In those days, Communist Party members in general, and particularly Hall, were usually the people with the drive to get things going. "Without the Communist Party, the [ILWU] would not have been the union it became," said Koji Ariyoshi, who remained a strong believer in communism (Maoist brand) to the end of his life. Ariyoshi thought Hall quickly lost his youthful radicalism. "I would say he lacked the development within himself to keep himself motivated, to continue the struggle," said Ariyoshi. "There are people who came up from the ranks, matured and developed and then began to lose their links with the rank and file, and that's what happened to Hall."

Ariyoshi said although Hall read all the time, he was not thoroughly grounded in Marxism-Leninism. "He wasn't that much committed."

Part 6
REVOLUTIONARIES AND COUNTER-REVOLUTIONARIES (1947–1949)

CHAPTER 36

Mookini, Izuka, and "The Truth"

Bob Mookini was the first ILWU leader in Hawaii to defect. Others followed during the time of the Red Scare: Ichiro Izuka, Francis Y. Moriyama, Amos A. Ignacio, Bert Nakano. All challenged Hall's leadership; all raised the issue of communism within the union; and all of them lost their fight. Izuka, Kawano, and Nakano were self-confessed former members of the Communist Party.

Robert Kahaleniau Mookini, Sr., tall and affable, was president of Local 152, the pineapple local. He decided to "throw off the yoke of false mainland leadership. . . . I, as a native-born Hawaiian, can no longer stand for their actions."

Mookini claimed that Hall did not bargain honestly during the 1947 pineapple negotiations and wanted "to utterly destroy" the industry. For what reason, he did not say. Mookini dreamed of taking the pineapple workers out of the ILWU and into the AFL Teamsters with himself as chieftain. He had no real support, though. He was a general without an army.

Hall was not troubled by Mookini or his name-calling. "We don't know of a single person Mookini has been successful in swinging," said Hall.

Bridges told Hall to move with caution and not to bring charges against Mookini "unless we have the real goods." Even then Bridges hesitated; he wondered what the repercussions might be among Hawaiians.

On June 3, 1947, the ILWU charged Mookini with misfeasance and malfeasance of duty. The ILWU said Mookini had openly opposed the union; had engaged in financial irregularity; and had "devoted an average of less than two hours a day to union activities." A five-member board[1] heard the case on June 20, 1947. Mookini did not appear. The board voted to expel him. Hall cabled Goldblatt. The revolt was nothing, a zephyr in a teacup, but it presaged trouble.

In 1947 red-baiting was a national pastime. Farrington told Allen that Hawaii was "not out of step" with the anticommunism crusade in Washington. The Truman administration was investigating government employees whose loyalty was suspect and Farrington said Truman was merely "stealing Republican 'thunder.' " "This is all part of the rising tide of sentiment against Russia and its purposes," Farrington explained.

In Hawaii the fires of anticommunism which Governor Stainback had kindled were burning brightly. Allen informed Farrington he had been told by the *Star-Bulletin*'s political writer Millard Purdy that Republican legislators, "backed by the GOP organizational leaders and some 'downtown bigshots,' " planned to step up the anti-Communist drive. It was part of their political strategy:

> The strategy is, [Purdy] believes, to project the Political Action Committee into the limelight as an organization of fellow-travelers, if not of actual reds, and to tar with the same brush all who have been supported or endorsed by the PAC for public office.

According to Stainback, Hall held the PAC "in the palm of his hand."

Other moves directed against the ILWU took place in secret. On July 27, 1947, a meeting was held at the home of industrialist Walter F. Dillingham. Present were Henry A. White and Elvon Musick of the pineapple industry; Claude Jagger, president of the Hawaiian Economic Foundation; and Lee Ettelson, a Hearst Publications editor whom the ILWU called "The Mysterious Stranger." The purpose of the meeting was to discuss the ILWU leadership. The group was convinced that the ILWU not only meant to destroy the loyalty of employees to their employers but was also trying to persuade its membership that the employer

---

1. Composed of Takeo Furuike (chairman), James Yamasaki, Thomas Kamisato, Ralph Baldonado, and Yoshinori Nonaka.

was "the natural enemy of the working man and woman." They all agreed that businessmen in Hawaii were not aware of the seriousness of the problem.

In September 1947, as part of his mission, Stainback spoke out at an AFL rally against Communists in the labor movement in Hawaii. "Stainback blasted hell out of us," Hall wrote Goldblatt. That same month a small incident took place which eventually had much greater impact on Hall and the ILWU than Stainback's assaults from a podium. Izuka, the onetime labor leader from Kauai, had an argument with Jack Kimoto about the Communist Party, a clash which so irritated Izuka that he planned to write an exposé of the Communist Party of Hawaii. The subject of the argument was an old refrain: the 1946 campaign for delegate to Congress, Farrington versus Borthwick.

The matter still rankled. Kimoto told Izuka that the Communist Party considered him a traitor to the working class because he had not accepted the Party order to support Republican Farrington against Democrat Borthwick. Kimoto said the Party hadn't attacked Izuka; Izuka had attacked the Party and thus he had violated Party discipline.[2]

Angrily, Izuka retorted that he had no choice but to let the public know "the truth." "The Communist Party was trying to take over [my] means of making a livelihood," he said. That was the reason Izuka gave for the publication of a 31-page, 13,000-word pamphlet—"The Truth about Communism in Hawaii"—which carried Izuka's name as the author. The ILWU didn't think he was capable of writing it. They believed it was ghostwritten and they were right.

Izuka said Fred Erwin, an AFL official on the West Coast, paid Paul Beam, a Honolulu advertising and public relations man, to write the first draft. Beam was the writer; Izuka supplied the information. "Beam wrote the first brief of the manuscript," said Izuka. "I found it was too shallow and not convincing enough. . . ."

He offered that first draft to Ray Coll, Sr., the *Advertiser*'s editor, but Coll refused to publish it. He was afraid he would be

---

2. Izuka resigned from the Communist Party on October 12, 1946.

sued for libel. Izuka then showed it to Arnold Wills, the NLRB man. Wills read it and offered some suggestions: "Don't exaggerate," he told Izuka. "You don't have enough information. Pinpoint the dates and times."

"Will you write it?" Izuka asked. Wills said that he would. "You must give me about a week." Then he sharply cross-examined Izuka as though he were a lawyer confronting a hostile witness. Based on Izuka's word, drafted by Beam, polished and sharpened by Wills, "The Truth" went to press. The pamphlet sold for twenty-five cents. It shocked the community. The question was: How true was "The Truth"? Hall called Izuka "a self-confessed liar," but Allen thought "The Truth" was "at least a fairly accurate portrayal of communism here."

Allen did a little digging. He called Henry "Hy" Holloway, president-manager of the Fisher Corporation, in whose plant the pamphlet was printed. Holloway told him Borthwick had phoned one day and asked to talk to a company salesman. Holloway assigned Charles Mulvehill. Mulvehill and Borthwick went into an office. Sitting there were Berman and Izuka. Berman introduced Mulvehill to Izuka and asked Mulvehill if the company could print a small pamphlet. Sure, said Mulvehill. Berman delivered the copy to Eddie Sakai, the printing superintendent. Sakai had the type set. Holloway told Allen that if he had read the pamphlet beforehand, he wouldn't have printed it. "I don't agree with some of the things it says and I don't want any complications."

Izuka said a total of 29,000 copies were printed—and distributed as follows: Hawaii Government Employees' Association, 11,000 copies; Teamsters Union, 6000; AFL, 2000; Elks Club, 2000; Kauai, 1500; the Big Island, 1500; the University of Hawaii, 1000; Bartenders' Hall, 1000; and the Samuel Amalu Hawaiian Organization, 1000. What was left went on general sale.

Alfred J. Kilantung, president of the Filipino Organization of Hawaii, who worked in the Industrial Relations Department of Castle & Cooke Terminals, asked Izuka to publish 10,000 copies in Ilocano at fifteen cents a copy. Izuka mailed 4700 copies in batches of 500 to Filipino groups on the Neighbor Islands and received $1490 from Arthur G. Smith, an American Factors lawyer, in payment for the Filipino edition. Izuka said he netted $1700 in all for his work.

Hall knew a piece of effective writing when he saw it. The pamphlet made its points clearly and was easy to understand. It was widely discussed. Copies appeared in Congress and in the schools; it was circulated on the plantations. David Thompson reported from Hawaii:

> Went to Olaa where membership meeting was still going on. Members had reported that lunas were showing them Izuka's smear sheet. Arakaki hit red issue hard—three languages. Group of Portuguese guys outside engaged me in conversation . . . real worried about the effect of pamphlet on rank and file. . . . Willie Baptiste said we had to sue for libel and "put Izuka behind bars." I explained that we had to face the real issue of whether to turn a deaf ear to these attacks.

"Have feeling that it will do a lot of harm if someone doesn't get to the members and straighten them out in a hurry," said Thompson. He thought it would be a good idea for someone to counterattack.

Hall agreed. He wrote a rebuttal which said Izuka's pamphlet was "written and edited, we have learned, by a recent law school graduate who has personal and selfish reason to hate the leadership of the ILWU." He didn't name the person, but he meant Ed Berman.[3] Hall claimed the pamphlet was part of "the boss plot against the union. . . . Izuka is merely a willing pawn in this plot." And Hall expected more attacks:

> The writer's denial that he is a member of the Communist Party—a denial which he has publicly made many times before—will not put a stop to the circulation of the lie, and our membership must expect it to continue. The bosses and their stooges are determined to use the issue of "communism" as a smokescreen behind which they can conceal their union-smashing attack against us.

---

3. Hall was wrong. Berman did not write the Izuka pamphlet. Izuka said, "Berman changed one or two sentences, but the main writing was done by Wills."

CHAPTER 37

The "Ignacio Revolt"

Amos Ignacio was a thin-faced Portuguese who led a short-lived rebellion against the ILWU leadership, a rebellion which has been called the "Ignacio Revolt." The revolt flared in December 1947 and petered out in a short time, but for a while it worried the union. It destroyed the careers of a small number of secondary labor leaders who had thrown in their lot with Ignacio, and it hurt the union's plans to raise sugar workers' wages.

Ignacio was born in Ookala on the Big Island; his parents were teachers. He had a high school education and went to work at Pepeekeo sugar mill in 1943. There he helped organize the workers, swearing them to secrecy. "If you got caught, you got fired," he said.

Ignacio was ambitious. He liked to take credit for organizing the union on Hawaii. "I was the spearhead and Jack Hall moved in and took all the glory," he said. He seemed destined for big things. Twice the union drummed up the votes that elected him to the Territorial House of Representatives (1944 and 1946).[1] Late in 1947, at age thirty-eight, he decided to break with the ILWU. He was then vice-president of the Big Island Division and a member of the Pepeekeo unit. He said it had been proposed that he become president of the union. He thought he could count on about thirty followers who were in leadership positions in the sugar locals. He even thought he had some strength on the other islands.

Ignacio explained his defection this way: "We started having doubts in our minds of [the ILWU] leaders' ulterior mo-

---

1. Ignacio ran for the Territorial Senate in 1948, but "the ILWU went after me," he said. "They lowered the boom," and he was defeated.

tives. . . . I was approached to sign up with the Communist Party. I told them to buy a one-way ticket to Moscow."

On paper he organized what he called "The Union of Hawaiian Workers (UHW)." He announced a slate of officers: himself, president; Akoni Pule, vice-president; Faustino Roldan, secretary-treasurer; and Jacinto Conol, second vice-president. David Thompson, then an ILWU International representative on the Big Island, tried to dissuade him. "He says his mind is made up," said Thompson. "[Ignacio] claims that the union has abused its power. Claims that there is not enough democracy in the union. Thinks he can get an immediate collective bargaining election. . . ."

On Sunday morning, December 14, 1947, an ILWU Big Island Executive Board meeting was held in Hilo. Thompson attended. The stakes were high; the atmosphere was tense. The delegates knew they could shatter the union, but "they were very disturbed by the red issue."

Ignacio suspended the regular order of business and announced he was resigning and leading his unit out of the ILWU to form an independent union. He said the reason was that the ILWU was "Communist-dominated; that he couldn't face his neighbors or himself while he was associated with it." Delegates from seven of the twelve Big Island sugar units voiced support for going independent.

Thompson spoke up. "Communism is not the issue," he said.

Many of us in the union had different beliefs, but we all have one common interest and that is to form a union of working people to win and hold for themselves what working people want. . . . The ILWU is not a Communist organization. It may be that some of the ILWU people are Communists, but the program of the ILWU is what the people make it.

This exchange took place:

Ignacio: Are there Communists in the ILWU?

Thompson: Frankly, yes there are. . . .

Ignacio: Are they a threat to the welfare of the workers?

Thompson: As far as communism is concerned in the U.S., I

don't think that the U.S. is willing to be a Communist country, next week or ten years from now. . . .

Thompson himself then asked the unasked question: "If Amos asks me if I am a Communist, I will tell him it's none of his business." He went on:

It is not a question to discuss in a union meeting. We came together to discuss union program. Do you think that I'm a Communist then I am not a good American? I fought in the last war for America and have a wooden leg now. . . .

If you form an independent union you are either going to play ball with the bosses or fight. If you fight, you are going to get the same treatment the ILWU is getting now.

Ignacio called a press conference next day. "4000 Sugar Workers Bolt on Hawaii," said the *Star-Bulletin*'s front page. Ignacio thought he had an ally in Kaholokula on Maui. He phoned Kaholokula that night, and next day wrote him a "Dear Joe" letter outlining the procedure to follow "in order to accomplish what we have set out as our goal, the ultimate destruction of the ILWU." First, he said, hold a membership meeting explaining the threat of communism and exposing the ILWU program which ultimately will "lead the workers to destruction." Then, he said, sign up all the members as proof that the UHW has a majority of workers so that the NLRB will be forced to call for a representation election. He warned that "rabble-rousers" from the ILWU would try to confuse them and discredit their action. "Good luck, fella *[sic]*, and let me hear from you soon," he wrote.

Ignacio thought all the pieces were falling into place. He was exuberant. "When I walked in here [his office] . . . I felt like tearing the walls down. . . . Wonderful. . . . I'm a free man again." He issued a small blue pamphlet titled "YES, Communism Is Un-American." It claimed that the "ILWU Bosses" preached class hatred, tried to dictate how union members should vote, centralized the union's power, and "took away our individual voices."

Ignacio called on Harry Kamoku, the Hilo longshore leader.

"Even though I had bolted, he was still a friend of mine," Ignacio declared. " 'Harry, join me,' I said. 'Amos, it would be suicide,' Kamoku said."

David Thompson, fearing that the house was in shambles, called on Nakano, the ILWU union leader in Hilo. Nakano was angry at the dissidents. "Stupid, selfish bastards," he said. But he, too, was worried. On election ballots at his unit (Local 155) at the Canec plant, union members had written insults: "Kiss my ass" and "Commie bastard."

Thompson drove to Olaa. There Arakaki talked about withdrawing the Olaa unit "if the whole island went independent." Thompson discovered the ILWU had no contacts at Naalehu, Pepeekeo-Honomu, Laupahoehoe, Hakalau, and Paauhau. He called for reinforcements in a hurry. "Try to get some of the good guys from the other plantations to knock off work and hit the road," he advised.

Hall sent over Labez and the Reverend Mr. Yadao. Labez, Yadao, and Thompson called on Kamoku. Kamoku said he didn't think a revolt was brewing on the Hilo waterfront. He told Thompson not to get excited, though later he admitted: "The news was a great shock to me—a complete surprise."

Dan Frias, president of the Pepeekeo-Honomu unit, told Thompson that the Filipinos and the older Japanese were "dead set" against communism and wanted an independent union or no union at all. To Thompson, who was under the gun, it appeared that dissension was widespread. He didn't realize that it was confined to a comparative handful and that the core of the union's strength—the rank and file—was loyal to the ILWU.

What had caused the commotion? he wondered. Perhaps a number of "old beefs and dissatisfactions" which Ignacio had taken advantage of—such as a day's pay,[2] consolidation of the units,[3] fear of a strike, and the red-baiting. Some of the membership were uneasy about Hall's feud with Stainback.

---

2. Robertson's plan to start on November 1, 1947, to collect a day's pay per month from each union member to build a reserve "fighting fund."

3. Consolidation of all the units into a single unit to strengthen the union, facilitate control from the top, and "tighten up" for the battles ahead.

Thompson frankly was worried. "My own assessment is that we have a very difficult situation in reaching the rank and file in those plantations where the leadership is decided and that it will be impossible to change the minds of some of the leaders," he said.

> All the enemy forces are very busy, and probably getting a lot accomplished while we are still not moving. . . . Our weakness is that even the guys who are "undecided" and not too damned militant about it, they are scared stiff of their rank and file and the red issue. . . .

Thompson proposed that the ILWU move fast, split into three groups, pick up all the rank and file members it could, and hold membership meetings at every plantation. Thompson also thought Goldblatt should come over. "Workers respect him because he is the guy who has negotiated all their biggest gains so far," he said.

> [Goldblatt] understands the situation in sugar best. Robertson would be a real red-herring at this point. Bridges does not have as much stature with sugar workers as Lou, and would be a target for the press.

He telephoned Goldblatt and Goldblatt decided immediately to come to Hawaii. A Territorial Sugar Workers Unity Conference was set for Hilo from January 3 to 5, 1948.

On December 19, Rania, Samson, and Arakaki debated Ignacio and Dan Frias at Pepeekeo, Ignacio's home base. After a long discussion, the members voted overwhelmingly to support the ILWU.

Laupahoehoe was the weakest link, Hall decided. "[Cipriano] Coloma [the unit president] is solidly behind Ignacio and had held camp-to-camp meetings obtaining approval of his action," said Hall. He conceded that Coloma was a capable leader and that it would be hard to convince his people he had made a mistake. Labez, Rania, and Samson talked to Coloma for an hour and a half but could not change his mind.

Rutledge turned up on the Big Island on December 20. According to Hall, Rutledge told Nakano he would join the ILWU if the union would denounce communism. "Cute, huh?" Hall said. "Nakano was somewhat taken in by this line, but I gave Dave [Thompson] strong instructions to tell our guys to stay the hell away from Rutledge because they are not able to handle him."

Suddenly support for Ignacio began "folding quite rapidly." Hall could see "daylight ahead" and was confident the ILWU would bring all the units in line before the sugar unity convention. "At the worst we can't lose more than one or two units," he said. He credited the turn in events to the Filipino leadership in the field on the Big Island and to the Oahu, Kauai, and Maui leadership.

At Hall's request, Kawano flew to Hawaii on December 24. He reported that Ignacio had "snowed under" a number of ILWU members, but "the boys did a good job of lining the men back into the ILWU." On the same day, Roldan, one of Ignacio's hand-picked officers, broke with him and issued a statement saying he had been misled. "Rick [Labez] phoned this morning," Hall reported. . . .

Izuka never did things halfway. He sent the Sugar Unity Conference a special delivery letter saying the ILWU had called him a "moron," a "renegade," a "self-confessed liar," and "other uncomplimentary names." Now he wanted a chance to reply. The conference opened on the morning of January 3, 1948, in the Hilo Armory. The subject: the Ignacio Revolt. Izuka's letter arrived at 10:45 AM. Kamoku wanted to keep Izuka out, but Goldblatt said to let him speak. At 2:41 PM Izuka got up on the platform and stayed there until 5:27 when the conference adjourned for the day.

He had no fear of being there in the lion's den. "I faced them like nothing because my convictions [were] so clear," he said. He spoke for half an hour and then the questions rained down on him: "Who was the ghost writer for the book? . . . Who pays your salary? . . . Why hasn't the FBI picked up the men you call Communists?"

He faced a "barrage of questions, accusations, catcalls,

laughs and mockery." Goldblatt said it cost five hundred dollars an hour to run the conference. "Mr. Izuka," he said, "you have been given democracy at great expense to the ILWU."

On the platform Izuka tried to field the hard shots. He said he sold his house for $13,000 to raise the money for his campaign against the ILWU leadership. "Nobody is behind me. . . . I am spending my own money."

Samson confronted him. "How many years were you a member of the Communist Party?" he asked.

"From 1938 to 1946," said Izuka.

"During those eight years, Mr. Izuka, did you or did you not plan to disrupt the U.S. government?"

"I did."

"You did!" exclaimed Samson in mock alarm. "Then how come you are still talking to me? They are supposed to put [you] in Alcatraz and throw away the key."

Izuka hung on. Hall grew restless. "I'm getting goddamned fed up after hours of talk by this little renegade," he said in a loud voice and came down from the platform.

"A question, Jack," Izuka pleaded. "Give me a question." Hall circulated among the delegates and wrote questions on slips of paper for them to ask Izuka.

Goldblatt, the keynote speaker, said he had been red-baited by professionals and that "it burns me . . . to be taken on by an amateur." The ILWU leaders on the mainland had undergone the same treatment ten years before, he said. "Communism is not an issue in the ILWU—it never has been and it never will be," he said. "We are union men and women working together for improved wages, better working conditions, better hours, better education for our families and a decent, regular life. This is the beginning and the end of the ILWU program. . . ."

Goldblatt said coldly, "We damned well don't intend to beg anybody to stay in the union. . . . We are not anxious to hold on to anybody's tails in the union. If they are anxious to go, it will be 'goodbye, so long'. . . ." He admitted that the Ignacio Revolt *had* hurt the union. "There is no kidding anybody. Damage has been done. You don't have the strength to back your demands." He rebutted the criticism that the ILWU was strike-happy. "That is not true."

> This union is opposed to strikes. We are against strikes because strikes cause suffering and hardship. The only time this union feels there ever should be a strike is when there is no other way of peacefully settling the thing.

Goldblatt said the time had come for the sugar workers to bite the bullet and make a decision: Are you in favor of staying in the ILWU: Yes or No?

For three days running he delivered some of his most rousing speeches and the outcome was a foregone conclusion: 5908 workers voted to stay in the union; 122 voted to leave. It was a ninety-eight percent vote. Bridges called it "a tremendous vote of solidarity."

The Ignacio Revolt was crushed but it did leave scars. Months later, Kenji Omuro, acting president of the Hawaii ILWU Division, surveyed some of the plantations. The situation at Naalehu "was not too healthy"; in the wake of the Ignacio affair, no one wanted to take on leadership roles. A new set of officers had to be elected at Pepeekeo-Honomu. At Laupahoehoe and at Kohala there were still Ignacio followers.

Ignacio kept hoping a miracle would happen. He approached management but the Employers Council refused to encourage him. Hall said: "Only a few companies, particularly C. Brewer . . . might be giving him support of some kind." Dwight Steele said Ignacio had come in to see him and told him he was having a thin time of it, but Steele would have nothing to do with him.

CHAPTER **38**
The Reinecke Affair

In the summer of 1947 the John Reineckes of Pahoa Avenue perceived some strange goings-on outside their house. The garbagemen were carefully dumping the Reinecke refuse into a separate box and carting it away. Reinecke asked for an explanation. The garbageman said he was told to keep their garbage separate; someone wanted it "gone over." He would not tell Reinecke who.

"I suppose," Reinecke surmised, "whoever is doing it expects to find Communist literature or 'incriminating' letters of some sort, though I am puzzled why they should go to so much trouble." He wrote the City and County Division of Refuse Collection and the mayor's office, but got no reply. The garbagemen continued to dump the Reinecke refuse into a separate box and haul it away for somebody's scrutiny.

Those were uneasy days. The Cold War was escalating; the nation was engaged in ferreting out Communists. Sometimes the pitch reached hysteria. Some people, in the phrase of the day, "saw reds under the beds."

On November 25, 1947, W. Harold Loper, superintendent of schools, brought charges against the Reineckes, both of whom taught in the public school system. In December they were suspended. Loper alleged they had violated the law which held that it was unlawful for a public schoolteacher to be a member of a secret society—that is, the Communist Party.[1] Reinecke taught at Farrington High School; his wife, at Waialae Elementary School. It took Governor Stainback eight months, but he finally got around to Reinecke, the author of the radical

---

1. Sec. 11641, chap. 281, Revised Laws of Hawaii 1935.

typescript paper which General Hull had given him in March.[2] One day Stainback decided to let the press know about the Reinecke tract, but without the word coming from him. He called in reporters and said: "Look, I can't tell you any of this, but if I walk out of the room and left this document on my desk and you saw it. . . ."

He walked out and Smyser of the *Star-Bulletin* saw Reinecke's name on the cover of the tract. He went to Farrington High and waited outside Reinecke's social studies class. Reinecke came out and Smyser asked him if he had written it. "He didn't say yes, and he didn't say no," said Smyser.[3] "Nothing except that he was a good teacher." Walton M. Gordon, the Farrington principal, said indeed Reinecke was "a very good teacher, one of the best we have at the senior level."

Reinecke called the charges part of Stainback's strategy to keep Hawaii from achieving statehood. He and his wife had never made any secret of their political views. Reinecke said Stainback was making a curiously belated discovery—namely, that there were Communists around. Stainback had not noticed them until suddenly it became expedient to do so.

> He cannot be so naive as not to know that the ILWU leaders who are called Communists in the Izuka pamphlet . . . were already called Communists two years ago [in 1946].
>
> At that time, when these men and the Governor got along politically, he could see no danger in them; he even appointed one of them [Hall] to office. But when they would not back his candidate for Delegate [Borthwick], and even found fault with his administration, they became an "insidious, foreign-controlled menace."

Riley Allen suspected that Stainback was motivated by a gut feeling against statehood: "I cannot help but feel that to a great many people the Governor's charges have a hollow ring." Allen said there was a report—a correct one, it turned out five months later—that Yoshiko Hall would be suspended from her job as a social worker with the State Department of Public Welfare.

---

2. "What Must We Do?"
3. "He didn't ask me if I wrote it," Reinecke said.

Mrs. Hall was on a customary six-month probationary period. She was, in fact, discharged on April 30, 1948. Newton R. Holcomb, the department director, said her work was not sufficiently good to qualify her for a permanent position and that he suspected her of being a member of the Communist Party.

Hall charged that the firing of his wife was Stainback's way of striking at him. He called the action "vindictive and political," a move against "those many honest people who refuse to dance to the sour notes of his lute."

The ILWU hired Gladstein to represent the Reineckes. Gladstein said the mild-mannered Reineckes were "just plain ordinary people who had never harmed a soul."[4] It was nonsense to think they would take orders to harm any of the thousands of children they had taught. There was a much more profound issue at stake, said Gladstein: civil liberty.

McElrath called the Reineckes "victims of the times" and said that was why the ILWU had taken up their cause. But Hall's heart was not in it; he feared the Reinecke case would weaken the ILWU. The case was "a byway," he felt, "and too much energy and effort would go into the struggle." He wanted the case brought to a head "as quickly as possible"; the less publicity, the better.

Goldblatt, on the other hand, felt they should use the Reinecke hearing as a forum for the union's defense of civil rights. Hall argued: "You're going to have a difficult job convincing me that your new position in the Reinecke case is correct. I can see no good in it at this writing."

Reinecke agreed that the ILWU supported him, "but with some reluctance." He said Hall gave the help "grudgingly. . . . It wasn't that Hall loved me less; he loved the union more. . . . They were afraid that if they were too firmly committed to defending us, they would run into a lot of criticism."

---

4. Koji Ariyoshi recalled an incident at a Communist Party meeting involving Reinecke, which he said showed how soft-hearted Reinecke was. A moth hovered around a light bulb. Reinecke caught the moth in his cupped hand, went outside, and released the moth unharmed.

I got the feeling on the part of the ILWU leadership that if we would resign from the school department, the Governor would not go ahead with his [campaign of] bias against the union. We were convinced we would be tried *in absentia*. We would be labeled Communists and not have any chance of presenting our position and of being judged on our merits.

Before the hearing took place, the Reineckes toured the Neighbor Islands to seek support. David Thompson met them at Kamoku's house in Hilo. He told them they ought to leave and "should have taken the advice of trade union officials . . . as to the real situation."

Reinecke replied that the union officials were mistaken. He had given out press releases about the trip, he said, and he was going to meet the people "even if we [the ILWU] 'sabotaged' him."

Thompson told Reinecke he couldn't stop him from speaking to the Local 142 Executive Board and Reinecke did speak. He and his wife, in fact, were well received; everyone signed the Reinecke petition. They collected thirty-eight dollars. Many union members asked them to return. They went on their way to the next stop, Olaa. "We got strong support from the people at Olaa," said Reinecke. "We got strong support in Hilo city and from Kamoku."

The Reinecke hearing before a six-member Territorial Commission on Public Instruction began in August 1948 and lasted for thirty-three days. School Superintendent Loper testified that he had once asked Reinecke: "Are you a Communist?" In reply, Loper said, "He didn't indicate that I had a right to ask such a question, but thought for a moment and said, 'In what sense do you ask that question?' "

Loper recalled that Reinecke told him that he did not advocate the overthrow of the government by force and violence. "I would be a fool to advocate anything of that sort," Loper quoted Reinecke as saying. Loper said that if Communists were allowed to teach in the public schools, "a vast majority of the public would lose confidence in its school system."

The Reinecke paper which General Hull had presented Stainback surfaced at the hearing. Reinecke said he wrote the tract only as an "intellectual exercise." He explained: "When I wrote this sketch I did not know a single member of the Communist Party. Obviously, therefore, it was not written and could not have been written as a plan for that party." The paragraph in the Reinecke tract that dealt with Boy Scouts also came to the attention of the hearing:

Question: Are you opposed to Boy Scouts?

Reinecke: By no means. I was a scout leader for one year when I was teaching at Konawaena School [1927–1928].

Reinecke testified that when he read Stainback's speech on Armistice Day, 1947, he knew he would "be the first marked for slaughter."

As the hearing ground slowly along, Hall said in exasperation:

[The Reinecke case] is going exactly as to my predictions. My only comment now is that if people were determined to get all the facts in the open regardless of consequences, it could have been done more positively and *cheaper* by a simple declaration.[5]

As expected, the commission found against the Reineckes. It decided that both had been properly dismissed. The commission revoked John Reinecke's teacher's certificate and found that both Reineckes were "not possessed of the ideals of democracy."[6]

Though he was now without a job, Reinecke would not ask Hall for help. He was a proud man. "I don't ask favors for myself," he said. "I never was told, but I got the impression that the top leadership—particularly Bridges—didn't want to have

---

5. Reinecke said he did not know what Hall meant.

6. In October 1976, the State Board of Education reversed the decision that dismissed the Reineckes and revoked John Reinecke's teacher's certificate. "Radical ideas are no longer so genuinely frightening as they were to many in 1948," a *Star-Bulletin* editorial commented.

outside intellectuals—particularly those who had been branded very publicly as Communists—working for the union. That's the way they thought."

The man who did hire Reinecke was Hall's arch-adversary. Reinecke worked for Art Rutledge for about a year and then Rutledge let him go, but only after Dave Beck ordered him to. When Beck, head of the West Coast Teamsters, was shorn of his power, Rutledge rehired Reinecke and employed him for a total of almost thirteen years. "That was very decent of him," Reinecke acknowledged.

Rutledge said Reinecke was the only person who ever invited him to join the Communist Party. "And that's why I have a soft spot for him," he laughed. "The other guys didn't want me."

CHAPTER **39**

Hall Applies Muscle

We are moving politically to take over the local Democratic Party and its convention in April [1948], including the Territorial Committee, the national committeeman and woman, and delegates to the national convention.
— Hall to Goldblatt, September 4, 1947

Hall did not take over the Democratic Party, but he tried. He recognized how weak the Democrats were and how he could capitalize on that weakness. To a large degree, the ILWU helped create the modern Democratic Party of Hawaii. ILWU members (such as Kawano) or people paid by the ILWU (such as Wilfred Oka) played a big role.

In 1947 there were Democratic precincts with no membership

at all and there were Democratic precincts with as few as five or seven party members. That made it easy to take over, said Kawano.

Late in 1947 Hall told Kawano that a "long-awaited meeting" was to take place that evening at Hall's home. Kawano was to bring as many people as he could.

"What's this long-awaited meeting all about?" asked Kawano.

"Well," said Hall, "the thing we have been planning for a long time. We are going to move tonight to try to work out the mechanics to move into the Democratic Party."

According to Kawano, Hall told the group at his home that they should become active in precinct work. They should try to get elected as county committeemen or committeewomen and as chairman or secretary of their precinct club. Above all, he said, try to get elected as a delegate to the Democratic Party convention:

> The thing to do is to be in a position where you can get into the caucuses and try to guide those politicians. And the way to do that he [Hall] stated was to try to help organize the Democratic Party because that seems to be the weaker one and the easier one to get into.

Oka was one of the most effective Democratic Party workers. He had a college degree; he knew hundreds of people whom he had taught at the Nuuanu YMCA; and he signed up new Democrats in batches. "He did a lot of legwork for me," said Jack Burns, who was trying to nurse his infant party along. Burns explained that Oka

> did a lot of running around. . . . Organizing precincts, putting those guys in, getting those guys, signing up those guys—in the ILWU, whom they could influence, and so forth. And that was the basic start [of the new Democratic Party] that we had until 1948 when we got the 442nd [the veterans] tacked in and I ran for office.[1]

Oka would call on his former YMCA students and say, "Hey, remember the things we were talking about? It's time we became

---

1. Burns ran for delegate to Congress in 1948 against Farrington and was beaten by a 3 to 1 margin.

first-class citizens." Then he would ask them to join the Democratic Party. The price: one dollar. Oka said the ILWU paid him fifteen or twenty dollars a week. The organizers made progress and fleshed out the bones. Because the ILWU had entered politics, said Kawano, "we have been able to revive the Democratic Party, make it more progressive, and now it [was] beginning to look like the people's party, and not the shadow of the reactionary Republican Party."

When election day came around, Kawano used to call in his longshoremen. He described the tactics:

> We used to knock off about 80 to 100 people to go around and help around the precincts . . . drum up candidates and one day . . . I think we had only about 80 people that morning. So I went down to McCabe [McCabe, Hamilton & Renny] in the morning and the trucks [were] already loaded ready to leave the truck yard. So I stopped the trucks and I yanked off about 50 or 60 people from those trucks to go out campaign.

Hall saw a chance to control the 1947 House of Representatives. Republican Representative Francis Aona of West Hawaii had died shortly after the 1946 general election and a special election was called in February 1947 to fill the position. "The reactionary forces of the territory," said Hall, "will be prepared to spend a lot of money in order to get a representative elected who will do their bidding. We should begin to move at once to obtain the support for a man we can count on."

Hall's choice of a candidate was Earl Nielsen, "if he is still solid with us." Nielsen had run as a Republican in the 1946 primary and lost. Approached by the ILWU, Nielsen now became "an ardent Democrat." Hall realized that if the Political Action Committee openly supported Nielsen, it would hurt him. It had to be done on the quiet. With PAC's underground support, Nielsen won—though by only sixteen votes. When the legislature convened, each party had fifteen seats in the House and it was a standoff. It remained that way for eighteen days.[2] Hall and McElrath lobbied at Iolani Palace; Hall warned that

---

2. William B. Stephenson, chairman of the Territorial Commission on Subversive Activities, called it "a struggle without parallel in the history of the territory."

any PAC-endorsed representative who broke ranks would be dumped in the next election.

The deadlock was broken when George Aguiar, a freshman Democrat fron Kauai who was fed up with the stalemate, voted Republican.

In 1947 Hall exerted all the pressure he could to get rid of Governor Stainback. He wrote a letter to Secretary of Interior Krug which was leaked to the press.[3] The *Advertiser* bannered the story:

HALL IN MOVE FOR T. H. POLITICAL POWER, SEEKS STAINBACK OUSTER

The story said Hall suggested that former Honolulu FBI man Robert Shivers, collector of customs, replace Stainback. Hall told Krug that the ILWU's support of Stainback for reappointment, which he had given hesitatingly in 1946, was a "serious mistake." He said Stainback had alienated the broad mass of Democratic voters and that four-fifths of Stainback's appointments had gone to Republicans.

The *Advertiser* called Hall's letter one of the ILWU's "boldest bids for power." An editorial commented:

The PAC polled and questioned candidates before the election. The PAC endorsed some candidates officially and threw the entire weight of the union against those not receiving its approval. The PAC practically took over the Democratic Territorial Committee. The PAC organized the Democratic membership of the House of Representatives, paralyzing the Legislature. . . .

Hall refused to comment on his letter to Krug. "The ILWU doesn't want to be in the forefront of this thing," he said. "Groups all over the community are interested in it."

Riley Allen certainly expressed an interest. Allen said the ILWU was "after Stainback's scalp" and that Hall was friendly with Shivers. According to Allen, Shivers was embar-

---

3. By Glazier, the ILWU representative in Washington, and by Hall and McElrath in Honolulu.

rassed by Hall's embrace. "Bob Shivers is much concerned because of the broad implications that he and the ILWU are tied up for political purposes," said Allen.

According to Allen, Stainback was pleased by Hall's attack on him. He felt the attacks would be discredited and he would gain by it. Allen had his own theory regarding Stainback's "shrill, stentorian shout" about communism. He said it stemmed from Stainback's wish to hurt the cause of statehood: "I have reason to believe that [Stainback] filled the ears of several Congressmen with his misgivings about the Muscovites and that his tactics are not only bred of animosity toward Jack Hall and the ILWU, but of his desire to delay statehood." At the other end of the line, Farrington, the man whose mission in life was statehood, replied: "I have identically the same feelings. . . ."

By spring 1948 Allen was deeply worried about Hall's power:

My impression is that the ILWU is getting a stronger and stronger hold, through its experience in organization work and in infiltration of its members into other organizations.

The anti-ILWU forces are apparently not organized and not sure of how to fight. The move of the ILWU into the Democratic party is an argument for unity and vigorous action by the Republican party.

The Democratic Party Territorial Convention was only a month away. "Some work is being done behind the scenes to attempt to patch up the differences," said Allen, "but the success so far is extremely doubtful."

The convention opened at McKinley High School auditorium on Sunday, May 2, 1948, and went on until 1:30 AM next day. Allen attended and watched the ILWU in action. Anytime the union wanted to press home a point, it was able to do so. "Jack Hall was much in evidence and inclined to throw his weight around," said Allen.

Allen talked to old-time Democrats, such as William H. Heen, who told him they realized they were outgunned and did not see much point in fighting the ILWU on the floor. "My observation is that the policies of the ILWU are opportunistic as far as personalities are concerned—its objective being primarily to serve the ILWU," said Allen.

Hall looked at politics with a cold and analytical eye. Allen and Farrington might believe statehood was just around the corner, but Hall knew better. He asked: What can be accomplished *now?* Well, the Democratic Party could petition Congress to amend the Organic Act and permit Hawaii to elect its own governor and judges. That was the best Hawaii could hope for for the next few years. "It is a foregone conclusion that statehood will be dumped," said Hall. He made his peace with the kingmakers in politics. On Maui, the man was Harold Rice. So what if Rice secretly was opposed to statehood "like his buddy, the governor"? He and Rice got along. Chances for another Democratic sweep there were good. Hall asked Koichi Imori to talk to Rice. Imori shrewdly asked Rice to "continue to give leadership" to the Democratic Party. A relationship was worked out with Rice and Hall went to Maui to draft, as he called it, "a modus operandi for the coming [1948] elections."

Hall predicted that in the 1948 elections the Republican campaign line would be "the usual red-baiting with a new twist to appeal to pro-statehood people." He meant the theory that the Republican Congress would grant statehood only if Hawaii elected a substantial majority of Republicans to the legislature. Hall took comfort in the Republicans' discomfort. "The Republicans are pretty well split," he said, "and many are beating a path to our door believing we don't mean what we say about straight backing for Democrats."

As a shrewd political analyst, Hall constantly assessed the union's political strength. In 1948 Kauai was a weak spot. "The leaders are too damn far ahead of the workers," he said. "They have failed utterly to follow the program laid out for them when Bob [McElrath] and I were over there for a week."

In the primary the union "took a shellacking" on Kauai. Hall went over to Kauai to tidy things up. "They responded damned quickly," he said, "after we got about 100 of the leadership together for the first night and political work is now being done on an enthusiastic and grassroots scale. I was able to mend a few of their fences and give them some measure of confidence.''[4]

It irked him that Kauai's ILWU leadership had managed to stir up resentment among small businessmen who were among the most loyal union supporters. It all started with the purchase of $15,000 worth of rice by the union from nonlocal sources. It turned out to be brown rice that nobody wanted. Aghast, Hall remembered the brown rice fiasco of the sugar strike. "Shades of 1946!" he exclaimed.

For all Hall's misgivings, the ILWU did fairly well in the 1948 general election. "We are luckier than we have a right to be," said Hall. It was still the era of Republican control of the legislature (nine to six in the Senate; twenty to ten in the House), but Hall was optimistic. "We have done enough fence-patching that we probably won't be crucified in the next session," he predicted.

The union had bounced back on Kauai and Maui and got its vote "back together" on Hawaii. "Even though it doesn't look so hot for the Big Island on the surface, precinct returns let the politicians know we still pack a pretty good vote," Hall said.

The union scored its biggest victory in the upset defeat of Republican incumbent Senator Clem Gomes by Democrat Manuel Aguiar on Kauai. "I really laid it into Gomes at our meeting and when the final results were in, we had turned the trick," said Hall.

On Oahu the Democrats carried four out of six seats in the Fifth District. The Fourth went straight GOP once more, but Vincent Esposito "pulled strong." "We dumped [James W. "Jimmy"] Glover for the Senate and [Herbert K. H.] Lee got in. Primarily because of the plantation vote," said Hall.

On the Big Island, Pule and Nielsen, with the ILWU's help, held onto their seats in West Hawaii and the plantation vote was strong. "The big Hilo vote knocked hell out of us," said Hall.

Jimmie Kealoha, a Republican, was elected Big Island chairman. Kealoha knew which way the wind was blowing. Hall said

---

4. Hall always had problems with Kauai—"The Maverick Island," Koji Ariyoshi called it.

Kealoha "promised me complete cooperation. . . . He said he wanted to stay in office and that he could see from the returns we could hold our own."

Although the Republicans retained control of the legislature, Hall could see possibilities. "We have some chance of influencing the following GOPers: [Norito] Kawakami, [Thomas] Sakakihara, [Takao] Yamauchi, [Alfred] Afat, and in some situations [Hiram] Fong. In the Senate we can do business at times with [Eugene] Capellas, [Francis] Silva *[sic]*[5] and [William J.] Nobriga."

On November 16, 1949, Hall submitted his resignation from the Democratic Party to Burns, the chairman of the Oahu County Committee. Hall said that some Democrats "have notoriously betrayed the principles and policies of the party." It was a grave mistake for the union to be tied up exclusively with one party. "There are a lot of phonies and extreme conservatives in the Democratic party," Hall told friends. "It is much more advantageous for us to be on the outside and influence elections. . . . To commit ourselves entirely to the Democratic party is wrong."

Burns sent his regrets. "This should clear the minds of those who have been saying that the ILWU has been dominating the Democratic Party," he said. He referred to Hall as just "a hardworking member of his precinct club," which amused some of the pols in town.[6]

Allen wondered what Burns could be thinking. "Mr. Burns does not give a complete description of Mr. Hall's activities in the Democratic party," he said. Harking back to May 1948, he recalled, "One has only to remember the Democratic Territorial Convention . . . effectively quarterbacked by none other than

---

5. Senator Francis Sylva of Kohala.
6. Years later Hall reminisced about the days when he tried to capture the Democratic Party. "Our union has always followed a program of independent political action except for a sorry period when some of us incorrectly thought we could pick up the dead carcass of a jackass [that is, the Democratic Party] and rejuvenate it into an intelligent, vigorous, loyal and honest animal that might lead the rest of us to progress, decency and a better life."

Jack Hall. He called the signals unerringly, and his forces on the floor carried them out swiftly and invincibly."

Allen said Hall's departure brought joy to the hearts of the Democratic Party's right wing. Maurice Sapienza, chairman of the right-wing Democratic Conference Committee, said he hoped others would follow Hall's example and take a walk.

None of this meant that Hall and the ILWU were through with politics. On the contrary, as a free agent, Hall could now maneuver more easily than before. "No, we haven't 'turned our back' on political activity," he said. "It's just that we have changed our methods of participation. . . . We are just as interested in politics as the next guy."

CHAPTER 40
Olaa '48

Chester J. "Chet" Meske was a city boy (from Milwaukee) who worked for the ILWU and was sent to Honokaa—a place he called "Siberia"—to help reorganize the Hamakua Coast in the wake of the Ignacio Revolt. Meske, a tall and solemn man of Polish descent, stayed from May through November 1948. He was a "lunger," as he called himself, a man who had spent five years recuperating from tuberculosis. When the rains came he was afraid that the weather and his seven-day-a-week job would bring on a recurrence of the ailment so he left. But he accomplished things.

It didn't take him long to find out what was wrong. "It is very obvious to me that the union is very weak because neither the local officers nor the business agents are close enough to the rank and file members," he said. As the union's International representative, Meske covered Ookala, Paauilo, Paauhau, Honokaa, and Kohala. Kohala was fifty miles from his base and all he could do was look in now and then. It was not an easy assignment for a *malihini*. He summarized:

> The Kohala leadership . . . resents any interference or assistance from "the outside." It's damn difficult to do a real job on five plantations, with two or three b.a.'s [business agents]not worth a damn. If this keeps up, we'll get nowhere (and Meske will lose more hair and end up in the nut house).

Meske lived in a hut in Honokaa; the sugar cane grew right up to the window. He washed his clothes in the kitchen sink. He had only a couple pairs of pants, a few shirts, and socks. Once a month he went to Honolulu for a talk with Hall.

Meske was appalled at the condition of workers' houses. Doors wouldn't close; roofs leaked; floors were rubbery with age. "I'd lean on a table and it would collapse," he said. He grew angrier. He went from camp to camp looking for grievances, writing them down on a clipboard, advising unit leaders. He never ignored a worker's complaint. He would stand and listen. He started holding Sunday meetings and he brought workers by bus to the Honokaa High School. There he would talk to them—in short sentences—and the words would be translated into Japanese and Filipino. He knew he was on trial before the silent men who watched him.

"I would wave my arms; try to express myself in the simplest way. . . . I held out one finger. I'd say: 'Alone, we are powerless. But put all the fingers together and they form a fist. With a fist we are powerful.' "

The silent men began to open up to the blue-eyed stranger. He looked around for young men willing to accept leadership roles. He found one such prospect in Yoshito Takamine, then twenty-one years old.[1]

---

1. Later, Big Island Division director and a state legislator.

In 1948 the sugar industry told the ILWU that Pioneer Mill and Olaa Sugar Company, both American Factors plantations, were in "desperate shape." If they were to stay in business, the employees would have to take a pay cut. At other "distressed" plantations on the Hamakua Coast—Onomea, Pepeekeo, and Hilo Sugar Company—management proposed pay cuts of eight cents an hour. At Olaa, William L. S. "Billy" Williams, the manager, sought a 17.2 percent pay cut. Goldblatt, speaking biblically, said Williams' chances of getting that kind of a cut were as slim as the chances of "a camel passing through the eye of a needle." He said the union might take a 5-cent cut at Olaa, but that was all. He turned out to be a prophet. (The basic rate then in the sugar industry was 78½ cents an hour, with the exception of Onomea where the ILWU, in September 1947, agreed to a base rate of 73½ cents.)

In June 1948, Steele asked Hall to negotiate a wage cut for the plantations. Hall suggested instead an industry-wide wage floor, but higher rates for the more productive plantations.

"An industry floor lower than 78½ cents?" Steele asked.

Hall heatedly responded: "I told him all hell would break loose if any wage cuts were insisted upon and that we were firmly convinced that they meant to take us on. We couldn't stop them, I said, but if we went down we were determined to have a lot of company."

Steele said that all the industry wanted to do was stay in business. Hall said the industry would have to present "compelling evidence before we would believe them." Hall knew he was playing with weak cards. The sugar workers would not support an industry-wide strike. They were concerned about "hanging on [to] their jobs." It did no good to tell the sugar workers that most plantations were making money. As McElrath said: "Their stock answer was: 'What you say may be true . . . but plantations are going out of business and more are threatening to go out. . . . Some of us are out of jobs and many more will lose their jobs if more plantations liquidate.' "

Hall said it looked "like a rough winter" ahead: plantations were tightening up; layoffs had started. Goldblatt, convinced that management wanted to liquidate Olaa and blame it on the union, told Hall to make Olaa a public issue. The ILWU distributed leaflets in three languages. Union leaders talked to small businessmen, ran ads in the *Hilo Tribune-Herald,* and broadcast over radio stations in English, Japanese, and Ilocano. It became a battle of figures and figures are dull. Not even ILWU members listened. Management seemed to be winning the war of words. "Too may figures have been tossed around on Olaa and too many of our members have become lost in these figures," said Meske.

Olaa went on strike on October 9. Hall, Kenji Omuro, T. C. Manipon, and Rania came for a visit and they didn't like what they saw: the Olaa workers didn't have the spirit that strikers had in the 1946 strike. Only 450 of the 1400 workers attended the meeting when strike action was discussed. Goldblatt said Olaa was "a long way from having the solidarity needed for a successful fight."

On October 10 Hall and Rania spoke to strikers who paid no attention. Then Manipon harangued them in Ilocano and they whooped and yelled and clapped and pounded on the floor.

Williams, the Olaa manager, was used to trouble; this was his fourteenth strike or work stoppage. He thought the strike was effective, but Meske was dubious. The strike fund was low.[2] Olaa workers felt abandoned. "They seem to feel that they are fighting a battle for the whole territory and everyone should dig deep," David Thompson said. Contributions came in slowly; sometimes as little as fifty cents a person. On the eighteenth day, strike committees were still only loosely organized with no effective soup kitchens, no education or recreation committees. Strike leaders bickered; a few workers were doing all the work. It looked to Meske as though the strike was a loser. Meske blamed the indifference on the other sugar workers. "An overwhelming majority of our members are still asleep and can't understand that Olaa's struggle is their struggle too," he said.

Jared Smith, the *Advertiser*'s elderly agriculture writer,[3] went

---

2. $6525, as of October 27, 1948.
3. He was then eighty-two.

to Olaa. He was an agrostologist, an expert on grasses, and sugar cane, after all, is a big grass. He was troubled by the thought that the cane was being neglected and that Olaa might go out of business.[4] He had been to Puna many times. More than forty years before, he had ridden horseback to Pahoa. Then farmers were planting coffee and rubber trees, not sugarcane.

Management agreed to mediate the Olaa strike and Ernest B. DeSilva, supervising principal of the Big Island schools, was named mediator. Hall told the ILWU division heads that there was little chance of a settlement unless the price of sugar increased. "The company just refuses to budge and is determined to smash us no matter how long it may take," he said gloomily.

Hall asked Goldblatt if a little "guerrilla warfare" with Amfac might get things moving—perhaps a one-day protest strike. "Our Amfac units are all tough ones and I think we could do it very successfully," he said. Hall went out with ILWU members on "bumming" expeditions for food and money. In Hilo they went door to door. On Lanai they collected $207 at one meeting. Some Lanai workers tossed ten-dollar bills in the pot. At Ewa Plantation the members voted to donate a dollar apiece through the checkoff; Waipahu forwarded five hundred dollars. The longshoremen sent a thousand dollars worth of foodstuffs.

The response heartened Hall. "It is my opinion that if the Olaa beef is doing nothing else, it is at least awakening the membership to the necessity for action," he said.

Olaa strikers mass-picketed the mill, the offices and camps, and the homes of supervisors and strikebreakers. "Our guys have been awfully damned tough in the picketing of homes," said Hall. The court granted the company an injunction to halt mass picketing. Someone turned on the ignition keys of thirteen plantation trucks and the batteries ran down. The company called it "sabotage." Hall warned the strikers against violence.

---

4. A total of 435 independent planters produced half the crop processed by the Olaa mill and they had a $2.9 million stake in the Olaa operation.

Hall told Steele he might as well concede that the union was in business to stay and draft a peace plan for Olaa. "He promised to stick his nose in at Amfac, although he has been far from welcome," said Hall.

Christmas was coming and the union prepared to give the Olaa children a bit of cheer. There were 740 children living in thirteen camps in Olaa. ILWU members donated fifty cents each to buy three gifts for each child.

Steele took a hand and finally progress was made. On December 16 the union and management settled the strike on the Onomea formula—basically, a five-cent wage cut.[5] The strike had lasted sixty-seven days. During that time sugar prices had risen two dollars a ton. That rise in price and a series of operational economies made the settlement possible, according to Williams.

The union called it a victory and announced it would toss a *luau* that "will rock the island." Hall said he had told management back in August that sugar prices were going to climb. Goldblatt said for the first time the union had taken on a liquidation fight and proved that "these threats of starvation can be licked."

Meske went home before the end of the strike. Hall wrote him that in addition to the settlement at Olaa, "we got a hell of a lot of other oral understandings that I only wish we had on other plantations"—such as severance pay for displaced employees who were not able to perform other work. "The company is falling all over itself trying to get in our good graces and if there is any substantial change in the price of sugar, they will quickly get back to the industry wage line."[6]

Hall said there never was such a victory *luau*—five cows, fifteen pigs, eight thousand *laulaus* (pork, beef, salt fish, taro tops,

---

5. Philip Murray, CIO national president, criticized Bridges because the ILWU accepted the wage cut. Bridges was then a member of the National CIO Executive Board. "Murray read me the riot act," he said. "He just dripped sarcasm all over the place. Made me feel like five cents on that whole deal."

6. At the January 1, 1950, contract reopenings, the Olaa and Onomea wage differentials were eliminated.

wrapped in ti leaves). Almost four thousand people attended, including management. "As Dave [Thompson] said, it was the goddamndest luau ever thrown and if there was anybody who didn't get drunk, it was his own damn fault."

In the middle of the Olaa affair Hall was also engaged in pineapple negotiations. There were dozens of problems: people to guide; decisions to make. The pressure built and for him there was one safety valve: drink. Toyomasa Oshiro, secretary-treasurer of Local 152, felt it was his duty to tell Bridges:[7] "During [the] current pine negotiations Brother Jack Hall has gone on a drunken spree for as long as a week and has failed to attend a number of important meetings when we most needed his advice and guidance."

Oshiro was troubled because Hall twice had told the union Pineapple Negotiating Committee he would meet with them at the Employers Council and had failed to show up. The first time Takeo Furuike, Local 152 president, reminded Hall of the session next day, but Hall didn't appear. The next time he was missing Oshiro went looking for him and "found him sleeping, as he had been drunk."

"What burns me up," said Oshiro, "is the fact that he made no effort to contact any of our committee members. . . ." Hall apologized and said it would not happen again. But Oshiro said it had happened before. "Brother Jack Hall has been guilty of the same offense during previous pineapple negotiations; that is, the last contract and the contract before."

Yet Oshiro held Hall in high regard:

He has done a lot for the union and has carried on negotiations to the satisfaction of the rank and file. I hate to think of the outcome when our members find out that he had been in a drunken condition during the crucial week of our negotiations.

7. Hall knew Oshiro had written Bridges (Oshiro sent him a copy of the letter), but never held it against him. In fact, he never mentioned the subject to Oshiro.

"You, as President of our International Union, have the responsibility of seeing to it that Jack is brought in line," he told Bridges.

> I feel very strongly that something must be done. . . . I think the whole organization in the territory is too loose. The local officers and the Regional Director [Hall] no doubt are aware of their responsibilities but they simply refuse to carry out their respective duties.

Bridges did not reply; he left the matter in the hands of Robertson, the director of organization. It was not the first time that Oshiro had complained. He felt the Hawaii leaders depended too much on the International. It came to the point, he said, where local leaders had lost their initiative and relied on the regional officers for help "no matter how small the problem."

Oshiro found fault with the regional officers for not reacting promptly to the threat posed by the Ignacio Revolt and by Izuka's pamphlet. "The top leadership of the regional office was so confused and bewildered that their reactions reflected a great deal upon the secondary leadership and the members as well throughout the territory." Oshiro said McElrath habitually failed to attend the regular Wednesday morning meetings of the four regional officers. "Brother McElrath is presently assigned to work with the sugar local. He is never to be found in his office or anywhere near the union hall. The first and best chance of locating him would be to inquire at his pet bars in town. . . ."

Hall's weakness was well known to his friends and they often came to his rescue. When Hall was missing during the 1947 pineapple negotiations, Okada played a hunch and found him at Ala Moana Park beach. "He had passed out," said Okada. During the Sugar Unity Convention, Hall was supposed to address one of the sessions and failed to show up. Okada went looking and found him in his room in the Hilo Hotel. "Everything fall on him," said Okada. "You see, the other guys, they talk like anything, but they all had to go to Jack Hall for everything. . . . Jack Hall took everything in those days."

Part 7
THE LONGSHORE STRIKE
(1949)

CHAPTER 41
A Chat on the Waterfront

In January 1949, Jack Kawano, president of the longshore local, had a friendly chat with Jack Guard, manager of McCabe, Hamilton & Renny stevedoring company, about a pay raise for longshoremen. They were earning $1.40 an hour. Sugar workers were getting 78½ cents. The employers claimed that for the type of work they did the longshoremen were the best-paid workers in the territory. But on the West Coast, ILWU longshoremen were earning $1.82 an hour. A 42–cent differential existed between Hawaii and the mainland. Same work, said the Hawaii long-shoremen; same ships; same cargo; same company.

On that basic issue—the difference in the pay rates—the 1949 longshore strike broke out. It was a strike that lasted almost six months, one of those elemental labor struggles that become landmarks. The strike tore at the fabric of the community, stirred up passion and hysteria, set people against people. It bankrupted some small merchants, caused large financial losses to industry and wage earners—and established the ILWU as an entrenched power.

The Hawaii longshore contract was to expire March 1, 1950, but Hall invoked the wage-reopening clause and asked for bargaining to begin February 1. That was the subject Kawano and Guard talked about. Guard was a friendly employer with concern for his workers. They liked him, confided in him, even borrowed money from him. Some Hawaiian longshoremen owed him as much as a thousand dollars.

Guard wanted to know what the union was going to ask for. Kawano told him he didn't know. But he said the employers better do something about the wage differential. He tossed the words off lightly; it was just a friendly talk. But he said if the employers didn't narrow the wage gap, the longshoremen would fight—"like the longshoremen on the coast have done." He said they wanted a substantial wage increase.

Guard offered Kawano some advice. He said not to ask for forty-two cents to bring Hawaii up to the West Coast scale in one crack. Ask for fifteen cents. That would be a reasonable start in cutting down the differential and later they could ask for more.

Fifteen cents? Kawano was skeptical. Fifteen cents, he said, won't settle the issue.

On January 26 Hall began the reopened talks with Philip P. Maxwell of the Employers Council. Hall asked either for thirty-two cents or that the wage be fixed by voluntary arbitration. On February 28 the employers countered with an offer of eight cents. Arbitration was repugnant to them. Arbitration, they said, meant "passing the buck" to a third party who had "no responsibility for the success or failure of an industry." The lines were hardening. "I think the waterfront employers welcome a longshore strike at this time and are ready to take us on and give us the works," said Robertson pessimistically.

No one deceived himself about the extent of the damage a dock strike would cause. "We recognize," the ILWU acknowledged, "that an interruption of shipping will be a serious matter not only for the people directly involved, but for all Hawaii."

On March 21 Hall told the waterfront employers they had until April 10 (later extended to April 30) to grant the 32-cent increase or agree to an outside arbitrator. Maxwell called this strike notice premature. After all, he said, only three negotiating sessions had been held. "It is rather like putting a sword over the negotiations."

On March 29 Hall instructed the ILWU Oahu Longshore Executive Board to draft a blueprint for a strike "in the event we have to hit the bricks." He wrote letters to the military commanders telling them that rumors that the ILWU would not handle military cargo in the event of a strike were false. On April 1 Fred Low, chairman of the union's negotiating committee, asked San Francisco to send Henry Schmidt over "due to the longshoremen's strike that is coming up."

"The Dutchman"—Schmidt was born in Holland of Dutch

and German ancestry—was an expert on waterfront strategy. For years he had worked on the San Francisco docks "shaking hands with the cargo," as he called it. Low said Schmidt was just the man to boost the morale of the longshoremen. Schmidt packed his bag and came over. He didn't think a shipping strike could last long. Maybe a month. How could the employers stand it? It would cost Matson alone twenty thousand dollars a day for every day the *Lurline* was tied up.

Goldblatt flew to Hawaii on April 20. Next day he and Hall met with the Strike Strategy Committee to find out how tough the longshoremen would be on the eight-cent wage offer by the industry.

Levi Kealoha of the Honolulu longshore local said the eight-cent offer meant a strike. Low said: "Hilo is on record for thirty-two cents or bust." Primitivo Queja of Kauai said if the offer was less than twenty cents, the Kauai longshoremen would reject it.

The two sides started meeting April 27 at the Moana Hotel, but time was running out. The deadline was midnight April 30. Late on the night of the thirtieth, the employers raised their wage offer to twelve cents. Goldblatt rejected it.

The strike began at one minute past midnight on Sunday, May 1. That day Goldblatt and Hall went to see "Pinky" Budge, president of Castle & Cooke, at his home in Kahala. Budge was cordial. First he showed them his garden and his orchids and then they talked business. Budge proposed that Goldblatt and Hall go back to the union members and recommend that they accept the twelve-cent offer. He was sure that if they did, the offer would be accepted.

Hall and Goldblatt spoke about a fifteen-cent offer they claimed the employers had made off the record.[1] Just add one penny to it, they said. Just one cent!

---

1. According to Hall and Goldblatt, shortly before the midnight deadline, management had made the fifteen-cent offer. Goldblatt said he told them if they raised the offer to sixteen cents, he would go to the membership and recommend that they accept. The West Coast longshoremen had settled for fifteen cents.

Russell Starr, chairman of the Stevedoring Companies Negotiating Committee, questioned whether any such fifteen-cent offer, off or on the record, had ever been made. Yukio Abe, secretary-treasurer of Local 136, angrily responded that the fifteen-cent offer was confirmed on June 3.

"He just wouldn't make a deal for sixteen cents so we could begin to close the gap with the mainland," said Goldblatt. Then, according to Goldblatt, Budge talked to them about the advantages of working in Hawaii: the weather was beautiful; people didn't have to buy winter clothing. "Living down here is a lot easier," said Budge.

"In what way?" asked Goldblatt.

"Well, they live in happier circumstances and in better weather."

At that point Goldblatt could not refrain from making an intemperate remark. He said, "In my many negotiations this is the first time I have ever heard anyone take God's gifts and put them on the paycheck."

He and Hall walked out and drove to Hall's house. "It's going to be a long strike," said Goldblatt.

CHAPTER 42

Message to Stalin: "Dear Joe"

In three days six ships were tied up. Hall cabled San Francisco that both sides were "bedding down for the long haul." It appeared there were ample food supplies, but at the first hint of a strike people began to hoard. They stashed away rice. Canned milk was in short supply even before the strike began.

On May 4 a four-column "Dear Joe" editorial appeared on the front page of the *Advertiser*. It was the opening shot in publisher Lorrin P. Thurston's war on the ILWU during the strike. Thurston wrote all the "Dear Joe" editorials—"every damn word," he said. "Dear Joe" was Josef Stalin, the Soviet dictator. The editorials charged that the Hawaii longshoremen were serving Stalin in a plot to destroy Hawaii's economy.

"What Are Your Next Orders, Joe? We Are Ready!" said the headline over the first "Dear Joe" editorial:

> Strike the ships. Two thousand men can and have tied up a community of 450,000 people. Every man who strikes is tying up hopes, job security, and welfare of 220 people. Good stuff? Five strikers tie up 1,100; 100 strikers, 22,000—and so on. Easy! Just like that. . . .

The "Dear Joe" editorials set the strident tone for the longshore strike. Thurston had tuned up in the 1946 strike. He despised Hall, Bridges, and Goldblatt. "I was a man of my own convictions," he said. "I guess I hated their guts."

At first "Dear Joe" infuriated the ILWU and then they began to treat the editorials as a joke. But in the community at large many people took them as gospel and applauded Thurston; a strong antiunion feeling was growing.[1]

On May 9 the *Lurline,* symbol of tourism in Hawaii, docked at Pier 11. She stayed there 157 days, 10 minutes, and 55 seconds. On May 10 cargo totaling 53,705 tons was tied up in strikebound ships. Two days later a Pan American Airways Clipper brought 12,000 pounds of food and supplies.

In mid-May, Goldblatt, who was in Hawaii, summed up the outlook: morale of the union members was high; organization was strong; discipline was tight; but tension was growing. In Goldblatt's view, the "employer fronts"—We, the Women, the Chamber of Commerce, businessmen's organizations—were leading the attack on the ILWU. He couldn't understand why, almost immediately, such an ugly mood had developed:

> I can't help but feel the employers sort of wandered into this one. Up to the deadline there was no feeling that the employers were particularly interested in settling. If anything, I got the impression, both in negotiations and from other sources, that they just made the as-

---

1. Because some people thought "Dear Joe" was Delegate Joe Farrington, Thurston had to explain in one "Dear Joe" editorial that the Joe he had in mind "lives in the Kremlin."

sumption that the union wouldn't strike no matter what developed. Some of the [industry] guys on top are convinced in their own mind that something like eight or twelve cents was a fair offer. . . . They just wouldn't believe us when we told them that the demands were serious.

He concluded that the two sides were simply miles apart. He didn't really believe the employers were thinking of any "deep-going plot to wreck the union" (despite ILWU propaganda to that effect). The employers merely wanted to go back to the "good old days" of low wages, he thought. He did realize that the strike would make or break the union:

The fact remains that as a union we either come through and prove to the membership down here that we're not just the tail end of organization or wages, or else we might just as well admit that what we can do for them is damned little. . . .

Goldblatt conceded that most of the community was on the side of the employers. The union could expect no help from Governor Stainback or even from Mayor Wilson, a friend of the ILWU. "The Governor is worthless and if anything will move against us if he gets the chance," Goldblatt predicted. "The Mayor is treading on eggs." Nor was he happy about George Hillenbrand, the federal mediator assigned to the strike. Goldblatt called Hillenbrand "utterly useless."

In Washington, Farrington was worried; the strike was bound to affect the chances for statehood and he was unable to do anything about it.

On May 10 Goldblatt and McElrath went to see Riley Allen. They tried to prevail upon him to advocate arbitration in his editorials. Allen would not commit the *Star-Bulletin* to arbitration or to any other course. He told them he hoped they would settle the strike "without name calling and without uproar." It was a little late for that; both sides already had started calling each other names.

Allen noted that the strike had already aroused much more emotion than any previous strike. Shortages of foodstuffs and supplies were reported; unemployment had started. Allen wrote Senator Morse that Hawaii's plight "grows hourly more serious.'' He asked that the federal government ship food and supplies to Hawaii on military ships. They could dock at Pearl Harbor "to avoid disorders on our own Honolulu docks.''

Stainback, the man in the middle, called the two sides in to discuss how to settle the strike. The union didn't trust him; Goldblatt thought he was feeling them out on a wage offer and playing the employer's game. "If he gets a chance to stick a knife into us, he will,'' said Goldblatt.

Looking on helplessly, people became alarmed and sent two thousand telegrams to President Truman urging him to intervene. The ILWU instructed Glazier, their Washington representative, to show congressmen the "Dear Joe" editorials.

All the time Thurston believed he was doing the right and courageous thing and that people were responding to him. But all the time events were conspiring to pull the knot tighter. Dairy workers and volunteers, under the protection of a court order issued by Federal Judge J. Frank McLaughlin, unloaded a thousand bags of feed from the *Hawaiian Citizen* at Pier 9. Bridges cabled Glazier that the use of a United States marshal to unload cargo showed that the federal government was "out to knife" the ILWU. He termed the move "the most flagrant use of strikebreaking we have ever seen" and asked Glazier to call it to the attention of Congress.

The Bar Association of Hawaii's Executive Committee asked for a federal investigation to determine whether the longshore strike was "a Communist strategy." Steele said there had been five major strikes on the coast in fourteen years and now the ILWU was making its biggest play for power. "This is it," said Steele. "We have always felt that the ILWU would not make its big move against the sugar, pineapple or miscellaneous industries, but on the waterfront where it can cut off everything coming into or going out of the territory."

Stainback appointed Circuit Judge Gerald R. Corbett to head an Emergency Food Committee. "No one is going to starve in Hawaii," Stainback assured the world. He cabled James P. Davis of the Department of Interior: "CANNOT EXAGGERATE DISASTROUS EFFECTS THAT A LONG CONTINUED STRIKE WILL HAVE.''

What should he do? Stainback considered the Hawaii ILWU leaders "card-carrying Communists," but at the same time he thought that Thurston and his "Dear Joe" editorials were "a lot of tommyrot." On May 26 Stainback recommended the setting up of a three-member fact-finding panel. Management agreed; the union refused. That same day Bridges, Schmidt, and Robertson were indicted by a federal grand jury in San Francisco.[2] "Another attempt to wreck the ILWU," said Schmidt.

The letters poured in on Stainback. A man named Raymond Uhl suggested that he draft the strikers into the militia. Someone advised him to recruit the Hawaii National Guard to man the docks.

Bill Stephenson, a professional red hunter, sent a letter to Stainback:

> As the goverment must well know, the ILWU has not operated as a labor union of the type which Americans have come to respect and which our laws are designed to foster and protect. The ILWU is ably directed by a small number of leaders, an effective number of whom as Communists do not have at heart the best interests of the United States or the Territory. Nor are they guided by the principle that their actions shall be directed to the betterment of the members of the union.
>
> The sole and sinister aim of Communist ILWU leaders is to further the ends of Russia. . . .

"Get the lead out, Governor," Mrs. A. W. Rasmussen wrote Stainback. James H. Anthony criticized Stainback for not doing enough against these "usurpers of the American way of life. . . . I hope that you will lie awake nights thinking; that your conscience will not let you sleep, for you should have a lot to think about."

K. L. Andrew wrote Stainback that this "foreign-born [that is, Bridges] S.O.B. from Australia, who should have been

---

2. Bridges on grounds that he had committed perjury in denying membership in the Communist Pary when he became a United States citizen; Schmidt and Robertson on charges of perjury and conspiracy to violate the naturalization laws when they stood up as witnesses for Bridges.

deported or hung *[sic]* years ago, has been babied along." Willie Wong sent Stainback a two-word message on a postcard: "Sir. Arbitrate." Frederick Hambrock of Philadelphia asked why Stainback couldn't deport Robertson, Goldblatt, and Schmidt.[3] He suggested: "Get them on income tax evasion, proof of citizenship, any damn trumped up charge to stop this uncalled-for-strike."

Major John L. Phillips of Temple City, California, said all strikes, lockouts, slowdowns, or interference with full production should be outlawed. "Only acts of God to be permitted." Wesley C. Keir of San Francisco wrote his message in purple ink. "This is a full scale rehearsal for insurrection to coincide with Russian attacks on the United States."

J. A. Conrow, Sr., of Memphis, Tennessee, took the precaution of hand-printing his letter—he said that a typed letter "might be intercepted by a secretary." He asked Stainback to acknowledge the receipt of his letter; "otherwise, I shall ask the FBI to trace and find just who intercepts your mail."

Dr. Kenneth P. Emory, an anthropologist at the Bishop Museum in Honolulu, wrote Stainback on museum stationery. He was "firmly convinced that the ILWU leaders are leading a foreign directed attack on the islands designed to wreck our economy." Dr. Samuel D. Allison, a Honolulu dermatologist, said he hoped the strike could be settled "without jeopardizing the gains made by the labor movement."

One citizen told Stainback to declare a state of emergency, put Hawaii under martial law, and arrest all striking union members and their leaders. "The leaders should be shot for treason within a half hour after reading this," he said.

Stafford L. Austin of Hilo praised Stainback for the "very steadfast and unfaltering manner" in which he was handling things. Mr. and Mrs. E. E. Black of Honolulu, vacationing at the Empress Hotel in Victoria, British Columbia, thanked Stainback for the "excellent way" he had protected their interests. Dr. H. L. Arnold, Sr., of Honolulu said that although he was a

---

3. Robertson presumably to his native Texas; Goldblatt to The Bronx; and Schmidt to his adopted San Francisco.

lifetime Republican, he had become an ardent admirer of Stainback. "The worthwhile people of Hawaii are definitely with you," he wrote.

An ominous message to Stainback was written on a postcard. It said: "There is a lot of talk around Washington that you are a Communist."

CHAPTER **43**
The Broom Brigade

The Broom Brigade began marching at 10:30 AM on May 31 in front of the ILWU headquarters at Pier 11. About three hundred women carried brooms with signs attached urging the ILWU strikers to go back to work. Nine out of ten marchers were *haoles*. They marched daily until mid-August and became a symbol of the 1949 strike; sometimes as many as four hundred women and thirty children took part.

From a car parked on the *mauka*[1] side of Queen Street that first day, Mrs. Mary K. "Girlie Hart" Robinson called over a loudspeaker: "Your leaders are deceiving you. Why don't you go back to work?"

"Why don't you *wahines* go home?" an ILWU picket shouted back.

To many, the women were heroines; to others they were buffoons. The ILWU claimed that some of them—they included, at times, such pillars of society as Louise Dillingham—came down in chauffeur-driven cars, took a turn or two on the picket line,

---

1. Inland, or toward the mountains.

and withdrew. "It was the only time most of the people in this community ever saw those *haole* women with a broom in their hands," said McElrath.

Mrs. Robinson said the women were doing a patriotic job. "We don't have to recruit them. They come here to march . . . because they know it is their duty to the people of the islands."

The Broom Brigade was the brainchild of Mona Hind Holmes, part-Hawaiian wife of a dairy industry executive. "I'll tell the truth," she said. "I was the founder." She had a small farm and had bought some cattle from the King's Ranch of Texas. The cattle were aboard one of the strikebound ships. Mrs. Holmes called the ILWU. "If you let those valuable cattle die, I'm going to sue you," she said in her frustration.[2] She talked it over with some other women whose feelings also ran high: Mrs. Robinson, president of We, the Women of Hawaii; Ruth Black, wife of construction man E. E. Black; and Corinne Von Wedelstaedt (Forde), executive secretary of the Hawaii Restaurant and Dispensers Association. "What we ought to do is go down there and sweep the ILWU into the harbor," said Mrs. Holmes angrily. "And that's how it all started." The word "sweep" launched the Broom Brigade.

Von Wedelstaedt, a high-spirited former model, took part enthusiastically. "I led the Broom Brigade," she said, speaking of opening day. "They were scared. They thought they were going to be killed."

She also led a half-hour demonstration on Merchant Street in front of the *Star-Bulletin* offices. She had decided that the paper was pro-ILWU.[3]

It was fun to picket, but the women thought of a better way to hurt the *Star-Bulletin*—by a boycott of advertisers. "Let's hit Joe Farrington where it will hurt him the most," they said. They called a meeting at McInerny's Fort Street store and met with several of Honolulu's leading businessmen. The women told the business executives they knew how to break the strike: stop ad-

---

2. The cattle did not die. They were landed unharmed.
3. One of the Broom Brigade's signs said: "Is the *Star-Bulletin* Edited by McElrath?"

vertising in the *Star-Bulletin*. The businessmen agreed to try it; they let their scheduled ads run but did not reschedule any.[4]

Attorney Garner Anthony wondered if there was a legal way to stop the strike. He read his law books, pondered, then sent Stainback a letter saying that in his opinion the territory could bring a bill in equity in circuit court to enjoin the strike. The basis for such a suit would be the allegation that the strike was a "concerted action on the part of the union against public health, safety and welfare." Such acts are unlawful, Anthony said. "While the court could not direct the employees to go back to the job, it could order them to cease and desist from striking."

In a follow-up memorandum to Stainback, Anthony had another thought: "A second cause might be added alleging that the strike is being fomented as a part of a plot to overthrow the government or as a means to that end. . . ." Anthony spoke as "an affected citizen." He offered his services to Stainback if Stainback desired them.

Others also were thinking of how to end the strike. Doc Hill had no law degree but he was shrewd. He sent Stainback a memorandum, prepared at his request by the Legislative Reference Bureau, which Hill thought could serve as the basis for drafting legislation to end the strike. "What I have in mind," Hill said, "is the enactment of legislation authorizing the Territorial Government to seize and operate the facilities used in loading and unloading cargoes during a strike or a work stoppage." In short, government operation of the docks. Stainback thought the idea was worth examining.[5] He tucked it away in the back of his mind. Meanwhile, he wanted to try something else first. He prepared to name a fact-finding board.

The islands were now held tightly in the grip of the strike. Corbett, chairman of the Governor's Emergency Food Committee, worked sixty hours a week. All sorts of shortages were reported. Poultrymen had to kill fifteen thousand chicks

---

4. Riley Allen said the boycott lasted about ten days—"then, one by one, they came back."

5. On Hill's letter he penciled: "To Att. Gen. for info & comment."

because they had run out of feed. Hospitals were short of the anesthetic cyclopropane and were reporting shortages of infant food, bandages, cotton balls, and sponges. The supply of embalming fluid was gone. Yeast was in short supply. Young Brothers needed wire hawsers for towing barges.

The navy transport *General Breckenridge* sailed from San Francisco with a relief cargo of medicine and yeast, and on June 7 Matson and the ILWU signed a memorandum of agreement which permitted relief supplies to be loaded aboard Matson's *Hawaiian Refiner* in San Francisco. The *Refiner* brought 11,150 tons of cargo ranging from salt to shrimp. ILWU longshoremen unloaded the ship at the prestrike wage of $1.40 an hour, but the union told Corbett it would not handle any more Matson relief ships. It accused Matson of cooperating "with certain persons and organizations" to try to break the strike. The ILWU also asked to place a union member on Corbett's committee, but he objected. He said he would not bargain with the union "over terms and conditions upon which the necessities of life will be brought to the people."

The strike had started to take a toll: some companies went on a 36-hour work week and employees took a ten percent wage cut. Sugar piled up in the pier areas. The Honolulu Council of Churches held special services to seek divine guidance for a solution to the strike. The Reverend Stephen L. Desha said the strike was wrecking the economy of Hawaii.

Allen gloomily surveyed the scene: "Hundreds of merchants are scraping bottom on non-food items and unemployment is rising at a rate which shows how seriously cut is the buying power of the people."

Thurston appealed to the Hawaiian longshoremen in a front-page editorial in the Hawaiian language with a headline which said: *"He Noi No Na Hawaii Oiaio."*[6] A Maui-born San Francisco longshoreman named Joseph Maldonado came to town to organize a breakoff group from the ILWU longshoremen. He taunted the ILWU by renting office space next to ILWU headquarters. Four days later Maldonado was beaten in a Pier 8 café.

---

6. "A Request from a True Hawaiian."

In Washington, Glazier, the energetic ILWU lobbyist, buttonholed senators, talked to the press, and grew increasingly irritated with Farrington. He said Farrington listened only to people from the Sugar Planters' Association. A stream of "vigilante type" letters was pouring into Washington, said Glazier. The writers urged congressmen "to get a witchhunt" started.

By now the strike had a national audience, and on the mainland the editorials were grim. The *St. Louis Globe-Democrat* said:

> [The strike] has forced adults, children and infants alike to vastly reduced rations . . . while the dock workers hold out for higher wages and Bridges' CIO musclemen patrol to see that none weakens to the cry of humanity. Mothers forage town desperately for canned milk for their babies.

Farrington saw President Truman and, according to Glazier, asked Truman to intervene, either through a Taft-Hartley injunction or by seizing the stevedoring industry under the provisions of the Shipping Act of 1916. Bridges and Goldblatt cabled Truman, saying they had learned that Senator Morse had called on him to ask that he appoint an arbitration board. Naturally, they approved. They denounced the double-page ads running in the *New York Times,* the *Washington Post,* and the *Washington Star* which castigated the ILWU.

> Through those mediums the employers have attempted to turn a simple demand for a wage increase, together with an offer that the dispute be arbitrated, into a pernicious plot against the Territory of Hawaii, the people of Hawaii, and the United States.

Truman shook off the plea to intervene; he said he had no authority to do so.

Cyrus Ching, the lordly[7] director of the Federal Mediation and Conciliation Service, offered his help. Glazier informed Bridges and Goldblatt but they were not impressed. Schmidt, who loved to quip, said in Hawaii there was now a second

---

7. He was six feet, seven inches tall.

"Big Five"—namely, Bridges, Goldblatt, Hall, McElrath, and Schmidt.

In Honolulu, the ILWU soup kitchen served 1300 to 1400 meals a day. Union members grew vegetables and went fishing and hunting. One day the Maui people brought over some deep-sea turtles and there was turtle soup for lunch. But strikes are not dinner parties: turtle soup was seldom on the menu and for many the fare was thin. Schmidt noted that "some strikers are much in need and are compelled to bring wives and children to [the] soup kitchen for meals. [The] union is paying house rent for needy families whenever the Territorial welfare department refuses to do so."

CHAPTER 44
Fact-Finding: The First Dialogue

On June 15 Stainback announced he had appointed a fact-finding board[1] and gave them seven days to conduct a hearing and present a recommendation for the strike's settlement. That seemed like a short time to Goldblatt. "To call it fact-finding . . . is a weird stretch of the imagination," he protested. Schmidt said it was a foregone conclusion the board would sub-

---

1. Members were: James L. Coke, former chief justice of the territorial supreme court; George Bicknell, director of the Veterans Administration; Ernest De Silva, supervising principal of the Island of Hawaii public schools; Newton R. Holcomb, director, Territorial Department of Public Welfare; and Dr. Harold S. Roberts, acting chairman of the University of Hawaii Department of Business and Economics.

mit a recommendation "which already has the full approval of the employers."

Allen contended the ILWU's tactics had alienated even the normal "neutrals." "Any reasonable proposal by the Governor's committee, buttressed by stated facts," he said, "will meet with general approval and support."

Goldblatt handled the union's case and Jim Blaisdell represented the employers. In his opening statement Goldblatt set the tone for sharp confrontation. He was a man who could talk. In fact, he sounded like a courtroom lawyer and at one point Judge Coke mistook him for one. Goldblatt challenged the board to make a finding of fact on the charge that the strike was Communist-inspired. "The union will be most eager to hear testimony and consider evidence on this issue; to cross-examine witnesses and to present evidence and testimony on its own behalf," he said.

Board member De Silva asked Blaisdell if, in fact, the alleged Communist plot was an issue in the dispute. Blaisdell replied: "Well, I could refer to our statement and you will find . . . it is conspicuous by its absence."

Goldblatt assailed the role of the press. "What are they trying to do?" he asked. "They are trying to conduct a murder trial of the ILWU." He doubted the union could get a fair hearing; he said he had examined the history of similar hearings in Hawaii and such chances were "exactly zero." In his opinion the hearing had been destroyed before it began. He may have talked too much, and the quick-witted Blaisdell parried. "One party to this fact-finding proceeding has stated that it is absolutely waste time, that it is done before it is started," he said. "If that is the fact," said Chairman Coke, "we may as well fold our tents and go home."

They were off to a ruffled start. Blaisdell said Goldblatt had launched a "well planned, deliberate and vicious" attack on the motives of the employers:

I have known Mr. Goldblatt for fourteen years . . . and . . . I have heard that speech, not here, but practically every place that I have encountered him and that particular speech has improved only in the eloquence of its delivery. . . .

Finally they hacked through the thicket of preliminaries and Goldblatt opened his case by saying that the heart of the matter was simple: Hawaii's longshoremen deserved equal pay with West Coast longshoremen for doing the same kind of work:

All they are trying to do is reestablish the differential which existed in 1945 when the differences between the Hawaii longshoremen and the West Coast longshoremen working on the same cargo and upon the same basis, on the same ships, as members of the same union, were only a dime apart.[2]

Next morning he called Fred Low, the Strike Committee chairman. "How long do you think they are willing to stay out?"

Three to six months, said Low.

How are the strikers getting along?

"Squeezing along," said Low.

"How long do you think you can keep squeezing?"

"As long as the others; the rest of the boys keep on squeezing too."

Then Goldblatt called Schmidt, who described longshore work: men loading and storing cargo; the winch drivers, the men "who work under the hook"; the four-wheel-truck drivers; the jitney operations; the men on the dock sorting and piling cargo.

Was this unskilled work? asked Goldblatt.

"Not at all," said Schmidt.

Suppose a winch driver was inept?

"The cargo would be smashed and the men that work in the hold would be killed or injured," said Schmidt.

Russell Starr, Blaisdell's first witness, said the ILWU's 32-cent demand was "completely unrealistic": "There was no

---

2. ILWU researcher Teddy Kreps said Hawaii longshoremen earned $11.20 in a regular eight-hour day. West Coast longshoremen earned $16.38 for eight hours. The West Coast dockers got six hours' pay at straight time and two hours at overtime.

justification for singling out a small group of about 2,000 man for a wage increase of 32 cents which was unheard of in terms of any mainland or local patterns of wage increases."

Compared to workers in similar jobs, said Starr, "the stevedores were the highest paid, not only from the standpoint of hourly rates, but because of more favorable overtime provisions." He explained that overtime constituted a large part of the longshoreman's pay. A longshoreman got straight time from 7 AM to 4 PM, Monday through Friday, but all other hours were overtime. Starr said a longshoreman needed skill to be a good winch driver, gang foreman, or leaderman, but the longshoremen doing manual labor needed no experience:

> I don't say that our men don't work hard. Our men work. They are not lazy. . . . But I will also say this: that there is more lost time in the longshore industry as a whole than in any other industry in the world. . . . That is the way these ships are built; that is the way cargo is stowed, but there is lost time.

On cross-examination, Goldblatt asked Starr if work on the waterfront was so attractive, why was there such a big turnover of personnel? "Why aren't the Japanese and Hawaiians rushing down to work on the waterfront?"

"I don't know," said Starr.

In his summation, Goldblatt said that according to the press, the radio, the employers, and the community at large, "never in the history of Hawaii has there been a just strike."

> Every strike, no matter for what reason, has invariably been condemned and invariably attacked with the same weapons, and invariably slandered and vilified and their leaders castigated.

In his summation, Blaisdell spoke of ILWU power and arrogance:

> Interesting! Interesting! How much goes into getting a contract and how little it means. . . . I don't know where you could go to find an example of more complete arrogance, a complete smugness, than [Goldblatt's] sense of righteousness of position. . . .
> The fact of the matter [is] the ILWU cannot be crossed. They

simply cannot be crossed. If they were not so powerful, it would lend itself to the example of a small and extremely spoiled child.

Blaisdell said he had been in Hawaii since 1943 and had watched the rapid growth of the ILWU. Once Hawaii was a place where unions were impotent, but not any longer. The long-shore strike, he said, was something new under the Hawaiian sun:

> This is a brand-new experience for the union and it is a brand-new experience for this community. Every port in the territory, which is the absolute life-line of the Territory of Hawaii, is closed. Whether they understand it or not, they [the people] don't like it and they speak up and they say they don't like it. . . .

The seven days of sound and fury came to an end and Judge Coke called the proceedings adjourned. He asked the two sides to leave the door open to a settlement; such a move would be welcomed as "the rainfall coming down."

The board submitted its report June 28, 1949, the fifty-ninth day of the strike, and recommended that the longshore wage be raised by fourteen cents—from $1.40 to $1.54 an hour, with eight cents retroactive to March 1, 1949. (The document had left a space blank for the wage figure. That figure was inserted at the last moment so that it could be kept confidential.)

The stevedoring companies said they would go along with the fourteen-cent recommendation; the longshoremen rejected it by an 826 to 59 vote.[3] Schmidt and Hall had told the longshoremen they could not recommend acceptance of the proposal. The employers could not reject the offer because the public would disapprove. The union could not accept because it would widen the wage gap with the coast. Steele urged the industry to reject the offer "to protect the [industry's] bargaining position." Budge of Castle & Cooke disagreed. The Big Five executives were afraid to affront Washington since Washington controlled the purse strings—sugar subsidies under the Sugar Act.

---

3. Bridges said the fourteen-cent figure haunted the union from then on. "We could never get over that," he said. He said the union should not have taken part in the fact-finding hearing.

CHAPTER 45

Hot Days, Hot Cargo, Hot Words

In July 1949, Mark Egan, managing director of the Hawaii Visitors Bureau, suggested a slogan for the Aloha Week Committee to lift the community's spirits. It was: "Out of the Trenches by Aloha Week."[1] Hotel occupancy was off thirty-six percent.[2] In San Francisco a wag had started a "Bundles for Hawaii" campaign. That made Egan feel terrible.

The Broom Brigade continued to march. "Hall's Belly Full, You're Empty," said a picketer's sign. One issue sounded loud and shrill: communism. Randolph Sevier, executive vice-president of Matson, said it was useless to throw "communist brickbats" at the ILWU. Cadagan of Hawaiian Pine said leveling charges of communism against the union "without producing the facts to prove them" settled nothing. Riley Allen wrote an article for the *Philadelphia Inquirer* saying the Communist issue had been trumpeted so loudly "that it has largely obscured the wage issue." Lorrin Thurston sent President Truman a telegram saying that if he wanted to see the new American life under Communist direction, then come to Hawaii. Senator William F. Knowland of California suggested that Truman order an airlift to Hawaii like the Berlin airlift. "We won't be smashed," said Hall. "No matter how much of their power is brought against us."

Negotiations were getting nowhere. One day the two sides met for thirteen minutes and adjourned. "This looks like the last meeting for a long time," Hall told Bridges. He described the

---

1. October 30 to November 7.
2. Up to July 7, 1949, 1119 visitors had come to Hawaii so far that year compared to 1749 for the same period in 1948.

siege: "Morale is excellent. The guys figure, 'We've been out two months. Let's stay out even another four months and get something worthwhile.' "

Judge McLaughlin signed an order permitting the American Can Company to unload tinplate from the *Hawaiian Citizen* at Pier 9. The ILWU offered to work the ship for $1.72 an hour. Otto Heine, the United States marshal, declined the offer and hired volunteers for $1.40 an hour; there were plenty to spare. ILWU pickets massed at dockside and the police arrested 106. The union paid a hundred dollars apiece to bail them out. Hall told Bridges the employers "will try anything to break the strike. . . . Longshoremen burnt up. . . ."

He made a request of the restless Bridges. He asked him *not* to come to Hawaii. "It's not necessary and would provoke a lot of wahine hysteria that would get the beef off on a different issue." Bridges ignored the advice and told Hall he was coming. He said he would arrive July 8 and was counting on ILWU members to protect him at the airport. "Keep the wahinis *[sic]* off me so that I may preserve my dignity and other things."

In an island community cut off from shipping, someone was bound to try to run in ships. On July 12 the Hawaii Stevedores, Ltd.,[3] started business with equipment rented from the struck stevedoring companies. They had no trouble recruiting workers for the old $1.40 wage. The ILWU charged that the territory had set up the company and hired strikebreakers.

Schmidt took a motorboat tour of his preserve, the Honolulu waterfront, and snapped pictures of men working the *Steel Flyer* at Pier 28. The sight galled him. "Scabs doing a bad job." But they were aboard ship; they were working; and that was not good for the morale of the strikers.

On July 16 Hawaii Stevedores work gangs were bused to Pier 29 where ILWU pickets awaited them. It was a meeting made for bloodshed. The police intervened, arrested ninety-six pickets, and charged them with disorderly conduct.

---

3. Officers were Ray Adelmeyer, a small businessman, president; and former delegate Samuel Wilder King, George Fujii, and Ray Pullen, vice-presidents.

At 6:30 AM on July 20, two or three hundred ILWU strikers and sympathizers stormed the Hawaii Stevedores' Ala Moana headquarters. There was a short, vicious fight with clubs, bottles, bricks, and knives and twenty-four men were injured, among them a policeman, three ILWU members,[4] and twenty Hawaii Stevedores employees. Four persons were hospitalized.

On July 26 six taxis drove up to the *Steel Flyer* at Pier 28 carrying thirty-three members of the Sailors' Union of the Pacific. ILWU pickets couldn't stop them. The sailors scrambled aboard ship, raised steam, and the ship, half loaded with sugar, set sail. "We are tired of this place and we're going home," said one of the sailors. Hall set a tail on the "hot cargo" ship. The *Flyer* docked in Philadelphia, but members of the International Longshoremen's Association—no friend of the ILWU—refused to unload her. Off she went to Brooklyn and there the ship unloaded her cargo of 6200 tons of raw sugar at a refinery. It was only a drop in the sugar bowl. In midsummer of 1949, some 400,000 tons of sugar were piled in warehouses and on docks in Hawaii.

The Hawaii Stevedores soon had competition which the ILWU welcomed. The union signed an agreement with eight companies[5] who used a fleet of barges and tugs and converted landing craft—a "splinter fleet." The operators agreed to pay the ILWU longshoremen either $1.72 an hour or $1.40 plus 42 cents to be held in escrow until the strike was settled. The first vessel, the *Mokupapa,* a converted LST, arrived July 25.

One of the original members of the splinter fleet was MEW Associates. The owners were Takaichi Miyamoto, proprietor of a liquor store; business executive C. Robert Weiller; and lawyer-embryo politician Othello Vincent Esposito. (The acronym MEW was made up of the first letter of their last names.) "I was the guy that helped break the back of Matson," said Esposito. "I was the guy that had the stevedoring company and brought the barges in and hired the ILWU."

---

4. More than three ILWU members were injured. Most injured longshoremen didn't want their name revealed to the police.

5. Meats, Inc., Eastern Iron & Metal Company, Ltd., Hawaii Northwest Products, Ocean Prince, Inc., Pacific Freight Forwarders, A. A. Smalin, South Seas Shipping, and MEW Associates.

The idea stemmed from a casual remark Esposito had made after a luncheon meeting at the YWCA. Businessmen were thrashing around for a way to bring cargo in. Esposito said that "if anyone had any brains . . . they'd hire a lawyer and go time-charter a ship." It was easy, he said. It seemed so simple he talked himself into it and then found it was not so simple after all. MEW Associates was not able to charter a ship. "Those companies over there [the West Coast] were afraid of Matson and no one would give us a ship," said Esposito.

MEW Associates chartered two large steel barges and two sea-going tugs *(Hercules* and *Monarch)* from Red Crowley's Puget Sound Tug & Barge Company of Seattle. Crowley feared neither man nor beast, but he did charge a fancy price. Esposito said barges normally rented for $133 a day, but he had to pay $999 a day.

The splinter fleet touched off an uproar, which Schmidt enjoyed. "The Chamber of Commerce is blasting hell out of everybody for participating," he said. The employers admitted that the splinter fleet was causing "tremendous dissension." Maxwell accused Employers Council members of quietly using the fleet themselves. One of the culprits, according to Howard Babbitt of C. Brewer, was the Dillingham Corporation. Lowell Dillingham was on the council's board of directors. "It was a very nasty situation," said Steele.

By now Bridges was ready to play to a nationwide audience. He wanted a hearing in the United States Senate with both the union and the employers summoned to appear. That would be "right down our alley," he said. He knew who the ILWU's spokesman would be: Harry Bridges. "In such an event I shall go to Washington to present the case for the union." He asked the Hawaii ILWU to gather material for him.

And it came to pass. Bridges met Blaisdell in the Senate Caucus Hearing Room on July 18 before Elbert D. Thomas's Committee on Labor and Public Welfare. Blaisdell spoke first. He said that once a parity wage with the West Coast was adopted, "there would never be any more bargaining in the

Hawaiian Islands. Our bargaining would be made on the West Coast or East Coast as the case may be.''

Blaisdell said longshoremen's pay had to match pay for similar work in Hawaii. That was the way things had always been, but now the ILWU wouldn't play the game.

"Why?" Blaisdell asked the senators.

"Why?" echoed Chairman Thomas.

"That rests in the mind of Mr. Bridges, Mr. Goldblatt, and some other people," said Blaisdell. "I do not know."

In his turn, Bridges said the strike was simply over the issue of wages: "Instead of treating it as a simple economic strike, they are blowing it up as a dangerous threat to the economy of the islands and they are trying to make it appear as a Communist plot. Neither charge is true."

Bridges said he hadn't come to Washington looking for help. "Just leave us alone. We will take the people on and whip them baldheaded before we get through."

Senator Robert A. Taft, coauthor of the Taft-Hartley Bill, asked Bridges why the union had rejected the fact-finding board's recommendation of a fourteen-cent wage raise. That would bring the longshoremen's basic wage to $1.54. Taft said the average wage of 14 million industrial workers in the United States was $1.20 an hour. "How would that [offer] break the union?" he asked.

It was inevitable that the communism issue would be broached. Senator Morse asked Bridges if he or any other ILWU member was trying to subvert Hawaii with Communist doctrine. Bridges replied that what infiltration the ILWU had done in Hawaii was merely to organize workers. He said the longshore employers were the same people who owned and operated all the basic industries in Hawaii—sugar, pineapple, and longshore.

"Mr. Bridges, do you deny the allegation that the motivation of the union and your leaders . . . is to communize the economic life of the islands?" asked Morse.

"Oh, absolutely. . . . Of course, that is ridiculous," said Bridges. "We are after a wage increase, nothing more and nothing less. If that is going to lead to communism, well, that is just too bad. . . ."

"Do you have any Communists as officers of your union?" asked Taft.

"Offhand, I do not know," said Bridges. "We do not run around and I do not inquire."

Senator Paul Douglas of Illinois proposed they take up a collection and rent a three-room suite in a hotel. He said to put Bridges in one room, Blaisdell in another, and conciliator Cyrus Ching in the middle room. Let them spend twenty-four hours together and thrash out a settlement. "I have a twenty-dollar bill that I would be willing to contribute toward a room."

He then asked Bridges if he would agree. Bridges knew a "grandstand play" when he heard one. He also knew the value of public relations, so he promptly said yes. Blaisdell, who had no instructions from his employers on the subject, "hemmed and hawed" and finally declined. Later he came back and interrupted Bridges' testimony to say he would accept. Bridges guessed that he had to call Hawaii to find out what to do.

Bridges was pleased with the day's work; he felt he had bested Blaisdell in the congressional arena.

Toward the end of July, Hall asked Burns, the Democratic Party Oahu County chairman, to go to Washington to help the union. Hall was afraid Truman would give in to mounting pressure and invoke a Taft-Hartley injunction against the ILWU. Burns said he couldn't go. He didn't have any money. Hall said, "Well, we'll find you some."

The ILWU arranged for Burns' air fare and sent him money in Washington. Burns stayed at an inexpensive hotel and got meals from island boys going to school in Washington. Burns took with him two photostatic copies of the McCabe and the Castle & Cooke Terminals financial reports for 1947 and 1948. He had visited Washington for the first time only that January "to let them know we had a Democratic Party out here." He knew no one in Washington but Farrington. He didn't even know where to begin.

He had a cousin in Falls Church, Virginia, who was in deanery work. She knew Father McGowan of the Catholic Welfare Council and introduced Burns to McGowan. They had a tenuous sort of link: both had gone to St. Benedict's College in Atchinson, Kansas (some thirty years apart). McGowan took a liking to Burns and got him an appointment with Secretary of Labor Maurice Tobin, "another fish-eater,"[6] as Burns happily noted.

Burns showed Tobin the photostats. He said the strike was a matter of wages: the differential between Hawaii and the West Coast. "All the boys wanted was to get within reasonable range of catching up," he said. Then Burns matched names on the companies' financial reports. "I told him: 'This guy on this list is related to this guy on this list. And this one on this list is related to this one here. . . . ' " Tobin said, "God, that's unthinkable."

Tobin called an assistant, who took Burns to see Philip Murray of the CIO. Murray introduced Burns to James Carey, the CIO secretary-treasurer, who turned him over to his assistant, Harry Read. Read said the CIO had no great love for Bridges, "but a labor dispute is a labor dispute, and we're not going to help anybody buck a labor dispute out."

Read made appointments for Burns to see Alex Campbell, chief of the Department of Justice's Criminal Division, and Frank Tavenner, chief counsel of the House Un-American Activities Committee. Burns asked why. Read said to get a postponement of the Bridges-Robertson-Schmidt trial and the appearance of the HUAC in Hawaii. "There's a real effort being made right now to push the trial up . . . and to push the hearings out there right now."

"Holy name!" said Burns. "In the middle of the strike that would guarantee to lengthen the strike."

Burns did call on Campbell, who put his feet on his desk and said, "Now let's you and me have a good visit." The result, according to Burns, was that Campbell promised "to hold the damned thing off [the Bridges trial] till December or so."[7]

Burns then went to see Tavenner. He reviewed the background of the strike and Tavenner asked him, "But what about

---

6. A Catholic.
7. The trial began November 14, 1949.

Communists in the ILWU?" Burns replied: "Sure, sure, all these guys were Communists at one time or another. I'm not going to argue that issue. But what the hell did they do, Mr. Tavenner? Where did they go?" He meant that he looked upon the ILWU leaders above all as trade unionists. Tavenner asked Burns to write a statement summarizing his views. Burns drafted a statement, had it typed in the White House, and gave it to Tavenner.[8]

Tobin called Cyrus Ching in New York to tell him about Burns, and Ching phoned Burns in Washington. That amazed Burns: a man as important as Ching calling him. "Who the hell am I? I'm nobody."

"Do you think if I got those guys away from there [Hawaii], they'd talk better sense?" Ching asked Burns.

"Well, they might," Burns speculated.

"Well, we'll try," said Ching.

---

8. The statement may have had some influence. The HUAC hearings in Honolulu were held off until April 1950.

CHAPTER **46**

The Territory Runs the Docks

On July 7 Senators Hill and Heen called for a special session of the legislature to deal with dock strike legislation. On July 14 Stainback asked for emergency legislation to end the strike. On July 26 the legislative session convened in an atmosphere of gravity and passed on first reading nineteen emergency labor dispute bills.

"We must ensure continued shipping," said Stainback. "We cannot do so unless the government itself takes over stevedoring operations."

The legislature passed the Dock Seizure Bill that put the territory in the stevedoring business. Representative Earl Nielsen called it "a strikebreaking bill." Doc Hill called it "wishy-washy." Senator Thelma Akana said, "Call it what you will, it will get cargo moving and that's what counts." On August 6 Stainback signed the bill. The ILWU announced it would challenge the constitutionality of the law.

Hall knew the bill would pass no matter what pressure he brought to bear. If he couldn't stop an old reliable like J. B. Fernandes from voting for the bill, how could he stop the others? "The Territorial Legislature has passed and the bigoted old man on the second floor of Iolani Palace [he meant Stainback] has signed a law which (they say) will break the strike," said Hall. The legislators were overlooking one thing, he noted. Trade union solidarity.

Bridges claimed the bill was rammed through: "No hearings are allowed. Bills are considered in executive session. They are even being passed without a copy of the final draft being in the hands of the legislators when they vote."[1]

On August 7 the Broom Brigade marched for the last time. The dock seizure law was on the books; they felt their work was done. They marched at Pier 11, five hundred strong, with brooms and placards at the alert and carried small American flags. Some wore a fresh hibiscus in their hair.

The Dock Seizure Act gave the territory the right to take over and operate the docks and hire stevedores at prestrike wages. The ILWU ordered its men not to work for the territory and sent word to the West Coast not to handle or sail ships to or from Hawaii. At 11:01 AM on August 10, James L. Friel, the Honolulu harbormaster, seized Castle & Cooke Terminals and Mc-

---

1. Not so, said Hiram Fong, Speaker of the House during the 1949 special session. "Everything was followed according to Hoyle," said Fong. "First, second and third readings of bills. Nothing was rammed through."

Cabe, Hamilton & Renny Stevedoring companies in the name of the territory. On that day nearly a thousand of Oahu's seventeen thousand unemployed queued up in front of the Aloha Tower to sign on as government stevedores. Even aliens could sign, if they had lived in the territory for three years. In a few days the territory signed up 1765 stevedores and then stopped recruiting; it already had more than enough.

The government stevedoring operation began at 8:05 AM on August 15 when Attorney General Walter D. Ackerman, Jr., and Ben F. Rush, director of the territory's stevedoring company, boarded the *Hawaiian Monarch* at Pier 9. They summoned the crew and told them that under the law it was illegal for them to walk off the ship.

Stainback saw no problem "in spite of Mr. Bridges and his cohorts trying to persuade union men not to work for the territory." There were plenty of stevedores, "many of them members of the ILWU." What worried Stainback was the ILWU's strength on the West Coast.

Hall said the territory could run "a million ships" to Gulf and Atlantic ports from Hawaii, but that would not break the strike so long as they couldn't bring sugar to the C & H refinery at Crockett, California. Stainback might declare the ports of Hawaii open, but Hall declared the strike already was won "hands down, and the stevedoring companies know it."

That the recruitment of volunteer stevedores had come off so smoothly surprised Steele. He saw hundreds waiting in line to sign up; no one laid a hand on them. "If it had been San Francisco, there would have been blood in the streets." They had signed up to work the ships, "in what was obviously a strike-breaking thing."

The ILWU passed out leaflets warning the government stevedores that the ships they were loading would not be unloaded on the coast. "And the chances of a Matson ship even getting to the coast are about the same as [the chances of] Jack Hall being appointed chief of police." Once the strike was over, they would be out of a job and treated "like social lepers."

The day the territory took over the stevedoring operation,

Riley Allen summed up the effect of the strike to date: no one had starved; a small number had been put out of business; some people had lost their savings. "But the creeping paralysis which started at the waterfront is spreading through the territory's general economy," he said.

> The feeling is that the strong grip which the ILWU has taken on Hawaii's waterfront is in itself an improper thing because the power which the ILWU possesses has been unfairly used, and because the ILWU, if unchecked, offers a still greater threat to the economic well being of the islands.

The ILWU mustered its strength. Bridges wrote to the maritime unions: "The Hawaiian employers have set up a dummy stevedoring concern for the purpose of recruiting scabs and working ships under heavy police protection. Government operation right here now means government strikebreaking."

From Washington, Glazier carried the message up and down the East Coast. In New York he left five thousand leaflets. He sent letters to ten key senators[2] calling their attention to the Dock Seizure Act, which he labeled a "government operation . . . polite language to describe government strikebreaking."

Though it protested loudly, the union knew the law could not break the strike. The ships couldn't sail to the West Coast. The ILWU sent out a conference teletype message to all ILWU locals:

> Although Hawaii employers say port of Hawaii is open, truth is that Hawaii strike is 80 per cent effective until employers can get Matson line operating normally. This means hauling sugar to refinery in San Francisco [that is, Crockett] and general cargo back to islands, and operating passenger steamer *Lurline*.

Hall said: "The strike is effective and costing them plenty of dough."

---

2. Wayne Morse, Claude Pepper, Elbert Thomas, Paul Douglas, Matthew Neely, George Aiken, Robert Taft, Hubert Humphrey, Lister Hill, James Murray.

Amid the hubbub, Bridges came to town. No Broom Brigaders met him, just Hall and twenty-five ILWU members. Next morning the *Advertiser* greeted him with another "Dear Joe" editorial which said that "not since the days when Kamehameha landed from Molokai would Hawaii have been able to welcome such a complete and absolute dictator. . . ."

If that bothered Bridges, he gave no sign. Natty in a gray double-breasted suit with a red stripe, he talked to reporters. He fascinated them: the blue eyes intense; the long bony nose which seemed to be sniffing; the voice, high pitched and penetrating, speaking in the strange yet hypnotic accent.

He told them that employers on the mainland thought Hawaii employers were "nuts, just plain nuts." As for the Dock Seizure Act, it was "scabbery," he said. "No one can outlaw union solidarity. Experts have tried to bust this union and failed, and Stainback is an amateur."

Bridges consented to being interviewed over KIPA radio in Hilo. He didn't mind taking on a trio of reporters. He knew he could hold his own.

Reporter Tom O'Brien, a fervent anti-Communist, asked Bridges to discuss communism. Bridges said it would take all night; there was no time for that.

"I think that's the basis of everything that's behind you, Mr. Bridges," said O'Brien. "When people think of Bridges, they think of that. You can't get away from it."

"Well, thanks to radio commentators, newspapers and other things," said Bridges.

But a lot of other people think of me in other terms. There's a lot of people who think of me in terms of increased wages; lot of other people think of me in terms of trying to bring some equality to people irrespective of their race, color, creed, nationality, language or beliefs.

"I'm a trade unionist," said Bridges. "That's all. Nothing more, nothing less. . . ."

On August 15 Attorney General Ackerman obtained a circuit court order restraining the ILWU from picketing at the docks.

Bridges felt he needed to make a dramatic protest. What better way than to picket on the docks himself? "It is possible within the next day or two I and some other union officials . . . will be arrested on the picket line," he wrote Glazier.

He needed an accomplice, preferably from the AFL. The choice was inevitable. Who better than Rutledge? Rutledge was willing. "Come on, Art," Bridges said. "This is our job. . . . Let's get out there."

On August 16 they marched up and down at Pier 9 for thirty-five minutes—just the two of them (and the photographers and reporters who had been tipped off). Bridges told the reporters he was picketing to bring "this stinking mess" to the attention of the Supreme Court. Rutledge said he was just exercising his right "of free speech." The AFL and CIO in Hawaii might be miles apart in their political thinking, he said, but as trade unionists they both agreed that the Dock Seizure Act was "a strikebreaking measure."

The gentlemanly John Young, deputy high sheriff, trotted alongside and while on the run read them the court order restraining them from picketing. He handed the summons to Bridges who thrust it in his pocket.

When Stainback signed the Dock Seizure Bill, Corbett assumed that his emergency relief committee was out of business. However, the ILWU offered to clear the *Refiner* again as a relief ship. When Corbett declined, the union said he wasn't interested in bringing in another eleven thousand tons of supplies. In fact, they said, he sounded as though he were determined to help break the strike.

Corbett replied that he had taken a neutral stand and was sorry "the boys felt the way they do."

However, we should take some comfort in the fact that we no longer need to feel left out; that we haven't been ignored by the union, which has now denounced the British Commonwealth, the National Administration in Washington, the Governor and his fact-finding committee, the Attorney General of Hawaii and almost everybody else.[3]

It was true: the ILWU felt it was fighting for its life and most of the world seemed allied against it.

The government stevedoring operations had moved briskly. The stevedores first unloaded the Panamanian flagship *Nortuna,* manned by an entirely nonunion crew. The ILWU had no control over them. By August 22 the stevedores were working the Isthmian Lines *Steel Scientist* at Pier 10; Matson's *Hawaiian Farmer* at Pier 31; Waterman Lines' *Maiden Creek* at Pier 20; Isthmian's *Steel Architect* at Kahului; and the Panamanian *Nortuna* at Nawiliwili. By the end of August, the stevedores had unloaded all ships in harbor and loaded ships bound for Gulf and Atlantic ports. The ILWU was powerless to stop them.

Government longshoremen also loaded the Matson freighter *Hawaiian Refiner,* which was scheduled to sail to the East Coast, but the crew walked off and the ship stayed on until the end of the strike. Seamen antagonistic to the ILWU—among them the Seafarers' International Union of the Pacific (SIU) and the Marine Engineers' Beneficial Association (MEBA)—manned Isthmian and Waterman Lines ships. They ignored the ILWU pickets. Bridges appealed to MEBA's president. He said the engineers were "helping to break our strike."

But the government stevedores did *not* load ships for the West Coast—all the ILWU had to do was alert the coast that a "hot ship" was coming. The *Lurline* and the six Matson C-3 freighters had to sit the strike out. "The fact is that Matson is 100 per cent tied up," said Schmidt. So it made no difference if Isthmian and Waterman sent ships to Hawaii. It made no difference if the government longshoremen loaded the ships and seamen sailed them out of port. Matson could not sail to the West Coast and that was why the ILWU won the 1949 longshore strike. "That's the main thing," said Bridges.

---

3. Corbett summed up his committee's work as follows: the navy brought a total of 21,081 tons of supplies; commercial vessels, working under eight contracts with the ILWU, brought 38,785 tons.

All sorts of people had grand ideas on how to settle the strike. In July, Philip S. Ehrlich, a Honolulu-born San Francisco lawyer, came to Hawaii on such a mission. Bridges asked Hall to talk to him. Hall, Henry Schmidt, and a man Ehrlich identified as Arthur Symonds[4] met him. They told him the ILWU would appreciate his efforts to try to bring the two sides together.

Hall introduced Ehrlich to Philip Spalding, C. Brewer's president. Ehrlich, in a missionary mood, said, "I worked for three solid weeks, day and night, to bring about a settlement of the strike." He said he had devised a plan whereby the ILWU would agree to "ten to twenty" years of labor peace. It involved the creation of a board of seven to nine members to resolve labor disputes. Half the board would be union representatives; the other half, management. The odd man would be "an impartial arbitrator."

Two days before he was scheduled to leave for home, Ehrlich presented his plan to industry representatives. They were not at all impressed. "[They] maligned and insulted me and accused me of being a labor stooge paid by the ILWU and coming to the islands to disrupt economic conditions," he said. Ehrlich was crushed. He had tried to do something for his native islands and had failed. What bothered him most of all was that he worked so hard he hadn't even had time for a swim at Waikiki.

---

4. He meant Myer Symonds.

CHAPTER 47

The Battle of Words

The ILWU fought a running court battle during the longshore strike. The legal warfare opened early in the strike (May 25) when the Dairymen's Association brought a libel action against the Matson freighter *Hawaiian Citizen* in order to breach the union picket lines and take 6388 bags of soybean feed off the ship.

The court battles reached a climax with a $3 million damage and injunction suit filed August 16 in Federal District Court by Bouslog & Symonds in behalf of the ILWU. The defendants ranged from Stainback and Ackerman and the seven stevedoring companies to the members of the legislature who voted for the Dock Seizure Bill.[1]

The injunction suit went to the heart of the matter: namely, was the Dock Seizure Act constitutional? That question never was answered. Harriet Bouslog contended that the act damaged the union irreparably and flew in the face of constitutional and federal guarantees. The territory responded that the damage inflicted by the strike outweighed "the inconvenience of the union."

On the federal bench were two judges who seldom saw eye to eye: the soft-spoken, liberal Delbert E. Metzger, the senior judge; and the caustic, rigid perfectionist J. Frank McLaughlin. Bouslog sought to disqualify McLaughlin for prejudice against the union but failed. Since it was obvious that the two judges would see the issues in a different light, they themselves tried to

---

1. One legislative defendant was John F. Duarte of Maui, who usually hewed strictly to the ILWU line. He said of the $3 million suit: "When [the ILWU] take over the territory, I'll work at a dollar an hour to pay them off."

get a third judge from the mainland to split the difference. They cabled William Denman, chief judge of the Ninth Circuit Court of Appeals in San Francisco, that an *en banc* session with three judges would be in the public interest.

Denman replied that he had no power to create such a court. So, sitting side by side, unreinforced, Metzger and McLaughlin tried the case.

Bridges was one of the witnesses and, as usual, he talked nonstop. "I'm just a windy guy by nature." He said the Dock Seizure Act would destroy the union's contract benefits and its bargaining power. "This is a yellow-dog contract[2] made into law. It's even printed on yellow paper." He claimed the act would destroy the unity of the ILWU. No union can live unless it is united. Solidarity: that is the essence of a union's strength. "Unless a union has the power to strike to back up its demands that union hasn't a chance. . . ."

Garner Anthony, whom Stainback appointed to handle the territory's case as a special deputy attorney general, tried to show that Hawaii was suffering grievously from the strike. Torkel Westly, the assistant tax commissioner, testified that Hawaii's gross income would drop by $18 million because of the strike. Earl W. Fase, deputy tax commissioner, said the strike had cut payrolls by $2 million a month.

The case spun out for sixteen days, and every step of the way was "vehement." Then, on October 7, the two judges declared that they could not agree. The ILWU had lost by a split decision. Judge McLaughlin said the Dock Seizure law (Acts 2 and 3) "are not obviously void on their face." Judge Metzger said Act 2, as amended by Act 3, was "patently invalid on its face."

Metzger saw the legislation as "territorial meddling in a labor dispute." McLaughlin saw it as a valid exercise of the territory's police power. Hall said the ILWU would appeal. "We expect a hands-down victory in the Ninth Circuit," he said.[3]

---

2. A contract form that requires the applicant to sign, as a condition of employment, the guarantee that he won't join a union.

3. The ILWU's appeal was dismissed by the Ninth Circuit Court on October 29, 1949.

Allen regarded the split decision as an ILWU setback, but he said Acts 2 and 3 "tread perilously close to the constitutional borderline, if, indeed, they do not overstep it." Thurston saw the decision as vindication of his own position. "Hawaii's ports will remain open, despite the Bridges Blockade," he said.

The decision turned out to be not entirely a legal setback for the ILWU. The territory did not press an injunctive suit it had filed against the union; nor did it pursue its case against Bridges for contempt (the picketing incident at Pier 9 involving Bridges with Rutledge in tow). Other injunctive suits against the union were also permitted to lie dormant.

The territory had won the right to man the waterfront with government workers. The strike went on.

All through that tense August the two sides fought it out across the bargaining table and got nowhere. They often were snappish:

Maxwell: The employers have had contacts with your union for eight years and we have had damn good relations with—

Bridges (interrupting):   They had the lousiest relations that they have had with any group of employers.

Maxwell: But over that time there have been good relations.

Bridges: Those good relations have ended. . . .

Steele: What the hell is the strike over?

Bridges: Wages.

Steele: How much?

Bridges: Enough to settle the strike.

During one meeting at the Employers Council Rutledge stuck his head in the door. "Somebody told me that you folks are pretty close together," he said. "If you are. . . ." That piece of innocence brought the house down and they enjoyed a good laugh.

Some days were acrimonious. When Bridges said that longshoremen "keep their mouths shut to hold their jobs," H. M. Robinson of Alexander & Baldwin reacted at once. "I think that is a kind of far-fetched statement," he exclaimed.

"It is not far-fetched," retorted Bridges.

"It is a far-fetched statement," said Robinson angrily. "I have worked . . . on the mainland and I know for a fact that you get a hell of a lot better treatment down here than you do on the mainland. Ask any company."

"Ask any longshoreman," Hall broke in.

"We have had longshoremen that have worked for us for many years," said Robinson. "They have worked for us before the two of you were born. And we have provided them with lots of steady employment."

"Lots of it at $20 a month," Hall scoffed. "I remember when your company made a profit of $2 million while they paid the workers about $1.25 a day." Hall recalled the day of the black-list on the waterfront. "What about me?" he said. "I went to every Big Five firm in this town when the war started, trying to find a job. I couldn't get one. I have only worked for one private firm in this territory, a brewery,[4] where there was a closed shop contract."

Plainly it was time for a third party to try to bring them together. The two sides sent a cable to Cyrus Ching of the Federal Mediation Service asking for his help. Ching invited them to meet with him in New York at 3 PM Wednesday, September 7, 1949. It was a summons. Neither side wanted to go to New York: Bridges preferred a hearing room in the United States Senate; the employers would rather have stayed in Hawaii. But the Employers Council said they would "even climb Pike's Peak" if they thought it would bring them closer to settlement.

The New York meetings were held in the tenth-floor office of the federal Mediation Service at 9th and 30th Streets on the grimy West Side. The sessions lasted from September 7 to 12. Ching was seventy-three—a shrewd, white-haired *haole* who had thirty-seven years of experience in labor negotiations. "I

---

4. Royal Brewery.

have no magic," he said. The two sides stayed in rooms and suites on the thirteenth floor of the aristocratic (and expensive) Plaza Hotel overlooking Central Park. "It's pretty much meet, eat, and meet some more."

Although the employers trusted Ching, they had misgivings about his chief deputy, William N. Margolis. He scared them but they tried hard not to show it.[5]

Negotiations opened on a harsh note: Bridges proposed arbitration; Steele rejected it. They were back to square one. Bridges said some employers in Hawaii were paying longshoremen $1.72 an hour. (He meant the splinter fleet.) He said the arguments of the stevedoring companies sounded like the arguments of employers in the Deep South who kept wages low.

"We are not like the Deep South," Steele snapped. "We pay the highest agricultural wages in the world."

"That's a lot of crap," said Bridges. "The poor bastards eat only fish and rice because that's all they can afford on their miserable wages."

It was hardly a promising start, but they meant to try hard. "Let's stay with it, day and night, if necessary," Bridges suggested.

The reporters gathered around Ching after the session. Puffing on a curve-stem pipe, Ching tried to sound cheerful. "I posed certain questions they might be turning over in their minds," he said. "I think both sides have come here with every idea of getting this thing settled."

Next day at a meeting with the employers, Ching conceded that the strike was not an ordinary one; it involved the entire economy of Hawaii. For a moment he played the role of devil's advocate and posed a question to Steele. Suppose that by the spring of 1950 the gap in wages between Hawaii and the West Coast had widened and the ILWU called another strike. What then?

Steele said he didn't think that would happen. "We have

---

5. At mediator-conducted negotiations often there is play-acting. In these negotiations Margolis played the role of the "heavy." "The 'bad man,' " said Babbitt. "Deliberately so. To try and weaken our position. [That was] the technique. Ching, of course, was the 'good guy.' "

estimated Harry's strength pretty well and we doubt he is in a position to run another strike next year," he said. They sparred:

Ching: Do you fellows think you have got Harry licked?

Steele: Frankly, we think he is losing the strike.

Ching: But Harry doesn't think he is licked.

Steele: He doesn't generally talk like it, but some of the things he says show evidence of losing. . . .

Ching: Harry thinks his position is pretty strong. He has no idea he is licked. Of course he may be bluffing.

Steele: My experience is that he does bluff—right up to the last minute. . . .

"There is still nothing concrete," Ching told the reporters.

In the session next day with the employers Ching spoke of the fourteen-cent raise proposed by the Stainback fact-finding committee. How could the employers offer anything less than that? he wanted to know. It would amount to an ILWU surrender; Bridges "isn't that kind of a guy."

Steele replied that the ILWU's posture was based on its assumption that the strike was eighty-five percent effective. But that was not so, he said; the strike was only fifty percent effective.

"But Harry has plenty of nerve and is very resourceful and if he goes down, he will go down fighting and he will make it plenty expensive," said Ching.

"They are still pretty far apart," Ching told the reporters.

Next day the employers shifted tactics and said they would offer fourteen cents "plus something (we don't know what) in March 1950 for an extension to March 1951."

"How about three cents," said Margolis, fishing.

"That might be a deal," said Steele.

"Better be more specific," suggested Margolis. "Harry thinks his own nuisance value in March 1950 is worth at least six cents."

"Some day he will learn that he is not able to sell his nuisance value," Steele replied.

Ching said Bridges believed the ILWU was in good shape. "He says he can get ten cents, plus pensions and a lot more in March 1950."

"He is bluffing and talking," said Steele. "He says the opposite in Honolulu."

"How about fourteen [now] and six [in March 1950]?" said Margolis.

Nothing doing, said Steele.

Margolis: If Harry made an offer of fourteen, plus five, would you gentlemen jump out the window?

Steele: We wouldn't take it.

Babbitt: Not a chance.

Ching: Bridges is resourceful.

Steele: Sure he is. His tactic is to keep trying—throwing punches—and to hope for an employer mistake.

After the day's session, the reporters closed in on Bridges. In Hawaii he had been "talkative, cocky, affable," but in New York he was "curt, morose, and aloof."

On September 12 Ching said he didn't want to waste any more time. "It looks to me as if both sides are more interested in licking the other than in reaching a settlement," he said. "We are just as far apart as when we started. We are right back to the question of money." He read a statement acknowledging defeat: "The parties remain so hopelessly far apart in their thinking that further mediation at this time would be of no avail."

A headline told it all: "Ching Says Talks End in Hopeless Deadlock."

CHAPTER 48
All Wars Finally End

The strike wore on. In San Francisco a wealthy business executive named Walter C. Buck called Bridges. Buck was a director and a large minority stockholder of Matson[1] and a man to be reckoned with. His father had been a founder of Matson and he himself helped direct Matson affairs. Buck was in his seventies but still full of drive and determined to end the strike. Matson ships lay idle; no stockholder could be happy about that.

Buck invited Bridges for talks at Mrs. Walter F. Dillingham's luxury suite in the Fairmont Hotel. "He'd have me down at 8 in the morning and we got to talking," said Bridges. Philip Davies, a San Francisco banker, and William Roth, chairman of the Matson board of directors, often took part.

Steele went to San Francisco on personal business and heard that Bridges was talking at the Fairmont with Buck and others. When one of the participants invited Steele to attend, he gladly came along. The scene amazed him: there stood some of San Francisco's big shipping executives clustered around a thin man with a high-pitched voice who was doing all the talking. The man on center stage was Bridges. He was holding his audience spellbound.

But what was he talking about? The big strike in Hawaii and how to settle it? Not at all. He was talking about the Kon-Tiki expedition and his theories about the movements of ancient peoples to the Pacific islands. "I've never seen such a beautiful job of seduction," said Steele.

By now the pressure on both sides was enormous. It was a war

---

1. Buck owned twelve thousand shares of Matson stock, three-quarters of one percent of the outstanding stock.

of attrition, said Goldblatt, a question of who would give in first. By September 25, some 505,025 tons of sugar, worth $61,108,025,[2] had piled up. Four of the Big Five (Brewer, Castle & Cooke, Alexander & Baldwin, and American Factors)[3] owned forty percent of the stock in Matson. Budge said Matson had lost $800,000 a month for five months.

The weakest link in the employer chain was Brewer. Just before the strike began, Brewer had arranged to buy blocks of stock which the Spreckels family held in Brewer plantations. That left Brewer in a weak cash position. Spalding, Brewer's president, became uneasy as far back as July and had held secret talks with Hall. He also had encouraged Ehrlich, the San Francisco lawyer, to come forth with a plan to end the strike.

But not only the big companies suffered. The longshoremen also were hurting. In a strike the people who suffer most are those on strike. The Territorial Department of Public Welfare stopped payments to longshoremen on strike and Hall wrote in protest to the Federal Security Agency in San Francisco. Longshoremen owed the butcher, the baker, the Waiahole *poi*-maker. They owed for doctor bills, for rent, for telephone bills. Ah Quon McElrath, ILWU social services coordinator, arranged with the Catholic diocese of Hawaii for deferment of tuition for the children of longshoremen. Mrs. McElrath also arranged for the deferment of payment for schoolbook rental and school fees for the children of longshoremen attending public schools.

An ILWU official wrote to Kamehameha School for Girls saying he could not pay the hundred-dollar tuition for his daughter and asked if she could be granted a scholarship. Longshoremen couldn't pay their loans and mortgages. Finance companies granted them extensions until the strike was over. A man named S. McFadden sent twenty dollars to the longshoremen.

---

2. Based on the New York spot price of $121 a ton.

3. Castle & Cooke directed the affairs of Castle & Cooke Terminals; Brewer, Hilo Transport & Terminal; Amfac, Ahukini Terminal; and Alexander & Baldwin, Kahului Railway and Kauai Terminals. McCabe, Hamilton & Renny had no "parent" and had little heft in decision making. A major part of McCabe's business was the handling of military cargo and this work went on through the strike.

Hall thanked him. "This is very generous of you in view of the fact that you are out of a job," said Hall.[4]

Steele and Bridges began informal talks in San Francisco; according to Steele, they did not negotiate. Steele relayed what was going on by phone calls to Maxwell and he, in turn, informed the Employers Council board of governors. On September 25 Bridges called Schmidt in Honolulu and said that he, Goldblatt, and Steele were talking and were "not too far apart."

By then word was spreading that the talks between Bridges and Steele had made "very good progress." A settlement was predicted "within a short period." Steele returned to Honolulu on September 29. Reporters asked him if he had talked to Bridges and he said, "I always talk to Harry when I'm in San Francisco. . . ."

Bridges came back to Honolulu on October 2, accompanied by Buck. "We went down to Hawaii together," he said later. "Buck started to knock heads together. We got together with Spalding." Spalding was one of the levers of power. The others were Budge of Castle & Cooke; Bell of Alexander & Baldwin; and Walker of American Factors.

To reporters Bridges said: "Yes, I feel cheerful, without going into details. . . ." At that point he was more than cheerful, for he already knew that the basic agreement had been worked out and he was sure Buck could twist enough arms to get it ratified. "The agreement was all worked out before we left here [San Francisco]," he said.

Bridges and Goldblatt started meeting with Steele at 10:30 AM October 2 at Steele's home in Kahala. They stayed until 7 PM. Next day the circle widened: Bridges, Goldblatt, Hall, and Schmidt; Steele and Maxwell. On October 4 the alternatives narrowed to two sets of figures: either a fourteen-cent wage raise then, and another seven cents in March 1950, with a contract extension to 1951; or a fifteen-cent raise and six cents the following March with a contract extension.

---

4. The longshore locals sought $33,600 in loans from the sugar units. Hall said the union was $150,000 in debt. Sugar units contributed a total of $20,000 from their unit treasuries.

For a moment the employers hesitated. It was tempting to think they might still win. After all, the government stevedoring operation had unloaded 100,000 tons of cargo in September—more than the total unloaded in September 1948. "Steele feels that if we could hold out for another three weeks we could write our own ticket because there are real signs of union weakness," said Brooks, the Employers Council research director. Some council members balked at granting a large raise to the longshoremen; they felt it would "betray the rest of the business community."

On October 5 the Employers Council board of governors held a special meeting. Lorrin Thurston, Henry White of the Hawaiian Pineapple Company, Lowell Dillingham of the Dillimgham Corporation, and Leroy Bush of Honolulu Construction & Draying spoke out against the fourteen-cent plus or fifteen-cent plus formulas. They said it amounted to surrender. But the "Big Four"—Spalding, Budge, Bell, and Walker—dwelt upon the losses the sugar companies and Matson were taking and they drove their point across.

On October 6 Schmidt sat writing a letter to a friend. Bridges had just left that morning by plane for the mainland and at the airport he had announced that the strike was settled. "Honolulu is in an uproar," Schmidt wrote. It had been such a long and grueling fight that he could not believe it was really over. Like the soldier in a foxhole, he kept hearing the guns in his mind although the guns had fallen silent. He doubted the strike was over, but as he sat writing, official word came: the strike *was* settled. Schmidt added a triumphant postscript: "The beef is over! And we win; there's no mistake about that. . . ."

The scene at Honolulu Airport that morning made for good theater. Bridges had arrived about eight thirty, bedecked with leis; he had called Steele before he set out for the airport and now he expected a return call. It would be confirmation that the strike was settled.

Hearing the rumors about an imminent settlement, the press had carefully planned its coverage. The night before, Douglas Lovelace and Leif Erickson of the Associated Press had visited

Hall in his home on Kau Way and he had given them a copy of the statement Bridges was to read. At AP's office Erickson punched an end-of-the-strike story on tape. All the office had to do was flip a switch and the story would go out. Erickson drove to the airport and stationed an office girl close by at a pay telephone with an open line to AP. The *Star-Bulletin* sent a fast-moving reporter, Moray Epstein.

Bridges dawdled while waiting for the call from Steele. A longshoreman who knew a settlement was in the offing shouted over to him: "Well, Harry, we'll expect you back in 1951. We'll really give 'em hell then."

At 8:40 AM passengers were told to board the flight to San Francisco. Bridges cocked a foot on a bench, pulled a sheet of paper from his pocket, and said: "Well, Steele hasn't called me, so here it is." He dictated:

> I have negotiated a settlement of the longshore strike in off-the-record discussions. I am recommending that the union accept it. . . . The settlement is for a wage increase of twenty-one cents an hour; fourteen cents on return to work, and seven cents payable on February 28, 1950. Eight cents is retroactive for the period from March 1 to the end of June this year. . . .

Erickson signaled his girl in the phone booth. She told the person waiting at the AP's end of the line. The tape started clattering out the news.

Epstein took Bridges' statement down and jumped for a phone. He read the statement to a rewrite man and within three minutes a *Star-Bulletin* reporter was reading the statement to the Employers Council for comment. At that very moment the employers were in session at the Alexander & Baldwin building to consider the terms of a settlement.

They were flabbergasted. Bridges had jumped the gun, they cried. The announcement was premature. Dick Nimmons, the Employers Council public relations officer, yelled "double-cross!" Steele was embarrassed. Here he was telling the employers he *thought* he could get them a settlement and Bridges had announced that the settlement already had been made. It was an uncomfortable moment but Steele explained, as casually as he could, that since they were close to agreement, he had told

Bridges he was confident the employers would go along. "But it shouldn't have been announced."[5]

Allen heard the employers' denial, but he sensed that a settlement must have been tentatively reached. He thought Bridges simply had "outsmarted the employers" by releasing the news first. The *Star-Bulletin* put out a first extra saying the strike had been settled but giving the employers' denial "appropriate weight." Less than two hours later the employers also announced the settlement. Their statement was "basically as Bridges had described" it, but phrased differently to put things in a different light.[6]

Russell Starr, who spoke for the employers, said they had agreed to a fourteen-cent raise and, in fact, had accepted that same figure three months earlier. "We will now accept it again to end the strike." The sixth paragraph of the employers' statement said: "To eliminate the possibility of a waterfront strike in Hawaii before June 21, 1951, twenty-one months from now, the companies will agree to an automatic wage increase of seven cents on March 1, 1950."

It was a case of two sides saying the same thing, but packaging it differently. To the employers it was a 14-cent wage raise; to the union it was a 21-cent raise. The ILWU assumed that anybody could add: 14 plus 7 equals 21.

Bridges boarded the plane and took off. Was his announcement premature?[7] He called it "merely a bit of strategy."

Allen thought the terms of the settlement were "a pretty stiff shock." He said the "little fellow" (the small employer) felt let down. He had been exhorted by the Chamber of Commerce and

---

5. Steele said: "It's one of the few times I've had any problems in my dealings with Harry because he's always been forthright and never cuts any corners or gone back on his word. In that case, he really did do something he shouldn't have."

6. The art of press agentry.

7. McElrath said the employers were supposed to call Bridges back. "They said they would get back to us. They didn't." Allen confirmed that the employers were supposed to call Bridges back. Allen said: "The settlement was actually reached about 4:30 Wednesday afternoon [October 5] and my information is that at that time Bridges agreed to a joint statement or simultaneous statement . . . and expected the employers would be ready by night, possibly for Bob McElrath's ILWU broadcast at 6:45."

the Employers Council not to break ranks; not to patronize the splinter fleet; and not to let the ILWU "dictate terms." Privately, Allen thought the ILWU had won a victory; but publicly, in his editorial column, he took another tack. "It is now clear that neither side gained a clean-cut victory," he said. Moreover, said Allen, the ILWU had not achieved its announced goal of "thirty-two cents or arbitration."

By now, 24,423 people on Oahu—17.6 percent of the work force—were jobless. Some companies had been forced to cut their employees' pay by as much as half. Food prices had climbed 6.6 percent; some small businesses had gone under. Research Associates of Honolulu estimated that the strike cost the islands $100 million. It was a nice round figure; no one really knew the price tag. The ILWU was satisfied. "The longshore strike guaranteed our survival. . . ."

On October 7, the day after Bridges pulled his coup, a 200-pound tavern worker celebrated the announcement of the settlement by drinking a quart of gin. He fell asleep on the edge of Pier 14 and rolled into the ocean. A watchman heard him calling for help; two policemen paddled out in a boat and hauled him in like a big *ulua*.

At 12:15 PM on October 23, 1949, the longshore strike officially ended. It had gone 177 days.

Part 8
THE TEMPER
OF THE TIMES
(1950–1952)

CHAPTER 49
Hall vs. HUAC

The House Committee on Un-American Activities came to town in April 1950 to investigate communism in Hawaii. Stainback and Farrington had prodded them and the 1949 strike gave them added zeal. Given the temper of the times, the trip was inevitable. Hall knew that he and the ILWU were the chief targets. "Plenty of witnesses have been lined up," he wrote Goldblatt, "including some people who will surprise you. About all we can do is to make reasonably sure no one goes to jail for perjury."[1]

He alerted people on what to expect. "We have done everything we can in preparation," he said. "Meetings will be held all over the territory . . . to discuss and explain the purpose of the hearings. . . . This is just one of those places where there isn't any place to duck, so we just have to stand up and fight. . . ."

Lorrin Thurston welcomed the hearings since he believed there was a plot to take over Hawaii. Riley Allen thought the hearings would be "a good thing": "Whatever the march of ex-Communists to the witness stand, it will be apparent that the power of the leftists has been rapidly waning after people got fed up on their economic tactics."

The HUAC chairman was Francis E. Walter, a Pennsylvania Democrat, who was restrained and quiet, but persistent. The committee's chief counsel was the inquisitor, Frank L. Tavenner. Hall was subpoenaed and for three days he sat on a bench in the foyer, reading magazines and books and waiting to be called.

Izuka, the pamphleteer, testified that there were 130 Communists in Hawaii and that Communists led the ILWU. He

---

1. Hall meant: Take the Fifth Amendment and refuse to answer questions.

reached back to the 1946 delegate's race, which never seemed able to leave the stage of history, to cite what he called a case of ILWU dictatorship of the membership. He said Hall's endorsement of Farrington over Borthwick was "a triple dose of castor oil forced down the throats of the workers."

On April 13 Hall was called as a witness. At 9:10 AM, he entered the packed chambers. He was wearing a gray-green aloha shirt his wife, Yoshiko, had made. The exchange was short and simple:

Tavenner: Mr. Hall, when and where were you born?

Hall: I was born in Ashland, Wisconsin, February 28, 1914.[2]

Tavenner: How long have you lived in Honolulu?

Hall: I established residence in Honolulu in, I believe, August or September 1935.

Tavenner: Mr. Hall, are you now or have you ever been a member of the Communist Party?

Symonds (representing Hall):   I advise my client not to answer the question upon the grounds that it might incriminate him.

Tavenner repeated the question and Hall replied, "On the advice of counsel, I refuse to answer on the grounds it might tend to incriminate me. I want to add, however, that I have filed with the National Labor Relations Board the customary non-Communist affidavit."[3] The witness was excused. It was 9:15 AM. Hall had been there only five minutes.

Twenty-six ILWU members, including Hall and McElrath, took the Fifth Amendment. Hall said the hearings were part of a plan "to smear and discredit the ILWU." If he had done

---

2. He was wrong. He was born in 1915.

3. After taking a stand not to sign the Taft-Hartley affidavits, the ILWU decided in February 1950 to sign, after all. They were afraid that if they didn't, the union would be raided by other unions. Hall said: "Unless we are in compliance . . . we have no legal rights to insist on and defend our rights . . . through the NLRB and the courts."

anything wrong, he said, he would have been brought to trial long before.

Hall blamed Stainback for the visit of the Un-American Activities Committee in Hawaii. He said Stainback hoped to lop off the heads of the union, but it would not work:

> The membership . . . has been through too much. They have faced the combined wrath of Hawaii's employers, spending tens of millions of dollars in attempts to smash them. . . . Our membership knows their gains—material, political and social—have come because their union and their leadership [are] honest and won't be intimidated by anyone.

Why didn't he answer Tavenner's questions? "A 'yes' or 'no' or 'don't know' answer could easily result in a perjury indictment with perjured witnesses against me," Hall claimed. "Witnesses against progressives these days are a dime a dozen." Hall said he had done nothing to be ashamed of. "My life will continue to be spent in the fight against oppression and for a better life for working people," he said.

What was the rank and file reaction to the HUAC hearings? Practically none, Hall decided.

> This doesn't mean that the issue is dead, far from it. The press—particularly Farrington's Star-Bulletin—the radio, the employer fronts and, I suppose, ultimately the AFL, the CIO . . . will be beating the drums. If the storm can be weathered any place, however, it will be weathered here. . . .

Still, to quell any "rumblings down below," the union had to embark on countermeasures. "This red issue will have to be hammered out in the June conference and followed up with a speaking tour of all units," said Hall. "We can't answer it forever with assertions of red-baiting, witch-hunting, etc. . . ."

One of the surprise witnesses at the HUAC hearings was Bert Nakano, the man badly wounded in the "Hilo Massacre." Nakano testified that he was "now strongly opposed to communism" and that Communists could not help labor, only hurt it. He told about his former Communist Party ties: he said he joined the Party in July 1946; John Reinecke gave him his Party card; he paid dues to Harry Kamoku.

Nakano said he testified because he felt he owed it to the members of his unit. "I thought the best thing was for me to clear myself." After the hearing he called a special meeting of his unit members and they backed him.

Hall was troubled by Nakano's defection; the man had suffered for the cause of unionism. Soon after the HUAC hearings, Hall called Nakano and asked him to come to Honolulu for a talk. Nakano flew to town. In his words:

> We sat down and he said, "Bert, Harry [Bridges] wants you to come out and say you made a mistake in testifying before the Un-American Committee."
>
> I said, "Jack, what do you think I am—a goddamned fool? After I testified, stuck my neck out, and say, 'I made a mistake going before the Committee.' . . . I'm no goddamned hypocrite! Furthermore, you got to start cleaning yourself too. This thing is holding up organizing. People are scared to join the ILWU."
>
> Then he says, "Well, Bert, I can't do that."

Another surprise witness was Kawano. Kawano didn't know what to do: Should he testify? Should he not? He called on Dan Inouye, the young lawyer and war hero, for advice. They arranged to meet; Inouye picked him up and they drove around Ala Moana Park for a while and "Silent Jack" did not say a word. Finally, he spoke up. He said he had been subpoenaed by the Un-American Activities Committee. "I think I should tell you, Dan, that I'm a member of the Communist Party," he said.

It was not the sort of confession one hears every day driving around Ala Moana Park, and Inouye, who was thinking of a political career, was startled.

"What do you think I should do?" asked Kawano.

"That's a personal question for you to decide," said Inouye. "If I were in your position, with my background, I suppose I would testify."

Kawano appeared before the committee but took the Fifth Amendment when he was asked about Communist Party activities and the names of Party members. He declared: "I am not a Communist." He meant—not at that moment. He had decided in November 1948 to drop out of the Party because by then he was convinced that the Party ran the ILWU. He had made a break with the union that he had served for fifteen years.

In the audience listening was Inouye. He said that when Kawano spoke, "people were cursing . . . and when he got all through, he stood up. And he came to me. Everyone was watching. And he hugged me. . . . Two of us embracing. And we walked out together. And I remember we went to the Mesmachi restaurant to have lunch."

Thirty-nine persons, including Hall, refused to testify. It was inevitable that they became known as the "Reluctant 39." They were served with warrants, charging them with contempt of Congress, and released on two hundred dollars bail. Hall thought the comparative modesty of the bail was significant; it showed that the indictments were returned merely "for the purpose of testing the law."

He gave his six-dollar check from the United States Treasury for appearing before the committee over to the Bridges-Robertson-Schmidt defense fund. He called his little joke "poetic justice (of a very limited nature, of course)."

In November 1949, the National CIO voted to try the ILWU and eight other affiliated CIO unions on charges that they were "consistently directed toward the achievement of the program or the purposes of the Communist Party rather than the objectives and policies set forth in the Constitution of the CIO." Hall sent Rania to the National CIO hearing in Washington in May 1950. He expected a "kangaroo court," and, as he predicted, the ILWU was expelled. A three-member committee heard the case. Bridges figured the verdict had been decided before the trial started. Paul Jacobs, a writer and labor specialist who prepared the case for the CIO, said he began writing the expulsion order while the trial was going on. The ILWU was now a maverick union, but that did not bother Hall or the membership. "We can take care of ourselves with or without the CIO," said Hall. "We were around long before the CIO and we'll be around when they are dead and gone." Expulsion did hurt, however. It made the union more vulnerable to red-baiting and made the members feel that somehow they were out of the mainstream of American labor.

In 1950 Hawaii held elections to name the sixty-three delegates to a convention that would write a state constitution. Hall took steps to ensure that the ILWU's voice would be heard. A key delegate he wanted elected was Harriet Bouslog. She had nerve; she had brains; and she was not bashful about making herself heard. Around her, Hall figured, his forces could rally.

One day Hall called Mitsuyuki Kido, a successful newcomer to politics. Kido had taught for sixteen years in Kalihi (eight years at Kalakaua Intermediate School and eight at Farrington High). He had run for the Territorial House in 1946, and, as a novice, he had led the ticket in the Fifth District. He had also led the ticket in 1948, so now he had a feeling of strength. He acknowledged that he had done well because of the ILWU. During the 1946 sugar strike, while the political campaigning was going on, union members took him from one stop-work meeting to another. The pitch was simple: "This is Mits Kido," they would tell the crowd. "He deserves your vote." It was easy as that: they set him up as a friend of the union. "And that's how I got elected," Kido said candidly. His contacts in Kalihi-Palama helped, of course, but it was the ILWU vote—the union "boxes," or rural areas where the union was strong—that gave him the big block of votes.

And now, at Hall's suggestion, Kido met him in lawyer Chuck Mau's office. "I want you folks to be aware of a position the union has taken," Hall said to Kido. "The union wants Harriet Bouslog elected at all costs because we want the union's position presented at all the hearings. So, Mits, we want you to team up with Harriet."

"What do you mean, 'team up'?" Kido asked.

"Well, I want you to take Harriet around to your school-teacher friends, and things of that sort."

In other words, wherever Kido went Harriet Bouslog was sure to go to give the impression that they were a twosome. Kido looked at Hall and said, "Well, Jack, I don't think I'd like to do that. I'm not interested in pairing with anybody. . . . I'll help Harriet whatever I can, but I won't team up with her."

Hall took it calmly. "Well, Mits," he replied,

you know that we don't think the election of one or two more liberals is going to help the convention in any way and we are going to make any kind of a deal we can to elect Harriet. Now, if your decision is final that you want to run by yourself and not pair up with Harriet, I want you to know that the union is going to make deals.

"We're going to play this game the way we think it's going to help us," said Hall.

"Fine," said Kido. They shook hands and departed. We're still good friends, Kido thought, and he wasn't too worried. After all, he had led the ticket twice . . . he was known . . . he was popular. But later he began to feel a twinge. "I had an uneasy feeling all along that everything wasn't all right."

In the primary election Kido ran fifth in a field of thirteen. Came the general election and he finished next to last and out of the running.[4] "Oh, wow! Did I get clobbered," he said. And now he realized what muscle the ILWU had. "I got snowed in every precinct in which I used to lead; all those plantation districts. . . . He [Hall] gave the word."

Hall drew a conclusion from the Constitutional Convention election results:

Voters are still anti-ILWU but not to the extent they were in 1948. They voted for candidates they considered to be a little left of center. The Republican machine candidates did not do very well; neither did the lunatic fringe and the Stainback crowd. Farrington's group, with the Rice clan, ran hog wild by and large.

Hall then delivered a one-sentence summary which could have stood as an ILWU maxim for years: "All in all, the election shows that we are a balance of power, but have one helluva time getting our own people in."

---

4. Harriet Bouslog also lost, although the ILWU "boxes" plunked for her.

One of the delegates elected to the convention was Frank Silva, Hall's old partner from Kauai. Silva was one of the Reluctant 39. Word had spread that convention delegates wanted to expel him for refusing to answer HUAC's questions. Hall wrote Sam King, president of the Constitutional Convention. "It would be tragic indeed," said Hall,

> if a convention responsible for the drafting of a constitution to protect and safeguard the rights of citizens in a new state should take such action. Certainly delegates to the convention, particularly those with a legal background, would not write a constitution under which a person would be held guilty until proven innocent. . . . We urge the Constitution Convention not to be stampeded by the unsupported testimony of professional informers. Mr. Silva, in taking his oath as delegate to the convention, swore that he is not and has not been, for a period of five years immediately preceding, a member of the Communist Party.

The convention convened in April 1950 and immediately focused on the Silva case. Silva spoke in his own behalf. McElrath wrote a short speech for him but, according to McElrath, Harriet Bouslog embellished it. McElrath, who was in the audience, listened to his own words being spoken; but when Silva came to the end of the McElrath draft, he launched into a fiery Bouslog-written addendum. McElrath was furious.

Arthur K. Trask, a lawyer and himself a man of strong opinion, asked that Silva be expelled "by reason of his contumacious behavior . . . toward the Constitutional Convention."

"Contumacious!" Silva called that a pretty big word and one that had little meaning for a working man like himself.

After eight hours of debate, the Trask Amendment to expel Silva passed, 53 to 7. Most of the delegates liked Silva; they knew his good war record. "They regarded him as a young man of sincerity and good character—but terribly tragically led astray," said Allen.

After the vote was taken, McElrath, always questing, slyly put a question to Flora Hayes, an amiable Hawaiian delegate: "Flora, I bumped into an odd word today. I don't know the meaning of it. Do you? It's 'contumacious.' " He spelled it.

"No, I've never heard of it," Flora Hayes admitted.

McElrath decided that ninety percent of the other delegates didn't know the word either. "She [and the others] had voted the guy out because he had committed an offense she had never heard of," he said.

CHAPTER **50**

"Standpatters" vs. "Walkouters"

For the ILWU in 1950, April was the cruelest month. The Constitutional Convention opened, at which they had only a modest say; the Un-American Activities Committee convened, with the ILWU as its target; and on Sunday, April 30, the Democratic Party held its Territorial Convention and the issue of the Reluctant 39, most of whom were ILWU members, tore the convention apart.

Hall accused Stainback of mounting a drive to capture the convention. "Unless Stainback is able to do so, he is through as governor," Hall claimed. He told the ILWU leaders:

> The governor's forces are making terrific headway and are packing the party with Republicans in Democratic clothing. This can only be offset if our leadership on the outside islands make sure that not a single vote is lost.

Hall instructed the ILWU to see to it that every unorganized precinct was organized and that delegates elected to the convention were in tune with the ILWU's viewpoint and would "not fold under the hysteria of the Un-American hearings." He gave the ILWU's Tom Yagi and Tom Tagawa the responsibility of lining up delegates and proxy votes. Proxies should go "preferably [to] ILWU leadership," he said.

As was natural, the Democrats had split into pro- and anti-Stainback groups. Hall pushed hard to strengthen the anti-Stainback forces, while organizers, such as Wilfred Oka, worked hard at the grassroots level. When the convention convened, the anti-Stainback group controlled the vote. Among them were fourteen delegates and two alternates who were members of the Reluctant 39.

Everyone knew a break was coming. It took place at the meeting of the Democratic Party's thirty-member Territorial Central Committee. Vincent Esposito, a Harvard Law School graduate, and Kido, the schoolteacher, were the contestants for the chairmanship. Kido had more supporters at the meeting, but "Espo," as he was called, had more proxies and more votes. The Kido group challenged the Esposito proxies of three ILWU members: Tom Yagi, Kameo Ichimura, and Bob Murasaki. All three were Reluctant 39-ers. The challengers claimed they were not entitled to offer proxies. "They were being pilloried," said Esposito.

The committee divided into the liberals, called "left-wingers," and the conservatives, or "right-wingers." It was a standoff; trouble was brewing. It came on schedule at the convention after Esposito had finished his hour-long keynote speech. He told the delegates that people who supported social or political change were called "radical" or "red." He told them not to be afraid of such name-calling. The Democrats, he said, must present a program of "social change for social good."[1]

When he finished speaking, Maurice Sapienza, a right-wing delegate, made a motion to drop the fourteen Reluctant 39 delegates. He read a letter written by Charles M. Hite, vice-chairman of the Democratic Central Committee, in which Hite warned Stainback of "the sinister and insidious infiltration into our [Democratic Party] ranks of communist influence."

---

1. At that stage in life Esposito was strongly supported by the ILWU. "We were brothers," he said.

Kawano denounced Sapienza's motion as an attack on labor and the ILWU. "He was wildly cheered," Martin Pence, a convention guest, noted.

> There was no answer from the right. [Harold] Rice of Maui said coldly there was no use staying around the convention anymore and he was going to leave and invited others to follow him out.
>
> There was no emotional surge and no firey *[sic]* language. The whole thing was not flaming. [Oren] Long stood up, turned to me and shook my hand and asked me if I was leaving and walked off.

The 91 delegates who took a walk controlled 118 of the 510 floor votes. It was inevitable that a pair of convenient terms emerged: the "walkout" group and the "standpat" group. The split was irreparable. "Those fellows walked out and they never came back," said standpatter Sakae Takahashi.

Allen, whose juices always flowed liveliest when politics heated up, cabled Farrington:

> DEMOCRATIC TERRITORIAL CONVENTION SPLIT SUNDAY AFTERNOON INTO TWO BITTERLY OPPOSED GROUPS AND EACH PROCEEDED TO ELECT OFFICERS ADOPT RESOLUTIONS ET *[sic]* PLATFORMS ELECT COMMITTEES STOP EACH DECLARES ITSELF THE DEMOCRATIC PARTY OF HAWAII. . . .

The standpatters named Burns as permanent party chairman and adopted resolutions against Stainback and in favor of Johnny Wilson for governor. For good measure, they also passed a resolution condemning communism. The standpatters were by far the stronger side. Allen called them the "Lau Ah Chew–Burns group" and said they included the ILWU members and other Reluctant 39-ers "cited by the HUAC." Both the walkout and standpat groups endorsed statehood, Allen reassured Farrington. He said the fight among the Democrats was now out in the open and in any case could do the Republicans no harm. He predicted that the "left-wingers" would be "slaughtered" at the elections.

A "new Democratic Party" emerged. The standpat group named Chuck Mau to head the Territorial Central Committee and replace the gentle Lau Ah Chew. They were a determined

force and they had a dream. Four years later the reconstructed
Democratic Party overthrew half a century of Republican rule in
Hawaii.

Many standpatters resented the label of "left-winger" since
they felt the word was so "closely allied in the public mind with
communism and disloyalty." Two officers in the group were
war veterans: Inouye and David A. Benz, a young businessman.
They issued a joint statement: "People like myself are in the
Democratic Party to make it the representative party of all
working people, clerks, merchants, farmers, and small businessmen, as well as labor."

They said that if labor hadn't come into the Democratic Party
in 1946, then small businessmen and white-collar workers
wouldn't have come in either. "There are two ways in which we
can fight communism," Benz said.

> You can stand on the sidelines and scream and make martyrs out of
> them. Or you can do what we have been doing since the Democratic
> convention—that is, abide by the rules and regulations of the party,
> yet fight all expressions of communism and extreme leftist senti-
> ment. . . . If the fellows who walked out on the convention had not
> walked out, our fight would have been easier.

Benz and Mau called on Allen to ask his advice on how to get
rid of the "left-wing appellation." Allen, who savored the role
of political statesman, told them that so long as they permitted a
number of "hostile witnesses" in their group (he meant members of the Reluctant 39), then the Democratic Party would be
looked upon as "leftist."

Whether the standpatters, led by Burns, heeded Allen's advice
or not, they did take steps to remove leftists from power. The
first person purged was Wilfred Oka, who was then the Democratic Party County Committee secretary. The County Committee turned Oka out of office by a 33 to 30 vote. Inouye, who had
Burns' blessing, replaced him.

Oka felt humiliated. He resented the way his ouster had come
about. "They put up the American flag," he said. "About six
guys got up and they quoted Americanism. . . ." Oka con-

fronted Burns after the meeting. "I'm talking about sportsmanship," he said.

> It could have been very simple. You could have seen me and said, "Wilfred, for the good of the party, please do not run." And you know what I would have said? "Jack, you are right. I'll step down. Get other people." Because it was no big thing. It was no . . . glamorous job.

The trial of the Reluctant 39 began on January 3, 1951, before Federal Judge Delbert E. Metzger. Thirty-eight were represented by Bouslog & Symonds; one defendant—Jack Kawano—was represented by his own attorney, Norman K. Chung. The thirty-nine cases turned on a case in Denver, Colorado, where Mrs. Patricia Blau had been cited for contempt for refusing to answer questions before a federal grand jury. Her conviction was overturned by the United States Supreme Court by an 8 to 0 vote. Metzger agreed with that decision. He had a low opinion of contempt citations.[2] On January 19 he ordered the acquittal of all thirty-nine defendants and cited as the key reason the Constitution of the United States, which, he said, "stands there like a Rock of Gibraltar." He said a person had the right to speak out or remain silent before a congressional committee, but he warned that the issue of communism was going to cause a lot of trouble for people in Hawaii. From the bench, Metzger delivered an opinion:

> The Communist Party, or any member of it, have their rights in courts of law of the land, according to the understanding of the Court as to the meaning of the laws, but we all know that the Communist Party . . . is in very ill standing throughout the United States. . . .

"So far as I am concerned," said Metzger, "people who choose to may belong to it, but I just merely express the hope

---

2. Howard K. Hoddick, who as acting United States Attorney handled the government's case against the Reluctant 39, said Metzger was "one of the kindest, most humane judges that ever sat on the bench. . . . [He] just wouldn't have any truck with contempt of Congress citations. And he threw them out."

that none of our local people are contaminated and brought into ill will of others in the community by association with the Communist Party.''

Metzger did not know it, but the trouble he spoke of was coming soon for seven Hawaii residents, including Jack Hall.

CHAPTER 51
"Silent Jack" Speaks

Jack Kawano's disaffection with the Communist Party was a long time in the making. He said four men "converted" him—Burns, Mau, Kido, and Ernest I. Murai. In Mau's opinion, Kawano was the sparkplug of the newly organized Democratic Party. "He was the one that just put the fire into everybody," said Mau. For a year the five—Burns, Mau, Kido, Murai, and Kawano—met many a Saturday night at a teahouse or at Mau's home. Sometimes Inouye and Sakae Takahashi came. They talked about how the Democratic Party could strengthen itself and wrest control from the Republicans.

Mau said he didn't know then that Kawano was a member of the Communist Party.[1] Mau said he, as a lawyer, was just trying to sell Kawano on Americanism. "So I used to talk about American history, the Constitution of the United States, I think for the first eight months. The last four months we talked about Russia. What kind of a system of government it was and so forth. And at the end, in front of the four of us, I asked him: 'And now you have heard both systems, which one do you like

---

1. No doubt Burns knew.

best?' '' He said Kawano opted for "the capitalist system in the United States."[2]

Kawano also approached Mau, as he did Inouye, when he was subpoenaed by the HUAC. Mau remembered him coming to his house at 9 PM on a Sunday to tell him. Mau told him he had nothing to worry about. "Just tell them you're not a Communist." Then, according to Mau, for the first time Kawano said: "No, but I am!"

Kawano told Mau he wanted to rid the union of communism. "I can't come out and tell them everything because I'd be useless to the union. . . . I'd like to stay in the union and fight them." Mau advised Kawano to tell the Un-American Activities Committee that he was not a Communist and "leave it go at that. Not answer anything else."[3]

Kawano said he attended his last Communist Party meeting in June 1949. During the longshore strike he was assigned to lobby at the legislature, "when my real position was supposed to be on the strike; with the longshoremen." He felt the union had shunted him aside.

He blamed Hall for his demotion. Kawano harbored a resentment against Hall, the *haole* from the mainland who had taken over after Kawano felt he had done the spadework. But times had changed. The ILWU had developed; it demanded leadership with a sophistication that Kawano did not have. The ILWU said Kawano refused to be chairman of the strike committee in the 1949 strike, "his logical responsibility as president of the local," and that Kawano did nothing to help the union win the 1949 strike. "Any assignment was ducked. He disappeared for days on end."

Kawano claimed that during the 1949 longshore strike the Communist Party tried to take the sugar workers out on strike

---

2. If indeed that was Kawano's preference of the moment it did not prevail for the rest of his life. In an interview in 1974, he said, "Even today I still believe what the Communists say about capitalism."

Question: You're a Socialist at heart?

Answer: I believe I am.

3. Which is what he did.

and he resisted. If the sugar workers went out, he said, then both they and the longshoremen would lose their strikes. According to Kawano, the Communists said he was talking like a good union man, but not like a good Communist.

At the ILWU International Executive Board meeting in Seattle on October 10, 1950, board member Kawano was absent. Goldblatt said he had resigned. The members wanted to know why. Kawano had served labor well; they were puzzled. Bridges said he had talked to Kawano. "He is personally disgruntled," said Bridges.

> He feels he has not been treated right. Quit cold during the Hawaii [1949] strike and as a result had the strike committee sore at him.
>
> Democratic Party politics and internal union politics enter the picture. Jack was opposed as president [of the longshore local]. Was not elected chairman of the strike committee. He seemed to feel there should be a job of some kind for him.

Ernie Arena said Kawano had urged the longshoremen to accept the fourteen-cent wage raise recommended by the Stainback fact-finding committee and had claimed the strike couldn't be won. It was moved and seconded that Kawano's resignation be accepted. The motion carried. Kawano was off the board.

When his term was up as president of the longshore local in November 1950, Kawano announced he wouldn't run for reelection.[4] For a time he went back to work on the waterfront; then he worked as a janitor for the International Theatre.

On February 10, 1951, Kawano released an exhortation calling on ILWU members to purge the union of "all Communists and those who follow the Communist line." He declared he once had been but was not now a Communist. . . .

> I joined the Communist Party because some individual Communists were willing to assist me organizing the Waterfront Union. . . .
>
> I decided to quit the Communist Party because I found that the primary existence of the Communist Party was not for the best interest of the workingman but to dupe the members of the union, to

---

4. The ILWU said: "If he had run, after his record during the strike, he would not have been elected."

control the union, and to use the union for purposes other than strictly trade-union matters. . . .

Kawano's statement was concise and startling. Hall thought that, just as Izuka had had help in drafting his pamphlet, so Kawano must have had help in drafting his statement. "Jack couldn't and didn't write that statement," said Hall.

But it was not easy to shake off Kawano's defection. He had been a power; many union members respected him. He had courage and even if he was stodgy and often mute, they knew he had fought for labor for a long time. Charles H. Saka, a Maui Division Executive Board member, spoke his mind: "Coming from a unionist of Kawano's integrity, and the fact that the ILWU has not answered him to my satisfaction, I find the matter quite disturbing. I am of the opinion that side-tracking the issue will result in grief come showdown in negotiations. . . ." Hall's response did not satisfy Saka. He resigned.

Another union official, Yutaka Niimi, secretary of Local 142, Unit 15, Wailuku, told Hall that he, too, was disturbed. Hall said he was happy to discuss the damage Kawano was doing to the union.

"I should like to raise one question with you," said Hall. "Just why is it that Kawano has waited until now, a few weeks before our [sugar] contract expires, to play stoolpigeon before the unAmerican committee? . . ."

On the scene in Hawaii, Goldblatt assessed the damage:

The Kawano attack, while it has created a certain amount of confusion which is inevitable, seems to have been handled very well and done no fundamental harm here. . . .

Allen saw it differently:

ILWU leaders here are trying to brush off Kawano's statement, but are finding it no easy job. But it is too much to expect that there will be an early or serious break in the ILWU. . . .

On July 6, 1951, Kawano testified in Washington before the House Un-American Activities Committee in a closed-door session in Room 226 of the Old House Office Building. Representative Francis Walter presided; Judge Mau attended. He was the only spectator.

Mau had encouraged Kawano to go to Washington. He told Kawano that after the way he had been treated by the union, "I think it's time to recant and really tell the whole story." Kawano said he was willing, but that Mau had to come with him. Mau said, "Okay, I'll try to make arrangements so you can have a hearing." He talked to business executive Ben Dillingham. Mau said he would pay his own way. Dillingham agreed to pay Kawano's plane fare and subsistence in Washington.[5]

Under friendly questioning before the HUAC (there was no cross-examination), Kawano testified that he had made a mistake in not speaking out during the committee's hearing in Honolulu. He said that when a HUAC investigator came to Hawaii in late July or early August 1950, he wanted to talk openly to him but Hall told him he would be "a rat" and that "my name would be mud from that time on."

In his statement Kawano reviewed the history of the Communist Party in Hawaii from the day in the spring of 1937 when Bill Bailey set up shop in his Emma Street room to the 1949 strike. He named names; he recited them, page after page. There was no one to challenge him. He said the Party was deactivated during the war, but revived in 1945 with the first meeting "held on the grass near the apron of Kewalo Basin." He said Charles and Eileen Fujimoto were assigned the job "to contact and recruit [members] into the Communist Party."

He spoke of the meeting of the Party's Executive Board in Hall's home on Oahu Avenue early in 1948 to discuss taking over the Democratic Party. "I believe the influence of the Communist Party in the Democratic Party is very strong," he said. He discussed the controversy over "coming out in the open"— that is, letting the public know who belonged to the Communist Party and who should get credit for the ILWU's success. He said the Fujimotos spearheaded the campaign to come out in the open and they were supported by Kimoto, Reinecke, Koji Ariyoshi, and Dwight James Freeman, a Party organizer who had been sent to Hawaii in 1946. "They met opposition from Hall,

---

5. Neither Mau nor Dillingham remembered the exact amount.

McElrath, and myself," said Kawano. Kawano argued that it would be bad to come out in the open.

Kawano told the HUAC that "in the beginning the Communist Party influence was practically nil. Today the influence goes pretty deep into the membership of the ILWU." He said the Party had the union tied up: "They made policies and important decisions for the ILWU. . . . They go so far as to line up candidates and campaign for those guys for office. They determine who is going to run as head of this local or head of that local. . . ."

Kawano acknowledged that Burns, Mau, Kido, and Murai had converted him.[6] "It was they who convinced me in such a fashion that led to the determination to break my ties with the Communist Party," he said.

The ILWU read Kawano's testimony, which was spread out in full in the newspapers, and called him a villain, a traitor, a man who for his own purposes sought to break the union leadership. McElrath saw him as the chief defector in a line of defectors: "We knew he had gone the way of other disgruntled individuals who didn't do their jobs yet thought the labor movement owed them a living. Kawano has joined others such as Izuka, Ignacio, Mookini, and Maldonado as a liar, informer and anti-labor tool."

What infuriated the union most of all was Kawano's charge that the Communist Party ran the union. "Kawano, as well as this [Executive] board, knows that he lies when he says anyone but the membership runs the union." McElrath characterized Kawano's testimony as "a mixture of lies, half-truths and distortions and will not fool the workers. As officers of this union we know of our own personal knowledge that the ILWU involves the finest traditions of democracy."

Mau had sat spellbound as Kawano testified. "There was nobody else there listening," he said. "That story was unveiled and it was so fascinating."

---

6. Burns thought well of Kawano all his life. "A hell of a human being," he called Kawano. "He made one mistake; got a bit misled, got a little bit pushed over the counter. . . ."

After Kawano finished speaking, Mau went to the office of the United States Attorney General to tell them something. He talked to a deputy who was in charge of Smith Act prosecutions and brought up the subject of "the emergency in Hawaii." What emergency? asked the deputy. The Communist threat, said Mau. The deputy smiled. "You don't have anybody but 'buck privates' in Hawaii," he said.

"What do you mean?" said Mau.

"The bigwigs [in the Communist Party] are in the mainland United States," the deputy said.

Mau asked where the Attorney General's office would file Smith Act cases. The deputy said the next trials were scheduled to be held in Los Angeles, Seattle, Chicago, and Denver. "Maybe then we'll have time for you."

"Gee, that will be another two, three years," said Mau.

"Sounds like it," said the deputy.

"Would you like to see another Pearl Harbor?" Mau dropped his bomb.

"What do you mean?"

"The Communists would be quite willing, if they can infiltrate into Pearl Harbor, the waterworks, the electricity company," said Mau.

Mau went on: "Be in a strategic position, if war ever came with Russia. They'd have people blowing up utilities and so forth. . . . If the citizenry should fall to the siren song of the Communists, we'd be very, very weak. . . . And Communists usually take over weak countries."

According to Mau, his words struck home. The deputy asked him to stay over in Washington until the next day. He said a staff meeting was scheduled for the next morning and he intended to bring Mau's warning to the staff's attention.

Next morning the deputy called Mau at his hotel. "We're going to Hawaii next," he said. He meant the government was going to start picking the defendants for a Smith Act trial in Hawaii.

The Number 1 target would be Jack Hall.

CHAPTER 52
Lanai '51: The Quiet Battle

Lanai is an unusual island, small (141 square miles), and isolated. Lanai City, the only town,[1] sits at 1600 feet elevation, "a single camp surrounded by pineapple fields." At night in the clear air the stars are sharp and brilliant. The wind blows much of the time and whistles a tune from the top of the Norfolk pines.

Lanai is devoted to one thing: raising pineapple. Once there were 14,000 acres in pine; Lanai grew 200,000 tons a year. At 4:30 AM the whistle blows on days when there is work in the fields and the small, hardworking Filipinos, who are the bulk of the laborers, get up for another day's work.

On Lanai in 1951 the workers struck for 201 days. At first there wasn't much about it in the papers and the ILWU accused management of "a conspiracy of silence." Though it may have been a quiet strike, it had great impact. The Lanai strike was an outgrowth of the union's defeat in pineapple in 1947. The employers, having won that battle, tried to take advantage of it. "They got cocky enough so that they finally made themselves a great big mistake," said Goldblatt.

The employers felt they were strong enough not to bargain with the union on an industry-wide basis—that is, one contract for the entire industry. Instead they wanted to bargain on a unit level: company by company, even plantation by plantation. "We all felt we were in a strong position and we ought to be able to negotiate on our own terms next time around," said Steele. "Maybe we'd even get the upper hand. . . ."

The industry set the pattern of unit bargaining and insisted

---

1. Population in 1976: 2200.

bargaining would be handled that way henceforth. The union had to accept. It was not strong enough to resist. Everything was settled—until Lanai. C. C. Cadagan, Hawaiian Pine vice-president, made the decision to bargain company by company. "We wanted to take them on and see if we could break up consolidated bargaining," he said.

In October 1950, the pineapple industry drove through a two-year contract which called for an eight-cent raise. Hall, who negotiated it, was bitter: "We will not soon forget that every single proposal of the union to give the individual workers more protection and job security was brushed off with monotonous regularity to the tune of, 'We are unable to grant the union's request.' "

All Hawaiian Pine ILWU units, except Lanai, ratified the contract. Lanai rejected it, 618 to 33. Goldblatt talked to the pineapple workers in Honolulu. He told them they didn't have the strength to shut down the whole industry and that was a fact of life. After the meeting a few members from Lanai asked to talk to him. They gathered in the parking lot outside the union hall. There was no place to sit; the men squatted on their haunches. The Lanai members wanted to know just one thing: Did they have the right to strike?

Goldblatt said, yes, they could strike but he warned:

One thing you won't be able to do—because there's no use lying to you—you're not going to be able to shut down the rest of the industry. If the company can manage to operate, if they can ship pineapple to the cannery . . . then to think that we will be able to double back and tell the cannery workers to forget the contract and pull out—it won't work. It won't win.

That did not seem to bother the men from Lanai. They asked what the union could do to help them if they went on strike. "The one thing we can do, we can help as best we can," said Goldblatt.

By that I mean we can try to get you some money; give your bumming committee a hand. We can go plantation by plantation . . . but if you go out, you know you're going to be out a long, long time. If you guys are thinking about a 30-day strike, or something like that is gonna win, forget it!

Goldblatt told them if they went out on strike, they would be out more than three or four months. There was no plot or scheme to strike Lanai. "We knew what the employers were doing," he said. "Everything was spelled out there. Nobody had to hit us on the head because it was going on right around us." The union was being "whittled to pieces," said Goldblatt. Moreover, the union was afraid that unit-by-unit bargaining might spread to sugar.

On February 27, 1951, some 752 Lanai workers walked off the job. They demanded a twelve-cent wage increase, a union shop, job security, and a review of the classification system. Their leader was the stolid and often silent Pedro de la Cruz. De la Cruz was the ILWU business agent on Lanai and chairman of the Strike Strategy Committee; he was tough and he was trusted by his men.

The strike took management by surprise. "I was floored when I heard about it," said Cadagan.[2] The workers prepared for a long strike. De la Cruz, the man they said couldn't talk, made himself perfectly clear when he explained how the men felt. "Not a single bit of that island is owned by the employees," he said. "Every damned thing, our homes and everything, belongs to the employer. Only our lives belong to us. . . ."[3]

The strike settled down into an endurance contest. The Filipinos hunted in the hills and fished. The union fed the strikers in a community soup kitchen. In May, Hall went over to Lanai and found morale to be good. Such tough men could stay out indefinitely but something troubled him. Even if they did, could they hope to win anything? Hall told Cadagan the Lanai

---

2. For years Steele thought Goldblatt had hatched the plan to strike Lanai: "It appeared to be such a brilliant strategy on the part of the union that I gave Goldblatt credit for it."

3. Company policy on owning land on Lanai changed in the mid-1950s. Workers were able to buy house lots and could even live on "Haole Hill" if they chose.

strikers were as uncontrollable as a wildcat. He even toyed with the idea of writing them off, according to Cadagan. Hall told Goldblatt the Lanai people indulged in some "pretty frustrated thinking."

> One brainstorm [said Hall] is to get the longshoremen to refuse to handle Hapco goods. Some of the other local leadership is also a bit frustrated and feel that we should "do something" to help Lanai in a physical fashion.
>
> I gave the Lanai leadership and all the local leadership a pretty critical analysis of the situation and with no holds barred in a meeting last Saturday [May 6, 1951]. . . . This has led to a little bit of the same old militant attitude by some of the leadership that has gotten them into constant trouble over the years and forced a lot of learning the hard way. . . .

Hall discussed Lanai with Jim Blaisdell, the employer's attorney, and Blaisdell dropped a "not so subtle" hint that Hawaiian Pine would take a strike through the summer without worrying about the cost. If the strike went on that long, Blaisdell said, there would be no need for harvesting gangs "for a long, long time."

Hall, the poker player, thought Blaisdell was bluffing, but he admitted the union couldn't afford to discount the threat "because Hapco might see some advantage of burning the house down." He told Blaisdell that if the company followed through with that kind of a "kamikaze program," the union would not confine the fight to Lanai alone—not "by a damn sight." At that stage Hall was trying to pick up "anything possible" in an effort to find a base for an early settlement.

No early settlement was possible and that was what lawyer Ronald B. Jamieson, who was appointed conciliator, found out. Hall told De la Cruz to cooperate with Jamieson and give him any information he wanted. "Convince him," said Hall, "of your determination to get job security and union security. Give him a clear understanding of attitudes of workers in relation to 'Snob Hill.' "

Jamieson was deliberate and painstaking (he made a good

judge), but he was not the man for the job. He was not a conciliator, Cadagan said. To Jamieson the Lanai strike was puzzling. The Wahiawa unit of Hawaiian Pine had signed the labor agreement; the company wanted to settle with Lanai on the same terms, but the Lanai workers rejected the offer.

"Why?" Jamieson wondered. "Why did the ILWU take one position at Wahiawa and a different position on Lanai?"

Hall said Jamieson made no useful suggestions to help settle the strike. Jamieson said he did, "but too few were acceptable to both sides." Hall ignored Jamieson and he and Cadagan signed a memorandum of agreement and thought they had the key to unlock the door. On May 26 Hall, Cadagan, Jamieson, and E. C. Rinehart, an Employers Council negotiator, met for a "victory" celebration at the Young Hotel. Hall did not dream the Lanai workers would reject the agreement. He was happy and relieved and insisted on Jamieson having a drink: whiskey and water. They all drank up.

Later, Cadagan drove Hall to his office. On the way they stopped and parked because Hall wanted to talk. "We sat in my car for two hours talking," said Cadagan.

> We talked about everything. That was when Hall told me he had been a member of the Communist Party and when they tried to dictate to him how to run the union that was when he broke with them. He said, "If Jack Kawano would tell the truth about me, that's what he would say."

Hall went to Lanai to ask the workers to ratify the memorandum of agreement. An out-of-doors meeting was held and Hall "hit the floor three times." The meeting lasted for hours. Hall's words were translated into Ilocano but, according to Cadagan, the translator added a few ideas of his own, saying, in effect, that "you don't have to do what Hall told you. Sugar will back us up."

A few days later word came back that the Lanai membership had rejected the agreement. "This was an extraordinary event in the ILWU and was not satisfactorily explained," Jamieson said.

Jamieson gave up on July 21. He said there was no likelihood of peace in any of Hawaii's major industries which the ILWU dominated. "I resigned as conciliator because there appeared to be nothing more for me in that capacity," he said.[4]

Goldblatt came over in August. He wrote Bridges that the two conciliators (George Hillenbrand and Arthur Viat), who took up the burden Jamieson had laid down, were "worthless." The strike was solid; support was coming in; and the crop was "going to hell." Goldblatt estimated the company was losing $250,000 worth of pineapples a day. It all showed the "full-blown insanity of the Big Five and their attitude toward bargaining," said Goldblatt. One thing was certain, he said: the Lanai affair "has knocked off any ideas" about company-by-company bargaining in sugar.

The strike already had stretched out longer than the 1949 longshore strike when Hall and Goldblatt one day got a call from Jim Blaisdell. "Look," said Blaisdell, "we want to get together to kick the gong around. How about the Tropics?"[5]

They met and, as was their custom, had a few drinks. Then Blaisdell said, "This Lanai pineapple thing has to be settled."

Hall said, "Well, we never wanted it to start. You're the guys who broke up the industry-wide bargaining."

Blaisdell said, "Why don't you tell me what will settle the damn thing?"

Goldblatt said, "All right, fine."

---

4. Five years later Jamieson testified before a U.S. Senate committee that Goldblatt had told him the Lanai strike was born out of hatred for the company and that the ILWU has threatened to reduce Lanai "to volcanic ash."

Goldblatt said he had explained to Jamieson that there were issues at stake in the Lanai strike which were not part of the normal labor contract: the housing situation, the superiority complex of management, "Haole Hill." "I said to him, 'There's only one possibility and that's to cut past it and get the thing into a different arena. As long as it stays in that narrow situation on one island, I don't see how in the devil the damned thing is going to be resolved. . . .' "

5. He meant the Waikiki Tropics. There was another Tropics in those days—the Ala Moana Tropics, across Atkinson Drive from the ILWU Memorial Hall.

If you jot these things down while I mess around, we'll make a deal. The Lanai settlement cannot be the eight cents. . . . What we want—there is an extra four or five cents. We'll take twelve or thirteen cents. That will settle Lanai.

But simultaneous with that, and the only way we can handle that, all the pineapple companies go back into industry-wide bargaining. And that means Del Monte, Libby, Hawaiian Pine, Maui Pine, and so forth and so on. They all come back into industry-wide bargaining.

We take all the contracts you've signed, . . . open them. We open them five months early and these guys get an increase over the eight cents of four or five cents. . . .

Blaisdell wrote it all down on the back of an envelope. They had another drink; he got up and said he'd call later. Next day he asked them to meet him at his home in Kahala. Hall and Goldblatt came. All of the industry was there—Henry White, L. Verne Haas from Libby, Jack Driver from Del Monte, Cadagan. Blaisdell was full of joy. He roared around the grounds on a motorcycle. He poured martinis. The place was noisy as a carnival. The atmosphere got so friendly that Goldblatt was prevailed upon to play the piano.

Then Blaisdell got around to the reason for the merriment. "Look, everybody is agreed," he said. "We have an understanding. We're all going back. We're going to sign a single agreement. Industry will be back together again. . . ." And he spelled it out, basically, as he had taken it down at the Tropics.

That was it: no written memorandum of agreement at that moment. Just Blaisdell's word. Hall and Goldblatt felt the keen edge of triumph. They were ready to go home, but "those guys wanted a party," said Goldblatt. "They got a party."

A poker game was started and Hall was drawn in. It turned out to be his lucky day. He won pot after pot. Pretending that because of his bad eyesight he couldn't see the cards, he would gape at them, holding them right under his nose. "Goddamn," he would say. "Let me take a look at them again." The whole thing was just "a big *shibai,*" said Goldblatt, who had been spectator to such playacting many times.

Hall went home with Goldblatt and his pockets were filled with greenbacks. They were late for dinner. Yoshiko was not entirely pleased. After dinner, Hall said he was still troubled about something. How would the Lanai strikers react to a settlement which benefited all the workers in the pineapple industry, and not just them alone?

"You watch, Lou," he predicted. "There will be some guys who are gonna say: 'The settlement is all right. We'll take it for Lanai only. The other people didn't fight for it. They're not entitled to it.' " He asked Goldblatt to go over to Lanai and break the news to them.

Goldblatt flew over. He stepped out of the plane at Lanai airport and "almost got knocked down." The wind? No. The smell of rotting pineapple. The smell of 100,000 tons of rotting pineapple. It smelled like a brewery. Almost seven months had gone by. "It was pure alcohol by that time." De la Cruz and Shiro Hokama, the unit treasurer, met Goldblatt. "Just smell that, Lou," they said happily.

The men gathered at the union hall to hear Goldblatt. He spelled it all out. One man jumped to his feet. "Hey, go over that again! You trying to tell me that these other workers get the *same* thing we get? Without striking?"

"That's right," said Goldblatt.

"No like."

Goldblatt patiently explained: sometimes somebody does the fighting and somebody else gains so they both can come out fighting together another time.

De la Cruz, the quiet man, sized up things. "Look, break it up now, fellows," he said. "We talk in a little while, huh?" They went out, found a place to sit, and somebody brought out a bottle of scotch. De la Cruz excused himself. He said he had to talk to key leaders.

Later, they reconvened the meeting and the same members who had said, "No like," now said, "Well, okay. If the union recommends it, we'll go along. . . ."

Goldblatt asked De la Cruz if he could take the last plane out that day. De la Cruz said sure. They could not take a ratification vote yet anyway; some members were out fishing. So Goldblatt left before the vote. At midnight the phone in his hotel room in Waikiki rang. It was Blaisdell. "What happened on Lanai?" he asked.

Half-asleep, Goldblatt said, "I don't know."

"What do you mean?" Blaisdell demanded. "I thought we had an understanding."

"Sure, we did," said Goldblatt. "I went over there, explained it. I think it will be all right."

"Goddamn it," Blaisdell exploded. "You got no business leaving there before the vote's taken."

"Maybe the best thing was to leave before the vote's taken," said Goldblatt. "Not to be looking down their necks. Just to walk away. Leave them alone."

The next morning De la Cruz called. "Okay," he said. He didn't like to waste words.

The strike ended September 14. Workers got a fifteen-cent raise: eight cents plus an additional seven cents which was negotiated for the entire industry.

In October Fujisaki flew over Lanai. The countryside looked like a cow pasture. No fertilizer had been applied; no weed control had been done. The weeds obliterated the lines between the fields in six thousand acres of pineapple. Some of the weeds were waist high and thick as a blanket.

Part 9
THE SMITH ACT TRIAL
(1952–1953)

CHAPTER 53

A Knock on the Door

At 6:30 AM on August 28, 1951, FBI agents knocked on the door of Jack Hall's apartment on Kau Way in Waikiki. They had come to arrest Hall for alleged violation of the Smith Act.[1]

The FBI also arrested six others and the defendants became known immediately as the "Hawaii Seven." The others were Reinecke, the discharged schoolteacher; Charles K. Fujimoto, a soil chemist who had announced that he was chairman of the Communist Party of Hawaii; his wife, Eileen, a former ILWU secretary; Dwight James Freeman, the Communist Party organizer who came to Hawaii in 1946; Jack Kimoto, for several years the head of the Communist Party in Hawaii and an employee of the left-wing *Honolulu Record;* and Koji Ariyoshi, former army lieutenant and editor of the *Record.*

Teddy Kreps, the ILWU research specialist, lived in the maid's quarters alongside Hall's place. Hall's daughter, Michele, who was called "Mikey," rapped on her door. "Momma sent me over," she cried. As Miss Kreps rocked the eight-year-old girl in her arms, she looked out and saw Hall in the custody of men wearing suits and ties.

"Where are you going, Jack?" she asked.

"To jail," said Hall. He managed to smile.

Mikey also alerted McElrath, who lived nearby. "They've just arrested Daddy," she said.

The FBI agents escorted Hall to their car and they passed the

---

1. The Alien Registration Act of 1940 which forbade the teaching or advocacy of the violent overthrow of the United States government. The author was Representative Howard Smith of Virginia. The Smith Act was amended in 1948 under the general conspiracy law and set punishment for conviction at a maximum five years in prison and a $10,000 fine.

street where McElrath lived. "Aren't you going to pick up McElrath?" Hall asked one of them. By then McElrath knew he was safe. If they had intended to arrest him, they would have done it at the same time they arrested Hall.

The night before his arrest Hall had been negotiating the final details in a sugar contract with Steele and Maxwell in a room at the Young Hotel. The talks had gone well; they were down the home stretch on wages and classifications. They intended to spend the night if need be to get everything "buttoned down." While they were talking Steele got a message from a source he trusted that "government people" (that is, the FBI) were downstairs waiting to arrest Hall. Steele sent back word asking that they hold off until the negotiators finished their session. Said Steele:

> I don't know whether that message got through, but the facts are that we didn't settle until late that night—3 AM, and we all obviously had a lot to drink and we went home and poor Jack was called out of bed with a hangover and a terrible thirst in the morning. . . .

The ILWU was furious. They called Hall's arrest a cold-blooded plot to smash the union. The Lanai strike was on; negotiations in sugar had reached a crucial stage. "The timing of his arrest," said the ILWU, "was no coincidence. . . . There was no question that the FBI and its agents figured that this would be the strategic moment to pick up Hall, torpedo negotiations, and force the union to settle for any terms offered by the employer."[2]

The defendants appeared that morning before United States Commissioner Harry Steiner for arraignment. Howard K. Hoddick, acting United States Attorney, asked for bail of from $75,000 to $100,000 for each. He said that amount was comparable to bail set for Smith Act defendants on the mainland.

---

2. Nonsense, said management. Maxwell said: "We didn't want him arrested. . . . If you deal with a guy who is straightforward and tells you the truth—no matter how tough he is—you're in a better position than you are with somebody you can't rely on."

Symonds, who represented the defendants, said such a large sum, in effect, would deny the defendants the right to bail.

"You have to take the charges into consideration," said Steiner, and he set bail for each at $75,000. He asked Symonds if they could raise it. The disheartened Symonds replied: "You'll have to give us time to make arrangements to rob a bank."

On the morning of Hall's arrest, the full ILWU Sugar Negotiating Committee met as usual. The fifty members voted unanimously to suspend negotiations until Hall could brief them. He was their brain; their spokesman. Steiner agreed to let Hall meet with them, but he ordered Hall to remain in the custody of United States Marshal Otto Heine. Hall saw the committee in Heine's office and waiting room on the third floor of the Federal Building. They all crammed into two rooms and Hall reviewed what progress they had made in the negotiating session of the night before.

The first move by the defense was to ask for reduction of bail, and Federal Judge Metzger granted Symonds' motion. Metzger agreed that it was unlikely the defendants would abscond and he cut the bail to $5000.[3] That cost Metzger his judgeship. In Washington, Senator Joseph C. O'Mahoney, a Wyoming Democrat, called Metzger's action "outrageous" and predicted it would "speedily terminate the judge's services."[4]

Hall wasn't surprised by his arrest; he more or less expected it. He knew about the Smith Act. He had studied comments on it in the left-wing National Lawyers Guild *Review*. He had read about the Foley Square Smith Act trial in New York.[5]

---

3. The federal grand jury recommended that Metzger raise the bail to $7500 from $5000 and he agreed. All seven defendants were people of modest means. Hall, at the time, was earning $100 a week.

4. Metzger's term ran out on September 28, 1951, and he was not reappointed. He was then seventy-six.

5. The trial before Judge Harold R. Medina of the top eleven Communist Party leaders in the United States, including Eugene Dennis, general secretary of the Communist Party of America. All eleven were found guilty on October 14, 1949, and all but one defendant (Robert Thompson, a war hero) were sentenced to five years in prison and a $10,000 fine. Thompson got a three-year sentence.

The decision to indict the Hawaii Seven was made in Washington. "Neither I nor the local United States Attorney's office selected those particular seven," said Hoddick. Two government lawyers came to Honolulu to present the cases before the federal grand jury—Larry Bailey, a senior trial lawyer, and Tom Donegan, both with the Justice Department. Hoddick said the seven were indicted because the evidence the government turned up indicated they were "the most active in the Communist Party in Hawaii at that time." Moreover, said Hoddick, "they were in a position . . . to do the most damage. . . ."[6]

On August 28, 1951, the FBI released biographies of the seven defendants. Hall's biography identified him "as being among those who formed the organization nucleus of the Communist Party movement in the territory. . . ."

Hall was resigned to a long and grueling trial. He knew that his job as a militant labor leader entailed risks—even the risk of going to jail. "I speak with authority on the matter of jails, having been in a few during the course of my years with the trade movement," he once said. After his indictment, he told the ILWU members:

> It matters little if I, as an individual, become the victim of hysteria and eventually wind up behind bars. I will have the satisfaction, at least, of having not compromised, in return for personal security, the principles which have guided me my entire life.

---

6. In time Hoddick came to regard the Smith Act prosecutions as wasted effort. In 1974 he said: "I've since had reconsiderations on that whole subject. I think personally that America would be where America is today if there had not been any prosecutions of the Smith Act cases."

CHAPTER 54

Preliminary Event

Delbert Metzger was the kind of judge who liked to keep a bottle of whiskey in his desk drawer in chambers and pour out a jigger for a friendly caller. He was the opposite of the strict J. Frank McLaughlin—in personality, in courtroom conduct, in judicial philosophy. During the preliminaries of the Smith Act trial they engaged in a tug-of-words: Metzger in his flat Kansas drawl; McLaughlin in his Massachusetts twang.

Hoddick tried to remove Metzger from the case for "bias and prejudice." He claimed bias showed itself in the way Metzger had reduced bail for the defendants and in his action in dismissing the case against the Reluctant 39. Metzger declined to step down. He said he would not be intimidated by anyone. "I don't have to obey anyone except my reason and my conscience."

Bouslog & Symonds challenged the makeup of the federal grand jury on the grounds that it was not a true cross-section of the community.[1] Metzger dismissed the jury as nonrepresentative of the community at large, but he did not dismiss the indictments against the Hawaii Seven. He told his reporter friend Louise Hollingsworth that the indictments were "perfectly valid—hell, yes."

At that point the regular change in assignment of judges came up and McLaughlin took over the criminal calendar. He asked Metzger to point out what section of the law gave Metzger the right to discharge the jury. "Regardless of what he says, I say

---

1. Reinecke filed an affidavit saying that of the 418 names on the jury panel, 276 came from Oahu's affluent Fourth District and only 54 from the "working man's" Fifth District; moreover, Caucasians made up 70 percent of the jury list, but only 19.7 percent of the total number of voters.

the grand jury is still intact and will report as directed," he said. McLaughlin, who had a flair for the dramatic, summoned Metzger to appear as a witness at the hearing challenging the grand jury's makeup. The prospect of a spat in open court between two federal judges titillated the town. "Hawaii is treated to the spectacle of a feud between two federal judges of equal rank in judicial matters," the *Advertiser* commented.

On the appointed day the courtroom was filled. On the bench sat the stern-faced McLaughlin in his black robe of office. On the witness stand sat the pink-faced Metzger wearing a dark suit with a small red orchid in the lapel. "According to the newspapers, you and I are feuding, are we not, as a result of this legal snarl?" said McLaughlin.

"No, sir," said Metzger. "There is no feud in this court. It takes two to make one."

"I'm pleased to hear that," said McLaughlin, and they took up the case. Metzger repeated his contention that the grand jury was nonrepresentative; McLaughlin repeated his ruling that the jury was legally constituted. Neither changed the other's mind; the indictments against the Hawaii Seven stood.

Hall was no ordinary client. He had the mind of a lawyer; he could read and absorb legal writing; and neither lawyers nor judges could intimidate him. He was often impatient with his own lawyers: no brief they wrote ever completely pleased him; no argument they made in court entirely satisfied him. He ordered Bouslog & Symonds to prepare a motion for a separate trial for him.

Symonds advised against it; it would do more harm than good, he said. The other six defendants also were against it. They said it would destroy their sense of unanimity. Hall was adamant. "I have reiterated our insistence the motion be separate [in] my case at least." He wanted to remove himself from the other defendants.

When Symonds finished a first draft of the motion, Hall rejected it. It fell far short of the ideas that he, Symonds, and Richard Gladstein had discussed in San Francisco—separation on the grounds that Hall's arrest "was an attack upon the union."

In addition to the motion for a separate trial, Bouslog & Symonds also filed an affidavit in the Ninth Circuit Court of Appeals to remove McLaughlin from the case. The affidavit claimed that McLaughlin "harbored bias and prejudice" against Hall and the ILWU. (McLaughlin told Symonds, and not in jest, that he was the "most affidavited" judge in the history of the United States judiciary.)

The decision to try to remove McLaughlin was not unanimous. Symonds wanted to keep him on the case and he summarized his feelings in a memorandum to Hall. He said in spite of his cavalier attitude the judge was "somewhat timid and has a fear complex."

> He has legal ability, but he is not a Medina [Judge Harold Medina, who presided at the New York Smith Act trial] and it is possible to stand up and face him and argue. . . . In a long trial in which he has such a deep-rooted hatred of communism and a fear that there is a Red under every bed, I feel it is possible he will lose his composure and inject into the trial his animosity. It is my experience that whatever he thinks shows on his face. He does not have a poker face. This, of course, would be helpful to us during the trial.

Symonds said he believed McLaughlin would commit judicial error which would result in a mistrial. Furthermore, he argued, it they got rid of McLaughlin, the government would bring in a judge from the mainland—a judge "picked by the Justice Department for the very purpose of trying a Smith Act case." An imported judge would be worse than McLaughlin, said Symonds.

But he was the only one among the defense who wanted to keep McLaughlin on and was "completely outvoted." His law partner, Harriet Bouslog, was totally opposed to McLaughlin and filed a supplemental affidavit of bias and prejudice against the judge. She felt he hated the ILWU and wanted to make his reputation as a judge in a Smith Act case.

Hall insisted that a separate petition be filed in his behalf against McLaughlin, "not only for his views on Communists and associates of Communists, but particularly on his bias and prejudice against the ILWU."

Symonds complied. But when Hall saw the draft of the motion, he disapproved. It didn't catch what he considered to be his main thrust—namely, that the Smith Act indictment was an attack on the union. "It seems to me the law office is capable of a much better job if it were given sufficient thought," Hall said. "It seems to me," he went on, "that in attacking the bias and prejudice of McLaughlin, we have an ideal opportunity to set the tenor of the case which is primarily, as I thought we had agreed, an attack on the ILWU, and secondarily, a civil liberties case. . . ."

Hall said the record could be built to show that the ILWU had been consistently labeled "Communist-dominated." Its leaders had been reviled as Communist sympathizers or Communists themselves. He pointed out that the ILWU constitution required that he, as a union officer, recognize Communists "as equal within the union, work with them and . . . defend their right to be Communists—all of which McLaughlin is biased and prejudiced against."

Gladstein agreed with Hall that Symonds' draft of the affidavit could be strengthened. It was, he said, "a little too labored and couched in more conclusionary phrasing than is necessary. . . . Lawyers are frequently prone to fall into legal straitjackets and thus miss a lot of meat that ought to go into such papers."

Gladstein advised Symonds to delete from the affidavit that part (page 6) which said that Hall "was or is a member of the Communist Party." He also questioned whether Symonds should even say that Charles Fujimoto, who had admitted the fact at a press conference called for that purpose, was a member of the Communist Party, or its chairman, or anything else in the Party. Why admit anything? Gladstein asked.

Gladstein also weighed the point of whether or not it would be a good idea to argue the motion of bias and prejudice against McLaughlin before the Ninth Circuit Court. From a public relations standpoint, he said, a setback would be serious; it would be construed as a "bad defeat" for Metzger.

On March 11, 1952, at his own request, McLaughlin was replaced as the Smith Act case judge. As the lawyers say, that made all arguments on the subject moot. McLaughlin said he asked to be relieved "in the best interests of the court" and not because he considered himself unqualified to hear the case.

While all this preliminary legal scrambling was going on, the ILWU was busy. The union examined the federal jury panel to find out all it could about prospective jurors for the Smith Act trial. These included three people from Molokai; George L. Butterfield, John W. Hoxie, and Charles T. Kawano. Hall told Regino Colotario, the ILWU business agent at Kulapuu, to find out as much as he could about the three—"the good, bad and indifferent"—so that the defense lawyers could decide if they should be permitted to serve. Hall asked Colotario to check such things as their fraternal organizations, their military records, what kind of books they read, their political views, and, naturally, what they thought of Hall and the ILWU. Hall had a special instruction for the case of Charles Kawano: find out if he was any relation to Jack Kawano.

The ILWU mounted a nationwide campaign to keep other unions informed. Jeff Kibre, who then represented the union in Washington, supplied the names and addresses of 250 union locals all over the country. Goldblatt sent each a pamphlet. "The real issue behind the indictments has been forced into the open," Goldblatt told them. He meant the union's claim that the federal government was out to destroy the ILWU.

The ILWU organized its home territory for all-out defense. Fujisaki was named territorial defense director. Hall thought he was gaining ground; community reaction was "constantly improving." Especially encouraging was the report that ILWU membership was "solid as ever." Hall confessed some fear in the beginning that his indictment might hurt; that union members might regard him with suspicion. But, according to Teddy Kreps, his arrest created "not a ripple on the rank and file."

The ILWU arranged testimonial dinners for Hall all over the

territory. Rania said he talked to ILWU members who told him: "Brother Rania, if [there's] a chance if Jack Hall go to jail, we can all go to jail, too? See if they can pick their pineapple and process cane then."

Hall wrote to trade unionists on the mainland to draw attention to the union's defense strategy. He spoke on the radio: "My almost seventeen years [in Hawaii] have been lived in a fishbowl. I am sure that I, more than any other individual, has had his activities watched, reported, documented and distorted. . . ."

There had been no question of his loyalty, he said, when Stainback appointed him to the War Labor Board and to the Honolulu Police Commission. As for overthrowing the government by force and violence: "If I were crazy enough to entertain such weird ideas, I would not be the regional director of this union—I would be a permanent resident of Kaneohe [State Hospital]. . . ."

It was obvious the case would go on for a long time. Hall told his sister, Mrs. Mildred Hall McIntyre, of Glendale, California, not to worry, "as it will be a hell of a time before any jail doors close upon me."

Goldblatt, who often played the role of prognosticator, analyzed Hall's indictment in the light of union-employer relations. He predicted the employers would say: "It's too bad Jack got himself into this mess. He's a nice guy, but he's got to take the consequences." Goldblatt also predicted the employers would assure the union that they didn't intend to take advantage of the situation, but he was not satisfied with a mere declaration of intent. He said Hall's indictment could not have been a surprise to the employers. Maybe they didn't pull the trigger, he said, but they helped load the gun.

Always quick to seek advantage, Goldblatt said Hall's indictment gave the Hawaii ILWU an opportunity to make demands of the employers. He said the ILWU should force them to issue a statement on their relationship with Hall and to appear as witnesses and testify on Hall's role in the union. "Where we can get up enough steam, we might even demand that the employers call on the Justice Department to leave industrial relations in Hawaii alone and drop the indictment."

CHAPTER 55

A Hunt for Legal Talent

McLaughlin was out; Metzger couldn't get reappointed to the bench; so who would be the judge to try the Smith Act case? For a time it seemed as though a mainland "importee" would get the assignment and then Jon Wiig, a Honolulu circuit court judge, was appointed to succeed Metzger.

Wiig was long and lanky, somber looking on the bench, with black hair and a pair of thick, energetic eyebrows. "The least Nordic looking Norseman I've ever seen," said Reinecke. He was, in Reinecke's words, "no legal gymnast."

Wiig was born in North Dakota and came to Hawaii in 1933. He was a former city and county attorney and had served as an officer in the navy. He was sworn in as Federal District Court judge on June 19, 1952; spent time on the mainland to familiarize himself with Smith Act cases; and talked to Judge Medina who had tried the New York case. In September 1952, Wiig took over his judiciary duties. He was ready for a siege, which is what the Smith Act trial turned out to be. "It was a pretty tense time," he called it.

Wiig was not Farrington's choice for the federal judgeship; Farrington preferred attorney Joseph Hodgson. He thought Wiig ought to stay on the circuit court bench. Allen didn't agree. Taking his cue from lawyer Russell Cades, Allen approved of Wiig. "He [Cades] likes both his knowledge of the law and his industry," Allen commented.

Nor was Wiig Jack Hall's choice for the job; Hall called Wiig "a reactionary" but conceded it would be hard to make a case against Wiig for bias and prejudice. "In fact, I think it is impossible from what we can recall thus far," said Hall.

Hall had a good memory (and the ILWU kept a complete file of clippings). He remembered Wiig from the 1946 election campaign. At that time Wiig was a candidate for the Territorial House from the Fourth District and publicly criticized federal negotiator Stanley V. White, the man who had declared that the sugar industry was not bargaining in good faith. Wiig said White ought to "go back to Washington where he belongs."

Hall also recalled that during the 1946 campaign Wiig opposed the "so-called radical unions." "We are the only one called radical and the only union of any consequence here so he must have meant us," said Hall.

In all this seriousness, two FBI agents helped provide a bit of comic relief. Richard Burress and James Condon, the two agents, called on David Thompson of the ILWU to pump him for information on Hall and the union. Burress and Thompson had one thing in common: they were both ex-marines. (According to Bridges, the FBI approached seventeen ILWU members during this period "to get our people to take a stand against the union.")

When they first came to Thompson's home on Ocean View Drive in Kaimuki on December 13, 1951, Thompson was not home. They saw him the next day and again on January 9, 1952. Thompson tipped off Hall and McElrath at once. It seemed like too good an opportunity to miss; they planned a little reception. McElrath moved the furniture around in Thompson's living room. He placed chairs for the FBI men so they would sit facing the radio console. He then planted a microphone in the radio and ran a wire out the window and down to a recording machine in the basement. Thus prepared, he, Thompson, and Teddy Kreps waited. The FBI men arrived on schedule. McElrath and Kreps scampered downstairs and shut the basement door. They sat and they listened. For comfort they had beer.

Thompson played his role like an actor. He encouraged the FBI men to talk and they were cooperative. One FBI man said: "We may be [J. Edgar] Hoover boys but we aren't selling [Hoover] vacuums. We don't want to give you the old Hoover treatment."

Much of the recorded conversation was gibberish, but one

point was clear: if Hall cooperated with them, he would be dropped as a Smith Act defendant. Said one agent:

> I mean, like you and I, we can talk all the year about Jack Hall, but we don't get anything accomplished. Same thing, he could be here and talk to us and we couldn't say, "Jack, if you so-and-so, we'll get the indictment dismissed." Or, "You won't have to go to trial; we'll back you to the hilt." What we could do would be to explain his position to the guy who regulates these indictments, who's going to press the thing and see if it couldn't be straightened out whereby it would be six instead of seven [defendants]. . . .

At one point an FBI agent asked Thompson what kind of a man Hall was. "Well, Jack is a guy as far as I'm concerned that's given the best part of his life for the labor movement," said Thompson.

> People say a hell of a lot of things about him, but I feel that Jack's honest, that he has given very freely of himself; he's a complex personality. . . . He's brilliant, works like a goddamn mule; gets more work done than any other six guys put together—and he's a rare thing. He's a great strike leader. . . .

At the second meeting Thompson told the FBI agents he had talked to Hall. Hall had told him he was certain the FBI knew he wasn't a Communist and that the FBI was trying to get him "to break the union."

"Oh, he's convinced of that, too, huh?" said one of the FBI men.

"Yeah," said Thompson, "and he said that you guys, you know everything that's going on around here and you know he's not a Communist." Thompson said Hall told him that the FBI wanted Hall and "that the other guys [the other six defendants] are 'window-dressing.' "

The FBI men concurred: Hall was indeed the prime target, they said. The other six defendants weren't in a league with Smith Act defendants on the mainland. "These would make poor Communists in the lowest cell in California but they're the guys who are the leaders of the Communist Party here and so we're stuck with them. . . ."

The words rolled onto the tape and McElrath sat down in the basement drinking his beer.

Even before he was indicted, Hall began to look around for local lawyers to help defend him. In late 1950 or early 1951 he talked to Vincent Esposito. How would he like to handle such a case?

Esposito told him he was only a novice and didn't think he could do a good job. "Furthermore, I was a kind of starving attorney [trying] to stay alive," he said to Hall. "I don't think I'm sophisticated enough politically to handle it."

Hall replied, "You can learn. You're a reader and you can learn. It isn't that complicated that you can't learn."

Esposito told Hall the Smith Act trial would take years—months of preparation, months of trial, months of appeal. It would be a life devoted to one case. It would cost a lot of money.

"How much?" said Hall.

"It would involve many tens of thousands of dollars for me to be your lawyer for two years, or three years," Esposito replied.

Then Hall explained that he did not intend for Esposito to be chief counsel. He meant to get a mainland lawyer to captain the ship. "Well," said Esposito, "I'm not sure that I want to be a cabin boy. . . ." Esposito declined the offer.

Hall even considered the man who had long been his adversary in labor negotiations: Wendell Carlsmith. He had come to admire Carlsmith. Carlsmith was like him in some ways. Both were hard workers; both could be ruthless. Both had hair-trigger minds. One day they met by appointment at Ciro's on Hotel Street. "Wendell," said Hall, "I want you to defend me."

Carlsmith was a Big Five lawyer. How could he defend in court a man of Hall's reputation charged with such a serious crime? As Carlsmith said to Hall, it was "not in the cards." In his practical lawyer's way he pointed out that he was building a law practice "which is quite adversary to you, and I am sure that the damage to my practice would last on into the next generation of my family."

To Hall that meant that Carlsmith thought he wouldn't be paid enough. He told Carlsmith the ILWU would make it worth his time. "We will pay you a fee that will make it unnecessary for you to practice. . . . We want you. I do! I want you," he said.

"Jack," Carlsmith replied. "I *can't* do it."

He did offer some free legal advice, however. He said that under no circumstances should Hall take the stand. "No one can take the witness stand, with the kind of public feeling there is in a case like yours, without getting into a legal perjury charge," he said. "They'd nail you on something; you unintentionally would make a mistake and they'd nail you." Hall said he had already got the same advice from his own lawyers.

Carlsmith told Hall to admit his Communist background. "And I would have done it all over the territory, in public," he said to Hall:

> Couple that with what I knew: that you had divorced yourself from the Communist movement. . . . Every juror in that box would have had the knowledge that you had renounced the Party. That would have been the best evidence. You have a perfect right to make these statements.

CHAPTER **56**
The Cross-Examiner

Gladstein, the chief defense counsel in the Hawaii Smith Act case, had a voice he could play like an organ. He knew how to organize a defense in court; he was a "master cross-examiner." He called the signals; he was the "quarterback."

Gladstein had been co–chief counsel in the New York Smith

Act case in 1949. At the conclusion of the trial, Judge Medina ordered all the defense attorneys to jail for contempt of court. Gladstein served six months (less one month off for good behavior) in the federal penitentiary at Texarkana, Texas.[1]

Symonds said "all the decisions were made by Richie." The other defense lawyers would express their views, he said, "but Richie ultimately was the one who made the final decisions as to what strategy should be used and tactics because, first of all, he had the support of all the defendants with the exception of Hall, when Hall wanted to disagree. . . ."

Hall hadn't wanted Gladstein to handle the case in view of the notoriety of the New York case and Gladstein's jail sentence. Moreover, he still harbored resentment against Gladstein for the fee that Gladstein's firm had collected in the Fair Labor Standards Act case of 1945–1946. Gladstein came into the Smith Act case knowing Hall opposed him:

> I knew also that Jack had broken with the other defendants for whom he had developed an ill-concealed disdain; and they, in turn, regarded him with open distrust. Indeed, Jack wanted in the worst way to have his trial severed from the others; inasmuch as the judge would not grant such a request, Jack tried to separate himself from the others by his observable conduct.

Gladstein said Hall wanted to focus the case on a trade union defense of himself and do away with politics. "Poor man!" said Gladstein.

> His was a tragically difficult position to be in, mainly because a political trial cannot be effectively or honorably defended by contending that it is non-political. It was my responsibility to provide a full and complete defense against the government's case which undeniably was a political case in every conceivable aspect. . . .
>
> Jack's behavior at that point in his life reflected a seething inner conflict between himself and others, between himself and his past, with a frustration that he felt at the helplessness in which he was be-

---

1. He was released from prison on September 30, 1952.

ing placed, at his rage with former close friends who had betrayed him and with their accusations and subsequent testimony.

Gladstein didn't want to take the case. It was Bridges who talked him into it. The ILWU also hired another experienced lawyer from the mainland, Abraham Lincoln Wirin of Los Angeles, to round out the team of Gladstein and Bouslog & Symonds. Wirin was general counsel for the American Civil Liberties Union for Southern California. Hall asked Symonds what the legal fees would be.[2] Symonds guessed the trial would last three months and cost about $25,000. He advised Hall to set up a budget of, say, $50,000 to pay for the cost of the trial.[3]

As the date of trial approached, McLaughlin moved to debar Gladstein from practicing in federal court because of his jail sentence. Now the defense had to shift its strategy momentarily from a defense of the Hawaii Seven to a defense of Gladstein.

Symonds said McLaughlin had known for six months previously that Gladstein was the attorney of record for the defense but the judge had done nothing "until the eve of the trial." For a while it seemed as though Gladstein was lost to the defense, and Symonds said they were prepared to go to trial "with or without counsel [Gladstein]."[4]

Bridges lent a hand to keep Gladstein on the case. He asked a confidant (whom he did not name) to talk to "certain people in the territory." The unnamed friend pointed out that the trial would have "an extremely bad effect" on island union-employer relations and upon industrial stability.

Hall cleared the deck. He assigned Andrew Salz, an ILWU

---

2. Reinecke said the ILWU paid most of the legal costs. An ad hoc committee, headed by his wife Aiko, collected a few thousand dollars. "It was ninety-nine percent a defense of Jack Hall," said Reinecke.

3. A Bouslog & Symonds report said the ILWU spent $109,970.15 from January 1, 1953, to December 13, 1953, alone. This included $86,521.90 for legal fees and costs. The trial began November 5, 1952; a verdict was reached June 19, 1953.

4. Gladstein was ordered in September 1952 to show cause why he should not be disbarred, but the show cause order was postponed until after the trial so as not to prejudice the defense's case.

research associate and International representative, to handle some of his union chores. Hall prepared the union membership for the trial. "A bunch of Lochinvars from out of the East are going to prosecute us and try to convince a jury that we should go to jail for five years and pay some outlandish fine," he said.

He harped on one theme: that he *and* the ILWU were on trial. He pointed to the union's record, as he saw it:

> We like to think, and we are sure most honest people will agree, that the great changes that have come about in our islands during the last two decades have come about largely because of what the working people have done through the ILWU.

Starting with the preliminary motions and on through the trial, the defense tried to separate the ILWU from the alleged conspiracy. Symonds said Hall wanted the defense to be solely a defense of the ILWU. Whatever the other defendants did had to be tied in with protecting the union. "And if they said anything or did anything that was not in that direction," then it was harmful to what Hall considered the government's prime target: "namely, to get the ILWU."

In other words, said Symonds, while the ILWU wasn't named in the indictment, Hall was. Hall's name was synonymous with the ILWU, "and he felt it was very important from a public relations standpoint—no one expected these [preliminary] motions to be granted—to publicize the fact that Jack Hall [was] saying, 'Look, the ILWU has nothing to do with this damned conspiracy.' "

The government also tried to build a strong team of prosecutors, but it had to deal first with a matter of internal politics. On hand for the case from the beginning were Hoddick and a special assistant, Rex A. McKittrick. Hoddick, a young Harvard Law School graduate, handled the preliminaries. He was then acting United States Attorney for Hawaii and hoped to get a full appointment, but soon he had a competitor for the job, A. William Barlow, a former navy officer.

Barlow and Hoddick fought briskly for the United States Attorney's job. Barlow had support from the Democratic National Committee; Hoddick, from the Justice Department. The struggle went on a long time and the two developed a distaste for each other.[5] When Barlow was finally confirmed on May 29, 1952, Hoddick had been acting United States Attorney for nearly a year and a half and had devoted much of his time to preparation of the Smith Act case.

Despite his personal feelings about Hoddick, Barlow agreed that Hoddick should continue to work on the case, but he added a proviso. He considered the case of such importance that he thought the Justice Department should bring in at least one of the department's major prosecutors—someone "thoroughly familiar with tactics employed by Communist defense in cases before [Judge] Medina." Barlow did not want Hoddick to be the chief prosecutor; he suggested instead someone who had handled the prosecution in the Los Angeles Smith Act case.

Hoddick agreed to carry on as special assistant. "I was deep enough in the case that I could not readily be replaced," he said.

Acceding to Barlow's request, the Justice Department appointed a New York lawyer, John C. Walsh, to be the chief prosecuting attorney for the Smith Act case, and another special assistant, Thomas Mitchell, was added to round out the prosecution's team. Walsh was then forty-seven, a veteran courtroom lawyer: handsome, pleasant, but not especially industrious. Reporter Keyes Beech talked to him. "His [Walsh's] reluctance to talk about the trial is matched only by his readiness to talk about himself," Beech wrote.[6]

Allen approved of Walsh's appointment and even took some of the credit for it. Both he and Farrington had tried to impress

---

5. "Barlow and I had been having a very stiff competition for the presidential appointment," said Hoddick. "I don't think we were very trustful of each other." Barlow agreed.

6. "The government attorneys caused me considerable concern," said Wiig. "Jack Walsh . . . very attractive man, a moderately good trial lawyer, but he wasn't in Gladstein's class. I knew that Jack Walsh came down here for the purpose of getting a conviction whether errors were made or no errors were made. . . . I had to watch carefully that no reversible error would be in the record."

the Justice Department "on the urgent need for such an appointment." Said Allen: "The convictions in the California red cases[7] show that with intelligence, skilled and persistent prosecution, these 'second stringers' can be caught in the mesh of their own intrigues."

The teams of lawyers were chosen; the thicket of motions was cleared away; the preliminaries were over. Wiig was on the bench. First, he had to reconsider McLaughlin's previous rulings and three other defense motions: (1) the attack on the makeup of the trial jury panel; (2) a motion for a change of venue (removal of the trial to another island, where, according to the defense, "hysteria" did not prevail); and (3) a plea for additional peremptory challenges. Wiig granted seven additional challenges; he denied the other motions.

Hall looked over the defense team—Gladstein and Wirin, Bouslog and Symonds—and pronounced them "a formidable array of legal talent." He studied the jury panel. "If the final jury drawn is half-way decent," he said, "we will probably have a fair chance of coming out okay. Community reaction is good and I think that we have a great deal of real support even though it is not too vocal outside the union ranks."

---

7. *United States* v. *Yates* et al.

CHAPTER **57**

The Seven-Month Siege

Not since the celebrated Massie case twenty years ago has any trial commanded such wide interest in these islands. For the "big wheel" among the defendants is burly, bespectacled Jack W. Hall . . . Hawaii boss of the ILWU.
—Keyes Beech in the *Chicago Daily News,*
September 2, 1952

Fourteen months after the arrests of the seven Smith Act defendants, their trial began in the high-ceilinged courtroom on the Diamond Head side of the third floor in the old Federal Building in Honolulu. In muggy weather, it took three days to pick the all-male jury.

In the beginning, before the strain of the seven-month-long trial set in, the atmosphere was Hawaiian-style and relaxed: "one may almost say, [an atmosphere] of informality." Gladstein marveled. He thought of the Smith Act trial in New York where four hundred policemen surrounded the building and every witness was guarded. In Honolulu spectators drifted in and out; they wore aloha shirts. Reinecke saw one man, wearing an orange-colored T-shirt, whose belly "cascaded over his belt buckle."

Walsh opened. He said the case was a giant "jigsaw puzzle," but that he would fit all the pieces together and show there was a "huge partnership in crime." He said the conspiracy extended "its branches or tentacles" all over the mainland and to the Hawaiian Islands. Walsh said Hall was not being tried because he was an ILWU official, but "on one issue and one issue alone"—violation of the Smith Act. He said the government would prove that Hall was a Communist Party member, a member of the Party's Executive Board, "and as such directed its activities in these islands."

In his opening statement, Symonds said "whether or not Jack was a member of the Communist Party has nothing to do with the charge. . . . As you know, the Communist Party of the United States is a legal party." Symonds continued: "We will show that every action taken by Jack Hall was for the exclusive purpose and with the only intent of improving and bettering conditions of the union members."

In large measure, the government built its case on the writings of Communist leaders. The prosecution contended that the overthrow of democratic states by force and violence was replete in Communist written works; that the defendants knew it and subscribed to it. Thus a large part of the testimony consisted of readings from Marx and Engels, Lenin and Stalin; many names cropped up that were unfamiliar in Kakaako: Kautsky, Trachtenberg, Kerensky, Zinoviev.

"When Walsh begins reading from Lenin and Stalin, the jury slumps back in weary resignation as he stumbles along like nobody they have heard since they listened to their high school schoolmates," Reinecke observed. On the days Walsh read from Communist writings, the courtroom had seats to spare. One day, within Reinecke's hearing, Walsh asked Wirin: "How long do you have to read this stuff to read it intelligently?"

Paul Crouch was the first government witness. He had formerly been a member of the Communist Party, had dropped out, and now testified as to the nature and goals of communism. The prosecution presented several such witnesses from the mainland: Crouch, John Lautner, and Daisy Cadan Van Dorn, an elderly woman whom Reinecke called "somebody out of 'Arsenic and Old Lace.' "[1]

The sessions went on most of the day. Hall was grateful for the recesses and for delays because they helped him catch up on his union work. He found it hard to attend court all day and do union business at night and in spare moments. He left home at 6 AM. His wife drove him to the ILWU office and he would get in a

---

1. Goldblatt called them "trained cobras."

couple of hours' work before he had to go to court at ten. It was a grueling life. Yoshiko Hall recalled: "It was certainly no party; meeting with the membership and keeping the union together when he thought the trial would split them. . . . I don't know how I survived it or how Jack survived it."

Day after deadening day, the trial went on. "The case is dragging along," said Hall.

Izuka was the third prosecution witness and now spectator seats were at a premium. Izuka was working as a chicken farmer on Kauai. He testified he first met Hall in 1937 when Hall and George Goto came to Kauai to help the longshoremen who had struck Kauai Terminals. Symonds, on cross-examination, sought to make the point that Hall had made use of the Communist Party as a means to help the cause of labor.

Question:	Mr. Izuka, while you were in the Communist Party on Kauai, the business part of the Communist Party meetings was spent in connection with improving labor conditions and building a strong union, is that not so?
Izuka:	I say that in the early stages, it is correct.
Question:	Now Mr. Izuka, is it not a fact that you didn't tell the members on Kauai that you were a member of the Communist Party because to disclose your membership might weaken the union and the employers might start attacking the union?
Izuka:	Yes, partly *[sic]* is correct.

When the defense wanted to know what he was paid to testify, Izuka said: $19.95 for air fare from Kauai; $6 for taxi fare from Port Allen to Lihue; the regular $4 witness fee; and $5 a day for food and lodging.

Hall was not impressed by Izuka. His testimony was a repeat of the recitation in "The Truth about Communism in Hawaii." "The judge wouldn't let us go into who paid him what, etc., except that we did get confirmation that [attorney] Arthur Smith gave him $1490," said Hall. He then summarized one of his main objectives:

> Everytime we have tried to get the ILWU on trial—and that's whenever we get the least semblance of an opening—the prosecution objects like hell and the judge sustains the government. It is obvious that the government is going to steer clear of the union and any of its activities.
>
> I have been trying to force the attorneys to get in a position to file a motion for mistrial so as to place the judge clearly and publicly on the prosecution's side, but all the lawyers except Harriet seem most reluctant to join the issue.

The opportunity came when Lautner, the government witness, testified. He said the Communist Party's purpose was to gain control of basic industries so that "in a national crisis, the Party would be in a position to paralyze the nation's economy." Gladstein and Wirin moved to strike the testimony from the record; Wiig denied the motion.

Thereupon Gladstein, Wirin, and Symonds, speaking in that order, called for a mistrial. They pointed out that the ILWU was the labor force in the basic industries in Hawaii and that Hall was the ILWU regional director. Hence, according to the Lautner theorem, Hall had control of the basic industries; he was a classic example of what Lautner called the Communist Party's "concentration policy." That policy, if Lautner was to be believed, was to "seize the basic industries in the islands" and "paralyze the economy. . . ."

Wiig denied the motion for a mistrial. Hall, in exasperation, claimed that the defense lawyers had mishandled the motion:

> I vigorously opposed the strategy, which was simply a maneuver that backfired and effectively estopped an overall motion for mistrial, tying in the judge and developing our basic theme that there can't be a fair trial in a Smith Act trial and that it is wired from the judge down. Harriet strongly supported my position and in fact was as vehement as I. Sy [Symonds], too, supported my position, but not too vigorously.

Hall issued a statement saying that Wiig's denial of the motion for a mistrial convinced him that a fair trial was impossible:

Judge Wiig is permitting the prosecution to seek my conviction and that of my co-defendants not on anything I or they ever said or did, but on what paid informers, imported from the mainland, say members of the Communist Party on the mainland, unknown to me, said or did. . . .

But if Hall saw Wiig as a judge who was too hard on the defense, Riley Allen saw Wiig as a judge who was too lenient. "Judge Wiig has at times shown a surprising readiness to yield to arguments or appeals of the defense," he told Farrington. He believed Wiig was leaning backward "to avoid a possible reversal." The defense lawyers were articulate and resourceful, Allen said, and they were "backed by writers and a radio commentator."[2]

Allen thought the defense team functioned smoothly. Hall, however, spoke of the rifts that had opened up: "There is pretty pronounced disagreement now on the conduct of the trial—even among the lawyers." In Hall's opinion, "Richie [Gladstein] is getting very difficult and, of course, most of the defendants hero-worship him and defer to his judgment—which in some situations is tinged with the romantic. . . ."

Gladstein had leased a house on Black Point Road in Kahala and every night he reviewed the case and planned the next day's work. Almost every Sunday he held a strategy meeting which the defendants and lawyers attended. At first Hall did not come; later he came as often as union work allowed him to.

"Gladstein was a guy who would lay out the play for the whole week at the Sunday meetings at Black Point," said Koji Ariyoshi. He explained Gladstein's *modus operandi:* "He had a loose-leaf binder. 'We're here at this point in the trial. I'm going to raise this question. I'm going to raise this objection on Monday. Wiig is against me so I can do little. Al [Wirin], you stand up and make this objection. I'm going to cite this.' "

Hall seldom spoke to any of the other defendants. "He'd walk in [the courtroom] and he'd walk out," said Symonds.

---

2. Morris Watson, *ILWU Dispatcher* editor, wrote a daily running story on the trial. McElrath attended daily.

"And he'd talk to Gladstein—alone. And everybody else was just like sheep." Reinecke agreed that Hall was cool toward the others. "He was looking at it from a different point of view than the rest of us," said Reinecke.

> He looked at it from the point of view of a man who had the responsibility for the major union in Hawaii. A man who is not going to turn his back on his pals, but who is no longer a Communist. . . .
>
> In his heart, he was not an anti-Communist. [But] I think he had had too many substantial differences with the Communist leadership on the West Coast. . . . I think that he felt that the Communist Party meddled too much with union affairs.

Reinecke studied the defense lawyers as thought he were studying a book. He thought Gladstein was extremely effective, though "a little doctrinaire." Wirin was dedicated, but "not a good courtroom lawyer." Symonds had good rapport. Harriet Bouslog? "She tends to talk too much," said Reinecke. The defense deliberately kept her out of court.[3]

Ariyoshi said Hall wanted to isolate himself from the other defendants. "He played it cool toward me," said Ariyoshi. "He didn't want to talk to me at first. He had already split from the [Communist] Party. . . . He thought the membership [of the ILWU] wouldn't understand the Communist issue. He was afraid they wouldn't support him."[4]

Wiig walked a tightrope. He made it a point not to go anywhere because he was sure to be harassed. The Smith Act trial was the topic of the day. "We went to a cocktail party at Ike Sutton's," said Wiig, "and everybody was talking about the trial. 'I hope they hang the sons of bitches,' they said. It got to be embarrassing. I'd walk down Merchant Street to M's Coffee Shop. 'Get them bastards, Jon,' somebody would shout."

Wiig said he had no trouble with the defense lawyers. "I al-

---

3. Bouslog agreed that her job was limited primarily to research. She resented not being allowed in court. "None of them would let me say a goddamned thing," she protested. "Oh, the male chauvinists."

4. Koji Ariyoshi said: "The Smith Act did a very good thing for Hall. Up to then people had a better image of Kawano than of Hall."

ways had a high regard for Myer Symonds," he said. "Gladstein was under wraps at that time. . . . He had just finished serving [time] in jail. He used decorum. He [was] extremely competent. Wirin—I'd have to slap down a little. . . . Sometimes he talked a little too much. I never let anybody get out of control."

On Sunday, December 14, 1952, Hall and Harriet Bouslog talked to union members at Honokaa on the Big Island about the Smith Act trial. The trial didn't make much sense to the average ILWU member: he figured the courts were out to get Hall. Hall urged Bouslog to forget legal terms and talk to them in simple English. He gave her some advice: "Look, Harriet, you're always talking in language that the workers don't understand. . . . We want these people to understand. We want to give them an idea what's going on in the trial. Try to talk in a way they'll understand."

Bouslog said she would try. She spoke for a rousing half hour, but of all the things she said three sentences were memorable because they haunted her for years and almost ended her legal career. She said at Honokaa the following:

> There is no such thing as a fair trial in a Smith Act case. All rules of evidence . . . have to be scrapped or the government can't make a case. . . . They just make up rules as they go along.

Hall liked the speech. He thought it had a nice ring to it. He hugged her.

In the crowd, unobserved by Bouslog, was a reporter, Yoshio "Yosh" Matsuoka, of the *Hilo Tribune-Herald*. He took notes and wrote a story.

On December 16 Wiig summoned Harriet Bouslog to court and asked her: "Did you say that some rather shocking things and horrible things were going on in this trial? . . . Did you say that all rules of evidence have to be scrapped or the government can't make a case and just make up the rules as they go along, or words to that effect?"

Bouslog nervously replied that she had merely paraphrased for the laymen the rules of evidence, and she proclaimed her innocence: "I think there is not one word of what I said at

Honokaa that in any way . . . shows contempt for this court; that my remarks were directed, as I said, primarily to the conduct of the prosecution in the Smith Act case. . . .''

Wiig was not appeased. He ordered United States Attorney Barlow to investigate the case. Bouslog's troubles had begun.

CHAPTER **58**

Witness Takes the Stand

Kawano told the same story to the Smith Act jury that he had told in Washington to the House Un-American Activities Committee. Then there was just one spectator—Chuck Mau. Now Kawano was home, speaking to the entire community about Hall, who watched him with hard-set mouth from twenty feet away. A reporter wrote: "He was not the same scowling, chip-on-the-shoulder waterfront organizer they called 'Silent Jack.' It was an older man whose story, told in a firm, low monotone, broken here and there by long pauses, had the quality of reminiscence.''

Kawano recalled how Bill Bailey came to town in 1937 and called the meeting in his room on Emma Street to organize the Communist Party of Hawaii. He told about George Goto who introduced him to Jack Kimoto and how Kimoto said he had been sent to Hawaii from the West Coast to set up Communist cells. He related how the Party went out of business during the war and was reborn late in 1945. He talked about how Hall gave instructions to infiltrate and take over the Democratic Party.

He went into detail on the visit of Archie Brown, the San Francisco Communist, who came to Hawaii in 1948 and pressed the Party "to come out in the open" and take credit for the advance of unionism. He quoted Brown as saying to him: "I have heard quite a bit about you. I want you to know that it is not all good. . . . It is guys like you, Hall and McElrath who are the guys sabotaging the progress of the Communist Party in Hawaii. . . ."

Kawano said he replied that Hall was doing more good for the Party and more good for the union "than anyone of the other people outside the labor movement and all of them put together."

He told of Hall's disagreement with the Communist Party, which had been "riding herd on him," and how, early in 1949, Hall had gone to the mainland for a showdown. He said Hall had come back "in a very happy mood" and told him that it was "all ironed out."

He discussed the longshore strike and repeated his accusation that in 1949 the Communist Party wanted to take the sugar workers out on strike, too, but that he had rejected the idea. After he had his lengthy say Gladstein took over and Kawano sat through nine days of cross-examination.

Gladstein directed his attention to 1949 and Kawano's quarrel with Hall. Kawano admitted he had "the beef with Hall" and said he had discussed it with a number of ILWU men: Joseph Akana, Julian Napuunoa, Ben Kahaawinui, Simeon Bagasol, and Frank Kalua.

"And you told them that the reason was because you wanted to take fourteen cents, whereas Hall held out for twenty cents. Isn't that right?" said Gladstein.

"Absolutely not," said Kawano.

Kawano said the reason for the "very, very great disagreement" with Hall was that Hall was "not trying to settle the strike in favor of the men, but in favor of the Communist Party."

Question: Is that so?

Answer: That is correct.

Question: In other words, at the end of 1949, you had the union's interests at heart, didn't you?

Answer:	I did.
Question:	You didn't think Mr. Hall had the union's interest at heart, did you?
Answer:	Sometimes I did not.

Gladstein accused Kawano of being a slacker during the 1949 strike; he said often the union couldn't find him.

Question:	They knew you were shooting pool?
Answer:	I shoot pool once in a while.
Question:	They knew you were playing golf instead of taking care of their grievances.
Answer:	I played golf once in a while. I shoot pool once in a while, and once in a while I played poker. Just like Jack Hall.

Gladstein asked Kawano about a meeting in August 1950 between Kawano and Timothy Flynn, CIO regional director for Northern California. Kawano said he had turned down an invitation from Flynn to work for the CIO.

Question:	You did state [to Flynn] that it was necessary to get rid of Hall. Didn't you?
Answer:	I stated it was necessary to try to eliminate Communist influence in the union.
Question:	You said he was a Communist.
Answer:	I did say that.
Question:	And you said it was necessary to eliminate Jack Hall in the union?
Answer:	As he followed the Communist line, yes.
Question:	This is what you told them?
Answer:	I told them that.

Under Gladstein's prodding Kawano said the 1949 strike was not Communist inspired: it had broken out simply over wages, he said. On re-cross-examination, Gladstein asked: "Didn't

[Hall] tell you that when you made a statement . . . about the union taking direction from the Communist Party that you were talking through your hat?''

''He never did,'' said Kawano.

''Didn't he say that that was slander to the union to say that the Communist Party ran it?''

''He did not.''[1]

The defendants did not take the witness stand. Their lawyers said they would be held in contempt of court if they refused to answer questions that would implicate others as members of the Communist Party. Kimoto and Ariyoshi wanted at least one of the defendants to explain what the Communist Party had been trying to achieve in Hawaii. If no one took the stand, said Kimoto, then union members would think the Communist Party had done something to be ashamed of and had something to hide.

Hall didn't want any of them to take the stand; he felt there was ''tremendous danger'' if they did.[2] Reinecke said only one person was qualified to take the stand: Hall. Reinecke opposed the idea of Charles Fujimoto, the Party chairman, testifying. He said Fujimoto had no prestige in the community and would ''just repeat clichés and make a bad impression.''

As the bulwark of its case, the defense called on fifty witnesses, more than half of them character witnesses. It was no problem getting people such as Senators J. B. Fernandes and John G. Duarte to testify. They were Hall's friends; they owed their political careers to him and to the ILWU. The problem was

---

1. Kawano never changed his mind.

2. Symonds said: ''As soon as a defendant got to the stand, the first question on cross-examination would be . . . 'What cell did you belong to? Name everybody who was a member of the cell.' And the court would order it to be answered because it would all be part of the conspiracy.

''And also it would mean that you would have to name every person in the islands that had any identification with the Communist Party . . . and if they refused to answer on the grounds that it didn't have anything to do with the case, then they were subject to contempt.''

getting people in The Establishment who knew Hall to testify in his behalf. Hall made the request of Neil Cadagan, the Hawaiian Pineapple Company vice-president.

"To what effect do I testify?" Cadagan asked.

"You'll answer questions about my character," said Hall.

"Don't forget you told me that you were a member of the Communist Party," Cadagan reminded Hall.

"I know that," said Hall. "It doesn't matter in this case. It's conspiracy to take over the government by force and violence and I have never been guilty of that."

Cadagan talked it over with his family. He had two sons at Punahou, a private school. "They were scared they would be crucified in school," said Cadagan. He dropped by Hall's office to tell him he couldn't testify.

"I'm sorry," said Hall, "but I understand."

Hall asked J. B. Guard of McCabe stevedoring company to testify and Guard agreed. Symonds briefed Guard on what he would be asked. Guard testified that he had known Hall for twelve or thirteen years and that Hall's reputation for honesty, integrity, and loyalty to the government was good. Guard said he had heard people call Hall a Communist and that he had been present when Hall's name came up, and "they probably called him every name in the book."

Mayor Wilson testified that Hall's reputation for loyalty was good. He said that Hall led 20,000 or 25,000 union members. "You mean to tell me that they wouldn't know that he is loyal?" said Wilson. "If he was disloyal, they would let him go. . . . I know in politics the moment a man makes a slip, he is only a one-timer. . . . They are watching you. You make a slip, they desert you."

Wilson said Hall had accomplished something Wilson himself had tried to do since 1911 and had failed—that is, organize labor in Hawaii. "He came along and he does what I was unable to do. So I take my hat off to him."

Willie Crozier, the gadfly of Hawaiian politics, put on a coat and tie and came to court to testify in behalf of Hall and Ariyoshi. Crozier said that by making collective bargaining work, Hall had carried out "Christian principles." As a result, he said, "the plantation worker doesn't have to take his hat off when he sees the boss now. The plantation worker can stand up like a man."

Attorney Charles M. Hite testified that Hall's reputation as to honesty and integrity was excellent, but "so far as his loyalty is concerned, my testimony must be negative in that I have heard every epithet known to man applied to Jack Hall throughout the community."

Anthony C. Baptiste, Jr., the Kauai County chairman, said Hall was honest and Hall's word was good. Senator Duarte said, "I feel he is a good citizen of the territory." J. B. Fernandes called Hall "an honest man and a square-shooter."

The defense tried to put the two talkative FBI men, Burress and Condon, on the stand and play "The FBI Tapes" of their chats with David Thompson. Wiig ruled that such evidence wasn't relevant.

In rebuttal the government sought adverse character witnesses, but Barlow and the FBI agents had trouble getting them.[3] "The Big Five were quaking in their boots over Hall," said Barlow.

Hall welcomed the testimony of any adverse character witness—Gladstein would get a chance to cross-examine them. Hall knew who two of them would be: Stainback and Samuel Wilder King. Stainback was eager to testify against Hall, but King was reluctant. He demanded first to see a list of Democrats who would testify against Hall.

---

3. The following declined to testify as adverse witnesses: attorney William B. Cobb (indicated it wouldn't be a good idea to get involved); Senator Wilfred C. Tsukiyama (pleaded the pressure of work in the closing days of legislature); attorney Russell Cades (never heard the defendants' reputations discussed); Mary Noonan, Oahu County Republican Committee chairman (did not want to testify); realtor Mitsuyuki Kido (could not testify as to the defendants' loyalty); Representative Yasutaka Fukushima (among his friends Hall had a good reputation for loyalty); Assistant Public Prosecutor Spark M. Matsunaga (had heard nothing about the reputation of the defendants); attorney Hiram L. Fong (his partners thought it best for him not to testify either for the prosecution or for Hall).

Barlow and Stephenson, chairman of the Hawaii Commission on Subversive Activities, called on King's son, Samuel P. King, president of the Bar Association of Hawaii. The son talked to the father. Young Sam King said his father always "referred anything legal" to him. He advised his father of "the parameters of the thing," and Governor King then made up his own mind to testify.

An FBI agent called on Jack Burns, then director of the Office of Civilian Defense, and asked him to testify. Burns said: "Okay, just expect me to answer the questions honestly. I've never lied on the witness stand yet. It's not gonna start now." Asked to explain, Burns said that during World War II, when he was working in police intelligence, he was told that Hall was "one helluva American."[4] The prosecution did not call Burns.

The FBI asked Judge Alva B. Steadman, president of Cooke Trust Company, to testify against Hall. Steadman said he had known Hall for years and if he were subpoenaed he would testify favorably for Hall. The prosecution did not call him. (When Hall asked Steadman to testify in his behalf, he declined.)

The FBI interviewed Captain Jack Bertram, manager of Kauai Terminals. Bertram said he would have to talk to his two bosses: American Factors and Alexander & Baldwin. (Each owned fifty percent of the stock in Kauai Terminals.) Chauncey B. Wightman, A & B vice-president, told Bertram he could testify, but, to his surprise, George Sumner, president of Amfac, said no. Sumner thought if Bertram testified against Hall, the ILWU would shut down the Kauai docks in reprisal.

The FBI called on disc jockey Hal "Aku" Lewis. Lewis was in a bind: he traveled in two different circles. One was made up of employers who believed Hall was disloyal; another was made up of newspapermen who believed Hall was loyal. Lewis said he didn't think he would make a good witness with that sort of background. The government didn't call on him.

The FBI, as well as Hall, asked Cadagan to testify. He said,

---

4. By Robert L. Shivers, the FBI chief; by L. Q. McComas, director of the Territorial Department of Labor; and by Colonels George W. Bicknell and Kendall J. Fielder of army intelligence.

"If I get on the stand I'll say . . . that [Hall] was always meticulous about keeping his word." The prosecution did not call on him.

The government recalled J. B. Guard who earlier had testified that Hall's reputation for loyalty was good. When Guard walked into the courtroom, the prosecution lawyers looked jubilant; they considered it a victory. The defense lawyers, who had no inkling he was coming back, looked worried and angry. As an adverse character witness, Guard testified that Hall's reputation for honesty and integrity was "above reproach." But, he said, judging from what he had heard around town, Hall's reputation as to loyalty was bad.

Under cross-examination, Guard said that people had castigated him for speaking out in Hall's behalf the first time around. "This is Moscow," one caller taunted him. Guard said he had discussed his original testimony four times[5] with Barlow and with McCabe's lawyer, Arthur Smith. He had read the transcript of his testimony, he said, and had decided to amplify it. The defense said pressure had been brought to bear on him to change his testimony.

Governor King testified that Hall's reputation for loyalty to the government was bad. "I consider that as a citizen he is not a very good citizen," said King. "That he does not seem to believe in the American system of democracy."[6]

Stainback testified that Hall's reputation for loyalty was "very bad." Stainback said the series of ILWU strikes in the 1940s "followed the Communist pattern, to keep a disrupted economy."

Gladstein asked Stainback if he hated Hall. "Not personally," said Stainback, "except that, if I think that a man was a

---

5. On April 14, 17, and 18 and on May 4, 1953.

6. Allen told Farrington that King's testimony resulted in "an immediate wave of favorable comment—notably among businessmen." Farrington replied that King had shown "real courage and leadership." He wrote Allen: "You will be interested to know that this comes as a result of your telephone call reporting to me your conversation with Bill Barlow in which he told you the prosecution was having difficulty on obtaining competent witnesses for the case. I communicated this to the president of the Bar Association [Samuel P. King], who, in turn, has been very active in meeting this problem."

traitor to this country, then I certainly don't have any love for that reason.''

Louis LeBaron, an associate justice of the Territorial Supreme Court, testified that feeling in the community against Hall and the ILWU started to heat up during the 1946 sugar strike and came to a boil during the days of the Reluctant 39. Nolle R. Smith, assistant director of tax research for the Chamber of Commerce of Hawaii, and Nils Tavares, former territorial attorney general, both testified that Reinecke's reputation for loyalty was bad. Since both knew Hall well, he couldn't understand why they didn't testify about him.

Businessman-politician Frank Fasi testified against Charles Fujimoto. Symonds offered to show that Fasi knew Hall best of all the defendants. If that was so, said Wiig, why didn't he testify about Hall's reputation?

Walsh, the chief prosecutor, replied that it was up to the government to decide against whom any character witness they summoned would testify.

On cross-examination, Gladstein asked Fasi if he had not taken part in strikebreaking during the 1949 strike. Fasi said, ''I can say unqualifiedly, no.''

Question: Did you not rent some equipment . . . to unload strikebound cargo on a vessel here?

Answer: No, I don't think so. . . .

Question: Did you tell Mr. Hoddick that you thought it would be good publicity for you in your political aspirations to be a witness here?

Answer: No, as a matter of fact . . . I told them that, no, that testifying, I realized, might kill me politically. The same thing I told the FBI in 1951, that I realized that my political future was at stake, and, realizing that, I was still willing to testify.

Listening to the adverse witnesses, Hall concluded the employers had laid down a policy not to get involved in the case. ''They have decided that no one officially connected with any of the firms where we have contracts or any of the agencies will testify against us," he said.

Instead they are cooperating with the prosecution to the fullest extent by getting prominent witnesses over whom they have complete control to appear. At the same time they are careful not to have a witness to testify against me who might open the door to a re-hash of industrial relations in Hawaii. . . .

"Nolle Smith knows me intimately for many years," said Hall,

yet testifies against Reinecke because over the years he has been a GOP Vitousek machine man[7] and a Chamber of Commerce . . . man since before the 1949 strike.

C. Nils Tavares testifies against Reinecke even though he can't remember the occasion he says he met him. He knows me intimately and personally for fifteen years and we have had plenty of battles.

Frank Fasi testifies against . . . Fujimoto to avoid being cross-examined. . . .

---

7. Roy A. Vitousek, for many years Speaker of the Territorial House of Representatives.

CHAPTER 59

A One-Dollar Bet

Almost two months before the Smith Act trial closed, the ILWU began to prepare its members for bad news. The union said the government had no case against Hall. The trial was an "antilabor vendetta," it said, but chances for an acquittal were slim. An ILWU memorandum said: "We should begin now preparing ourselves and our ranks for the worst, to the end that we can come out fighting—fighting mad."[1]

It took twelve and a half days for the opposing teams of lawyers to sum up. Hoddick spoke for almost ten hours in a two-day period and he got a sore throat. In his summation, Gladstein

> leaned on the lectern and chatted with the jurors, shouted at them, whispered to them, winked conspiratorially at them, and squinted at them.
>
> He rapped his knuckles on the lectern, dragged it across the floor, abandoned it, wrote on a blackboard, sneered at the prosecutors, fingered his mustache, bounced, paced the floor and lectured on the law.

During the lengthy arguments, Wiig felt a pain in the chest and was afraid he might collapse on the bench. During recess he lay down on a couch in his chambers. "I was scared," he said. He had his chest X-rayed and the pain eased. But as a precaution, when he started to read the instructions to the jury (seventy-one points that took two hours), his brother, Dr. Laurence Wiig, sat in the front row and kept an eye on him.

---

1. "I made it quite clear to all of the defendants and their lawyers that in my opinion we stood a small chance to hang the jury as to Eileen [Fujimoto], Jack and Koji," said Gladstein.

The case went to the jury at 4:08 PM on June 17, 1953. The jurors had been sitting for thirty-two weeks; they had listened to eighty-three witnesses and had heard an outpouring of more than three million words. Wiig told them to bring razors, toothbrushes, and a change of clothing.

The town speculated about the verdict. Allen thought the trial would result in a hung jury; he surmised that one or two of the jurors might be pro-ILWU. He related to Farrington a bit of gossip going around: the "reliable report" that Hall himself expected a hung jury. Allen said there was a "widely held opinion" that under Gladstein's tenacious cross-examination most of the prosecution's adverse character witnesses had made "rather a mess of it." In a broadcast on June 16 McElrath said Prosecutor Walsh couldn't find anyone who would bet on a conviction. "If he can't get a conviction, it seems he'll settle for a hung jury," said McElrath.

The jury deliberated sixteen hours and seventeen minutes and announced it had reached a verdict. The lawyers and the defendants were summoned. Hall and his wife watched the twelve men as they walked to the courtroom. His face was grim. "When they come back so fast, it ain't good, kid," he said to Yoshiko. She clung to his arm.

Robert Nakamura, the foreman, announced the verdict: all guilty.[2] Although he had guessed what was coming, Hall was shaken. He pressed his lips tightly together. "It's only the beginning," said Gladstein. He meant that the appeals would go on for years.

Despondent, Hall and his wife went home. Some of the ILWU office staff had attended court that day and Priscilla Shishido, Hall's secretary, recalled:

> Someone asked me whether we should visit the Halls or whether they would want to be alone. I said, "Now is the time to show they have friends." Rags [Mrs. Shishido's husband, Mitsugi] and I arrived bearing liquid gifts. We found a very dejected family but in no time at all their home, both floors, [was] filled with people. . . .

---

2. The defense heard that "two or three" jurors held out for a while for acquittal of Hall, Ariyoshi, and Mrs. Fujimoto.

Most people were happy with the verdict, including, according to Allen, those who had nothing in common with employers "except the strong desire to see Hawaii rid of Bridges, Hall and their gang." Summarizing the trial, Allen said most people believed that membership in the Communist Party "firmly binds the member to the theories and practices of the party and that these theories and practices include and in fact basically teach . . . overthrow of government by force and violence—if it can't be done by stealth and infiltration."

Farrington approved of the verdict. It was proof, he said, of the growing appreciation of the menace of communism. He told Allen that one of statehood's most vocal foes, Senator Hugh Butler of Nebraska, was delighted: "Butler feels so strongly about the verdict in this case that he is telling some of his friends that the jurors 'won statehood for Hawaii.' "

The ILWU walked out in protest over the verdict. The *Advertiser* called the walkout "one of the ugliest demonstrations of bad citizenry on record."[3]

The date for sentencing was July 3. Hall expected the "full book": a maximum sentence. That morning he and the other defendants delivered prepared statements. Hall leaned on a lectern and read his statement in a high, clear voice from a yellow legal tablet. He said he felt no sense of guilt. "As Your Honor knows," he said,

> there is no direct evidence or testimony in the record . . . that I ever uttered a single word to anyone at any time urging or recommending that our government be overthrown, with or without force and violence.

Hall said he had read very few of the Communist publications that were introduced in evidence. He was not proud of that fact, however, because "all intelligent persons should seek to acquire

---

3. The Ft. Pierce, Florida, *News-Tribune* commented: "A stooge of Harry Bridges, heading up the ILWU in Hawaii, was convicted as a Communist conspirator, along with six more goons in the same union. . . . So what happens? . . . Over 26,000 member of the ILWU go on strike and tie up the port of Honolulu."

as much knowledge as possible and from every available source. . . ." Hall continued:

> I am compelled to point out that no direct evidence was offered in this case that I was a member of the Communist Party during the three-year period preceding the indictment. . . . The prosecution well knows I was not a member of the Communist Party when they got their indictment and they know I am not now. . . .

Hall said the purpose of his life—"and I believe I have been loyal to that purpose"—was to do all he could "to advance the interests of the working people, the weak, the oppressed." He said he had made mistakes, but they were honest mistakes.

> If in living my life in pursuance of this purpose, I have created some enemies, I have gained many friends, real friends. These friends are my only real worth except the respect of those who condemn me yet concede my integrity of purpose and honesty.

His voice rose, and he looked up with an angry look:

> I bitterly resent any implication or inference that my life—my deeds, my words, my pen—has been but a fraud, a cover-up for some future potential teaching or advocacy of the overthrow of the government. This weird twisting of my life and purpose [does] not square with the facts. . . .

On the bench, Wiig, his voice a whisper, asked Hall if he was surprised by the verdict. Hall said he was. "I had hoped that there were enough men of courage on the jury to stand up against the fear that prevails in this community. . . ."

Wiig asked Hall if he had told Barlow that should the jury return a guilty verdict against him, "Harry Bridges will come to Honolulu and tear this building apart, brick by brick."

Hall flushed. He had run into Barlow in the elevator and indeed he had made the remark; but in jest, he said.

"That was a joke?" Wiig asked Hall.

"Yes, and there have been many more like it," said Hall. "In retrospect . . . it doesn't seem like such a good joke."

Wiig agreed.

During the lunch-hour recess, Hall wrote to friends and thanked them for sending letters in his behalf to James K. Mattoon, the federal probation officer. "While they may not do any good, at least they mean a great deal to me," he said. Just before court reconvened, Hall bet a newsman one dollar that he would get the maximum prison term. He collected his bet. Hall and the other five men who were defendants were sentenced to five years in prison and fined five thousand dollars. Mrs. Fujimoto was given a three-year sentence and fined two thousand dollars.

David Thompson, who was in the courtroom, groaned when he heard the sentences. He clenched and unclenched his hands.

Wiig said he handed down maximum sentences because he was satisfied that "the conspiracy . . . was a highly dangerous one." He doubled each defendant's bail to fifteen thousand dollars. Shortly after court adjourned, Hall walked into the office of William F. Richardson, Jr., chief clerk of the federal court, and soon Toyomasa Oshiro, the ILWU office manager, arrived with the extra bail money for Hall in bundles of fifty and hundred-dollar bills. The money came from the union's defense fund.[4]

Hall expected to go to prison. One day he was looking at Wendell Carlsmith's collection of the Admiralty Edition (eight volumes and maps) of Captain Cook's three voyages to the Pacific. "Wendell," said Hall, "I want you to do one thing for me. I'll probably have to go to jail. Will you let me have, volume by volume, as I read them, your set of Cook?"

Carlsmith told him that as a rule he never let his originals out of his office. "But with you—certainly."

What did the Hawaii Smith Act trial accomplish? Three opinions:

Symonds: "The government was interested—not so much in sending anybody to jail—the government wanted to expose

---

4. The other six defendants spent a week in the city and county jail in Iwilei. They were freed on bond on July 10. Julius Rosenstein, an 87-year-old sculptor, and three others (Stephen P. Sawyer, Harriet Bouslog's husband; Fusae Kimoto, Jack Kimoto's sister; and Charles T. Wakida, a carpenter) posted ninety thousand dollars worth of real property.

anybody who had any connection or any dealing or any alliance or any agreement with the Communist Party whether they were Communists or not, so that they could be destroyed by the publicity. . . ."

Hoddick: "We do know that as a result of the prosecutions there was an education of the American people as to what communism is about. There was also a decided, insofar as they kept statistics, a decided drop in known members of the [Communist] Party and its affiliated groups for a number of years. . . ."

Willis Butler, Hall's close friend: "The greatest irony in the Smith Act is that [Hall] already had split ideologically from the Party. He knew it and they knew it, but he was on trial."

Part 10
THE MIDDLE YEARS
(1954–1959)

CHAPTER 60
Naalehu '54: The Feisty Lathe Operator

Hall and the other Smith Act defendants had been convicted, and their appeal now ground along slowly in the mills of the judiciary system. Smith Act conviction notwithstanding, Hall by now enjoyed good relations with most employers he dealt with. They knew they had to live with him; they trusted him; some were even fond of him.

Such a man was Cadagan of the Hawaiian Pineapple Company. One day he told Hall he was not trying to run the union's business, but he had a suggestion to make. In the pineapple canneries almost every regular worker had a skilled job; they were the backbone of the bargaining unit. But, according to Cadagan, these top-grade workers felt put upon. The union seemed primarily concerned with the lower-rate employees and with across-the-board pay raises. This had the effect of narrowing the wage scale and hurting the pride of the skilled workers. Cadagan had a solution. He offered to "toss in a good-sized chunk of dough" by offering percentage increases and reclassification. He said this would eliminate the complaint of the skilled cannery workers, especially those in the top grades.

Hall said thanks; he saw nothing wrong with considering an offer from management. It was an example of the new mood in union-management relations and Goldblatt seized upon it. He suggested that Hall call on the heads of companies the union dealt with: such men as Jack Driver, Vernon Haas, Stu Milligan. "There has been a change in the situation," he said. A few years earlier things were different: then the ILWU membership would have been suspicious of any suggestion of friendlier relations with management.

"We don't think these dangers exist today," said Goldblatt. "We think that a program of more cordial relations with the company does not militate against continuing growth of the rank and file." Not that cooperation would mean the end of problems. They would go on as long as union and management sat on opposite sides of the bargaining table. But it was time to let the community know the role the union played, said Goldblatt. If a worker got more, he spent more; and that benefited Hawaii. It was a simple fact of life. Goldblatt thought that this information, properly released, would have a "tremendous impact" on the merchants and professions in the community.

But in the spring of 1954 something happened at Hutchinson Sugar Company on the Big Island that was to undermine Goldblatt's strategy. One rainy Saturday afternoon a lathe operator named Haruo Tachibana decided to attend a union meeting in Hilo. Tachibana was one of only two lathe operators in the mill, however, and his supervisor had warned him not to take off. (The other lathe operator had already been given permission to go to the meeting.) But the mill was closed for the day; no cane was being ground. Tachibana went to Hilo and the company suspended him for a day.

When he learned of the suspension, Tachibana lost his temper. He shouted, threatened, laid hands on Robert Wilkinson, the assistant mill engineer, and challenged Wilkinson and John Harmon, the mill superintendent, to fight. He thought the punishment was unfair. He had worked at Hutchinson for twenty years—ever since he had finished the eighth grade at Naalehu school at fifteen.

Tachibana had his tantrum and the company fired him. Suddenly, a little thing had boiled up into a big thing. The ILWU tried to head it off. "It is our opinion that the case should not be blown up," Goldblatt cautioned, "particularly in view of some of our suggestions for an overall compaign which we believe ought be be undertaken in the islands." He meant the new relationship he hoped was blooming between union and employer.

Bridges called Jim Blaisdell and asked him as a personal favor to see if they couldn't solve the problem at Naalehu "without going to battle." He suggested calling in Sam Kagel, a veteran West Coast labor mediator, for "single-shot arbitration that might prevent the situation from hardening." He suggested reinstating Tachibana without back pay and putting him on probation.

Blaisdell tried to play the role of peacemaker; he talked to Steele at the Employers Council and to Alan S. Davis, C. Brewer's president. (Hutchinson was a Brewer plantation.) Blaisdell got nowhere. It was a matter of principle, said Davis; management had the right to discharge an employee for cause without consulting the union. Blaisdell informed Bridges. Sorry, he said.

On April 22, 1954, some 317 employees at "Hutch," as people called the plantation, walked out. Davis said the company would "not bow to . . . threats and surrender." The ILWU sent over rice; the union set up soup kitchens. The men organized fishing and hunting parties. Battle was joined: the case of the lathe operator had touched off a full-scale strike. By May 8 it looked as though a long strike was in the making and the words everyone dreaded to hear were spoken: "It looks like another Lanai."

The ILWU said Tachibana was just one of "a long list of grievances" against Hutchinson's management. Hall said Tachibana was a "very quiet guy, not a hot-head. He must have taken a lot before he blew up."

The union singled out a source of complaint: the plantation manager, James S. Beatty. Jim Beatty was a big man with white hair and piercing blue eyes. He looked like central casting's picture of the old-style plantation manager; he wore riding breeches and boots, kept his tie neatly tucked in his shirt, and wore a straw hat to shade his face. A reporter described him as

an austere man, aloof, but not the haughty whip-cracker that has been painted in the ILWU stories of "Beattyism."
He demands that a job be done right. He believes that only one

man can run a plantation at a time. He is a plantation manager from the old school, but he is no martinet.

It was McElrath who coined the word "Beattyism." He liked to use words that had a bite to them.

"What is 'Beattyism'?" McElrath asked and answered his own question:

> Beattyism is a whistle or a roar instead of courteously calling a person. Beattyism is an "I'm the boss" attitude and "You'll watch your step if you want to keep your job around here." Beattyism is a militaristic approach to labor relations.

McElrath gave Beatty a title: "King of Naalehu."

Beatty counterattacked. He was not the kind of man built for whipping. He told his employees they were being shuffled around like checkers on a checkerboard. It was a foolish strike that could only hurt them, he said. And for what?

> Ask yourself this question: will I get more wages, or benefits or anything else when the strike is over? Is the strike for more wages? No. Is the strike for more benefits? No. Is the strike for better working conditions? No. Is the strike for any reason that will help me? No.

Beatty was not fond of the union; he could not stomach McElrath, but he trusted Hall. "If [Hall] said he would do a certain thing, he would do it and he would live up to it," said Beatty. So he and Hall made a date and met at the Young Hotel. They killed a quart of Old Crow and talked about what they could do to end the strike. "They [the ILWU] had their necks out and were defeated and were trying to figure out how they could get out of it gracefully," said Beatty.

But there seemed to be no easy solution: Tachibana was fired. "Now and forever!" as Beatty put it. He would not take him back. Beatty said he had laid down the law to his own management personnel, so why shouldn't the same law apply to employees? "I told all my supervisors not to touch anybody no matter what happened. I'd fire the man who touched an employee." Tachibana had cursed and laid hands on a supervisor so he fired him and that was that.

Beatty said he didn't want a strike; Hall didn't want a strike; the workers didn't want a strike. It was a strike *nobody* wanted.

The days passed and the strike went on. Management did some secretive "fertilizing by moonlight." The two sides appeared to be rooted to the ground. It took until mid-August, in fact, for them to work out a compromise. They met at last in a converted railroad boxcar next to the union's soup kitchen and thrashed out the terms: Tachibana was out; so were Mr. and Mrs. Alfred S. Hansen. (Hansen was the company's industrial relations director; his wife edited the company house organ.) It was a tradeoff. Hall urged the Naalehu membership to accept. They did and the strike was over. At 6:30 AM on August 30, 1954, once again the work whistle blew. It was a cheerful sound. The strike had gone on for 128 days.

"We are so relieved," said Mrs. Ashina Akamu, a worker's wife. "Four months is a long time." In Naalehu, a town of two thousand, the plantation was the whole economy. If the plantation shut down, the economy died.

Both sides claimed victory. Tachibana said, "The attitude of the company was the main issue. That has changed." The ILWU guessed that the company lost $400,000. Beatty said "the Tachibana cane" made for a beautiful crop because it had four extra months to grow. "We now had age on our cane," he said.

Riley Allen said it was a strike that nobody won.

CHAPTER 61

The Democratic Sweep

In 1954, with a shove from Hall and the ILWU, the Democrats seized control of the legislature for the first time in fifty-four years. The ILWU gave Republican Neal Blaisdell the support to defeat a brash young man of politics, Frank Fasi, for mayor of Honolulu; tried but missed by only 890 votes to elect Burns over Betty Farrington for delegate to Congress; and helped elect six Democrats (for the seven seats) to the Honolulu Board of Supervisors.

Hall sent a jubilant cable to ILWU headquarters:

DEMOCRATS SWEEP HAWAII TAKE SENATE 9 TO 6—2 REPUBLICANS IN OUR CAMP TAKE HOUSE 20 TO 8[1]—1 REPUBLICAN IN OUR CAMP STOP DUMP FASI ELECT BLAISDELL BY NARROW MARGIN STOP DUMP MANY . . . REPUBLICANS STOP AUDITOR *[sic]* DELEGATE RACE FARRINGTON STOP BURNS LOSING LESS THAN 300 VOTES RECOUNT EXPECT. . . .[2]

Hall attributed the Democratic sweep to the ILWU and the resentment of government employees against the King administration. His cable concluded: "BEST RESULTS HISTORY OF ILWU AND EVERYBODY KNOWS WHY."

He had carefully prepared for the elections, sensing that the time was ripe to defeat the Republicans, and he had campaigned for a strong labor turnout. In a speech in Hilo, he said, "A union has got to use its vote and it uses its economic strength,

---

1. The correct figure was 21 to 8.
2. A recount was not sought. Hall's figure was incorrect.

with no defection, to put into office men and women who are committed to easing the economic situation in the territory."

It annoyed Governor King to see Hall lead the fight against him. In fact, he accused Hall of political blackmail. Here was this arrogant man, said King, who only recently had been convicted of what "in effect is treason to the United States," taking upon himself the right to speak for organized labor. Hall's outspokenness also vexed Riley Allen, who said the ILWU and its small sister union, Henry Epstein's United Public Workers, were out to elect legislators who would do their bidding.[3] Allen disputed the claim of ILWU power at the polls. Had not the union suffered defeat in 1952 when it went all out to back Delbert Metzger in the race against Farrington for delegate?[4] In his opinion, the union was "less powerful politically" than it had been before. "This is the result of the trial and conviction of Jack Hall. . . ."

Events conspired against the Republicans. On June 4, 1954, sugar workers celebrated ten years of organizing effort with a rally at Waipahu Plantation ball park. Among the guests were Judge Alva E. Steadman, president of Cooke Trust Company, and Robert R. Trent, executive secretary of the Hawaiian Sugar Planters' Association. Steadman addressed the rally, saying that labor peace was possible only if both labor and management respected each other's rights. "We are in the same boat economically," he said.

In his speech Hall said that in a decade "tremendous change" had taken place and he gave management its share of the credit:

---

3. Epstein, a power in labor and politics for more than thirty years, arrived in Hawaii in 1947. Both Hall and Epstein were militants, but with a difference in style. Hall was bold; Epstein, quiet. They usually saw eye-to-eye on politics, but not always. Hall helped Epstein from the beginning and in the early days the ILWU subsidized the UPW to a degree: Hall gave the UPW free office space at Pier 11 and the use of ILWU office equipment.

Hall liked the smart, efficient Epstein. He liked the idea of "a little sister union." Over the years the UPW thought of joining the ILWU, but Hall said, "You're doing all right the way you are."

4. Metzger lost by a vote of 67,748 to 58,445. With ILWU support, he carried the Neighbor Islands and Oahu's Fifth District.

And while the morass out of which we have climbed is not a pretty one, we are not bitter about the past or against those who were responsible for the suffering and the indignities of those days.

It is to the credit of the men of industry in Hawaii that with but few exceptions they have changed with the times.

Relations are maturing and mutual respect and fair dealings are the order of the day.

The rally at Waipahu troubled Allen, who noted that Trent and Steadman had appeared willingly on an ILWU-sponsored program—"a fact," said Allen, "that Jack Hall and Bob McElrath and other ILWU spokesmen will not fail to emphasize."

On Saturday, June 19, 1954, Farrington died of a heart attack in his office in Washington. Betty Farrington ran for her husband's unexpired term. To the consternation of Jack Burns, Metzger was prevailed upon to run against her in the special election held July 31, 1954. "I didn't want Metzger running," said Burns.

But the smart guys around here said you got to have opposition anytime there's an election. You shouldn't leave vacancies at the top of the standard. . . . That may be true, but you don't necessarily try it 100 percent. . . . But they insisted and talked old Metzger into it and Metzger got clobbered. . . . [5]

Betty Farrington knew she would receive a "sympathy vote." Burns knew that was bound to happen, too, but Allen saw the vote in the July election as an "overwhelming" victory for Mrs. Farrington—a blow to the ILWU—and he envisioned another victory for her in the November election "by another impressive majority." He did not appreciate the growing appeal of the Democratic Party and he underestimated the ILWU's drive and organizing ability. That fall the union was hard at work. "We are all busily engaged in political action and have done a tremendous amount of work in putting out direct mailing of more than

---

5. By a vote of 43,195 to 19,951.

a quarter of a million pieces of campaign literature (not in the name of the union, however)," said Hall.

For Goldblatt's benefit, Hall outlined the union's political strategy:

> The Democrats generally have listened to our advice on how to handle the red-baiting issue and have taken the position that loyalty oaths, investigations, etc., will not destroy communism, but conditions which give rise to Communist thinking are matters that must be gotten after. These include the elimination of unemployment, etc., etc., all matters which the Republicans have failed miserably to resolve during their half century of control.

It was not unusual by now for Republicans to come to Hall for union backing and, as a *quid pro quo,* promise to support the ILWU's legislative programs. "In addition and more important," said Hall, "they have advised me that should their vote be crucial in the organization of the House, that they would be willing to vote in any Democratic Speaker that we designate."

The ILWU was in the best shape politically it had ever been. Hall foresaw Democratic control of both Houses in the 1954 election, but he underestimated how large the control would be. He also predicted (incorrectly) that Burns would beat Mrs. Farrington;[6] the odds "are excellent," he said.

Hall had always opposed Frank Fasi, the maverick politician; the 1954 election was typical. Fasi came from East Hartford, Connecticut, and had served during the war with the marines on a dot of an island near Tarawa in the South Pacific. For a time he was stationed on Kauai and in 1946 he returned to the islands. He got into the building and salvage business, but his heart was always in politics. He started his political career in 1950 running

---

6. Betty Farrington got 69,466 votes; Burns, 68,576. Burns' supporters blamed Hall for his defeat. "He didn't do enough," said Takaichi Miyamoto. Mike Tokunaga, co-committee manager with Dan Aoki of the Burns campaign, said Hall contributed no money. "We ran completely out," Tokunaga said. "We figured we needed about $3000 to win. . . . Dan and I went down to see Jack Hall. . . . We asked him for the money. He told us there was no use spending money on Jack Burns. . . ."

for the Territorial House. He lost, but it was clear he had a lot of promise if he could only wait. But Fasi was an impatient man.

In 1952 he beat Johnny Wilson for the job of Democratic National Committeeman. Wilson was the darling of the ILWU and the defeat of the old man (he was then eighty) rankled Hall, who never masked his feelings about people. If he didn't like you, you knew it. Hall disliked Fasi; he considered him an opportunist. He summed up his opinion of Fasi:

> He is the usual young, ambitious and somewhat ruthless guy that's trying to make a name for himself and acquire worldly goods.
>
> He is anti-ILWU and active in veteran's affairs mostly through the VFW. He came to Hawaii as an ex-GI, got into . . . surplus . . . with his veterans' preference and apparently has made a pretty good hunk. His credit rating is supposed to be pretty good but I wouldn't let him hold the money in a crap game. . . .

Hall claimed Fasi had obtained the votes he needed to win the national committeeman's election "by meeting the expenses of the more penurious [convention] delegates."[7] *Caveat emptor,* said Hall. Let the buyer beware.

When Fasi made his first bid for mayor of Honolulu in 1952, Hall stepped in to oppose him. In a radio talk, Hall called Fasi "the ambitious young man":

> Frankie boy . . . got his urge to run for mayor in some divine or supernatural way. He says he had no intention of running because his wife was very ill. However, his plane for the mainland started out so many times and turned back so many times that he was just so, so tired that Providence must have been trying to urge him to run for mayor when he got rested so he just up and filed.

In politics, said Hall, "like in war, all is fair, including bunkum."

Fasi knew the political facts of life. He was aware of the ILWU's strength but he defied Hall anyway. "Fearless Frank,"

---

7. The ILWU alleged that in the 1952 race for national committeeman Fasi paid the convention expenses of Albert Tani from the Big Island; in return, they claimed, Tani gave Fasi sixty-seven proxy votes.

he was called. In his Labor Day speech in 1952, Hall had assailed the Democratic administration—Governor Oren E. Long and President Truman. Fasi replied, saying the Democratic Party of Hawaii would be far better off if Hall and the ILWU got out of the party and stayed out. "They have been holding a Damocles sword over the head of every candidate who doesn't cut the ice with them," said Fasi. He called the ILWU leadership "vicious"; they were bent, he said, on controlling candidates to further "their own selfish interests."

In the 1952 Democratic mayoralty primary Wilson defeated Fasi by 3365 votes. (Wilson beat Neal Blaisdell in the general election.) But Fasi's defeat merely fanned his ambitions. He was tenacious; he had enormous confidence. He waited for the next time around, and by April 1954 he predicted: "I will be the next mayor of Honolulu." His prime targets, said the ILWU, were Wilson and the ILWU, and not in that order of priority.

As the 1954 primary approached, "Friends for Frank Fasi," his political organization, distributed leaflets which pointed out that a voter could split his ticket: cast his ballot on the Republican side for legislative and supervisor candidates, and on the Democratic side for city administrative offices. It was an invitation to Republicans to cross the line and vote for Fasi against Wilson in the primary:

Question: Can I vote in the Republican Primary for House of Representatives, for senators and for supervisors, and also vote for Frank Fasi for mayor?

Answer: Yes! Vote only on the Republican side of the territorial ballot and only on the Republican side of the supervisors ballot. Vote only on the Democratic side of the County officers ballot. Your vote will be Republican on the two ballots and Democratic on one ballot—perfectly all right. . . .

Question: Can I just vote for Frank Fasi on the County officers ballot and no one else?

Answer: Yes!

On election day, an estimated ten thousand Republicans crossed over and voted for Fasi and he beat Wilson by 1102 votes. But in the general election Republicans crossed back over and Fasi lost to Blaisdell in a close race—47,704 to 45,240.[8] "The odds were too much—even for me," Fasi consoled himself. He knew who had tilted the scale against him: Jack Hall.

In Congress the opponents of statehood dwelt on the political power of the ILWU. Allen briefed Mrs. Farrington on how to deal with them. He and Nils Tavares, chairman of the Hawaii Statehood Commission, presented her with a primer on how to argue the case. Allen listed these main points:

- The claim that the ILWU dominated Hawaii.

Allen's answer: The ILWU was the biggest and most powerful union in Hawaii, "but, repeatedly, on showdowns the ILWU has failed in its political objectives." It failed in 1949, said Allen, when it undertook to paralyze the harbor and the legislature passed the Dock Seizure Act and reopened the waterfront.

- The claim by Representative John R. Pillion of New York, one of the most vitriolic of the antistatehood group, that Neal Blaisdell's victory over Fasi in 1954 was a victory for the ILWU.

Allen's answer: "It is not denied that the ILWU played some part in Blaisdell's election, but it was not the controlling factor." Blaisdell had a lot of appeal, said Allen. He was a local man; he had served two terms in the Territorial Senate; he was popular and a former athlete.

- Pillion's charge that the 1954 election was, in fact, an overwhelming victory for the ILWU.

Allen's answer: The ILWU sustained two big defeats in that election: in the delegate's race Mrs. Farrington defeated Burns, and in the mayoralty primary Fasi beat Wilson.

---

8. Proof that Republicans "jumped the fence": the total vote for Fasi and Wilson was 47,446. But the total vote for the two candidates for city auditor was 37,643.

• Pillion's charge that Hawaii's tolerant atmosphere nurtured the seeds of communism the same way the islands' mild climate nurtured exotic plants.

Allen's answer: "Repeatedly, on a showdown, the ILWU has sustained defeats in the fields of politics as well as economics." As an example, he pointed to the 1950 referendum when the state constitution was ratified, over ILWU opposition, by a plurality of more than 55,000 votes; 3 to 1, said Allen.

There were far shriller voices than Allen's taking on the ILWU in those days. Territorial Senator Ben Dillingham enlivened a dull Saturday morning at the legislature with a thundering speech. He charged that the Democratic majority elected in 1954 was under the thumb of "treacherous" ILWU leaders. His voice booming, he cried out:

> It is an outrage to see the [ILWU] leadership dictate all the policies of the Democrats. It is a real fact. What the leadership say, right or wrong, damaging or not.
>
> It is time that the people of the territory woke up to this urgent fact. . . . These people are called "agrarian reformers"—nice people. McElrath "is a swell little fellow. . . ."
>
> It's time we woke up and found out who we are dealing with. The people should know that the only thing that stands between ourselves and chaos is the position of the governor. If he were subject to the pressure of the ILWU, we would be closer to a satellite of the Soviet Union than a territory of the United States, and I'm not kidding.

CHAPTER 62
Juneau Spruce

In 1949 ILWU longshoremen of Local 16 in Juneau, Alaska, illegally struck the Juneau Spruce Corporation, a lumber company, and set in motion a wave that traveled all the way to Hawaii. Juneau Spruce obtained a $750,000 court judgment against Local 16 and the ILWU International. With accumulated interest piling up daily, the judgment ran in excess of a million dollars. Juneau Spruce was serious business: lawyers for the company went to court to attach ILWU assets, including those of Local 142 in Hawaii. Juneau Spruce also had its comic side: for months the union kept its assets hidden and Goldblatt ran the International's business "out of his hat."

It all began with the wildcat strike. Local 16's strike had gone on for six weeks before the International even knew about it; then Juneau Spruce filed charges of unfair labor practice, alleging that Local 16 had engaged in a secondary boycott. The NLRB dismissed the suit; Juneau Spruce filed suit in the Federal District Court for Alaska under the Taft-Hartley Act and thereupon obtained the $750,000 judgment.[1]

The case was appealed and made its way up through the Ninth Circuit Court of Appeals and to the United States Supreme Court: on January 7, 1952, the Supreme Court affirmed the decision. At that time it was the largest judgment ever awarded a corporation in such a suit against a trade union; it was also the first time that such a suit had reached the highest court in the

---

1. Juneau Spruce was just one of a number of cases filed against the ILWU for alleged violation of the Taft-Hartley Act. In 1953 there were ten suits filed against the ILWU for a total of $7,768,500. Some were settled out of court; some were dropped; and some the union won. The years 1951–1953 were difficult ones for labor.

land. Naturally, the ILWU saw no cause for jubilation over this distinction. The union noted wryly that the Supreme Court decision was unanimous and that it had been written by Associate Justice William O. Douglas, "sometimes considered liberal."

To collect, Juneau Spruce took the case to California and obtained a court order attaching the assets of the International. But the ILWU International had no treasury and no reserve fund. "All the ILWU has as an entity," said the Local 142 Executive Board, "is a few sticks of furniture and current per capita collections upon which it operates." Judgment was entered in the Federal District Courts in San Francisco and Honolulu and garnishee summonses were served on banks in San Francisco and Honolulu which handled union funds, on ILWU Locals 6 and 10 in the Bay Area, and on Locals 142 and 155 in Hawaii.

The case came up before Judge McLaughlin. "A fishing expedition," Hall called it—lawyers Easter-egg hunting. McLaughlin "froze" Local 142's assets and Hall bridled:

Apparently, they think that Hawaii is a gold mine that is more productive than any in Alaska, because the members here have over a period of years built up substantial funds for their own security and protection. Apparently, also, because they think that the Federal Court here is a friendlier atmosphere in which this alien corporation can come in and pick up a few bucks.

The ILWU tried to settle out of court for $75,000 to stop "the harassment and intimidation." Goldblatt dealt with James P. Rogers, a partner of Manley B. Strayer, the Portland firm which represented Juneau Spruce. Goldblatt thought he had a deal. At two o'clock one morning in San Francisco he and Rogers shook hands on a $75,000 settlement. He told Rogers the International would have to borrow the money. It was agreed, according to the union, to pay $25,000 thirty days after dismissal of the suit and the $50,000 balance at the rate of $10,000 a month for five months.

Next morning Goldblatt and Rogers went to Gladstein's law offices on Market Street to sign the papers. Rogers said, "I'd better check with my office first." Goldblatt listened to him over the phone; he heard the deal unraveling as Rogers spoke. Rogers' partner turned it down.

On February 28, 1955, his birthday, Hall testified before Judge McLaughlin in the Juneau Spruce case. Howard Hoddick, the former acting United States Attorney and special prosecuting attorney in the Smith Act trial, handled the case for the company. Hoddick had subpoenaed the ILWU's financial records. He told the court the only way to make sense out of the union's accounting system was to have an audit made. "We don't argue that they haven't kept records," said Hoddick. "It is just that they have kept so many of them and that they are so intertwined [the local and the International] and interrelated that you can't get an accurate picture."

Local 142, for example, owned the ILWU International headquarters building on Golden Gate Avenue in San Francisco (purchased for $25,000 in 1949 when the International was strapped for cash).

Hall testified that the ILWU in Hawaii shouldn't have to pay for a far-off litigation arising out of a set of circumstances that Hawaii knew nothing about and had no control over. He said he had discussed with Bridges and Goldblatt the subject of disaffiliation by Local 142 from the International so that the Hawaii ILWU could not be a party to the Juneau Spruce suit. Goldblatt told him he didn't blame him.

Then they got around to the topic of the day: "Where is the International keeping its assets . . . its cash receipts—at the present time?" Hoddick asked.

"I don't know," said Hall. "They are not in Hawaii."

Indeed at that moment it required all of Goldblatt's considerable ingenuity to stay one jump ahead of the court-appointed referee who was seeking out the International's assets. As Goldblatt explained, "We were in this 'cops-and-robbers' act with the employers and with Juneau Spruce, in particular, because we had to see to it that assets disappeared." And, miraculously, they did. Like a magician and his rabbit, Goldblatt managed to make the union's assets disappear. Said Goldblatt:

A number of things were done. For example, we exonerated all per capita and then we'd collect the per capita in dues. I remember George Andersen coming back from Hawaii one time and he had picked up $60,000 in cash.

What to do with $60,000? "Why don't you put it in your savings [account]?" Andersen suggested.

"No, I don't want to do that," said Goldblatt. "It would be even more suspicious."

So the money was kept in his house over the weekend. He had an arrangement with the bank:

I'd give them a list. And I'd give them a list of cashier's checks and in some cases paying people two or three months in advance. Or paying off bills in advance. . . . And I would get a call that all the cashier's checks were ready. I'd walk down to the bank with the cash. Put out the money. Pick up the cashier's checks. Drop them in the mail. In that way, we sort of operated out of our hat.

All the time the Juneau Spruce affair was cooking on a front burner, a court case involving the union was simmering at the back. The case was an outgrowth of the Fair Labor Standards Act overtime-pay case which Gladstein and the ILWU had won in 1946 with a million and a half dollar settlement. This related case *(Maneja et al.* v. *Waialua Agricultural Co., Ltd.)*[2] involved the definition of an agricultural worker under the FLSA. Waialua sought a declaratory judgment in Federal District Court to the effect that its operations were exempt from the FLSA's overtime provisions. By counterclaim, Waialua employees (Maneja and thirty others) sought to recover unpaid overtime for work performed between November 20, 1946, and September 14, 1947. The suit, filed by the Honolulu law firm of Anderson, Wrenn & Jenks, moved from federal court to the Ninth Circuit Court of Appeals and then on up to the United States Supreme Court. It had been all but forgotten.

One day Hall phoned Goldblatt. "Remember the [Waialua] case?" he said.

2. 349 U.S. 254, 1955.

Goldblatt said sure he did, but he didn't want anything to do with it. "We're through with that," he said. "We don't want any more money. If the attorneys can collect something, fine," said Goldblatt. "Let them take on the job of distribution of funds. Plus, we'll have all kinds of trouble if we have to distribute the money. Only some guys will get it and some guys won't and some guys will get a fair amount and some guys will get nothing. . . ."

"No," said Hall, "that's *not* what I'm talking about." He told Goldblatt the employers had decided that if the ILWU was interested in an immediate settlement of the Waialua case out of court, "they're prepared to make us an offer right now."

Goldblatt asked what good that did. Hall said, "Don't you have Juneau Spruce hanging around?" Goldblatt said yes.

Don't you see? said Hall. A tradeoff. Trade them the settlement in the Waialua case for the Juneau Spruce judgment. Take the money from one to settle the other. And, incidentally, said Hall, it doesn't look as though we're going to win a judgment in the Waialua case.

Goldblatt sprang instantly alert. What were the employers willing to pay to settle the Waialua case out of court? he asked. Hall said he thought they could be pushed to at least $250,000. (The sugar companies eventually paid $355,000 including lawyer's fees.)

Goldblatt talked to Gladstein, who had argued the Waialua cases before the Supreme Court. Gladstein didn't think their chances were very good: "Win some; lose some." Goldblatt asked Gladstein what he thought about Hall's suggestion of a tradeoff before the court ruled. Fine, said Gladstein; go ahead.

Goldblatt phoned the Juneau Spruce lawyers. He told them they had forty-eight hours to make up their minds if they wanted to accept $250,000 to settle the case out of court. "It makes no difference to us," he said casually. "We can continue on the merry chase."

The lawyers called their client, the Dant brothers, owners of Juneau Spruce. Jack Dant was tired of the case and tired of lawyers. Here he had a big judgment but couldn't collect and ILWU longshoremen in Juneau were engaged in a slowdown. Dant told his lawyers to take the $250,000. The lawyers called Goldblatt back. "All right," they said. "It's a deal."

"And that's exactly the way it worked out," said Goldblatt. "The 250,000 bucks were paid. Juneau Spruce got it. . . . That case was dropped. It was all settled."

As Hall surmised, the Supreme Court ruled against the ILWU and in favor of Waialua Agricultural Company, which meant that the sugar companies would not have been obliged to pay anything at all.[3] The employers felt it was more prudent to settle out of court for a nominal sum than run the risk of a judgment against them that might go as high as $5 million.

Asked what he thought of that line of reasoning, Hall said, diplomatically: "No comment." In private, he was amused.

The ILWU local leadership naturally agreed to the tradeoff and Hall decided that so long as the majority approved, "minority individuals can't legally quarrel with the settlement." It would have been impossible to try to distribute the settlement equitably, he said. Each worker's "share" would have amounted to less than one dollar for each year of service.

"Could we not then advise the plantations that this was our 'equitable' distribution method of settling all claims and then have each member sign a waiver against receiving any money?" Hall inquired of Gladstein.

Hall met with the thirty-one sugar workers in whose names the case had been brought. He had to convince a few "hardheads" among them to sign the waivers.[4]

The Juneau Spruce settlement delighted Bridges. "The fact that the idea originally came from you in Hawaii has really been terrific," he said. At the Local 142 convention in September 1955, Bridges thanked the Hawaii membership—"and most especially . . . Brother Jack Hall. . . . The whole idea originat-

---

3. The officers and lawyers for Juneau Spruce and the ILWU signed a memorandum of agreement for $250,000 on April 2, 1955. The Supreme Court ruled against the ILWU in the Waialua Agricultural case on May 23, 1955. It took until July to collect waivers to be signed by ILWU workers, but that was fairly routine. The "exchange" already had been set in motion. Eventually 10,000 waivers were turned in to the lawyers.

4. Hall said there were "three or four" negative votes at HC & S.

ed down here and as we all know, we were able to finally come out of it and honestly say Juneau Spruce didn't get any ILWU money. . . ."

To the delegates that was the best part of all.

CHAPTER **63**
Hall the Politician

Betty Farrington had squeaked through to victory in the delegate's race in 1954, and Hall was determined to defeat her in 1956. First, though, he wanted to talk to her and see what he might extract. In May 1956, he broached the subject with Kibre, the ILWU's man in Washington. He agreed that the voteless office of delegate was merely "a service operation," yet it did have some value. "Frankly, we would have no hesitation making the same sort of deal with her that we had with her husband in the early days," said Hall.

By that he meant that for her part of any bargain they might strike, Betty Farrington's paper, the *Star-Bulletin,* "would *again* [Hall's italics] become fair and unbiased in its news handling of matters involving or affecting the ILWU." Hall did not say what the *quid pro quo* might be.

"I suggest that you keep her well-buttered up and at the right time suggest that she have a session with me," Hall wrote Kibre. "She knows me well enough to know that I would protect her in a situation even if nothing came of our conversation."[1] Shortly

---

1. Betty Farrington denied that she knew Hall personally. She said she had *no* correspondence with him. She said she only met Hall once in her life—at the Waikiki Tropics one night when George Martin of the ILWU introduced Hall to her.

after, Hall told Kibre that there was no use preparing a bill of particulars against the *Star-Bulletin*. "Betty is aware of the paper's attitude in the last five or six weeks," said Hall. "The Bulletin is so obviously anti-ILWU that the Honolulu Advertiser, the morning competition, appears as leftist as the [ILWU] Dispatcher in comparison."[2]

In June or July of 1956, Bridges called on Betty Farrington in her office in Washington. She clearly recalled the occasion: Margaret Turner, her secretary, rushed into her chambers in alarm and announced:

"Oh, *he's* out there in the front office. Can't let him in."

"Who?" said Mrs. Farrington.

"Harry Bridges!"

Show him in, said Mrs. Farrington. She and Bridges talked for two hours. She said Bridges offered her the support of the ILWU in the 1956 delegate's race; that he offered to contribute $250,000 toward her campaign; and that he offered to sponsor a testimonial dinner for her in Honolulu.[3] She said she declined his offer of support or a testimonial dinner and told him she could not accept "a penny of his money."

"Harry, I couldn't possibly do that," she said. "If you will just leave me alone and not endorse me, and don't endorse Jack Burns—just leave us both alone—I'll get enough votes on my own from your boys to get elected."

Her account of the meeting with Bridges filtered down to Hawaii. Hall told Bridges that Mrs. Farrington "in her desperate bid for re-election has reported, in a distorted fashion, on your talks with her." Hall said Mrs. Farrington implied that she had been offered the support of the ILWU, indignantly refused it, and that was the reason why the ILWU endorsed Burns.

Hall had been committed to Burns for a long time; he liked

---

2. In Betty Farrington's opinion, the *Star-Bulletin,* under Allen's editorship, was always fair and impartial in its treatment of the news.

3. Bridges' version of the meeting: "I sure as hell know that her story about my meeting with her and offering $250,000 to finance her campaign against Jack Burns just did not happen! . . . when it comes to endorsements on any national or local candidates, such endorsements are strictly up to the decision of the local unions—not the International."

the tall ramrod, former police captain. The two got along well. "He's an all right guy, a practical politician, and will be a refreshing experience," Hall told Kibre. "He keeps his word and levels. He is an important Catholic layman but a staunch defender of the ILWU. He has many friends among members of Congress. . . ."

Support for Farrington was dwindling; support for Burns was growing, Hall contended: "Dillingham, Doc Hill, Hung Wo Ching,[4] and many of Betty's former supporters are for Burns and have made fairly substantial contributions to his campaign. We have been doing a lot of money-raising from non-ILWU sources."

The GOP was impotent, said Hall. "[Governor] King has wrecked . . . the Republican Party."

> It is about as effective as the pre-1946 Democratic Party and we are back practically to a one-party system again. If it were not for the ILWU support of Republican House members, the Democrats would have overwhelming veto over-riding power in the House as well as the Senate. . . .

With the ILWU's total commitment, Burns defeated Farrington by 82,067 votes to 66,732. Hall called it a "resounding defeat" and said it exceeded his expectations.

On Saturday, November 10, 1956, eight hundred members and guests of the ILWU gathered at a dinner at the Kewalo Inn across from Fisherman's Wharf in Honolulu to honor Hall. Among the guests were some politicians, including Edward N. Sylva, the territorial attorney general. Sylva looked out of place. He was a Republican, a Harvard Law School graduate, and a staunch anti-Communist. He not only was the highest legal officer in the territorial government, but he had served as the first chairman of the Territorial Commission on Subversive Activities and had headed the commission of the Department of Public Instruction that had passed on the loyalty of the Reineckes.

---

4. Mrs. Farrington said Hung Wo Ching never supported her. His brother, Hung Wai Ching, did help her to run her campaign.

Sylva was a prize exhibit and the ILWU made it a point to introduce him around. He met Bridges and told him: "I'm happy to meet a fellow Republican."[5]

Sylva's audacity created consternation among the ranks. Early that following Monday, King angrily summoned him into his office, delivered a twenty-minute lecture, and demanded his resignation. Sylva refused and King fired him. "Strange are the ways of Hawaii," Hall mused.

Riley Allen said Sylva had been guilty of bad judgment—"impulsive, it seems to us"—and he applauded King's swift retaliation. Sylva explained that he regarded the Saturday night affair as merely a labor organization meeting. The rank and file had invited him, so he attended. "I met a lot of union men there," he said. "I talked to them. I shook hands with them. And I made friends with them." What was wrong with that? The time had come for better relations between labor and the community. "We have to move to them," said Sylva. "There has been too much wall-building between ourselves and the ILWU—and communism. We sit on top of the wall and throw invectives at those on the other side. This is no solution. We must bridge the gap."

As for the ILWU, he said, there were plenty of "ex-Communists" in the union, "but no real live Communists." Hall knew a plug when he heard one. "I'm sure Mr. Sylva had sufficient information to know what he's talking about," Hall said blandly.

On the heels of the Sylva episode came the Eastland Committee to investigate, once more, communism in Hawaii. Burns did his best to discourage them from coming. Hall said not only would the visit hurt the cause of statehood, but it was "even against [Democrat] Eastland's best interests . . . because Hawaii as a state would widen the Democratic control of the Senate and House."

Hall thought one more "all-out effort" might bring statehood:

---

5. Shortly before, Bridges had registered as a Republican, thereby flabbergasting both Democrats and Republicans.

Perhaps even a number of Southern Senators can be brought along if they were assured it would not mean more Republican Senate votes. . . . Burns is also going to introduce a bill for an elected governor and if we can't get statehood, at least we should have a chance to get Sam King. Incidentally, anything we can do to have him replaced should be done.

Hall speculated that the Eastland Committee was coming either for a junket and to influence local politics or else they were "playing for substantial stakes." He thought they might be after Symonds and Harriet Bouslog—the start, perhaps, of a move to disbar them. He noted the business executives ("our fine friends from the summit," he called them) who were raising funds for the anti-ILWU organization called IMUA, the Hawaii Residents Association.[6] Among them, he said, were George Burgess of the Hawaiian Pineapple Company,[7] H. C. Eichelberger of Amfac, Thomas G. Singlehurst of the Bishop Trust Company, and Ed Schneider of the Bank of Hawaii.

The Eastland Committee arrived and Senator James O. Eastland, the chairman, a man from Mississippi, took an office in the basement of Iolani Palace. His chief counsel was Robert Morris, a chubby man who wore a bowtie.

Morris phoned Symonds and said Eastland wanted to see him. Symonds went over to the palace. Eastland sat smoking a cigar. Morris said to him, "Senator, this is the lawyer, Symonds, I was telling you about."

Eastland said nothing. He didn't look up.

Morris said to Symonds: "I've checked on you and you're well liked here. The judges and the lawyers all think well of you. You can be a help to the committee. So, if you will assist the committee—you won't have to appear on the subpoena."

Symonds replied: "Mr. Morris, I think I have nothing to cooperate with you about and I think you're talking to the wrong person."

---

6. IMUA's stated purpose was to combat subversive activities.

7. Cadagan, a Hawaiian Pine vice-president, told his company not to contribute to IMUA. He said it was "just plain foolish" to try to negotiate with the ILWU in good faith and at the same time contribute to an organization which maligned the ILWU.

"Symonds, you haven't heard the last of this," said Morris.

Symonds walked out. Eastland never said a word. He just smoked his cigar.

The committee hearings went over familiar ground. Lieutenant General (Retired) John W. "Iron Mike" O'Daniel, a member of IMUA, testified that in his opinion Communists controlled the sugar workers and stevedores. O'Daniel said that when he had been commanding general of the United States Army in Hawaii from September 1952 to April 1954, he conducted practice alerts every three months to guard against "a Communist takeover." He visualized an uprising in Hawaii, "simultaneously with an attack from outside."[8]

On the day McElrath was subpoenaed, the Senate hearing chambers were packed.[9] Morris interrogated him.

"Name . . . address . . . ?"

"Robert McElrath . . . 2407 St. Louis Drive."

"Occupation?"

"I decline to answer. . . ."

A hush, then a titter swept through the room. McElrath tapped with his right foot on the floor.

Then, one question after another:

"Are you a Communist . . . ? Were you ever a Communist . . . ? Were Communist meetings held at your house?"

"Same answer. . . . Same answer. . . . Same answer."

There was a grimness about the proceedings that made the spectators feel ill at ease. "It was a cold, chilly day, but you left the hearing chambers with sweat on your face."

Symonds was subpoenaed. He said he was born in Sydney, Australia, in 1909 and came to the United States with his parents in 1920.[10] Symonds took the Fifth Amendment.

Kibre wrote from Washington that neither the *New York Times* nor the *Washington Post* paid any attention to the

---

8. An uprising in Hawaii? That was too much for Governor King, who was also a witness. "I cannot go along with General O'Daniel," he said.

9. Hall was not subpoenaed. His appeal in the Smith Act conviction was pending.

10. "Same year as me," said the irrepressible Bridges. "It was a plot."

Eastland Committee hearings in Honolulu. The hearings had their moment in the local press, then disappeared. "They didn't prove a damn thing!" said the ILWU.

CHAPTER **64**

The Last Act of the Smith Act

"We have just begun to fight," Hall said soon after his conviction in the Smith Act case. But as the legal process dragged along (it went on for four and a half years), he began to lose confidence and could see the shadow of a prison cell. He wanted no sympathy: "Spend no time feeling sorry for me," he told ILWU members.

What pleased him most was the support of ordinary members. Sometimes it was a kind word, a smile, or even a friendly wave of the hand. Sometimes it was a kind deed. Tomas Sadoyat of Kapulena, Hawaii, sent him a box of fresh vegetables. That touched him. "They will never lick our kind of a union," Hall told Sadoyat.

Judge McLaughlin tightened his restrictions on Hall's travels. He required that Hall's lawyer submit a motion in court and notice to the United States Attorney whenever Hall wanted to leave Oahu.[1] Jim Blaisdell told Hall in confidence that some employers were betting Hall would be behind bars by the time the major contracts expired in two years. He said he assumed the

---

1. McLaughlin ruled that Hall could go deep-sea fishing with Doc Hill off Hilo but had to stay within the three-mile limit. A puckish copyreader wrote a headline: "Hall Can Go Deep-Sea Fishing—But Not Too Deep."

union knew that. Hall said it certainly did; the union wasn't dumb. He told Blaisdell the union meant to make the employers "pay extra for a longer agreement because of it."

Hall's second child, a son, Eric Mitsugi, was born June 21, 1954. Soon after, Hall told Bridges he wanted to attend the International Executive Board meeting on the mainland if McLaughlin would permit him. He said he needed to get away; the Smith Act conviction lay hard on him, and union chores never ceased. "The trip will do me good," said Hall. "I know that I should get away from everything for a few weeks and it is impossible for me to get any real rest here. In fact, I have been jumping around like a bee in a skillet and not getting too much sleep with the baby either. . . ."

The union carefully considered who should handle Hall's appeal. Goldblatt's first choice was a reputable San Francisco lawyer named Herbert W. Clark. Hall agreed and he wrote Clark that he had confidence the lawyer could give him the best possible representation—"and I certainly need it." Clark accepted but then backed out because of the pressure of other work.

Goldblatt approached other talented lawyers in San Francisco and Los Angeles, but none was willing. Gladstein recommended Garner Anthony, saying Anthony would make "a genuine impact" on the court, but Hall was not enthusiastic about Anthony.[2]

Goldblatt came to Hawaii and found signs of near despair that Hall's days of freedom were numbered. Something drastic had to be done, said Goldblatt, or the ILWU in Hawaii was in trouble. He told Hall:

We are giving thought to mapping some kind of program . . . which will make mighty clear to the employers, our political enemies, and anyone else, that any funny idea that they have that there will be any payoff for them in the event you are put in jail just will not work out that way—to the contrary, we are getting things geared up so that if

2. Anthony never was offered the job.

that unhappy event comes to pass, our enemies will have sufficient cause for regret. . . .

Bridges and Goldblatt asked Telford Taylor of New York, the lawyer who had been the chief American prosecutor at the Nuremberg trials, to take Hall's appeal, and Taylor accepted. He had handled the appeals in two of the Bridges cases. Goldblatt was pleased. He called Taylor "an enormous asset" and told him the ILWU was under fire only because of the union's "record of achievement" in Hawaii.

Taylor read the briefs and commented:

> It is apparent . . . that the principal arguments to be advanced in behalf of Mr. Hall do not relate to the nature and aim of the Communist Party, but to the degree, if any, of Mr. Hall's culpable connection with the Communist Party under the provisions of the Smith Act.

Taylor said he "would be unwilling" to argue that the Communist Party did not embody a conspiracy to advocate the overthrow of the government by force and violence:

> If such arguments were to be advanced on behalf of Mr. Hall, it would have to be done by someone other than myself. However . . . it appears from the briefs that this contention does not enter into the appeal. . . .

Taylor said he would charge the same basic fee as he did in the last Bridges case he handled; that amounted to fifteen thousand dollars for about five weeks' work. He estimated Hall's appeal would take eight weeks—say, a fee of about twenty thousand dollars plus expenses.

Goldblatt asked Taylor to go to Hawaii and suggested that Hall introduce him to a number of ranking executives, including all the Big Five presidents: Budge of Castle & Cooke, Mac-Naughton of C. Brewer; Russell of Davies; Bell of Alexander & Baldwin; and Sumner of American Factors. He provided for Taylor's information his own commentary on some of the other executives he thought Taylor should talk to. Goldblatt described them this way:

Paul Fagan, owner of the Hana Maui Hotel, who "became persona non grata with many of the big interests as a result of the position he took during the 1949 longshore strike in favor of a settlement."

Asa Baldwin, manager of HC & S, because "while he personally does not head the agency, he is probably the dominant influence. He participated as a member of the recent sugar employers' negotiating committee. Our relations with his company have been good."

Jack Guard, manager of McCabe, Hamilton & Renny, who "has always been friendly to the union and testified as a character witness for Jack, but later under pressure in effect withdrew his testimony."

Buster Burnett, head of Kahului stevedoring on Maui, and Stu Milligan, of management personnel at HC & S, because they "can reflect the community attitude sort of one level below such people as Fagan and Baldwin."

John Murphy, head of labor relations for Castle & Cooke, "which is still the dominant agency of the Big Five." Murphy, said Goldblatt, is "somewhat in the same category as Burnett and Milligan, but quite obviously more of a 'theoretical' thinker in matters of policy of the Big Five."

Dwight Steele, president of the Employers Council, who "is careful to reflect the opinions of the people he represents."

> He will disclaim any connection with the prosecution of Jack Hall and may even express his opposition to the case itself. He will also go to great pains to make clear that it is a matter outside of their relations with the union. He would still be worthwhile to press to find out what . . . the employers in Hawaii intend to do to disclaim any tie-up with the case—which the membership still believes exists. . . .

Taylor arrived April 18, 1956. Hall met him at the plane. "I want to develop my own understanding of the case and the people involved in it," Taylor said. He took Goldblatt's advice and went to see "everybody worth seeing."

By now two years had passed since Hall's conviction and it bothered some people that he was still free as air and conducting union business unrestrained. In Washington Representative Francis E. Walter, who had brought the first Un-American Activities Committee hearing to Hawaii, and Secretary of Labor James P. Mitchell were surprised to learn that the sugar and pineapple companies still dealt with Hall. Senator John M. Butler of Maryland called for an investigation of the "shocking" delay in deciding the Smith Act appeal. Senator William E. Jenner called the delay "a deplorable thing."

Taylor, representing Hall, and Rex A. McKittrick, representing the government, argued Hall's appeal before the Ninth Circuit Court in San Francisco on July 12, 1956. Taylor portrayed Hall as a "minor-league Communist who never played the Marxist game very seriously." Jack Burby, who covered the hearing, kept seeing faces and hearing voices from three years before:

> It was a ghost of a trial which ended in June of 1953 in convictions of all seven defendants. The attorneys conjured up names of witnesses that sounded familiar, the way that characters in an old book do. There were no faces to go with them. None of the defendants was in the tiny, marble-pillared courtroom to hear the appeals.

Taylor argued that membership in the Communist Party did not constitute a violation of the Smith Act. He said Hall was never a paid functionary in the Party and "held only the most lowly Party positions." The evidence showed, he said, that Hall was interested in the Communist Party for what help it could give him in organizing labor in Hawaii. There was no evidence that "ever manifested itself by deed or word" that Hall wanted to overthrow the government. Taylor conceded that Hall was controversial, "but there is no question about the energy and devotion with which he has given himself to the cause of unionism, and no doubt about the success that has attended his efforts." Would such a person seek to overthrow the government under which he had reaped such success? asked Taylor. "The accusation simply does not make sense. . . ."

McKittrick argued that Hall had led the Communist Party in Hawaii for a long time:

From 1937, when appellant Hall first brought Communist Party literature to longshoremen on the island of Kauai, until the eve of the indictments, appellant and other leaders of the Island [Communist] Party exerted every effort to indoctrinate recruits and the Party members in the islands in the principles of Marxism-Leninism.

From the beginning, said McKittrick, Hall, Reinecke, and Kimoto led the organizing of the Party. McKittrick said after the war the Communist Party grew from a handful into a force of 180 to 200 members, "many of whom were leaders in unions organized in the basic industries in the islands." He concluded: "The evidence shows that Hall was a Communist conspirator first and a trade unionist second. . . . Uncontradicted evidence shows that he surrounded himself in the appointive positions under his supervision with leading members of the Island Party. . . ."

Bridges sat listening and scowling. O. P. Soares, a Honolulu lawyer, also was there, but incognito. Instead of his customary white linen suit, he wore dark blue.

The Ninth Circuit Court held up its ruling until the United States Supreme Court rendered an opinion in the Los Angeles Smith Act appeal which would set the precedent.[3] On June 17, 1957, the Supreme Court, by a 6 to 1 vote, reversed the Los Angeles convictions and ruled that the Smith Act did not prohibit the advocacy and teaching of the overthrow of the government —provided it was not accompanied by overt action. Teaching, the court held, was an abstract principle protected by the First Amendment. The court also held that the three-year statute of limitations applied to Smith Act cases and the statute had run. (The government had argued that the offense was ongoing and that therefore the three-year statute of limitations did not apply.)

Hall took delight in the verdict and double delight in the chagrin of his adversaries. "The IMUAites are . . . apoplectic,"

---

3. *Yates et al.* v. *United States,* 354, U.S. 298, 299, 1 Fed. 1356 (1957).

he said. But even with the Supreme Court decision as a precedent, seven months went by before the Ninth Circuit ruled in the appeal of the Hawaii Seven. Hall became impatient: "Irritating as hell to not know where they stand," he said.

On January 20, 1958, the Ninth Circuit Court reversed the Honolulu Federal District Court conviction and acquitted the Hawaii Seven. Next day a reporter visited Hall's home on Kahala Heights. A party was going on. Steaks were broiling over the charcoals in a barbecue pit. "Louis Goldblatt . . . lying in his shorts, was broiling under the sun. Drinks were being served. Toasts were being said. . . ."

Hall lay on a couch, "at least temporarily at peace with the world." He was barefoot; his hair was crew-cut; he wore a skivvy shirt and a pair of khaki slacks. "We knew it was going to happen" was all he would say. It was a moment to savor and it came six and a half years after Hall was arrested in his apartment on Kau Way early that August morning in 1951.

The proceedings against Harriet Bouslog for her outspoken remarks at Honokaa didn't get under way until well after the Smith Act trial was over. On December 2, 1954, Bouslog met with the Ethics Committee of the Bar Association of Hawaii. On July 8, 1955, the committee filed formal charges against her in the Territorial Supreme Court and recommended that she be disciplined for unethical professional practice. On April 6, 1956, the Territorial Supreme Court ordered her suspended from practice in all territorial courts for a year. On June 9, 1958, the Ninth Circuit Court upheld the decision by a 4 to 3 vote. The court's majority opinion said that if Bouslog had shown a little humbleness, she might have helped her cause:

> But so long as she conceives that she has a right to litigate in a given case by day and castigate by night (or at recess) the very court, the honored place in which she is working . . . she does not deserve to practice law.

A dissenting minority opinion, written by Judge Walter L. Pope, said:

Suspending one person like Harriet Bouslog Sawyer from the practice for one year is not merely the imposition of punishment on her. In upholding this judgment this Court serves notice on all lawyers everywhere to hold their tongues, to watch their speech, lest some court hold criticism of a State or Federal prosecutor's procedures to be ground for disbarment.

Against the advice of Bridges, Bouslog insisted on taking an appeal up to the Supreme Court. Bridges and George Andersen of the Gladstein firm tried to talk her out of it during a meeting of the three at the Waikiki Tropics.

"We were trying to persuade her to cop a plea . . . to save her license," said Bridges.

> She said: "I won't!" I admire her for that. . . . She was crying. I said to George [Andersen], "Come on, let's knock it off. . . ."
>
> We were putting the pressure on her to kick her into line. This was George and I. Her best pals. Our major concern was to save poor Harriet. She said, "I'll take it on. I've got to make a trip." And she went to Washington.[4]

On June 29, 1959, the Supreme Court by a 5 to 4 vote overturned Harriet Bouslog's suspension from practice. The court concluded that there was not enough in the record to support the charge. Bouslog celebrated with a magnum of her favorite beverage, Mumm's champagne. "I have always felt my position would be vindicated," she said. "I will be more careful about what I say in the future, but I will never keep my mouth shut when I can open it to help out. . . ."

---

4. "She was up before the Supreme Court and she won it," said Bridges. "So she proved us wrong again."

CHAPTER 65

Sugar '58: "The Aloha Strike"

Hall called Cadagan one day late in 1957 and said he wanted to talk to him about sugar. Cadagan said he didn't know anything about sugar; he was a pineapple man. But he met Hall anyway. By then they were old friends.

Hall said he was worried that a sugar strike was coming and that it would be stupid. "I'm afraid these sugar people are going to break themselves," he said. "I wish they had some sense. I'm worried about losing jobs through a foolish strike."

The ILWU had warned long in advance that 1958 was going to be "a sugar year." As far back as 1954 the union began collecting one dollar per month per member to start a war chest. By 1958 the sugar units had $835,000.

Hall said the sugar workers had "a miserably low" standard of living. "True," he said, "it's higher than in other sugar producing areas . . . but that doesn't make it right. It's not right that sugar workers can only command, if he is in basic labor grades, $1.12 an hour."

Bridges told Steele that the union was willing to negotiate a one to three-year sugar contract and did not want to strike "unless forced to do so—and only after every reasonable attempt to compromise has been exhausted." Said Hall: "We are no kamikaze union. . . . We don't like to take chances where it is not necessary."

But the two sides were like two trains heading toward each other on one track: a crash was inevitable. Both sides began to argue their case in public. The union produced charts and figures to show how sugar workers' productivity had climbed over the years. Bridges alerted the ILWU on the West Coast "to hammer home the fact that longshore is going to be mobilized in full around sugar. . . ." The industry campaigned over the radio and on television. With the consent of the union, plantation managers spoke to ILWU members. A routine developed: managers spoke for twenty minutes; then the union members applauded, as Hall had asked them to do. They were polite, unemotional, and unconvinced.

Hall looked at sugar prices and liked what he saw. "Aren't [they] fantastic?" March futures on large shipments of Philippines sugar on January 16, 1957, were quoted at $131.50 a ton. Refined sugar was at its highest price in thirty-three years. The world price of sugar was only twenty-five cents per hundred pounds less than the domestic price. Cuban inventories of sugar were low.[1] "The year 1957 looks like a helluva good year," said Hall. "We'll have to get ours." Goldblatt cautioned that the sugar negotiations would be as crucial "as any in the history of the union." Hall agreed. He said the industry had a "new and subtle line": sugar was unstable; profits were low; the outlook was uncertain. "So far, no red-baiting," said Hall.

Negotiations began December 9, 1957, with a strike deadline set for February 1, 1958. The ILWU asked for a 25-cent across-the-board wage raise. The companies said they couldn't afford it. Maxwell, chairman of the Sugar Companies Negotiating Committee, said a 25-cent increase would jack labor costs up by $10 million a year. Net profit in 1956 from sugar operations on all twenty-six plantations was only $7½ million, he said. "The increase you propose is far beyond the capacity of the plantations and therefore will be impossible of achievement."

Goldblatt replied that profits from sugar operations alone were deceptive; they didn't include all the operations the companies profited by. "The agency system," Goldblatt said, "is a 'cream separator' and these same functions that are performed by the agency can be performed by any plantation . . . at least 75 to 80 percent of that agency's profit comes directly out of these plantations."

On January 28 the union backed away from its 25-cent de-

---

1. Cuba supplied one-third of the 9½ million tons of sugar the United States then consumed annually.

mand and said it would consider "something less." Management countered with an offer of a four-cent wage raise. The union rejected it. The two sides were far apart; a strike was certain.

At 12:01 AM on February 1, 1958, some 13,700 sugar workers walked off the job. The union was prepared for a long strike. They had their fat strike fund. They stockpiled rice, meat, oils, staples; sent men into the mountains to hunt wild sheep, goats, and pigs; sent out fishing parties. They tended vegetable gardens and set up soup kitchens that served more than eleven thousand meals a day (average cost: ten cents a meal). They were old hands at organizing and at conducting a strike.

A model strike machine functioned at Olaa. Arakaki was in charge and he had a $26,000 strike fund. He had updated the strike "manual" of the 1946 sugar strike. The union ran soup kitchens at Olaa, Mountain View, and Pahoa and operated a commissary. Fishing crews brought in three hundred pounds of fish a day. Arakaki mobilized the entire community. He had carpenters, mechanics, plumbers, electricians. He went to the chicken farms, the cattle ranches, and the truck farms and told the farmers and ranchers that he had a lot of idle men who would help them in return for produce and meat. They made a deal. The union members tended and harvested crops, mended fences, repaired coffee sheds. They did maintenance on mechanical equipment.[2]

Arakaki issued commands like a general. The men didn't question him; they carried out orders. "You could appeal, but in the meantime you carried them out," said Arakaki.

The strike was solid. The union even enjoyed more sympathy than Hall had expected. But he knew that as the strike went on, feeling for the strikers would fade. Neither side called for mediators, but the federal government sent them anyway: Earl J. Ruddy and the old Hawaii hand, George Hillenbrand. Hall was not impressed. He said the mediators were "bumbling around, but, of course, will be of no real value in the situation."

---

2. They cleaned Slim Holt's property at Warm Springs and he gave them six head of cattle, slaughtered and ready for butchering.

Ruddy and Hillenbrand tried for eighteen days and then left. They had accomplished nothing.

William F. Quinn, then thirty-eight, the second youngest governor in Hawaii's history,[3] now sat in Iolani Palace. Quinn was something refreshingly new among Republican governors. He was a lawyer; bright, personable; an amateur actor, a singer. The ILWU watched him with interest. They thought he might even shake up the Grand Old Party. They were happy that Sam King had not been reappointed by the president of the United States.

Quinn knew he had to do something about the strike and he called on Dr. Arthur M. Ross, a University of California economist and industrial relations specialist. Ross arrived on March 25.

Bridges noted that the sugar industry had not opposed Quinn's attempt to get negotiations restarted and he laid down a course of action for Hall: Don't go back over the ground already covered; don't get involved in discussion of the cost of producing, marketing, and transporting sugar because that could only work to the industry's advantage.

> Our best argument is still that the industry is shut down, the shutdown is backed by strong reserves we can throw into action at any time. . . . The ranks are solid, even though the going might be tough, and the strike is going to remain solid for a long time to come. . . .

Bridges said the ILWU refused to subsidize the sugar industry any longer. "They are just as well off letting some plantation fold, as keeping the whole shebang going by accepting wages from the industry based upon the arguments that some plantations can only afford to pay low wages."

The employers knew what it would take to settle the strike, said Bridges. "Eighteen cents . . . would settle things in a hurry, or would be a big step in that direction." Ross spent a week try-

---

3. George Robert Carter was appointed governor of Hawaii on November 23, 1903, at age thirty-six.

ing to pull the two sides closer. He did not succeed and departed, on March 31, "lambasting both parties."

On April 22 management offered a fifteen-cent wage increase on a two-year contract and the union voted it down. On May 7 the union proposed a sixteen-cent increase for the first year and a seven-cent increase the second year on a two-year contract. The industry turned it down. Quinn suggested fact-finding. Goldblatt told Hall to tell Quinn "point-blank" that fact-finding was out. The phrase had been anathema to the ILWU ever since the Stainback fact-finding commission of 1949.

Goldblatt said it was sugar that had built Hawaii and sugar workers were entitled to share in the good life. He said the Big Five dipped into the sugar bowl to pay everyone: the agencies, shipping companies, suppliers, bankers and brokers, trucking companies, merchants. "It's okay with us if all these activities live off sugar . . . but the first job of the industry is to provide something that begins to resemble a living wage for sugar workers." They were "low man on the totem pole," said Goldblatt.

By May, the fourth month of the strike, there was a strain; but for the most part the union was still in good shape. Hall thought most units could last financially through July. "A few can last longer without help."[4]

The sugar industry threatened to close plantations which were not profitable. Hall warned the industry:

> Once a sugar company announces or threatens liquidation, the union will raise new demands which must be satisfied by both the industry and the company considering liquidation before there will be any termination of the strike at any company.[5]

Murphy of Castle & Cooke cautioned that if the strike lasted until June 15, Ewa Plantation would harvest only thirty thou-

---

4. It cost $250,000 a month to run the strike during the summer months, said Hall. The Territorial Sugar Strategy Committee in May had $130,000 on hand. In addition, there was $300,000 in pineapple and longshore funds available, and accounts, "such as the political fund," available on a loan basis.

5. Demands such as: the right of employees at a plantation that closed to apply for a job with any of the sugar companies; the right of free transportation home; full vesting rights under the pension plan; and a $250 termination bonus for each year of service.

sand tons of cane in 1958 and 1959. (Normal production was fifty thousand tons.) The company then would have to lay off ten percent of the work force after the 1959 harvest and would lose $560,000 in 1958 and $1,387,000 in 1959. Murphy said the union was trying to destroy the sugar industry. Hall retorted: "The fact that they'll lose tens of millions to avoid giving workers a decent wage is no never mind."

Quinn asked Joseph P. Finnegan, director of the Federal Mediation and Conciliation Service in Washington, for help. Finnegan sent Hillenbrand and Ruddy back into the fray, accompanied by Arthur C. Viat, regional director of the mediation service's San Francisco office. They arrived on May 14 but they, too, failed.

Twice Quinn had tried federal mediation, and he also had brought Ross in to mediate "right in my office"—all in vain. That meant if it were going to be done, he had to do it himself. As in any long strike things began to get tense. "Finally, they were beginning to have violence on the [picket] line," said Quinn. "The money in the union fund was gone;[6] the cane was dying. So I called them in—hell, I hadn't had any experience."

Quinn summoned Hall and Steele. "I don't want to talk to your committees," he said. "I want to talk to Boyd MacNaughton[7] and Harry Bridges. . . . Let me talk to the people who are going to make the decisions."

They came to his office: Bridges, Hall, and Slim Shimizu, head of the union's Strike Strategy Committee, on one side; MacNaughton, Steele, and Maxwell on the other. The horse-trading began in earnest; the wage gap narrowed. They came down to the crucial stage. At that point, according to Quinn, they were just a quarter of a cent apart—"and this is absolutely true"—when Bridges and MacNaughton balked. Each said he had gone as far as he was going to go.

Quinn flared. "Look, this is ridiculous," he said, and he warned:

What I'm going to do—tonight—I'm going to go to every TV station and I'm going to get on the radio and I'm going to tell everybody in

---

6. Not according to Hall.
7. President of the HSPA, as well as president of Brewer.

this territory how you people are hung up with the whole community suffering, and all of these people seriously damaged by this—for a quarter of a cent on the wage line.

Quinn did go on radio and he announced his recommendations for a settlement. It was a three-year contract with a sixteen-cent across-the-board wage increase plus an additional seven cents on June 1, 1960, eight months before the end of the contract. It was the first three-year contract without a reopening clause in the history of the Hawaii sugar industry. Both sides accepted. At 3:47 PM on June 6, 1958, the strike ended. It had gone on 128 days—longer than the 1946 sugar strike. Hall said the strike cost the industry more than $50 million; the industry had lost more than a quarter of its annual crop.[8]

Bridges said the companies "walked into that one. They were stupid. That [strike] could have been avoided." Maxwell agreed that the companies had bumbled. "I think probably we more or less did," he said.

So confident was the union during the strike that Hall put men back to work on some plantations "in order not to destroy their jobs." Under direction of union strike committees, they irrigated and kept the cane alive.[9] The union called it "The Aloha Strike."

"That strike need not have occurred if the employers had put on the table for additional wage adjustment the money they would not admit they had coming back in surcharge rebates from Matson, but which we knew was coming back," said Hall.

---

8. Donald Maclean, president of California & Hawaiian Sugar Refining Corporation, said Hawaii delivered 764,125 tons of raw sugar in 1958, as against 1,082,938 in 1957.

9. It was hard to explain that strategy to the men, said Bridges. "But once we got the thing going and the guys swung into it, they got the idea. You know, they were patting themselves on the back—making wages, and [donating] fifty percent of it to the soup kitchens or the strike fund; screwing the employers." (Bridges was wrong: it was twenty-five percent of the wages, not fifty.)

CHAPTER 66

One Sunday at Paula Drive

Eight Democratic representatives[1] met with Jack Hall at his home on Paula Drive on Sunday, January 25, 1959, to plot the defeat of Vincent Esposito and Tom Gill for the leadership of the Territorial House. It was the kind of political show that Hall loved to direct. He had talked it over with Charley Kauhane, a man alternately in and out of favor with the ILWU. Hall was concerned that Esposito and Gill would "ostracize" legislators sympathetic to the ILWU. Kauhane, a rough and tumble fighter, said he could take care of himself.

Seven House members took their cue from Kauhane, and Hall pointed out that if these eight Democrats ("The Outcasts," Kauhane called them) lined up with the eighteen Republicans in the House, that would make twenty-six votes: a bare majority of the fifty-one representatives. Wasn't it worth trying? Hall asked.

The Sunday meeting was arranged. "We needed some assistance and advice from Hall," said Representative George Okano. "We made the request to see him" and they spent the day.[2] Hall told them if they stuck with the Republicans, they could beat the Esposito-Gill forces. It was a simple matter of addition; Esposito didn't have the votes. Hall asked nothing in return; no *quid pro quo*. "Nothing like that," said Okano. It

---

1. Present were Charles E. Kauhane, George M. Okano, and John C. Lanham of Oahu; Pedro de la Cruz of Lanai; Yoshito Takamine and Akoni Pule of Hawaii; David K. Trask, Jr., of Maui; and Manuel S. Henriques of Kauai.

2. From 9:30 AM to 4:30 PM.

would be enough for him if he placed some of his people in positions of power on the committees. Besides, he didn't like Gill and Esposito; they were too independent for him.

The Territorial Senate organized with no problem; Herbert Lee was named Senate President. But the House ran into trouble. Esposito, a young man who had great political ambitions, had won the speakership in 1956 by a single vote over Elmer F. Cravalho of Maui. The ILWU had supported Cravalho and jettisoned their old friend, Esposito.

Gill, Esposito's chief lieutenant, was chairman of a prelegislative committee on land reform, the big issue of the campaign. Like Esposito, Gill was a bright, young man, but he had two considerable debits: he was both sharp of tongue and uncompromising. At a House Democratic caucus Gill ignored the Kauhane faction who protested Gill's proposed House rules. Kauhane accused Gill of "bracketing" the committees—that is, placing Esposito-Gill people in control of the important committees.

"Those are the rules," Gill insisted. "If you don't like them, you can fight them on the floor of the House. Aloha."

Angrily, Kauhane retorted: "I am not bound by a decision made by eighteen Democrats."

Kauhane studied a copy of the Republican plan to organize the House which gave Republicans proportionate representation on the committees. The Republicans wanted the right to select their own committee assignments; they were against a proposed rule to give the majority leader and the vice-speaker a vote in each House committee. Kauhane signed the plan and made friends. He then started talking coalition with the Republicans. Representative Sam King, arch-foe of the ILWU and Hall, asked: "But can you trust Charley Kauhane?" Yasutaka Fukushima, a fellow Republican, said he thought they could.

Confident that he had the votes, Esposito refused to bend. Eddie DeMello, the ILWU lobbyist, and McElrath called on Esposito in his office in the Hawaiian Trust Company building. "We were asking for three things: chairman of the Labor Committee, which I think we deserved; a member on the Finance

Committee; and a member on the County Committee," said DeMello.[3]

Suddenly the door burst open. "Gill came busting into Vince's office. He asked Vince, 'What's this guy doing here?' Vince told him, 'They're meeting with us. Asking for some appointments.' Gill said, 'They'll get nothing.' Vince said, 'I'll continue this with you people. I've got to check with the boys.' "

"They said they'd get back to us and they never did," said McElrath. "They met privately and organized their House without talking to us. They thought they could shove it down our throats."[4]

DeMello reported to Hall and the ILWU Political Action Committee. He waited for Esposito to call. A week went by; two weeks. No call came. DeMello phoned Esposito's home. Esposito's wife, Joyce, said her husband was at the Ala Moana Tropics or the Tahitian Lanai. DeMello found him at the Tahitian Lanai, in the company of Gill and Dr. John Stalker of the University of Hawaii.

What about it? DeMello asked. Esposito said, "I talked to the boys and the boys won't do it. They feel we've got the votes and can organize the House the way they feel."

DeMello replied, "If that's the case then we're finding another man for Speaker." It was then, he said, that the idea of a coalition took shape:

> We had a meeting that day and for many days and some of the meetings lasted until three in the morning. Hall directed the meetings. He had the experience and the know-how. So we made a deal with eighteen Republicans and we got eight Democrats. . . . Jack was always involved. When I needed him to talk to people, he

---

3. McElrath remembered their requests as slightly different: the Labor, Finance, and Judiciary committees.

4. Esposito said McElrath, DeMello, and George Martin of the ILWU offered to support him if he gave the ILWU legislators control of Finance, Land Reform, and the County committees. "You can be Speaker again under those conditions," he quoted McElrath as saying. He told them no.

was there. I used his prestige and ability. In most cases he would convince them.

Hall felt Cravalho was a natural to join the coalition. They arranged to meet at the Waikiki Tropics one evening. Hall asked Cravalho if he wanted a drink. "A screwdriver," said Cravalho. Hall came right to the point: he said they were lining up a coalition of Democrats and Republicans to knock off Esposito and Gill. Would Cravalho join?

"No, I'm not interested," said Cravalho. "I don't want to be in a coalition." He said the only thing he wanted was to be chairman of the Finance Committee again because he thought he had done a good job as chairman in the past session.

Hall got angry. "You're just hot-headed about it," he snapped. "It can't work."

"Okay, it can't work," said Cravalho.

Hall got up; Cravalho got up. They both walked out. "It was the shortest meeting I've ever had with anybody," said Cravalho. "We didn't even finish our drinks."

When Esposito saw the forces lined up against him, he tried to do something about it. It was too late. The Republicans had struck a bargain with the "Kauhane Eight." A reporter who watched the goings-on blamed Gill: "He's an inflexible guy and his unwillingness to give up some of the power as head of both Judiciary and Land Reform caused a lot of resentment among both Republicans and Democrats."

Gill, on his part, said the way he proposed to organize the House was exactly the way it had always been done—that is, until Hall intruded. "They got the word [from Hall] and slipped over to the other side," he said.

In dismay Democrats David McClung and Tadao Beppu watched their party coming apart. "The so-called Esposito group was so intractable," said McClung.

They wouldn't recognize that when you've got two roughly equal numbers and two factions that you ought to get together and say,

"Let's split up the political pie in terms of organizing and get on with the business." And they weren't willing to do that. . . .

McClung and Beppu broke with the Esposito-Gill forces and started talking to the Kauhane group. "We listened to Kauhane's attitude, which was really the same as Gill's," said McClung. "You know, 'Give us the whole pie. The hell with the rest.' "

The battle was joined on the floor of the House. Esposito, who did not dream that a coalition could be welded between Democrats and Republicans, lost the showdown vote, 28 to 22. Ray Adams of Maui and, in the end, Cravalho joined the Kauhane Eight, along with the Republicans, and Cravalho won the speakership. Esposito fought hard. "Let the ship go down with all guns firing," he proclaimed.

When it became obvious that Esposito had lost, Gill went up to a number of Republicans, shook their hands, and said, "How does it feel to be in bed with Jack Hall?" In his mind's eye was the memory of the Republican politicians who had stood on the platform and accused the Democrats of being in league with the "red menace": namely, Hall and the ILWU. "And now they were in bed with the ILWU," said Gill. "All of a sudden— kaplunk! There they were with their two feet sticking out. So I asked them: 'How does it feel, boys?' Of course, they didn't like it."

In Gill's view, the Kauhane Democrats were beholden to Hall. The ILWU's attitude toward politicians was really a simple thing, he said, and he could state it tersely:

When they needed something that was important to them, they wanted it. That's it! Other things; no big stuff. But if you ever said to them, "Now wait a minute. What is this you want and why?" Then you're a phony. You're out.

"It's their *modus operandi*," said Gill. "Once you understand it, you don't have any problem with it."

From Washington, Delegate Burns sent Cravalho a telegram congratulating him on his victory over Esposito. It was hardly the most diplomatic thing to do at that moment. Esposito, Gill, and McClung, who had in the end voted for the Esposito combine, were furious.

For Esposito the defeat was wormwood; it ended his political career.[5] Ironically, once he had been a good friend of the ILWU leaders; in fact, Goldblatt was a special friend. Goldblatt used to stay with him when he came to Honolulu; they talked away many a night. Esposito admired all three ILWU leaders—Hall, Bridges, and Goldblatt. "It was a heady wine to see how much they knew about things," said Esposito.

> I was astounded to know how much they knew about the Big Five, about the sugar industry, about economy. I was a legislator and a lawyer and I didn't know one-tenth what they knew.
>
> They were absolutely brilliant people. There is no question in my mind that those two men [Hall and Goldblatt], without a law education, knew far more law than I did. And I was a pretty good law student.

When Esposito first ran for the House in 1950, the ILWU had supported him. The falling out came, he said, after a series of incidents. He refused to give McElrath a secret copy of a report by the Hawaii Commission on Subversive Activities which, he said, he was sworn not to release until it was made public. He declined to act as a junior counsel for Hall in the Smith Act trial, and he hesitated to testify as a character witness for Hall in that trial.

"Let's you and I talk," he said he replied when Hall broached the subject of testifying. The exchange, according to Esposito, was short and bitter:

Hall:	I'm only asking you if you're going to testify for me in the Smith Act trial.
Esposito:	I'd like to talk to you first. I'd like to ask you some questions.
Hall:	Well, fuck you.

5. He later won election to the State Senate, but the defeat in the House "upset the timing" for advance in politics.

"Wow!" said Esposito. "Here I was sort of their drinking partner." He could single out the incident that, finally and irrevocably, shattered their friendship. One night he, Hall, Bridges, and Goldblatt sat drinking in a Waikiki tavern. Bridges started talking about lawyers and said there wasn't an honest one in a carload. "They got into a full-blown discussion about lawyers," Esposito recalled. He tried to defend his profession. He said there were good lawyers and bad lawyers just as there were good labor leaders and bad ones. "There's nothing sacred about you and your class," he told them. The argument heated like iron in a forge and "got into one swearing, angry, drunken, mean thing," said Esposito. "It went on till 1 o'clock . . . and, boy, the flavor of that was really ugly."

In the course of the invective, Hall denounced Esposito and his liberal politics. "You can't trust a liberal because you don't know what he's thinking," said Hall.

> You're not dependable. I'd rather do business with a prostitute than with a liberal. At least I can buy them and I know how they're going to vote. You—I'll never know how you vote. You're one of those smartass liberals.[6]

Thus ended the friendship. Esposito was sad about it. They were such *exciting* people to talk to, he said.

Hall informed Goldblatt about the part he had played in the defeat of Esposito. "Congratulations on the highly effective job done re one Mr. Esposito," Goldblatt replied. "I have a feeling this might put an end to one opportunist's climb to power and glory on the back of former friends."

On the day he was defeated, Esposito decided to confront Hall and ask him why he had engineered his downfall. He knew no other way to do it except face to face. That evening he

---

6. Despite Hall's denunciation of him, Esposito retained a lifetime admiration of Hall. "He had in him a sort of sense of greatness," said Esposito. "He looked at things in a big way. A very unusual, facile, bright mind with a fantastic memory to go with it. . . . [He had] a kind of singleness of purpose. He was first, last, and always—drunk or sober—morning, noon, and night . . . a true labor unionist and really a true leader of his union."

phoned Hall at his home. "This is Vince Esposito," he said. "I want to talk to you."

Startled, Hall said, "When?"

"Right now."

"You want to come up to my house right now?"

"Yes, I'd like to sit down and have a few drinks with you."

He came, without invitation, up the hill to Hall's house. He knocked, walked in, sat down. Hall made him a strong drink. Esposito poured some of the bourbon back into the bottle and made himself a modest drink. "You realize you're diluting the bottle," Hall laughed.

One of Hall's relatives was there. They sat and drank and "talked all around the subject." Esposito never did get around to saying what was on his mind; he never asked Hall, Why did you do it? The answer really was simple and, of course, Esposito knew it: Hall wanted the ILWU to have the power in the legislature that he believed it was entitled to.

Finally, many words and many drinks later, Esposito said thanks, goodbye, and started for the door. "Hall got up and walked to the door with me and practically fell on his face," said Esposito.

CHAPTER **67**

The Glow of Statehood

Burns laid down the strategy of separating the Alaska and Hawaii statehood bills and letting Alaska have first crack. If the strategy worked he was a hero; if it failed he would look like a fool. He asked Hall about it. Hall recognized the risk, but he approved. "I made the decision . . . because that's the only way it was going to be done," said Burns.

He and Delegate E. L. Bartlett of Alaska discussed the Alaska First strategy at Thanksgiving Day dinner in 1956 at Bartlett's home. They decided to try to convince the majority in Congress to agree. As Burns explained, "You got to know a little bit of history. The trouble is, people won't use history and it repeats itself."

> Every state that got into the union came in damn near in tandem, bringing in different shades of opinion and balancing things off. If they were going to bring in two Republicans, they wanted to bring in two Democrats. . . .

Alaska was to be the Democratic state; Hawaii, the Republican state. The politicians' reasoning was that Hawaii had gone Republican for more than fifty years (conveniently forgetting the Democratic surge that started in 1954).

Committed to his course of action, Burns told Senate Majority Leader Lyndon B. Johnson that he was willing to get up on the floor of the House and make a motion to recommit the Hawaii statehood bill and let Alaska go first. Johnson, the hard-boiled politician, said, "How in hell can you do that?"

"Well, Senator, it is reasonably simple," said Burns. "I think that we have very smart constituents who will understand what I am doing, but beyond that, can you tell me another way Hawaii can get statehood?"

"No, I can't," said Johnson.

"Well, okay, that's the way it goes then," said Burns.

He unveiled the plan for local consumption at the Princess Kaiulani Hotel in 1957, saying that if he had to permit the Alaska bill to go through first "and throw Hawaii out . . . I was going to do it." The words stirred strong reaction: to some statehood zealots it sounded like surrender. "I mean, I started getting letters—what they were going to do to me," said Burns.

Hall knew Burns was risking his political career "because, if it had not worked, I am afraid that he personally would have taken the blame for the fact that Hawaii did not get statehood."

The Statehood Act passed on March 12, 1959. By then the steam had gone out of the fight against it. In fact, the bill went through the Senate in less than four hours. Any of the fourteen senators who voted against the bill could have filibustered for four hours, but they chose not to. The bill went through the House in less than twenty-three hours. Hawaii was in—there was just the formality of a presidential signature—and the ILWU International officers sent congratulations to Hall:

THIS OCCASION MARKS ANOTHER RESOUNDING VICTORY FOR OUR UNION AND ITS FRIENDS AND SUPPORTERS IN HAWAII AND ELSEWHERE. . . . THE ENEMIES OF STATEHOOD HAVE ALWAYS BEEN THE ENEMIES OF THE ILWU. . . .

With statehood Hall's dreams swelled: the ILWU's political power was bound to grow; it now could help elect a governor; help send people to Congress who had a vote. He was in the Big Leagues now. There was no question about whom Hall wanted in the governor's chair: "We all feel very strongly here that Jack Burns should run. . . . No other Democrat can be elected and even if he could, the importance of governorship for this first term outweighs all other considerations." And he outlined what a governor could do: "My God, just the opportunity to clean up the judiciary, let alone police commission, university regents, Department of Public Instruction, etc., is sufficient reason for electing a real liberal to the top state post."

The first elected governor would make more than five hundred appointments. Hall wanted a say in those appointments.

In April 1959, the ILWU held its thirteenth Biennial Convention in Seattle and Hall introduced Burns. He said he first had heard of Burns in 1935 when seamen came ashore and started organizing labor in Hawaii. The word was that Burns was "a good cop."

Hall told the convention delegates that in 1945 Secretary of Interior Ickes prodded Governor Stainback into appointing "working men" to boards and commissions. It was then that Stainback named Hall to the Police Commission. Hall said he later forced Chief of Police Gabrielson, "who had been shoving people around in those early organizational days," to resign. Hall said he had pressed for Burns' appointment as police chief, but "I didn't quite have the votes on the committee." He became friendly with Burns and "watched him struggle to build, together with us, a political movement representative of the people of Hawaii and not just a few large business concerns."

Burns was a humble man, said Hall, but a man of courage. He took defeats, kept trying, and finally, with the help of the ILWU and "many others in the community," was elected a delegate to Congress "who believed in working people and in statehood." Jestingly, Hall said he now had a problem on his hands: the plebiscite to ratify the Statehood Act would take place July 27, 1959. On July 28 Hawaii would elect two United States senators, two representatives, and the governor. How would he address Burns following the election? As "Senator Burns" or as "Governor Burns"? "I can assure you of one thing," said Hall, "that the vast majority of the people of Hawaii will elect him to either office he seeks. . . ."[1]

The compliments finished, Burns slipped on his spectacles and began to read his speech. He never was a great speaker. He often rambled; he spoke in a dry monotone; he was not the kind who can kindle a fire. But this time he said something that ignited his audience and reverberated 2600 miles away in Hawaii:

> And as we analyze the situation in Hawaii and give proper credit where credit is due, I am going to make a statement that I have made before in Hawaii:
>
> That the foundations for democracy in Hawaii were laid by the ILWU! [loud applause] because they freed the working man of the plantations . . . from the economic and political control of management; because they enabled him to realize that they had dignity, that they were citizens who had a right to participate in such little government as we had. . . .

The news services picked up the speech; it became known as the "ILWU-brought-democracy-to-Hawaii" speech, and it enraged conservatives. They interpreted it to mean that Burns was under Hall's thumb; otherwise, why should he publicly make such an effusive declaration of fidelity?

"Mr. Burns' entire political history has been one of alliance

---

1. Burns preferred to run for the Senate but bowed to Democratic Party wishes and ran for governor.

with the ILWU," said Philip Maxwell of the Employers Council.

> In May, 1948, he was nominated for his first major political office, the chairmanship of the Oahu Democratic Party County Committee, by Ernest Arena, longtime ILWU business agent. I cannot believe that this nomination was accidental. . . . Does anyone believe that the ILWU gives this kind of support without expecting—and getting—something in return?

William H. "Bill" Ewing, managing editor of the *Star-Bulletin,* said the ILWU "made [Burns] what he is today. He would never have got there without the support of the ILWU. And, of course, Harry Bridges. He is their boy."

The air was heavy with condemnation; Hall had to respond.[2] He placed a full-page ad in the Sunday paper, which said:

> The ILWU has never asked Mr. Burns for a political favor. It has supported Mr. Burns because he was not and is not in the pocket of any special interest group—employers or otherwise. . . .
>
> We have no commitment from Mr. Burns on who is to be appointed to any governmental post. We have neither asked for the appointment of any individual nor even suggested to him a single name for consideration.

Despite the controversy over Burns' speech, Hall predicted he would win the election by fifteen thousand votes.[3] He predicted that Kido, Burns' running mate, would beat Jimmie Kealoha by three to five thousand votes; that Republican Hiram Fong would

---

2. Aware that the Seattle speech had cost him votes, Burns did what many a politician does: he "amplified" his remarks. In a speech to the ILWU Local 142 convention six months after the Seattle speech and a month after the first statehood elections, Burns said: "It is a FACT *[sic]*—an undeniable, incontrovertible TRUTH—that until the laborers of the plantations were organized into a union, the word democracy had no meaning to the more than 24,000 workers who worked on the plantations. . . ."

3. Hall underestimated Quinn, who had come up with what Democrats called a "campaign gimmick": the "Second Mahele." This was a plan to sell public lands on the Neighbor Islands with a limit of one acre to a family. Prices would start at about fifty dollars an acre and be allocated through public drawing. The reference was to the Great Mahele of 1848 when King Kamehameha III divided land among the royalty, the *alii,* and the commoners.

beat Democrat Frank Fasi by five thousand votes in the race for one seat in the United States Senate; that Democrat Oren Long would beat Republican Wilfred Tsukiyama by fifteen thousand votes for the other Senate seat; and that Dan Inouye would win over Charles H. Silva by twenty thousand votes in the race for a seat in the United States House of Representatives.

The election results stunned Hall. Quinn beat Burns by 4138 votes; Kealoha beat Kido by 15,596 votes. Inouye won by more than 60,000 votes, but Tsukiyama lost to Long by only 4577 votes. There was some consolation for Hall: Fong, strongly backed by the ILWU, defeated Fasi by 9514 votes.

Some Democrats blamed Hall for Burns' defeat. They said he concentrated too much on beating Fasi and not enough on electing Burns. Many Democrats blamed Burns himself for his defeat; they said he spurned their help until it was too late. "A lot of people who were close to Burns felt that because he had helped engineer statehood . . . he was a shoo-in and didn't need help from a lot of quarters," said McClung. Gill said, "It got within two weeks of election and then—that's when Quinn was pulling his Mahele bit—[Burns] sent a message out: 'What can you do?' " Said Gill:

> All he had to do was ask. Vince [Esposito] went out. Sakae [Takahashi] went out. We made speeches, attended rallies. They did their best, but there was only a week.
>
> He lost it by spitting on . . . this island [Oahu]. He thought the ILWU would take care of the island.

Embarrassed, Hall tried to explain the Burns defeat. "No one can single out any reason," he said. He attributed part of the cause to the press, which, he said, misrepresented Burns' Seattle speech. He admitted the speech hurt Burns.

Fasi knew who to blame for his own defeat: Hall and the ILWU. He had campaigned in the Democratic primary against Bill Heen much the same way he had campaigned against Wilson in the 1954 mayoralty election: Youth versus Age. He defeated Heen, but in the general election there was that tough "kid from Kalihi," Hiram Fong, to contend with. And Hall, of course, the power broker. "His power is fantastic," said Fasi.

He was able to force Kauai County Attorney, my campaign manager [Toshio Kabutan], to stop any active work on my behalf. He forced rank and file ILWU unit leaders who supported me actively in the Primary Election to campaign for Fong. The results were startling. Kauai gave me 3,576 votes in the primary to 1,649 for Heen and 1,592 for Fong.

The General Election gave me 4,322 to 5,337 for Fong. Kabutan . . . had predicted I would take the island by 2,500 votes before Hall's intervention. In one precinct, as an example, my primary vote of 150, as against a combined total of 92 for Fong and Heen, dwindled to 55. Fong got 252.

Maui was even worse. We had counted on taking the outside islands by at least 4,000 votes. Instead, we lost them by 6,000 votes—all in ILWU areas and that more than spelled the difference! . . .

Fasi pursued the office of mayor of Honolulu for sixteen years before he won election. In 1967 he raised more than half a million dollars in campaign funds by holding a $100-a-plate "birthday party." He had more than enough to wage a strong campaign in 1968. Before the election he went to see Hall. "It looks as if I'm going to be elected mayor," he said. "I didn't come here to solicit your help and I wouldn't change my opinion any more than there will be a second Immaculate Conception."

Hall laughed.

"I just wanted to tell you," Fasi went on, "that if I'm elected, the union, as one of the biggest unions representing workers in the island, will be listened to and have a voice in my regime."

Hall said thanks.

The ILWU, as usual, fought Fasi in 1968 and supported his opponent, Republican D. G. "Andy" Anderson. "We have known Frank Fasi for more than twenty years and have always considered him as two-faced and opportunistic," said a letter from the ILWU leadership to the members. Though the ILWU opposed Fasi and the rest of labor and the business community were divided over him, and Fasi got only lukewarm support from his own party officials, yet he beat Anderson by 94,264 to 78,499 votes. Fasi's effectiveness over television and his rapport with low-income groups did it. He won 2 to 1 in Kalihi and Kapalama, for example.

The child Jack Hall.

Young militant labor leaders in 1940: Mutt Arashiro, Yasu Arakaki, Johnny Brun, Jack Hall, Jack Kawano, Masao Yotsuda, Johnny Elias, "Big Ben" Kahaawinui, Bert Nakano, Harry Kamoku, unidentified person, and Louis Welch. *(City Photo)*

Hall in 1944, shortly after he became ILWU Regional Director. *(Star-Bulletin Photo)*

Hall during the period of "sweetness and light" before the 1946 sugar strike. *(Photo Hawaii)*

Some of the labor team of 1946–1947: back row, Henry Gonsalves, Teamsters business agent; Bob Mookini, ILWU Local 142 president; Harriet Bouslog with a hibiscus in her hair; a jaunty Art Rutledge; and Jack Hall. Front row, a youthful Dave Thompson, Amos Ignacio, and Rudy Eskovitz of the Marine Cooks & Stewards. *(ILWU Dispatcher Photo)*

A moment to savor: Gladstein hands over the $1.5 million FSLA check to Hall, with Kawano and Okada looking on. *(ILWU Dispatcher Photo)*

Sugar workers' wives and children march through Hilo on the first day of the 1946 sugar strike. *(ILWU Photo)*

Goldblatt speaking to striking long-shoremen in 1949.

Goldblatt eulogizing Hall in 1971. *(Graphic Pictures Hawaii)*

Broom brigaders confront longshoremen in 1949 strike. McElrath, right, listens in. *(Star-Bulletin Photo)*

Hall addresses a testimonial picnic on Kauai in
1952. *(ILWU Dispatcher Photo)*

Symonds confers with Hall during the HUAC hearings in 1950.

Hall poses in 1958 with marlin caught off the Kona coast. *(ILWU Dispatcher Photo)*

Hall in black tie and business suit at the Aloha United Fund annual meeting in 1968. *(Advertiser Photo by Ron Jett)*

The game is over: McElrath, top photo, reads his poem-eulogy to Hall. Bottom photo: red carnation leis cast in the water. *(Photos by David Thompson)*

Part 11
THE MELLOWING YEARS
(1960–1969)

CHAPTER **68**

Mechanization

*At 1:12 p.m. on Jan. 8, the operator in the cab
of a 60-foot gantry crane at Pier 29-A hoisted
cargo-container box No. 10239 from the deck
of the Hawaiian Farmer.*

*He jockeyed the 24-foot aluminum box over
the ship's rail and set it down on a flatcar
alongside the dock as easily as you'd drop an
egg into an eggcup.*

The operation took 4 minutes, 47 seconds.
—Honolulu Advertiser,
January 18, 1959

The ILWU early on realized that mechanization was inevitable and there was no use fighting it. Recognizing that it had to use mechanization to its own advantage, the union studied the subject in the careful way it always studied complex problems. The most efficient ports in the world, such as Rotterdam, were investigated. Lincoln Fairley, the ILWU's director of research, methodically collected material and, of course, it was available to Hall.[1]

"We told the industry, 'We will cooperate in automation changes, provided you agree to share the benefits with the workers,' " said Hall. He knew that ideas for automation which had been on drawing boards would "find their way into industry." It would mean drastic reductions in the work force—in

---

1. The basic difference in Hawaii and West Coast longshoring was that Hawaii did not use longshore gangs dispatched from a union hall (or more accurately from a joint management-union hall). Each Hawaii stevedoring company hired its own regular crews and kept a casual list of standbys.

sugar, in pineapple, and on the waterfront. Goldblatt saw trouble ahead:

> The union took the position from the beginning that the responsibility for those workers rested squarely on the industry and the fate of these workers was a subject of collective bargaining, and that unless we could make provisions . . . to take care of these people, who were replaced by the machine, we were going to run into more difficulties, which might make the 1946 strike look like rather a minor thing.

Prudently, the union began to prepare. Starting in 1952 the ILWU made it worthwhile for longtime workers to leave the sugar industry voluntarily and go back home. "In this way the work force was shrunk from the top, instead of cut from the bottom and laying off younger family men who had less seniority," said Hall. The incentives to repatriate were separation pay and allowance. A worker could go home "with sizeable amounts of American dollars, which vastly expanded in purchasing power in the Philippines." Hall said money that would have gone to active employees was used to buy pensions for older workers so they could leave. At the same time the union also negotiated what Hall called "the best medical plan in the nation for retired workers."

Hall discussed mechanization with Fred Simpich of Castle & Cooke and Ben Dillingham of Oahu Railway & Land Company. A joint Matson–Castle & Cooke–OR & L team undertook to research the problem of how to conduct stevedoring operations more efficiently. Hall told Simpich the union wanted its share of the savings:

> I warned him that while we believed in the principle of increased efficiency providing we got our share of the benefits, that the introduction of new techniques had to be timed with a situation where it would not bring layoffs and less than forty hours of work per week. . . .
>
> I said it was far better to let attrition reduce the size of the work force, break up the gangs to fill the deficiencies in other gangs, delay ship turnabout temporarily and pay out extra overtime to a reduced work force rather than be faced with desperate rank and file opposition later. . . .

The ILWU, meantime, considered other tactics. Goldblatt played with the idea of eight hours' pay for a seven-hour workday in exchange for an agreement which would permit the stevedoring companies unlimited use of waterfront machinery and the right to shift men around as they saw fit.[2] Bridges considered a six-hour workday. It was always a part of his idea of the shape of things to come.

Mechanization was inevitable and what labor and management were approaching was the establishment of a mechanization fund through which workers would share in the benefits of new waterfront techniques. Hall proposed that the employers pay for such a fund through a ten-cent-a-ton tax on inbound and outbound cargo. The employers, however, opposed any kind of tax; they also opposed the idea of "sharing savings." Hard bargaining went on for a long time and finally the two sides worked it out. A Mechanization and Modernization Fund (known as M & M) went into effect in Hawaii in 1960. The industry put up $450,000—$150,000 for the year that ended June 15, 1960, and $300,000 for the year ending June 15, 1961.

The M & M fund guaranteed a longshoreman thirty-two hours of straight time a week, or $90.24 (based on the straight-time wage then of $2.82 an hour)—that is, a guaranteed income of $4692.48 a year. If a stevedore lost his job but could transfer to the West Coast, the agreement gave a family man an $850 travel allowance and a single man $325. It provided supplemental severance allowance to older workers and a bonus of up to $6077 or his regular pension benefits, whichever was greater. It also permitted workers to repatriate voluntarily and take a lump-sum payment of their pension equities. "Some left with as much as $20,000," said Hall.

To pay for M & M, the industry devised a formula based on a combination of tonnage handled by the stevedoring companies

---

2. The thought amused Paul St. Sure, president of the Pacific Maritime Association. Tongue in cheek, St. Sure said that when new machinery was installed on the docks, the ILWU demanded that all workers get skilled pay. "The rest of the gang comes along to witness the operation—and stays on as a witness." This amounted, in essence, to giving the onlookers "expert witness pay." Goldblatt had to laugh.

and man-hours of workers employed. "The mechanization fund approach is the most logical one we can devise to cushion the impact of improved cargo handling methods on longshore and to give the men some share of the benefits of these improved methods," said Hall. Goldblatt called the plan that Hall negotiated "a very healthy and constructive agreement." He said he meant to apply some of its features to the West Coast agreement.[3]

The mechanization plans both in Hawaii and on the West Coast did not please all the longshoremen. Nor did it especially please Bridges. Some longshoremen felt they were giving up too many rights; that the agreement gave the employers too free a hand. In some cases (as in Hilo) it cut the work force drastically. On the West Coast the vote on M & M was a good clue to its reception. It was accepted by a vote of 6267 for and 3331 against.[4]

What did M & M accomplish? A paper prepared for President Nixon's Pay Board in 1972 concluded that on the West Coast from 1960 to 1970 "on the order of $900 million to $1 billion worth of man-hours were 'saved' due to an increased productivity." The report said during that period West Coast employers paid out $63.5 million in benefits.[5] Longshore labor costs dropped sharply at a time when labor costs in the rest of the economy generally were rising steadily. Bridges did not challenge the Pay Board report.

Hall believed in "full services" for ILWU members: in-

---

3. Hall negotiated what Hawaii labor historian Edward Beechert called "a very interesting" contract. One "ingenious feature" was a plan whereby longshoremen were taken to the Neighbor Island ports as needed.

4. M & M played its role and then went out of existence. Instead of M & M ILWU longshoremen have a guaranteed annual income, according to Bernard T. Eilerts, a Hawaii Employers Council president. On the West Coast in 1977 the longshoremen were guaranteed at least thirty-four hours' average work over a four-week period; in Hawaii, thirty-six hours, said Eilerts. "The object was accomplished—to reduce the people in the work force," he said. "It's no longer an issue."

5. The report did not cover Hawaii. The Employers Council said it had no figures on Hawaii, but that savings and benefits probably were proportionate to the West Coast.

surance, health, education, social work, welfare.[6] He had decided as early as the late 1940s that union members should have their own insurance and medical plans. He talked to Paul G. Pinsky, a San Francisco insurance consultant and former member of the left-wing faction of the CIO, whom Hall had known since 1945. Pinsky and his partner, Bernard Berkov, set up an improved medical insurance plan for pineapple and longshore workers.

With the help of Pinsky and Berkov the ILWU entered the insurance field. The union sold auto insurance to its members at ten percent less than private company rates. Saburo Fujisaki, director of the ILWU Membership Service Department, handled administration of the union-negotiated health, dental, and pension plans; he was assisted by the union's social worker, Ah Quon McElrath. "In the field of prepaid medical and hospital care, the objective of the union is to cover the entire bill for our people," said Fujisaki.

For example, Fujisaki said, in 1966 the sugar workers' medical-hospital plan covered 10,500 workers and more than 20,000 dependents. It provided for almost complete medical care, including drugs, at a monthly cost to the workers ranging from $1.65 for a single person to a maximum of $6 for a married worker with six or more dependents.

---

6. In 1971, a network of 2561 elected ILWU unit officers, stewards, and membership service committeemen functioned at 185 different companies with union contracts. Each unit had its own elected officers, stewards, and membership service committees (sports, publicity, medical and pension plans, and welfare).

CHAPTER **69**

The Nixon Caper

The 1960 presidential election was something special for the ILWU. That year Hall tried to elect Richard Nixon president. Of course, it was presumptuous to think little Hawaii could elect anyone president, but Hall occasionally was a visionary. He delivered in person to Nixon a plan by which he said Nixon could win the labor vote on the mainland and, at the same time, win the election. He predicted that the ILWU would lead Nixon to victory in Hawaii. "Our members have a pretty good record of following our recommendations," he said.[1]

Hall was angry with John F. Kennedy, Nixon's opponent, because, according to Hall, Kennedy had made "a deal with the AFL-CIO." The ILWU had called a special meeting of the International Executive Board to consider whom the union would endorse for president. The ILWU had a policy: endorsement for president had to be unanimous; one dissenting vote would kill it.

Kennedy was anathema to the ILWU. As Bridges explained:

Kennedy had declared war on the ILWU as such. And on me. And Hoffa [Jimmy Hoffa, Teamster Union president, whom the Kennedy administration had investigated for corruption]. . . . Kennedy in a cold-blooded way . . . had to have some villains to campaign upon and he made [us] the villains. . . .

The ILWU Executive Board did not endorse Nixon unanimously; some members couldn't swallow the idea. Nixon had earned a reputation for being antiunion that went back to the start of

---

1. Hall came close; Nixon lost in Hawaii by only 115 votes.

his congressional career in 1946. But Hall was determined to fight Kennedy and line up Local 142 against him. "My mind is made up . . . (but, of course, I will follow the union program whatever it is)," he said. "As an individual, I fail to see how any member of an ILWU family, how any member of a Teamster family or for that matter any unselfish members of any trade union can vote for John F. Kennedy."

On August 4 Nixon came to Hawaii, accompanied by United States Senator Hiram Fong. Nixon was scheduled to speak at 8:30 PM at the Waikiki Shell. That day Goldblatt and Hall were talking politics at Hall's house. Hall mentioned that he had been invited by Fong to meet Nixon. Why not go? said Goldblatt.

"There's no purpose going down to meet him just to shake hands," said Hall. He worked the thing over in his mind for a moment and then snapped to attention. "Let's give him something," he said.

Good idea, said Goldblatt. They decided to write a message, put it in a sealed envelope, and hand it to Nixon. "If any reporters ask any questions—no answer," said Goldblatt. The sealed envelope itself "creates all the mystery you want. You can't have any more than that." The message they wrote said if Nixon took a position that labor's problems should be solved by labor and that he intended to appoint a Secretary of Labor who would not interfere in the affairs of labor unions, then he would win labor votes; and with enough labor votes, he would win the election. Hall reasoned that such a declaration by Nixon would tilt the labor vote for him in the big labor states like Pennsylvania and Illinois. "All he needed [to win] was those two big states," said Goldblatt. "Both of them heavily union states. . . ."

The message written, the envelope sealed, Hall asked his wife to drive him and Goldblatt to Kapiolani Park. He told her to take a roundabout route. Mrs. Hall laughed.

"Just like cops and robbers," she said. Why all the secrecy? Hall told her sombody might have "gotten wind of it." She drove them down and parked; they were right on time. Hall intercepted Nixon near the bandshell entrance. A reporter described the scene:

Mr. Hall, a bespectacled, towering six foot-two incher whose personal hallmark is a casual hula shirt,[2] accosted Mr. Nixon as he walked from his motorcade into the park with Senator Hiram L. Fong. He introduced himself and handed Mr. Nixon a folded sheet of paper.[3]

They exchanged a few words. Hall told Nixon that Kennedy had made deals with AFL officials. "You're in the AFL or you're not recognized," Hall told Nixon.

Nixon asked Hall a question or two about the ILWU's influence in Hawaii and said he would study Hall's message. Mission completed, Hall and Goldblatt rejoined Mrs. Hall. They went to the Waikiki Tropics, had a drink, and went home.

Hall pressed his campaign against Kennedy and the union went all out to beat him. "How can you possibly hand Kennedy a gun and ask him to shoot at us?" Hall said.

ILWU support gave Nixon a 3300-vote lead on the Neighbor Islands but Kennedy took Oahu. It was the old pattern of voting once again. The election was so close that at first it appeared Nixon had won. Later, the recount showed that Kennedy was the winner.

Though he had lost, Hall was satisfied the ILWU had shown its strength. With the exception of Hawaii, in the states where the ILWU had membership—Alaska, Washington, Oregon, and California—Kennedy had been beaten. The ILWU liked to think it carried weight.

"At least we accomplished the 'mission,' " said Hall. "If we had sat on our . . . hands, Kennedy would have carried both states [Hawaii and California]."

---

2. Aloha shirt.
3. Incorrect. A sealed envelope.

CHAPTER 70

Artful Art

> *To Lou Goldblatt I was the only thing in the*
> *way to their having full, complete sway of the*
> *entire state. If they've got transportation and*
> *hotels, they've got everything.*
> —Arthur Rutledge

In 1956, the ILWU International tried to work out an agreement between the Hawaii ILWU and Rutledge's Teamsters. On the mainland the two unions had a warm relationship: why not in Hawaii? Goldblatt talked it over with Hoffa, the Teamsters International president, and with Larry Steinberg, Hoffa's administrative assistant. They decided to start small in Hawaii: to stop baiting each other, not to interfere with each other's organizing programs, and to organize cross-town trucking. They also agreed to organize all plants industrially with the proviso that trucking companies which primarily handled sugar and pineapple belonged to the ILWU.

Hall was not optimistic. Neither was Rutledge. Each heartily mistrusted the other, but they had their orders from above and Hall said he would try. "Rutledge is the kind of individual where relations will always be on a tenuous basis," said Hall. Rutledge was equally suspicious. In his mind he retained the image of his first meeting with Hall—the time when he came to Hall for help in the bartenders' strike and Hall had exclaimed: "We can take over!" Rutledge had kept his guard up. "Anytime they [the ILWU] make a pact, it's to get in bed with you," he said.

For months they stumbled along. Then, at Hall's suggestion, they held a "Unity Breakfast" in the Mauna Kea Room of the Princess Kaiulani Hotel. (At Hall's suggestion, Rutledge paid the tab.) Everyone seemed friendly; the air was heavy with promise. "It was unity all over the place and shows some hope of paying some future dividends," said Hall. "Obviously, Art is under some sort of general instructions from Hoffa to work with us."

In May 1957, they announced a pact of mutual assistance. The *Advertiser* took a photo of unity and harmony: the rare sight of Hall and Rutledge sitting amiably alongside one another. They drafted plans—they would make staff personnel available; they would select targets; they would organize the unorganized. They even coined a slogan: "Let's make Honolulu a union town." Bridges called the pact "a signal achievement."

But the community was skeptical. Hall and Rutledge in a togetherness act? An *Advertiser* editorial said the pact was meant to keep Rutledge and Hall on public display and to "scare the pants off unorganized workers and the people who give them jobs."

Robertson came over, looked things over, and told Bridges the unity program was slowly "beginning to click." Hall disagreed; nothing much was happening, he said. "Sad situation, but factually, Art is not going to let anybody get in a position of having any real following."

For his part, Rutledge kept probing for mines and booby traps. "I am no fool," he said. If he didn't keep his guard up, said Rutledge,

> it would be no time before the ILWU would be trying to push me out and seeking to run the Teamsters movement in the islands. . . . If any deal is worked out, the ILWU won't keep their word and will use it for whatever purposes will help the ILWU.
>
> They would not work with me even if they agreed to and so I am not going to have anything to do with it. . . .

"They [Hall and Goldblatt] consistently underestimated the fact that I can think a little bit, too," said Rutledge. The 1957 unity pact came to naught.

In 1959 leaders of the Teamsters and the ILWU were ready to try again and met in Los Angeles to talk it over. The first draft of a new unity pact was signed July 29, 1959, and Rutledge came up with a catchy word: "JOB," which stood for Joint Organizing Board. "We had beautiful stationery set up and everything," said Rutledge.

The pact defined jurisdiction: Teamsters could sign up drivers of all commercial vehicles, except trucks owned or leased by sugar and pineapple companies. The pact also dealt with politics: neither the Hawaii Teamsters nor the Hawaii ILWU could take a position on a national election until their respective International had laid down the policy. On local elections, the two would consult with each other. If they disagreed on choices, and before either took a stand that "might cause a blowup," they would refer the matter to the International. Any dispute they couldn't resolve would go topside to Hoffa.

They agreed to help each other organize, but they dodged a big point: which union—the ILWU or the Hotel Workers— would have jurisdiction over Neighbor Island hotels? The ILWU said the outside islands were an ILWU preserve. According to Rutledge, Hall told Einar Mohn of the West Coast Teamsters that "jurisdiction over all the other islands, it's all ours."

Problems mounted. Hall said the ILWU should move into the construction field on the Neighbor Islands because workers there preferred the ILWU to the AFL-CIO. On Maui, Yagi, the ILWU division director, said AFL-CIO leadership was "incompetent and not giving sound direction to the rank and file."[1]

Rutledge insisted that, as an act of good faith, the ILWU hand over three Honolulu trucking companies to the Teamsters —Y. Higa Trucking Service, Allied Van Lines, and Honolulu Transport and Warehouse. Hall said all right, but the company employees strongly resisted. He commented: "I really don't believe [Rutledge] wants the ILWU-Teamsters relationship to be anything more than staying out of each other's jurisdiction for fear that his personal control over his membership might be weakened. . . ."

---

1. Goldblatt proposed that the ILWU organize the Neighbor Island construction industry and then, in six months or a year, as part of the unity agreement, turn the workers over to the AFL-CIO.

The pact was hopeless, Hall told Bridges. "We just can't get [Rutledge] to do anything on carrying out our understanding and while I keep pressing him, he is all over the lot and won't do anything definite about new organizing."

Clearly it was time for Goldblatt, the man who smoothed things over, to take a hand. On the mainland the ILWU-Teamster pact worked to their mutual advantage, said Goldblatt. It was the only way to coordinate negotiations, tie up the loose ends in independent contracts, and seal up "all escape hatches by the employers." Joint negotiations were necessary. Wasn't it worth the effort to try to work things out in Hawaii, "even though it might not be a smooth running affair?"

It troubled Goldblatt to see Hall's attitude toward Rutledge. "The kind of flexibility for which we are deservedly famous when it comes to maneuvering in negotiations or strike situations is suddenly absent," he said.

> In its place is a quick hardening, bitterness and recriminations, whether directed against Rutledge or against the International, because things aren't being done. I can't see how on one hand we can make a decision to pursue an alliance with the Teamsters, which from an overall trade union point of view, is naturally sound, and on the other hand become so quickly irritated if any kind of a hitch develops.

He urged Hall to push through the transfer of the three trucking companies to the Teamsters; he told Hall to do "two-three-four times" as much as Rutledge to make the pact work.

Hall replied that he was trying to turn over the trucking companies. He knew how important it was to the "national picture," but he was having trouble. He said Rutledge wouldn't take orders from any Teamster official, except maybe Hoffa. "Meanwhile, we struggle along and won't let it go."

The three trucking companies finally were transferred to the Teamsters. Hall said the workers showed "intense hatred of Art," but Hall told them the ILWU would not take them back even if they voted against Rutledge in an NLRB representation election. Some Honolulu hotel workers belonging to Rutledge's union wanted to come over to the ILWU. Hall said that to show his goodwill he told them to stay with Rutledge's Hotel Workers. He also refrained from criticizing the Teamsters. "In fact, at meetings with tour drivers we have made it clear that the Teamsters is a damn good union, but Rutledge is the problem."

Though he and Rutledge kept drifting further apart, still they kept up the illusion of unity. At a meeting on August 8, 1960, Hall and Rutledge signed yet another draft of their pact. They agreed upon a joint organizing card; two thousand of them were released to Hall for printing. They assigned Joe Blurr of the ILWU as field director to take over organizing and Paul Steinberg, Teamster executive Larry Steinberg's son, as administrative assistant. Young Steinberg set up an office in Rutledge's Unity House. They struggled again to define who had jurisdiction over what and they arrived at a conclusion: where jurisdiction was clearly defined, contracts could be signed by the individual unions; where both unions were involved, then a joint contract was to be signed. It was all *shibai,* a sham. The irresistible force, Jack Hall, had met the unmovable object, Art Rutledge.

Through it all Goldblatt somehow managed to sound cheerful. "My own feeling is that the agreement can work," he said. He envisioned either a statewide or at least an islandwide (Oahu) contract in cross-town trucking. "It would also provide one of the major keys to organizing in other fields," he said. He told Larry Steinberg he hoped that jurisdiction over Neighbor Island hotels "doesn't get thrown into the pot." That jurisdiction belonged to the ILWU, he said.

But by the fall of 1960 it was clear the pact had failed. Paul Steinberg phoned Joe Blurr and told him so. He also put it in writing. He said the working agreements under the pact "have been indefinitely suspended."

Blurr replied: "The fact is that Local 996 [Hawaii Teamsters] has refused to honor the agreement. . . . If there is any 'suspension' of the pact, it has been suspended by Local 996." Blurr said ILWU officers had been trying for months to reach Local 996 by letter and even by telegram—"all of which remain unanswered."

The JOB was over and done with.

Rutledge loved to tweak Hall's nose. One day, without telling Hall why, he ordered a single picket set up at Pier 2 where Matson's *Hawaiian Trader* was unloading. Hall called Rutledge. The Teamsters' switchboard stayed open for ten minutes, then cut Hall off. He was fuming. When the ILWU operator raised the Teamsters' switchboard again, the operator told her Rutledge had left the building. He ducked Hall all day.

Hall angrily informed Goldblatt. " 'It's Me, O Lord'[2] . . . crying out in the wilderness of Hawaii. That God damn *[sic]* Rutledge is going to drive us all nuts unless the Teamsters do something about him or let us take the gloves off."

Rutledge said he had sent out the picket to help the West Coast Teamsters in a jurisdictional dispute in San Pedro, California, with the ILWU and "to give the public notice that we have traditional jurisdiction in Hawaii."

Hall's complaint was taken up by Goldblatt, who spoke to the Teamsters. Goldblatt said the ILWU would not tolerate "the deliberate gimmicking and the crap pulled by Rutledge." Things had reached the point where Hall and the others were "getting ready to march."

The Teamsters promised to tell Hoffa about the rascal Rutledge. Furthermore, said Goldblatt, when Paul St. Sure, president of the Pacific Maritime Association, heard that a Matson ship had been capriciously picketed, he would be "fit to be tied. After all, that's a sacred cow."

Surely Rutledge would be punished, thought Goldblatt. "Methinks a smart guy was smart once too often." Nothing came of it, though. Rutledge ran his own show and Hoffa was far away.

---

2. The title of artist Rockwell Kent's autobiography.

CHAPTER 71

The Hall-Burns Affair

In 1962 Hall and the ILWU played a major role in electing Burns governor. In his twelve years in office, Burns always could count on the union's support. He was a close friend of Hall's. They didn't even have to do much talking to each other; often just a few words were enough to reveal their thinking.

Hall introduced Burns to the Local 142 convention in 1961 as a friend of the union "in good weather and bad . . . in victory and defeat."[1] The ILWU raised more than ten thousand dollars for the Burns campaign of 1962, but more important they sent their troops to knock on doors and talk to people and work up enthusiasm for Burns.

Burns' opponent was Governor Quinn, who had surprised and beaten him in 1959 despite the ILWU's support. Quinn's former running mate, Lieutenant Governor James K. "Jimmie" Kealoha, challenged Quinn in the Republican primary and left an opening for Hall to exploit. The ILWU quietly campaigned for Kealoha; they decided he would be an easier opponent for Burns than Quinn, though, as Hall admitted, support for Kealoha was "spotty." Kealoha himself wondered if the ILWU was really giving him any help at all. "They didn't fight me," he said, "but they didn't do any supporting."

On October 5, the night before the primary election, Kealoha, a Hawaiian-Chinese, spoke at a rally in the Hilo Armory. He said, almost wistfully, that "it would be wonderful if a local boy who is non-Caucasian could be elected governor." He didn't

---

1. Burns described himself at the time as an "unemployed politician. My golf game is really improving—I shot a 79 yesterday."

know Quinn was there; in any case, he thought he was just dropping a harmless remark.

Quinn didn't think it was so harmless. When it came his turn to speak, he said that after the 1959 election,

> I think the friends of my friend Jimmy[2] persuaded Jimmy that he should seek the office of governor irrespective of our relationship or the public welfare and they urged my friend Jimmy to start working toward that end three years ago. I think my friend Jimmy succumbed to their wooing and blandishments. . . .

Quinn said Kealoha had turned against Quinn's land program (the promised "Second Mahele"), for which they had campaigned. "Jimmy has even repudiated me because I don't have the right color skin. And my skin has not changed color since 1959," said Quinn. He could not keep the bitterness out of his voice. In the audience Kealoha listened sadly. He felt Quinn had treated his little ploy about a local boy "as a racial thing."

Kealoha lost the primary by almost fourteen thousand votes.

On October 15 Hall met with Jack Reynolds and Robert Hasegawa of the AFL-CIO and with Rutledge to talk about the general election. Hall also saw Burns that day and talked to Kealoha. Something was troubling Hall. With few exceptions, he said, the ILWU secondary leadership had "climbed on the Democratic bandwagon without obtaining the type of commitments which are necessary." Hall meant that the union did not get promises from the other Democratic candidates for office to support Burns. Burns had been beaten once by Quinn; some ILWU people thought it might happen again.

However, labor was united: the AFL-CIO, the Teamsters, the United Public Workers, and the ILWU were all pulling together for the "Big Five"—the three Democratic candidates for Congress (Inouye for the Senate; Gill and Spark Matsunaga for the House); Burns for governor; and William S. Richardson for lieutenant governor. Even Hall and Rutledge were in agreement.

Shortly after the October 15 get-together, union leaders met

---

2. Kealoha preferred the spelling "Jimmie."

with the "Big Five" Democratic candidates at Rutledge's Unity House. Present were Reynolds, Hasegawa, Akita "Blackie" Fujikawa, and Jim Dooley of the AFL-CIO; Rutledge was there, and so were Hall and McElrath. Hall said he, Rutledge, and Reynolds stressed the Burns campaign above all else. As Hall put it: "Reynolds, Art and I made it quite clear to the assembled five that we were supporting the slate on the basis of the understanding that the slate would support each other and that we expected to take a hard look at the situation before the general election."

After their little chat Hall asked Burns in private how his campaign was coming along. Burns did not sound enthusiastic. He confirmed, "rather reluctantly," that Inouye was working only in areas where he wouldn't antagonize his own people.[3] "Large numbers of Inouye workers are only supporting Inouye," said Hall. Of the five Democratic candidates, said Hall, Gill was doing the best job—"particularly in taking on Governor Quinn, which the other congressional candidates are studiously avoiding."

Overlooking nothing in pursuit of a Burns victory, Hall invited Kealoha over for a talk. He said it went well:

> I was able to get Kealoha and his campaign manager together at my home with Burns and his campaign manager and Eddie [DeMello] and Joe [Blurr] and I, and confirmed an understanding that Jimmie's workers, wherever he has personal control over them, and he does in at least 75% of the cases, will go all-out for Burns.[4]
>
> In return for this aid, it is agreed that the Burns forces will use all of their influence to make Jimmie the Executive Secretary of the Hawaiian World's Fair Committee which is a fulltime job for the next three years.

Despite Kealoha's pledge, Hall was still concerned that the ILWU had obtained "no real commitments" from legislative

---

3. Quinn disagreed with that assessment. He said Inouye went all out campaigning for Burns.

4. Kealoha said he did not personally campaign against Quinn in the general election, but his supporters did.

and city-county candidates "for special support for Jack [Burns]." Nevertheless by now he was confident enough to place a small bet on Burns: the bettor gave him five thousand votes.

Quinn knew he was in trouble. He assumed that in 1959 the ILWU hadn't gone all out to oppose him; they hadn't taken him that seriously. Now it was different. Hall was leading the drive for a Burns victory. It didn't take binoculars to read the signs. In 1962 Quinn had the same friends in the plantation towns and camps that he had had in 1959; but when the same Quinn political posters went up, they were slashed or torn down. "The message got through and I lost all that support," said Quinn.

Burns beat Quinn decisively.[5] The Democrats swept the board. The "Big Five" Democratic candidates won easily. The unfulfilled Second Mahele promise had backfired. Kealoha people had helped Burns; the Democrats had run a good campaign. But it was the labor vote—especially ILWU strength—and the vote of the Japanese-American community that defeated Quinn.

Hall collected his bet. Finally, his friend Burns was in the governor's chair. That was good, he said, "but we've never had any problems we felt any politician could settle. He [Burns] didn't ask for anything and we don't expect anything."

Rutledge saw Burns on the night of the election, "trembling" with emotion over his victory. That night Rutledge got a call from Hall to meet him at Jim Dooley's house. Reynolds was there, along with Hall and Dooley. Rutledge said Hall presented a list of candidates whom the ILWU proposed for appointment to boards and commissions.

As soon as he got there, he could see Hall's maneuver, said Rutledge. " 'What about this commission . . . ?' [Hall] wants to get the jump on everybody—so he goes down the list." Rutledge told Hall he didn't come there prepared to make recommendations for appointments to board and commissions. He had no choices of his own in mind. He was letting it go by default. "This was Jack—the politician," said Rutledge. Indeed Hall did have the subject of appointments in mind. He told the Local 142 Executive Board shortly after the election that he

---

5. 114,308 to 81,707.

would meet with AFL-CIO officials to discuss Burns' appointments. "We have to quickly decide what particular areas we are interested having our people participate [in] and the names of the people who are entitled to participate," he said.[6]

Once Burns was in office Hall's usual contact with him was over the phone. They met now and then. They did not ordinarily write each other. On the night of April 30, 1963, Hall and DeMello saw Burns in his office and he told them he would sign the two bills the legislature had passed that day, bills in which the ILWU had a special interest.[7] Hall described what happened at the meeting:

> [Burns] also proposed that he and I spend a half-day together a week or so after the legislature closes on May 3 going over all of the appointments he is considering making and not just those that may come from the ILWU.
>
> This will give us a real opportunity to express our views on some of the more conservative elements he has been pressured to appoint to the Democratic party organization.

"All in all, 1963 seems to have been a pretty good year for the ILWU in Hawaii both politically and economically," Hall said with satisfaction.

His power was at a peak, and his old adversary, Frank Fasi, who in 1962 had lost a bid for election to the United States House of Representatives, acknowledged it. "When you talk about Hawaiian politics today, you have to bow to the Mecca—the fountainhead of political power, John Wayne Hall," said Fasi. "For, say what you will, Jack Hall is the most powerful single political figure in Hawaii today. I say that from personal experience and long years of observation."

---

6. Henceforth ILWU members were named in generous measure to boards and commissions, state, county, and civic, which Hall and Burns both believed was only the union's just deserve.

7. One was the Little Norris-LaGuardia bill (the so-called "Frank Silva Bill"), which placed a five-year limit on personal history questionnaires for state employees and members of state boards and commissions; the other was the unemployment compensation bill, which called for increased contributions from employers.

Hall replied: "Every time some politician can't get elected, he finds someone to blame. I'm very happy the people of Hawaii have not seen fit to elect [Fasi] to public office."

Hall's political choices sometimes puzzled people. Why did he support Republican Hiram Fong, whose views often ran counter to many principles the radical ILWU stood for? "It's simple," said Hall. "He can't get elected without us. So he'll do what we ask him to do—within reason."

In 1962 the ILWU backed Gill for the United States House of Representatives; in 1964 Hall wanted Gill to stay in the House and not challenge Fong for his seat in Senate. He liked having a senator he could call on. Long before the 1964 campaign, DeMello wrote Gill that the ILWU Election Campaign and Legislative Committee had endorsed him and Fong for reelection to the seats they held. DeMello said the union was impressed with Gill's record in the House; "except for Medicare," however, the union also thought Fong had an excellent record. DeMello said Fong was part of a liberal Republican group and a key member of the Senate Judiciary Committee and, as such, he had been helpful in killing bills the ILWU disliked, such as wiretapping. He hoped Gill would see things his way. Hall sent a copy of DeMello's letter (which Hall probably composed) to Fong and added: "It would help things all around if you would support medicare and keep Goldwater[8] the hell out of Hawaii."

Hall knew Fong's reelection wouldn't be easy, "even without a Goldwater albatross around his neck." He told Kibre in Washington to impress upon Fong the need to disassociate himself from Goldwater and Kibre did. He also said for public consumption that Fong was not a Goldwaterite.[9] Said Kibre:

> We know Hiram is not 100% for the ILWU. We don't see eye to eye with him on many issues. We do know that he carried out every commitment he made to this union. . . . As far as the ILWU is concerned, Fong delivered the goods.

---

8. Republican Senator Barry Goldwater of Arizona was a presidential candidate.

9. Fong said of Goldwater: "He was nominally of my party and I supported him. But we didn't agree on a lot of issues."

"Hiram did us several favors," McElrath explained. "His word was good. Hard to get, but when you get it he carried it out. Sort of like Doc Hill. . . ."

In Hall's opinion, Fong was "one of the great champions of the U.S. Senate," an assertion that liberals in Hawaii reckoned was hyperbole. That didn't mean, said Hall, that although the ILWU endorsed Fong for election that it agreed with everything he said and everything he voted for. "And on some things we are in very sharp disagreement and it would be a mistake to hide that because it should be out in the open." Hall called Fong "a protector of civil liberties." He said Fong's vote killed wiretapping "when the entire Kennedy crowd was pushing like hell for it." According to Hall, Fong's vote in the Senate Judiciary Committee also killed a bill to screen waterfront workers which the union opposed. "A key vote in committee can be a helluva lot more important than a vote on the floor," said Hall.

All very well, but how to sell Fong against Gill? Hall had a problem. To union people Gill had credentials: he was an outspoken critic of Republican conservatism. He had the solid backing of Rutledge and the AFL-CIO. Hall knew that the AFL-CIO Committee on Political Education and Gill would be "slamming [Fong] every minute." Hall thought he might force a crack in the lineup for Gill; maybe he could convince Jack Reynolds, who was high in the AFL-CIO hierarchy, of the "importance of the kind of work Hiram has been doing."

Reynolds told him he had tried to discourage Gill from running for the Senate, but he admitted he had no influence over him. Few people did. Gill was his own man, like it or not. Hall fished around for campaign material for Fong. He asked Kibre to let him know the number of times Gill had addressed the House of Representative, on what issues, and for how long.[10]

Out of the blue State Senator Nadao Yoshinaga challenged Gill in the Democratic primary. Hall never asked him; Yoshinaga just leaped in on his own. "Hall must have been shocked

---

10. Fong's television campaign concentrated on his assertion that Gill was an "absentee congressman." The central theme of Fong's TV spots was the showing of an unoccupied chair, purportedly representing the "absent" Gill.

when I announced," said Yoshinaga. "I never talked to him about it."[11]

Hall seized on Yoshinaga's entry as a ploy. "We're going to unofficially and quitely push for Najo . . . in order to get as sizeable [a] vote as possible against Gill," he said. From 1951 to 1958 Yoshinaga had worked for Bouslog & Symonds on his home island of Maui. Yoshinaga was smart, militant, and unpredictable. He sometimes gave the Democrats hell as well as the Republicans. Nevertheless he was a labor man and he assumed the ILWU would quietly support him, "but I don't think they would throw Hiram out completely."

Rutledge learned about Hall's endorsement of Yoshinaga and professed indignation. "[Hall] thinks his members will jump through any hoop he holds up," said Rutledge. He said he knew what Hall had in mind: if Yoshinaga won the primary, Hall would dump him even though he was an ILWU man, and support Fong in the general election. "I find it hard to believe [Yoshinaga] would allow himself to be used as a stooge to put over a Jack Hall–Hiram Fong double play," said Rutledge. Gill came up with one of his own salty phrases: he said Hall "bean-balled Nadao."

Gill beat Yoshinaga in the primary by almost a 2 to 1 margin. ILWU support was impotent. Fong defeated Gill in the general election by fourteen thousand votes. ILWU support, the Republican vote, plus the power of television advertising, Fong's "local boy" image, and the Neighbor Island vote did it for him.

---

11. In fact, Yoshinaga and Hall never conferred on anything. "Jack Hall never asked me nothing *[sic]*. He never asked me not one time; let alone legislation or union matters," said Yoshinaga.

CHAPTER 72
The "Green Desert"

> Interviewer: *Hall got bored with Hawaii by 1959.*
> Goldblatt: *He got bored before that.*

> *Things here are in good, boring shape.*
> —Jack Hall

In 1959, a newspaper story said Hall would be reassigned to the mainland.[1] Hall felt he had to deny it. The story had been floating around for at least six months, he said, but it was not true. As proof, he said, he and Yoshiko planned to remodel their home on Paula Drive. "It is true," said Hall, "that my job as representative of the national officers in the islands has lost much of its challenge. Remember I came to Hawaii in 1935 when much needed to be done to make Hawaii a more democratic community. . . ."

Hall sent the clipping to Goldblatt with a comment: "No harm done—not that I wouldn't like to get the hell out of here for a year or so before I completely stagnate." For Hall, Hawaii had become a "Green Desert": lovely to look at, but destitute in large measure of mental stimulation. It was a place where a person with a meditative frame of mind suffered.

Hall enjoyed Goldblatt's visits. They renewed him. "Lou the Lash," he once called Goldblatt; Lou the Stimulator; Lou who came with a big bag of tales to unpack. Hall would seize on him as the Ancient Mariner seized hold of the Wedding Guest.

---

1. The story ran in the *Advertiser* on January 3.

"Jesus Christ! What have you heard now?" he'd exclaim. "Got any stories?"

Goldblatt, spinner of tales, seldom disappointed. He loved to "talk story." Usually it was something racy: something to savor and have a good laugh over; something out of the routine and that made it doubly welcome.

For Hall's life had fallen into routine. He lived simply. He got up early and started making coffee. While the coffee was boiling, he went upstairs and shaved. He usually prepared breakfast for the family—the hearty breakfast he liked: eggs, ham, bacon or sausage, toast, coffee, fruit. Often, a papaya. He dressed in slacks, loafer shoes, and an aloha shirt. His wife drove him to work. He got there before 7:30. He liked to work by himself in the office before anybody came; in the early hours he would wade through his work.

If he had a speech to write, his wife sometimes drove him to the office as early as 2 AM. Often he worked at home late at night with pencil and yellow legal tablet. Sometimes he brought home his special typewriter with big letters.

In his correspondence he was a stickler for proper language. He liked lean prose that came straight to the point. He wrote out the important letters, putting in big commas so his secretary could not miss them. He excelled at dictation. He liked efficient people around him and detested mediocrity. He tackled problems immediately; there was no place in his life for "the half-ass mañana attitude which prevails in Hawaii."

On free days Hall would spend hours in the kitchen. He'd start early; he might be there till noon, chopping vegetables, preparing dishes. Sometimes he took all weekend to prepare a dish. He was good with lamb and stews, marinated meats and chicken, and seafood. He cooked fish in shoyu and spices. Though he liked to go fishing, the fish he cooked was usually caught by somebody else. Cooking relaxed him; it was therapy. But his mind—Hall's restless mind—worked on while he prepared dishes. Yoshiko Hall often caught him making notes.

Hall sometimes did the laundry and hung the clothes out to dry. That astonished Ayako Kaneda (Nitta), a Japanese girl who lived with the Halls from 1964 to 1968. At home in Japan, men didn't cook or do the laundry. That was women's work.

Hall loved music—from the hot licks of the great jazzmen to the Beethoven Ninth. A picture emerges:

> It was something to watch him come home after some of those seemingly endless [negotiation] meetings, put on one of his favorite records, pull up a chair and just about bury his head in the loudspeaker. You could almost see the music folding over him, blanketing out the tensions of the day.

He collected Fats Waller "platters," as he called them. He loved the blast of Louie Armstrong's golden trumpet. When the jazz blew hot, Hall sat enraptured; nodding, swaying, tapping his feet to the beat.

Hall went to opera especially because it was a chance to be with a friend, Leo Lycurgus, manager of the Volcano House hotel on the Big Island. Hall and Lycurgus exchanged books. He told Lycurgus that Will Durant's *Story of Philosophy* was his favorite book. They never talked about union affairs, but Hall sometimes discussed philosophy. He said that a man who worked with his hands should have dignity and be respected. He should be able to develop mentally and come to enjoy good things: read good books, listen to good music.

Hall was moody. He could sit for hours in silence. "So many times so silent in the house," said Miss Kaneda. "He didn't mind sitting in the same place all day."

"Jack was the only person who could sit here for hours and not say a word," said Willis Butler. Sometimes on Sunday he spent the day at the Butlers' home on a quiet street in Kailua. He swam in the pool, drank beer, slept on the *punee*. He listened to music. It was a place of refuge; no one could track him down there.

Hall's lack of a college education sometimes bothered him. He felt uncomfortable among intellectuals, though he himself had an intellectual cast of mind and was fluent and well read. He drank with his union brothers, played poker with them, joked and talked easily with them, but he was not one of them. "He was a little—aloof?—that's too strong a word," said Butler.

Every morning Hall, the diabetic, took a shot of insulin. He kept it in small bottles in the refrigerator; each bottle had its own needle attached. He knew the sugar content of all foods—and of all drinks. For, happy or unhappy, content or discontented, restless or at peace, Hall drank. It was the comforter. Yoshiko would try to stop him when he had too much. "I tried everything I could to get him to stop. . . . But I couldn't do it without getting him angry at me."

Mrs. Hall said that when Hall took part in labor negotiations, he would stop drinking.[2] "He could exercise that kind of discipline over himself," she said. Dr. Butler confirmed that Hall could stop drinking for months. Speaking of Hall's drinking, Butler said that

> he lived with it. He coped with it to the end. He wasn't destroyed by it. When you think of alcoholism, you think of somebody who is totally disabled. Jack was never really disabled by his drinking. For a few hours or a day at a time, he would have problems.

Some people thought differently. Bridges, for example, called Hall "a problem drinker." Eric Hall, who loved his father, was hurt when he saw him drink too much. "We used to hide the bottles around the house," said Miss Kaneda. Hall never punished his son, she said. "He would just watch him and didn't say anything except about school work."

Sometimes Hall called on his half-brother, Bobo Hall, to punish Eric. "Spank him," he would say. He used harsh language, yet he cared deeply for his son. "There was great affection between the two of them," said Bobo. "Jack would come in and mess his hair and then kiss him. . . . He would talk to him as an equal. He would never talk down to him. He would do that

---

2. Carlsmith said the same. Maxwell and Randolph Crossley, who often sat across from Hall at negotiation sessions, said it was not true. Tangen said: "Jack always drank a lot. And he's one of the few guys who didn't drink under pressure. . . . [He could go] a week or ten days and never take a drink."

with other children, too.'' Hall also had a good relationship with his daughter, Mikey. ''The kids adored him,'' said Mrs. Hall.

Hall's two children (there was an 11½-year difference in their ages) were precocious and took part in conversations with their elders on all topics. They were not sent out of the room when people came to call. ''They were extremely intelligent children,'' said Bobo Hall, ''but they could get kind of [ungovernable].'' Said Eddie Tangen, a friend of the family:

> There was no indoctrination of those kids in terms of making them completely understand what socialism was. And neither Jack nor Yoshiko ever set out to make super-leftists out of their kids. The kids had an awful lot of exposure to people. His house was wide open. All the members of the union leadership coming over, and other people coming over there. Those kids were never excluded. Those kids would grow up with a tremendous amount of respect for both their father and their mother. . . .

Hall liked to swim and hike. Carlsmith used to invite him to his ranch on the Big Island.[3] Hall didn't ride or shoot, but he liked to go along with Carlsmith when he hunted goats and sheep. Once they saw a Sentinel goat in silhouette a thousand yards away on top of Hualalai. Hall thought it was too long a shot. Carlsmith had a powerful scope on his rifle. He said, ''Jack, you will know if I hit it—it will go over backwards. If I scare it, it will go forward.'' Hall watched through binoculars as Carlsmith squeezed off the shot. ''My God!'' Hall exclaimed. ''You hit it.''

Though he enjoyed going along on a hunting trip, Hall hated the sight of blood. He got sick if he saw an animal in pain or run over. There was an antidote: a slug of Jack Daniel's whiskey. ''He was able to take pain himself,'' said Butler, ''but he couldn't stand to see other people hurt.'' Ayako Kaneda agreed: ''He was a very soft person and it wouldn't show outside.''

Hall developed into a good speaker. Organizations ranging

---

3. The 105,720-acre Puuwaawaa Ranch, which borders Parker Ranch on the south. It was then owned by Donn and Wendell Carlsmith and Lowell and Ben Dillingham.

from the Rotary Club and B'nai B'rith to the National Association of Accountants and the United Methodist Church invited him to speak. He wrote his own speeches. (A half-hour speech would take about six hours.) Once he was invited to enroll in the National Security Seminar of the Industrial College of the Armed Forces, a gathering sponsored by the Chamber of Commerce. The chamber seemed an illogical host for a left-wing unionist. "Must be getting too damned respectable," Hall grumbled.

Once he addressed seventeen leading bankers and investment counselors on the subject of state and city-county bonds, and they listened attentively. "Very well received," said Hall gratified. Then the thought struck home: here he was, the boogeyman to The Establishment in the late 1940s and early 1950s, addressing bankers. "I'm getting respectable—can't even go barefoot in the park anymore."

He was busy in civic affairs. He served as a member of a three-man committee which selected Lowell S. Dillingham, president of the Dillingham Corporation, as chairman of the first Aloha United Fund; he was a director and member of the steering committee of the Hawaii Visitors Bureau; he was president of the Hawaii Council for Housing Action (HCHA).

He began to attend community functions. On occasion he even wore a dark suit and black tie. The days when he had to wield a pair of chopsticks fast so he could get his share of the contents of the communal rice bowl were long gone.

Always there were union negotiations. At one point the ILWU was negotiating twenty-two contracts. Hall was assigned eleven. A sugar contract ran out January 31, 1966: "The industry is so fat," said Hall. "Yum, yum."

He fished aboard Ray Cravalho's boat *Maria* off Kona. He took Eric fishing for the first time when the boy was seven. That day Hall caught a thirty-pound *ono* off the Penguin Banks and Eric cranked in five small *ahi,* said Hall. One day Hall caught a 270-pound marlin while fishing aboard the *Lani Kai* off Kona. It took forty minutes to boat the fish.

One weekend he and Eric went sailing with one of Hall's friends from Los Angeles, Jack Baskin. It was a rough trip and old seaman Hall got battered. "I'm covered with bruises, sunburned and aching," he said. "The millionaires can have their sport."

Michele, his daughter, married John L. Burton, a California legislator, and in 1964 Hall became a "grand daddy." "It is better to be a grandparent than a parent," he philosophized. "You can enjoy the kids and when they get too bad leave them with the parents. I took some pictures of Kimi. . . . Although she is only ¼-Hall, the intelligence comes through. . . ."

Hall had a special relationship with Dr. Butler. Though he had reservations about doctors in general, "he was intelligent enough to not hem and haw when he found a doctor that he could trust," said Butler.

For a time Hall took oral medication for his diabetes. When it became clear that he had to take insulin shots, he learned how to administer them. Said Butler:

From that time on he not only gave himself his shots . . . but he would even regulate his dose of insulin from day to day and week to week, according to what his urine was showing [his blood sugar count] and according to whether he knew he had violated the rules of his diet to some extent.

Hall also suffered from gout and hypertension. He had hay fever; sometimes his desk was covered with handkerchiefs spread out to dry.

In September 1960 he nicked his finger while doing yardwork and the finger became infected and wouldn't heal. Butler sent him to the hospital and it was discovered that his blood sugar count, which at normal is 100, had climbed to 235. "The most I had previously was 135," said Hall. Butler wanted to put him on a drug, Orinase, but Hall talked him into letting him first try a strict diet. At the end of the week his blood sugar count had dropped to 189; then to 135. Hall stayed on the diet. "No starch, no sugar, and not a drink for seventeen days today," he wrote Goldblatt in triumph. "I'm beginning to feel that I don't like people who drink. Now down to a trim 198 [pounds], about ready to play left end for California. Anyway, I'm feeling damn good and busy as hell."

Goldblatt was worried about Hall's health and told him he

was glad he was dieting and losing weight and even managing without liquor. "However, I can't very well accept your growing hostility toward anyone who can still take a drink," he joked. He predicted that Hall would go back to drinking.

Six months later Hall's blood sugar count again jumped alarmingly. Butler ordered him "incarcerated"—Hall's own word for it—in Kaiser Hospital for examination and rest. Hall explained the seriousness of his condition:

> [Butler] tells me that a couple of more points change in the ratio of acetone in my blood could have sent me into a permanent coma. Seems as though when diabetes has insufficient carbohydrates to feast upon, then the fat tissues are attacked and this creates acetone. Drinking seems to accelerate the process. . . .
>
> My diabetes was run back as bad as it had ever been, and, of course, I was completely run down with fatigue, both physical and mental. . . .

Butler put him on a new drug to help promote weight loss. He took twenty pills a day, had to have lots of rest, and "*no* booze, at least for the next three months." Said Hall: "I join Joe Blurr in the temperance league. (Now we only have to get McElrath hospitalized for a week and we have it made.) I'll have difficulty being tolerant after about two weeks, but I'll try. . . ."

In December 1964, Hall made another trip to the hospital; again it was diabetes. He underwent another complete checkup: "Barium, ugh!" he exclaimed. He had to spend a week at home. There was some cheerful news after the lab tests: "I don't know how it happens after the life I have led but everything is okay—blood pressure, heart, chest, liver, etc.," he said. "My diabetes is back in control and I hope I can keep it that way."

On the night of April 18, 1968, Hall underwent an emergency operation at Kaiser's for a ruptured appendix. Because he was a diabetic, the danger of infection was much more serious than with a nondiabetic patient. Peritonitis set in. Hall spent thirty-three days in the hospital. On the day his brother Bobo visited him he felt so miserable that "he wanted to die." Hall lost thirty pounds during that siege and had to stay home for several months to recuperate.

CHAPTER 73

Hall vs. Bridges

The ILWU knew how to keep a secret. Bridges and Hall became antagonists, but not many people outside the union knew it. To have made that fact known would have hurt the union, so the union held its tongue. To the public the ILWU's top leaders presented an image of unity, but within the portals there was dissension. What started out between Hall and Bridges as simple dislike grew into hostility. During the last years of Hall's life he and Bridges were enemies and lashed out at each other.

Bridges said Hall was power-hungry but by the time he realized it, he couldn't do anything about it. "I should have fired him," said Bridges. "Later, it was too late; he was too strong. You couldn't fire him."

The union's top leadership divided into two sets of adversaries: Bridges and Robertson versus Goldblatt and Hall. One aspect of their quarrel grew out of a difference of opinion on how to conduct labor negotiations; they were disparate personalities and conducted union business differently.

"I just thought that [Hall and Goldblatt] favored this high-falutin' type of unionism that depended upon fancy negotiations and figuring on top and being good at figures and these are the things that produced contracts," said Bridges. "The basic rank and file strength of the workers, which is what counts, is forgotten, see? And the workers are taught mistakenly that what produces a good contract is fancy negotiations, especially by haole people with college degrees."

A picture was created, said Bridges, of Hall the Achiever. Hall did not deliberately seek to create such an image. "Let's just say it evolved that way and other people did it," said Bridges.

And [Hall] knew that I was kind of laughing at him. . . . And, of course, the way he'd say: "So, what about you . . . ? You're the bastard. I don't give a damn what they say about me."

I said, "My line is the goddamned, lousy newspapers—they made me." They never tried to build me up as a great hero around here. Even in the lousy union either. . . . I said, "I never pretend I'm anything but a no-good bum. I've got no goddamn contention of wanting to be a pillar of society or any of that horseshit."

Local 142 wielded a lot of power. Bridges could not overlook it; 142 represented thirty-five percent of the membership of the union and it voted *en bloc.* Hall held the Hawaii vote tightly together. He was skilled at caucusing. Local 142 quickly became a solid force in the union. Anyone who wanted to run for International office had to get 142's support and had to reckon with Hall.

Bridges said it was only natural that in the public's mind Hall, the regional director, was identified with the success of the ILWU in Hawaii. "All right," said Bridges, "you can't separate that. . . . [He's] absolutely part of it." Bridges said Hall was trusted and had earned a reputation for honesty and ability. ("Okay; couldn't argue about that.")

Robertson called Hall a dreamer. "Hall liked to sit down and write up a story," said Robertson. "He had the ability to do that; so few of us have: the ability to put the situation and his thoughts . . . on paper."

Robertson said Hall's greatest shortcoming was his lack of confidence in others and that it reflected an inferiority complex. He claimed Hall failed to develop local leadership, especially among Filipinos. Robertson said in the early days he often had to carry the burden for Hall. "Look, too many times I had to pinch-hit for Jack Hall when he was supposed to be with me at an organizing meeting . . . particularly on the outside islands when he was sloppy drunk, or in a goddamn bar, or in his hotel room," said Robertson. And, Robertson continued: "During the period I was over there in the early days forming a union [for five months in 1947] . . . he was a sick man. He should never drink. He was a diabetic."

But just as Bridges did, Robertson also gave Hall credit for the ILWU's success in Hawaii. "I don't want to take that from him. I'm telling you, he didn't develop leaders to follow," said Robertson.[1]

> He was a behind-the-scenes, shrewd, crafty politician, and used the labor movement as a club to accomplish his ends. And now that's as clear and straightforward as I can put it. But he made a great contribution as an individual to the upbringing of the movement. I'm not going to take that away from Jack because it's there and a lot of people loved him, but they didn't know him like I did.

The correspondence between Bridges and Hall often reflected their growing disenchantment with each other. Sometimes just a phrase in a letter struck sparks. In mid-1964, Hall wrote Bridges a note saying he and Yoshiko were coming to San Francisco on vacation. Hall remarked, more or less as an aside: "Naturally, the entire trip will be at our expense."

Somehow that annoyed Bridges. "Lay off the needle about paying for your trip," he replied. "All the officers and staff take their vacations at their own expense."

Hall raised the bicker a decibel. "Don't be so sensitive about non-existent needles—none was intended," he countered.

In 1965 Hall took issue with mediator Sam Kagel on the long-shore negotiations and said he no longer had confidence in arbitration to resolve basic trade union issues. In the future, said Hall, he would rely on direct collective bargaining. Again the flint was there to strike fire. "When and where did you ever get the notion that we ever had such confidence in resolving basic trade union issues by arbitration?" Bridges snapped. "Never in the history of this union to my knowledge, so maybe apparently I have been asleep, or slipping or something."

> What gets me [said Bridges] is this super-duper position of—never, never fool around with arbitration. It just seems to me that not too

---

1. Didn't develop leaders? The Hawaii labor historian Edward Beechert has pointed out that each of the islands developed its own leaders. Hall had to work with people who had their own island power base. "A person less committed would have taken advantage of the situation and tried to manipulate things," said Beechert. "Given all the diverse personal involvement, Hall still was able to get them to work as a unit. It was a tribute to Jack that he used his power very carefully. He was a good union man: a brilliant, outstanding union man."

long ago we called on the rank and file in Hawaii to put up one hell of a fight for the principle of arbitration. That is, voluntary arbitration.

I hold no brief for Kagel or any other arbitrator, but I am not going to allow a personal beef with the arbitrator to blind me to the use of arbitration when some gains can be made and we have nothing to lose by using the device. . . .

The quarrel was joined. Hall replied that he had no feeling about Kagel that warranted Bridges' outburst. "I am not subjective," said Hall. "Sam didn't do very well by us, particularly in the fringe areas." Hall then challenged Bridges' contention that "not too long ago" (during the 1949 strike), the union had fought for the principle of arbitration:

It is true that *sixteen* years ago we put up a fight for arbitration, but that is a helluva long time ago under completely different circumstances. . . . I am incensed at you even suggesting that I would use the rank and file to "play along with personal beefs." I have no personal beef with any arbitrator. Thanks for your views although I don't share them.

He took the trouble of sending a copy of his letter to Goldblatt, not through regular ILWU channels, but to Goldblatt's home near San Francisco.

In the late 1960s Hall thought Bridges might resign on account of age. (Bridges was then over sixty-five.) Hall repeatedly vowed he would never run against Bridges and that so long as Bridges wanted to remain union president, he would not contest it. Bridges believed him.

How then to approach so delicate a subject as a Bridges resignation? Hall wrote Bridges:

While I am certain that the entire membership would support your continuing as president of the union for life, there are so many rumors flying around that we hope you can put them to rest by advising us whether you intend to seek re-election at the next convention and if elected whether you intend to serve the full term.

"In Hawaii," said Hall, "we consider the question of leadership succession when you eventually retire extremely important to the nation."

Bridges did not see fit to reply to Hall by letter. He answered him in person at a Local 142 Executive Board meeting in Honolulu in December 1968. Was he going to run again? Answer: Yes. For a full term? Yes. "I will surely not be a candidate in 1971—why will I stick around that long?" said Bridges.[2]

Local 142 proposed in 1968 that the ILWU constitution be amended to provide for three International vice-presidents—one from the West Coast longshoremen locals, one from the West Coast warehouse locals, and one from Hawaii. The Hawaii vice-president would be Hall. Since it was a plan designed both to raise Hall's status and power and reduce Bridges', he could hardly have been expected not to resist. Bridges attacked the proposal at a Local 142 Executive Board meeting. "We are a trade union, but we are drifting more and more into being a corporation and business union," he said. He charged that the plan was concocted by Local 142 and Local 6 of the San Francisco Bay area to create special jobs for Hall and for Charles "Chili" Duarte, president of Local 6. That plan would split the union, Bridges claimed.

It was old hat, he said. The plan had first been offered five years previously; now it was revived as something new. The union didn't need extra full-time vice-presidents. "That they are unnecessary is proven by the fact that they will pinch-hit as regional directors," said Bridges. "I have been told if I shut up, my job will be free. Now I have reached a point at my age [that] if I want to get personal I get personal. This [plan] is tailored for two people."

Hall replied to the rebuke. "I don't think anybody can say there is a job in this union I am not competent to handle," he said.

I think we are getting some sand thrown in our eyes. . . . We never got an answer as to how this proposal is going to cause any splits in this union. As a matter of fact, unless something is done to change the present structure, we are going to have a split and it is going to be a split between the black people and the rest. . . .[3]

---

2. The ILWU retired Bridges and Goldblatt in 1977.

3. Hall was talking about black longshoremen in the ILWU, especially those in Local 10 in San Francisco.

Others arose to take on Bridges. "Harry said a lot of things which boiled down to the idea that everybody else in the top leadership is crooked or [has] some phony ambition or jealousness and Harry is the only guy in their way," said David Thompson. He then raised a point that was seldom spoken about outside the union confines—namely, the tension between Bridges, on the one hand, and Hall and Goldblatt, on the other. He said Bridges' "personal conflict with Jack and Lou" had clouded his judgment.

George Martin, the Big Island ILWU Division director, said there was "a personal feud, which is a shame," between Bridges and Hall (and Duarte). "I have admiration for you and your record," he said to Bridges, "but I think it is sad when you come before the 142 Executive Board and fight something we worked so hard to present." Martin went on:

> We believe this will give us representation directly to the International office, but you are so suspicious. . . . If you take the position you are going to split the union—you carry a big club if you insist on this—you will split the union.

The Local 142 Executive Board heard Bridges out, then voted unanimously against him.

Bridges returned to the fight at the International Executive Board meeting in December 1968. He said the ILWU's membership was at low ebb, the lowest point since 1940. Adding two more officers would increase costs of running the union by forty thousand dollars a year. "There is no work for additional officers, except as advanced in the proposal," he said. "That is, to have them act as regional directors."

Saburo Fujisaki, a Hawaii member of the International board, said Local 142 did not believe the proposal would split the union. "We feel that the union is getting into all kinds of problems and there should be a broadening of leadership," he said.

Antone J. "Tony" Kahawaiolaa, Jr., another board member from Hawaii, said: "We want to be recognized for the work we have done in Hawaii. We like Jack Hall and want to give him that recognition. We still want him back there and not away from the state of Hawaii."

Goldblatt said he saw nothing wrong with expanding the union's top leadership. Hawaii made up a large part of the ILWU, he said. Moreover, its structure differed from the mainland's: it included sugar, pineapple, longshore, hotels, bakeries, cowboys, auto mechanics, and more—all in one union. In Hawaii the ILWU had ventured into civic activities. "If ever there was a union in the U.S. that has tried to be part of the community, it is the local in Hawaii," said Goldblatt.

But the three-vice-president plan antagonized some of the board members from the mainland: "Somebody is trying to make a job for somebody. . . ." "It seems aimed at outvoting the longshore forces and will cause a split."

Bridges said that if the board insisted on the two extra vice-presidents, he and Robertson would resign at the next ILWU International convention. As he listened to the wrangling, Robertson was appalled. "I am deeply disturbed because for the first time in many years the team at the top is breaking up and there are differences of opinion."

Death resolved the crisis. On January 4, 1969, Duarte died. Robertson announced he would not run for office again and Hall announced he would run for Robertson's job.[4] The matter was tidily dealt with at the International Executive Board meeting in March 1969. Fujisaki said Local 142 was withdrawing its proposal because of opposition to it. He announced Hall's candidacy and said Hall would move to San Francisco.

A board member commented: "After all the work Jack Hall has done, if I were a member of Local 142 I would vote against letting him go." Well, said Fujisaki, it was only a few hours to Hawaii from the mainland. If Local 142 needed Hall back in a hurry, they could quickly get him back.

---

4. Robertson said: "I have done my darndest to get [Bridges] to step out when I do, but he told me to go to hell."

CHAPTER 74

"I'm Only in Back"

> *Not too many people would stand up against Hall. That's the trouble.*
> —Newton K. Miyagi, Local 142 secretary-treasurer

Newton Miyagi, the man who "controlled the money" and coordinated the ILWU's political activity, kept out of sight. He operated with a telephone and often was regarded as the power behind the throne. If anyone told him that he laughed. "I'm only in back; that's where I want to be," he would say.

The son of a Waipahu plantation supervisor, Miyagi started to work on a plantation at sixteen and became an ILWU business agent in 1948 and secretary-treasurer of Local 142 in 1952.

Miyagi and Hall had differences, and at one of the union elections Hall tried to oust Miyagi but failed. "We had quite a bit of misunderstanding over certain programs," Miyagi said. Those programs usually involved money. The most violent disagreement, according to Miyagi, came over Hall's hardheaded support of a newspaper, the *Hawaiian Reporter,* which lasted only twenty-one months but was costly. "All told, I'd say a quarter of a million dollars went down the drain," said Miyagi.

Hall believed in newspapers. He loved to read them; he had great respect for the power of the printed word. And in 1957 he decided to launch a newspaper. He and McElrath were not happy with Koji Ariyoshi's *Honolulu Record;* it was not the kind of paper Hall wanted. "It turned out not to be a community paper," said McElrath. The prospectus (which McElrath wrote) promised a liberal paper with few editorials. Instead Ariyoshi constantly wrote editorials with a heavy left-wing slant. "Every paper had an editorial column and half the news stories were editorialized," said McElrath. "[Ariyoshi] never got out of the caves of Yenan."

That wasn't what Hall wanted. "We are pushing a newspaper in order that other people in this community can get the truth about the major issues that confront our nation and our state," he said. "Get the truth on the so-called controversial issues." Hall asked Morris Watson, editor of the *ILWU Dispatcher*, for advice on publishing a newspaper. Watson thought it an "exciting idea," but he cautioned that it should not be a trade union paper or a left-wing paper. "It should be lively, hard-hitting, and never be guilty of dullness," he said.

Watson told Hall not to try to fool anybody about who was backing the paper: tell the public right off, he said, "and then let the paper gain prestige and confidence on its own."

Miyagi was not enthusiastic about publishing a paper, but he told Hall he would not fight the project. The union bought printing equipment and shipped it over; Hall hired a man from the mainland named William Friel as editor. Volume 1, No. 1 of the *Hawaiian Reporter* came out on June 18, 1959. "We want a truly independent and liberal paper," Hall instructed Friel: a paper the community would accept.

It never came off; the paper was a lost cause from the start. It didn't take long for Hall, a man with an eye for journalism, to see it. After nine issues he was disheartened. "I don't think it is any secret that the make-up and content have been disappointing, not only to us but to other people," he said.

What troubled Miyagi was that in the minds of many ILWU members, the paper had become "Miyagi's program." Well, he consoled himself, "you can't blame the membership. When it came to money—"

Hall tried to boost the circulation. He hoped to reach twenty thousand copies, the point at which the paper was expected to make a profit.[1] Hall sent Fujisaki out to talk ILWU members into buying the paper. David Thompson and Koji Ariyoshi spent two weeks on Kauai and two weeks on Maui, going house to house, canvassing for subscriptions. In January 1960 the ILWU solicited public sales of *Reporter* stock and the stock was

devalued from $5 to $2.50 par value. (There were 49,000 shares
of stock outstanding; the ILWU held 29,925. Delbert Metzger
had 75 shares and the remaining 19,000 were to be sold.)

But the cause was hopeless; the paper lacked a point of view
and it lacked appeal. It "doesn't have orientation, policy, color
or genuine interest," Goldblatt summed it up. There was no way
to overcome the public's lack of confidence; everyone knew it
was "the ILWU's paper." Nor could Hall shake the public's
identification of the paper with the *Honolulu Record.* It was
hard to sell advertising; the cash position was desperate; but
Hall, against Miyagi's advice, kept trying to turn the corner. If
the paper folded, he feared, it would be looked upon "as a
defeat for the union."

Hall fired Friel[2] and Marion Sexton, another professional
journalist, took over as editor. "If Sexton can do a job, advertising and circulation-wise, we will take another look at the
editorial situation," said Hall. "If he doesn't, we'll probably
call it quits."

He hated to admit defeat, but after ninety-two issues Hall
gave up. He tried to find consolation for the money spent: he
claimed the *Reporter* had helped improve the two Honolulu
dailies. It served as an "antidote to the employers' monopoly of
public information in Hawaii," he said.

In 1963, when Hall and Miyagi were not at all friendly, Miyagi
had his closest call for reelection and it was Hall who quietly led
the fight to defeat him. "Jack was getting annoyed at my making certain decisions," Miyagi explained. "The Cuban thing and
so on. All this was building up [so] that Jack felt that maybe I'm
going too far with making up my own mind without consulting
others." (In 1960 Miyagi had visited Castro's Cuba, was impressed with the Socialist government, and told the newspa-

---

1. It reached a high of 11,700.

2. Koji Ariyoshi described the *Hawaiian Reporter* this way: "Friel wanted
cheesecake and Waikiki shots. He told me, 'I played it safe. I was not going to
get myself smeared.' "

pers: "Cuba has a real people's government and the people are for it.")

In 1962 Miyagi denounced President Kennedy's blockade of Cuba to force the Soviet Union to remove long-range missiles from the island. ILWU members, who are as patriotic as anybody, supported the president and denounced Miyagi. Some told him to resign. (Rutledge, who knew a winning hand when he saw it, sent Miyagi a one-way ticket to Havana.)

Miyagi's opponent in the 1963 election for secretary-treasurer was Seiko "Shirley" Shiroma. Hall supported Shiroma; so did Joe Blurr and Fujisaki. Samson and Damaso backed Miyagi, as did the key man in the election—Tom Yagi of Maui. The tally sheets came in early from Oahu, Kauai, and Hawaii and it was anybody's race. Then Yagi arrived with the Maui vote in his pocket. He talked to Miyagi before he went to see Hall and told Miyagi: "No problem, Maui County." Maui had always been a Miyagi stronghold. Miyagi won the election by 750 votes.

Then Yagi told Hall. There was a group of Japanese labor leaders in the ILWU building that day, eating and drinking at a reception. "When Jack heard the results, he came storming out of there," said Miyagi. Hall went down to the reception room and started drinking.

For a time he and Miyagi did not speak to each other; they resorted to writing notes to each other. Miyagi couldn't understand why Hall wouldn't sit down and talk to him. He wondered why Hall wouldn't shoulder the blame for the failure of the *Reporter*. "Why couldn't he say, 'Look, I'm sorry. I made a mistake,' " said Miyagi. An apology from Hall? "That I could never get out of Jack."

In 1965 Hall proposed a fifty-cent raise in per capita tax of union members and Miyagi opposed it. He thought twenty-five cents was enough. He asked Hall what he needed the fifty-cent increase for. "Organizing, organizing, and so on," was the reply. Local 142's Executive Board asked Miyagi's opinion. The moneyman said he was against a fifty-cent raise, and although he didn't attend in person, the ILWU convention in Vancouver voted Hall's proposal down. In a pique, Hall stayed in his room at the Bayshore Hotel and drank.

When Hall came home he said to Miyagi: "You're pretty good. You don't have to be there and your program is already laid down."

"When I think I'm right," replied Miyagi, "I'm going to express my feelings." It all puzzled him. Why didn't Hall sit down and talk things out with him? "I wouldn't have been bull-headed," he said.

Miyagi believed that one of Hall's weaknesses was blind loyalty to friends. Over the years Hall had a good relationship with his old comrade-in-arms McElrath. Hall regarded McElrath as smart and able, but sometimes indecisive and lazy. "They really got on fairly well," said Goldblatt.

> Jack felt that McElrath had performed a real service in the union in the early days when the going was very rough. . . . I know that Jack used to get a little irritated with him because Bob had a tendency of disappearing. I'd generally write and simply say: "Look, if you don't straighten out and fly right—well, that's that." But, by and large, Jack and Bob remained close friends.

For eleven years (1948 to 1959) McElrath was the "Voice of the ILWU" over radio. As such, he served as a lightning rod for the union and often took the abuse of the public and the employers. Sometimes the abuse was savage: "We all considered him a rash, egotistical little nincompoop," said Slator M. Miller, who for years was a sugar industry official. By 1957 the ILWU wondered if McElrath's hard-line broadcasting was winning friends for the ILWU. Was he reaching only listeners who already were in the ILWU camp, Goldblatt asked, "and those who listen in so as to work up a good hate for the evening?"

Bridges asked whether the ILWU shouldn't reexamine its radio program. Hall replied that he was already doing that. He said he found that both the English and Filipino language broadcasts had lost listeners. By now the harshness had gone out of the relationship between union and employers. Both had softened their voices and relaxed. "In line with our policy of toning down because of our understandings with the employers, we have turned the [radio] program over primarily to community use," said Hall.

In January 1959, Hall told Goldblatt the ILWU English radio program was "pau" (finished). He reassigned McElrath to help him negotiate contracts and "get off the public relations gambit." Hall said: "No cloak and dagger after the first of the year."

"Has McElrath fallen out of favor in the union?" a reporter asked Hall.

"No," said Hall. "Public relations has fallen out of favor with the union, not McElrath. McElrath is doing a good job in his new assignment and I'm satisfied with his work. He is doing negotiating and organizing and internal work."

It didn't take long for Hall to decide that the switch from public relations and radio work to straight union work was good for McElrath. It improved his attitude and his sense of responsibility, said Hall.

CHAPTER 75
The "Fair-Haired Boy"

On November 22, 1963, Hall spent the day at home talking to Eddie Tangen about a job he wanted Tangen to take. They were old friends; Tangen had met Hall in 1938 on Kauai.

Tangen was a former seaman, a labor organizer, and former secretary-treasurer of the Marine Cooks and Stewards. He had dropped out of the labor movement and for a time ran a resort in Northern California. He was lucid (some said glib), a dark-eyed man with thick black eyebrows that met across the bridge of his nose. Over the years he saw Hall many times. Tangen helped the ILWU in the 1946 and 1949 strikes.

Hall told Tangen he needed him to help organize white collar workers. He said the job was too much for him to do in addition to his other work and there was no one else in the union he could call on.

"We need the sophistication and ability of Tangen," Hall informed Goldblatt. He conceded there was a problem: it was going to be hard to explain to union members that not a single person in Local 142 was qualified for the job. It was also hard to convince Bridges and Robertson; they strongly opposed Tangen's appointment. "We wanted some people who were non-haole," said Bridges.

> I promised those guys years ago that we were at the end of importing mainlanders. It was like an imperialist domain down there. . . . They couldn't get their thinking away—that was kind of a colonial impression, and that included Hall.

"If at this late date we have to send another fucking haole from the mainland over there to give those people leadership, then we've been derelict in our duty," Robertson said.

Hall defied them both; he insisted upon Tangen coming over as an International representative and he had his way. Tangen arrived February 1, 1964. "I made up my mind years ago to come back—and I did," he said. Tangen began organizing hotel workers, but Goldblatt had other plans for him and one day he discussed them with Tangen and Hall at Hall's home. Goldblatt said that the bad old days were gone and the union no longer had to fight for its life. Now was the time to pay attention to the quality of life in Hawaii. What kind of state should it be? What kind of planning should be done? Shouldn't the union get involved in planning?

They agreed the union should. It meant taking a new tack: the ILWU, which had fought for wages, hours, and conditions, now intended to fight for good planning. "A lot of unions think only in terms of collecting dues," said Hall. "We're a different type of union."

The result was the Malama Project.[1] The ILWU began to take

---

1. Hawaiian for "to take care of; to preserve."

a stand on planning and community beautification, and Tangen became involved up to his bushy eyebrows. "This little egg laid by Goldblatt, hatched by Hall and served to me has turned into a full-scale poultry operation," he commented.

Strange things began to happen and strange fellowships were forged. One morning ILWU members planted gold trees along the Pali Highway. The Outdoor Circle, whose mission it was to pretty up the city, was delighted. "We think it's unusual, but we're awfully happy," said Mrs. Harold Erdman, the Outdoor Circle president. The town was amazed and some people were skeptical: what did gold trees have to do with union pork chops? Asked if she thought the ILWU had an ulterior motive, Mrs. Erdman said: "Ulterior motive? What could it be? I think they would like to see this turned into a lovelier place."

The ILWU announced it was against the filling in of Salt Lake in Honolulu to make a golf course. Tangen badgered the city council to set a height limit of forty feet for construction on the slopes of Punchbowl. He called Waikiki "an architectural jungle" and deplored its chaotic development. Suddenly the ILWU was committed to planning. It went about it in the same determined way it went into negotiations at the bargaining table. "While it appears that our image is more community-directed than it has been in the past, it doesn't mean any change in the basic objectives of the union," said Hall.

"You may wonder why the ILWU is poking its nose into the issue of Waikiki," said Tangen. He went on to explain: "It's because we have an obligation to our members and the people of this community to preserve Hawaii's natural beauty. We've got to stop those fast buck artists from lousing up the rest of Hawaii."[2]

Tangen said the ILWU wanted Hawaii to be "just as much a paradise" for the union's 23,000 members and their families as for the tourists. "We are going to try to persuade the state and county governments that planning is the most serious problem facing us today," Tangen said.

---

2. On September 17, 1975, Goldblatt looked out the window of his hotel room (Room 1930 in the Ilikai) at the solid wall of high rises covering Waikiki. "But what did we accomplish?" Goldblatt said sadly.

In a special message to its members, the union elaborated:

> We have found it necessary from time to time to remind our employers, and sometimes ourselves, that we are working in order to live, not living in order to work.
>
> The time has come for our community to apply the same perspective to its beaches and other areas of outdoor living and enjoyment, which are threatened with destruction, spoliation and restriction. . . .

The union had pushed the right button; planning was an idea whose time had come. The public applauded so loudly, in fact, that Hall professed to be startled. "The papers played it up and we were amazed at the response," said Tangen.

> We have been contacted by politicians, professional groups, public committees and individuals representing nearly every phase of planning in the state. We had assumed some shots would be taken at us and expected to be told to stick to our sugar, pineapple and docks and keep our noses out of things we are not experts at. . . . However, to date, we have not received one bitch. On the other hand, we have been praised and our support solicited.

Tangen had become the "fair-haired boy" and the tough old union suddenly was a hero. It was hard for Hall to take. The ILWU has "added a new dimension to its stature," said the *Advertiser*. The *Maui News* said: "The News found itself standing shoulder-to-shoulder with the ILWU."

Because the union was treading on unfamiliar ground,[3] the ILWU decided to hire an expert—preferably one with a national reputation—to chart the course. Goldblatt thought of Lewis Mumford, an internationally known expert on city planning.[4] He wrote Mumford, saying, "We need a person . . . whom we can trust and who generally agrees with our position on development." Would Mumford come to Hawaii?

---

3. Tangen admitted: "We didn't know a damn thing about this field. . . ."

4. In 1938, at the request of the Honolulu City and County Parks Board, Mumford had surveyed Honolulu and in September of that year had issued his report, "Whither Honolulu?" It said, in effect, that Honolulu could be a thing of beauty and a joy forever, provided proper planning were done.

Evidently he could not, but he recommended a former student of his, Allen Temko, a member of the Center for Planning and Development Research at the University of California at Berkeley. Temko was a nationally recognized critic of architecture and urban planning. The ILWU hired him, paid him a $2000 fee plus expenses, and asked him to prepare a "white paper" on the subject of planning for Hawaii. "We're going to be as serious about planning as we are about politics," said Tangen.

Temko briefed Hall on what he planned to study: How good were the architectural design and planning of the hotels? Did the tourist industry misuse the beaches and shorelands? What was the social and economic strategy of the tourist industry? Overriding these questions was Temko's long-range premise that "good planning makes for good business, and conversely, greedy and tawdry development might well be ruinous for Hawaii."

Temko, with the fascinated Tangen in his wake, started moving across the landscape. He roamed the Big Island from Kamuela to Keauhou Bay. He went over to Maui and looked at the Maui Pineapple and Land Company's project at Honolua and at Amfac's Kaanapali project. He reviewed the Campbell Estate's plans for Kahuku, the northwest corner of Oahu. He looked at the hotels in Waikiki built along the edge of the water. "What is this mad concept that you have got to build hotels two inches from the sand?" he asked. "We're concerned about keeping the beaches open for all Hawaiians, not just ILWU members."

"Allen Temko—we love you!" the smitten *Advertiser* exclaimed.

There was also a desperate need for low-cost housing for workers, and Hall realized the ILWU could solve the problem only by acting in concert with others. He devoted a great deal of attention to housing. He believed it was part of his job; part of his "wider view" of what a union leader should do. That is why in the 1946 sugar contract he insisted that rents be placed on a cash basis rather than provided for through perquisites; that a "no eviction" policy be instituted; and that rents be frozen at existing rates. As a result, for years sugar workers lived in plantation housing for from $12.50 to $45 a month. Rents also were frozen for pineapple workers.

With rents frozen it was not sound policy for the plantations to stay in the housing business. They wanted out and discussed it with the union. In the early 1950s the union permitted companies to phase out the housing—if a suitable alternative was provided. One such alternative was the sale of house lots by the companies to the workers at low prices.

"The union sat down with the companies to work out land sales, site improvement, the movement of existing homes, or the packaging of new home construction and financing," said Leonard Hoshijo, ILWU housing coordinator. "As a result thousands of agricultural workers, often thought of as the low man on the totem pole, have been able to purchase comfortable homes and lots in fee at lower than market prices."

The ILWU developed a group of experts on housing who represented the union in working with government, churches, clubs, and with other unions and employers to develop house lots for sale to working families. They also went to work on family projects and rental housing for the elderly. The ILWU members shared in the benefits.[5]

In 1966 Hall was the moving force in the organization of the Hawaii Council for Housing Action (HCHA). At the time, he was at the height of his power and prestige and was able to bring together big business, the churches, and government leaders to serve voluntarily on the nonprofit HCHA board of directors. The HCHA members[6] inspected the ILWU's low-rent St. Francis Square Housing Project in San Francisco. Hall asked lawyers, architects and builders, and officials of the Big Five to render service gratis to help plan housing. He expected big things

---

5. The ILWU housing program continued after Hall's death. In 1974 housing became a statewide program coordinated at the Local 142 level. With the old plantation houses deteriorating, the union organized nonprofit corporations to sponsor government-assisted rental projects to serve hotels, sugar, and general trades workers. Housing for workers was one of the ILWU's greatest accomplishments.

6. Jack Palk of Oceanic Properties; Aaron Levine, vice-president of the Oahu Development Conference; the Rev. Larry Jones; Temko; and Hall.

to happen. In fact, he thought the prospects were so good that he wrote Goldblatt:

> The project is catching the imagination of everyone around here including state and city with full cooperation all around. Even the HRA [Honolulu Redevelopment Agency] executive secretary, Lee Maice, who was very cold at first now wants to lead the parade to do a project that is really socially useful.

One of the low-cost housing projects Hall was interested in for union members was Kukui Gardens[7] on North King Street in Honolulu. Hall raised forty thousand dollars in seed money from ILWU members. As a possible source of interim financing, he considered the ILWU–Pacific Maritime Association pension fund (which then consisted of $19 million to $20 million in corporation bonds yielding from 2¾ to 5 percent interest) and also the insurance companies which held ILWU pension funds. The HCHA bid on Kukui Gardens, but to Hall's chagrin Clarence Ching (Loyalty Enterprises, Ltd.) won the bid. Hall thought the HCHA bid was "far superior" and he wrote all four of Hawaii's members in Congress, saying Ching would ask them to use their influence with the Federal Housing Authority and the Department of Housing and Urban Development to obtain clearance for the project. "I would hope that you permit the federal agencies to act on Mr. Ching's 'foundation' and plans without political pressure from your office," Hall said.[8]

Bridges became uneasy about Hall's role in the HCHA. What was it costing the ILWU? he inquired of Miyagi. "What I would like to do," said Bridges, "would be to ascertain from your books and records how much money the International and the local spent so far on the housing project for architects, consultants, travel expenses, etc." He asked for just the facts, "without raising any questions about anything being off color about arrangements."

---

7. Not to be confused with Kukui Plaza.

8. Kukui Gardens, built by Loyalty Enterprises, turned out well. "Still one of the best rent situations in town," said Robert Devine, at one time an HRA official.

The answer came not from Miyagi but from Hall. He told Bridges expenses totaled twenty thousand dollars up to November 23, 1966. "Harry, this letter is kind of long but worthwhile if it helps clear the air," Hall wrote.

Nobody is going to make a buck off this project with people as determined as Wilcox [Allen C. Wilcox, Jr., an Alexander & Baldwin vice-president], Palk and others in our executive meeting committee to make it really non-profit. We are using everybody's brains, including lawyers, but no pay except coffee and doughnuts at council meetings.

Hall worked hard at it, but the HCHA did not accomplish as much as he and Tangen had hoped.[9]

Hall's quest for low-cost housing went back to the mid-1950s when he tried to arrange with construction executive William Blackfield to build houses on Oahu. He had been impressed with Blackfield's project at Olomana on the windward side. There Blackfield built three hundred houses on leasehold land under agreement with the Kaneohe Ranch Company. The houses cost $9000 to $10,000; land rent was $125 a year. The problem was the familiar one on Oahu: land and financing.

Castle & Cooke had land at Pohakupu near Kailua on Oahu, and Hall discussed a project there with Blackfield. The idea was that Blackfield would build homes at cost plus ten percent for overhead. Blackfield's profit would come from a percentage of the leasehold rent, paid over the 55-year duration of the lease. The homes were expected to cost ILWU members about ten thousand dollars for a three-bedroom house of 1000–1100 square feet.

But despite all that Castle & Cooke and Goldblatt could do,

---

9. The HCHA's record for 1966–1976; Hale Ole, a 150-unit condominium at Pearl City, Oahu; Hale Mohalu, 111 one-bedroom, one-story units in Kahului, Maui; Makalapa Manor, 122 townhouses and apartments in Aiea, Oahu; Kauluwela No. 1, 126 one- and two-bedroom apartments in the Kauluwela district of Honolulu; Kauluwela No. 2, 84 three- and four-bedroom apartments; Keola Hoonanea, 175 one-bedroom units in Kauluwela.

There was more: Waimanalo Apartments, 80 apartments in Waimanalo Village; Waimanalo Banyan Tree, 122 apartments; Malulani Hale, 150 one-bedroom apartments on North Kuakini Street, Honolulu; and four Model Cities programs, which totaled more than 300 units in Kalihi-Palama and Waianae.

Hall could not arrange for financing for more than sixty units and he dropped the plan. "We never put it together," Blackfield recalled. "He wanted to do it very badly."

Tourism began booming after statehood. Tourism meant hotels and hotel rooms meant jobs, "especially [for] our children who can't look to our old economic bases—sugar, pineapple and military employment—for jobs," said Hall. "It is quite obvious that tourism is everybody's business, even though you can't sometimes see its effect on your paycheck."

In 1964 Hall was named to the Hawaii Visitors Bureau board of directors as the labor representative. Hawaii needed capital from the mainland to invest in the hotel industry and Hall lent his support. "The ILWU politically and economically is doing everything possible to encourage investment, which means jobs for you," he told Oahu construction workers. Gratified, he watched the hotels go up and the tourism industry expand. "New joints organized every week and the hotel situation looks better every day," he said. The tourism field "is opening like a budding rose." In 1966 he predicted that by 1970 Hawaii would be host to a million visitors a year who would spend more than $450 million.[10]

The ILWU concentrated on organizing the Neighbor Island hotels and left the Oahu hotels to Rutledge. By 1967 the prospects seemed dazzling:

> Minus the 5,000 jobs Rutledge now controls on Oahu and approximately 3,000 jobs in small units of family motels, etc., we have a near future project of over 30,000 jobs in hotels. This does not include approximately 2,000 tour drivers and employees of major restaurants not connected with hotels.

Hall asked ILWU members directly employed in the tourist industry to subscribe two dollars each to the HVB fund; those not directly employed in tourism were asked to contribute twenty-five cents each. "This is not charity," he said. "This is an investment in the economic security of all who live in Hawaii regardless of where they are employed."

---

10. In 1970, some 1,748,970 visitors came to Hawaii and spent $550 million.

CHAPTER 76
Politicians and Others

> *There are two things in a politican's mind. First is to get elected and second is to get reelected.*
> —Jack Hall

One day in 1959 Hall, Yagi, the ILWU Maui Division director, and Elmer Cravalho, Speaker of the House, met at the Wagon Wheel restaurant-bar on Kalakaua Avenue to discuss Cravalho's political future. He had been Speaker since earlier that year when the Hall-directed coalition of Democrats and Republicans defeated the Esposito-Gill forces. Cravalho wanted to leave the legislature and run for Maui County mayor against the incumbent, Democrat Eddie Tam. Cravalho made his points quickly and neatly, as was his custom.

There were two versions of what happened next: Cravalho's and Yagi's. Yagi said Hall looked at Cravalho coldly. "I don't want you to run against Tam," he said. "I want you to stay on as Speaker of the House. You have a big job ahead of you. . . . You run for chairman—over my dead body!"

Yagi sat stunned; Cravalho was speechless. Hall shoved his chair back, got up, and walked out. His face was set; his mouth tight and hard. Later, Yagi saw him and said, "You know, you put me in a spot. Why didn't you tell me about it beforehand?"

"Tom, he has a bigger job to do," Yagi said Hall replied. "The Speaker's job is the bigger job. Elmer performed a terrific job for the ILWU."

Cravalho remembered the episode differently: Hall was not abrupt or angry, he said. Hall calmly pointed out that for the good of the community he preferred that Cravalho stay in the legislature. As Cravalho recalled it:

> He went through all the factors and the needs of the community and where he needed strong leadership, at least in one level of the legislature. He said, "We prefer—if we had our druthers. . . ." It was not abrupt, nothing like that.

Cravalho said that over the years the ILWU had always supported him; they had respect for each other. Was there any *quid pro quo* in return for the ILWU's support?

"Never," said Cravalho.

"Could Hall order you around?"

"No."

"Did he ever order you around?"

"Never, NEVER. . . . Nobody gets in that position," said Cravalho.

On occasion, he said, he even incurred Hall's wrath. In 1959, said Cravalho, Hall "cursed me up and down for not going with that [anti-Esposito] coalition originally." In 1960, Cravalho supported Kennedy for president, which riled Hall.

Hall didn't have to use his muscle often in the legislature because many of the union's pet projects were bills most Democrats favored. But if need be, he could "exert raw power." In 1961 the union pushed across a cut in the sugar and pineapple excise tax rate from two percent to one-half of one percent. Of course, Hall knew that part of the savings to the companies would be passed on to the ILWU members. But Tom Gill, the House Majority Leader, fought the cut. "They went to the floor," Gill said. "They had the votes. . . . I was getting my ass kicked. They were all lined up and they got their cut."

That was another occasion when Cravalho opposed Hall. Said Cravalho:

> Of course, there were those who said I voted "no" because I knew I had the votes anyway. But I voted against it. I can recall some of them told me when I got home they were going to have the [ILWU] membership out there at the airport to picket me. . . . I said, "Can't be helped. That's the way I feel. I don't think there is any justification for [the tax cut]."

Hall drove through the tax relief, as he called it, in one swoop, instead of nibbling away a small bite at a time. "The several and continuing millions in the coffers of these two industries we expect them, of course, to share with their employees," said Hall. (The savings to the companies amounted to $7 million to $8 million a year.)

Representative David McClung charged Hall with a "narrow and selfish" attitude. McClung proposed suspending further tax cut benefits for the sugar and pineapple companies for five years. Hall replied that the general excise tax was a regressive tax (as, he said, any schoolboy knows), and "so long as we have such taxes, it is patently unfair and discriminatory to charge the manufacturers of sugar and pineapple products more than other manufacturers—and especially without regard to the profitability or lack thereof of any particular company."

He suggested to McClung a way to obtain additional revenue: "Increase the rate on corporate and individual income at higher levels," he said.

The maximum rate on corporate income now is only 5½ percent on income in excess of $25,000. The extremely healthy profits of many island corporations, including a considerable number of sugar companies, could stand a much higher income tax rate, especially on incomes in excess of $250,000 annually.

Late in 1964 the Governor's Advisory Committee on Taxation, of which Hall was a member, recommended that taxes be raised by $34.2 million, including a twenty percent increase ($24.2 million) for the State General Fund. It seemed like a broad leap; State Tax Director Edward J. "Ed" Burns, the governor's brother and cochairman of the advisory committee, filed a minority report opposing it. The plan included an increase from 3½ to 4 percent in the sales tax. Rutledge called that idea "vicious." Hall, however, approved the plan in a letter to ILWU members and he received community support. The *Star-Bulletin* commented: "Mr. Hall, who bosses a well-run outfit, knows taxes will have to be raised and that everybody ought to pay a share."

In 1961 Speaker Cravalho ordered a House Select Committee to investigate a report of undue ILWU pressure exerted on Maui officials. The incident which touched off the investigation was the delay in the award of a contract to build the Wailuku War Memorial–Convention Hall. The committee held four hearings in the chambers of the Maui County Board of Supervisors in Wailuku.[1] County Chairman Eddie Tam, along with Yagi, Regino Colotario, and Tai Sung Yang of the ILWU, were among the witnesses called.

The committee reported that at a meeting (no date given) at the Hotel Iao Needle, ILWU officials suggested that F & M Contractors, Inc., low bidder on the job, withdraw its bid for site preparation and that Thomas T. Tanaka of Honolulu, second low bidder, be awarded the contract.

On February 16, 1961, according to the committee, Yagi and other ILWU officials met with the Maui Board of Supervisors at the ILWU Hall on Lower Main Street in Wailuku and urged the supervisors to award the contract to Tanaka. "According to the ILWU, their only interest was a monetary savings to the people of Maui," said the committee report.

On February 21, 1961, ILWU officials called on Tam at his home to discuss the contract. "Chairman Tam . . . states that this was one time when the union should allow board members to make their own decisions," said the committee. During one visit with Tam, according to the committee, Yagi indicated that Hall wanted to see the award of the contract deferred. Nevertheless, the Board of Supervisors voted 4 to 3 to award the contract to F & M Contractors. "The influence of the ILWU is clearly set forth in the pattern of events," said the committee report, which drew these conclusions:

> The hearings . . . pointed out that the immediate question of the award of the contract in the instant case has proven to be only the focal point in what appears to be a perplexing problem in the County of Maui—the apparent all-pervasive influence of the ILWU over the actions of County officials. . . .

---

1. On April 12, 13, 17, and 18, 1961.

In the case of the contract in question, your Committee feels that the local leadership of the ILWU went beyond the bounds of propriety in its activities. . . .

Your Committee believes that one of the purposes of the ILWU is to win out in an organizational battle with AF of L–CIO for the right to represent employees of the construction trades on Maui. Such a victory would be enhanced if F & M Contractors, Inc., one of the largest construction firms on the island, could be deprived of this contract. The inter-union battle is a matter of common knowledge on Maui. . . .

In 1966 Hall supported Governor Burns' hand-picked candidate for lieutenant governor, Kenneth F. Brown, against Gill in the Democratic primary election. Hall called Gill "brash" and said he would destroy Hawaii's economic security. "We must have a lieutenant governor who will not frighten those people who want to help us build our economy," said Hall.

Brown had built-in disadvantages—he was a recent convert from Republicanism and hardly the type to appeal to liberal Democrats—but Burns couldn't stand Gill. The selection of Brown over Gill did not sit well with many ILWU members and they deserted in substantial numbers during the primary, one out of four voting for Gill.

Gill beat Brown in the primary, 90,891 to 38,416. "We are disappointed but we are not soreheads," said DeMello. It was a humiliating defeat and some ILWU members never forgot it. Miyagi called it "one of the worst mistakes [Hall made]. . . . I can't get it off my mind—the endorsement of Kenny Brown for lieutenant governor."

It was Hall who taught the ILWU how to play politics. Hall said the union was politically independent. "Neither political party, Democrat or Republican, gave us the finest labor laws in the nation," he said.

It was the political pressure exercised at the right time and right place by ILWU lobbyists, and by our few devoted political friends. It was the respect that all politicians have—newspapers to the contrary—of our ILWU's ability to hold its vote that made these laws possible.

Hall said it was not unusual for an unfriendly politician to make his peace with the union after an election demonstrated the union's strength.

Of course, the union was motivated by self-interest, said Hall.

That's our job as trade unionists. To take care of the membership. Once we have done that, we generally find time to help out programs which are in the interest of the larger community, such as education. . . . And on occasion . . . we have used our political influence as a pressure group, and that's what we are, to aid our employers even when they were kind of reluctant to accept our help because they were too cautious.

"We play politics," said Tangen. "We just happen to do it a little better [than the others]."[2]

In the early 1960s Hall looked around at the young Democrats who controlled the politics of Hawaii. "Who are the Democrats around here mostly? A bunch of young lawyers and small businessmen all on the make for a quick buck," he told reporter A. M. Rosenthal of the *New York Times.*

It's harder to deal with them than with the big employers, Republicans. We get more commitments from the established employer groups. We have a community of interest. The small businessman, all he wants is higher prices, fair trade, a quick buck, guaranteed profits.

---

2. What did the ILWU accomplish politically? The union has been credited with leading the fight for improved labor, economic, social and educational legislation in Hawaii. Of course, it had the help of other unions: the AFL-CIO, the Hawaii Government Employees' Association, and the United Public Workers, and the support of the liberal community.

The union challenged and upset anti-labor laws: the criminal syndication law, the anti-picketing law, the assembly and riot act. The ILWU initiated or gave support to legislation on taxation, civil service, government organization, education, culture and the arts, public welfare, health delivery service, no-fault insurance, housing, public utilities service, programs for the elderly, child-care, youth services, consumer protection, planning and economic development, tourism, promotion of agriculture, conservation, immigrant services.

The ILWU campaigned against capital punishment; in favor of legalized abortion, the abolishment of loyalty proceedings and personal history statements for state employment.

"We are all for free trade," said Hall. "Except in the sugar industry," he amended the statement. "Self-interest," he said
with a smile.

Rosenthal's story was picked up by the Honolulu newspapers
and Hall felt compelled to amplify his statement. He said that
basically the young Democrats were "more interested in themselves, in getting ahead, than they are in the program, policies
and platform of the Democratic party. They vote in their own
interest. . . ."

Though he looked forbidding, Hall was approachable and as
a power broker his advice was often sought. He told T. C. Manipon, newly appointed to the Kauai Police Commission, to establish a reputation for fairness. Hall said that when he was on
the Honolulu Police Commission, he made it a practice never to
do a small favor. "I never 'fixed' even a traffic ticket," he said.
"Ticket fixing is too cheap a use of your power as a commissioner. Save the power for when you really need it in something
big like a strike."

J. Frank McLaughlin, who lost his seat on the federal bench
after statehood, sought the ILWU's support to regain it. He appealed to Miyagi, who passed the word on to Hall. McLaughlin
had been a hard-line foe of the ILWU, but Hall nevertheless
weighed the request in his usual cool way. There were two seats
open on the federal bench and Hall assumed that the chief con-
tenders were Jon Wiig, the Smith Act trial judge, and A. William Barlow, the former United States Attorney.

McLaughlin didn't have the endorsement of the Bar Association of Hawaii: the bar said he lacked judicial temperament. He
had infuriated a number of lawyers by the iron-fisted way he ran
his court. It would have been simple to rule against McLaughlin,
but Hall sympathized with him. "Since his removal from the
bench . . . he has been a lost soul," said Hall. "Harriet
[Bouslog] wants him opposed, but then she doesn't have any
political savvy anyway. It has always been my experience that
our best friends are those who fought us, were dumped and then
regained community position with our help."

Hall decided that the ILWU should try to help McLaughlin
regain his seat on the bench. "He sure is a helluva lot better guy

for us than A. William who has the best chance after Wiig," Hall said.

Hall had not liked Harriet Bouslog ever since she became affluent through buying stocks and real estate. He sent Goldblatt a newspaper clipping that told of her dealings in Pioneer Mill Company stock. Hall said she had been buying Pioneer Mill stock since 1948. "Remember when she said trade union lawyers shouldn't make more money than trade union officials?" Hall wrote Goldblatt.

> Some of the executive board guys are pretty sore when they recall the dough [Local] 142 put up in her disbarment proceedings—under the mistaken impression that she needed that financial help (although they weren't told by any of the officials that she needed such help). Sy [Symonds] is sore about the publicity, too. Of course, Harriet has been making quite a few bucks in real estate transactions and while the book value of her Pioneer stock is $80,000 and worth twice that much, it probably cost her about $25,000. . . .

Goldblatt said Hall's feelings about Harriet Bouslog sprang from her alleged violation of the unwritten ILWU "code of ethics." He said she had used information she heard discussed by Hall and himself; that sort of activity was taboo.[3] Goldblatt said he didn't blame Bouslog for doing well: she had waged valiant battle in court for the ILWU; she had fought the good fight on behalf of little people who couldn't afford to pay her a fee. She liked the life-style she had grown accustomed to. "God knows she earned it," said Goldblatt.

---

3. Goldblatt said Bouslog had listened to a conversation in Hall's home between Hall and Goldblatt about Pioneer Mill plantation. The gist was that although Pioneer Mill at the moment was in poor financial shape, its vacant lands would grow fine crops of sugar once management finished clearing the rocks. Goldblatt said if anyone wanted "to make a killing" they'd buy Pioneer Mill stock and that's what Bouslog did.

Bouslog said she did not take advantage of the conversation. She said her stockbroker, Tom Pires, recommended that she buy Pioneer Mill stock and so she did. It was simple as that.

CHAPTER 77
"Live and Let Live"

Hawaii mellowed in the 1960s: the ILWU was tolerated and even admired; Jack Hall stood at the height of his power. "It was much easier when we had no friends," he said, almost nostalgically. His friend Burns was in Washington Place; his people were well represented on the state boards and commissions and in the public forum. Hawaii was prospering.

At such a satisfying moment Hall sat for an in-depth interview.[1] Topics ranged from Tom Gill ("I want his future to come to an end") to the priorities of the day ("This bothers me. What are the goals of the union movement in Hawaii today? Just more of everything? . . . This is disturbing to some of us who came into the union movement with some social objectives, to lift the downtrodden and so on").

Near the end of the interview, Hall, in an expansive mood, leaned forward and said:

> You know, once I wanted socialism but I don't any more. It isn't practical. The American people will never accept it. Most Americans want to be millionaires and engage in free enterprise. Success is measured in dollars.
>
> Even in socialist countries they have had to modify their standards and objectives. It isn't realistic. You have to be a pragmatic person. When I was young, I believed socialism was the answer to unemployment, depression and poverty. I don't believe that any more.

Like Burns' speech in Seattle in 1959 Hall's remarks made waves. The reaction embarrassed him and he responded immediately. He said the article made him sound "more 'mellow'

---

1. With Gardiner B. Jones of the *Advertiser*.

than I have considered myself to be." Nor did he think he had changed as much as the interview indicated:

Certainly in my lifetime I agree that "socialism" is "impractical" in America but that doesn't mean I agree a socialist organization of a country's economy is bad. It has proven successful in a number of countries. It has been and still is my belief that socialist organization of their economy is the only real hope for the impoverished working people in the under-developed countries of Asia, Africa and Latin America.

"Also," said Hall, "while 'Class War Is Out' in Hawaii, as the [Jones] article headlined, a class struggle goes on every day at the bargaining table over who is going to get what share of the pie, else there would be no unions."

For eight years (1959 to 1967), with what Hall called "insignificant minor exceptions,"[2] labor peace generally reigned in Hawaii. Hall said that was because the employers had learned to respect the union. Mediators played their part in keeping the peace. The Federal Mediation and Conciliation Service was always on call, but the mediators with the most influence were the ones brought in to handle a special case—men such as Sam Kagel from San Francisco, Nathan Feinsinger from Wisconsin, and a Honolulu lawyer, Bert Kobayashi. Such mediators could maintain an independent attitude. They didn't have to worry about their job.

Mediation is an art, said Kagel. "You can't take a course. To be successful you've got to get to the jugular vein. . . . That's

---

2. The chief "minor exceptions":

   1. The 44-day strike at the *Advertiser* and *Star-Bulletin* in 1963. The ILWU represented the circulation departments. Hall, McElrath, and Ah Quon McElrath taught the members of the American Newspaper Guild how to organize. Under the guild contract the pay of some reporters as much as doubled.

   2. The 83-day "fire-fight" in 1965 between the ILWU and George Murphy, owner of Murphy-Aloha Motors. Hall called Murphy "ruthless" and "harder than nails." Murphy said the ILWU was "the most strike-happy union in the United States."

   3. The ILWU's 61-day strike against the pineapple industry in 1968, the longest industry-wide pineapple strike.

the difference between one mediator and another.'' Sometimes a mediator resorted to the dramatic. Dwight Steele called Feinsinger ''a ball of fire.'' Steele described the University of Wisconsin professor as the kind of troubleshooter the president would send out to Hawaii who in a few days ''would work out something and announce a settlement.''

For years Kobayashi, first as state attorney general and then as Supreme Court associate justice, took part as a labor mediator in almost every major strike or threat of a strike. Kobayashi didn't want the job, but Burns thrust it on him and he developed his own formula for success: ''In mediation if you don't have a feel for the people in front of you, you can never understand them. Human relationship is the key to successful mediation.''

At times Goldblatt and McElrath thought Kobayashi was overly sympathetic to management; and in the beginning, before they began to feel at ease with Burns, management was suspicious of any Burns appointee. At one session an ILWU member, a fellow Nisei, said to Kobayashi coldly: ''You don't appreciate our problems. You were born with a silver spoon in your mouth.''

Kobayashi bristled. ''If you think just because I'm the attorney general I'm a rich man, then you're stupid,'' he said. ''And if you want to test me physically—if you want to stand up and slug it out with me, we'll slug it out.'' There was an interested spectator watching that exchange: Goldblatt. He wanted to see how Kobayashi would handle himself.

When he first became a mediator, Kobayashi worried about the balance of power; he thought management was too strong. But after a few years he felt that the pendulum had swung: now the unions held the balance of power. ''I hope we can prevent management and unions between them from destroying things we have fought for,'' he said.

The ILWU also wanted a balance of power. ''If any union wants a strong Employers Council, it's the ILWU,'' said Hall.

It is vastly better for us to deal with pros than with guys who are running around in circles. We prefer a strong employer to a weak one. A weak employer makes our job more difficult. The employees think they have a patsy. The ILWU is strong enough to impose any demands if it did not have a sense of responsibility. . . . We could bring down the temple any day, but when we do so we destroy ourselves.

When an outsider, such as Kagel, was brought in to mediate, the union and management each paid half the bill. Fees usually ranged from three hundred to five hundred dollars a day.[3] "I consider my fees very reasonable," said Kagel. "Jack [Hall] never raised any question about them."

Kagel was wrong, though: Hall did object. Kagel charged $2500 for handling the longshore negotiations in November 1961. Bridges, always a careful man with a dollar, advised Hall to write Kagel a "rip-snorting" letter of protest. Hall wrote Kagel:

> You should know that the workers here and the officials of Local 142 are horrified and incensed by the size of your bill.
>
> Local 142 is not a lush corporation. Only 1,600 members were involved in the situation which utilized your efforts. The amount you billed us for mediation and what we now anticipate for arbitration will be a heavy drain on the finances of the Local. In fact, Local 142 only budgets $20,000 for all negotiations in *all* industries each year.

Kagel said his mediation efforts resulted in a "satisfactory" settlement. Hall took umbrage. "I don't know who it was satisfactory for—certainly not the union," he told Kagel. "It was the employers who were taken off the hook, in my judgment, not us." Hall sent a copy of his letter to Bridges. "Damn good letter," said Bridges. "A little weak tho *[sic]*."

---

3. The price quotation was for 1974.

CHAPTER 78
Feig the Fearless

> *I got a lot of guts. I stood and fought them. I never got scared. . . . I know I won my point.*
> —Isaac Feig

Isaac Feig of the ILWU was five feet four and weighed 134 pounds. After he underwent an operation on his duodenal ulcer, he weighed 120. But he had drive and sublime faith in himself and he challenged Hall at the height of Hall's power and he won. Somehow he made it all sound like David challenging Goliath.

Feig came from Salmague barrio, Cabugao, Luzon, with the first group of Filipino workers in 1946. He arrived in January; his wife and daughter came in July. He was a tailor. His father had died when he was in grade school and he tried to educate himself. Almost as soon as he was assigned to HC & S's Camp 2 at Puunene, he began to take an interest in union matters—not casually, like most workers, but with enthusiasm. He talked up unionism; he helped other workers fill out their work papers. He was even an organizer of sorts. He went faithfully to every union meeting. "I never missed one," he said.

He worked for two and a half months as a hoe weeder and then applied for a job in the warehouse. By studying at night he earned a high school diploma. Feig wanted to move into a leadership post in the union. In 1963 he ran for business agent and it was then that the trouble began.

Feig complained to the United States Department of Labor that there were violations of the election law. The department ordered a second election and Feig put his own locks and seals on the election boxes at the Wailuku Sugar Company balloting place. Yagi told him he had violated the union constitution. Feig replied: "If I did anything wrong, I wish you would call the police."

Yagi reported the incident to Hall, who called it a clear violation: "This guy usurped control of the division balloting committee and got himself a bunch of locks and put extra locks (for which he alone had the keys) on every ballot box and manufactured his own seal, saying this was done under the Labor Management Act, which is a lie." Hall accused Feig of trying to incite a revolt among the Filipino members against union leadership. "Throw this man out because of what he is doing to the union," Hall said.

But to many union members, and especially Filipinos, that seemed like drastic punishment. Even Hall admitted that the charges against Feig were "*manini,*"[1] but he said, "if we permit racism to grow in this union, we're going to be destroyed. This is the real issue this guy is guilty of."[2]

A five-member trial committee set a date for a hearing. Attorney James King of Bouslog & Symonds was assigned to make sure the union handled Feig's case in accordance with the union constitution and the Landrum-Griffin Act. "We will probably keep the case extremely narrow—not go into a lot of crap on the side but just the technicality of what he did," said Hall.

> Somebody tries to take over on his own and figures he is bigger than the balloting committee then we should do something about it. . . . I hate to see anybody deprived of his membership in this union, but here we have a guy who did all these things to destroy the union so we have to do this.

As a Filipino member of the union, Carl Damaso, Local 142 president, said he supported the charges against Feig. "This guy doesn't trust anybody," said Damaso.

The ILWU decided that Hall should be the one to file charges. "I thought inasmuch as there was so much conflict in the elec-

---

1. Trifling.
2. Feig denied it.

tion that we better have somebody who wasn't in this [the Maui] division prefer charges,'' said Hall. ''We decided perhaps I should be the one to do it because it might cause less of a racial split.''

Feig's trial was held in June 1964 in Wailuku. While the full Wailuku Sugar Company balloting committee testified, outside the union hall ILWU pickets marched in support of Feig. They carried signs that said: ''We're Behind You, Isaac.'' Hall invited the picketers in. As the chief witness against Feig, he accused him of ''disgraceful and unconstitutional conduct.'' The trial committee voted to expel Feig. The Maui Executive Board heard his appeal and sustained his ouster, but the fight had only begun.

Feig circulated petitions among the five thousand Maui ILWU members asking for his reinstatement. He worked hard; he created an image: the little guy versus the big union. He aroused strong feeling among Filipinos; at Pioneer Mill he won reinstatement by a 378 to 33 vote.

Hall said the Pioneer Mill vote was an isolated case. ''I'm sure this guy will be thrown out—the whole issue will wash away very nicely,'' he said. He was right: the membership did turn down Feig's appeal for reinstatement, but only by a slim margin—288 votes.[3] Feig fought on: the next arena was the courts. He solicited donations to pay for his legal fees; he went to politicians for help. He sold Portuguese sausage and sweet bread to help raise money. He hired a Honolulu lawyer, Frank D. Padgett, who filed suit in Feig's behalf in Federal District Court against Local 142.

In his court petition, Feig alleged that the union had violated the Landrum-Griffin Act and claimed that his expulsion was a move to silence his criticism of the Maui leadership. He was cocky; he immediately sent his application for membership and his initiation fee to the union. (The union returned his application, saying it was premature.)

But it was plain that the ILWU didn't want to go to court; the publicity was hurting the union. In July 1966, King, the ILWU

---

3. 2037 to 1749.

lawyer, wrote Padgett, Feig's lawyer, saying that the union would reinstate Feig if he would drop the suit.

The case was settled out of court on September 30, 1966, through an exchange of letters between King and Padgett. Two years had gone by. Feig was reinstated as a fully paid-up member of the union and the union paid the court costs. Feig had to pay his lawyer seven hundred dollars.

Still full of fight, he wanted to file a damage suit against the union, which the ILWU would have fought, but Padgett talked him out of it. "Since it was proved that I was vindicated, I was satisfied," said Feig. Miyagi wrote him a letter officially reinstating him. Feig did not give up hope that he might still win leadership rank in the union, and in 1967 he ran for business agent at large. Though he lost, he showed he still had considerable support.[4]

---

4. The tally: John Arisumi, 2876 votes; Mamoru Yamasaki, 2553; Feig, 962. Feig took early retirement in 1969 with a $100-a-month pension which he had to supplement by working as a yardman.

Part 12
DOWNHILL ALL THE WAY
(1969–1971)

CHAPTER 79
Leaving

In April 1969 Hall was nominated to replace Bob Robertson as an ILWU International officer. It was the realization of Hall's dream for years—to take on a new challenge.

Robertson called himself "the plough horse of the ILWU." Hall, as the new vice-president–director of organization, meant to move at a far brisker pace. He was "raring to go." He thought there was a lot of organizing to do. "Of course, I have lots of ideas," he said. His nomination was no surprise; he had decided to run for the office as soon as he heard that Robertson was retiring.

Damaso nominated Hall at the ILWU Convention in Los Angeles, calling him "a real giant." Hall listened in embarrassment. When it came his turn to respond, he remarked: "My ears are kind of burning from the nice things that were said." In a reminiscing mood, he harked back to the day in 1932 when he left Los Angeles, a boy of seventeen in a time of depression, and roamed around looking for a job. "I ended up going to sea," he told the delegates.

> And in the 1934 strike I was in the Sailor's Union and at that time, as the [West Coast longshore] strike was winding up, the Sailor's Union officials were opposing the settlement of the strike by arbitration.
>
> I was one of the rank-and-filers that helped get Harry [Bridges] into that meeting and convinced the rank and file that the Sailors should accept arbitration and settle the strike. . . . At that time I was more or less convinced that there were two people that could walk on water. And one was Harry Bridges. . . .

He ended his acceptance talk by saying that Bridges would go down in history "as *the* trade unionist of the Twentieth Century."

The nomination "by acclamation with no opposition" gave

Hall quiet satisfaction. Going into the convention, he had the endorsement of every ILWU regional caucus: Canada-Northwest, Columbia River–Oregon, Northern and Southern California, and Hawaii. There was still the formality of an election, but that was just a numbers game; there was no opposition. Hall ran for one vice-president's job; Bill Chester ran for another (vice-president–assistant to the president). Yet, like smart politicians, they both ran hard. "My campaign fund—while nothing like what Chester plans—is in pretty good shape," said Hall, "although we have not asked a single member for a contribution nor do we intend to. Neither have any of our employers offered any money to get rid of me (illegal under the Landrum-Griffin [Act] anyway). People we do business with—politicians, banks, etc.—have responded generously."

Tangen did the selling job in Hall's behalf. He wrote the ILWU locals up and down the West Coast. "I can guarantee that he's got a good head and is ready and willing to sit down and discuss program with everybody," said Tangen. "Even though we'll suffer a loss when Jack leaves, the gain of the national union will make it worthwhile."

In his usual methodical way, Hall prepared himself for his new assignment. He asked Chester, then regional director for Northern California, and William Piercy, regional director for Southern California, to arrange a tour for him of the locals. He asked for the names of all the major unorganized companies in Southern California, the nature of their business, and the number of their employees.

The election was cut and dried. Hall "led the ticket." He received 28,865 votes; Chester got 26,699; and Bridges, running unopposed, got 28,682.

The first order of business in Hawaii was to pick a successor to Hall. Five names were mentioned: George Martin, Yagi, Tangen, McElrath, and Miyagi. McElrath was chosen. Bridges had a one-word explanation: "Compromise," he said.

The seven-member Local 142 Executive Committee, which made the recommendation, was composed of the four division directors (Martin of the Big Island, Yagi of Maui, José Corpuz of Oahu, and Fred Taniguchi of Kauai) and the three Local 142 executive officers (President Damaso, Vice-President Samson, and Secretary-Treasurer Miyagi). Yagi voted *kanalua;*[1] Martin voted for himself; and the other five voted for McElrath.

Hall made the announcement that McElrath would succeed him. He said the ILWU National Organizing Committee (Bridges, Goldblatt, Hall, and Chester) approved McElrath unanimously because of the man's "proven ability and loyalty to the union and its principles over more than twenty-five years."

Robert Gunsky, the Employers Council president, said McElrath would have to fill "some awful big shoes." McElrath would have to prove to the industrial community that he had the same "integrity of words and actions" Hall had. The news of Hall's impending departure caused uneasiness among management, and Hall tried to allay their fears. No one was indispensable, he said. The union was in good shape; it could carry on without him. He was not abandoning Hawaii. "Whenever they need me, I'll be back." As special reassurance to Senator Fong, Hall wrote that, of course, he also would come back "for major political problems such as the next election."

Hall resigned as director and executive committee member of the Hawaii Council for Housing Action; director and officer of the Hawaii Visitors Bureau; from the Aloha United Fund; and as an alternate on the board of directors of the Waikiki Improvement Association.[2]

He passed the word on to Rutledge through their mutual friend Sook Moon, a trucking company owner: "Tell your fat friend [he meant Rutledge] he can have it all now."

---

1. Doubtful.

2. Hall's public and community service record includes the following major assignments:

1944–1945: Hawaii War Labor Board and Hawaii War Manpower Commission. 1945–1965: Honolulu Community Chest. 1946: Honolulu Police Commission and Territorial Labor Appeal Board. 1963: Governor's Advisory Committee on Taxation and Finance and Governor's Maritime Advisory Board. 1964: Mayor's Finance Advisory Committee. 1965–1969: Director, Hawaii Visitors Bureau. 1966: President, Hawaii Council for Housing Action. 1966–1969: Vice-President, Aloha United Fund; Vice-President, Hawaii Visitors Bureau; Executive Board, Industrial Relations Research Association. 1967–1969: Hawaii State Harbor Task Force. 1968: 1968 Constitutional Convention, Public Information Committee; Waikiki Improvement Association. 1968–1969: Board of Directors, National Housing Conference.

"Moving after fifteen years in the same house is a great problem," said Hall. "We have to arrange to sell our house, then rent for a while while we find a house we want to buy. . . ."

The ILWU prepared an aloha party for Hall at the Honolulu International Center and more than a thousand guests came. Hearing speakers praise him, Hall again felt ill at ease. "So many nice things have been said about me in the past two weeks. It's embarrassing."

It has a real quality of unreality. It's not me they're talking about. It's almost the exact opposite of the things I heard about myself during the six months I spent in Federal Court [the Smith Act trial]. It didn't sound like me then, and it doesn't sound like me now.

On the eve of his departure, the editorials were effusive. The *Advertiser,* Hall's enemy in the old days, said:

It does not exaggerate to say that more than any other man, Hall helped bring industrial democracy to these islands as they moved from feudalism and paternalism to the sophisticated and broadly affluent society of today. . . .

The State Senate passed a resolution wishing Hall well. It bore the signature of Senator Eureka Forbes, an adversary of Hall's, along with the others. That endorsement stumped Hall. "I wondered what I had done wrong to warrant her approbation," Hall said. Then he read a news story which said Mrs. Forbes signed the resolution because she was glad to see him leaving. "I feel better now," said Hall.

As his final written communication as regional director, Hall saluted Hawaii: "Mahalo to friend and foe alike," he wrote. "They have made Hawaii interesting and exciting for me."

He may have sounded cheerful but there was a shadow darkening the future. Hall had Parkinson's disease.[3] Dr. Butler suspected it after an examination in April 1969, two months

---

3. Parkinson's disease, sometimes called *paralysis agitans,* is a degenerative disease of the thalamus, one of the basic nuclei at the base of the brain. The victim suffers from stiffness of muscle and from tremors. The cause is unknown. It does not interfere with the thought process, but it often causes the victim to become depressed.

before Hall left Hawaii. There were just a few symptoms at first: Hall had trouble buttoning his clothes; he had some loss of balance, some stiffness in his walk. But he was always somewhat inept physically, according to Butler, and the symptoms might have gone unnoticed and "passed for his usual clumsiness." Then things began to happen: Hall almost blacked out once or twice for no apparent reason; his limbs trembled.

Butler found that Hall had poor circulation in one of the carotid arteries of the neck. He told Hall either he was in the early stages of Parkinson's disease or he had an arteriosclerosis plaque in the carotid artery. He advised Hall that as a first order of business he should get a thorough medical examination in San Francisco.

CHAPTER **80**

Ailing

The Halls bought a three-bedroom house on Yerba Buena Avenue in San Francisco which had a maid's room and separate bath. They had no maid, but perhaps they might find another charming foreign student to stay with them, such as Ayako Kaneda, the Japanese girl. San Francisco State University was only a mile away.

"We are finally set in our new home and happy—although I live out of a suitcase most of the time," Hall wrote his Hilo friend, Leo Lycurgus. He was on the go. "My job should be designated 'Director of Re-Organization,' not Organizing," he said. He and Chester traveled around to the locals to discuss organization, jurisdiction, and the "recapturing of work we have lost."

Hall had a number of suggestions. He proposed shifting the emphasis to organizing in harbor areas, "where basic longshore muscle can be brought into use." He suggested mergers of

ILWU units: Local 6 of the Bay Area and Local 11 of San Jose; Locals 9 and 19 in Seattle; and the smaller warehouse locals and longshore locals in the Northwest. He thought there was a potential for organizing in Alaska. He suggested bringing the Hawaii Government Employees' Association into the ILWU and said the HGEA and the United Public Workers should merge.

During one rush of work he was out of town twenty-five out of sixty days. To take a break he rented a cabin in the Sierra for a week. "It's not Puuwaawaa[1] but it is nice to get away for a while and get acquainted with the family," he said.

He felt like a displaced island boy. People on the mainland seemed cold to him. "They are not as honest and forthright as in Hawaii," he said. "The only thing I really miss about Hawaii are the many close friends I left behind, like you and Leo," he wrote Nick Lycurgus, Leo's brother. He wrote Samson, the Local 142 vice-president: "Dear Sammy: Still missing the warmth of Hawaii, not the weather so much, but the people." He told Samson he was working his way into the job but did not have a free hand under the union constitution.

Heeding Butler's advice, he underwent a multiphase medical examination at Kaiser Hospital on Geary Boulevard. "Not exactly personalized but very efficient," he commented. He was a good patient. "Except for being pretty tired, I feel pretty good because my work is challenging," he wrote Butler. "I've cut down insulin to twenty-five units on my own because I was getting too many insulin reactions in the late afternoon, especially that required a quick sugar intake to stop the trembling, etc."

He went from Kaiser's to the care of a number of physicians; months passed; and one day Dr. S. Malvern Dorinson, a specialist in physical medicine and rehabilitation, broke the news to him that he knew was inevitable. He sent the word on to Butler: "You were on the right track in dia[g]nosing my current medical condition when I saw you last April [1969]. The verdict (which I more or less expected) was Parkinson's disease."

Hall read everything he could find about Parkinson's and, as he did with diabetes, he became an expert, in a layman's way, on

---

1. Carlsmith's ranch on the Big Island.

the disease. "I am now having an appointment next week with a neurologist for treatment," he wrote Butler. "My guess is first a go at [the drug] L-dopa—I hope one of the side effects is the well publicized one."

What he meant was that sometimes L-dopa brought on an increase in the sex drive. Hall wrote ILWU librarian Priscilla Shishido, with a twinkle in his eye: "You know it is supposed to have some interesting effects. We shall see." He told Butler that if L-dopa didn't work, he might have to undergo a brain operation. "Only the left side seems to be affected—leg drags, trembling left hand and weak voice."

He tried to remove the curse of Parkinson's and put the people he cared for at ease. "It is not a death sentence," he wrote Mrs. Shishido. He said that Dr. Tom Burton, the paternal grandfather of Hall's grandchild Kimi Burton, had suffered from Parkinson's disease for seven years, but was still practicing medicine in his seventies. "He has been on L-dopa for the last year and gets around fine," said Hall.

He began to refer to Parkinson's disease by the initials "P.D.," as though it were an old friend. He wrote Mrs. Shishido a second time to emphasize that Parkinson's was "not a death sentence, but it is a little confining."

Hall came back from a trip to Canada and was ordered into Mt. Zion Hospital in San Francisco for another series of tests. He underwent head X-rays and an EEG (electroencephalograph), which records brain waves. Samples of spinal fluid were taken. He submitted to the tests with patience, even with humor. "The conclusion was that there was no tumor which [the doctor] would have liked to find because he loves to operate."

By then he had been on L-dopa (four grams a day) for some time. He had no trouble walking, but he always felt tired. "There is no trembling of the left hand but it is still weak and I will get rehabilitation exercises," he said.

He began to use a bicycle exerciser to build his strength, and he dreamed about going hiking again at Point Reyes National Park on the California coast and perhaps, with luck, even venturing with backpack into Desolation Valley near Lake Tahoe. There was a bright side: for a while at least, diabetes, his steady companion through the years, was under control. He had been dieting carefully, and for one stretch of three weeks he had not taken a drink.

On November 15, 1969, Hall took part in the "mobilization" demonstration in San Francisco against the Vietnam War. It brought back the memory of the uncomfortable march he and thirty-eight others had made down Kalakaua Avenue on May 30, 1965, in the first antiwar demonstration in Hawaii.[2] "It's a lot more comfortable with 200,000 people than with 100 walking through Waikiki," Hall wrote.[3]

Antiwar demonstrators wanted to know why the ILWU didn't refuse to handle war materiel if indeed it was against the war. The Bay Area waterfront was booming. The union had "jobs coming out of our ears," said Bridges. "I know it's blood money, but people that were desperate for jobs and work—I can understand them not thinking of it that way—they go to work. But it certainly disturbs our middle-class and intellectual friends and they talked to me about it. . . ."

David Thompson asked Hall if either he or Goldblatt could come to Hawaii to appear on a television panel on Vietnam. Hall sent Thompson's letter to the International officers and Bridges returned it with a memorandum attached which said: "I would say this is a waste of time and money." He initialed it "H" for Harry.

Hall wrote Thompson: "Under the circumstances, I don't think it worthwhile to pursue the matter further because it would result in a split between the officers." He was deeply disturbed by the union's lack of firmness on Vietnam. "Where is the ILWU?" he demanded. "Still isolated from the Moratorium—but on the wrong side these days."

That was one of his differences with Bridges. Now that they both worked in the same building, the old gray loft at 150 Golden Gate Avenue, the grudge between them grew fat. Bridges ridiculed Hall's ideas; he seemed to have a "demonic"

2. The ILWU opposed the Vietnam War but said it could not refuse to handle war cargo because "there was not broad enough support from the rest of the labor movement and they would have been isolated and replaced in that work, the union beaten and weakened without changing national policy. . . ."

3. "Jack was timid," said Butler. "He was embarrassed at exposing himself."

feeling for Hall. And Hall did not try to disguise his contempt for Bridges.

One of the issues that divided them was the move by Bridges to join the International Longshoremen's Association (ILA) of the East Coast. Hall was against it. Bridges believed there was only one way to guarantee the ILWU's future: a tie-up with the ILA or with the Teamsters Union. "Things are confused here as ever with Harry determined to fragment the union so he can take the longshore section back to the AFL-CIO through the ILA—I don't think he will be able to make it," Hall wrote Mrs. Shishido. There were bitter exchanges at the International Executive Board meetings. Hall spoke angrily of "Harry's wheeling and dealing."

In September 1969, Hall returned to Hawaii to help Burns get reelected in 1970. He had been gone only a few months but the union greeted him like a long lost friend. He glowed in the warmth of the welcome for the "coast haole." He told the Local 142 convention that it was a depressing time. Taxes ate up the working man's paycheck; American cities were rotting at the core; the country was engaged in a shameful war.

"There's a lot of criticism of the Burns administration," he said.

> To put it bluntly, they call it an administration of the budda-heads [Nisei] and the ILWU and there's going to be a vigorous campaign to try to unseat the present administration and replace it with one that has a lot of beautiful ideas but if they were put into effect I don't know how we'd eat. . . .

Hall said the Burns administration had given the ILWU the chance to take part in the levels of administrative government that controlled the state's growth:

> It doesn't mean that we control it; it means simply that we have a direct voice in the highest council, and I think we should all stop for a minute and think out what would happen if there were a new administration and where the ILWU would stand in all this.

He said he recognized the threat posed by Burns' opponent, the sharp man, Gill. The ILWU could survive a Gill victory, said

Hall. "We may have to crawl back into our storm shelter for a while but we know how to do that—we've done it in the past under Mahope Joe's [Governor Joseph B. Poindexter] and martial law and under Ingram Stainback's so we'll survive. . . ."

Hall returned to Hawaii in April 1970, still concerned about Burns' reelection. If the ILWU didn't hang together, he said, Burns "will go down the tube" in the September primary election.

CHAPTER 81
Dying

> *Naturally, everyone wants to keep living as long as possible and never gives up the hope that maybe a breakthrough will come. I know that I would be frightened and at the same time sad that I had wasted so much of my life and have not done a hundred things that I should have done before and just ran out of time to complete.*
>
> —Jack Hall to a woman dying of cancer

Time *was* running out. Hall went on trying to work. Some days it was a struggle just to get up. He lurched when he walked; his left leg dragged. Sometimes it took him minutes to move a few feet.

Out of politeness a friend asked him on one of his bad days: "How are you, Jack?"

"All right," he said gruffly, his mouth set in a tight line. He didn't want sympathy; he didn't want anybody to ask him how he felt. It was obvious he was not well. Many days Yoshiko begged him not to go to work. He went anyway.

Oreste's bar on Jones Street was a haven; Phil the bartender, a friend. Hall's favorite drink was vodka and grapefruit juice. There were two San Francisco watering places frequented by the ILWU: Oreste's and nearby Harrington's. Bridges and his allies preferred Harrington's; Hall, Goldblatt, et al. went to Oreste's.

Hall planned a trip in September 1970 to Hawaii, then up to Alaska and on down to the Pacific Northwest on union business. It seemed like a precarious venture for a man in his condition and Yoshiko pleaded with him not to go. He was stubborn. "Someone has to do it," he said.

"It was a disaster," said Mrs. Hall. "I knew it was going to be a disaster. . . . You couldn't talk him out of it."

Hall flew to Hawaii on September 4. His friends who hadn't seen him since the previous April were shocked. To get into a car, he put in his right leg and then, pulling his left leg with his right arm, he hauled himself in. One morning he had breakfast at the McElraths'. He couldn't handle the spoon to eat his papaya. He couldn't comb his hair. He couldn't tighten his belt. (McElrath later bought him a pair of suspenders at the Liberty House.)

Butler picked him up at his hotel[1] in Waikiki and brought him home to the quiet of the Butler house in Kailua. He spent the afternoon. Butler put on his favorite music—"The Gettysburg March" rang out again. Hall sat in a big easy chair in the living room and listened to the music. He didn't say much. When it came time to go, he couldn't get out of the chair. Butler had to help him get up. Hall walked over to the living room table, put his hand in his pocket, and couldn't take it out again. It seemed trapped. Butler had to take hold of his hand and lift it out of his pocket.

Katsuto Nagaue, the man who had taught Hall how to read a financial report, visited him. It was a sad encounter. "He looked terrible," said Nagaue. "As he sat there talking, spittle came out of his mouth." Nagaue was stricken by the sight. "I'm dying, Kats," said Hall. Nagaue could say nothing. What was there to say?

Priscilla Shishido was crushed. Hall seemed to have lost the will to live.

---

1. The Ambassador on Kuhio Avenue.

McElrath assigned Honolulu longshoreman Lawrence Kelley to help Hall. Kelley accompanied him for about a week and Hall was glad to have him. "He was more helpful than a Kelly Girl," said Hall. "I wouldn't have made it without him."

Kelley slept in an adjoining room at the hotel. He helped Hall dress and undress; he helped put him to bed. One night Hall fell out of bed and the alert Kelley heard the sound and came in.

Kelley said that Hall was half-paralyzed on the left side and walked dragging his foot. "He never complained about his illness. He was still trying to do a job," said Kelley.

McElrath drove to the hotel to pick up Hall and Kelley and drive them to the airport. He went up to Hall's room and helped him put on his socks. On the plane to Anchorage Hall got stuck in the rest room and couldn't get out. The ever watchful Kelley came to the rescue.

In Alaska, with Kelley at his side, Hall managed to get his business done. Then they flew to Seattle and Hall went to North Bend to attend a union meeting at a community college. On the morning of September 14 he tried to get out of bed, became dizzy, and fell against the sharp edge of the headboard and cracked two ribs.

He managed to get dressed and though he suffered through the morning session, he sat it out. At the lunch break, as he was walking down the concrete steps, he caught his heel and started to pitch forward, "making like a Moiseyev dancer."[2] As he told it: "I finally got my feet under me and avoided the fall which would have been disastrous. It didn't take too much from a few guys, particularly Jason Johnson, of North Bend, to convince me to get my ass back to S.F. [San Francisco] and my doctors."

On September 16 Hall was readmitted to Mt. Zion Hospital where he underwent "brain scan, x-rays, EEGs, spinal punctures, etc." The tests showed he did not have a brain tumor. It was his old affliction, Parkinson's disease.

The drug L-dopa nauseated him—"like morning sickness for pregnant women," he said. Yet following the trip to Hawaii and Alaska, for a while he felt better. "I am not strong but I can walk without difficulty, get dressed, etc. alone," he said.

---

2. A troupe of Russian dancers.

On December 1, 1970, Hall went to Vancouver, British Columbia, to attend an ILWU International Executive Board meeting. He intended to go on from Vancouver up to Alaska. Again Yoshiko begged him not to go. She took him to his doctor, expecting the doctor to rule against the trip, but to her amazement he told Hall it was all right for him to travel. "In face of that, there was nothing I could do to dissuade him from taking the trip," she said.

As she feared, the trip was a nightmare: "Vancouver turned out to be snowing, raining, hailing and generally all hell bent weather-wise and Jack had a tough time. Also, some one, I still don't know who, had his G.P. [general practitioner] call him in Vancouver and advised him against going to Alaska."

Hall attended board meetings from December 2 to 4. His mind was alert and he gave lucid reports on the status of organizing in California and the Pacific Northwest. He also spoke on the subject close to his heart—politics in Hawaii: "We had a political alliance with the HGEA in Hawaii during the last election that helped clean up the legislature," he said. "The HGEA is very happy to work with us. . . ."

Bridges discussed the risk entailed in taking government workers into the union. They were "a special breed of cats" who would not strengthen the union, he said. Hall said that he, too, had mixed feelings about taking in government workers. "If it were not for the Hawaii law which makes the relationship of Hawaii government employees the same as private workers, I would have turned them down. I've turned down government workers before."

Hall said he and Johnny Parks, the ILWU regional director for the Northwest, were going to Alaska for a few days. Bridges asked why. "To see if we can get those ports back," said Hall.

"For the past thirty years Alaska has had potential and we have 400 to 500 members there," said Bridges. "To get fourteen guys in this port and fifteen guys in that port isn't worth fiddling around."

Vancouver exhausted Hall and he called off the trip to Alaska. He came back to San Francisco "in very bad shape." Yoshiko met him at the airport on a dark day that matched her mood. She took him to the doctor, and in her outspoken way, she protested "about Jack not getting anywhere with his medication and living by the book."

On December 10 Hall went back to Kaiser Hospital for examination by an internist, a neurologist ("the top guy at Kaiser"), and a therapist. The next day Bridges announced that Hall was sick and might be away for some time.

An iron routine began for Yoshiko. She spent her days at the hospital. She came home at six or six thirty in the evening and had no time for anything except shopping for groceries and doing the laundry. The ordeal whittled her to seventy pounds.

Hall was kept in the hospital for ten days. He had trouble walking. He was down to 160 pounds; his clothes no longer fit. He had suffered a severe setback and yet after he was home for a few days, he was "much better, concerned about what's going on in the rest of the world. . . . We are not going to have a funeral right away," said Yoshiko.

Friends rallied by his side. Damaso assured him that "everyone in Hawaii wanted him to get well." Arena, his old pal from back in the 1940s who now worked in San Francisco, came calling. Hall's children, Michele and Eric, comforted him. Mikey "has been a dream of a daughter and friend—she is simply great," said Mrs. Hall.

Yoshiko took instructions in therapy technique to help Hall get his "sea legs" back. If he could get around by himself, she hoped, then her life would be on a "bit more even keel." Hall spent a happy Christmas Day. Mikey took pictures of him laughing and playing with his grandchild Kimi.

On New Year's Day Hall did not feel well and stayed in bed. Around noon he said he wanted something to eat. He had not eaten breakfast and that alone disturbed Yoshiko. He always enjoyed a good breakfast. She prepared a fancy sandwich for his lunch. She wanted to make the tray look attractive so she went out in the yard and found a big, purple-centered fuchsia, "a particularly pretty one," and put it on the tray alongside the sandwich. She turned music on and she and Eric went into Hall's bedroom to chat with him and keep him company while he ate. "For a guy who likes his breakfast so much, it seems strange—" they said, making conversation.

Suddenly Hall began to vomit. He realized something catastrophic had happened: he had suffered a massive stroke.

Yoshiko and Eric tried to lift him to take him to the hospital, but they could not. In their agitation, they didn't think of the obvious thing to do: call an ambulance. Instead, Eric phoned Arena. When Arena got there, Hall was pale but conscious. There were a few steep steps from the bedroom to the second floor landing and then the flight downstairs to the door. It would have been impossible to carry him. Arena called an ambulance. The attendants put Hall in a wheelchair, took him downstairs, and drove to Kaiser Hospital on Geary.

Hall's doctor wasn't there. A staff doctor handled the case. It was an emergency—they didn't have time to get Hall's chart out. Yoshiko briefed the doctor on her husband's medical history. She said he was a diabetic and that he suffered from Parkinson's and was on L-dopa. The doctor ordered intravenous feeding. Yoshiko thought her husband was in shock from not eating; a diabetic must eat regularly.

An attendant wheeled Hall into a room flooded by the light of a big overhead lamp. Yoshiko went along. Hall thought he was in an operating room; he was supposed to have a prostatectomy done and he thought they were going to operate right then. "They're going to cut me open," he said in alarm to Yoshiko. "Don't let them operate on me now. I'll have it done next week, but not now."

She assured him they were not going to operate. "They're just giving you IV [intravenous feeding]. Don't worry."

He relaxed and gave her a kiss. "See you later, Jack," she said and left the room. That was the last time she saw him alive.

Yoshiko stayed at the hospital until eight that evening. She and Eric stayed up all night, they were so worried. In the morning she kept phoning the hospital but could not reach Hall's doctor. She became alarmed. At about one that afternoon she and Eric drove to the hospital.

When Yoshiko walked up to the receptionist, the woman was unable to speak. Yoshiko knew then that her husband was dead. He had died late at night. Yoshiko saw Hall's doctor in the corridor and in her anguish she screamed at him.

CHAPTER 82
Mourning

"ASTONISHED AT BROTHER HALL'S DEATH," Tomitaro Kaneda,[1] president of the All Japan Maritime and Dock Workers Union, cabled from Tokyo.

"Thanks for all the help, Brother Hall. We won't forget," said Jack Copess, business manager of the Hawaii Boilermakers Union, Local 204.

"He played a historic role in the labor and political life in Hawaii," said Bridges. "The results of his life work can be found among the tens of thousands of families who moved into better lives because of his work as a trade unionist."

"If there is any guy who shook the volcanoes loose of their ashes, Jack Hall did," said Goldblatt. "He changed the whole history of the islands."

"We had many differences as to methods," said Rutledge. "He believed he could accomplish much through politics while I believed in direct action."

"Jack was one of the greatest labor leaders that Hawaii will ever know," said Grunsky, president of the Hawaii Employers Council.

H. N. Trevedi of the Municipal Corporation of Greater Bombay wrote: "Dear Shri[2] Bridges: Hall was a towering trade union leader of the time. What a loss and what sorrow to be snatched away at 56."[3]

The magazine *The Nation* said:

---

1. Ayako Kaneda's father.

2. Hindi for "Mr."

3. Hall would have been fifty-six on February 28, 1971.

Hall and his union . . . taught the Islands Establishment that they knew more about how best to run the economy, how to govern the territory and later the state, how to achieve racial and ethnic unity, than did the militant management of a quarter of a century ago. . . . Communities, regions, states and powerful individuals should be a bit more circumspect about whom they kick around, especially when "radical" and "subversive" ideas are involved. Ideas that enrage the Establishment may be the very ones desperately needed, even for the prosperity of the Establishment.

From 10 to 10:15 AM on January 7, 1971, 41,000 government workers in Hawaii and 23,000 ILWU members stopped work to pay tribute to Hall. Longshore Local 10 in San Francisco and Local 13 in Wilmington, California, closed down their ports for twenty-four hours.[4] In Hawaii, ILWU members gathered outside their shops and offices and at pierside.

Local 142 sent a leaflet to its members: "Jack had brains, guts, honesty, and above all, faith in working people. . . . Sick as he was the last years, dragging his big body along, Jack worked . . . till he died. . . ."

A thousand people gathered the night of January 7, 1971, at the Honolulu International Center to eulogize Hall. Michele, Hall's daughter, had written Bridges not to come: he was not welcome. McElrath phoned Sid Roger, the *ILWU Dispatcher* editor, and told him to tell Bridges to stay away. Roger told McElrath to tell Bridges himself.

Bridges came and sat on the speaker's platform but he did not speak. He felt it was insulting to try to keep him away. Goldblatt delivered the eulogy.

The family requested that no flowers be sent and the ILWU asked that those who wished to do so should make donations to the Eric Mitsugi Hall Scholarship Fund.[5]

Roger wrote the obituary for Hall which appeared in the *Dispatcher*. He took the material from the two Honolulu dailies,

---

4. In honor of Hall and Bill Gettings, regional director of the Pacific Northwest, who had also died recently.

5. The drive raised $24,000. Rutledge gave $1000.

from the ILWU files, and from his own knowledge of Hall. Bridges told him the obituary was full of lies and distortions.

"The material about his life I got from Local 142," Roger replied. "I didn't invent it."

"Dave Thompson wrote it," Bridges said, angrily. "It's full of lies. How come you mentioned about Hall being a major organizer of the union? He didn't organize a damned thing. How come you didn't mention Chet Meske and Frank Thompson?"

"Because they didn't just die," retorted Roger.

January 20, 1971, was one of those splendid days which Hawaii is blessed with. The sun shone brightly, the sea was sparkling, the tradewinds blew.

Twelve men[6] went out that morning on the catamaran *Ale Ale Kai* to scatter Hall's ashes. They boarded the boat at the Hilton Hawaiian Village, not far from where Hall had once lived when that strip of beach was known as "Submarine Alley."

McElrath had written a tribute, "Sailor Remembered," a fifteen-line eulogy to Hall in verse.[7] He had recalled the poem "Eagle Forgotten," Vachel Lindsay's hymn in honor of John Peter Altgeld, a prolabor governor of Illinois. McElrath started to read his lines but was overcome with emotion. Tangen stepped up and finished the reading for him.

Bobo Hall, Jack Hall's half-brother, cast into the ocean the ashes he had kept in a cardboard box at home. Damaso and McElrath each dropped a red carnation lei into the water. The catamaran pulled about and sailed past the drifting leis as the mourners poured into the ocean a bottle of Jim Beam whiskey and a bottle of Smirnoff vodka. Somehow that gesture seemed appropriate to them and it broke the tension.

---

6. John "Bobo" Hall, David Thompson, Mac Kageyama, Jack Dykes, Toyomasa Oshiro, Ben Vea, Mitsugi "Rags" Shishido, Fujisaki, Tangen, Damaso, McElrath, and Yagi.

7. The first two lines:

Sleep softly . . . sailor not forgotten . . . under the foam. Time has its way with you there and the sea has its own.

ACKNOWLEDGMENTS

The story of Jack Hall and the ILWU could not have been told without the help of librarians. The writer will always remember with gratitude the late Priscilla Shishido, who made the Hawaii ILWU library one of the finest union libraries in the country. She helped inspire the writer with a taste for research into the topic which she herself found endlessly fascinating: the story of Hall.

Special thanks are due to the two librarians at Anne Rand Library, Marjorie Canright, former chief librarian who retired, and Carol Schwartz, her successor, and to Betty Yanagawa of the Hawaii ILWU library and her former assistant, Ellen Furukawa. The writer is also grateful to Sonja Tyau, research librarian at the Hawaii Employers Council library; to Mrs. Robert Van Niel, assistant documents librarian, government documents collection, Gregg M. Sinclair Library at the University of Hawaii; and to the ever cheerful and always helpful librarians at the Hawaii News Agency: Beatrice Kaya, chief librarian; Margaret Iwamoto, assistant librarian; and Ella Tom, Kiyoko Bowman, Mildred Kuniyoshi, Nancy Hall, Shari Kageyama, Deanne Norton, Sharon Moore, Mildred Young, and Dana Lynn Ebinger.

The writer owes a special debt to Agnes Conrad, director of the Hawaii State Archives. Upholding the finest traditions of her profession, she was not content merely to allow the writer to labor in the vineyards of the State Archives, but she also gave him suggestions on *what* to seek out to make his book richer and fuller.

The writer is also grateful for their special help to June Gutmanis for her work on the index, to Tsuneko Scoops Kreger for her proofreading work, and to Don Yoder of Covelo, California, for his editing.

Grateful acknowledgment is made to the following for permission to quote from the sources listed:

Doubleday & Company, for four words from *Democracy in America,* by Alexis de Tocqueville, copyright © 1969, by J. P. Mayer, copyright © 1966 in the English translation by Harper & Row; Atheneum House, Inc., for five words from *The Making of the President,* by Theodore H. White, copyright © 1961; University of Hawaii Press, for a paragraph from *Hawaii's War Years, 1941–1945,* by Gwenfread E. Allen, copyright © 1950, reprinted by Greenwood Press, 1971; Farrar, Straus & Giroux, Inc., for four words from *The Aloha State,* by Ben Adams, copyright © 1959, by Hill and Wang; Hastings House, for two sentences from *Wisconsin: A Guide to the Badger State,* copyright © 1954; Houghton Mifflin Company, for fifty-three words from *Turbulent Years* by Irving Bernstein, copyright © 1969.

To J. Garner Anthony, for permission to quote from his *Hawaii under Army Rule,* Stanford University Press, copyright © 1955; to Alexander MacDonald, for permission to quote from his *Revolt in Paradise,* published by Stephen Daye, Inc., copyright © 1944; to Joyce A. Matsumoto (Najita), for permission to quote from her "1947 Pineapple Strike," University of Hawaii Industrial Relations Center, August 1958; to Virgilio M. Felipe, for permission to quote from his historical paper, "The Vibora Luviminda and the 1937 Puunene Plantation Strike," University of Hawaii, May 1, 1970; to Thomas Lawrence O'Brien, for permission to quote from his publication, "The Plot to Sovietize Hawaii," printed by the Hawaii News Printshop, copyright © 1948.

SOURCES

The bedrock for this book is the ILWU's official correspondence on Hawaii—including several thousand letters which Jack Hall wrote and received as ILWU regional director in Hawaii and later as ILWU vice-president–director of organization in San Francisco. The union opened its Hawaii file to the writer at the Anne Rand Library at ILWU International Headquarters in San Francisco and at the ILWU Memorial Foundation on Atkinson Drive in Honolulu.

Others made letters available. The writer saw correspondence Hall had with John E. Reinecke, Jack Kawano, Dr. Willis Butler, Ichiro Izuka, Priscilla Shishido, and James W. Cooley, a pre-World War II labor organizer. Letters are cited in the notes with the name of sender and recipient and the date—for example, Hall to Goldblatt, December 5, 1960.

That wealth of letters was supplemented by more than two hundred interviews the writer conducted with people who played a role in this story. (Interviews are cited in the notes with the last name of the person interviewed—for example, Bridges.) Some interviews were short: a chat over the phone; a chance meeting on the street; an encounter on a plane. But many interviews were long and the questions carefully prepared. The chief interviews were taped. ILWU officials, from Harry Bridges and Louis Goldblatt on down to the men in the fields, granted interviews and were consistently helpful. David E. Thompson, ILWU director of education, talked informally with the writer at least thirty times. Robert McElrath, a former ILWU regional director and Hall's comrade since 1938, granted five one- and two-hour-long interviews which were taped. Bridges, the founder of the union and longtime president, gave a five-hour taped interview; so did Goldblatt, the former International secretary-treasurer.

The employer representatives who dealt with the ILWU also were helpful. They all had keen memories of the years of confrontation. The Hawaii Employers Council permitted the writer to go through, page by page, the bulky transcripts of the negotiations carried on before and during the strikes of the late 1940s and early 1950s.

Many politicians who dealt with Hall talked freely to the writer. Many of his friends (and foes) of yesteryear also discussed him. The late Governor John A. Burns called the writer one afternoon, and as Burns sat signing papers in his office, he asked in his brusque way, "What are we talking about?"

"Jack Hall and the ILWU," the writer said. Then for two hours Burns spoke into a tape recorder (which he furnished) on his memories of Hall and the politics of Hawaii.

Others also helped generously. Edward D. Beechert, Jr., professor of history at the University of Hawaii, permitted the writer to copy Beechert's interview with Hall, the only taped interview with Hall that came to the writer's attention (cited in the notes as Beechert tape). The writer owes Professor Beechert a further debt. He provided a valuable critique of the manuscript and his suggestions for deletions, additions, and corrections immeasurably strengthened the work. He also sat for an interview to expand on his notes and permitted the writer to make full use of the material (cited in the notes as Beechert interview).

Charles P. Larrowe, Michigan State University professor and author of *Harry Bridges: The Rise and Fall of Radical Labor in the U.S.,* gave the writer his original notes on Hall which he took in an interview in 1964.

Yoshiko Ogawa Hall, Hall's widow, provided the only personal memorandum Hall left behind. It is a report (cited as Hall Diary) which Hall prepared for the use of his lawyers during the Smith Act trial to account for his whereabouts from the time he first saw Hawaii (1932) up until the time he joined the ILWU (1944). Mrs. Hall also made available for the writer's inspection the few mementos Hall kept: his seaman's discharge papers, some of his books, his record collection. Hall kept very little; he was not, as his wife observed, sentimental.

In time Hall became an accomplished speaker; many of the original drafts of his speeches, which he himself wrote, are in the

ILWU Atkinson Drive library. Often they were typed on a special typewriter with large letters and they bear his copyreading marks.

The ILWU made available the minutes of all the ILWU International Executive Board meetings, going back to 1934, and the ILWU Local 142 Executive Board meetings. The writer also had access to minutes of local unit Executive Board meetings. The ILWU furnished the minutes of the union's International conventions and the Local 142 conventions.

Hall was a prolific writer; he was a man with newspaper ink in his veins. He wrote for, and for a time edited, the old *Voice of Labor.* He edited the *Kauai Herald* and the *Herald,* both sharply outspoken labor papers. Many of his pieces were signed. He never was obtuse; a reader knew exactly what he was driving at.

Hall was a defendant in the Hawaii Smith Act trial (cited in the notes as Smith Act). The case went on for months; the appeal went on for years.

Hall was the spokesman for the ILWU in Hawaii and he often talked over the radio. The radio scripts and the columns of the two Honolulu dailies, the *Advertiser* and the *Star-Bulletin,* are rich sources of information. The writer also made use of the following publications: *Garden Island,* the *Maui News,* the *Hilo Tribune-Herald,* the *Honolulu Record,* the *Hawaiian Reporter, The Voice of the ILWU, ILWU Dispatcher,* the *San Francisco Chronicle,* the *San Francisco Examiner,* the *San Francisco Call-Bulletin,* the *Hawaii Hochi,* the *Portland Oregonian,* the *New York Times,* the *Washington Post, Time* magazine, *The Nation, The Congressional Record.*

During the 1940s Philip A. Brooks worked for the Hawaii Employers Council as chief researcher. Brooks attended labor negotiation sessions and kept notes in Phillips Code, a kind of shorthand that telegraphers used. Brooks wrote a Doctor of Philosophy dissertation in 1952 titled "Multiple-Industry Unionism in Hawaii." It details the Hawaii employers' viewpoint in dealing with the ILWU and is an excellent source of information.

In 1960 Joyce Lea Walker, then a student at the University of Hawaii majoring in speech therapy, chose Hall's Labor Day speeches as the topic for a master's thesis. She asked Hall for an interview and a rapport was established. She interviewed him six times. Walker's thesis, which bore the formidable title "A Rhetorical Analysis of the Epideictic Speeches of Jack Hall, Regional Director of the ILWU for Hawaii," came out in June 1961. It is a good source of information on Hall.

Another former University of Hawaii student, Thomas Michael Holmes, wrote a doctoral dissertation, "The Specter of Communism in Hawaii, 1947–53," submitted in August 1975. The work recreates the strained atmosphere of the times.

The writer knew Hall from the early 1950s until Hall left for San Francisco in 1969. For several years in the mid-1950s the writer covered the ILWU as part of the labor beat for the *Honolulu Advertiser.* He often saw Hall in his office on the second floor of the ILWU building. Feet propped on his desk, relaxed and lucid, Hall spoke freely with him. The writer had learned something about the man: namely, not to waste his time with idle chatter. He had his questions well framed; he shot them out at Hall as if out of a rifle; and when he finished asking the questions, he said, "Thanks, Jack. Goodbye."

INTERVIEWS

Takumi "Taku" Akama, John K. Akau, Jr., Harry Albright, Herbert C. Alexander, William G. "Bill" Among, J. Garner Anthony, Daniel T. "Dan" Aoki, Yasuki "Yasu" Arakaki, Matsuki "Mutt" Arashiro, Ernest L. "Ernie" Arena, Koji Ariyoshi, Howard C. Babbitt, Simeon L. Bagasol, William J. "Bill" Bailey, A. William Barlow, Daniel "Danny" Beagle, James S. "Jim" Beatty, Edward D. Beechert, Jr., Ronald Y. "Ron" Bennett, David A. Benz, Dr. Morton E. Berk, Edward Berman, E. E. Black, William Blackfield, Louis B. Blissard, Harry Boranian, Douglas Boswell, Nobi Bouslog.

Harry Bridges, Noriko "Nikki" Bridges, Archie Brown, John Brun, Buck A. Buchwach, John A. Burns, Dr. Willis P. Butler, Cornelius C. "Neil" Cadagan, C. Wendell Carlsmith, Revels H. Cayton, Moses D. Claveria, William B. Cobb, Elmer F. Cravalho, Randolph Crossley, William H. "Willie" Crozier, Carl Damaso, Edward C. "Eddie" DeMello, Benjamin F. "Ben"

Dillingham II, Nelson K. Doi, Bernard B. Eilerts, John Elias, Henry B. Epstein, O. Vincent Esposito, Elizabeth Pruett "Betty" Farrington, Lindsay Faye, Isaac Feig, Nathaniel Felzer.

C. J. "Charlie" Fern, John B. "J. B." Fernandes, Hiram L. Fong, Corinne von Wedelstaedt Forde, Juliette Mae Fraser, Mrs. Basilio B. Fuertes, Sr., Yoroku Fukuda, Noboru Furuya (George Goto), Thomas P. Gill, Louis B. Goldblatt, Albert Grain, Edward J. Greaney, Jr., Robert R. Grunsky, Jean Gundlach, Mrs. Hazel L. Hall, John Junior "Bobo" Hall, Yoshiko Hall, Mabel Hamamura, Thomas H. Hamilton, Shurei Hirozawa, Howard K. Hoddick, Shiro Hokama, Mona Hind Holmes, Leonard Hoshijo, Amos A. Ignacio, Koichi Imori, Daniel K. Inouye, Ichiro Izuka, Walter Johnson, Sam Kagel, Frederick K. "Fred" Kamahoahoa, Jr., Isaac Kekaulike "Chicken" Kamoku, Charles E. Kauhane.

Jack H. Kawano, Joseph E. "Joe Blurr" Kealalio, James K. "Jimmie" Kealoha, Lawrence K. "Larry" Kelley, Jr., Mitsuyuki "Mits" Kido, Denichi Jack Kimoto, Shunichi Kimura, Samuel P. King, Bert T. Kobayashi, Beatrice Krauss, Robert G. "Bob" Krauss, Theodora Charlene "Teddy" Kreps, Ricardo Labez, Roy J. Leffingwell, Bernard H. Levinson, Hal "Aku" Lewis, Frederick Tam "Fred" Low, Leo Lycurgus, David C. McClung, Ah Quon McElrath, Robert McElrath, Mildred Hall McIntyre, Aaron Marcus, James K. "Jimmy" Mattoon, Chuck Mau, Philip P. Maxwell, Chester J. "Chet" Meske.

John H. Midkiff, Sr., Thomas B. "Tommy" Miles, Slator M. Miller, Newton K. Miyagi, Takaichi Miyamoto, John Troup Moir, Jr., Benjamin "Ben" Morimoto, Yoshikazu Morimoto, Robert Moyle, Dr. Ernest Murai, Stephen "Steve" Murin, John F. Murphy, Katsuto "Kats" Nagaue, Haruo "Dyna" Nakamoto, Bert H. Nakano, Lelan Nishek, Nellie Nishihara, Ayako Kaneda Nitta, William R. "Bill" Norwood, Wilfred M. Oka, Hideo "Major" Okada, George Okano, Jack Osakoda, Robert C. Oshiro, Toyomasa Oshiro, Mrs. Emma "Mama" Ouye, Omi Oyama, Masaro "Mel" Ozaki, Edwin "Eddie" Paaluhi, Jack K. Palk, Mrs. Earl R. (Ruth) Parmeter, Martin Pence, Paul G. Pinsky, Alfred Preis.

William F. "Bill" Quinn, Aiko Reinecke, John E. Reinecke,

Mrs. Charles A. (Patricia) Rice, William S. Richardson, Edwin Clark "Bill" Rinehart, Joyce Roberts, James Riley "Bob" Robertson, Mary K. Robinson, Sidney Roger, Edward Rohrbough, Arthur A. "Art" Rutledge, Rachel Saiki, Andrew J. "Andy" Salz, Harriet Williams Bouslog Sawyer, Henry Schmidt, Phillip Schrader, Edward S. "Ed" Sheehan, Mitsuo "Slim" Shimizu, Masaru Harry Shimonishi, Mitsugi "Rags" Shishido, Priscilla Yadao Shishido, Frank G. Silva, Barry Silverman, Adam A. "Bud" Smyser.

Dwight C. Steele, Harry Stroup, Mrs. Paul Sveda, Myer C. Symonds, Frank Takahashi, Sakae Takahashi, Tokuichi "Dynamite" Takushi, James T. Tanaka, Eddie Tangen, Jack Teehan, David E. Thompson, Frank E. Thompson, Lorrin P. Thurston, Mike N. Tokunaga, Arthur K. Trask, David K. Trask, Jr., Daniel W. Tuttle, Jr., Unsei Uchima, Charles Velson, Hajime Ghandi Warashina, Mrs. Edward Watase, Maxie Weisbarth, Robert Wenkam, Jon Wiig, Thomas S. "Tom" Yagi, Masao Yamada, Nadao Yoshinaga, Masao Yotsuda, John Young.

CORRESPONDENCE

William F. Bailey, Albert W. "Al" Bates, James P. Blaisdell, Harry Bridges, Roy Cummings, Richard Gladstein, Louis B. Goldblatt, Yoshiko Hall, Ronald B. Jamieson, Grover Johnson, Jack Kawano, Charles P. Larrowe, Mrs. John A. "Aunt Lily" Larson, Bert H. Nakano, Mrs. Paul Sveda, Frank E. Thompson, Jon Wiig.

BIBLIOGRAPHY

BOOKS

Adams, Ben. *Hawaii: The Aloha State.* New York: Hill and Wang, 1959.

Allen, Gwenfread. *Hawaii's War Years.* Honolulu: University of Hawaii Press, 1950.

Anthony, J. Garner. *Hawaii under Army Rule.* Stanford: Stanford University Press, 1955; Honolulu: University Press of Hawaii, 1975, paperback ed.

Bernstein, Irving. *Turbulent Years.* Boston: Houghton Mifflin, 1971.

Brooks, Philip A. *Multiple-Industry Unionism in Hawaii.* Boston: Eagle Enterprises, 1952.

Cariaga, Roman R. *The Filipino in Hawaii.* Honolulu: Filipino Public Relations Bureau, 1937.

Coffman, Tom. *Catch a Wave.* Honolulu: University Press of Hawaii, 1973.

Daws, Gavan. *Shoal of Time.* New York: Macmillan, 1968; Honolulu: University Press of Hawaii, 1974, paperback ed.

De Caux, Len. *Labor Radical.* Boston: Beacon Press, 1970.

Fuchs, Lawrence H. *Hawaii Ponoi: A Social History.* New York: Harcourt, Brace, 1961.

Johannessen, Edward. *The Hawaiian Labor Movement.* Boston: Bruce Humphries, 1956.

Johnson, Hayes and Nick Kotz. *The Unions.* New York: Pocket Books, 1972.

Kuykendall, R. S. *The Hawaiian Kingdom.* Vol. 2. Honolulu: University of Hawaii Press, 1966.

Larrowe, Charles P. *Harry Bridges: The Rise and Fall of Radical Labor in the U.S.* New York: Lawrence Hill, 1972.

Lens, Sidney. *The Labor Wars.* New York: Doubleday, 1973.

MacDonald, Alexander. *Revolt in Paradise.* New York: Stephen Daye, 1944.

Pratt, John Scott Boyd, Sr. *The Hawaii I Remember.* Kaneohe, Hawaii: Tongg, 1965.

Quin, Mike. *The Big Strike.* Olema, Calif.: Olema Publishing Co., 1949.

Simpich, Frederick, Jr. *Anatomy of Hawaii.* New York: Coward-McCann, 1971.

Wakukawa, Ernest K. *A History of the Japanese People in Hawaii.* Tokyo: Dai Nippon Printing Co., 1938.

OTHER SOURCES

"Alexander & Baldwin, Inc., Seventy-five Years a Corporation." *Ampersand* (Honolulu), June 30, 1975.

Anthony, J. Garner. "Report on the Status of Civil Government in Hawaii." Mimeographed. Honolulu: September 20, 1943.

"Are Unions Losing Their Clout?" *U.S. News & World Report,* October 4, 1976.

Beechert, Edward D. "Racial Divisions and Agricultural Labor Organizing in Hawaii" University of Hawaii Industrial Relations Center, 1977.

Billings, Richard N. and John Greenya. "Power to the Public Worker." Washington: Robert B. Luce, 1974.

Blaisdell, James P. "Industrial Stability in Hawaii." Talk given in Honolulu to the Social Economic Trends Committee of the Hawaii Education Association on February 21, 1946.

Brissenden, Paul F. "The Great Hawaiian Dock Strike." *Labor Law Journal,* April 1953.

Buchwach, Buck A. "Hawaii, U.S.A.—Communist Beachhead or Showcase for Americanism?" Honolulu: April 1957.

Cariaga, Roman R. "Filipinos on an Hawaiian Sugar Plantation." A treatise. Honolulu: 1936.

Congdon, Charles Franklin. "Background and History of the 1946 Hawaiian Sugar Strike." Master's thesis, Columbia University School of Business, 1950.

"Constitution and Bylaws of ILWU Local 142 (Consolidated Longshore–General Trades–Pineapple–Sugar–Tourism Union), Chartered: September 1, 1952, As Amended to October 1, 1971." Honolulu: n.d.

Davenport, John. "A Heretical View of Labor Unions." *Fortune,* February 1974.

De Toledano, Ralph. "Joe Rauh's Counterattack." *National Review,* December 20, 1974.

English, Richard. "We Almost Lost Hawaii to the Reds." *Saturday Evening Post,* February 2, 1952.

Felipe, Virgilio M. "Hawaii: A Pilipino Dream." Master's thesis, University of Hawaii, 1972.

Gray, Francine Du Plessix. "The Sugar-Coated Fortress—II." *New Yorker,* March 11, 1972.

"Hawaii '75: Annual Economic Review." Honolulu: Bank of Hawaii, 1975.

"Hawaii: Sugar-Coated Fort." *Fortune,* August 1940.

"Hawaii's Sugar Islands." Honolulu: Hawaiian Sugar Planters Association, 1975.

Henderson, C. J. "Labor—An Undercurrent of Hawaiian Social History." Talk given in Honolulu to the Social Science Association on May 9, 1949.

Hodge, Clarence L. "Hawaii Facts and Figures, 1942–1945." Honolulu: Chamber of Commerce, 1946.

Holmes, Thomas Michael. "The Specter of Communism in Hawaii 1947–53." Ph.D. dissertation, University of Hawaii, 1975.

"Housing Statistics for Hawaii, 1973." Statistical Report 99, State of Hawaii, Department of Planning and Economic Development, 1974.

Ige, Thomas H. "Working Conditions and Workers' Wages." *Monthly Labor Review,* December 1955.

Iwasa, Warren. "Shaping Our Understanding." *Hawaii Observer* (Honolulu), November 19, 1974.

Izuka, Ichiro. "The Truth about Communism in Hawaii." Honolulu: 1947.

Jacobs, Paul. "Harry, the Gag Man." *New Leader,* July 6, 1964.

Jacobs, Theodore J. "Review of *The Company and the Union* by William Serrin." *New York Times Book Review,* March 18, 1973.

Kagel, Sam and John Kagel. "Using Two New Arbitration Techniques." *Monthly Labor Review,* November 1972.

Kempton, Murray. "Three Men of Labor." *Harper's,* May 1973.

Kerr, Clark and Lloyd Fisher. "Conflict on the Waterfront." *Atlantic,* September 1949.

Kurita, Yayoi. "Employers' Organization in Hawaii." *Labor Law Journal,* April 1953.

"Land Use and Ownership Trends in Hawaii." Statistical Report 98, State of Hawaii, Department of Planning and Economic Development, 1973.

Lee, David B. "Where Is Hawaii Heading?" *Honolulu Magazine,* November 1974.

Lenin, Vladimir Ilyich. "What Is to Be Done?" In *The Essential Works of Lenin,* edited by Henry M. Christian. New York: Bantam Books, 1966.

Lind, Andrew W. "Modern Hawaii." Honolulu: University of Hawaii Industrial Relations Center, 1967.

McElrath, Robert. "Hawaii's Experience: A Model of Enlightened Agri-Business Labor Relations." Talk given in Honolulu to the International Association of Government Labor Officials on July 6, 1970.

Matsumoto (Najita), Joyce A. "The 1947 Hawaiian Pineapple Strike." Honolulu: University of Hawaii Industrial Relations Center, 1958.

Morris, George. "Review of *Harry Bridges: The Rise and Fall of Radical Labor in the U.S.* by Charles P. Larrowe." *World Magazine,* March 23, 1973.

"The Mysterious Stranger." Honolulu: ILWU, 1947.

Nakasone, Henry I. "Propaganda Techniques Employed in IMUA and ILWU Radio Broadcasts." Master's thesis, University of Hawaii, 1956.

O'Brien, Thomas L. *The Plot to Sovietize Hawaii.* Honolulu: Hawaii News Printshop, 1948.

Pendleton, Edwin C. "Reversal of Roles—The Case of Paternalism in Hawaiian Labor Management Relations." Honolulu: University of Hawaii Industrial Relations Center, 1962.

Perlman, Mark. "Organized Labor in Hawaii." *Labor Law Journal,* April 1952.

Pincetich, John. "The Agency System 1948." Unpublished article written for *Wall Street Journal,* 1948.

Raskin, A. H. "Is the Picket Line Obsolete?" *Saturday Review World,* October 19, 1974.

Reinecke, John E. "Feigned Necessity." Unpublished manuscript on Hawaii's attempt to obtain Chinese contract labor (1921–1923), 1967.

_____. "A History of Local 5: Hotel and Restaurant Employees and Bartenders International Union (AFL-CIO), Honolulu, Hawaii." Honolulu: University of Hawaii Industrial Relations Center, 1970.

_____. "Labor Unions of Hawaii." Chronological checklist. Honolulu: University of Hawaii Industrial Relations Center, 1966.

_____. "Memorandum on Military Control of Hawaiian Labor." Mimeographed. Honolulu: 1944.

"Reports of the President, Treasurer, Auditor, Committee Chairmen." Honolulu: Chamber of Commerce, 1945.

Richstad, Jim Andrew. "The Press and the Courts under Martial Rule in Hawaii During World War II—From Pearl Harbor to Duncan V. Kahanomoku." Ph.D. dissertation, University of Minnesota, 1974.

Roberts, Harold S. "Labor Relations: Patterns and Outlook." *Monthly Labor Review,* December 1955.

Sheed, Wilfrid. "What Ever Happened to the Labor Movement?" *Atlantic,* July 1973.

Shoemaker, James H. "Labor in the Territory of Hawaii." Bulletin No. 687, U.S. Bureau of Labor Statistics, 1939.

Sumner, George. Talk on labor-management relations in Hawaii given to the Hilo Kiwanis Club on August 26, 1955.

Taylor, Frank J. "Labor Moves In On Hawaii." *Saturday Evening Post,* June 26, 1947.

Thompson, David E. "Agricultural Workers Made It in Hawaii." *Labor Today,* October–November 1966.

———. "ILWU Works for Better Public Schools." *Educational Perspectives* (University of Hawaii), December 1966.

Walker, Joyce Lea. "A Rhetorical Analysis of the Epideictic Speeches of Jack Hall, Regional Director of the ILWU for Hawaii." Master's thesis, University of Hawaii, 1961.

"The Water Saga of Central Maui." *Ampersand* (Honolulu), Fall 1974.

Weingarten, Victor. "Raising Cane." Honolulu: ILWU, 1946.

Wentworth, Edna Clark and Frederick Simpich, Jr. "Living Standards of Filipino Families on an Hawaiian Sugar Plantation." Honolulu: Institute of Pacific Relations, 1936.

"What the Marxists See in the Recession." *Business Week,* June 23, 1975.

CONGRESSIONAL HEARINGS

U.S. Congress, 75th, 2nd Session, Joint Committee on Hawaii. *Hearings Relative to a Study on the Subject of Statehood, Honolulu, October 6–22, 1937.*

U.S. Congress, 79th, 1st Session, Hearings Before the Joint Committee on the Investigation of the Pearl Harbor Attack, Part 28, Held at Fort Shafter, Honolulu, September 8, 1944.

U.S. Congress, 79th, 2nd Session, House Subcommittee of the Committee on the Territories. *Hearings on Statehood for Hawaii, Held in Hawaii, January 7–18, 1946.*

U.S. Congress, 80th, 2nd Session, Senate Subcommittee on Territories and Insular Possessions of the Committee on Public Lands. *Hearings in Washington on a Bill to Enable the People of Hawaii to Form a Constitution and State Government, January–April 1948.*

U.S. Congress, 81st, 1st Session, Senate Committee on Labor and Public Welfare. *Hearing Held in Washington on July 12, 1949, on the Hawaiian Labor Situation.*

U.S. Congress, 81st, 2nd Session, House Committee on Un-American Activities. *Hearings Held in Honolulu, April 10–12, 1950.*

U.S. Congress, 81st, 2nd Session, Senate Committee on Interior and Insular Affairs. *Butler Minority Report.* Washington, May 1–5, 1950.

U.S. Congress, 81st, 2nd Session. *Report on Hawaii Civil Liberties Committee.* House Report No. 2986.

U.S. Congress, 82nd, 1st Session, House Committee on Un-American Activities. *Hearings Regarding Communist Activities in the Territory of Hawaii—Part 4.* (Testimony of Jack H. Kawano in Washington July 6, 1951, pp. 1–53.)

U.S. Congress, 83rd, 1st and 2nd Sessions, Senate Interior and Insular Affairs Committee. Washington, June 29–30 and July 1–11, 1953, and January 7–8, 1954.

U.S. Congress, 84th, 2nd Session, Senate Subcommittee to Investigate the Administration of the Internal Security Act and Other Internal Security Laws of the Committee on the Judiciary. *Hearings on the Scope of Soviet Activity in the U.S., Held in Honolulu, November 16 and 30, 1956, and December 1, 1956.*

U.S. Congress, 86th, 1st Session, House Committee on Interior and Insular Affairs. *Hearings in Washington on HR 50 and HR 888, Providing for the Admission of the Territory of Hawaii into the Union as a State, January 26–28, 1959.*

LEGISLATIVE HEARING

Territorial Legislature, 23rd Session. Senate Sitting as a Committee of the Whole, March 22, 1945, on SB 72.

REPORTS

Report of E. J. Eagen on the Hawaiian Islands. From Hearings before the House Committee on Labor Board and the Wagner Act, May 3, 1940. [Cited as Eagen Report.]

Congressionai Report on Statehood for Hawaii. Submitted by the Subcommittee of the Committee on the Territories of the House of Representatives, February 22, 1946.

Report of Proceedings before (Governor Stainback's) Emergency Fact-Finding Board, June 16–17, 1949.

Report on the "Hilo Massacre," submitted to Gov. J. B. Poindexter by Attorney General J. V. Hodgson on September 9, 1938. [Cited as Hodgson Report.]

State Legislature, General Session, 1961. Select Committee Report No. 17, Re: HR 45, HD 2, concerning the investigation of alleged violations of the County of Maui and the City and County of Honolulu, Honolulu, May 8, 1961.

U.S. National Labor Relations Board 20th Region: In the Matter of Honolulu Longshoremen's Association and Castle & Cooke Inc., and Honolulu Stevedores, Ltd. Case No. XXC-55, April 1937. Trial examiner: George O. Pratt. [Cited as Pratt Report.]

NOTES

ABBREVIATIONS

Adv.	*Honolulu Advertiser*
HEC	Hawaii Employers Council
ICON	ILWU International convention
IEB	ILWU International Executive Board meeting
LCON	ILWU Local 142 convention
LEB	ILWU Local 142 Executive Board meeting
S-B	*Honolulu Star-Bulletin*
VOL	*Voice of Labor*

PROLOGUE: NO MONUMENT, NO PLAQUE

"don't want to write": Rutledge. Teddy Kreps, an ILWU research expert who was in Hawaii from 1948 to 1953, said the same. "Neither Harry [Bridges] nor Hall cared about how they went down in history," she said.

not sentimental: Yoshiko Hall.

moving eulogy: Hall's tribute to the late Rev. Emilio Yadao of the ILWU and to Gertrude Damaso, wife of Carl Damaso, Local 142 president.

ashes sat: John Hall.

Hall's early days: Goldblatt, McElrath, Reinecke, Berman, Bailey, and others. Also *Kauai Herald* and *Voice of Labor*.

biggest power broker: Gill, Esposito, Quinn.

"face lighted up": Reinecke.

"We simply believe": Hall's speech, "Labor's Role in Politics," Honolulu, June 11, 1963.

"Reward your friends": labor chieftain Samuel Gompers.

"Organized pressure": Hall's speech, "Labor's Role in Politics."

did not threaten: Kido.

promises to be kept: McElrath.

did not like independents: Gill, Esposito.

Burns scolded him: Aoki, Oshiro.

paths ran parallel: Oshiro.

skilled negotiator: Steele, Maxwell, Babbitt, Cadagan.

"IBM machine for a brain": John Hall.

confronted management: Goldblatt, McElrath.

"We have to unite": Local 142 pamphlet, "Stop-Work Tribute to Hall," January 5, 1971.

Hall's personality: Yoshiko Hall, McElrath, Ayako Kaneda Nitta, Dr. Willis Butler, Mrs. Butler, Goldblatt, Bridges, Frank Thompson, David Thompson, Reinecke, Mrs. Reinecke, Berman, Imori, Weisbarth, Frank Silva, Rachel Saiki, and others.

Hall's drinking: Yoshiko Hall, McElrath, Butler, Dr. Morton Berk, Omi Oyama, Rags Shishido, Goldblatt, Bridges, Robertson, Newton Miyagi.

Hall's two great friends: Rags Shishido.

ballooned to 260: Hall to Duarte, April 29, 1963.

"Four drinks at 300": Goldblatt.

Hall's ailments: Butler. Also Hall's death certificate (State of California, Department of Public Health, No. 3801, January 2, 1971).

kept struggling: Roger.

"quick, clean mind": Butler.

talked like a lawyer: Symonds.

learned on a grapefruit: Yoshiko Hall.

reading Communist literature: Weisbarth, Goto, Berman, Kawano, Izuka.

never wavered: Goldblatt, Bouslog.

"Left on trip": "Hall Diary," p. 1.

hard-core: Berman, Weisbarth.

never left the Party: David Thompson.

name-dropper: David Thompson. Symonds said the same.

gourmet cook: Yoshiko Hall, McElrath, Goldblatt. "Hall loved to cook, but he hated to clean up," said Mrs. Mitsue Thompson, David Thompson's wife.

loved music: Yoshiko Hall, Goldblatt, Butler.

"The Gettysburg March": Butler. Jazz expert Ferd Borsch identified the piece.

changing a light bulb: Yoshiko Hall.

trained in accounting: Nagaue.

keep a checkbook: Yoshiko Hall.

mathematical wizard: Goldblatt, Bridges.

couldn't drive: Yoshiko Hall.

more than four inches: Dr. Michihiko Hayashido, Kaiser Memorial Foundation Hospital in Honolulu.

poker player: Kawano, Steele, Goldblatt.

hated chitchat: Yoshiko Hall.

intolerant of incompetence: Goldblatt, McElrath.

not hard on his help: McElrath, David Thompson.

gambler's instinct: McElrath, Thompson.

"Thirty days in jail": Goldblatt.

"bored, bored, bored": Bouslog.

"pragmatic": David Thompson.

genuineness about him: Labez.

up until three: Yoshiko Hall.

distrusted intellectuals: Yoshiko Hall, Butler, McElrath, Reinecke, Esposito, David Thompson.

"Better an avowed enemy": McElrath.

ungainly: Butler.

appealed to women: Bouslog.

couldn't dance: Yoshiko Hall.

liked to swim: Yoshiko Hall.

Hall was shy: Hall to Reinecke, May 19, 1969. Also Butler.

felt naked: Hall to Butler, November 26, 1969.

enthralled by music: Goldblatt, Mrs. Nitta.

wrapped in thought: Butler, Mrs. Nitta.

were adversaries: Yoshiko Hall, Michele Hall Burton. Also, letters in the ILWU file: Hall to David Thompson, January 21, 1970; Hall to Priscilla Shishido, March 24, 1970; undated memorandum in envelope dated October 14, 1969, from Hall to Mrs. Shishido, Ah Quon and Robert McElrath, and David Thompson.

"blare of trumpets": Noriko Bridges, Harry Bridges' wife.

"knocked down ducks": David Thompson.

Hall complained: Bridges.

laughed at Hall: Bridges.

bigger force: Thompson.

carried on feuds: Gill; Esposito; Beechert tape, p. 19. Also Hall to Secretary of Interior Julius A. Krug, September 23, 1947.

racial antagonism: McElrath.

Hall versus Miyagi: Miyagi.

"wrote notes": Miyagi.

his best friends: Steele, Murphy, Cadagan, Babbitt.

trusted him: Cadagan, Murphy.

"turn Hawaii around": Goldblatt's eulogy to Hall, Honolulu, January 7, 1971, p. 8.

"to be respected": Goldblatt.

CHAPTER 1: THE BITTER YEARS

Hall's birth: For years Hall thought he had been born in 1914. He found out "to his delight" that it was in 1915. (Priscilla Shishido to Zalburg, memorandum, February 15, 1974.)

   The official biographies released by the FBI on the seven defendants in the Smith Act trial referred to Jack Wayne Hall "also known as Howard Wesley Hall and John Wayne Hall" (*S-B,* August 28, 1951). The FBI said Hall was born as "Howard Wesley Hall." The FBI was wrong. Howard Wesley Hall was an elder brother who died in infancy. Hall's name was Jack Hall, not John Hall. "I am glad to know that my name is still Jack Wayne Hall—at least according to the family Bible," he wrote his sister Mildred on May 22, 1952. "I was shocked to find I had an alias."

"December until April": from *Wisconsin: A Guide to the Badger State* (Hastings House, N.Y.: Writer's Project, Works Progress Administration, 1941), p. 391.

Hall's boyhood: Yoshiko Hall, Mrs. Mildred Hall McIntyre of Los Angeles, his sister; John Hall, his half-brother; Mrs. Hazel L. Hall of Los Angeles, his stepmother; and letters from his Aunt Lily: Mrs. John A. Larson of Klamath Falls, Oregon.

mother's suicide: Yoshiko Hall, Mrs. Larson, John Hall.

in flu epidemic: Yoshiko Hall.

account of suicide: Mrs. Larson to Zalburg, September 9, 1975.

story of gas fumes: ibid. Also letter from Mrs. Larson to Priscilla Shishido (February 26, 1971).

Percy: Mrs. Hazel Hall, Mrs. McIntyre, John Hall, and Mrs. Earl R. Parmeter of Ashland, Wisconsin. Also letters from Mrs. Larson to Zalburg, June 5, 1974, September 9, 1975, and January 24, 1976.

used strop: Hall to Riley Allen, September 4, 1940. Hall wrote: "Now, I don't spank very easily. In fact, even my father had somewhat of a task with me when the occasion required such procedure. But the razor strop was an advantage I was consistently unable to overcome."

"up the bottle": Bailey to Zalburg, November 4, 1975. Hall often told people he left home on account of his father. "His father racked him up. At 16 he shipped out," said Frank Silva.

labor was a racket: John Hall.

skipped four semesters: Mildred Hall McIntyre.

B minus average: A copy of Hall's scholastic record at Huntington Park High School was made available to the writer through the courtesy of Lloyd C. Reslock, supervisor, Student Records Department.

"long drink of water": Mrs. McIntyre.

from age twelve: Hazel Hall.

[footnote] "a traitor": Yoshiko Hall.

"grandmother says": Hazel Hall.

"wonderful grandmother": Hall's Commencement Day talk at Hawaii Technical School, June 7, 1967, p. 3.

"exciting Islands": ibid.

CHAPTER 2: THE GREEN BACKDROP

"carpenter's mate": from "Motion for a Separate Trial for Hall," a petition filed by Bouslog & Symonds in Federal District Court in Honolulu, November 31, 1951.

"It was daybreak": *ILWU Reporter,* April 2, 1951.

feeling of "escape": interview of Hall by Ed Sheehan, January 10, 1969. Sheehan made his notes available to the writer.

"Orient had impact": from "Random Notes on Jack Hall," prepared by Priscilla Shishido in January 1971, shortly after Hall's death.

twenty-four men bunking: Walker, "Rhetorical Analysis," p. 18.

"in time for excitement": Beechert tape, p. 1.

dodged tear gas: Walker, "Rhetorical Analysis," p. 18. Among mementos left behind by Hall is his 1934 strike clearance card (SUP No. 49), signed by Secretary George Larsen and stamped: "Loyal Record Clear."

"going after scabs": Beechert tape, p. 1. Hall met Bridges during the 1934 strike and said he helped bring Bridges to an SUP meeting. (16th ICON, Los Angeles, April 7–12, 1969, p. 420)

joined Sailors' Union: Hall's union card: No. 4106. On February 7, 1938, Hall and fellow labor organizer James Cooley were suspended for ninety-nine years by the SUP for "having organized and represented the Inland Boatmen's Union of Hawaii, a CIO affiliate and a dual union to the SUP."

liner *Mariposa:* Hall Diary, p. 1. Hall told Beechert mistakenly that the ship was the *Monterey.*

"with gear flying": Hall to Oliver Hodges, East Hamilton, Ontario, March 3, 1959.

"had good fortune": from Hall's Labor Day speech, September 5, 1955, p. 1.

Cayton had given Hall: Cayton.

deserted ship: Hall Diary, p. 1.

Weisbarth met him: Weisbarth. Weisbarth's own reception in Honolulu was not auspicious. On the day he came home (August 6, 1935), a plainclothesman met him at the dock and told him to see Chief of Police William Gabrielson, a strong antiunion man. He did. Gabrielson warned him: "Your best bet is to get back on that ship and get out of town." "In a pig's ass," Weisbarth retorted. "This is my home town. I'm going to stay here." (Weisbarth interview)

wrote and distributed: Hall Diary, p. 1.

"remember Jack Guard": ibid.

sweatshop days: February 6, 1936. (The issue erroneously printed the date as "January 6"), and *VOL,* March 25, 1937.

seamen were left-wing: Hall's Labor Day speech, September 5, 1955.

every political hue: Berman.

sailed for twelve years: from *Who's Who on the Island of Hawaii 1938* (Hilo, Hawaii: John A. Lee, 1938), p. 8.

started movement: Beechert tape, p. 2.

"sleep union": Chicken Kamoku. Hall described Harry Kamoku as "warm, friendly, generous, self-educated, devoted, selfless, fun-loving, joking, satirical." (Hall's Labor Day speech, Hilo, September 3, 1962, p. 1)

"Madman Kamoku": Rachel Saiki.

work fifteen: Paaluhi. Stevedore employers said longshore work could not be performed efficiently if it were broken up and that loading and unloading had to go on without interruption.

elected president: *Who's Who on the Island of Hawaii 1938,* p. 8. This was the first legitimate longshore union in Hawaii. "They took part in the strike of 1936 and won the right of sole bargaining agent for the port of Hilo, the first organization in the territory to receive such right." (*VOL,* November 10, 1938)

donated space: Kealoha.

[footnote] copper plate: Roman R. Cariaga, *The Filipino in Hawaii* (Honolulu: Filipino Public Relations Bureau, 1937), footnote, p. 37.

loaned typewriter: Kamoku.

Bodie's description: Weisbarth, Berman.

"typewriter going": Weisbarth. Hall gave seamen credit for starting the drive to organize the Hawaiian Islands. "To those wandering workers—to those [for] whom a ship's forecastle is home—belongs the credit for instilling the spark of organization in island labor." (*Kauai Herald,* June 16, 1941)

CHAPTER 3: THE VOICE OF MILITANT UNIONISM

had tuberculosis: Weisbarth.

raised forty dollars: *VOL,* November 4, 1935.

ten dollars a week: *VOL,* January 16, 1936.

seamen, liberals: Hall Diary, p. 1.

"has become famous": *VOL,* November 4, 1935.

"not all Don Blanding": *VOL,* April 4, 1936.

"dangerous to think": *VOL,* January 6, 1936.

odd jobs: Hall Diary, p. 1.

read Communist literature: Hall Diary, p. 1.

"get a quarter": Beechert tape, pp. 4–5.

knew the gang: Hall Diary, p. 1.

to make a living: Berman.

interest whetted: Berman. Robert O. Griffin, who ran the Police Records Division, resigned from the force in July 1935. (*S-B,* July 12, 1935)

"planted roots": Berman.

hands full: Bridges, Goldblatt.

"strategic position": Berman and Weisbarth to Bridges, June 8, 1937.

"oligarchy of sugar": Berman to Bridges, October 4, 1937.

"workers against themselves": Berman to Meehan, October 4, 1937.

"time is ripe": Berman to Meehan, October 26, 1937.

Meehan replied: Meehan to Berman, January 3, 1938.

CHAPTER 4: ON THE WATERFRONT

Hall's trips: Hall Diary, pp. 1–2. Dates are based primarily on Hall's seaman's discharge papers.

served twenty-four days: from Hall's Honolulu police record. There are three incidents: (1) a 24-day sentence for assault and battery on the Matson guard; (2) a ten-dollar fine for use of profanity on February 15, 1937—Hall called strikebreakers "You [censored] scabs!"; (3) Hall's arrest at dockside on February 4, 1938, during the Inter-Island Steam Navigation Co. strike.

watery guava: Reinecke to Zalburg, September 13, 1975.

helped prepare leaflets: Hall Diary, p. 2.

"malcontents": *S-B,* December 4, 1936.

Hall's itineraries: Hall Diary, p. 2.

information about Cooley: Weisbarth, Berman, and Cooley's widow, Mrs. Angela Cooley of Honolulu. Cooley was killed in action over New Guinea on February 7, 1943, as an aerial gunner aboard a bomber of the 321st Air Bombardment Squadron. "He could have sat out the war here, but he wanted action," said Mrs. Cooley.

1100 seamen: Beechert tape, p. 4.

"Gorotuki": Judge Shunichi Kimura recalled the word being used.

"put a roof over": Hall's Labor Day speech, Honolulu, September 1, 1952, p. 4. Hall called Alencastre "our only real friend."

fed a thousand: *S-B,* November 6, 1936; *VOL,* November 9, 1936.

quietly contributed: Beechert tape, p. 6.

Hall was chairman: Hall Diary, p. 2.

painful acquaintance: ibid.

Burns knew: Burns.

"If you did any beating": Burns.

"seamen's faction": Hall Diary, p. 2.

Only 240: Kawano to Bridges, February 4, 1938.

leaving forty: ibid.

"Who wants to be": Beechert tape, p. 4.

intimidation, bribery: from Hall's Labor Day speech, Honolulu, September 5, 1955, p.1. Also his Labor Day speech, September 1, 1952, p. 3. In the 1952 speech he said: "The employers fought us with labor spies, with goons, with guns, with the press, with everything at their command."

"We were working": 29th annual ILA Convention, San Pedro, California, May 4–19, 1936, p. 76.

"Miss your foothold": Chang to Bridges, January 21, 1937.

"If the employers": 30th annual ILA Convention, Pacific Coast District, Seattle, May 11, 1937, p. 25.

"No impartial person": Pratt Report, p. 32.

"Every morning about 6": Pratt Report, p. 9.

Eagen spent: Eagen Report, pp. 615–623.

dominated by Big Five: Eagen Report, p. 5.

"more slave than free": Eagen Report, p. 33.

"too preposterous": *S-B,* May 3, 1940.

"a distortion": AP, May 11, 1940.

"gratuitous contribution": *S-B,* June 8, 1940.

didn't notice: Hall Diary, p. 2.

Kawano's background: Kawano.

as little as five or ten dollars: from 1st ICON, Aberdeen, Washington, April 4–17, 1938, p. 181.

lived in a shack: Reinecke.

Hall slept: Reinecke.

dues collecting: Kamahoahoa.

"Morale is weakening": Kawano to Bridges, February 4, 1938.

"absolute mistake": Bridges to Kawano, May 31, 1939.

Kawano asked: Kawano to Bridges, May 19, 1939. At that time ten persons employed in an industry could apply to join the ILWU. Charter fee was $15. ILWU International per capita tax was twenty-five cents a month; district per capita tax was ten cents, both payable to San Francisco headquarters. (Meehan to Melville Holmes, of Matson and Dollar Lines clerks union, April 22, 1938)

sent five hundred dollars: Kawano to Meehan, August 9, 1940.

"We beseech you": Kamahoahoa to Bridges, September 25, 1940.

Chapter 5: Maui '37: The Last Racial Strike

Hall's itinerary: Hall Diary, p. 3.

Bailey's background: Bailey; Berman.

"do political work": Bailey.

invented a tale: Bailey.

red bunting: Bailey.

"flag of working class": from Kawano's testimony, Smith Act, p. 6300.

called a meeting: Bailey.

Hall wasn't there: Bailey to Zalburg, July 18, 1975. In the Smith Act trial there was this colloquy (p. 7701):

> *Hoddick:* With reference to this meeting in Bailey's room—was this on Queen Emma Street?
>
> *Kawano:* Yes.

given a white card: Smith Act, pp. 6301–6302.

"a big Commie": Bailey.

"revolutionary duty": Bailey to Zalburg, November 4, 1975.

Fagel's background: Berman; *VOL,* April 8, 1937; and Virgilio M. Felipe, "The Vibora Luviminda and the 1937 Puunene Plantation Strike," a historical paper for History 424, University of Hawaii, May 1, 1970.

slept on deck: Bailey.

Bailey's wardrobe: Bailey to Zalburg, July 18, 1975.

met at dockside: Bailey.

did politicizing: Bailey to Zalburg, November 4, 1975.

good crowds: *VOL,* April 22, 1937.

"meeting was held": ibid.

lunas laughed: ibid.

tried to persuade: Hall Diary, p. 3; Berman.

books ineptly kept: Hall Diary, p. 3.

"can of beans": Bailey to Zalburg, November 4, 1975.

strike broke out: annual report of Hawaiian Commercial & Sugar Co., Ltd., for year ending December 31, 1937. Report said net profit of HC & S for 1937 was $1,683,944.91, compared to $1,992,941.41 in 1936.

"sharpening cane knives": Claveria; Beechert interview.

workers' demands: Reinecke's column in *Honolulu Record,* September 7, 1950.

"tear down mill": *S-B,* May 20, 1937.

"Mules Get Hour": Bailey.

Machine-gun headline: *VOL,* May 6, 1937, p. 1.

hired a hundred deputies: *VOL,* April 29, 1937; AP, May 26, 1937.

one-third did not go out: HC & S annual report, p. 4.

dropped hoe: Felipe history paper, p. 20.

Fagel and eight others: *Territory* v. *Fagel,* et al., Case No. 1996, Criminal No. 14288, 1937.

lawyers seldom defended: Eagen to NLRB, Washington, D.C., March 19, 1937. Eagen, the NLRB director for Seattle, wrote: "Not a first class lawyer in the islands will take a labor case."

Johnson's role: Johnson to Zalburg, April 26, 1974. He enclosed pages 30 to 34 (handwritten) of his memoirs, which included the Hawaii adventure.

won slight raise: Fagel claimed a fifteen-percent raise, "but this was not substantiated." (*VOL,* July 23, 1937) Damaso said the Filipinos won a wage raise and that management agreed to recognize the union. "But it didn't last long." Damaso was blacklisted and never again worked on a plantation. "They accused me of being the instigator of the strike." (Damaso interview)

Wells advised industry: Edward D. Beechert, "Racial Divisions and Agricultural Labor Organizing in Hawaii," pp. 9–10.

wanted to avoid spectacle: ibid., p. 10.

chose to serve: *S-B,* January 14, 1938.

"Sometimes to be in jail": *VOL,* October 28, 1937.

"haven't got a lawyer": Bailey.

Chapter 6: Kauai: The Special Island

strike of April 1937: Hall Diary; 1st ICON, Aberdeen, Washington, April 4–17, 1938; Izuka, Goto, Weisbarth; Izuka research paper, "The Labor Movement in Hawaii (1934–1949)," University of Hawaii, April 11, 1974.

sent Hall and Goto: Hall Diary, p. 3. Also Beechert tape, p. 5; Goto, Weisbarth.

The repercussions of that seemingly unimportant strike were enormous, according to Hall. He said: "After the collapse of the 1937 Maui plantation strike . . . there occurred an event of much historical importance in Hawaiian labor history. The longshoremen at Port Allen, Kauai, without any outside instigation except occasional whispered conversations with seamen on the vessels anchoring there, suddenly went on strike . . . because of accumulating grievances and low pay—pay as little as 28 an hour. They called the sailor's hiring hall in Honolulu and asked for help in setting up a union. I was sent.

"A local union was set up. An American trade union began to grow. It survived many struggles. It sent organizers into the sugar and pineapple plantations to organize without regard to race, creed and color or language. It achieved the first collective bargaining agreement in the history of the pineapple and sugar industries, first at Kauai Pineapple Co. and later at the McBryde Sugar Co. It launched independent political action for workers in the islands, breaking up the stranglehold of plantation management and defeating entrenched plantation dominated politicians." (Hall to the Social Action Committee of Congregational Churches, Honolulu, June 25, 1960, p. 3)

"Here are tickets": Goto.

"go back to work": Izuka said John Waterhouse, president of Alexander & Baldwin, came to Kauai on April 23 and gave the Port Allen workers pay for overtime and that ended the first brief strike. (Izuka research paper, p. 321)

back in steerage: Hall Diary, p. 3.

August 1937 strike: report by Tsuru Ogashi, delegate from Local 1-35, Port Allen, at 1st ICON, p. 177.

"five pounds of meat": 8th LCON, Honolulu, September 27–30, 1967, p. 84.

"blow him down": Morimoto.

Shear the rabble-rouser: Izuka, Weisbarth, Arashiro, Goto.

talking to cane fields: Beechert tape, p. 6. Hall said: "We had a few unionists, soap-box unionists, who'd blast off with a few union records and talk to the cane fields and villages, but the people were frightened in those days."

"like Santa Claus": Brun.

seniority clause: 1st ICON, p. 177.

got sixteen dollars: Silva.

Watase Hotel: The hotel had five rooms upstairs, three down. It was owned originally by Masami Watase and ownership passed to his son Edward. (Mrs. Edward Watase interview) The property has since changed hands.

lot of talking: *S-B,* June 21, 1969.

"have to level": interview of Hall by Joyce Lea Walker, May 26, 1960.

"lots of meetings": Beechert tape, p. 10.

two changes: Silva.

tempting target: Threats were made against Hall, which was not unusual for a militant labor leader in those days. Hall said: "There were two occasions when they [unidentified] were out to knock me off on Kauai that have been confirmed by informed sources." (Beechert tape, p. 15)

Hall told A. E. P. Wall, *Advertiser* Sunday editor: "I was also on the receiving end of some violence on Kauai. They were after me with a gun and they almost got me once." (*Adv.,* June 20, 1965)

Shurei Hirozawa of the *Star-Bulletin* wrote: "One night during the 1940 dock strike, a thug pulled a .45 on [Hall] in a bar but a quick-thinking barmaid turned off the lights and hid him under a steam table in the kitchen." (*S-B,* June 21, 1969)

The writer could find no witnesses or documentary proof of any of these alleged incidents. Shimonishi and McElrath said that during the 1940–1941 Ahukini dock strike, a man by the name of Naito pulled a gun on Hall in a bar in Hanapepe. The waitress turned off the lights and Hall escaped through the kitchen. (McElrath and Shimonishi interviews)

A fracas did take place in a Hanapepe bar involving Hall that is partially documented. It occurred on February 5, 1941, during the Ahukini strike. A group of AFL seamen ran into three CIO men: Hall, Brun, and Shimonishi. According to Brun, one of the AFL men pointed to Hall and said: "There's the guy that's holding us up."

Brun said Hall cracked a beer bottle on the table and warned the seamen: "Anyone comes for me you won't recognize him tomorrow." Brun said the wife of a truck driver from Port Allen hit him (Brun) and Shimonishi over the head with a beer bottle. He said the barmaid switched off the lights, the owner called the police, and that ended that. (Brun interview)

The *Garden Island* carried an account of the affray. The story identified no one by name; nor did it state the name of the place in which the incident occurred. The story said that the CIO man "least loved by the AFL [Hall, apparently] barricaded himself in a corner under a table . . . out of harm's way . . . like a turtle in a shell." The story said an AFL Auxiliary (the truck driver's wife) swung a beer bottle and hit two CIO men on the head. (*Garden Island,* February 11, 1941)

"did they leave?": Silva.

fell into a hole: Brun.

"Mr. Hall's mission": *Garden Island,* November 7, 1939.

"Look at this!": Ozaki.

"idiotorials": *Kauai Herald,* March 14, 1941.

"read this": Yamada.

"borrow" a chicken: 8th LCON, p. 84.

in county jail: *Garden Island,* January 27, 1940; also Izuka. The plaintiffs were Faustino Respicio, Paul Ventura, and Maximiano Ancheta. Hall filed a counter-charge of assault and battery. A news story said: "Mr. Respicio said he asked them [Hall and his companions] to be quiet and that Mr. Hall angrily broke down their adjoining door." (*S-B,* December 13, 1939)

"Ichi's here": Izuka.

"great days": 8th LCON, p. 84.

CHAPTER 7: 1938: YEAR OF VIOLENCE

"Hilo Massacre": A massacre, of course, is a slaughter. No one was killed during the episode which took place August 1, 1938, at the Hilo docks, so the name is a misnomer.

The authority on the "Hilo Massacre" is a 53-page (single-spaced) report submitted to Governor Poindexter by Attorney General Joseph V. Hodgson on September 9. Hodgson and Edward N. Sylva, the deputy attorney general, spent August 4 to 8 in Hilo with a staff. They interviewed 242 persons, collected photographs, moving picture film, shells and pellets. The Hodgson Report laid no blame but recommended that a grand jury investigate the shootings.

The authoritative report on the Inter-Island strike of May 26–August 15 is a 50-page (single-spaced) account prepared by the Hawaii Educational Association Social-Economic Plans Committee (undated). Chairman of the committee and writer of the report was John E. Reinecke. Much of the material was gathered by Lillian Givens, Shizuyo Kawamoto, and Alice Smith.

The report said (p. 44): "From the point of view of union organization, few events could have been more opportune than the Hilo shooting. A movement draws inspiration from its martyrs."

The employers recognized the impact of the incident and its value to the cause of labor. "[In] ILWU folklore [it] came to be known as the 'Hilo Massacre.' " (Brooks, *Unionism in Hawaii,* p. 67)

major role: Hall Diary, p. 4. Berman also credited Basil Mayo, Folinga Faufata, and Ben Kahaawinui with helping to organize the IBU. (Berman interview)

alternately worked: Hall Diary, p. 4.

ship was strikebound: *S-B,* February 5,7,8, 1938.

incident at Pier 13: *VOL,* February 10, 1938.

mood was ugly: Taylor testifying at his trial. (*S-B,* March 5, 1938)

"Get out": Taylor.

clamped armlock: Norwood.

poked Taylor: Norwood.

held incommunicado: Beatrice Krauss, Reinecke.

"quite a beating": Norwood in Smith Act, p. 10154. Also Norwood interview.

failed to appear: Krauss, Reinecke.

lectured the group: Krauss, Reinecke.

showed them the statute: Krauss, Reinecke.

"committing stickups": Smith Act, p. 10136.

six witnesses: *VOL,* March 10, 1938.

acquitted Taylor: *S-B,* March 5, 1938.

On May 26: Hodgson Report, p. 8; Reinecke Report, p. 25.

closed shop: Hodgson Report, pp. 5, 8. Inter-Island seamen's wages ranged from $67.50 a month for a wiper to $110 a month for a chief cook. The IBU asked for wages ranging from $80 for a wiper to $140 for a chief cook. (Reinecke Report, p. 13)

Berman described a seaman's life: "They had a barrel of lomi salmon and a barrel of poi and they'd go into the messhall and take it out of this barrel. . . . They had very bad food, very bad conditions." (Berman interview)

A resolution adopted December 16, 1938, by longshore Local 1-37 said members working for Inter-Island made an average of $9 a week; those working for McCabe made $5 a week; and those working for Honolulu Stevedores made $15 a week.

within twenty-four hours: *VOL,* June 3, 1938.

Welch's conviction: Reinecke Report, p. 30.

"Dynamite Plot": Reinecke Report, pp. 34–35. Hall Diary, p. 5. The Reinecke Report (pp. 5–6) said Wilson was "distrusted by both AFL and CIO unionists as a knave or a fool, or both."

"raided unions": Berman, "The Truth about the AFL–CIO Fight in Hawaii," pamphlet (mimeographed), 1937, p. 24.

Mayo asked: *S-B,* July 22, 1938.

"Mahope Joe": William H. Ewing, a *Star-Bulletin* editor, said Crozier gave the name to Poindexter. (*S-B,* February 23, 1972)

events of July 22: Hodgson Report, pp. 9–11; *Hilo Tribune-Herald,* July 22–23, 1938.

meeting of board: Hodgson Report, p. 12; *Tribune-Herald,* July 28, 1938.

"assure you": Hodgson Report, p. 12.

"don't know what may happen": *Tribune-Herald,* July 28, 1938.

Inter-Island announced: Hodgson Report, p. 13.

Hasselgren asked: Hodgson Report, p. 13.

noted the effect: Hodgson Report, p. 14. Hodgson detailed the pellets used (p. 51): buckshot, soft lead, .34 inch in diameter and weighing 1 $\frac{3}{16}$ ounces. "The killing or wounding potentialities are about equivalent to nine shots from a .32 caliber revolver." Birdshot: hard lead (chilled), .11 inch in diameter and weighing 1 $\frac{3}{18}$ ounces. "At close range, say within ten yards, this cartridge would be dangerous for humans. Up to 50 yards, it would cause serious wounds in humans. . . ."

plans published: Hodgson Report, pp. 14, 16.

"Japanese Army?": Hodgson Report, p. 16.

Kamoku warned: Chicken Kamoku.

sixty-nine officers: Hodgson Report, p. 21.

details of shooting: Hodgson Report, pp. 25–48.

"push us aside": Hodgson Report, p. 27.

threw thirteen grenades: Hodgson Report, p. 28.

threw them back: Chicken Kamoku.

shouted insults: Hodgson Report, pp. 12–13.

Warren's gun: Hodgson Report, p. 6.

"You people": Hodgson Report, p. 35.

"so excited": *Tribune-Herald,* August 1, 1938.

order to fire: Hodgson Report, pp. 36–38.

twenty-two shots: Hodgson Report, p. 46.

fifty people were hit: Hodgson Report, pp. 48–50.

"spun me around": The Hodgson Report (p. 49) described Nakano's wounds: "Pellet entered through rear and passed through femural artery and vein and went out on other side in front. This caused gangrene of toes. . . . Also shot through back of left leg. Also shot through left arm shattering bone between elbow and wrist. . . ."

"shot us down": *VOL,* August 4, 1938.

"evidence not sufficient": *S-B,* September 20, 1938.

"total failure": Reinecke Report, pp. 47–48.

Kawano versus Berman: McElrath said Berman was right. "Some strikes you lose."

Hall on Kauai: Hall Diary, p. 4.

"When strike began": *VOL,* August 18, 1938. About half the longshoremen were Hawaiian. (Reinecke Report, p. 5.) Reinecke shared Hall's opinion at that time about Kawano. The Reinecke Report (p. 5) called Kawano "a young man of strong character and intelligence." The report also applauded Berman as "a man of education as well as strong native intelligence . . . an able speaker, a forceful personality, he was naturally the outstanding leader of the strike."

CHAPTER 8: A START IN POLITICS

Progressive League: Hall Diary, p. 5.

"play politics": Morimoto.

"make people aware": Brun.

mass of legislation: Hall in *VOL,* May 12, 1938.

Fernandes' victory: *VOL,* November 10 and December 1, 1938.

Rice "the kingpin": He was called "the grand old man of politics." (*S-B,* August 28, 1964) He served in the Territorial Legislature for thirty-four years.

on the beach: the old Rice home is now the site of the Kauai Surf Hotel.

in steerage: Crozier; Hall Diary, p. 5.

"You and I": Crozier.

League grew: Hall to Reinecke, November 13, 1939; Hall to Cooley, June 12, 1940.

spent time at Iolani: *Kauai Herald,* September 20, 1940.

"like mountain goats": Hall in *VOL,* May 12, 1939.

labor's only friend: ibid.

wrote campaign speeches: Fernandes.

cast in gloom: Hall Diary, p. 5.

target to take on: Izuka research paper, p. 212. Fern said: "Hall was what you'd expect him to be. Everything was wrong in Hawaii. He was anti-Establishment. It was a Commie line but also a union-leadership line." (Fern interview)

thirty or thirty-five dollars: Hall to Reinecke, June 17, 1940.

walked three and a half miles: Alexander. He said his *haole* neighbors despised him for working for Hall.

owner was Izuka: Izuka; *Kauai Herald,* July 26, 1940.

"intend to be partisan": *Kauai Herald,* July 12, 1940.

sip or two: Alexander.

not best paying guest: Alexander.

"N. K. Jui": Reinecke. He used a nom de plume because he was afraid of the repercussions against him as a public school teacher writing for a radical labor newspaper.

"all the rumors": Hall to Reinecke, June 17, 1940.

"If we Orientals": *Kauai Herald,* July 26, 1940.

"Security for thousands": *Kauai Herald,* May 5, 1941.

CHAPTER 9: YOUNG MAN WITH A MISSION

"gallon of sake": Hall to Reinecke, November 13, 1939.

"for first time": *VOL,* May 26, 1939.

"Bell let us talk": Hall said Bell gave workers the first guaranteed wage in the agricultural industry in Hawaii—twenty-five cents an hour. (Beechert tape, pp. 8–9)

called "The Kremlin": Imori.

job paid: Imori.

hand-to-mouth: Reinecke, Berman.

"loved his whiskey": Reinecke.

legendary lover: Imori.

attend Party school: Hall to James W. Cooley, secretary-treasurer, Brewery Workers' Union of the Hawaiian Islands, September 4, 1939. Also Izuka and Smith Act, pp. 1124–1125. Izuka testified that the Party school began September 19, 1939. It was held at 121 Haight St., Party headquarters in San Francisco. Hall's letter to Cooley confirmed the date. Hall and Izuka sailed August 25; Hall worked as scullion aboard ship. He returned to Hawaii October 11. (Hall Diary, p. 5)

"stood up to speak": Hall to Cooley, September 4, 1939.

pleaded with Henderson: Hall Diary, p. 6.

"too many problems": ibid.

Hall was intelligent: Reinecke.

Silva affair: Silva; *Kauai Herald,* July 26, 1940; Hall to Reinecke, May 29, 1940.

"Hitler-like": *Kauai Herald,* July 26, 1940.

"case built up": Hall to Reinecke, May 29, 1940.

applied pressure: ibid. Hall mentioned "the subtle hand of J. B. Fernandes moving out there."

Patterson and Mukai: ibid. Tongue in cheek, Hall commented that Patterson and Mukai were "exceptionally good 'friends' of Mr. Baldwin."

"long-standing injustice": Hall to Goldblatt, February 25, 1957.

CHAPTER 10: AHUKINI: THE RACES COLLABORATE

Ahukini strike: 4th ICON, Los Angeles, April 7–14, 1941, p. 208; Hawaii Employers Council Research Reports, February 1950, no. 292, "A History of Longshore Negotiations in Hawaii before 1949"; *S-B,* May 8, 12–13, 1941.

bound to succeed: Shishido, "Random Notes on Jack Hall," p. 2.

"where the principle": 8th LCON, Honolulu, September 27–30, 1967, p. 84.

Makua docked: 4th ICON, p. 209.

"first clear case": Shishido, "Random Notes," p. 2.

"decision not to handle": Hall Diary, p. 6.

met irregularly: ibid.

Communist-inspired: *Garden Island,* July 30, 1940.

"no tears shed": *Garden Island,* March 25, 1941.

rented skating rink: Izuka. Also Virginia Stevens, unpublished manuscript on Hall, 1946.

planted taro: Izuka.

assessed themselves: *S-B,* June 21, 1969.

"into company trap": Izuka research paper, p. 58.

"kill with kindness": O'Brien to Bridges, April 15, 1941.

Guerts flew: Bridges.

"We didn't win": 8th LCON, p. 84.

"we have won something": *Kauai Herald,* November 1, 1940.

"Company still dizzy": Hall to Reinecke, June 17, 1940.

hired Hall and Ozaki: Ozaki, Fernandes.

fell into routine: Reinecke.

go to India: Thompson.

Yoshiko Ogawa episode: Yoshiko Hall; the Reineckes; David Thompson; Hall Diary, p. 7.

brought girl home: Thompson, Yoshiko Hall.

wearing a kimono: Yoshiko Hall.

"fell in love": Aiko Reinecke.

"always treasure": Hall to the Reineckes, May 19, 1969.

"for people who think": *Herald,* July 4, 1941.

"axes to grind": ibid.

"medal for Loujo": *Herald,* July 18, 1941. The name "Loujo" is a contraction of Louise and Johansen. Hollingsworth was prominent on the scene as a *Star-Bulletin* court reporter from 1924 to 1962. A salty, outspoken woman, she loved babies, cats, the radical labor movement, and struggling young lawyers, probably in that order of priority.

"imperialistic squabble": Hall in *Herald,* September 12, 1941.

condemned strikes: *Herald,* November 10, 1941.

"Employers . . . are discovering": ibid.

"pilau haole": Ozaki.

"We have not grasped": *Herald,* November 10, 1941.

spoke at Aala Park: *Herald,* November 24, 1941.

to involve Cariaga: McElrath; Hall Diary, p. 8.

"Evil days": *Herald,* November 24, 1941.

CHAPTER II: A BRIGHT SUNDAY MORNING

early one Sunday: McElrath.

Kimoto's background: Kimoto.

voyage of *Lihue:* McElrath.

[footnote] doubted that Hall: O'Brien to Bridges, September 20, 1941.

youthful rashness: Frank Thompson to Goldblatt, September 10, 1944. Thompson said McElrath was "somewhat irresponsible."

Both had dates: McElrath.

"bales of cotton": McElrath.

string barbed wire: McElrath.

Hall went to work: Hall Diary, p. 8. He was exempt from military service because of his eyesight.

hated painting: Yoshiko Hall. In her unpublished manuscript on Hall, Virginia Stevens wrote: " 'Suji *[sic]* down and paint 'er tomorrorrroooo.' Hall will never forget the painter deckhand's cry. Working at this job, hating it. . . ."

fired after argument: Hall Diary, p. 8.

asked to arrest Hall: Hall's speech at Annual Territorial Joint Conference of Hawaii ILWU Locals 136, 142, 150, and 155 in Honolulu, February 2, 1952, p. 3.

"that voluminous file": ibid.

Bicknell interceded: from a "Motion for a Separate Trial for Hall," p. 1.

McComas liked Hall: Hall Diary, p. 6.

Shivers cleared Hall: Hall's speech at the Joint Conference of ILWU Locals, p. 3.

libation was meager: Reinecke.

moved to South Vineyard: Hall Diary, p. 8.

bag of laundry: Reinecke.

"like a detective": McElrath.

"never kidded myself": *Herald,* March 9, 1942.

"No-Good Haole": *Herald,* March 9, 16, 23, and 30, 1942. McElrath said
    Bishop was "Oscar."
wear a jacket: Nagaue.
"inspectors and missionaries": Nagaue.
"It's Jack's job": *Victory,* April 22, 1942.
loaned Hall books: Nagaue. One was *Principles of Accounting* by H. A. Finney
    and Herbert E. Miller; another was *Cost Accounting* by W. B. Lawrence.
in charge of division: Hall in his column, "Looking Things Over," Hawaiian
    edition of *The Dispatcher,* August 1, 1944.
traveled all over: Nagaue.
learned how inept: Yoshiko Hall.
"technique of ducking it": Goldblatt.
He was jubilant: Nagaue.

CHAPTER 12: THE MILITARY BLOCKADE

Military Blockade: The authoritative study on military rule in Hawaii during
    World War II is *Hawaii under Army Rule* by J. Garner Anthony. Anthony
    served as territorial attorney general from October 1942 to December 1943. He
    said (p. 203): "Thousands of persons were convicted in provost courts, some
    with trials and some without, and sentences were imposed without regard for
    the limitations of law in the offenses involved and for offenses unrelated to
    military security."
    Another helpful publication which deals with the heavy hand of the military
    during the war is the Ph.D. dissertation submitted by Jim Andrew Richstad to
    the Graduate School of the University of Minnesota in June 1967: "The Press
    under Martial Law."
General Order No. 38: It said: "1. All wage rates to be frozen as of December 7,
    1941, for all employees on the Island of Oahu, so long as they remain in the
    same classification." The order was signed by Lieutenant Colonel Thomas H.
    Green, executive of the Judge Advocate General's Department. Unless they
    could obtain permission from their employers, plantation workers could not
    travel from island to island. Hence they were bound to their job.
fine of $200: punishment is described in General Order No. 91 (March 31, 1942)
    under Section (C), Paragraph (2). Provost courts did a big business. In 1942
    one Honolulu provost court handled the cases of 22,480 people. The disposi-
    tion: 22,121 were found guilty and fined a total of $532,539.50; 943 were sent
    to county jail and 710 to Oahu Prison. (*Hawaii under Army Rule,* p. 52)
"Obey, or be punished": Federal Judge J. Frank McLaughlin in *Kam Koon
    Wan* v. *E. E. Black,* 75 F. Supp. 553, p. 561 (1948).
unfair share: James H. Shoemaker, "The Economy of Hawaii in 1947," U.S.
    Department of Labor Bulletin 926, p. 26.
"carpetbagger": Alexander MacDonald, *Revolt in Paradise,* p. 83.
[footnote] approached 10,000: Gwenfread Allen, *Hawaii's War Years,* p. 377.
    The Hotel and Restaurant Employees and Bartenders International was a
    good example of how union membership shrank during the war. In 1939 the
    union had 40 members. By the end of 1941 it had 640. In November 1943 it
    had 64. (John E. Reinecke, "A History of Local 5," p. 12)
"Man on Horse": McElrath.
"virtually abdicated": Anthony to Stainback, memorandum, December 1, 1942.
"emancipation of Hawaii": *Hawaii under Army Rule,* p. 27. Also Richstad
    thesis, p. 98.
"fat of land": *Hawaii under Army Rule,* p. 108.

quart of liquor: A bottle a week did not suffice Hall. "That would just whet his appetite," said Reinecke.

"butter, Kleenex": *Hawaii under Army Rule,* p. 108.

"straighten out": Anthony.

support from Farrington: Anthony.

"supine acquiescence": *Hawaii under Army Rule,* p. 45. The ILWU pledged it would not strike during the war and it didn't. "Strikes are treason in this war," said Bridges. (6th ICON, San Francisco, March 29–April 2, 1945, p. 66)

few lawyers: Anthony.

"that sort of hooey": Dillingham at hearing before Joint Committee on Investigation of the Pearl Harbor Attack, 79th Congress, 1946, pt. 28, p. 1444.

"subject to criticism": Sevier to Kawano, August 19, 1942.

council was "a joke": O'Brien to Bridges, January 28, 1942.

"rudely shattered": ibid.

"borrowed" workers: ibid.

"keep locals together": ibid.

"No leadership": Kawano to O'Brien, September 30, 1942.

"troublemaker": Izuka research paper, p. 67.

"Lock 'em up": ibid.

distributed leaflets: ibid., p. 68. During the war there were only three strikes in Hawaii. The work loss was about a thousand man-days of work, according to W. H. Loper, chairman of the Hawaii Employment Relations Board. (Hearings before the Subcommittee on the Territories, House of Representatives, 79th Congress, 2nd Session, Honolulu, January 7–10, 1946, p. 128)

Following Party orders: Izuka research paper, p. 68.

custody of Hall: Hall to Annual Territorial Joint Conference of Hawaii ILWU Locals, pp. 3–4.

He was in touch: Hall Diary, p. 8.

finishing touches: ibid.

[footnote] "We are pledged": 5th ICON, San Francisco, June 4–10, 1943, p. 7.

plan to Mead: Kawano to Mead, undated.

response of stevedoring companies: *Revolt in Paradise,* p. 142.

"Memorandum on Military Control": Hall, Rutledge, and Arnold L. Wills, director of the NLRB's Honolulu office, supplied the information.

Rutledge was named: "A History of Local 5," p. 14.

"bayonet up your ass": ibid., p. 13. Instead of the word "ass," the text is censored with three asterisks. There was no mistaking the part of Rutledge's anatomy that was threatened, however.

CHAPTER 13: TWO WHO PERSISTED

"There isn't any: "A History of Local 5," p. 14.

McElrath shipped out: McElrath's testimony at Iolani Palace, April 17, 1950, before HUAC, 81st Congress, 2nd Session, Report No. 2887, p. 3.

organized drydock: McElrath before HUAC; McElrath interview.

son of Italian: Arena.

McElrath was deferred: McElrath.

"a stabilizing effect": McElrath.

"looked for bulls": McElrath.

assigned radio job: McElrath. He once said: "I sold more radios in this town [than anyone] because of those broadcasts."

"Make Rat": Kimoto.

Bridges didn't speak: McElrath.

Wills portrait: Gill, Yoshiko Hall, Steele, Rutledge, Berman, Kawano, Izuka, Arakaki, McElrath.

Norman Thomas socialist: Gill.

"like scared rabbits": Wills over radio KHBC, Hilo, January 30, 1939.

"keep records": Gill.

"Those fancy lawyers": Gill.

"Lord of Creation": Wills to Honolulu Rotary Club, September 12, 1950.

"boss is a bastard": ibid.; Robertson.

[footnote] "bum advice": Thompson to Goldblatt, April 1, 1946.

"thoroughly negative": Will's Rotary Club speech.

visited Hall: Yoshiko Hall.

[footnote] wanted to hire: Izuka, McElrath. "spit my salary": Izuka research paper, p. 113.

"give you credit": Izuka.

"You'll never make a good Communist": *S-B* editorial, "He Changed Hawaii," January 4, 1971.

disillusioned: Reinecke.

using workers as a base: Gill.

"secret, conspirational": open letter (undated) from Wills "to each and every non Communist member of the ILWU" on the subject "The Mysterious Stranger Unmasked."

CHAPTER 14: RUTLEDGE THE IRREPRESSIBLE

along with Babe Ruth: Rutledge.

[footnote] Rutledge background: "Report of the Immigration Examiner," a petition filed in U.S. Federal District Court in Honolulu on June 19, 1953, and signed by James J. Kelleher, naturalization examiner.

bench warrant: "Report of the Immigration Examiner."

"going to write it up": Rutledge.

hearing of March 21, 1935: "Report of the Immigration Examiner."

"nothing to it": Rutledge. He said he assumed that his father had been naturalized and so he was the son of a citizen. As for the prohibition charge, Rutledge said: "I was in the liquor business sooner than the law allowed."

arrested twenty-three times: "Report of the Immigration Examiner."

"gesticulating": Rutledge.

"general without an army": Rutledge.

"a perfect setup!": Rutledge.

"Mr. Irresponsible": Hall to Goldblatt, October 23, 1958.

"cannibal union": Rutledge letter (undated) to Policy Committee of Western Conference of Teamsters.

"get in bed with you": Rutledge's feelings about Hall were expressed in a letter to Dave Beck, Teamster International vice-president, on March 19, 1946. He said: "The other night I had a long talk with Jack Hall, who is a member of the Police Commission and Regional Director of the ILWU. I have known him since 1938 and have gone through some tough times with him, having been broke together etc. He pointed out that their program is to take over, in true commy fashion, anyone who gets in the way, including myself. . . ."

"Hatfields and McCoys": Al Goodfader in *Adv.,* June 22, 1961.

supported the *Herald:* Rutledge; Hall Diary, p. 8. Speaking of 1941, Hall said: "[I] was very close to Rutledge at this time." (Hall Diary, p. 7)

members asked Rutledge to take over: Rutledge; "A History of Local 5," p. 7.

ninth-grade education: Rutledge.

"Edward G. Robinson": Dale Richeson in *S-B,* May 22, 1960.

hotel organizing: "A History of Local 5," p. 9.

turn to typewriter: Rutledge. The ILWU said in a pamphlet (mimeographed), sent to all members of Rutledge's Unity House unions on December 16, 1954, that Rutledge "was always welcome to help and advice from ILWU and he took full advantage of ILWU friendship.

> "For example, after he pulled the HRT and the hotel strikes in 1951, he came running to the ILWU for lessons in strike strategy. As everyone, including employers, knows, ILWU gave all-out support to HRT and hotel workers to win their strikes. . . ."

"mild revolution": *S-B,* August 31, 1943.

Rutledge wept: *S-B,* August 1, 1947.

"double-talk artist": Frank Thompson to Goldblatt, July 22, 1946.

"During sane moments": ibid.

"with such shenanigans": ibid.

We, the Women episode: Rutledge; *S-B,* July 23, 1946.

"wants to paralyze": *S-B,* July 25, 1946.

CHAPTER 15: KAWANO SENDS A PLEA

organized Waiakea: Hall Diary, p. 8; Kawano, Nakano, Rutledge. Also letters of Kawano and Nakano to Bridges and Goldblatt.

"plantations are ripe": Nakano to Goldblatt, November 30, 1943.

Start with mills: Kawano to Goldblatt, February 25, 1944. Also memorandum from Kawano to Bridges and Goldblatt dated "Feb.-March, 1944." Kawano said: "These plantations are the backbone of political reaction in the territory. Therefore, the men in the plantations must be organized sooner or later and it might as well be now." (Kawano to Bridges, January 28, 1944)

help of camp police: ibid. Also Kawano to Bridges, January (no day) 1944, and Kawano to Bridges, January 28, 1944.

dogfight coming: Kawano to Bridges, January (no day) 1944.

rented a hall: ibid.

33 ⅓ cents: "Feb.-March, 1944" memorandum.

meant Rutledge: Kawano to Bridges, January (no day) 1944.

"an opportunist": "Feb.-March, 1944" memorandum.

Kawano, Rutledge, and Hall got together: Hall Diary, p. 8; Kawano and Rutledge interviews.

everything "on wheels": ibid.; also Kawano to Bridges, in letter dated "March-April, 1944."

talked to Kimoto: Kawano.

"Come on down": Kawano.

"Bridges didn't want them": Rutledge. Rutledge said: "But the [Communist] Party did. Those people who were in the Party got together because they wanted the basic industry for political control and the word was sent over here that they got *[sic]* to do something. The Party line took precedence over the economic questions because that was the thing that caused them to start organizing over here."

thousand dollars apiece: Nakano. "Rutledge reneged," said Nakano.

wrote press release: Hall Diary, p. 8.

"situation demands": *S-B,* December 14, 1943.

fired him: *S-B,* December 13, 1943. Also Rutledge, Kawano.

"What do I do now?": Kawano to Bridges, "March-April, 1944."

Hall helped Rutledge: Hall Diary, p. 8.

losing per capita: Kawano to Bridges, "March–April, 1944."

let matter slide: *S-B,* March 10, 1944.

"with aid of Rutledge": Kawano to Bridges, January 28, 1944.

Gutsch report: Gutsch to Bridges, February 11, 1944.

"hasn't the head": ibid.

"more than ever convinced": Goldblatt to Kawano, December 8, 1943.

sent applications: Goldblatt to Nakano, December 8, 1943.

"let us handle": ibid.

taken graduate work: Goldblatt.

"If Lou came over": Kawano to Bridges, January (no day) 1944.

"want a good organizer": ibid.

He looked around: IEB, Chicago, February 11, 1944, p. 17.

CHAPTER 16: THE "MISSIONARIES" COME TO HAWAII

sparkplugged the buildup: Goldblatt to Kawano and Kamahoahoa, April 12, 1945.

Kawano walked over: Osakoda.

money from treasury: Kawano to Goldblatt, April 20, 1944. Also Beechert, p. 11.

pull men off: Kawano.

eight selected: Nakano.

ten dollars a day: Meehan to Goldblatt and Robertson, April 21, 1944. Also Tanaka. Fukuda thought they got six dollars a day plus transportation, room, and board.

Kawano named Fukuda: Kawano. He said that Communist Party members objected to Fukuda's appointment as head of the longshore organizing team because Fukuda was not a member of the Party. Kawano said he chose Fukuda because "to me, Fukuda was the most trustworthy."

 Kimoto, the Party head at the time, said he doubted that anyone raised objection to Fukuda. He said he didn't even know any of the longshoremen so how could he know their politics? (Kimoto interview)

On departure: Kawano to Goldblatt, April 20, 1944.

sleeping off a drunk: Kamahoahoa.

shot craps: Osakoda.

registered at Okino: Tanaka.

"You ain't kidding": Osakoda.

"missionaries": longshore organizers told people they were just doing "a little missionary work." (Ben Adams, *Hawaii: The Aloha State,* p. 81)

in town four hours: Osakoda quoting Nakano.

uneven match: Osakoda.

Hall came down: Tanaka.

borrowed Doc's truck: Kealalio.

all went well: Kealalio, Osakoda, Fukuda, Tanaka, Elias.

Osakoda slipped in: Fukuda.

wearing leggings: Osakoda.

"Scotch Coast": a common term for the Hamakua Coast where Scotsmen reigned on plantations for years. At one time five of the Big Island plantation managers were of Scottish descent: Alexander Fraser, Hilo Sugar Co.; James Fearn Ramsay, Honomu; James Munro Ross, Hakalau; Andrew Thomson Spalding, Pepeekeo; and Robert Allen Hutchinson, Laupahoehoe.

flashed billfold: Arakaki.

"We corrected that": Beechert tape, p. 11.

"ripe for organization": Kawano to Goldblatt, February 25, 1944.

sent them off: Kawano to General Richardson, March 23, 1944.

"Sooner or later": Osakoda.

drive up in a taxi: Fukuda.

plan with Takahashi: Osakoda, Takahashi.

Hagon episode: Fukuda, Osakoda, Kawano.

"want to be locked up?": Fukuda.

wrote Richardson: Kamahoahoa to Richardson, March 23, 1944.

Hall wrote statement: Hall Diary, p. 8.

"unidentified strangers": Richardson to Kamahoahoa, March 31, 1944.

"their true identity": ibid.

"Send 3000": Kawano to Goldblatt, February 11, 1944.

"Rush applications": Kamahoahoa to Goldblatt, March 28, 1944.

"To date Local 137": ibid.

"spent over $5000": ibid. Kawano told Meehan that the longshore local spent
    $7000. (Meehan to Hall, March 2, 1952) Hall put the figure at about $5000.
    (Beechert tape, p. 11)

CHAPTER 17: THE "MISSIONARY" WORK GOES ON

One Sunday: Okada.

picking up cane: *Adv.,* November 5, 1972.

"gonna organize": Okada.

"who no scare": Okada. "Castner was a real fighter," said Okada. Ogawa died
    September 7, 1964.

"I hear you folks": Okada.

Kapu signs: Fukuda.

a friendly man: Okada, Kawano.

protected the Japanese: Okada.

sixteen hours a day: Midkiff.

only one thing: Kawano.

[footnote] ten cents more: Midkiff, Warashina.

"You know, boys": Okada.

lights were out: Okada. Also *Adv.,* November 5, 1972.

"hustle the other leaders": Okada.

"Go ahead and organize": Okada.

"smashed by military": Hall to Goldblatt and Robertson, October 23, 1944.

"practically demolished": Frank Thompson to Goldblatt, July 21, 1944. Also
    Izuka research paper, p. 64.

Hall blamed Fitzgerald: Hall to Lincoln Fairley, director of ILWU research de-
    partment, March 23, 1948.

tie-up of military: ibid. Goldblatt said the ILWU in Hawaii was in a state of
    "suspended animation" during the war.

threatened elderly Japanese: Hall to Fairley, March 23, 1948.

"did it single-handed": Elias also helped organize Waipahu, Aiea, Ewa, and
    Waimanalo plantations. He left Hawaii in 1951. "That was the time the labor
    movement was getting respectability and making deals under the table," he
    said. "There were leaders laying around and not giving service to the member-
    ship. Jack [Hall] was already lining up his Little Caesars. I couldn't stand
    that." (Elias interview)

signed up 284: Frank Thompson to Goldblatt, November 28, 1944.

"something has to be done": Nakamoto. His nickname, "Dyna," short for "Dynamite," was bestowed upon him because of his energetic personality.

kept a garden: Nakamoto.

getting nineteen cents: Beechert tape, p. 11.

CHAPTER 18: MEEHAN PICKS HALL

description of Meehan: Reinecke.

gave him $2250: Meehan to Goldblatt, April 21, 1944.

arrived March 17: Meehan to Hall, March 2, 1952.

"here in the interests": *S-B,* March 25, 1944.

episode with colonel: Meehan to Goldblatt, March 19, 1944.

"When the Big Five learns": Meehan. The exclamation mark is Meehan's.

$4.50 a day: Meehan to Goldblatt, April 29, 1944.

"leave a buck tip": ibid.

"any white man": Meehan to Goldblatt, March 19, 1944.

stayed with Reineckes: Reinecke.

"a concentration camp": Meehan to Goldblatt, April 4, 1944.

six hundred paid dues: Meehan to Goldblatt, April 21, 1944.

"I find him capable": ibid.

"seldom in his office": Meehan to Hall, March 2, 1952.

sat voiceless: ibid.

looked down: Kawano.

"along for the ride": Meehan to Hall, March 2, 1952.

"I found Kawano lazy": ibid. A question naturally arises: Why did Meehan alter his opinion about Kawano so drastically? Meehan told Hall he had a negative feeling about Kawano all along. Why didn't he say so? His reply: "Because [Kawano] stood in high regard with the workers and I did not believe it would be in the best interest of the union to make such a report because of the dissension it might cause." (Meehan to Hall, March 2, 1952)

"like a Buddha": Rutledge.

"confidence of people": Meehan to Goldblatt, April 21, 1944.

set up a $1500 budget: minutes of the meeting of the joint Executive Board, trustees, and officers of ILWU Local 1-37, Honolulu, May 12, 1944.

"someone who will stay": ibid.

Meehan-Kawano exchange: ibid.

make Reinecke statistician: ibid.

never informed: Reinecke.

"could be induced": Meehan to Goldblatt, April 21, 1944.

"minimum of persuasion": Hall to Goldblatt, June 15, 1944.

salary of seventy-five dollars: Goldblatt to Seth Levine, CIO Maritime Committee, Washington, D.C., August 7, 1945.

CHAPTER 19: HALL TAKES OVER

seventeen-page letter: Hall to Goldblatt, June 15, 1944.

"our job to educate": ibid.

"couple of dollars": ibid.

most effective control: ibid. Hall said: "We were able to elect Hawaii's first independent legislature." (Hall to Goldblatt, November 27, 1944, and Hall to Goldblatt and Robertson, October 23, 1944)

"far to the left": Hall to Goldblatt, June 15, 1944.

failed by twenty-two votes: ibid.

"waste time": Hall to Goldblatt, June 15, 1944.

not get bogged down: Goldblatt to Hall, July 8, 1944.

"not interested in knockdown": ibid.

Winn's description: Carlsmith. Also *S-B* editorial, December 27, 1946.

Blaisdell's description: Bridges, Goldblatt, Carlsmith, Steele, E. C. Rinehart. Rinehart said: "He had the ability to charm a group of men out of their skin."

heavy artillery: Beechert interview.

Carlsmith's background: Carlsmith; anonymous sources.

"way to do business": Steele. Mediators also had to be good drinkers. That applied to William F. Quinn, when, as governor, he took part in mediation sessions. "It's a damn good thing I had a healthy capacity at that time in the Moana Hotel when I sat there and matched, drink for drink, and I was thinking that if I'm going to keep my trustworthiness and my rapport and their confidence in me, I can't say, 'No, I'm not going to have a drink with you.' And so I sat there and had them." (Quinn interview)

did not hit it off: Hall to Goldblatt, October 3, 1944.

"hair-down" talk: Hall to Goldblatt, December 14, 1944.

"let's get together": ibid.

"playing second fiddle": ibid. In a letter to Zalburg, dated August 30, 1977, Steele derided the thought. "It's hard for me to believe that," he said.

[footnote] "don't believe that": Hall to Goldblatt, December 14, 1944.

"no need to pay him": ibid.

control over policymaking: Goldblatt to Frank Thompson, November 14, 1944.

"island interests": ibid.

"absolutely adamant": ibid.

"every bit of pressure": ibid.

"any genuine friendliness": Hall in *Hawaiian Dispatcher,* December 5, 1944.

"in for a fight": ibid.

CHAPTER 20: THOMPSON THE ORGANIZER

came to town July 8: Thompson to Goldblatt, July 14, 1944.

first of many: Yoshiko Hall.

talked to 250: Thompson to Goldblatt, July 14, 1944.

put in a notebook: Labez.

in yellow legal tablet: McElrath.

"have allready elected": Thompson to Goldblatt, July 18, 1944.

"worked so hard": ibid.

"at opportune time": Hall to Goldblatt, July 15, 1944.

didn't take a bath: Yoshiko Hall.

five feet eleven: Thompson.

"no relation": *Hawaiian Dispatcher,* July 3, 1944.

ruthless: "Hearings before the Joint Committee on Hawaii," 75th Congress, 2nd Session; Senate Con. Res. 18, relative to statehood, October 6–22, 1937, pp. 95–103.

Also Eagen Report, p. 7. Eagen testified that in 1935 Thompson ordered Garnett Burum, manager of the Seamen's Institute of Honolulu, to arrange to "dump" (beat up) Weisbarth. Carlsmith said: "They caught him [Matson's Thompson] red-handed . . . in that stevedoring thing in Honolulu." (Carl smith interview)

maternal grandfather: Thompson.

"Fancy Dans": Thompson.

"lot of ground": Thompson to Goldblatt, July 18, 1944.

"puts in a day's work": Thompson to Goldblatt, September 2, 1944.

"all over hell": Thompson to Goldblatt, July 18, 1944.

ILWU members on waterfront: Thompson to Goldblatt, September 2, 1944.

"Kawano is a hard worker": Thompson to Goldblatt, December 7, 1944.

Owens episode: Thompson to Goldblatt, August 8, 1944.

Maui labor picture: Thompson to Goldblatt, August 19, 1944.

"rulers" of the island: *VOL,* May 6, 1937.

called on Baldwins: Thompson to Goldblatt, August 19, 1944.

signed up nonagricultural: Thompson to Goldblatt, September 2, 1944.

"PAC campaign": ibid.

bawled McElrath out: Thompson to Goldblatt, September 10, 1944.

"would scare anybody": ibid.

Walsh affair: Thompson to Goldblatt, September 10, 1944.

[footnote] "a lot cheaper": McElrath.

"find some way": Thompson to Goldblatt, September 10, 1944.

confrontation with Walsh: Thompson to Goldblatt, February 20, 1945.

"Hanapepe": Thompson to Goldblatt, August 23, 1944.

phoned Bridges: Thompson to Goldblatt, November 13, 1944. The call was on November 9.

"Winn has been boasting": ibid.

two keys: Goldblatt to Thompson, November 24, 1944.

"Hall gets pretty worried": Thompson to Goldblatt, November 13, 1944.

played hooky: Thompson to Goldblatt, September 3, 1944.

"Plenty of steaks": ibid.

"A tropical paradize": Thompson to Goldblatt, July 18, 1944.

CHAPTER 21: THE ILWU GATHERS STRENGTH

"make a real dent": Hall to Goldblatt, August 22, 1944.

"not a political party": ILWU handbills (undated).

"politicians are scared": Hall to Goldblatt, August 22, 1944.

registered their people: Hall to Shigeo Takemoto, president, Local 144, Unit 3 (Wailuku Sugar Co.), August 10, 1944.

"Mobilize every member": Hall to Frank Takahashi, president, Local 144, Unit 2 (Puunene), August 10, 1944.

"Labor isn't sitting": ibid.; also Hall in *Hawaiian Dispatcher,* September 24, 1944.

"rigorous" bill: Hall's testimony before Territorial Senate sitting as a Committee of the Whole, March 22, 1945, p. 23.

under Smith-Connally: Hall to Kaholokula, July 27, 1944.

goal of $10,000: ibid.

going to fire him: Kaholokula to Hall, July 26, 1944.

"Hogwash": Hall to Kaholokula, undated.

"Take no steps": Hall to Kaholokula, August 10, 1944.

"rolled up majority": Hall in *Hawaiian Dispatcher,* October 17, 1944.

"hold our vote together": ibid. Hall cited the results in Keaukaha and Waiakea Homesteads in Hilo. In the race for county chairman, Democrat Clem A. Akina, backed by the ILWU, defeated Republican Samuel M. Spencer, an incumbent for twenty-two years.

outlined the strategy: Hall to Kaholokula, October 10, 1944.

Hall exulted: Hall to Goldblatt, November 27, 1944. Also Hall to Fernandes, November 11, 1944. "It looks as if we have elected an independent House to go with a progressive Senate," said Hall. "Now comes the job of preventing someone from buying the results."

fifteen of nineteen: Hall to Goldblatt, November 27, 1944.

"tin pants are uniform": ibid.

"hard work begins": Hall to Ignacio, November 11, 1944.

"promises cheaper": Hall to Henriques, November 11, 1944.

owned his election: Hall to Goldblatt, March 6, 1945. Hall said Henriques "has repeatedly pledged his support."

come before February 15: Hall to Henriques, February 8, 1945.

arrive on fifteenth: Henriques to Hall, February 10, 1945.

"looking to you": ibid.

"demonstrating to enemies": Hall to Arakaki, November 13, 1944.

"most important committees": Hall to Ignacio, November 11, 1944.

"Our political strength": ibid.

"VICTORY!": *Hawaiian Dispatcher,* January 23, 1945.

"job to consolidate": ibid.

"A wonderful job": Hall to Goldblatt, January 19, 1945.

"puts all workers": ibid.

not a sugar year: Goldblatt to Hall, June 27, 1945.

nice to get cash: ibid.

some "elbow-bending": Hall to Goldblatt, January 19, 1945.

"provided security": Brooks, *Unionism in Hawaii,* p. 24.

checkoff a good thing: ILWU Longshoremen's Bulletin 25, October 11, 1945, which said: "The union must have a dues-collecting system that is consistent and businesslike; otherwise, the elected officers spend all their time collecting dues and neglect to accomplish the other necessary work that must be done. . . ."

$125 a year: Hall to Goldblatt, August 7, 1945.

seven cents an hour: Brooks, *Unionism in Hawaii,* p. 105.

"best deal we could obtain": Hall to Goldblatt, August 7, 1945.

[footnote] by flashlight: Shishido, "Random Notes on Jack Hall," p. 5.

"fight for more": Hall to Goldblatt, August 7, 1945.

"most disturbing feature": Goldblatt to Hall, August 20, 1944.

"importance of racial unity": minutes of conference on problems in Hawaii, held in October 1945 in San Francisco, pp. 10–11.

getting tired: Frank Thompson to Goldblatt, September 17, 1945. Thompson said: "Jack Hall is a very tired guy and needs to be taken away from these islands for about two months. His worst fault is that he has taken too much upon himself and at present is weary."

"real weaknesses": Goldblatt to Thompson, August 18, 1945.

"dig up the booze": ibid. Goldblatt also warned the *haoles* in union leadership not to speak pidgin English, which they were not expert at. "Generally, it is taken as though we were poking fun at them," he said.

"one-phrase answers": Thompson to Goldblatt, September 17, 1945.

"talked to me plenty": ibid.

CHAPTER 22: THOMPSON VS. ARAKAKI

report on membership: Thompson to Goldblatt, March 5, 1945. Wills said: "When controls were lifted, workers flocked into the unions by the tens of thousands." (Wills, "The National Labor Relations Act," a statement submitted to the Judiciary Committee of the Territorial Legislature on April 23, 1943, p. 2)

unhealthy pattern: Goldblatt.

building up treasuries: Thompson to Nakano and Ignacio, September 24, 1945.

"instead of strike fund": ibid.

wouldn't go along: Thompson to Goldblatt, September 24, 1945. Goldblatt said it wasn't just consolidation that "got under Arakaki's skin." In some cases units organized by the ILWU wanted to "move right now . . . strike right now." Goldblatt said the leadership was not going to do it. He told the members:

" 'You either follow the directions of the union or find yourself another union.' It was just that cold because we knew that once you tackle the employers, unless you have that kind of strength behind you, top to bottom, field to mill, you couldn't win. That sooner or later the split would take place, either industrially, island by island, or race by race. All these things had to be coopered up and patched up to make sure it didn't happen." (Goldblatt interview)

[footnote] "to prevent splitting tactics": Beechert, "Racial Divisions," pp. 30–31.

didn't like Hall's handling: Thompson to Goldblatt, October 1, 1945.

found out about meeting: ibid.

both him and Hall "removed": ibid.

meeting had taken place: Leoncio Velasco and Yukinori Fujioka to Bridges, January 18, 1946.

"oust any *haoles*": ibid.

"laid down the law": Thompson to Goldblatt, October 1, 1945.

"hot-headed boys": Goldblatt to Thompson, October 11, 1945.

Goldblatt came over: Thompson to Goldblatt, January 7, 1946.

"acts very nervous": Thompson to Goldblatt, December 28, 1945.

incident at Japanese school: ibid. It took place December 18, 1945.

"dictatorial, fascistic": Fujisaki to Robertson, December 20, 1945.

"shoved everything down": ibid.

"qualifications secondary": ibid. Hall said: "We, of course, enforced multi-racial leadership, irrespective of abilities, which bothered some people because they thought it wasn't democratic—guys like Yasu Arakaki. . . . But you can't survive without multi-racial leadership." (Beechert tape, p. 13)

"might as well come home": Thompson to Goldblatt, January 16 and January 18, 1946.

"addle brains": Thompson to Bridges, January 18, 1946.

was jeopardizing future: Velasco and Fujioka to Bridges, January 18, 1946.

"Hitlerite dictator": ibid.

Arakaki sent telegram: It is not in the ILWU file. Arakaki said he had no recollection of it, but probably did send it. Bridges' telegram makes it clear he did.

overplayed his hand: Thompson to Goldblatt, January 21, 1946.

"Please remember": Thompson to Goldblatt, January 23, 1946.

"you have to understand": Thompson to Goldblatt, February 4, 1946.

"They wondered why": ibid.

"the trouble with Arakaki": ibid.

thankless job: Thompson to Jacinto Conol, September 1945.

"Like an excursion": Thompson to Goldblatt, April 29, 1946.

"Not bad kau-kau": ibid.

CHAPTER 23: THE POKER PLAYER

went to Gladstein: Gladstein to Zalburg, November 8, 1976.

wanted to sue: *Hawaiian Dispatcher,* August 1, 1944. Hall wrote: "Your editor spent two years in wage-hour enforcement—over a year in charge of the Wage and Hour Division of the Territorial Department of Labor. He is more than casually acquainted with the problems involved here."

legally shaky: Gladstein to Zalburg, November 8, 1976.

take on the Big Five: ibid.

"enormous effort": ibid.

received a telegram: Goldblatt.

[footnote] Gladstein firm: Gladstein to Zalburg, November 8, 1976.

there until January 6: memorandum by Goldblatt, January 9, 1946.

settle for $10 million: ibid.

"It was quite apparent": ibid.

offer was $1 million: Goldblatt memorandum.

a lot more coming: Goldblatt.

settlement for $1,500,000: Goldblatt memorandum.

"absolutely clear": ibid.

fee was outrageous: Yoshiko Hall. She said: "He felt Richie [Gladstein] was getting too much of a fee. . . . Jack never got over it and neither has Lou [Goldblatt]."

[footnote] "companies paid $1,500,000": Gladstein to Zalburg, November 8, 1976.

[footnote] "less than $25,000": ibid. Hall said the Gladstein firm got $135,000; the union got $135,000; and $30,000 went into a "cost fund" to pay for distribution of the FLSA money and any further legal fees. Total cost of distributing the funds came to slightly less than $15,000. (Hall to Goldblatt, May 27, 1948)

"numerous other problems": Hall to Bouslog & Symonds, memorandum, January 15, 1947.

"A real cleanup": Goldblatt to Hall, January 12, 1946.

"mark off the cards": Goldblatt to Hall, February 15, 1946.

began to wish: Hall to Goldblatt, February 7, 1946.

"a lot of bickering": Thompson to Goldblatt, May 13, 1946. An example: Antone Crivello, a watchman at Onomea Sugar Co., kept his pay envelopes and estimated he had 9120 hours of overtime during the war. He said he was paid $125 and protested to Hall who told him it was a local matter and he couldn't do anything about it. (O'Brien, *Plot to Sovietize Hawaii,* pp. 11–12)

as much as eight or nine hundred: Kawano.

court of last resort: Goldblatt.

CHAPTER 24: THE MEN FROM THE BARRIOS

"packed like sardines": Frank Thompson to Goldblatt, February 4, 1946.

"never a dirtier ship": ibid.

"raising hell": Hall to Goldblatt, February 7, 1946.

"sweetness and light": ibid. There was in fact a short period during which the ILWU and the employers appeared to be friendly. Goldblatt told Blaisdell that the 1945 longshore agreement, which had been settled through collective bargaining, could set a precedent. (Goldblatt to Blaisdell, June 8, 1945) The era of "sweetness and light" ended with the 1946 sugar strike.

"flex their muscles": Hall to Goldblatt, February 7, 1946.

handled in Washington: Beechert interview.

[footnote] "if it can be demonstrated": Hall to Stainback, May 31, 1945.

"godfather": Hall to Goldblatt, February 7, 1946.

militant crew: Slator Miller. Also Frank Thompson to Takahashi, May 27, 1946.
"We had organized them en route, which was important," said Goldblatt.

passage was sixty-five dollars: Miller.

Ilocanos considered best: "The Ilocanos have a sturdy, rigorous, hardened-to-the-soil attitude toward work and a resolve to persevere until they have realized their goal of saving, which fit in snugly with plantation efficiency. They prefer . . . a heavy job with good pay to a 'white collar job' with less remuneration." (Roman R. Cariaga, *The Filipino in Hawaii,* p. 25)

"bass his ass": Baldovi to Goldblatt, February 6, 1947.

"Very soon working": Baldovi to Robertson, undated. Letter was received June 17, 1946.

taste the sweetness: Conol to Robertson, September 4, 1945.

except Maui Pineapple: Brooks, *Unionism in Hawaii,* p. 122. Brooks called the ILWU's failure to organize Maui Pine "a blur on its otherwise complete unionization record."

"every nickel": Hall to Goldblatt, April 8, 1946.

asked for fifteen: Hall to Goldblatt, February 27, 1946.

"Harry . . . pointed out": Goldblatt to Hall, March 5, 1946.

"A light vote": Goldblatt to Hall, March 18, 1946.

thirty percent effective: Hall to Goldblatt, April 8, 1946.

"not ready for a fight": ibid.

"made every pitch": ibid.

"super-duper cult": Hall to Goldblatt, June 11, 1946.

CHAPTER 25: THE BATTLE PLAN

tested the ILWU: Brooks, *Unionism in Hawaii,* p. 129.

demands modest: ILWU pamphlet titled "Strike Deadline Nears" (undated). There were twenty-seven issues at stake that ranged from terms of agreement and wages to the perquisite fund and housing.

"$25 million housing fund": Goldblatt. He said: "We didn't say that that [fund] was around. We just said, 'Look, you owe it to us.' And incidentally we didn't expect to get a goddamned dime. . . . Look, we're in a beef. Throw in some of these demands. You can always yank them out at the last minute. Christ, the employers thought they won one of the biggest victories in the world when we dropped that and got something else." (Goldblatt interview)

"phantom fund": from Sugar Industry of Hawaii pamphlet titled "The Truth about the Sugar Strike," August 1946.

over $21 million: ibid. An industry memorandum (undated) said 44.8 percent of the cost of producing sugar went to labor. An HSPA financial statement for 1945 showed that the sugar industry earned a total net income of $4,386,424.44.

All six sugar factors made money in 1945 except F. A. Schaefer & Company, operators of Honokaa Sugar Co., which lost $387,392.15. Net income after profits of the other sugar factors was as follows: C. Brewer, $852,603.19; Alexander & Baldwin, $1,017,322; American Factors, $939,357.75; Davies, $340,714.65; Castle & Cooke, $1,623,918.

"did not embark lightly": ILWU pamphlet, "Strike Deadline Nears."

"When labor asks": *Adv.,* August 23, 1946.

strike was coming: The sugar industry claimed that the 1946 strike was "preordained.'' It felt that at that stage in life the ILWU had to show its strength to impress its own people and solidify them. The theory was that a union which never takes strike action is a weak union.

The ILWU disputed this. Goldblatt said the whole background of plantation life made the strike inevitable. ''It was 'preordained' only in the loosest sense of the word,'' he said. ''When you talk about something like this being preordained, then it takes almost a complete ignorance of things you had going.''

''escape San Francisco'': *Adv.,* December 14, 1968.

to end perquisites: Hall to Goldblatt, July 25 and August 12, 1946. Also Sugar Negotiating Committee Bulletin No. 2, August 3, 1946.

come to the rescue: Hall to Goldblatt, August 9, 1946. Goldblatt told Steele the price of sugar was going up; he got the word from Washington. ''Therefore, you ought to loosen up,'' he told Steele. Steele said the employers discounted his word. ''And as often happened, it turned out that Lou was right and we were wrong,'' said Steele. (Steele interview)

''a cent per pound'': Hall to Goldblatt, August 9, 1946.

man the utilities: Steele to Hall, August 10, 1946.

''turned over to committee'': Hall to Goldblatt, August 9, 1946; Hall to Steele, August 12, 1946.

''damndest strike'': Hall to Goldblatt, August 9, 1946.

''do not seem to realize'': Hall to Goldblatt, July 25, 1946.

''All our energy'': Hall to Goldblatt, August 12, 1946.

tally was 15,406: Hall to Goldblatt, August 6, 1946.

either he or Bridges: Hall to Bridges and Goldblatt, cable, August 12, 1946.

Strikes are battles: Commenting on the 1946 sugar strike, Stainback said: ''Strikes are like wars. The weapon of last resort. Like wars, the non-combatants endure as great or greater hardship than those in actual combat. Like wars, both sides sustain heavy losses, and no one wins.'' (*Adv.,* October 16, 1946)

Hall said: ''No one knows better than a worker the cost of a strike. He knows, as do all our members and leadership, that a strike is not a plaything. It's not something that can be turned on and off like a faucet. It is real and grim.'' (*Hawaiian Dispatcher,* March 22, 1946)

24-member committee: Frank Thompson to Goldblatt, August 5, 1946.

''voice and vote'': ibid.

$50,000 a day: ILWU report, August 3, 1946.

purchased radio time: Hall to Goldblatt, August 12, 1946.

''a bang-up job'': ibid.

hire Berman?: ibid.

booklets to sixty thousand: HSPA Bulletin No. 4 to plantation managers, August 23, 1946.

''All our efforts'': ILWU report, August 3, 1946.

Thompson told them: Thompson to Goldblatt, July 28, 1946.

''long drawn-out battle'': ibid.

Fujisaki advised: ILWU Daily Communications Report, June 29, 1946.

arranged with Labrador: Strike Strategy Committee report, August 19, 1946.

obtained ten-acre plot: Daily Communications Report, August 7, 1946.

Kauai polled its members: Daily Communications Report, August 21, 1946.

Ewa agreed: Thompson to Goldblatt, August 19, 1946.

sent out questionnaires: example cited was sent to Local 148, Olaa, on August 1, 1946.

"The major task": minutes of Strike Strategy Committee meeting, August 6, 1946.

"Apparently Ignacio": Hall to Goldblatt, August 12, 1946.

"strike can't lose": *Adv.,* September 7, 1946.

"If industry can show": *Adv.,* August 27, 1946.

"free ride": Brooks, *Unionism in Hawaii,* p. 140.

"People on other side": minutes of August 28, 1946, negotiating session.

"If it would do any good": ibid.

"well in advance": Brooks, *Unionism in Hawaii,* p. 141.

"Two and a half years": Robertson to Hall, cable, September 1, 1946.

sent night cable: Bridges and Robertson to Hall, September 1, 1946.

go for broke: Richard T. Nimmons, an Employers Council executive, quoted a Filipino sugar worker as saying: "If they got us out on strike and don't get what we are asking for, then the hell with the union. . . . This strike will make or break the union." (Nimmons' memorandum, August 27, 1946)

CHAPTER 26: THE RICECAPADE

"100% effective": *Adv.,* September 2, 1946.

never taken part: Hall press release, September 14, 1946.

"on a lark": Maxwell. Perhaps he did not realize the total commitment of the sugar workers. An illustration: The Koloa, Kauai, unit (Local 149, Unit 3) had 510 members, all on strike duty, as follows: on picket lines, 230; committees, 91; union police, 63; gardening, 46; utilities, 44; dairy-livestock, 14; medical, 12; fishing-hunting, 7; sanitation, 3; transport, 2; watchman, 1. That adds up to three more members than they actually had; or, as is probable, a few did double duty. (*The Centurian,* November 7, 1946, the local's mimeographed newspaper, printed in English and Ilocano)

fishing parties: minutes of Territorial Strike Strategy Committee, October 10, 1946.

"a man who leaves": ibid.

weakness was rice: Hall to Goldblatt, August 5, 1946.

arranged for purchase: Hall to Goldblatt, July 31, 1946.

put pressure on the government: ibid.

"ought to run down": Goldblatt to Hall, July 26, 1946.

"WITHOUT RICE": Hall to Goldblatt, August 5, 1946.

increase rice quota: Hall to Bouslog, September 18, 1946.

"uppermost in minds": David Thompson to Lincoln Fairley, September 11, 1946.

release for sale: Hall to Stainback, September 26, 1946.

"to prevent starvation": Robertson to Krug, cable, September 27, 1946.

"starving the workers": Robertson to Hall, October 4, 1946.

reporting shortages: minutes of Hawaii Island Strike Strategy Committee, October 7, 1946.

ate breadfruit: Okada's report (undated).

"sail relief ship": Schmidt to Robertson, October 7, 1946.

"eat whiskey?": Schmidt in a talk in Hilo, October 26, 1946.

worried about Filipinos: minutes of Strike Strategy Committee meeting at Olaa, September 7, 1946.

"a buck in their pocket": Goldblatt.

"break ranks": Goldblatt.

"very dedicated": Goldblatt.

place non-Filipinos: Labez, ILWU communiqué, October 8, 1946.

"change the whole system": Labez interview.

Deluge editors: Labez, ILWU communiqué, October 6, 1946.

Virginia Woods: Goldblatt.

"brown rice for peasants": Goldblatt.

get 5000 to 10,000 bags: Frank Thompson to Goldblatt and Hall, October 4, 1946.

"keep your pants on": Thompson to McElrath, September 26, 1946.

had to be on deposit: Woods to Hall, cable, October 15, 1946.

4487 bags: Woods to Goldblatt and Hall, October 17, 1946. The rice aboard the *Gill* was consigned as follows: 1496 bags to Local 142 (Hilo) and 997 bags each to Locals 144 (Wailuku), 149 (Lihue), and Pier 11 (Honolulu).

"RAISING HELL": Hall to Robertson, cable, November 13, 1946.

"do not want brown": Hall to Woods, cable, November 15, 1946.

rice thrust on them: Goldblatt.

"Spike this rumor": Labez, ILWU communiqué, October 8, 1946.

"roasting three dogs": O'Brien, *Plot to Sovietize Hawaii,* p. 11.

CHAPTER 27: THREE BOTTLES OF FOUR ROSES

"most powerful weapon": Charles F. Congdon, "Background and History of the 1946 Hawaiian Sugar Strike," p. 15.

using sewer water: ILWU Daily Communications Report, September 4, 1946.

At Olaa: Employers News Bulletin, No. 4, September 6, 1946.

in front of supervisors' houses: Carlsmith phoned the information to Vern Spackman, HSPA industrial relations director, at 11:45 AM, September 9, 1946.

"don't want violence": ILWU Communications Report, September 3, 1946.

"threatened and coerced": *Adv.,* September 12, 1946.

"gangsterism": Brooks, *Unionism in Hawaii,* p. 144.

five strikebreakers: *ILWU* v. *Walter D. Ackerman, Jr.* et al., Civil No. 828; opinion filed December 27, 1948, in U.S. Federal District Court in Honolulu, pp. 18–22.

"cat-calling": *Adv.,* September 17, 1946.

"a plantation judge": David Thompson's report, September 18, 1946.

"A Lawless Judge": ILWU leaflet, undated.

"scurrilous attack": *S-B,* October 12, 1946.

Gladstein fought: David Thompson said: "Gladstein and Hall flew over and Gladstein made an ass of the judge in his own court." (Thompson to Harry A. Steingart, San Francisco, September 24, 1946)

[footnote] Gladstein wrote it: 19th ICON, Honolulu, April 19–23, 1971, p. 249.

didn't care much: Goldblatt.

"If we can't picket": Goldblatt.

two thousand strong: Thompson to Steingart, September 24, 1946.

started to dry up: Thompson to Robertson, September 19, 1946.

verbal combat: Management Bulletin No. 6, September 20, 1946.

exchange at bargaining table: David Thompson's notes, September 18, 1946.

"handful of malcontents": summary record of sugar negotiations, Castle & Cooke, October 25, 1946.

"sticking in you": ibid.

"other HSPA bigshots": Thompson's notes, September 13, 1946.

"the big *uluas*": ibid.

"not yield an inch": ILWU Communications Report, September 14, 1946.

meeting at Commercial Club: Goldblatt.

"one lousy dozen": Goldblatt.

"you flubbed it": Goldblatt.

"premature meeting": open letter from White, October 21, 1946.

"losing $343,000 a day": *Adv.,* October 21, 1946.

"house organ for sugar": ILWU Communications Report, September 12, 1946.

asked to boycott: *Adv.,* October 8, 1946.

anti-Semitic: Kealalio said that during the 1946 strike "the Jew-baiting there was terrific." (7th ICON, San Francisco, April 7–11, 1947, p. 163)

"well-known 'red scare' ": Hall to all locals and units, October 30, 1946.

[footnote] "Communist-Fascist technique": Coll over KGU radio, October 9, 1946.

"made up of bosses": Hall, October 30, 1946.

Hill offered milk: ILWU Communications Report, September 6, 1946.

hired Lewis: Lewis; McElrath radio script, April 25, 1955; Gene Hunter, *Adv.,* November 11, 1973.

"We are not sorry": Hall in open letter from Local 145, Unit 3, Waianae, October 18, 1946.

wired Truman: cable, September 27, 1946.

knew Feinsinger: Goldblatt to Hall, December 13, 1946.

[footnote] total of $18,719.99: report by Okada (undated).

"a tremendous victory": Hall, November 15, 1946.

"a remarkable victory": Brooks, *Unionism in Hawaii,* p. 160.

frightened employers: ibid.

"created general awe": ibid. Babbitt said the employers were alarmed over the ILWU's success. "This was going to mean the death of the small ones [plantations]," he said. (Babbitt interview)

CHAPTER 28: ON-THE-JOB TRAINING

"I had butterflies": LEB, Honolulu, February 10–11, 1961, p. 61.

An incident took place: Murphy. Murphy said his mission was to persuade management that its business was to make money and not fight the ILWU. "We had to work together. We had to give and take. . . . I think Hall came to understand this and agreed with this finally." (Murphy interview)

"I'm going home": Murphy.

"the way the Romans operated": Murphy.

"a unanimous basis": Steele.

plantations are different: Steele, Maxwell.

plenty of rain: Maxwell. Because of the rain the Hamakaua Coast plantations were "sitting in the catbird seat," said Maxwell. Hall said: "Brewer was hurting so bad they forced a settlement in '46. . . . They took a hell of a beating." (Beechert tape, p. 13)

steal signals: Steele. Both sides had fun twitting each other. Murphy once told McElrath that the FBI had planted an informer inside the ILWU. Later, he and Jack Fox, a Castle & Cooke public relations man, embellished the story by starting the rumor that the man planted inside the union was McElrath himself. It was just nonsense, of course, but they enjoyed a chuckle over it. (Murphy interview)

"nonverbal communications": Steele.

"less sword-rattling": Steele. Steele said: "I felt from the early days that Hall played it pretty straight and I guess the simplest way to put that is if I had a chance in the late 1940s and early 1950s to substitute someone else in Jack's role in the ILWU, I don't think I would have suggested a change." (Steele interview)

Babbitt said of Hall: "He grew tremendously. He was eager to get the last few cents out of the employers, but as time went on he became thoroughly aware of the economics of both sugar plantations and the waterfront. And I think he tempered his demands." (Babbitt interview)

decided by mid-1945: Brooks, *Unionism in Hawaii,* p. 135.

"clean up" perquisites: Murphy.

Goldblatt has reminded: Brooks, *Unionism in Hawaii,* p. 160.

"Just as long as": Goldblatt over radio KGU, November 16, 1946.

"heart of economic power": 7th ICON, San Francisco, April 7–11, 1947, p. 171.

"Had a new type": ibid., p. 27.

"minimize job action": Hall, ILWU communiqué, November 21, 1946.

"a hardheaded Scotchman": Frank Thompson to Goldblatt, January 22, 1945.

CHAPTER 29: THE UNPLEASANTNESS AT PIONEER MILL

Bridges' ulcer: He had four-fifths of his stomach removed in 1949. (Minutes of 1949 longshore negotiations, August 18, 1949, p. 257)

involved 1067 workers: Hall to Aurelio Quitiano, general counsel on labor, Philippines Consulate, Honolulu, December 23, 1946.

violated memorandum: ibid.

job was to manage: ibid. Hall said Moir had a reputation "of being the most difficult manager in Hawaii to deal with."

"from top to bottom": Frank Thompson to Goldblatt, January 22, 1945.

only *haole* boy: Moir.

"neglected to tell": Moir.

union members attacked: *Adv.,* December 16, 1946.

"He water; he get hurt": ibid.

"a face-saver": Goldblatt to Hall, December 13, 1946.

to invoke formula: Hall to Quitiano, December 23, 1946.

"dickering back and forth": Moir.

"jumped ship": Moir said the Jack Hall of Port Allen days (1937–1941) was a "rabble-rouser."

tired of cabbage soup: Moir.

kicked him in shins: Moir.

"haven't had a meeting": Moir. Moir said: "Without a meeting, Bridges told them they were going back to work. They were taking direct orders from Bridges and didn't have a meeting. So much for your democratic union."

back to work: ILWU communiqué, December 31, 1946.

pleaded nolo: ibid.; *Adv.,* December 29, 1946.

"opinion of counsel": *Adv.,* December 29, 1946.

more than $50,000: Hall to Quitiano, December 23, 1946.

CHAPTER 30: FARRINGTON AND THE 1946 ELECTION

"You Communist!": Mrs. Farrington.

puzzled ILWU members: Kimoto.

castigated the union: Hall's opinion of the *Star-Bulletin* changed over the years. For example, on September 4, 1940, he wrote editor Allen: "As one who has usually agreed that the news columns of the *Star-Bulletin* are objectively written—though I cannot say the same for its editorials. . . ."

"a good union": Mrs. Farrington.

"wouldn't have gotten otherwise": Mrs. Farrington.

meeting in Miller's gym: Crozier.

pipeline to Hawaii: Allen wrote at least a letter a week to Farrington while Farrington was a delegate (1943–1954). The letters are dated and usually, but not always, coded (24-B, for instance).

came to office every day: Howard Case interview. Case, a Honolulu newspaperman for sixty-five years, served on both the *Advertiser* and the *Star-Bulletin.* He was a long-time *Bulletin* city editor. He said: "My lasting impression of R. H. A. [Riley Harris Allen], gained from an association of 34 years, is that, as an editor for nearly half a century, he never stopped working." Allen died in 1966 at eighty-two. Case died in 1977 at eighty-three.

"willing to fight": Allen to Farrington, July 26, 1946, 131-B.

"not formidable": ibid.

"make every effort": ibid.

not an officer in PAC: Hall to Stainback, November 19, 1946.

"Balderdash": Allen to Farrington, November 13, 1947, 175-C.

"ache for statehood": Hall's Labor Day speech, September 1, 1947, p. 3. He said: "And never for a second forget that statehood for Hawaii is our most important political objective."

Allen said some businessmen were against statehood. He said they had a fear, "exaggerated though it may be—that 'some day we may be living under a Japanese governor.' " (Allen to Carl E. Brazier of the *Seattle Times,* April 21, 1947)

could talk to Farrington: McElrath. He said: "He would listen. By listen I mean he would hear Jack out and give consideration to what Jack said. But he certainly didn't jump when Jack pressed a button."

"endorse on that basis": McElrath.

"romancing with PAC": *Adv.,* October 1, 1946.

[footnote] to develop union leadership: McEuen to ILWU unit officers and stewards, January 12, 1948.

"sold out his conscience": *Adv.,* November 2, 1946.

"looked Hall in eye": ibid.

"on-the-platter votes": Berman.

It rankled him: Thurston. Asked why, he said: "I guess it was largely because I hated their guts. . . . I think [the ILWU] did more harm than good."

"Fires being kindled": Coll spoke over KGU radio on the night of October 10, 1946. He and Thurston discussed what he was going to say. Thurston said Coll always saw eye-to-eye with him. "Ray never went into any policy that I didn't write or that we didn't discuss thoroughly and that I didn't approve."

"If we endorsed": *Adv.,* November 4–6, 1946.

lost her appetite: Mrs. Farrington.

"became evil one": bylined story by Mrs. Farrington, *S-B,* August 21, 1969.

"A bank takes money": Mrs. Farrington.

"a different type of game": Hill in a taped interview with Edward D. Beechert and Louis P. Warsh at Keauhou Bay, Hawaii, on February 27, 1970. The writer is grateful to both for permission to use this material.

"father confessor": ibid.

"Two or three ILWU leaders": ibid.

"with the date left blank": Frank Thompson to Goldblatt, July 29, 1946.

"What a character": ibid.

"passively" endorsed: Beechert and Warsh interview.

"working class electorate": David Thompson to Lincoln Fairley, August 1, 1946.

"Too few people": ibid.

twenty out of thirty-four: *Adv.,* November 8, 1946.

CHAPTER 31: THE PINEAPPLE STRIKE OF 1947

"into the trap": ILWU pamphlet, "Steward on the Job." July 25, 1947.

Hall-Goldblatt phone call: This conversation was recorded by a secretary in the ILWU's San Francisco office. Usually the ILWU kept in touch by letter. "We don't trust phones or wires for important items," Goldblatt said. (Goldblatt to Hall, May 10, 1947)

negotiations under way: with Hawaiian Pineapple Co., California Packing Corp., Libby, McNeill & Libby, Maui Pineapple Co., Baldwin Packers, Kauai Pineapple Co., Hawaiian Canneries Co., and Hawaiian Fruit Packers.

"Red-baiting": Hall elaborated: "The Elks have started a radio program on 'The Red Menace.' The Catholics have one, too. . . . The Teamsters Union [that is, Rutledge] is getting a good reception, too. Radio programs are playing them up as 'gentlemen.' The Teamsters have a $20,000 fund and are talking in terms of a raid on the canneries."

"Let them release profit figures": for the year ending May 31, 1946, Hawaiian Pine earned a net profit of $2,366,886 on net sales of $28,239,192; for 1947, $1,673,090 on sales of $28,936,500; and for 1948, $2,357,883 on sales of $33,896,922. (Moody's Industrials, 1947–1949)

longshore getting 30: on January 3, 1947, the longshoremen got a thirty-cent raise.

caught off balance: Goldblatt to Hall, December 13, 1946.

"not going to take a licking": ibid.

"a natural letdown": Hall in a confidential report to regional office department heads, locals, and unit officers, February 7, 1947.

"not driving through": Goldblatt to Hall, January 28, 1947.

"setback": Hall to Goldblatt, February 6, 1947, telephone call.

pineapple was weak: Brooks, *Unionism in Hawaii,* p. 165.

Less than thirty-five percent: Matsumoto, "The 1947 Pineapple Strike," p. 14.

"weren't in shape to fight": Goldblatt to Hall, January 28, 1947.

"I have in mind": ibid.

Push "like blazes": Goldblatt to Hall, February 14, 1947.

"If the rank and file": ibid.

"conciliatory but tough": Hall to Goldblatt, February 3, 1947.

"looking for a weak spot": Hall in ILWU Newsletter (mimeographed), February 25, 1947.

"nickel offer": Brooks, *Unionism in Hawaii,* p. 166.

"Woolworth offer": ILWU press release, May 14, 1947.

"Five copper pennies": Report to Pineapple Industry Negotiating Committee, February 18, 1947.

"deliberately misrepresented": HEC minutes of pineapple negotiating session, June 11, 1947.

"not tossed in sponge": McElrath to Virginia Stevens, March 31, 1947.

"Is there a point?": Steele, HEC Annual Report for 1948.

"sound like Cassandra": Goldblatt to Hall, March 18, 1947.

"a very good guy": Hall to Goldblatt, May 19, 1947.

designated Bassett: HEC minutes, May 16, 1947.

"hit the ceiling": Hall to Goldblatt, May 19, 1947.
would not grandstand: HEC minutes, May 13, 1947. Allen said Bassett "wielded the English language as the rapier of an agile duelist." (*S-B* editorial, January 27, 1954) Neither Allen nor Farrington was fond of Bassett. In 1952 when Neal Blaisdell ran against Johnny Wilson for Honolulu mayor, Farrington suggested that the best slogan he had heard for the Blaisdell campaign was: "Let's get the little Bassett out of City Hall." (Farrington to Allen, May 7, 1952)
"If they get away with their plans": Goldblatt to Hall, April 3, 1947.
send Bridges a cable: Goldblatt to Hall, May 21, 1947.
"driving hard": Goldblatt to Hall and Schmidt, April 30, 1947.
"every likelihood": ibid.
assessed union's strength: Hall to Goldblatt, May 12, 1947.
when best to strike?: ibid. The strike was called at the wrong time. "The peak season is a highly inopportune moment for a strike because it is then that union control is diluted by the presence of the unorganized seasonal workers who comprise about 50 per cent of the total work force." (Matsumoto, "The 1947 Pineapple Strike," p. 14)
"industry wants a strike": Hall to Goldblatt, May 16, 1947.
"unfavorable repercussions": Farrington to Allen, May 31, 1947.
outlook grim: Hall to Morimoto, June 23, 1947.
called it "disappointing": *S-B*, June 4, 1947.
repeated ILWU demands: HEC minutes, June 9, 1947.
planned a lockout: HEC minutes, June 11, 1947.
union hatchetman: Feinsinger used the word. (HEC minutes, June 11, 1947)
"function is not to negotiate": ibid.
Tanigawa's petition: June 11, 1947.
"a major dislocation": Stanley M. Miyamoto of Waialae School, June 16, 1947.
"fail to come that far": Goldblatt to Bridges, July 7, 1947.
loss of a major portion: cable from Washington, June 25, 1947.

CHAPTER 32: FIVE EXHAUSTING DAYS

"honest broker": Feinsinger's description of himself. (HEC minutes, July 7, 1947)
description of Feinsinger: Murphy, Maxwell, Babbitt. Murphy said the one word best describing Feinsinger was "acute."
"all kinds of tricks": Maxwell. He said one of Feinsinger's favorite ploys was to hand each side a sealed envelope with a message. For example, he might ask each side to let him know privately if they thought he was doing a good job.
one of the toughest cases: HEC minutes, July 15, 1947.
machinery set up: HEC minutes, July 8, 1947.
settlement imminent: Feinsinger to Steele and Bridges, July 11, 1947.
All that was left: ibid.
"I was directed": McElrath didn't recall who gave him the order.
handed a document: Feinsinger to Steele and Bridges, July 11, 1947.
double-crossed: HEC minutes, July 14, 1947.
"ILWU recklessly plunged": *S-B*, July 11, 1947.
"couldn't hold members": Crossley.
"Bridges believed me; Hall didn't": Crossley didn't have a high regard for Hall. "Lots of people say [Hall] was a man of his word. I found that if you could pin down what his word was, you had a chance of making it stick. . . . No matter how much he had to drink, he could still talk and he could still function. Sometimes he'd go to sleep at the meeting. He'd just lean back; his eyes

were closed. But if you'd try to trick him, he would snap to. His recovery ability was fantastic." (Crossley interview)

"before it was timed": HEC minutes, July 15, 1947.

couldn't deliver: ibid.

"in throes of a strike": Feinsinger to Steele and Bridges, July 11, 1947.

"Time will aggravate": ibid.

strike (or lockout): for years the ILWU used the term "lockout" to describe the 1947 walkout. Management said: "Even Mr. Bridges . . . this year [1948] repeatedly referred to last year's work stoppage as a strike." (Pineapple industry review of 1947, January 23, 1948)

On the first day: Matsumoto, "The 1947 Pineapple Strike," p. 10.

[footnote] industry employed: HEC minutes, July 7, 1947.

fifth day of strike: Matsumoto, "The 1947 Pineapple Strike," p. 11.

"not shaping up": Schmidt.

"I was on the scene": Bridges. It's not clear how strongly Hall was in favor of the strike. Robertson and Murphy said Hall definitely was for the strike. Oshiro of the pineapple local said he couldn't remember. Okada said Hall was against the strike.

"no monkeyshines": HEC minutes, July 15, 1947.

"window dressing": Brooks, *Unionism in Hawaii,* p. 180.

[footnote] "won't strike for pineapple": David Thompson.

incident of July 11: Rhoda V. Lewis, acting territorial attorney general, in a report to Governor Stainback, July 12, 1947.

incident of July 12: ibid.

incident of July 14: ibid.; also opinion filed in *ILWU* v. *Ackerman,* p. 26.

incident of July 15: Lewis's report and Ackerman case, p. 27. Police records show that on Oahu 116 persons were arrested in connection with the strike and charged with unlawful assembly and other charges. "Very turbulent days," said a *Star-Bulletin* editorial (July 17, 1947).

Some of the cases dragged on for years. For example, twenty-two men pleaded nolo contendere on September 10, 1953, in connection with the strike and were fined a total of $2750. In the case of the beating of the two truck drivers, twelve men were fined $125 each and another man forefeited $100 bail. In the Fernandez case, six defendants were fined $125 each. (*S-B,* September 15, 1953)

"Men have been beaten": Pineapple Industry to Oren Long, July 15, 1947.

"Lockout Won!": ILWU leaflet (undated).

"atmosphere of calm": *S-B,* July 15, 1947.

"Mistakes were made": *S-B,* July 16, 1947.

"Lucky to get out": Hall to Clifford D. O'Brien, northwest director, National Labor Bureau, Seattle, July 17, 1947.

Allen worried: Allen to Farrington, July 17, 1947.

drag sugar and longshore: *Adv.,* July 16, 1947.

"little talk of wages": Brooks, *Unionism in Hawaii,* p. 180.

"We'll do the talking": notes by Elvon C. Musick, president, Pineapple Growers Association of Hawaii, July 18, 1947.

"must have protection": HEC minutes, August 4, 1947.

"not going to take chances": ibid.

Plan A or Plan B: ibid.

"debacle": Goldblatt's word. Brooks called the strike "a severe loss for the union" and said it would be "hard for the union to live it down." (Brooks, *Unionism in Hawaii,* pp. 184, 187)

"One impression is indelible": Crossley reporting to pineapple industry, August 26, 1947.

"dug in their pockets": Omuro to Robertson, July 26, 1947.

Four years later: the 1951 Lanai strike.

CHAPTER 33: BOUSLOG & SYMONDS

several hundred: Bridges, Symonds, Bouslog.

couldn't find anyone: Symonds.

Bridges cast an eye: Bridges.

He liked her: Bridges, Bouslog.

Bouslog's background: Bouslog.

notified December 11: Bouslog.

seventy-five dollars a week: Bridges. He said: "She was perfectly satisfied [working for the ILWU in Washington] because she was a dedicated gal. She didn't want any part of practicing any goddamned bourgeois law. She wanted to stay there and represent and fight for the workers." (Bridges interview)

ninety dollars when she left: Bouslog.

"COME URGENTLY": Hall to Bouslog, cable, October 21, 1946.

wahine lawyer: McElrath radio script, January 18, 1956.

"Nobody's going to jail": Bouslog.

Symonds' background: Symonds.

"a kind of law clerk": Bridges.

"No one's going to jail": Symonds.

liked to tell jokes: Bouslog.

"do all the negotiating": Symonds.

financial arrangement: Bridges, Symonds, Bouslog.

rented an office: Bouslog, Symonds.

"We were very close": Bouslog.

"You may recall": Bouslog to Andersen, November 30, 1946.

worked eighteen hours: Bouslog.

push the cases: Bouslog.

chartered a plane: Bouslog.

had an agreement: Bouslog.

began to cry: Moir.

sentence was concurrent: Moir, Bouslog.

"written in Moscow": Bouslog.

heard *en banc: ILWU* v. *Walter D. Ackerman Jr.,* Civil Nos. 828 and 836, U.S. Federal District Court for the District of Hawaii.

"terror into workers": ibid., court opinion, p. 12.

"labor movement is unpopular": ibid., p. 79.

eighty-four percent: ibid., p. 92.

"other men a lot better": ibid., p. 93 (p. 312 of the transcript of case before Cristy).

Pombo-Cristy exchange: ibid., p. 290.

"marvelous Judge Metzger": Bouslog. Metzger's liberal interpretation of the law made him a folk hero to the ILWU. Not to Allen, however. He once said of Metzger: "He is coming to regard his pronouncements as more important than the Ten Commandments and the Sermon on the Mount." (Allen to Farrington, February 1, 1951, 32-G)

Ninth Circuit Court reversed ruling: 87 Fed., 2nd 860, February 28, 1951.

Rehearing denied: May 25, 1951.

Certiorari denied: October 22, 1951.

more representative: Bouslog.

sued Wirtz: Bouslog.

"Through sheer gall": *Adv.,* July 22, 1970.

fighting lawyers: Kawano. He said that "if you have a case and you cannot afford to lose the case, then the lawyer to get is either Bouslog or Symonds, because they work for a cheap fee, and work like the dickens, and usually win the case." (Hearings before the HUAC, 82nd Congress, 1st Session, July 6, 1951, pp. 50–51)

Majors and Palakiko: Bouslog saved James E. Majors and John Palakiko from the gallows. They were under death sentence for the rape-murder of Mrs. Therese Wilder and were scheduled to be hanged at 8 AM on September 22, 1951.

Bouslog got Associate Justice Louis LeBaron out of bed the night before and presented a petition in court at 10 PM. The hearings lasted until 3 AM. LeBaron ruled against Bouslog but gave her a stay of execution and the right to appeal. The stay was rushed to Oahu Prison and Warden Joe C. Harper got it at 4:25 AM.

Bouslog took the case on up to the U.S. Supreme Court. On August 15, 1954, Governor King commuted the death sentences. Fifteen years later the two men were released from prison. The case helped bring about the abolition of capital punishment in Hawaii. (Bouslog in *Adv.,* July 22, 1970)

seldom praised lawyers: Bouslog, Symonds.

merely tolerated: Symonds.

disliked Bouslog: Yoshiko Hall, Butler. Mrs. Hall worked for twenty years as Bouslog's secretary and ran the office of Bouslog & Symonds.

"made that clear": Symonds.

couldn't stand each other: Bouslog, Symonds.

CHAPTER 34: STAINBACK'S CRUSADE

"crusade against communism": Eastland Committee: Senate Committee on the Judiciary; Hearings to Investigate the Administration of the Internal Security Act, 84th Congress, 2nd Session, 1957, p. 2287.

one day in March: ibid., p. 2284.

"well-known Communists": ibid., p. 2285.

"Strange as it may seem": ibid., p. 2284.

gave Stainback a typescript: ibid., p. 2286.

"silly piece of writing": *Hawaii Observer,* October 13, 1976, p. 20.

[footnote] borrowed the title: Reinecke.

"make a speech": Butler Committee: Senate Committee on Internal and Insular Affairs; Hearings, Statehood for Hawaii, 83rd Congress, 1st and 2nd Sessions, 1953–1954, p. 531.

"We are not free": Eastland Committee, p. 2287.

"most fruitful field": *S-B,* November 11, 1947. Stainback said: "I shall immediately take steps to unearth these [Communist] activities . . . expose and dismiss territorial employees who are involved. . . ."

For two years: Eastland Committee, p. 2287.

Stainback's background: ibid., p. 2283.

had a law degree: Most fellow lawyers regarded Stainback as a good lawyer. (Anthony, Bouslog interviews) So did Allen. "The Governor is, I have been told by his legal confreres, a good lawyer." (Allen to Farrington, December 1, 1947, 197-C)

hard to believe: Butler Committee, p. 514.

"How could you": ibid.

"We didn't know": ibid., p. 517.

"not slightest notion": ibid., p. 535.

Stainback-Watkins exchange: ibid.

Littrell's recommendation: Littrell to McIntyre, November 14, 1941.

Ickes' reaction: Ickes to McIntyre, November 28, 1941.

"did not seem politic": ibid.

Stainback himself didn't like: Anthony, McElrath.

"We recognize all weaknesses": Hall to Bouslog, May 28, 1946.

"enviable position": ibid.

"in behalf of members": Hall to Krug, May 28, 1946.

lukewarm support: Allen to Farrington, May 31, 1947, 93-C. Allen commented on Stainback's "dilatory and grudging performance on statehood."

"in the best interests": Farrington to Allen, March 19, 1946.

"a great governor": ibid.

CHAPTER 35: THE BURNS CONNECTION

Hall a Party member: Burns.

She made it a point: Burns.

a simple man: Kawano, Kimoto, Oshiro. All used the same word to describe Burns.

sympathetic to change: Burns.

"used Party cells": Burns.

[footnote] exaggerated the role: Beechert, in an editorial page article, *Adv.,* October 27, 1976.

"Who is going to help?": from University of Hawaii's "Oral History Project," sponsored by the Chinn Ho Foundation, Tape 9, p. 21.

taken note of Burns: Hall to Kibre, November 14, 1956.

get rid of Gabrielson: Gabrielson was fired in 1946 when Hall was on the Police Commission. McElrath said: "I happen to know that Jack Hall wrote the chief's resignation." (McElrath radio script, November 30, 1955)

used anybody: Hall's speech at Annual Territorial Joint Conference of Hawaii ILWU Locals, Honolulu, February 2, 1952, p. 3. He said he "drew the line at no one—and no group. . . . I met and worked through and with Communists, Democrats, Republicans and non-partisans; with Catholics, Protestants, Buddhists and atheists; with politicians and government officials; with businessmen, big and small; with professionals and farmers; with AFL, CIO, Independent and, yes, company unions."

"Labor has accepted": Hall in *VOL,* June 16, 1938.

"closer to Wobblies": Beechert tape, pp. 14–15.

"first, last and always": Bouslog.

Reinecke was experienced: Kimoto. Attorney General Edward N. Sylva called Reinecke the "political philosopher of the Communist Party of Hawaii." (Butler Committee, p. 352)

"by Moscow gold": Kimoto.

in parked cars: Kimoto.

CHAPTER 36: MOOKINI, IZUKA, AND "THE TRUTH"

tall, affable: Maxwell's description.

"throw off yoke": *S-B,* May 24, 1947.

"utterly destroy": ibid.

general without an army: *S-B,* May 28, 1947.

was not troubled: ibid.

"don't know a single person": Hall to Goldblatt, May 19, 1947.

"have the real goods": Bridges to Goldblatt, June 2, 1947.

misfeasance and malfeasance: Oshiro, Local 152 secretary-treasurer, to Goldblatt, July 3, 1947.

financial irregularity: Hall to Goldblatt, cable, May 23, 1947.

"less than two hours": Oshiro to Goldblatt, June 2, 1947.

"not out of step": Farrington to Allen, March 28, 1947.

"backed by GOP": Allen to Farrington, March 22, 1947, 43-C.

"in palm of his hand": Butler Committee, p. 518.

meeting at Dillingham home: HEC minutes, July 27, 1947. Ettelson was a former managing editor of the *San Francisco Call-Bulletin*. An ILWU pamphlet on Ettelson, called "The Mysterious Stranger," (December 27, 1947) alleged that Ettelson was "imported for the purpose of breaking, weakening or watering down" the ILWU (p. 3). It said Ettelson's mission was to evaluate the employers' program of "creating a red scare and an atmosphere of hysteria about communism and identifying all union leaders with communism" (p. 6).

　　Ettelson denied he came to Hawaii on a union-busting mission. (*S-B,* January 10, 1948) He said he merely produced a "routine report anyone would make on handling public relations. . . . That thing [the ILWU pamphlet] is silly. It is very flattering to be made out as important as that."

"Stainback blasted us": Hall to Bridges, Robertson, Bulcke, and Goldblatt, September 4, 1947.

argument with Kimoto: Izuka research paper, "The Labor Movement in Hawaii," p. 110.

considered him traitor: ibid., p. 111.

had no choice: ibid.

"The Truth about Communism": The pamphlet, dated November 15, 1947, does not state the name of the publisher. The flyleaf identifies Izuka as an active trade unionist and leader of labor from 1937 to 1942, vice-president of ILWU Local 1-35 from 1939 to 1941, and president of the local from 1941 to 1942.

Erwin paid Beam: Izuka research paper, p. 112.

took draft to Coll: ibid.

"Don't exaggerate": Izuka interview.

"Give me a week": ibid.

How true was "The Truth"?: There are obvious errors; some of the people Izuka accused have claimed he was wrong. Some of his accounts of events were not correct.

　　There can be no doubt there were Communist Party members in Hawaii and in the ILWU. Nor can there be any doubt that Party members played the major role in helping build the union. But what were their motives? Was it to carry out the orders of the Soviet Union? History proves that is nonsense. Was it to help working men and women? History proves that to be true.

"self-confessed liar": Hall to the membership, December 31, 1947.

"a fairly accurate portrayal": Allen to Farrington, cable, November 21, 1947.

Holloway account: ibid., memorandum, November 21, 1947.

"I don't agree": ibid.

distributed copies: Izuka research paper, p. 128.

mailed 4700: ibid.

received $1490: Smith Act, p. 1640.

netted $1700: ibid., p. 1637.

Hall knew effective writing: David Thompson.

copies in Congress: Farrington to Allen, December 1, 1947.

copies in schools: *S-B,* January 5, 1948.

"Went to Olaa": Thompson to Hall and Robertson, November 24, 1947.

"recent law graduate": Hall to ILWU membership, December 31, 1947.

"writer's denial": ibid. Hall signed the Taft-Hartley affidavit on February 27, 1950. It said: "I am not a member of the Communist Party or affiliated with such party. I do not believe in, and I am not a member of, nor do I support, any organization that believes in or teaches the overthrow of the United States government by force or by illegal or unconstitutional methods." (Smith Act, p. 11191)

[footnote] Berman did not write it: Berman, Izuka.

CHAPTER 37: THE "IGNACIO REVOLT"

hurt union's plans: Goldblatt to Bridges, December 30, 1947. Goldblatt wrote: "The situation in sugar has been seriously disrupted and dangerously weakened by the Ignacio move, not just in terms of people who are affected but just as much in the weakening of confidence and the confusion that has penetrated the loyal units."

McElrath discounted the seriousness of the revolt. He said: "The fact showed that fifteen or sixteen persons had quit the union. . . ." (McElrath radio script, December 13, 1956)

Reinecke said the Ignacio Revolt "was no tempest in a teapot. It damned near cracked the teapot." (Reinecke interview)

Ignacio's background: Ignacio.

announced a slate of officers: Ignacio's pamphlet, "YES, Communism Is Un-American," Hilo, December 17, 1947. On the back cover, Akoni Pule, UHW temporary vice-president, was quoted as saying: "I hope the full meaning and significance of the Union of Hawaiian Workers will be absorbed by the godless Kremlin in Moscow."

The ILWU forgave Pule and supported him for years in office. McElrath explained: "He always voted the way we considered to be the right way." (McElrath interview)

"his mind is made up": Thompson to Goldblatt, Robertson, and Hall, December 15, 1947.

"disturbed by the red issue": ibid.

Delegates from seven units: ibid. Two units (Kohala and Onomea) sent no delegates.

"Communism is not the issue": minutes of Hawaii ILWU Division Executive Board meeting, December 14, 1947.

Thompson versus Ignacio: ibid.

"fought in last war": ibid. Thompson served with the marines on Guam and Iwo Jima. At Iwo, as a first lieutenant in K Company, 3rd Marine Division, he and another marine carrying radios jumped into a bomb crater sheltering ten other marines. The Japanese dropped a 120-mm mortar shell into the hole, killing eight and wounding four, including Thompson. He lost his right foot below the knee, and in the course of long hospitalization he underwent 217 skin grafts. (Thompson interview)

"4000 Sugar Workers": *S-B,* December 15, 1947.

phoned Kaholokula: Ignacio to Kaholokula, December 16, 1947.

"destruction of ILWU": ibid.

"Good luck, fella": ibid.

"When I walked in": Ignacio to Yoshikazu Morimoto, as quoted in Thompson's letter of December 15, 1947 to Goldblatt, Robertson, and Hall.

preached class hatred: Ignacio's pamphlet.

called on Kamoku: Ignacio.

"Stupid, selfish": Thompson to Goldblatt, Robertson, and Hall, December 15, 1947.

"if island went independent": ibid.

ILWU had no contacts: ibid.

"a complete surprise": Kamoku report, January 3, 1948.

"dead set": Thompson to Goldblatt, Robertson, and Hall, December 15, 1947.

"My own assessment": ibid.

[footnote] a day's pay: The program quickly ran into trouble. Goldblatt said it was "over the head or beyond the reach and understanding of at least half the membership." (Goldblatt to Bridges, December 30, 1947)

Goldblatt should come: Thompson to Goldblatt, December 15, 1947.

phoned Goldblatt: Thompson.

debated Ignacio: Hall to Bridges, December 21, 1947.

"Coloma is behind Ignacio": ibid.

talked for an hour and a half: Hall to Goldblatt, December 22, 1947.

"Cute, huh?": ibid.

"folding rapidly": Hall to Bridges, December 21, 1947.

"At the worst": Hall to Goldblatt, December 22, 1947.

"snowed under": Kawano memorandum, December 22, 1947.

"Rick phoned": Hall to Bridges, December 24, 1947. Hall said that Jacinto Conol, one of Ignacio's original supporters, "gave us all the information on what was going on." (Beechert tape, p. 14)

never did things halfway: Reinecke.

called him a "moron": minutes (mimeographed) of United Sugar Workers ILWU Local 142 Territorial Sugar Conference, Hilo, January 3–5, 1948.

let him speak: minutes of Sugar Conference, January 3, 1948, p. 1.

At 2:41: *Adv.,* January 4, 1948.

"Who was ghost writer?": O'Brien, *Plot to Sovietize Hawaii,* p. 49.

"barrage of questions": *Adv.,* January 4, 1948.

"Nobody is behind me": minutes of Sugar Conference, January 3, 1948, p. 7.

Izuka-Samson exchange: ibid.

"I'm getting fed up": O'Brien, *Plot to Sovietize Hawaii,* p. 49.

"A question, Jack": ibid., p. 50.

"it burns me": minutes of Sugar Conference, January 3, 1948, p. 15.

"Communism is not an issue": ibid., p. 17.

"don't intend to beg": ibid., January 4, 1948, p. 15.

"There is no kidding": ibid., p. 20. Goldblatt said the union was in "absolutely no position to strike at this time even around the demand for arbitration." (Goldblatt to Bridges, December 30, 1947)

strike-happy: minutes of Sugar Conference, January 5, 1948, p. 14.

Are you in favor?: ibid., p. 7.

5908 workers: *S-B,* January 20, 1948.

"a tremendous vote": Bridges to Rania, cable, January 20, 1948.

"not too healthy": Omuro to Rania, May 18, 1948.

"Only a few companies": Hall to Goldblatt, June 17, 1948.

Ignacio had come to see him: ibid. Ignacio went to work as shift sugar boiler supervisor at Honokaa Sugar Co. on October 18, 1948. He worked for

Honokaa for twenty-four years and retired November 15, 1972. He was then sixty-five. At the time of his retirement he was boiling house superintendent. (Ignacio interview)

Kaholokula was tried *in absentia* on May 30, 1948, on charges of dereliction of duty and negligence of office. (Koichi Imori to Robertson, June 1, 1948)

CHAPTER 38: THE REINECKE AFFAIR

strange goings-on: Reinecke to Morris Watson, August 28, 1947.

"I suppose whoever": ibid.

Loper brought charges: Many people of goodwill were genuinely troubled by the idea of an avowed radical teaching school. Typical was the writer of a published letter who signed with the initials "F. S." The letter said: "The Reineckes . . . are school teachers and are in a position to indoctrinate the susceptible minds of the students. They are supposed to teach, not disrespect, but a reverence for America." (*S-B,* December 9, 1947)

"I can't tell": Smyser.

"didn't say yes": Smyser.

"a very good teacher": *S-B,* November 14, 1947.

never made a secret: Reinecke press release, November 29, 1947.

"cannot be so naive": *S-B,* December 1, 1947. Reporter Keyes Beech said: "Today, as he talks of Communists, Governor Stainback sounds like a man who for a number of years has been sleeping in a nest of hornets and, to his horror, has just found out about it." (*S-B,* August 22, 1947)

"have a hollow ring": Allen to Farrington, November 28, 1947, 195-C.

"work not sufficiently good": *Adv.,* April 1, 1948. Two grounds were cited: (1) that Mrs. Hall's services were not up to standards; (2) that it was in the interest of the public not to continue her services beyond a probationary period as there was strong belief she was either a member of the Communist Party or closely associated with it.

"vindictive and political": ibid.

"plain ordinary people": Gladstein on KULA radio, August 20, 1948.

"a byway": Bouslog.

"difficult convincing me": Hall to Goldblatt, July 31, 1948.

"taken the advice": Thompson work report, April 2, 1948.

"if we 'sabotaged' him": ibid.

"Are you a Communist?": Reinecke hearing, August 9, 1948, p. 7.

"a fool to advocate": ibid., p. 8.

"a vast majority": ibid., p. 27.

"intellectual exercise": Reinecke hearing, September 10, 1948, p. 1.

"Are you opposed?": ibid., p. 21.

"marked for slaughter": ibid., p. 56.

"exactly as my predictions": Hall to Robertson, August 16, 1948.

"not possessed of ideals": *S-B,* October 30, 1948.

[footnote] "radical ideas": *S-B,* October 9, 1976.

Beck ordered him to: Reinecke. Reinecke said he saw the correspondence between Beck and Rutledge.

CHAPTER 39: HALL APPLIES MUSCLE

ILWU helped create: Many people said the union deserved the major share of the credit for organizing the modern-day Democratic Party. Among them were Governor Burns, Chuck Mau, Mitsuyuki Kido, Kawano, Oka, and grassroots organizer Tokuichi "Dynamite" Takushi.

Smyser said the ILWU came close to gaining control of the Democratic Party machinery; certainly the union had strong representation at the precinct level. "If they had taken control, it does not mean they would have controlled the elections," said Smyser. "They still would have been opposed all along the line." (Smyser interview)

easy to take over: Kawano's testimony, Smith Act, p. 6593.

"long-awaited meeting": ibid., p. 6628.

"work out mechanics": ibid., p. 6639.

"The thing to do": ibid., p. 6593.

" 'Hey, remember' ": Oka.

fleshed out bones: McElrath to Hall, November 15, 1947. McElrath wrote: "The job is just about completed in the Fifth District with Lau Ah Chew, Charlie Kauhane on holding committee and electing members to County Committee. Suggest that immediately your return [Hall was on the mainland] we hold a meeting with Marshall McEuen, Oka, Kawano, etc. to get the situation on a more solid administrative foundation."

"We have been able": Kawano to Robertson, June 3, 1948.

"The reactionary forces": Hall to Carl Fujimoto, December 26, 1946.

"if he is still solid": ibid.

"ardent Democrat": O'Brien, *Plot to Sovietize Hawaii,* p. 18.

it would hurt him: Hall to Fujimoto, December 26, 1946.

Hall and McElrath lobbied: Eastland Committee, p. 2725. Allen said: "PAC was active, and obviously trying to hold the fifteen Democrats in line." (Allen to Farrington, March 22, 1947, 43-C)

Aguiar was fed up: Smyser.

[footnote] "a struggle without parallel": Eastland Committee, p. 2725.

Advertiser bannered: on October 21, 1947.

"serious mistake": *S-B,* October 22, 1947.

"alienated broad mass": ibid.

"boldest bids": *Adv.,* October 21, 1947.

"The PAC polled": *Adv.,* October 24, 1947.

"ILWU doesn't want": *S-B,* October 21, 1947.

"after Stainback's scalp": Allen to Farrington, October 21, 1947, 150-C.

Stainback was pleased: ibid.

"shrill, stentorian shout": Allen to Farrington, October 25, 1947, 156-C.

"I have reason": ibid.

"identically the same feeling": Farrington to Allen, October 30, 1947.

"My impression is": Allen to Farrington, March 30, 1948, 50-D. "At heart Riley was a pretty conservative guy," said Smyser. "He thought that communism was a menace," but not to the extent that it would be a reason for not granting statehood. (Smyser interview)

"work is being done": Allen to Farrington, April 29, 1948, 68-D.

"Hall was much in evidence": Allen to Farrington, May 3, 1948, 73-D.

"My observation": Allen to Farrington, May 5, 1948, 77-D.

Hall looked at politics: DeMello, McElrath, Tangen. "He was my teacher," said DeMello. In an interview McElrath explained the ILWU approach to politics:

Question: Do you ever extract promises from candidates you say you'll support?

Answer: We choose to call them commitments and sometimes we have [obtained them] in the past and I assume we will continue. . . .

Question:	Does the ILWU have a political fund? Money you could give politicians to help them out?
Answer:	No.
Question:	If I came to you as an individual and said, "Can you help me with some money . . . ?"
Answer:	We never use union money. It's against the law. . . . I have and Jack [Hall] have got money from individuals that are liberal and would like to help out in an election and made that money available.
Question:	It isn't union money?
Answer:	No, no. We couldn't touch that. Now we have a political action fund which is voluntary, but that can only be spent by union workers for transportation, printing, sample ballots. *Kau-kau* for people that are working; gas and oil allowances. But we don't give it to the politicians. . . .
Question:	Did Jack Hall call all the shots in politics?
Answer:	No. His advice was listened to and generally accepted.

"foregone conclusion": Hall to Imori, April 21, 1948.

"like his buddy": ibid.

"continue to give leadership": Imori to Hall, Robertson, David Thompson, and Meske, April 22, 1948.

"a modus operandi": Hall to Robertson, July 31, 1948.

"usual red-baiting": Hall to Robertson, September 8, 1948.

"Republicans are split": ibid.

"too far ahead": Hall to Goldblatt, November 1, 1948.

"responded quickly": ibid.

"Shades of 1946!": ibid.

"luckier than we have a right": Hall to Goldblatt, November 5, 1948.

"pack a good vote": ibid.

"we turned the trick": ibid.

"big Hilo vote": ibid.

Kealoha "promised": ibid.

"chance of influencing": ibid.

"betrayed the principles": Hall to Burns, November 16, 1949.

"a lot of phonies": Kido interview.

"should clear minds": *S-B,* November 22, 1949.

[footnote] "dead carcass": Hall's Labor Day speech, September 3, 1962, p. 7.

"One has only to remember": *S-B* editorial, November 18, 1949.

follow Hall's example: *S-B* editorial, November 19, 1949.

"haven't 'turned our back' ": Hall to Curtis Aller, April 27, 1949.

CHAPTER 40: OLAA '48

called "Siberia": Meske to Robertson, Hall, David Thompson, Rania, and Kenji Omuro, August 27, 1948.

a "lunger": ibid., November 16, 1948.

"union is very weak": ibid., May 22, 1948.

"resents interference": ibid., August 27, 1948.

lived in a hut: Meske.

went from camp to camp: *Voice of the ILWU,* June 1977.

"wave my hands": Meske.

picked Takamine: Beechert interview; Takamine.

in "desperate shape": Hall to Goldblatt, June 17, 1948.

pay cuts: *S-B,* August 3, 1948.

might take five-cent cut: ibid. The ILWU assigned researcher Teddy Kreps to analyze Olaa's financial condition. She decided the reason for Olaa's financial crisis was a $3 million overdraft for "capital investment and expansion." Kreps said Olaa made a profit every year from 1941 through 1947, but had not paid a dividend since 1937. (Kreps to Symonds, memorandum, October 25, 1948)

The Olaa Sugar Co. annual report for 1948 said Olaa lost $645,285.27 that year because it could not produce 10,000 tons of sugar between October 10 and December 20, while the strike was on.

"a camel passing through": *S-B,* August 3, 1948.

"lower than 78 ½ cents?": Hall to Goldblatt, June 17, 1948.

"hell would break loose": ibid.

wanted to stay in business: Hall to Goldblatt, June 21, 1948.

"hanging on their jobs": Fujisaki to Robertson, June 3, 1948.

"Their stock answer": McElrath to Robertson, July 6, 1948.

"a rough winter": Hall to Goldblatt, June 21, 1948.

wanted to liquidate: Goldblatt to Hall, August 29, 1948.

distributed leaflets: Hall to Robertson, September 8, 1948.

Management winning: Fujisaki to Robertson, October 16, 1948.

"Too many figures": Meske to Robertson, October 28, 1948.

didn't have spirit: Fujisaki to Robertson, October 14, 1948.

"long way from solidarity": Goldblatt to Bridges, October 12, 1948. Goldblatt said the events of 1947–1948 showed how weak labor was in Hawaii. He said: "In the case of the ILWU, we are barely coming through with our skins, as in sugar; or making some slight gains, as in longshore; and being generally on the defensive in almost every situation."

whooped and yelled: Thompson to Robertson and Hall, October 12, 1948.

his fourteenth strike: Thompson to Robertson and Hall, October 20, 1948.

"seem to feel": Thompson work report, October 27, 1948.

as little as fifty cents: Meske to Robertson, October 28, 1948.

"majority still asleep": ibid.

Jared Smith's trip: *Adv.,* October 15, 1948.

"refuses to budge": Hall to ILWU division heads, November 16, 1948.

"guerrilla warfare": Hall to Goldblatt and Robertson, November 15, 1948. Hall commented that "there appears to be something phoney in the proposals of both Pioneer Mill and Olaa which relates to some finagling on control. Both plantations are owned by a large number of stockholders with the agency [Amfac] holding not more than 20 per cent of the stock, which may well be that they would like to see these two plantations forced to the wall in order to scare out the small stockholders and seize control of the companies." (Hall to Robertson, confidential memorandum, August 16, 1948)

"bumming": Hall to Goldblatt and Robertson, October 20, 1948.

"awakening the membership": Hall to Goldblatt and Robertson, October 21, 1948.

"guys have been tough": Hall to Goldblatt, November 6, 1948.

called it "sabotage": Hall to Goldblatt, December 1, 1948.

"stick his nose in": Hall to Goldblatt, November 5, 1948.

Christmas party: Fujisaki to Robertson, December 11, 1948.

Steele took a hand: Hall to Goldblatt, December 8, 1948.

prices had risen two dollars a ton: Olaa annual report, 1948. Also *S-B,* December 16, 1948.

"rock the island": Hall to Goldblatt, December 16, 1948.

"threats of starvation": Goldblatt to Hall, December 22, 1948.

"oral understandings": Hall to Meske, December 29, 1948.

never such a luau: Thompson work report, December 20, 1948. The ILWU never forgot Meske's short but vital role. Hall wrote him: "You will be pleased to know that from Kaiwiki through Honokaa there are less than 20 non-union members. . . . Paauilo had 100 per cent membership and only 5 are out of the union at Honokaa. . . . All four units are in rough, tough fighting shape which proves that the foundation you built through the long months in Siberia was a sound one." (Hall to Meske, December 27, 1951)

"who didn't get drunk": Hall to Meske, December 28, 1948.

felt it was his duty: Oshiro to Bridges, December 21, 1948.

"gone on a spree": ibid.

[footnote] never held it against him: Oshiro.

"found him sleeping": Oshiro to Bridges, December 21, 1948.

"guilty of the same offense": ibid.

held Hall in high regard: ibid. Oshiro said: "I think that Jack was one of the greatest guys—very sharp mind. Easy to work with. He wasn't the kind to say, 'I'm the king.' He let you run your show." (Oshiro interview)

"feel very strongly": Oshiro to Bridges, December 21, 1948.

"no matter how small": Oshiro to Bridges, June 16, 1948.

"leadership confused": ibid.

"Brother McElrath": Oshiro to Bridges, September 16, 1948.

CHAPTER 41: A CHAT ON THE WATERFRONT

a friendly chat: Kawano to Bridges, January 20, 1949.

same work, same ships: the basic argument put forth by the ILWU. The union contended that "colonialism" still existed in Hawaii.

Brooks said the ILWU chose to strike the longshore industry rather than the sugar industry because the union was strong in longshore and weak in sugar. (Brooks, *Unionism in Hawaii,* pp. 188–189) McElrath disagreed. He said the sugar industry had no control over prices, but longshore was "a straight pass-on industry." The sugar industry could not afford pay raises at that time, he said. (McElrath interview)

tore at fabric: *S-B,* September 1, 1971. Smyser said: "[The 1949 strike] polarized the island community, raised emotions higher than in World War II, and brought events to the very brink of civil strife."

established the ILWU: 9th ICON, Honolulu, April 2–6, 1951, Report of Officers, pt. 1, p. 2. The report said: "The strike was a long and bitter test of every fibre of our organization in Hawaii and the eventual victory meant the achievement of the same kind of recognition and status that was won by the Mainland longshoremen in the 1934 strike."

as much as a thousand dollars: Hall to Goldblatt, March 18, 1949. Hall said: "This loan business is an old technique of Guard's to get a ring in the guys' noses."

"like longshoremen on the coast": Kawano to Bridges, January 20, 1949.

Ask for fifteen cents: ibid.

offer of eight cents: minutes of longshore negotiations, February 28, 1949.

"passing the buck": press release of Stevedoring Companies of Hawaii (un-dated). It said that historically an arbitrator in a labor dispute was always a "compromiser" and that arbitration "destroys free collective bargaining."

"welcome a strike": Robertson to Goldblatt, February 18, 1949.

"recognize that an interruption": longshore negotiation minutes, March 21, 1949.

"like putting a sword": ibid.

"in the event": Hall's memorandum to ILWU Longshore Executive Board, March 29, 1949.

letters to military commanders: Hall wrote on March 31, 1949, to the following: Rear Adm. C. H. Morris, commandant, 14th Naval District; Maj. Gen. S. L. Parks, commanding general, U.S. Army, Pacific; and to Brig. Gen. Robert F. Travis, commanding general, U.S. Pacific Air Command.

"due to strike coming up": Low to Bridges and Goldblatt, April 1, 1949.

Maybe a month: Schmidt to Watson, August 13, 1949.

$20,000 a day: ibid.

Kealoha, Low, and Queja opinions: confidential memorandum of minutes of ILWU Longshore Negotiating Committee, April 21, 1949.

raised to twelve cents: *Adv.,* May 1, 1949.

Goldblatt rejected it: Waterfront Report No. 8, May 16, 1949. This was one of a series issued by the Stevedoring Companies of Hawaii.

went to see Budge: Goldblatt.

spoke about fifteen-cent offer: Goldblatt. Also Hall's Labor Day speech, September 5, 1955, p. 7.

[footnote] Abe responded: Abe to Starr, July 2, 1949.

"living down here": 9th ICON, pt. 1, p. 162.

CHAPTER 42: MESSAGE TO STALIN: "DEAR JOE"

six ships: *Adv.,* May 3, 1949.

"bedding down": Hall to Glazier, cable, May 3, 1949.

"Dear Joe": Many employers decried the "Dear Joe" editorials. "I think it did more harm than good," said Maxwell. "Even the employers regarded old Thurston as a kind of screwball." (Maxwell interview)

Two thousand men: 1700 were on strike, according to the Territorial Bureau of Research and Statistics.

stayed 157 days: *S-B,* June 1, 1960.

brought 12,000 pounds: *S-B,* May 12, 1949.

[footnote] "lives in Kremlin": *Adv.,* May 10, 1949.

"employer fronts": Goldblatt to Bridges, May 12, 1949.

"can't help but feel": ibid.

make or break: ibid.

"treading on eggs": ibid.

"utterly useless": Goldblatt to Glazier, May 7, 1949.

Farrington was worried: Farrington to Allen, May 13, 1949.

went to see Allen: Allen to Farrington, May 11, 1949, 120-E.

more emotion: ibid.

"hourly more serious": Allen to Morse, June 2, 1949.

"If he gets chance": Goldblatt to Glazier, May 7, 1949.

two thousand telegrams: *Adv.,* May 14, 1949.

show "Dear Joe" editorials: Goldblatt to Glazier, May 13, 1949.

unloaded a thousand bags: *Adv.,* May 29, 1949. Aaron Marcus of Dairymen's

Association said that cattlemen, their relatives, and friends unloaded the feed in forty-eight hours by working around the clock. (Marcus interview)

"out to knife": Bridges to Glazier, telex (undated).

"a Communist strategy": *Adv.,* May 25, 1949.

five major strikes: Steele to Low (undated).

"This is it": *Adv.,* May 25, 1949.

"No one is going to starve": *Adv.,* May 26, 1949.

"CANNOT EXAGGERATE": Stainback to James P. Davis, cable, May 6, 1949.

"card-carrying Communists": Stainback to Undersecretary of Interior Oscar L. Chapman, August 11, 1949.

"a lot of tommyrot": Allen to Farrington, June 16, 1949, 151-E.

union refused: *Adv.,* May 30, 1949.

"attempt to wreck": *Adv.,* May 27, 1949.

"a lot of talk": Mrs. Chester Brown to Stainback, June 9, 1949.

CHAPTER 43: THE BROOM BRIGADE

marching at 10:30: Harry Stroup in *Adv.,* June 1, 1949. Stroup said a carnival spirit prevailed and union picketers mildly poked fun at the women.

ninety percent *haole*: ibid.

"Your leaders": *Adv.,* June 1, 1949. Other signs read: "Get Honest Leaders"; "Don't Let Your Union Leaders Kill Hawaii": "We Need A Clean Sweep"; "Eh, Balala, Come With Tita." ILWU counterpickets carried signs that said: "Big 5, Let's Share The Profits" and "Get The Facts From The Union."

heroines: Steele said the women picketers were a clue to the public's feelings about the strike. "I think it did help us in the long run." (Steele interview)

   McElrath disagreed. He said he thought the Broom Brigade "really helped us." (McElrath interview)

"a broom in their hands": McElrath.

"don't have to recruit": *Adv.,* June 10, 1949.

talked it over: Mrs. Holmes; Mrs. Robinson; Mrs. Forde; E. E. Black.

demonstration on Merchant Street: Mrs. Forde. Also Allen to Farrington, June 2, 1949, 136-E.

"Let's hit Farrington": Mrs. Forde.

meeting at McInerny's: Mrs. Forde.

[footnote] "Edited by McElrath?": McElrath.

agreed to try: Mrs. Forde.

sent Stainback a letter: Anthony to Stainback, June 3, 1949.

"concerted action": ibid.

[footnote] lasted ten days: Allen to George S. Dale, American Newspaper Publishers Association, August 1, 1949.

"While the court": Anthony to Stainback, June 3, 1949.

follow-up memorandum: Anthony to Stainback, June 7, 1949.

"A second cause": ibid.

"an affected citizen": Stainback didn't agree with Anthony. Anthony himself later (Anthony interview) had second thoughts about the "second cause"—that is, that the strike was a plot to overcome the government:

Question: Did you really mean that?
Answer: No, I don't think there was anything to that.

"What I have in mind": Hill to Stainback, June 9, 1949.

worked sixty hours: Corbett to Stainback, July 13, 1949.

kill fifteen thousand chicks: Corbett to Stainback, June 1, 1949.

Hospitals were short: Corbett to Stainback, June 10, 1949. Also E. B. Weidknecht, Hotel Import Co., to Stainback, June 8, 1949.

embalming fluid: C. L. Wilbar, Jr., president, Territorial Board of Health, to Stainback, June 9, 1949.

yeast in short supply: Corbett to Stainback, May 28, 1949.

needed hawsers: Young Brothers to Stainback, July 22, 1949.

navy transport sailed: *S-B,* June 2, 1949.

accused Matson: ILWU communication, July 11, 1949.

"terms and conditions": *Adv.,* August 7, 1949.

Some companies: *S-B,* June 4, 1949.

Sugar piled up: *S-B,* June 6, 1949.

Desha said: *Adv.,* June 6, 1949.

"Hundreds of merchants": Allen to Farrington, June 8, 1949, 141-E.

Thurston appealed: *Adv.,* June 11, 1949. In 1949, ten to fifteen percent of the longshoremen were Hawaiian.

Maldonado came: ibid.; also Schmidt to Watson, June 14, 1949.

beaten in a café: *Adv.,* June 15, 1949. The assailants were convicted. Maldonado was expelled from the union.

listened only to planters: Glazier to Hall, June 8, 1949.

"vigilante type": ibid.

"vastly reduced rations": *St. Louis Globe-Democrat,* June 28, 1949.

asked Truman to intervene: Glazier to Hall, June 8, 1949.

Morse had called: Bridges and Goldblatt to Truman, cable, June 27, 1949.

denounced double-page ads: Glazier to Bridges, telex, June 24, 1949. The ads ran on June 23 in the *Times* and *Star* and on June 24 in the *Post.* Author Charles Larrowe said Thurston paid for them. (Larrowe's book, *Harry Bridges,* p. 276)

"Through those mediums": Bridges to Truman, June 27, 1949.

no authority to do so: Glazier to Hall, June 8, 1949.

Ching offered: Glazier to Bridges and Goldblatt, telex, June 3, 1949.

second "Big Five": Schmidt to Howard Bodine, ILWU Coast Labor Relations Committee, June 23, 1949.

serving 1300 meals: Schmidt to Local 10, San Francisco, June 16, 1949.

deep-sea turtles: *S-B,* August 19, 1949; also Schmidt interview. The Maui people brought over fifteen 250-pound turtles.

"some strikers": Schmidt to Local 10, June 16, 1949.

CHAPTER 44: FACT-FINDING: THE FIRST DIALOGUE

appointed a board: Glazier gave the ILWU credit. He said the union had talked "confidentially" to the conciliation service. (Glazier to Bridges, June 17, 1949)

"to call it fact-finding": minutes of "Reports of Proceedings before Emergency Fact-Finding Board," Honolulu, June 16-24, 1949, p. 49.

"already has approval": Schmidt to Bodine, June 23, 1949.

"any reasonable proposal": Allen to Farrington, June 15, 1949, 150-E.

mistook him for lawyer: Fact-Finding Board transcript, p. 116.

"will be most eager": ibid., p. 28.

"conspicuous by absence": *New York Times,* June 18, 1949.

"trying to conduct": Fact-Finding Board transcript, pp. 53-54.

"exactly zero": ibid., p. 59.

"waste time": ibid., p. 64.

"fold our tents": ibid., p. 65.

"I have known": ibid., p. 321.

"All they are trying": ibid., p. 96.

[footnote] earned $11.20: ibid., p. 252.

"Squeezing along": ibid., p. 144.

"cargo smashed": ibid., p. 188.

"completely unrealistic": ibid., p. 333.

"stevedores highest paid": ibid., p. 339.

"I don't say": ibid., p. 404.

"never a just strike": ibid., p. 668.

"Interesting!": ibid., p. 694.

proceedings adjourned: ibid., p. 732. The record consists of 732 pages of transcript; 51 union exhibits of 200 pages; 49 employer exhibits of 343 pages; 9 board exhibits, citations, and references; documents and national fact-finding reports.

recommend fourteen cents: Fact-Finding Board report, p. 38.

left space blank: Brooks, *Unionism in Hawaii,* p. 196.

Hall told the longshoremen: *Adv.,* July 1, 1949.

"protect bargaining position": Brooks, *Unionism in Hawaii,* p. 197.

CHAPTER 45: HOT DAYS, HOT CARGO, HOT WORDS

"Out of Trenches": *S-B,* July 16, 1949.

"Bundles for Hawaii": *San Francisco News,* August 1, 1949. "Nobody is starving," said reporter Keyes Beech. "Celery is $1.25 a stalk. So nobody eats celery. Potatoes were 25 and 28 cents a pound during one shortage but are down to 8 cents." (*Chicago Daily News,* August 18, 1949)

"Hall's Belly": *Adv.,* July 2, 1949. Mrs. Hall said her husband always donated his salary—"the total amount"—to the union when the ILWU went on strike.

"communist brickbats": Allen to Farrington, June 30, 1949, 159-E.

"without producing facts": Allen to Farrington, July 7, 1949, 166-E.

"largely obscured": *Philadelphia Inquirer,* June 28, 1949.

life under Communists: Thurston to Truman, cable, July 8, 1949.

Knowland suggested: UP, Washington, July 8, 1949.

"We won't be smashed": *Adv.,* July 22, 1949.

"last meeting": Hall to Bridges, July 5, 1949.

"Morale is excellent": ibid.

McLaughlin signed: *Adv.,* July 9, 1949. "Thank God for McLaughlin," said an *Advertiser* editorial (July 9).

"will try anything": Hall to Bridges, cable, July 1, 1949.

"provoke hysteria": Hall to Bridges, July 5, 1949.

"preserve my dignity": Bridges to Hall, July 6, 1949.

ILWU charged: ILWU to all longshore and ship clerks locals, July 25, 1949.

"scabs doing": Schmidt to Local 10, July 18, 1949.

clubs, bottles: *Adv.,* July 21, 1949.

"tired of this place": *Adv.* July 30, 1949.

"hot cargo": *S-B,* July 30, 1949.

refused to unload: ibid.

MEW Associates: Esposito.

[footnote] members of splinter fleet: Schmidt to Glazier, memorandum, August 30, 1949.

had to pay $999: Esposito. "We don't enjoy this barge shipping," said Sundai

Choi, treasurer of Hawaii Bakery Supply Co. "Costs are terrific." (*S-B,* September 3, 1949)

touched off an uproar: *Adv.,* September 9, 1949. Brooks said the splinter fleet was a "major element contributing to the ultimate capitulation of the stevedoring companies." (Brooks, *Unionism in Hawaii,* p. 222)

"The Chamber of Commerce": Schmidt to Bodine, September 2, 1949.

"tremendous dissension": Maxwell.

"right down our alley": Bridges to Schmidt, July 7, 1949.

Bridges met Blaisdell: Thomas Committee: minutes of Hearing on Hawaiian Labor Situation before Senate Committee on Labor and Public Welfare, 81st Congress, 1st Session, 1949.

"never be any more bargaining": Thomas Committee, p. 59.

wouldn't play game: ibid., p. 79.

"Instead of treating it": ibid., p. 101.

"whip them baldheaded": ibid., p. 108.

"How would that": ibid., p. 107.

trying to subvert: ibid., p. 130.

"We are after": ibid., p. 132. Bridges defined a left-wing union as a union "that believes its officers should be easy to remove and should function under a setup where their wages and expenses are no more than the highest paid . . . worker that is a member of the union." At the time Bridges was getting $145 a week plus expenses.

"Do you have any Communists?": ibid., p. 132.

"I have a twenty-dollar bill": ibid., p. 121.

"grandstand play": Bridges.

"hemmed and hawed": Bridges to Hall and Schmidt, July 18, 1949.

bested Blaisdell: ibid.

Hall asked Burns: Burns.

"we'll find you some": Burns.

"that's unthinkable": Burns.

"but a labor dispute": Burns. Burns was wrong if he thought that Murray and the National CIO helped the ILWU during the 1949 strike. Hall said bitterly: "Will any longshoremen ever forget during that strike that our sister CIO unions and the National CIO failed to send a single message of moral support, let alone a dirty 50-cent piece out of the hundreds of thousands of per capita dollars we sent them?" (Hall in Labor Day speech, September 4, 1950, p. 2)

The ILWU got support from the Marine Cooks and Stewards and from the Marine Firemen. They did not get support from the Sailors' Union of the Pacific. (Schmidt to Watson, memorandum, May 9, 1949)

"Holy name!": Oral History Project, Chinn Ho Foundation, Tape 8, p. 24.

"have a good visit": Burns.

"I'm nobody": Burns.

CHAPTER 46: THE TERRITORY RUNS THE DOCKS

special session: *Adv.,* July 8, 1949.

Stainback asked for legislation: *Adv.,* July 15, 1949.

grave atmosphere: *Adv.,* July 27, 1949.

"must ensure shipping": *Adv.,* July 15, 1949.

"strikebreaking bill": *Adv.,* July 27, 1949.

"wishy-washy": *Adv.,* July 29, 1949.

knew bill would pass: Schmidt to Bridges, July 29, 1949.

old reliable: Fernandes said: "I voted for the Dock Seizure Bill. [Hall] never asked me why. He knew I believed in that. He never said a word." (Fernandes interview)

"bigoted old man": Hall in *ILWU Reporter,* August 10, 1949.

rammed through: Bridges to Glazier, August 15, 1949. Bridges said the Dock Seizure Act prolonged the strike. "We won the strike all right, but it took a few extra months to do it." (Bridges testifying at hearing before Senate Committee on Labor and Public Welfare, Washington, April 29, 1953, p. 4)

marched for last time: *Adv.,* August 8, 1949.

right to take over: The act called for four things: (1) The governor could proclaim a state of emergency; (2) he could take over the stevedoring companies and designate a government agency to operate the docks in the name of the territory; (3) strikers and stevedoring company personnel got preference in hiring; (4) companies received fair compensation. The territory deducted all expenses, insurance, and taxes, plus one quarter of one percent of the gross.

Friel seized: *S-B,* August 10, 1949.

Ackerman boarded: Bridges to Glazier, August 15, 1949.

"in spite of Bridges": Stainback to Oscar Chapman, August 11, 1949.

"many members of ILWU": ibid. Captain C. F. May, national president of the AFL Masters, Mates and Pilots, said ILWU members in the pineapple canneries handled tinplate brought in by ship and that ILWU sugar workers handled fertilizer. (*Adv.,* August 24, 1949)

Brooks commented: "In Hawaii, the ILWU was very weak, so weak in fact that its members, especially of the sugar and pineapple locals, scabbed in great numbers." (Brooks, *Unionism in Hawaii,* p. 244)

"What worried Stainback": UP, San Francisco, August 19, 1949.

"a million ships": Hall in *ILWU Reporter,* October 5, 1949.

won "hands down": ibid., August 24, 1949.

"like social lepers": ILWU pamphlet, August 19, 1949.

Allen summed up: *S-B* editorial, August 15, 1949.

"The feeling is": *S-B* editorial, August 25, 1949.

"The Hawaiian employers": Bridges to Samuel Hogan, MEBA president, August 4, 1949.

"government strikebreaking": Glazier to ten senators, August 18, 1949. Senator Taft replied: "It is intolerable that one man [Bridges] can bring about this condition." (Taft to Glazier, August 31, 1949)

"Although Hawaii employers": ILWU teletype conference, August 4, 1949.

"costing them plenty": *ILWU Reporter,* October 5, 1949.

"nuts, plain nuts": *Adv.,* August 6, 1949.

KIPA interview: Bridges was interrogated on the night of August 8 by Jim Wallace and Ron Bennett of the *Hilo Tribune-Herald* and Tom O'Brien of the Hawaii press. Wallace asked why Hall dictated to the ILWU membership in Hawaii. Bridges said: "Jack Hall does not dictate for the union here or anywhere else. Neither does Bridges or any other officer of the union. The membership run the union." (Transcript of interview, p. 4)

"But a lot of other people": ibid., p. 21.

obtained court order: First Circuit Court, Equity No. 5128, August 15, 1949.

"next day or two": Bridges to Glazier, August 15, 1949.

"this stinking mess": *S-B,* August 16, 1949.

"right of free speech": ibid.

"boys felt that way": *Adv.,* August 14, 1949.

world seemed allied: IEB, San Francisco, November 11–13, 1949, pp. 12–13. Bridges said: "The other side hit us with everything in the book. They had such a lynch spirit in the islands that it was dangerous even to walk down the street. . . . The governor of Hawaii passed a phony law. . . . From Washington they were backing the governor."

[footnote] Corbett summed up: Corbett to Stainback, final report, November 21, 1949.

review of stevedoring operations: Schmidt to Bodine, August 20, 1949.

powerless to stop: IEB, San Francisco, November 11, 1949, p. 13. Bridges said: "When they passed the phony law over there, they were able to recruit enough scabs to load the ships and our ability to stop the ships from being loaded was nil."

"helping to break": Bridges to Samuel Hogan, August 4, 1949.

"hot ship" coming: Consider the "hot pine" barge. Hawaiian Pineapple Co. loaded the barge at Lanai and it was towed by nonunion employees of Isleways, Ltd., a Hawaiian Pine subsidiary. The barge with $800,000 worth of pineapple was towed first to Tacoma, where ILA longshoremen refused to unload it. The "frustrated barge," as the ILWU called it, then went around Puget Sound. Airplanes followed its unhappy course. Finally it was towed up the Columbia River past the Bonneville locks to The Dalles and there an attempt was made to unload it. (9th ICON, Honolulu, April 2–6, 1951, p. 7)

At The Dalles a single picket (Fred Low, of Hilo) patrolled the waterfront. Matt Meehan, the ILWU's man in Portland, sent longshoremen to The Dalles. They arrived while town people were unloading the cargo. Some of Meehan's men were armed with axes, sledges, knives, and rocks. They broke through the police lines. "Get those finks!" they shouted. Six men were hurt. The unloading stopped. (UP, The Dalles, September 26 and 28, 1949)

"100 per cent tied up": Schmidt to Bodine, August 10, 1949.

Ehrlich mission: Ehrlich to Budge, April 15, 1958; Bridges and Steele interviews; *Adv.,* August 15, 1969.

Hall, Schmidt, and Symonds met him: Ehrlich to Budge, April 15, 1958.

"worked three solid weeks": ibid.

"maligned me": ibid.

CHAPTER 47: THE BATTLE OF WORDS

running court battle: The lengthy legal fight is detailed in Paul F. Brissenden's "The Great Hawaiian Dock Strike," pp. 231–279.

Dairymen's libel action: *Dairymen's Association, Ltd.,* v. *S.S. Hawaiian Citizen,* U.S. Federal District Court, District of Hawaii, in Admiralty, No. 413.

$3 million damage: *Longshore and Allied Workers of Hawaii, Local 136, of the International Longshoremen's and Warehousemen's Union,* a voluntary unincorporated association and labor union, et al. v. *Wilfred C. Tsukiyama,* individually and as President of the Senate of the Territory of Hawaii, et al. Civil No. 930. Named as defendants were Tsukiyama and fourteen other territorial senators; Hiram L. Fong, speaker of the Territorial House, and twenty-three other territorial representatives; Governor Stainback; Attorney General Ackerman; the seven stevedoring companies; and others.

[footnote] "a dollar an hour": *Adv.,* August 17, 1949.

caustic perfectionist: *Adv.,* September 6, 1949.

cabled Denman: Brissenden, "Dock Strike," pp. 258–259.

"a windy guy": *Adv.,* September 1, 1949. Bridges was the star attraction. The court was jammed and people lined two deep against the walls waiting to get in and hear him. (*S-B,* August 31, 1949)

"yellow-dog contract": *Adv.,* September 1, 1949.

suffering grievously: *Adv.,* September 13, 1949.

"vehement": *ILWU* v. *Tsukiyama,* "Ruling upon Motion for a Preliminary Injunction," September 28, 1949, p. 2.

"not obviously void": ibid., pp. 8–9.

"patently invalid": *Adv.,* September 29, 1949.

"territorial meddling": *ILWU* v. *Tsukiyama,* "Ruling upon Motion," p. 10.

a valid exercise: ibid., pp. 11–12.

"hands-down victory": *Adv.,* September 29, 1949.

ILWU setback: *S-B,* September 30, 1949.

Thurston saw: *Adv.,* September 30, 1949.

injunctive suit: *Territory of Hawaii,* by W. D. Ackerman, Attorney General, v. *International Longshoremen's and Warehousemen's Union, Local 136, Longshore and Allied Workers of Hawaii; Jack W. Hall, Robert McElrath, Emilio C. Yadao, Levi Kealoha, Yukio Abe, and John Doe 1 to John Doe 100,* Equity No. 5128.

case against Bridges: The territory filed a petition on August 18 against Bridges and Rutledge to show cause why they should not be punished for contempt.

territory won right: The Dock Seizure Act was never again invoked during Hall's lifetime. At each legislative session during Hall's regional directorship, legislators friendly to the ILWU introduced legislation to wipe off the books the amended Dock Seizure Act (Act 209, approved in May 1951, which followed Acts 2 and 3), but they never succeeded.

Maxwell-Bridges exchange: HEC meeting, August 17, 1949.

Steele-Bridges exchange: ibid.

"somebody told me": HEC meeting, August 18, 1949.

Robinson-Bridges exchange: HEC meeting, August 19, 1949.

"What about me?": ibid.

time for a third party: HEC meeting, August 30, 1949.

a summons: Brooks, *Unionism in Hawaii,* p. 229. Also Richard F. MacMillan in *Adv.,* September 7, 1949.

"climb Pike's Peak": Employers Council release, August 30, 1949.

"I have no magic": minutes of joint session of employers and union with Ching. (September 7, 1949, p. 1). Ching alternately met with each side separately and then in joint session.

stayed at Plaza: *S-B,* September 9, 1949.

"meet, eat, and meet some more": ibid.

He scared them: Ching, September 8, 1949. Babbitt also said they were leery of Margolis.

opened on a harsh note: Ching, September 7, 1949, p. 1.

"not like Deep South": ibid., p. 4.

"let's stay with it": ibid.

"getting this thing settled": *Adv.,* September 8, 1949.

Ching-Steele exchange: Ching, September 8, 1949, p. 2.

"nothing concrete": *Adv.,* September 9, 1949.

fourteen-cent raise: Ching, September 8, 1949, p. 4. Babbitt told Ching he didn't understand the situation in Hawaii. "It doesn't make sense to have longshoremen get more than teachers, truck drivers, etc.," he told Ching. (ibid.)

"isn't that kind of a guy": Ching, September 9, 1949, p. 2.

"plenty of nerve": ibid.

"pretty far apart": *Adv.,* September 10, 1949.

shifted tactics: Harry Weitig of the New York office of Theo. H. Davies phoned Hawaii every day at 5:30 PM, New York time.

"might be a deal": Ching, September 10, 1949, p. 2.

"He is bluffing": ibid., p. 4.

"Would you jump?": ibid., p. 5.

"curt, morose": *Adv.,* September 11, 1949.

"interested in licking": Ching, September 12, 1949, p. 1.

"hopelessly far apart": ibid., p. 13.

"Hopeless Deadlock": *S-B,* September 12, 1949.

CHAPTER 48: ALL WARS FINALLY END

Buck called Bridges: Bridges. Buck's role in settling the strike generally was regarded as important. Bridges said: "I left here with Buck and we went down and finally got the thing straightened out. Buck's pressure had a lot to do with it."

Goldblatt said: "[Buck] was enormously important."

There was a minority dissenting opinion. Murphy said he did not think much of Buck's efforts. "There are people who emerge out of the air in a strike and they go away."

"down at 8": Bridges.

Davies and Roth: *San Francisco Chronicle,* October 7, 1949.

invited Steele: Steele.

who would give in: *ILWU Dispatcher,* October 14, 1949.

505,025 tons: *S-B,* October 1, 1949.

$800,000 a month: Brooks, *Unionism in Hawaii,* p. 152.

Brewer's weak cash position: ibid., p. 253. Brewer's precarious financial position was noted by Bridges, Babbitt, McElrath, Maxwell, and Murphy.

wrote in protest: Hall to Arthur Miller, Federal Security Agency, San Francisco, August 16, 1949.

arranged with diocese: A. Q. McElrath to Father McDonald, superintendent of Catholic schools, August 23, 1949.

arranged for deferment: A. Q. McElrath to W. Harold Loper, superintendent of schools, August 24, 1949.

wrote Kamehameha School: letter to Pauline Fredericks, principal, August 17, 1949.

sent twenty dollars: Hall to McFadden, July 29, 1949. Hall sent the letter to McFadden in care of the Honta store in Kaaawa.

began informal talks: *Adv.,* September 30, 1949.

"not too far apart": Schmidt, memorandum, September 26, 1949.

[footnote] sought $33,600: requests were made in separate letters (undated), and on September 9, by Mamoru Yamasaki, secretary of Local 136.

[footnote] $150,000 in debt: Hall to Charles V. Kershaw, Camden, N.J., December 1, 1949.

[footnote] contributed $20,000: LEB, United Sugar Workers, Camp Erdman, Oahu, January 19–20, 1950, p. 12.

"very good progress": *San Francisco Call-Bulletin,* September 29, 1949.

"within a short period": INS, September 29, 1949.

levers of power: Brooks, *Unionism in Hawaii,* pp. 250–253.

"I feel cheerful": *Adv.,* October 2, 1949.

"agreement all worked out": IEB, San Francisco, November 11, 1949, p. 13.

meeting with Steele: Steele; Brooks, *Unionism in Hawaii,* p. 256.

unloaded 100,000 tons: *Adv.,* October 5, 1949. The harbor was jammed with shipping. A headline said: "Island Waterfront Tonnage Nearing Non-Strike Normal." (ibid.)

"if we could hold out": Brooks, *Unionism in Hawaii,* p. 259.

"betray the rest": ibid., p. 260.

special meeting: ibid., pp. 260–263.

"Honolulu in uproar": Schmidt to F. T. Moore, ILWU Local 13, Wilmington, Calif., October 6, 1949.

doubted the strike was over: ibid.

"beef is over": ibid.

bedecked with leis: *Adv.,* October 7, 1949.

Bridges had called Steele: Allen to Farrington, October 7, 1949, 193-E.

visited Hall: McElrath.

with an open line: McElrath.

fast-moving Epstein: Allen to Farrington, October 7, 1949.

"really give 'em hell": Brooks, *Unionism in Hawaii,* p. 263.

"Steele hasn't called": *Adv.,* October 7, 1949.

"I have negotiated": *S-B,* October 6, 1949.

Erickson signaled: McElrath.

within three minutes: Allen to Farrington, October 7, 1949.

At that very moment: Steele.

announcement premature: Steele.

"double-crossed" them: Allen to Farrington, October 7, 1949. Maxwell said the Bridges settlement "differed slightly from our position, but the settlement stuck." (Maxwell interview)

he was telling the employers: Steele.

"shouldn't have been announced": Steele.

"outsmarted the employers": Allen to Farrington, October 7, 1949.

"as Bridges had described it": ibid.

agreed to a fourteen-cent raise: Stainback felt the settlement followed the recommendation of his fact-finding board. He so cabled Secretary of Interior Krug on October 6, 1949.

"accept it again": *Adv.,* October 7, 1949.

[footnote] "settlement was reached": Allen to Farrington, October 7, 1949.

"pretty stiff shock": ibid.

"It is now clear": *S-B* editorial, October 25, 1949.

24,423 people: E. B. Peterson, director, Territorial Department of Labor, quoted in *S-B,* October 15, 1949.

cut by as much as half: *Adv.,* October 7, 1949. Brooks summed up: "Many people have been inconvenienced; no one had starved; few had been seriously hurt; and Bridges demonstrated that though the government of Hawaii may have run the docks of Hawaii, Bridges ran commerce between Hawaii and the Pacific Coast. (Brooks, *Unionism in Hawaii,* p. 267)

Bridges said the 1949 strike didn't hurt Hawaii. Hall agreed. Maxwell disagreed. (*Adv.,* March 21, 1963)

cost $100 million: *Adv.,* October 6, 1949.

"guaranteed our survival": 9th ICON, Honolulu, April 2–6, 1951, Report of Officers, p. 2.

a quart of gin: *Adv.,* October 8, 1949.

had gone 177 days: the strike lasted from May 1 to October 24. Work resumed on October 25 and 26. Mahukona on the Big Island was strikebound for another month; work resumed there on December 8.

CHAPTER 49: HALL VS. HUAC

prodded them: When Farrington learned that the ILWU was under investigation by the National CIO for alleged Communist leanings, he pressed Rep. Francis Walter, HUAC's chairman, to bring the committee to Hawaii. (Mrs. Farrington interview)

Hall said the ILWU supported Farrington in 1946 "for good, sufficient and honest reasons," but that since then Farrington "has returned to the fold of the Big Five." (Hall over KHON radio, November 6, 1950)

ILWU opposition in 1950 did not hurt Farrington. He readily beat his opponent, William B. Cobb (Farrington, 71,271 votes; Cobb, 40,612). Stainback induced Cobb to run and promised him financial support. Cobb said he kept the promise. (Cobb interview)

"Plenty of witnesses": Hall to Goldblatt, February 13, 1950.

"Whatever the march": Allen to Farrington, March 29, 1950, 65-F.

reading magazines: *S-B,* April 13, 1950.

"a triple dose": *S-B,* April 11, 1950.

Hall-Tavenner exchange: transcript of Hearings before the Committee on Un-American Activities, House of Representatives, 81st Congress, 2nd Session, 1950, p. 1538.

only five minutes: *S-B,* April 13, 1950.

twenty-six ILWU members: Hall, Kawano, McElrath, Yukio Abe, John Akana, Yasuki Arakaki, Ernest Arena, Edward Hong, Kameo Ichimura, Koichi Imori, Douglas Inouye, Benjamin Kahaawinui, Frank Kalua, Jr., Levi Kealoha, Marshall McEuen, Yoshito Marumo, Robert Murasaki, Julian Napuunoa, Tadashi Ogawa, Hideo Okada, Ruth Ozaki, Mitsuo Shimizu, Frank G. Silva, Frank Takahashi, Ralph Tokunaga, and Thomas S. Yagi.

The other thirteen were Esther M. Bristow, Dwight James Freeman, Pearl Freeman, Charles Fujimoto, Adele Kensinger, Denichi Kimoto, Stephen Murin, Wilfred Oka, John Reinecke, Jeanette Nakama Rohrbough, Rachel Saiki, Shigeo Takemoto, and Ralph Vossbrink.

"smear and discredit": Hall in a statement, April 14, 1950.

[footnote] "unless we are in compliance": Hall in *ILWU Reporter,* July 12, 1950.

"been through too much": Hall statement, April 14, 1950.

"A 'yes' or 'no' ": ibid.

practically none: Hall to Glazier, April 25, 1950.

"rumblings below": Hall to Goldblatt, May 13, 1950.

"now strongly opposed": *S-B,* April 18, 1950.

"for me to clear myself": Nakano. On December 23, 1952, Nakano's local (155) voted to disaffiliate from the ILWU. (Nakano to Robertson, December 24, 1952) Nakano said he wanted to be "free from suspicion" of Communist taint. (*S-B,* December 29, 1952) The majority of the local worked at the Canec Division of the Flintcote Company in Hilo.

In 1955 the ILWU beat Nakano by a single vote in a representation election. In 1957, with the help of the AFL-CIO, the ILWU defeated Nakano's attempt to recapture the right to represent the 283 employees of Flintcote, by a 211 to 56 vote (*S-B,* July 4, 1957) Nakano went to work for the AFL-CIO Operating Engineers in Hilo.

Kawano called Inouye: Inouye, Kawano.

"I'm a member": Inouye.

thinking of political career: Burns.

"I am not a Communist": *S-B,* April 19, 1950.

decided in 1948: Kawano.

served for fifteen years: letter from Kawano to delegates, 9th Biennial ILWU Convention, Honolulu, April 5, 1951.

"purpose of testing": Hall to Yagi, Silva, Ichimura, Shimizu, Murasaki, and Takahashi, October 11, 1950.

gave six-dollar check: Hall to Goldblatt, May 13, 1950. The HUAC concluded that Charles Fujimoto was chairman of the Communist Party of Hawaii, but that the Party was "actually headed by Jack W. Hall." (*S-B,* January 20, 1951)

> Hall said Rep. Walter was not telling the truth. "Members of the Communist Party will find the UnAmericans' report both amusing and entertaining," he said. (Ibid.)

voted to try ILWU: *ILWU Dispatcher,* November 11, 1949. Bridges said: "When one really moves to find out what the shooting is all about, it is that the ILWU is fully controlled by its rank and file. . . . This the National CIO does not allow. . . ."

"kangaroo court": *S-B,* May 15, 1950.

began writing expulsion order: Paul Jacobs, *The State of the Unions* (New York: Atheneum, 1963), p. 90.

"We can take care of ourselves": *S-B,* May 15, 1950.

union more vulnerable and out of mainstream: Larrowe *Harry Bridges,* p. 325.

Hawaii held elections: primary election, February 11; general election, March 21. The Constitutional Convention opened April 4 and went until July 22, 1950. (Hawaii State Archives)

a key delegate: Kido.

Kido's background: Kido.

"I want you folks": Kido.

"Well, Mits": Kido.

[footnote] plunked: a political term meaning to vote for one candidate alone and no others, thereby adding weight to that vote.

"I got snowed": Kido was one of the organizers of the Democratic Party. He said the ILWU came into the party after the war "lock, stock, and barrel." Later, Hall told him that it was a mistake for the union to be tied to one party. "It's not in the interest of the union," Hall told Kido. (Kido interview)

Hall drew a conclusion: Hall to Goldblatt, February 13, 1950. Hall predicted the state constitution would be "of a decidedly reactionary nature." (Hall to Glazier, April 25, 1950) The ILWU opposed the constitution but it passed by 3 to 1 margin.

"balance of power": Hall to Goldblatt, February 13, 1950.

"It would be tragic": Hall to King, April 14, 1950.

McElrath wrote the speech: McElrath.

"his contumacious behavior": *S-B,* April 21, 1950.

"They regarded him": *S-B,* April 22, 1950.

"voted the guy out": McElrath. Silva was stubborn. In 1960 he was given a job by Kauai County Chairman Tony Baptiste as a laborer in the waterworks. But Silva refused to take the loyalty oath as required, lost his job, and could not be paid for the four months he had worked. "My reason for not signing was that it was inconsistent if I took one action in 1950 [at the Constitutional Convention] and then another in 1960. . . . I would look like a hypocrite." (Silva interview)

> For years—pressed by Hall—"Frank Silva bills" were introduced in the

legislature to modify the loyalty oath provision and the personal history requirements for public job-seekers (and to pay Silva for his work). It came to pass that any bill that sought to limit personal history declarations for job-seekers became known as a "Frank Silva bill."

Act 304, passed by the 1967 legislature, finally gave Silva the right to collect his long-overdue pay. It came to $998.07 with six percent interest.

CHAPTER 50: "STANDPATTERS" VS. "WALKOUTERS"

"Unless Stainback is able": Hall to Fred Low, Bert Nakano, Wataru Kawamoto, Blackie Kinoshita, Yoshikazu Morimoto, and Takumi Akama, March 31, 1950.

"preferably [to] ILWU": Hall to Yagi, March 31, 1950.

Oka worked: Oka.

fourteen delegates: Holmes, "Specter of Communism," p. 230.

challenged the proxies: Kawano Hearing: Hearing before the Committee on Un-American Activities, House of Representatives, 82nd Congress, 1st Session, July 6, 1951, p. 50. Also Esposito interview.

drop 39-ers: Holmes, "Specter of Communism," p. 232.

"sinister infiltration": Hite to Stainback, January 27, 1948. This letter was marked for identification as Plaintiff's Exhibit No. 154 in the Smith Act trial.

"wildly cheered": Pence's hand-written notes on the convention, dated May 2, 1950, which he made available to the writer.

ninety-one walked out: Holmes, "Specter of Communism," p. 232.

"Those fellows walked": Right-wing Democrats of that day often were careless about whom they called "Communists." They applied the term indiscriminately. Takahashi, a twice-wounded 100th Battalion company commander, was a victim. When he first ran for office in 1950, he was labeled "a Communist" by people in Kaneohe who mounted a campaign against him. (Takahashi interview)

"CONVENTION SPLIT": Allen to Farrington, cable, May 1, 1950.

"Lau Ah Chew–Burns group": ibid.

"new Democratic Party": *Adv.*, May 1, 1950.

gentle Lau Ah Chew: Esposito's adjective.

"allied in public mind": Smyser in *S-B*, May 23, 1950.

"People like myself": ibid.

"two ways we can fight": *S-B*, September 2, 1950.

"left-wing appellation": Allen to Farrington, May 23, 1950, 82-F.

"hostile witnesses": ibid.

first person purged: *S-B*, May 12, 1950.

trial of Reluctant 39: *United States* v. *Yukio Abe,* Criminal No. 10,355; *United States* v. *John L. Akana,* Criminal No. 10,336; and other consolidated cases.

turned on the Blau case: Holmes, "Specter of Communism," pp. 259–260.

"like Rock of Gibraltar": ruling by Metzger in *United States* v. *Abe.*

"The Communist Party . . . have their rights": ibid.

"So far as I am concerned": ibid.

CHAPTER 51: "SILENT JACK" SPEAKS

"converted" him: Kawano, Burns, Mau, Kido, and Takahashi. Also Kawano Hearing, p. 52.

met for a year: Mau.

"I can't come out": Mau.

blamed Hall: Kawano said he harbored no ill will toward Hall. (Kawano interview) In the Smith Act Trial, this exchange took place between Gladstein and Kawano on the witness stand (Smith Act, p. 7233):

Question:	You hate Jack Hall, don't you?
Answer:	I don't. There is no reason.
Question:	You have expressed to people on a number of occasions that you deeply hate him.
Answer:	During 1946—
Question:	First, answer me, yes or no?
Answer:	Now, no.
Question:	You did at various times express to different people that you deeply hated Jack Hall, didn't you?
Answer:	At one time, yes, I did.

demanded leadership: David Thompson. Holmes makes the same point: "There is considerable evidence that as the ILWU grew more complex, as it became an established entity rather than a struggling union looking for a foothold, Kawano's usefulness to the union diminished." (Holmes, "Specter of Communism," p. 284)

"assignment was ducked": statement (mimeographed) by Local 136 Executive Board and adopted at stop-work meeting, August 3, 1951.

take sugar workers out: Kawano Hearing, p. 46. Also Kawano interview.

"personally disgruntled": IEB, Seattle, October 11, 1950, p. 1.

Kawano wouldn't run: *S-B,* November 21, 1949.

worked as janitor: Kawano. He said pressure was put on his employers and he was fired.

"I joined the Communist Party": Kawano's press release, February 10, 1951.

[footnote] "If he had run": ILWU stop-work meeting, August 3, 1951.

"Jack couldn't": *S-B,* February 10, 1951.

"of Kawano's integrity": Saka to Yagi, May 23, 1951.

"I should like": Hall to Niimi, July 6, 1951.

"The Kawano attack": Goldblatt to Bridges, August 14, 1951.

"trying to brush off": Allen to Farrington, February 14, 1951, 43–G.

Dillingham agreed: Dillingham.

"my name would be mud": Kawano.

named names: Kawano Hearing, pp. 8–17, 26–32, 35–39, 44–46.

meeting "held on the grass": ibid., p. 27.

"I believe the influence": ibid., p. 37.

"coming out in the open": ibid., pp. 41–43. Also Kawano interview.

"met opposition": ibid.

"They made policies": Kawano Hearing, p. 49. Kawano said Hall chafed under Communist Party interference and that late in 1948 or early in 1949 Hall went to San Francisco for a showdown. According to Kawano, it was settled that Hall would take orders only from the ILWU International. If there were any problems—that is, any conflict between the ILWU International and Party orders—then the matter would be settled by the Communist Party headquarters in New York. (Kawano Hearing, p. 48. Also Kawano interview)

"they convinced me": Kawano Hearing, p. 52.

"We knew he had": *S-B,* July 31, 1951.

"knows that he lies": ILWU white paper on Kawano, August 3, 1951.

[footnote] "hell of a human being": Burns. No one in the history of the modern labor movement in Hawaii, except Hall and Rutledge, aroused such controversy as Kawano. A quarter of a century after his defection from the union, feelings about him still were uncompromising. A sampling:

Crozier: "A courageous fighter for Justice and Fair Play *[sic]*." (Crozier to Kawano, December 22, 1974)

McElrath: "Kawano was mediocre. On everything [Hall] just brushed Kawano aside." (McElrath interview)

Elias: "He [Kawano] was terrific." (Elias interview)

Berman: "A man [Kawano] who could not communicate. [He] didn't have what it took to assume leadership." (Berman interview)

Reinecke: "He [Kawano] was a tower of strength to the union for several years." (Reinecke interview)

"mixture of lies": *S-B,* July 31, 1951.

conversation with deputy: Mau.

Chapter 52: Lanai '51: the Quiet Battle

"a single camp": Bulletin No. 1, Lanai Unit 7, Local 152, June 25, 1951.

200,000 tons: Phillip Schrader, plantation manager.

"conspiracy of silence": *S-B,* June 25, 1951.

made the decision: Cadagan. "It wasn't a good idea. It left us wide open," said Cadagan.

"We will not soon forget": Hall in *ILWU Reporter,* November 1, 1950.

"Not a single bit": 10th ICON, San Francisco, April 6–11, 1951, p. 466. "There are no privately owned homes on this island," said the Lanai Unit 7 bulletin. "The 'top brass' are all whites, and no dark-skinned individual could be promoted to a superintendent's post, no matter how capable and efficient he is."

Hall said a number of Lanai workers were abruptly discharged in 1949. He claimed that Hawaiian Pine gave them notice on a Friday afternoon, flew them off Lanai on the following Monday, gave them a "jolly public relations banquet" on Tuesday, hung paper leis around their necks, and then shipped them off to the Philippines on Wednesday. (Hall in a talk at the Hawaii Technical School on June 7, 1967)

as a wildcat: Cadagan.

"frustrated thinking": Hall to Goldblatt, May 9, 1951.

"not so subtle": ibid.

"burning house down": ibid.

"anything possible": ibid. Hall was convinced that Hawaiian Pine was willing to lose the summer crop. "The firm is exceedingly arrogant and filthy with money." (Hall to John F. Conway, Portland, Ore., May 17, 1951)

"Convince him": Hall to De la Cruz, March 6, 1951.

strike was puzzling: Jamieson to Zalburg, October 24, 1975.

no useful suggestions: Goldblatt. Hall said: "Mr. Jamieson . . . did practically nothing to bring about a settlement." (Hall over KHON radio, December 4, 1956)

"too few acceptable": Jamieson to Zalburg, October 24, 1975.

thought they had the key: Cadagan.

"We talked about everything": Cadagan.

"hit the floor": Cadagan.

"an extraordinary event": Jamieson to Zalburg, October 24, 1975.

"I resigned": ibid.

[footnote] Jamieson testified: from transcript of Hearings before the Subcommittee to Investigate the Administration of the Internal Security Act, U.S. Senate, 84th Congress, 2nd Session, November 16–30, December 1, 1956, pp. 2368–2372.

$250,000 worth: Goldblatt to Bridges, August 14, 1951.

"knocked off any ideas": ibid.

"How about the Tropics?": Goldblatt.

"If you jot down": Goldblatt.

Playacting at poker: Goldblatt.

"You watch, Lou": Goldblatt.

100,000 tons: figure was agreed upon by Cadagan, by Schrader, the 1976 plantation manager, and by the Hawaiian Pineapple Co. Schrader said the company salvaged 60,000 to 70,000 tons of pineapple.

like a brewery: Shiro Hokama.

"pure alcohol": Goldblatt.

"Just smell that": Goldblatt. To the Lanai workers it was the smell of victory: a successful strike.

"No like": Goldblatt.

"What happened?": Goldblatt.

settlement terms: *ILWU Reporter,* September 19, 1951.

cow pasture: ibid.

thick as a blanket: Hawaiian Pineapple Co. annual report for fiscal year ending May 31, 1952, p. 5.

CHAPTER 53: A KNOCK ON THE DOOR

Hall's arrest: Kreps, Yoshiko Hall, McElrath, Steele. Also 10th ICON, San Francisco, April 6–10, 1953, pp. 54–55.

Fujimoto had announced: Smyser's testimony, Smith Act, p. 6285.

"Momma sent me": Kreps.

"To jail": Kreps.

"just arrested Daddy": McElrath.

"Aren't you going?": Steele. Why wasn't McElrath arrested? One theory is that having indicted Hall, the government would seemingly be engaged in overkill by indicting McElrath too.

everything "buttoned down": Steele. Hall handled negotiations all through the pretrial stage, the trial itself, and the appeal. Steele said he didn't think the Smith Act case hurt employer-union relations and he gave Hall credit for it. "In '46, '47, Jack was a pretty bitter, skeptical guy, but by the time of the Smith Act trial, I think he had really matured. . . ." (Steele interview)

sent back word: Steele.

"torpedo negotiations": 10th ICON, pp. 54–55.

deny right to bail: *S-B,* August 28, 1951.

They all crammed: 10th ICON, p. 55.

called "outrageous": *New York Times,* August 30, 1951.

read *Guild Review:* Hall to George Martin, December 1, 1950.

[footnote] Medina trial: *United States* v. *Dennis,* 183 F. 2nd 201.

"Neither I nor": Hoddick. Gladstein said Hall's indictment "represents the government's determination to break up the ILWU. . . . The lumping together of Fujimoto and Hall in this case must be understood as an effort on the part of the administration to increase its chances of succeeding in the attack on the union. Otherwise, it would have been simpler for the prosecution to indict, not Hall, but the union, that the government is after. . . ." (Gladstein to Bridges, memorandum, November 14, 1951)

In rebuttal, Hoddick said Gladstein was attributing a sinister purpose to the government's indictments. He said: "I think that the motivation of the government, though perhaps mistaken, was certainly bona fide and they were trying to do the job they were sworn by their office to do." (Hoddick interview)

"organization nucleus": *S-B,* August 28, 1951.

[footnote] "I've since had": Hoddick. "Looking back, we probably wasted a lot of time," said Hoddick. "The [Smith Act] trial was too thin, if there was any trial at all. But we believed it at the time."(Holmes, "Specter of Communism," p. 339)

"speak with authority": *ILWU Reporter,* August 23, 1950.

"It matters little": *ILWU Reporter,* December 19, 1951. The official charge against Hall and the other defendants was that from April 1, 1945, they conspired with the Communist Party leadership to violate Section 2 of the Smith Act by "conspiring (1) unlawfully, wilfully, and knowingly to advocate and teach the duty and necessity of overthrowing the government of the United States by force and violence and (2) unlawfully, wilfully and knowingly to organize and help organize the Communist Party of the United States of America as a society, group and assembly of persons who teach and advocate the overthrow and destruction of the government of the United States by force and violence."

CHAPTER 54: PRELIMINARY EVENTS

kept a bottle: Bouslog.

"don't have to obey": *S-B,* August 30, 1951.

challenged makeup: Union Defense Committee, ILWU Locals 136, 142, 150. "Chronology of Hall's Trial," p. 1.

[footnote] Reinecke filed: *S-B,* February 12, 1952.

"perfectly valid": *S-B,* February 13, 1952.

"Hawaii is treated": *Adv.,* February 20, 1952.

"you and I feuding": *S-B,* February 21, 1952.

Hall often impatient: Bouslog, Symonds.

"reiterated our insistence": Hall to Goldblatt, October 9, 1951.

"most affidavited": Symonds.

"He has legal ability": Symonds to Hall, memorandum, December 3, 1951.

"completely outvoted": Symonds.

"not only for his views": Hall to Bridges, November 7, 1951.

"It seems to me": Hall to Bouslog & Symonds, memorandum, November 9, 1951.

"too labored": Gladstein to Bridges, memorandum, November 14, 1951

"bad defeat" for Metzger: Gladstein to Bouslog & Symonds, March 5, 1952.

"best interests of court": *S-B,* March 17, 1952.

"good, bad, indifferent": Hall to Colotario, February 19, 1952.

Kibre supplied names: Kibre to Goldblatt, February 28, 1952.

Fujisaki was named: Fujisaki to Toshi Shirasaki, chairman, Local 142, Unit 3, Olaa, February 3, 1952.

"constantly improving": Hall to Glazier, March 24, 1952.

"not a ripple": Kreps to Glazier, September 4, 1951.

testimonial dinners: Hall wrote thank-you notes; for example, a personal letter to Unit 11, Paauhau, Hawaii, April 5, 1952.

"Brother Rania": 10th ICON, San Francisco, April 6–11, 1953, p. 173.

"My almost seventeen years": Hall over KHON radio, March 21, 1952, p. 6.

"jail doors close": Hall to Mrs. McIntyre, May 22, 1952.
"too bad Jack": Goldblatt to Hall, March 11, 1952.
"get up enough steam": ibid.

CHAPTER 55: A HUNT FOR LEGAL TALENT

Wiig on bench: The writer covered six sessions in the latter part of the trial. John F. "Jack" Burby covered the trial for the *Advertiser.*
"no legal gymnast": newsletter from the Reineckes to friends during the Christmas season of 1952.
sworn in June 19: Wiig in report to Social Science Assn., Honolulu, October 7, 1957.
preferred Hodgson: Farrington to Allen, January 28, 1952.
approved of Wiig: Allen to Farrington, January 25, 1951. (This letter was misdated; he obviously meant 1952.)
"a reactionary": Hall to Goldblatt, June 17, 1952.
"go back to Washington": *S-B,* October 23, 1946.
"We are only ones": Hall in a speech at Kalama Park, Wailuku, as reported in *S-B,* March 30, 1953.
two FBI agents: Burress and Condon came to Hawaii in July 1951. (Burress's testimony, Smith Act, p. 9987)
both ex-marines: Thompson.
"to get our people": IEB, San Francisco, March 6–7, 1952, p. 6.
came on December 13: Smith Act, p. 9987.
planned a reception: Thompson, McElrath, Kreps.
moved furniture: Thompson, McElrath.
"Hoover boys": transcript of first "FBI Tape," p. 16.
"six instead of seven": ibid., p. 4.
"People say a hell of a lot": ibid., p. 9.
talked to Hall: second "FBI Tape," pp. 1–2.
"window-dressing": ibid.
"poor Communists": ibid., p. 9.
approach to Esposito: Esposito.
approach to Carlsmith: Carlsmith.

CHAPTER 56: THE CROSS-EXAMINER

"master cross-examiner": Reinecke's words.
"quarterback": Koji Ariyoshi.
been cocounsel: Gladstein to Zalburg, November 8, 1976.
hadn't wanted Gladstein: Bridges to Hall, October 3, 1952.
harbored resentment: Yoshiko Hall.
"I knew also": Gladstein to Zalburg, November 8, 1976.
"tragically difficult": ibid.
Gladstein didn't want the case: Bridges.
last three months: Symonds to Hall, July 21, 1952.
shifted its strategy: Symonds to George Andersen, September 13, 1952.
[footnote] Bouslog & Symonds report: from *Star-Bulletin* Bureau, Washington, December 13, 1953.
"until the eve": Symonds to Wirin, September 12, 1952.
"with or without counsel": Symonds to Andersen, September 22, 1952.
"certain people": Bridges to Hall, October 3, 1952.
[footnote] ordered to show cause: *S-B,* September 10, 1952.
"A bunch of Lochinvars": Hall over KHON radio, October 24, 1952, p. 2.

"We like to think": ibid., p. 3.

"And if they said anything": Symonds.

Hoddick handled: Hoddick.

support from Democrats: *Adv.,* March 30, 1951.

support from Justice Department: ibid.

developed a distaste: Hoddick; and informal talk with Barlow, who declined to sit for a formal interview.

Barlow finally confirmed: *S-B,* May 29, 1952.

Hoddick should continue: Allen to Farrington, cable, May 23, 1952. Allen said he and Barlow had talked that morning in Allen's office.

handsome, pleasant: Reinecke's words.

not industrious: Hoddick, Symonds.

"His reluctance": *Chicago Daily News,* September 2, 1952.

"convictions in California": Allen to Farrington, August 7, 1952, H-97.

had to reconsider: Wiig in essay to Social Services Assn., October 7, 1952.

"a formidable array": Hall to Harold Kramer, executive secretary, North California Trade Union Committee to Repeal the Smith Act, San Francisco, October 30, 1952.

CHAPTER 57: THE SEVEN-MONTH SIEGE

three days to pick jury: The original twelve jurors were a good cross-section of Hawaii's population: a part-Hawaiian credit clerk, a Japanese auto parts salesman, a Chinese bookkeeper, a Russian dock guard, a *haole* plantation superintendent, a Korean-Hawaiian accounting clerk, an unemployed Chinese sales clerk, a Japanese electrician, a Japanese insurance agent, a part-Hawaiian engineer's aide, a part-Hawaiian electric lineman, and a Portuguese-Hawaiian athlete and salesman.

atmosphere "of informality": newsletter from Reineckes during Christmas season 1952.

four hundred policemen: ibid.

belly "cascaded": ibid.

"jigsaw puzzle": Smith Act, p. 3.

"partnership in crime": ibid., p. 14.

"one issue": ibid., p. 27.

"whether or not": ibid., p. 63.

"We will show": ibid., p. 55.

government built its case: 10th ICON, San Francisco, April 6–11, 1953, p. 58. The ILWU viewed the Smith Act case this way: "The prosecutor reads from books. The reading goes on for weeks and months. They pick out the purple passages in books about Russian revolution, economics, Karl Marx, Lenin or any other authors they can find. The prosecution then proceeds to try to prove that individuals had knowledge of these books. Finally, they call for conviction on the grounds that knowledge of these books is equivalent to teaching the overthrow of the government by force and violence."

"Walsh begins reading": Reineckes' Christmas letter.

"How long do you": ibid.

"Arsenic and Old Lace": ibid.

grateful for recesses: Hall to Goldblatt, January 13, 1953.

left home at 6 AM: Yoshiko Hall.

"case is dragging": Hall to Goldblatt, December 9, 1952.

Izuka first met Hall: Smith Act, pp. 1430–1437.

Symonds-Izuka exchange: ibid., pp. 1544, 1568.

$19.95 from government: ibid., p. 1615.

"judge wouldn't let us": Hall to Goldblatt, December 9, 1952.

"in national crisis": Smith Act, p. 4047.

moved to strike testimony: ibid.

"concentration policy": ibid., p. 4042.

"seize basic industries": ibid., p. 4079.

denied the motion: ibid., p. 4086.

"I vigorously opposed": Hall to Goldblatt, December 30, 1952.

"Wiig is permitting": *Adv.,* January 8, 1953.

"a surprising readiness": Allen to Farrington, February 2, 1953, I-19.

"avoid possible reversal": Allen to Farrington, January 24, 1953.

"pronounced disagreements": Hall to Goldblatt, December 30, 1952.

"Richie is getting difficult": ibid.

leased a house: Gladstein to Zalburg, November 8, 1976.

cool toward others: Reinecke, Symonds, Ariyoshi. Also Gladstein to Zalburg, November 8, 1976.

"didn't want to talk": Ariyoshi said Hall's left-wing bent was "fuzzy" and his knowledge of Marxism-Leninism limited.

walked a tightrope: Wiig.

forget legal terms: Bouslog.

"Look, Harriet": Bouslog.

"no such thing": from transcript of "In the Matter of the Disciplinary Proceedings against Harriet Bouslog Sawyer," No. 15,910, June 9, 1959, Appeal in the United States Court of Appeals for the Ninth Circuit, p. 12.

hugged her: Bouslog.

took notes: transcript of disciplinary proceedings, p. 12.

"Did you say": ibid., p. 35.

"there is not one word": ibid.

CHAPTER 58: WITNESS TAKES THE STAND

"not the same scowling": *Adv.,* February 3, 1953.

Bailey came: Smith Act, pp. 6295–6298.

Goto introduced him: ibid., pp. 6309–6311.

went out of business: ibid., p. 6525.

infiltrate Democrats: ibid., p. 6592.

Archie Brown story: ibid., pp. 6777–6789.

"I have heard": ibid., p. 6784.

more good "than anyone": ibid., p. 6786.

"riding herd": ibid., p. 6816.

"in a happy mood": ibid., p. 6817.

take sugar workers out: ibid., pp. 6829–6832.

"take fourteen cents": ibid., p. 7196.

"great disagreement": ibid., p. 7197.

"shooting pool": ibid., p. 7201.

invitation from Flynn: ibid., p. 7232.

"You did state": ibid., pp. 7232–7233.

not Communist inspired: ibid., p. 7615.

"Didn't he tell you": ibid., p. 7934.

would be held in contempt: Symonds.

wanted to take stand: Kimoto, Ariyoshi.

[footnote] never changed: Kawano.

something to be ashamed of: Kimoto.

"tremendous danger": Reinecke.

"just repeat clichés": Reinecke. (Both Charles and Eileen Fujimoto declined to be interviewed by the writer.)

request of Cadagan: Cadagan.

"Don't forget you told me": Cadagan.

"never been guilty of that": Cadagan.

Guard's testimony, Smith Act, pp. 9509–9511.

Wilson's testimony: ibid., pp. 10300–10315.

put on coat and tie: Burby in *Adv.,* March 27, 1953.

Crozier's testimony: Smith Act, p. 9453.

Hite's testimony: ibid., p. 9091.

Baptiste's testimony: ibid., p. 9175.

Duarte's testimony: ibid., p. 9149.

Fernandes' testimony: ibid., p. 9132.

put FBI men: ibid., pp. 10019–10059.

evidence wasn't relevant: ibid., p. 10059.

had trouble getting witnesses: Hoddick. Also Farrington to Allen, May 1, 1953.

[footnote] declined to testify: documented evidence was made available to the writer on all the cases cited here. The source asked to remain anonymous.

Hall welcomed testimony: Hall to Bridges, March 4, 1953.

King was reluctant: Samuel P. King.

"referred anything legal": King.

"expect me to answer": John A. Burns Oral History Project, Tape 9, p. 12.

"one helluva American": ibid. Burns said he let Hall and Ariyoshi know he would testify in their behalf as a character witness, but they decided not to "throw him to the wolves."

called on Steadman: source who asked to remain anonymous.

interviewed Bertram: Wightman.

called on Lewis: source who asked to remain anonymous. Lewis could not remember the incident.

asked Cadagan: Cadagan.

prosecution looked jubilant: *Adv.,* May 5, 1953.

worried and angry: ibid.

"above reproach": Smith Act, p. 10070.

reputation as to loyalty: ibid., p. 12071.

Guard read transcript: ibid., p. 12078.

"This is Moscow": ibid., p. 12079.

"not a very good citizen": ibid., p. 11772.

Stainback's testimony: ibid., pp. 11813–11943.

reputation "very bad": ibid., p. 11813.

"followed Communist pattern": ibid., p. 11847.

[footnote] "immediate wave of comment": Allen to Farrington, May 1, 1953, I-68.

[footnote] "real courage": Farrington to Allen, May 1, 1953.

"was a traitor": Smith Act, p. 11943.

LeBaron's testimony: ibid., pp. 12842, 12849.

Smith's testimony: ibid., p. 12448.

Tavares' testimony: ibid., p. 12809.

Symonds offered to show: ibid., p. 12748.

why didn't he testify?: ibid., p. 12744.

up to government: ibid., p. 12751.

"can say unqualifiedly": ibid., p. 12787.

"Did you not rent?": ibid., p. 12788.
"might kill me politically": ibid., p. 12796.
"They have decided": Hall to Goldblatt, May 13, 1953.
"Instead they are cooperating": ibid.
"Nolle Smith knows me": ibid.

CHAPTER 59: A ONE-DOLLAR BET

"antilabor vendetta": unsigned memorandum in ILWU files, April 30, 1953.
sore throat: Hoddick.
[footnote] "made it clear": Gladstein to Zalburg, November 8, 1976.
"leaned on lectern": *Adv.,* June 9, 1953.
felt a pain: Wiig. He was sick that Easter, too.
bring razors: *Adv.,* June 18, 1953.
"reliable report": Allen to Farrington, June 21, 1953.
"When they come back": *S-B,* June 19, 1953.
"only the beginning": *Adv.,* June 20, 1953.
"Someone asked me": Priscilla Shishido's "Random Notes on Jack Hall," January 1971, p. 4.
[footnote] "two or three jurors": Bouslog. Also Gladstein to Zalburg, November 8, 1976.
"rid of Bridges": Allen to Farrington, June 21, 1953.
"Butler feels strongly": Farrington to Allen, June 25, 1953.
"ugliest demonstrations": *Adv.,* June 24, 1953.
expected "full book": Hall to Yagi, July 3, 1953.
leaned on lectern: the writer covered the story.
"As Your Honor knows": from transcript of sentencing in Smith Act case, p. 71.
[footnote] "stooge of Bridges": *Ft. Pierce News-Tribune,* June 23, 1953.
"I am compelled": Smith Act sentencing, p. 72.
"I was not a member": ibid. Hall said "The government knows . . . that at least Jack Hall isn't a Communist now, because more than two years ago [on February 27, 1950] . . . Jack Hall signed an affidavit under the Taft-Hartley law in which he swore that he was not." (1st ICON, Honolulu, October 15–18, 1953, pp. 14, 16)
"loyal to that purpose": Smith Act sentencing, p. 72.
"If in living": ibid., pp. 72–73.
"I had hoped": ibid., p. 75.
"tear this building apart": ibid.
"many more like it": ibid.
"While they may not": Hall to Yagi, July 3, 1953.
bet a newsman: the writer heard him.
Thompson groaned: the writer sat behind him.
"conspiracy was dangerous": Smith Act sentencing, p. 92.
Oshiro arrived: the writer saw him.
[footnote] other six defendants: *Adv.,* July 11, 1953.
expected to go to prison: Yoshiko Hall, Reinecke, Carlsmith.
"I want you to": Carlsmith.

CHAPTER 60: NAALEHU '54: THE FEISTY LATHE OPERATOR

Cadagan's suggestion: Hall to Goldblatt, December 27, 1953.
"change in situation": Goldblatt to Hall, April 8, 1954.

"more cordial relations": ibid.

rainy Saturday: *S-B,* April 22, 1954.

shouted, threatened: ibid.; and *Adv.,* April 29, 1954.

"It is our opinion": Goldblatt to Hall, April 8, 1954. Bridges added a "shirt-tail" to Goldblatt's letter saying he had asked Blaisdell "to see what could be done."

"single-shot arbitration": ibid.

"not bow to threats": *S-B,* May 12, 1954.

"another Lanai": *S-B,* May 13, 1954.

"list of grievances": *S-B,* May 12, 1954.

Beatty's description: *Adv.,* June 7, 1954.

"What is 'Beattyism?' ": McElrath radio script, April 3, 1954, p. 3.

"King of Naalehu": ibid., April 28, 1954, p. 1.

shuffled like checkers: Beatty to Hutchinson employees, May 1, 1954.

"Ask yourself": ibid.

a quart of Old Crow: Beatty.

"fertilizing by moonlight": Robert Moyle. Moyle worked for Brewer for thirty-four years as a statistician.

met in a boxcar: *S-B,* August 28, 1954.

terms of agreement: McElrath radio script, August 27, 1954, p. 1.

"We are relieved": *S-B,* August 28, 1954.

"Tachibana cane": Beatty's phrase.

nobody won: *S-B* editorial, September 1, 1954. The Hutchinson Sugar Plantation Co.'s annual report for 1954 (p. 1) said that 16,016 tons of sugar were harvested—a loss of production of 5000 tons. Net profit for 1954 was $64,867, compared to a net of $150,572 for 1953.

CHAPTER 61: THE DEMOCRATIC SWEEP

"DEMOCRATS SWEEP": Hall to ILWU headquarters, cable, November 3, 1954.

"BEST RESULTS": ibid.

"A union has got": *S-B,* September 7, 1954.

"treason to United States": *Adv.,* September 8, 1954.

do their bidding: *S-B* editorial, September 8, 1954.

"less powerful politically": Allen to Ralph J. Donaldson, chief editorial writer, *Cleveland Plain Dealer,* January 14, 1954.

[footnote] arrived in 1947: Epstein.

[footnote] "you're doing all right": Epstein.

"in same boat": *S-B,* June 5, 1954.

"tremendous changes": ibid.

"a fact that Hall": Allen to Farrington, June 4, 1954, J-102.

"sympathy vote": Mrs. Farrington.

"overwhelming" victory: Allen to Mrs. James E. Payne, Colorado City, Texas, September 9, 1954. Colorado City was Allen's birthplace.

"busily engaged": Hall to Goldblatt, October 27, 1954.

"Democrats generally have listened": ibid.

"should their vote be crucial": ibid.

odds "are excellent": ibid.

Fasi's background: *S-B,* May 22, 1952. Also Brian Casey's column, *Adv.,* November 19, 1961.

A lot of promise: The writer often covered the young Frank Fasi.

If he didn't like you: Goldblatt. "If he was tight with you, you knew it. You didn't have to question or look over your shoulder." (Goldblatt's eulogy to Hall, January 7, 1971, p. 7)

"the usual young, ambitious guy": Hall to L. B. Thomas, Coast Labor Relations Committee, San Francisco, July 8, 1952.

Caveat emptor: Hall had three years of Latin in high school.

"ambitious young man": transcript of Hall's radio talk, October 3, 1952, pp. 8–11.

"Fearless Frank": a sobriquet often applied to Fasi. He said the ILWU never forgave him for testifying as a government adverse character witness in the Smith Act case. (*S-B,* May 21, 1969)

[footnote] Tani's expenses: ILWU Local 142 election campaign material titled, "Lest We Forget," a union look at Frank Fasi, July 15, 1959, p. 1.

Fasi would not sit for an interview. He said: "They [the public] are so conditioned to regard Hall and Burns as heroes that it won't do any good to try to discuss them." (Fasi in a chat with the writer in front of the Young Hotel on Bishop Street on April 5, 1975)

assailed the administration: transcript of Hall's speech, September 1, 1952, p. 6. Hall called Oren Long "a fastidious, precise little man . . . as deadly as a black-widow spider." He faulted Long for his failure to help resolve the Lanai strike of 1951. Hall sometimes engaged in overkill and this was an example. Long was mild and inoffensive, with no great drive and no taste for entering a bitter labor-management quarrel.

"holding a Damocles sword": *S-B,* September 8, 1952.

"vicious" leadership: Fasi radio speech, September 30, 1952, published in *Adv.,* October 1, 1952.

"I will be next mayor": *S-B,* April 4, 1954.

Fasi's prime targets: McElrath radio script, September 14, 1954, p. 3.

could split his ticket: *S-B,* September 30, 1954.

"odds were too much": *S-B,* November 3, 1954.

briefed Mrs. Farrington: Allen to Mrs. Farrington, February 23, 1955, 38-B.

[footnote] "jumped the fence": McElrath radio script, October 4, 1954, p. 1. Political analyst Dan Tuttle estimated that one-third of those who crossed over deserted Fasi in the general election. (Tuttle interview)

"repeatedly on showdowns": Allen to Mrs. Farrington, February 23, 1955, 38-B.

ILWU sustained two defeats: ibid.

"treacherous" leaders: *Adv.,* April 3, 1955.

booming voice: The writer covered Dillingham's speech.

CHAPTER 62: JUNEAU SPRUCE

$750,000 judgment: Hoddick; Goldblatt; report from Hall to ILWU Local 142 Executive Board, January 28, 1955, p. 1.

including those of Local 142: *Juneau Spruce Corporation* v. *ILWU,* et al., Civil No. 1401 in the United States Federal District Court for the District of Hawaii (1955).

"out of his hat": Goldblatt.

gone on for six weeks: Hall's report to LEB.

On January 7, 1952: LEB, January 23–25, 1952, p. 1.

[footnote] a number of cases: Beechert interview.

"sometimes considered liberal": LEB, January 23–25, 1952, p. 1.

no treasury: *Business Week* magazine, February 6, 1954, p. 113, and February 12, 1955, p. 138.

Judgment was entered: Hall's report to LEB, p. 1.

before Judge McLaughlin: *Juneau Spruce* v. *ILWU.*

"fishing expedition": Hall's report to LEB, p. 4. Hall said the same thing in a more Hawaiian manner of speaking: "Apparently, they feel it's a happy fishing grounds here and small-mesh hukilau nets are permitted." (LEB, January 28–29, 1955, p. 10)

"a gold mine": Hall's report to LEB, p. 3.

tried to settle: ibid.; Goldblatt; and *Juneau Spruce* v. *ILWU,* p. 11.

dealt with Rogers: Hall's report to LEB, p. 3.

to pay $25,000: ibid.

"I'd better check": Goldblatt.

"We don't argue": *Juneau Spruce* v. *ILWU,* p. 211.

owned International building: ibid., p. 6.

discussed disaffiliation: ibid., pp. 41–42.

didn't blame him: ibid., p. 43.

"Where is the International?": ibid., p. 46.

"Remember the case?": Goldblatt.

"they're prepared to make": Goldblatt.

companies paid $355,000: Hoddick; also *S-B,* April 15, 1955.

"Win some; lose some": Goldblatt.

"continue merry chase": Goldblatt.

tired of lawyers: Goldblatt.

engaged in slowdown: Hoddick.

[footnote] agreed to settle: *S-B,* April 15, 1955; Bridges to Hall, April 25, 1955; Hall to Livingston Jenks, July 18, 1955.

agreed to the tradeoff: Hall to Gladstein, May 2, 1955.

"Could we not then advise": ibid.

[footnote] "three or four" negative: Hall to Gladstein, May 31, 1955.

"idea came from Hawaii": Bridges to Hall, April 28, 1955.

"especially Brother Hall": 2nd LCON, Hilo, September 21–24, 1955, p. 12.

Chapter 63: Hall the Politician

"have no hesitation": Hall to Kibre, May 3, 1956.

"fair and unbiased": Hall to Bridges, October 29, 1956.

"keep her well-buttered": Hall to Kibre, May 3, 1956.

"paper's attitude": Hall to Kibre, May 16, 1956.

Bridges' visit: Betty Farrington.

offered $250,000: Betty Farrington.

"just leave me alone": Betty Farrington.

[footnote] Bridges rebuttal: Bridges to Zalburg, March 15, 1977.

"an all right guy": Hall to Kibre, November 14, 1956.

"Dillingham, Doc Hill": Hall to Bridges, October 29, 1956.

"wrecked the Republican Party": Hall to Kibre, November 14, 1956.

"resounding defeat": ibid.

some politicians: *Time* magazine, November 26, 1956, p. 21. *Time* said: "The union's sizeable vote is sending politicians scurrying high and low after ILWU support."

staunch anti-Communist: At the 1954 statehood hearings before the Senate Interior and Insular Affairs Committee, Sylva testified: "There is no question that the leadership of the ILWU is Communist to the core." (p. 167 of transcript) "happy to meet": *S-B,* November 12, 1956.

[footnote] registered as Republican: "I happen to be a registered Republican," Bridges told the Local 142 convention in September 1957.

"Strange are the ways": Hall to Kibre, November 14, 1956.

"impulsive, it seems": *S-B* editorial, November 14, 1956.

"met a lot of union men": *S-B,* November 19, 1956.

"Mr. Sylva has information": ibid.

"all-out effort": Hall to Kibre, November 14, 1956.

"for substantial stakes": Hall to Goldblatt, October 18, 1956.

"our fine friends": ibid. To IMUA members the most frustrating part of all was the ambivalent feeling many people had for Hall. IMUA expressed it this way: "Many persons are pleased to deal with or support Jack W. Hall, labor leader, but imply that they detest and would not deal with Jack W. Hall, the Communist." (Report of the Territorial Commission on Subversive Activities in 1955, p. 16)

"this is the lawyer": Symonds.

"you haven't heard": Symonds.

"a Communist takeover": O'Daniel's testimony, Eastland Committee, pp. 2232–2233.

McElrath-Morris exchange: *Adv.,* December 1, 1956.

[footnote] "I cannot go along": Eastland Committee, p. 2251.

"a cold, chilly day": *Adv.,* December 1, 1956.

neither paid any attention: Kibre to Hall, December 4, 1956.

[footnote] "It was a plot": *ILWU Dispatcher,* December 20, 1956.

"didn't prove": ILWU's "Speaker's Guide for Reporting on the Eastland Hearings," undated, p. 5.

CHAPTER 64: THE LAST ACT OF THE SMITH ACT

"just begun to fight": *S-B,* September 9, 1953.

"Spend no time": 2nd LCON, Hilo, September 21–24, 1955, p. 71.

"never lick our kind": Hall to Sadoyat, April 2, 1954. Hall said: "The smartest guys in the world at the top of any organization aren't worth a damn without the backing of the men on the job."

tightened restrictions: Hall to Goldblatt, April 24, 1954.

"pay extra": Hall to Goldblatt, April 27, 1954.

[footnote] "Hall Can Go": *S-B,* April 10, 1954.

"trip will do me good": Hall to Bridges, July 23, 1954.

"I certainly need it": Hall to Clark, July 28, 1955.

"a genuine impact": Goldblatt to Hall, August 26, 1955.

Hall not enthusiastic: Hall to Goldblatt, August 29, 1955.

signs of near despair: Goldblatt to Hall, August 2, 1955.

[footnote] never offered: Anthony.

asked Taylor: Goldblatt to Taylor, September 15, 1955.

"an enormous asset": Goldblatt to Hall, August 2, 1955.

"It is apparent": Taylor to Goldblatt, September 21, 1955.

"and would be unwilling": ibid.

about $20,000: ibid.

asked Taylor to Hawaii: Goldblatt to Hall, April 17, 1956.

Goldblatt's commentary: ibid.

"I want to develop": *S-B,* April 19, 1956.

"everybody worth seeing": Hall to Goldblatt, April 23, 1956.

still dealt with Hall: *S-B,* February 27, 1956.

"shocking" delay: UP, Washington, February 5, 1957.

"a deplorable thing": *S-B,* June 21, 1956.

"minor-league Communist": *Adv.,* July 13, 1956.

"lowly Party positions": Taylor's appeal brief, p. 20. (In the United States Court of Appeals for the Ninth Circuit, No. 13,915, *Fujimoto* et al. v. *United States* . . . additional brief for appellant Jack Wayne Hall)

"ever manifested itself": ibid., p. 25.

"no question about energy": ibid., p. 48.

"does not make sense": ibid.

"From 1937": Appellee's brief, p. 78; written by Louis B. Blissard, U.S. Attorney for Hawaii, and Rex A. McKittrick, special assistant to the U.S. Attorney.

From the beginning: ibid., p. 201.

"evidence shows": ibid., p. 235.

Bridges sat listening: *Adv.,* July 13, 1956.

Supreme Court reversed: AP, San Francisco, January 20, 1958. The court ruled that mere membership in the Communist Party was not sufficient grounds for a Smith Act conviction and that "preaching abstractly" was not a crime under the Smith Act.

"IMUAites apoplectic": Hall to Goldblatt, June 20, 1957.

"irritating as hell": Hall to Goldblatt, February 25, 1957.

Steaks broiling: *Adv.,* January 21, 1958.

"temporarily at peace": ibid. Hall claimed the Smith Act trial "strengthened the union. . . . Now there's a tremendous loyalty in the union for the leadership and I think for me personally." (Beechert tape, p. 17)

review of Bouslog case: AP, San Francisco, June 9, 1958.

"But so long as": from transcript of "Disciplinary Proceedings against Mrs. Bouslog," p. 21.

"suspending one person": ibid., p. 42.

meeting at Waikiki Tropics: Bouslog, Bridges.

not enough in record: *New York Times,* June 30, 1959.

"I have always felt": *S-B,* June 29, 1959.

"I will be more careful": *S-B,* September 25, 1959.

CHAPTER 65: SUGAR '58: "THE ALOHA STRIKE"

called Cadagan: Cadagan.

"a foolish strike": Cadagan.

collecting one dollar: *S-B,* March 28, 1959.

had $835,000: Hall's report to 3rd LCON, Honolulu, September 25–28, 1957, p. 38.

"miserably low": ibid.

"unless forced": Bridges to Steele, March 20, 1956.

"no kamikaze union": *Adv.,* March 3, 1957.

"to hammer home": Goldblatt to Hall, March 2, 1956.

"Aren't [they] fantastic?": Hall to Goldblatt, January 17, 1957.

crucial "as any": Goldblatt to Hall, January 21, 1957.

"new, subtle line": Hall to Goldblatt, January 24, 1957.

"The increase you propose": Sugar Industry report, February 3, 1958.

"cream separator": Goldblatt at 3rd LCON, p. 49.

"something less": Sugar Industry report, February 3, 1958.

a long strike: Hall to Kibre, January 6, 1958.

stockpiled rice, meat: ILWU strike publication (undated).

model strike machine: Arakaki.

strike was solid: Hall to Kibre, February 6, 1958.

[footnote] cleaned Holt's property: Arakaki.

"bumbling around": Hall to Kibre, February 6, 1958.

tried for eighteen days: *S-B,* June 7, 1958.

watched Quinn with interest: McElrath radio script, August 16, 1957, p. 4.

not opposed Quinn: Bridges to Hall, memorandum, March 21, 1958.

"just as well off": ibid.

"Eighteen cents would settle": ibid.

offered fifteen-cent increase: *S-B,* June 7, 1958.

tell Quinn "point-blank": Goldblatt to Hall, April 29, 1958.

"low man on totem pole": ibid.

"A few can last": Hall to Goldblatt, May 8, 1958.

[footnote] It cost $250,000: ibid.

"Once a company announces": ibid.

harvest only 30,000: Hall to Bridges and Goldblatt, May 13, 1958.

destroy the industry: ibid.

Finnegan sent Hillenbrand: *S-B,* June 7, 1958.

terms of contract: Sugar Industry report, June 8, 1958.

cost more than $50 million: Hall's talk to National Association of Accountants,
     October 14, 1960, p. 7.

[footnote] Maclean's figures: *S-B,* March 13, 1959.

"not to destroy": Hall in talk to Social Action Committee of the Congregational
     Churches, Honolulu, June 25, 1960, p. 5.

"need not have occurred": Hall's talk to National Association of Accountants,
     p. 7. Many plantations took heavy losses. Some figures: Grove Farm,
     $4,500,000; HC & S, $784,652; Olaa, $953,908. (*S-B,* June 7, 1958, and
     January 3, 1960)

CHAPTER 66: ONE SUNDAY AT PAULA DRIVE

met at Hall's home: Gill, Esposito, Kauhane, Okano; also *S-B,* February 3,
     1959.

talked to Kauhane: Kauhane.

[footnote] Present were: *S-B,* February 3, 1959.

"Those are the rules": *S-B,* February 20, 1959.

"I am not bound": *S-B,* February 19, 1959.

signed the plan: Kauhane.

"can you trust Charley": Kauhane.

Esposito refused to bend: "I never believed the Republicans would [form a
     coalition]—headed by Sam King, of all people," said Esposito.
          Hall called the coalition "a sort of emancipation proclamation" which
     freed the ILWU from the strong ties it had with the Democratic Party. (*Adv.,*
     March 24, 1959)

DeMello called: DeMello, McElrath, Esposito.

reported to Hall: DeMello.

"I talked to the boys": DeMello.

[footnote] "You can be Speaker": Esposito.

"an inflexible guy": *Adv.,* February 20, 1959.

"Let the ship go down": *Adv.,* February 20, 1959.

"Once you understand": Gill. Hall said of Gill: "Look at Tom Gill. . . . The
     guy's got a tremendous voting record; very bright guy, but we know that from

the time he first got into politics, he's fought everything this union stands for; associated with Rutledge, associated with the AF of L, associated with a group that doesn't like the rough way we play, I guess. . . ." (Beechert tape, p. 19)
were furious: Gill, McClung.

[footnote] "upset the timing": Esposito.

"can't trust a liberal": Esposito.

[footnote] "a sense of greatness": Esposito said Hall was "the most powerful guy in the islands. . . . The Governor, any legislator, including the Speaker and the President, didn't hold a candle to him for power. . . ." (Esposito interview)

"Congratulations": Goldblatt to Hall, February 27, 1959.

showdown with Hall: Esposito.

CHAPTER 67: THE GLOW OF STATEHOOD

Hall approved: Burns.

Thanksgiving Day dinner: 13th ICON, Seattle, April 6–13, 1959, p. 282.

told Lyndon Johnson: ibid., p. 286.

"reasonably simple": ibid.

"if it had not worked": ibid., p. 281.

twenty-three hours: ibid., p. 284.

sent congratulations: Bridges, Goldblatt, Robertson, and Germaine Bulcke, cable, March 12, 1959. They had worked hard on the wording: the draft is in the ILWU files with a number of crossed-out words.

"We all feel": Hall to Kibre, March 18, 1959.

Hall introduced Burns: 13th ICON, pp. 280–281.

"didn't have votes": ibid., p. 281.

"I can assure you": ibid., p. 282.

"foundations for democracy": ibid., p. 284.

"Burns' entire political history": *Adv.,* July 1, 1959.

"made him what he is": *S-B,* July 27, 1959.

"ILWU has never asked": *Adv.,* July 26, 1959.

[footnote] "It is a FACT": 4th ICON, Honolulu, September 23–26, 1959, p. 31.

win by fifteen thousand votes: Hall to Morris Watson, July 7, 1959. Hall's confidence probably was based on Burns' solid victories in 1956 and 1958 in the delegate's race. He beat Mrs. Farrington in 1956 by 15,335 votes and Farrant Turner in 1958 by 14,317 votes.

[footnote] "gimmick": from Burns' "Current Biography," February 1972.

Democrats blamed Hall: Mike Tokunaga. Tokunaga, Democratic Party leader, said: "Most people thought Burns was a cinch [to win]. A poll taken in April 1959 showed that Burns was behind, "but I could not convince anybody that it was an uphill fight."

concentrated too much on Fasi: Tokunaga.

Many Democrats blamed Burns: Oshiro. From 1961 on, Oshiro helped direct Burns' election campaigns.

"No one can single": 4th ICON, p. 97.

"kid from Kalihi": Fong's description of himself. (*Adv.,* June 29, 1959)

"His power is fantastic": Fasi to Paul M. Baker, chairman, National Democratic Party, Washington, August 19, 1959.

raised over half a million: *Hawaii Observer,* July 28, 1977, p. 13.

"It looks as if": Fasi in an informal chat with the writer on June 20, 1975, in his office in City Hall.

"We have known": ILWU letter to membership, October 30, 1968.
labor divided: *S-B* editorial, November 29, 1968.

CHAPTER 68: MECHANIZATION

"We told the industry": Hall's Commencement Day talk at Hawaii Technical
    School, June 7, 1967, p. 11.
"find their way": Goldblatt at 14th ICON, Honolulu, April 3–7, 1961, p. 158.
reductions in the work force: see Table 1.
"union took position": Hall's Commencement Day talk, p. 159.

Table 1

ILWU MEMBERSHIP* IN HAWAII
By Island and Industry for 1951, 1955, 1966 & 1976

Year	Island	Industry					
		Sugar	Longshore	Pine	General Trades & Others	Tourism	Total
1951	Hawaii	5,919	230	--	--	--	6,149
	Maui	3,672	190	2,051	40	--	5,953
	Kauai	3,514	123	353	155	--	4,145
	Oahu	3,049	1,150	1,694	420	--	6,313
	Total	16,154	1,693	4,098	615		22,560
1955	Hawaii	5,478	235	--	291	--	6,004
	Maui	3,149	191	2,102	175	--	5,617
	Kauai	3,483	152	603	180	--	4,418
	Oahu	2,889	1,173	2,619	626	--	7,307
	Total	14,999	1,751	5,324	1,272		23,346
1966	Hawaii	3,274	64	--	646	681	4,665
	Maui	2,281	138	1,776	411	264	4,870
	Kauai	2,442	57	232	374	347	3,452
	Oahu	1,908	1,016	3,641	1,789	--	8,354
	Total	9,905	1,275	5,649	3,220	1,292	21,341
1976	Hawaii	2,516	101	--	1,243	1,960	5,820
	Maui	1,957	88	1,583	744	1,712	6,084
	Kauai	1,849	42	--	315	914	3,120
	Oahu	1,475	700	2,979	2,823	--	7,977
	Total	7,797	931	4,562	5,125	4,586	23,001

*Actual membership, including those sick and on leave or layoff; does not include
membership figures for Local 160 (a small local of supervisory, security and professional
employees). Some workers shown here under "General Trades and Others" are assigned
to other industrial groupings for Local 142 administrative and election purposes.

Source: ILWU files

"shrunk from top": ibid.

"with sizeable amounts": Hall in a talk to Conference on Human Resources, Honolulu, February 1–2, 1967, p. 6.

"I warned him": Hall to Goldblatt, March 5, 1957.

seven-hour workday: Goldblatt to Hall, May 20, 1957.

[footnote] "expert witness pay": ibid.

six-hour workday: Bridges to Hall, memorandum, May 23, 1960.

ten-cent tax: Hall to Bridges and Goldblatt, August 10, 1959.

employers opposed any tax: from Memorandum of Agreement on M & M, p. 1. Agreement was entered into on July 14, 1960. A copy was made available to the writer by an employer executive.

put up $450,000: ibid., Attachment 4, Mechanization Fund Agreement, p. 1.

guaranteed thirty-two hours: ibid., Exhibit B, Wage Supplementation, p. 10.

$850 travel allowance: ibid., Exhibit A, Supplemental Service Allowances, p. 6.

"as much as $20,000": Hall to Conference on Human Resources, p. 7.

"mechanization fund": *S-B,* July 10, 1960.

"very healthy": *S-B,* August 7, 1960.

didn't please Bridges: LEB, December 5–6, 1968, p. 15.

vote on M & M: Goldblatt to Hall, December 14, 1960.

[footnote] went out of existence: Eilerts.

"$900 million saved": "Productivity in the West Coast Longshore Industry," Technical Paper No. 10, prepared by the Office of Economic Policy and Case Analysis and submitted to the Nixon Pay Board on March 14, 1972.

$63.5 million in benefits: ibid.

did not challenge: Bridges to Zalburg, April 11, 1977.

talked to Pinsky: Pinsky.

[footnote] no figures on Hawaii: Eilerts.

improved medical plan: Pinsky; David Thompson in *ILWU Reporter,* May 16, 1956.

ten percent less: Thompson in *ILWU Reporter.*

"cover entire bill": Fujisaki to 7th Annual Western Conference of Foundations of Medical Care, Honolulu, June 22, 1966.

CHAPTER 69: THE NIXON CAPER

predicted Nixon victory: AP, August 5, 1960.

"a pretty good record": ibid.

"a deal with AFL-CIO": ibid. Goldblatt said the ILWU felt "there is a fix between Kennedy and the top brass of the AFL-CIO." (Goldblatt to Watson, August 8, 1960)

[footnote] lost by 115 votes: AP's final tally showed Kennedy had 92,410 votes; Nixon, 92,295. The race was almost that close nationwide. That was why Goldblatt said the ILWU "came awfully close to electing a president." (Goldblatt interview)

earned a reputation: In 1950 an ILWU pamphlet said: "When [Nixon] ran for Congress in 1946, he handed out 25,000 white plastic thimbles labeled: 'Elect Nixon and Needle the PAC [labor's Political Action Committee].' "

"My mind is made up": Hall's Labor Day speech, September 6, 1960, p. 12.

"just to shake hands": Goldblatt.

"Hall, a bespectacled": Gladwin Hill in *New York Times,* August 6, 1960.

went to the Tropics: Yoshiko Hall.

"hand Kennedy a gun": *Adv.* and *S-B,* October 9, 1960.

"accomplished the 'mission' ": Hall to Goldblatt, November 17, 1960.

CHAPTER 70: ARTFUL ART

Goldblatt talked with Hoffa: Hall to Robertson, May 1, 1956.

not optimistic: Hall to Goldblatt, May 16, 1956.

Neither was Rutledge: Rutledge.

"Rutledge is the kind": Hall to Goldblatt, May 16, 1956.

"Anytime they make a pact": Rutledge.

"It was unity": Hall to Goldblatt, February 27, 1957.

pact of mutual assistance: memorandum by Hall, May 9, 1957. Goldblatt said things looked good. (Goldblatt to Hall, May 20, 1957)

took a photo: *Adv.,* May 9, 1957.

make staff available: summary of joint meeting, June 10, 1957.

"signal achievement": Bridges to all ILWU locals, May 21, 1957.

"scare the pants off": *Adv.,* May 15, 1957.

"beginning to click": Robertson tore off a corner of a sheet of paper and sent Bridges the message, which was received in San Francisco on June 7, 1957.

"Sad situation": Hall to Goldblatt, September 5, 1957.

"I am no fool": Rutledge spoke to a person identified by the ILWU simply as "our lawyer friend." This person told the ILWU what Rutledge had said. A copy of the memorandum containing Rutledge's allegations was submitted in a letter from Hall to Goldblatt, July 22, 1959.

met in Los Angeles: Hall to Goldblatt, June 3, 1959.

a catchy word: Rutledge.

define jurisdiction: draft of agreement, June 13, 1959.

"cause a blowup": ibid.

move into construction: Hall to Goldblatt, November 13, 1959.

"incompetent and not giving": Yagi's statement (undated) was contained in a letter from Jack C. Reynolds to Goldblatt, February 16, 1960.

Rutledge insisted: Hall to Goldblatt, October 23, 1959.

[footnote] proposed ILWU organize: Goldblatt to Reynolds, March 4, 1960.

"I really don't believe": Hall to Goldblatt, October 23, 1959.

"We just can't get": Hall to Bridges, December 3, 1959.

"all escape hatches": Goldblatt to Hall, April 27, 1960.

"The kind of flexibility": ibid.

"national picture": Hall to Goldblatt, May 1, 1960.

"Meanwhile, we struggle": ibid.

"intense hatred": Hall to Goldblatt, October 20, 1960.

to show goodwill: Hall to Goldblatt, July 27, 1960.

"a damn good union": ibid.

struggled to define jurisdiction: JOB meeting, August 15, 1960.

"My own feeling": Goldblatt to Lawrence Steinberg, September 2, 1960.

"indefinitely suspended": Paul L. Steinberg to Kealalio, November 17, 1960.

"any suspension": Kealalio to Steinberg, November 21, 1960.

a single picket: *Adv.,* March 11, 1961; also Rutledge. The incident occurred March 10, 1961.

ducked Hall all day: Hall to Goldblatt, March 13, 1961.

" 'It's Me, O Lord' ": ibid.

"give the public notice": *Adv.,* March 11, 1961.

"deliberate gimmicking": Goldblatt to Hall, March 13, 1961.

"ready to march": ibid.

"Methinks a smart guy": ibid.

CHAPTER 71: THE HALL-BURNS AFFAIR

played a major role: Bob Oshiro, Democratic Party chairman. He said: "The union that had the biggest weight in our society [was the ILWU]. They were the ones, I would say, that led to the victory [in 1962]."

often just a few words: Oshiro. Burns said the same. "Each could read the other guy's thoughts," said Oshiro.

"good weather and bad": 5th LCON, Honolulu, September 27–30, 1961, p. 28.

more than $10,000: ILWU memorandum printed in *S-B,* August 15, 1963. The memo said that in 1962 the ILWU knew that Burns didn't have much money and that the ILWU "would have to help him financially."

[footnote] "unemployed politician": 5th LCON, p. 29.

support for Kealoha was "spotty": *S-B,* October 17, 1962.

"would be wonderful": *Adv.,* October 6, 1962.

Quinn was there: Kealoha.

"my friend Jimmy": *S-B,* October 6, 1962.

"a racial thing": Kealoha.

met with Reynolds: Hall to Goldblatt, October 15, 1962.

"on Democratic bandwagon": ibid.

pulling for "Big Five": Hall to Goldblatt, October 22, 1962.

"Reynolds, Art and I": ibid.

"rather reluctantly": ibid.

"I was able to get": ibid.

"no real commitments": ibid.

placed a small bet: ibid.

knew he was in trouble: Quinn.

analysis of campaign: Smyser, *S-B,* November 17, 1962; Gardiner Jones, *Adv.,* November 9, 1962.

"He didn't ask for anything": *Adv.,* November 9, l962.

meeting at Dooley's house: Rutledge.

"Jack—the politician": Rutledge.

"have to decide quickly": LEB, November 11–15, 1962, pp. 2–3.

night of April 30, 1963: Hall to Goldblatt, May 1, 1963.

[footnote] Little Norris-LaGuardia: ibid.

"proposed that he and I spend": ibid.

"bow to Mecca": *S-B,* December 11, 1962; *Adv.,* December 11, 1962.

"someone to blame": *Adv.,* December 12, 1962.

"fountainhead of political power": The ILWU led the fight for the following major pieces of labor legislation:

1. Little Wagner Act (1945), which protects the rights of agricultural workers to organize and bargain collectively.
2. Hawaii Workers' Compensation Act. Benefits went from $20 a week (1944) to two-thirds of average weekly wage ($166.70 in 1976) for a maximum of twenty-six weeks.
3. State Wage and Hour Law. The minimum wage was 40 cents an hour in 1945; $2.40 in 1976.
4. Unemployment insurance, including coverage for agricultural workers (1975). Hawaii's agricultural workers won coverage because at the time they were the only organized agricultural workers in the nation. In 1978 benefits were payable for a maximum of twenty-six weeks at $126 a week.
5. Industrial Safety Laws (1955, 1965).

6. Little Norris-LaGuardia Act (1965), which prohibits *ex parte* restraining orders (orders issued without a hearing) against strikers or picketers.
7. Temporary Disability Insurance Act (1970), which provides to the claimant fifty-five percent of the average weekly wage.
8. Antistrikebreaking law (1964), which prohibits government employees from working for an outside employer when the employer is engaged in a labor dispute.
9. State Commission on Manpower Development and Full Employment (1965).
10. Hawaii Public Employment Relations Act (1970), which authorizes public employees to engage in collective bargaining and go on strike.
11. Prepaid health care provided for by the employer (1974).
12. State Employment Program (1975).

"It's simple": unpublished interview of Hall in 1964 by author Charles P. Larrowe.

union impressed with Gill's record: DeMello to Gill, January 23, 1964.

"help things all around": Hall to Fong, January 23, 1964.

"Goldwater albatross": Hall to Kibre, July 27, 1964.

impress upon Fong: Hall to Kibre, July 2, 1964.

not a Goldwaterite: Kibre in ILWU press release, October 26, 1964.

"one of great champions": 9th LCON, Honolulu, September 8–13, 1969, p. 14.

"Kennedy crowd was pushing": Larrowe interview of Hall.

"key vote in committee": ibid. Fong said: "[Hall] asked for things. Certain things we could do. Certain things we could not do. . . . I always kept my word with him." (Fong interview)

"slamming him": Hall to Kibre, July 27, 1964.

"work Hiram has been doing": Hall to Kibre, November 5, 1963.

tried to discourage Gill: Hall to Kibre, November 7, 1963.

times Gill addressed the House: Hall to Kibre, cable, September 11, 1964.

Hall never asked him: Yoshinaga.

"push for Najo": Hall to Kibre, July 27, 1964.

smart, militant: *Adv.,* June 1, 1961; *S-B,* September 15, 1965.

"throw Hiram out completely": Yoshinaga.

"jump through any hoop": *Adv.,* September 18, 1964.

"bean-balled Nadao": *S-B,* October 6, 1964.

CHAPTER 72: THE "GREEN DESERT"

This chapter is based upon interviews with Yoshiko Hall, John Hall, Ayako Kaneda Nitta, Dr. and Mrs. Willis Butler, Bridges, Goldblatt, McElrath, David Thompson, Tangen, Carlsmith, Rags Shishido, and others. Michele Hall Burton and Eric Mitsugi Hall, Jack Hall's children, declined to be interviewed.

"good boring shape": Hall to Goldblatt, October 11, 1958.

story floating around: *Adv.,* January 5, 1959.

"It is true": ibid.

"No harm done": Hall to Goldblatt, January 5, 1959.

"Green Desert": Goldblatt's phrase.

enjoyed Goldblatt's visits: Goldblatt.

"Lou the Lash": salutation of letter, Hall to Goldblatt, April 6, 1950.

"What have you heard": Goldblatt.

lived simply: Yoshiko Hall.

made coffee: Mrs. Nitta. Ayako Kaneda came to live with the Halls at age eighteen. She was the daughter of Tomitaro Kaneda, president of the All-Japanese Dock Workers Union (Zenkowan) in Tokyo. She studied for a year at Hawaiian Mission Academy and then for three years at the University of Hawaii. The Halls footed the bill. "They supported me 100 percent," she said. Yoshiko Hall considered Ayako "a daughter." (Nitta and Yoshiko Hall interviews)

dressed in slacks: series on Hall by a visiting newspaperman, Leverett Chapin, *S-B,* January 24, 1958. Chapin called Hall "very easily . . . Hawaii's most controversial citizen."

drove him to work: Yoshiko Hall.

before 7:30: Yoshiko Hall; also David Thompson and Chapin.

waded through work: Goldblatt, Thompson.

early as 2 AM: Yoshiko Hall.

excelled at dictation: John Hall.

liked efficient people: Goldblatt, McElrath, David Thompson.

detested mediocrity: McElrath.

tackled problems: Goldblatt, McElrath.

mañana attitude: Goldblatt.

hours in kitchen: Yoshiko Hall, Mrs. Nitta.

took all weekend: Yoshiko Hall, Mrs. Nitta.

good with lamb: Leo Lycurgus.

marinated meats: Mrs. Nitta.

with seafood: Yoshiko Hall.

caught by somebody else: Mrs. Nitta.

did the laundry: Mrs. Nitta.

loved music: Yoshiko Hall, Goldblatt, Lycurgus.

"bury his head": Goldblatt's eulogy to Hall, January 7, 1971, p. 4.

collected Fats Waller: Yoshiko Hall. The writer inspected part of Hall's jazz collection. It included: Red Nichols and His Five Pennies, Jack Teagarden, Benny Goodman, Glenn Miller, Coleman Hawkins and His Quartet, the Art Tatum Trio, Woody Herman, Sidney Bechet, Billie Holiday, Louis Armstrong, and Fats Waller.

When jazz blew: Goldblatt.

friend Leo: Yoshiko Hall.

should have dignity: Lycurgus.

kept in refrigerator: Mrs. Nitta.

knew sugar content: Yoshiko Hall.

happy or unhappy: Mrs. Nitta.

loved his father: Yoshiko Hall, Mrs. Nitta.

hurt when he saw him: Mrs. Nitta, Paul Pinsky.

called on Bobo: John Hall.

precocious: John Hall. Michele Hall Burton told the writer at a dinner in her mother's house in San Francisco on the evening of June 16, 1973, that the children of radical parents know each other all over the country. They have a rapport with each other; she called them "red-diaper kids."

invited him to the ranch: Carlsmith.

"You hit it!": Carlsmith.

hated the sight of blood: Yoshiko Hall, Mrs. Butler.

a slug of Jack Daniel's: Mrs. Butler.

Hall's speeches: Walker, "Rhetorical Analysis," pp. 135–169.

invited to enroll: Hall to Goldblatt, December 5, 1960.

"too damned respectable": ibid.

"Very well received": Hall to Mrs. John F. Larson, Klamath Falls, Ore., March 3, 1965.

"can't even go barefoot": ibid.

selected Dillingham: Hall to Dillingham, November 3, 1965. Hall called Lowell Dillingham "a determined, dedicated and hardworking person."

president of Hawaii Council for Housing Action: Hall was the first president. Realtor Jack Palk was the second. Palk said Hall was the driving force. (Palk interview)

wore black tie: *Advertiser* photo (undated) taken by Ron Jett showed Hall at the annual meeting of the Aloha United Fund in 1968.

"Yum, yum": Hall to Pauline Rosenthal, Venice, Calif., January 5, 1966.

fished aboard *Maria:* on January 18, 1960.

took Eric fishing: Hall to Pinsky, October 30, 1961.

caught marlin: Hall to Goldblatt, June 25, 1958.

"covered with bruises": Hall to Baskin, July 23, 1965.

a "grand daddy": Hall to John L. Burton, September 2, 1965.

"better to be a grandparent": Hall to Shirley Sveda, Ashland, Wisc., July 6, 1965. Mrs. Sveda was Hall's cousin.

gout and hypertension: Butler.

hay fever: David Thompson.

nicked his finger: Hall to Goldblatt, November 23, 1960.

climbed to 235: ibid.

"not a drink for seventeen days": ibid.

"growing hostility": Goldblatt to Hall, November 30, 1960.

"incarcerated": Hall to Goldblatt, May 15, 1961.

"[Butler] tells me": ibid.

"I join Joe Blurr": ibid.

"Barium, ugh!": Hall to Kibre, December 29, 1964.

a week at home: ibid.

"after life I've led": Hall to Goldblatt, December 31, 1964.

emergency operation: Hall to James Mergens, June 18, 1968.

thirty-three day in hospital: Hall to Benedict Wolf, June 13, 1968.

wanted to die: John Hall.

lost thirty pounds: *Adv.,* June 28, 1968. It took six hours with an ice pack to bring Hall's temperature down. "There was a time when I wasn't sure I'd make it," Hall said from his hospital bed. (*Adv.,* May 19, 1968)

CHAPTER 73: HALL VS. BRIDGES

Image of unity: Bridges.

were enemies: It was common knowledge among ILWU staff members during the year and a half (June 1969 to December 1970) Hall was at ILWU headquarters in San Francisco. Such views were expressed to the writer by Barry Silverman, ILWU director of research, and Danny Beagle, editor of the *ILWU Dispatcher.* ILWU officials in Hawaii, of course, were well aware of the tense relationship.

lashed out: Yoshiko Hall, DeMello, John Hall. Yoshiko Hall said: "Jack felt, I think, that there was no need for him to be diplomatic and save the feelings of Harry, and he didn't expect Harry to be that way toward him. So, probably harsher words were said than were necessary."

"should have fired": Bridges talking to the writer on May 29, 1975, in his office in ILWU headquarters in San Francisco.

held Hawaii vote; skilled at caucusing: Beechert interview.

"trip at our expense": Hall to Bridges, July 6, 1964.

"Lay off the needle": Bridges to Hall, July 16, 1964.

"Don't be so sensitive": Hall to Bridges, July 21, 1964.

no longer had confidence: contained in a letter from Bridges to Hall, August 19, 1965. Kagel called Hall "one of the most capable [labor] representatives I've ever seen. . . . He had an excellent brain. What amazed me was how thoroughly he knew his stuff." (Kagel interview)

"where did you get the notion": Bridges to Hall, August 19, 1965.

"I am not subjective": Hall to Bridges, August 24, 1965.

a copy to Goldblatt: Hall gave instructions to that effect.

Bridges was over sixty-five: Bridges thought he was born July 28, 1901. But when he went back to his birthplace in Australia for a visit after forty years, parish records showed he was born in 1900. (Noriko Bridges)

believed him: Bridges.

"While I am certain": Hall to Bridges, November 13, 1968.

Was he going to run?: LEB, Honolulu, December 5–6, 1968, p. 16.

"I will surely not": ibid.

"We are a trade union": ibid., p. 15.

special jobs: ibid., p. 23.

"if I shut up": ibid.

"I don't think anybody": ibid., p. 19.

"Harry said a lot of things": ibid., p. 21.

"a personal feud": ibid., p. 23.

"I have admiration": ibid.

"no work for additional officers": IEB, Vancouver, B.C., December 16–17, 1968, p. 9.

"We feel that the union": ibid., p. 10.

"want to be recognized": ibid., p. 15.

"If ever there was a union": ibid., pp. 15–16.

"Somebody is trying": ibid., p. 11.

"It seems aimed": ibid.

he and Robertson would resign: ibid., p. 15.

"deeply disturbed": ibid., p. 17.

resolved the crisis: IEB, San Francisco, March 11–12, 1969, p. 27. Bridges said it wasn't a crisis; merely democratic give-and-take. He said when it came to letting members have their say, there was no union like the ILWU. "We have autonomy bordering on anarchy!" (ibid., p. 23)

Local 142 was withdrawing proposal: ibid., p. 28.

move to San Francisco: ibid., p. 34.

[footnote] "done my darndest": ibid., p. 30.

"work Hall has done": ibid., p. 35.

could get him back: ibid.

CHAPTER 74: "I'M ONLY IN BACK"

"controlled the money": Miyagi.

coordinated political activity: McElrath to Rev. Clemmon King, Waimanalo Beach, September 23, 1960.

operated with telephone: the writer heard him during a taped interview in his office on December 8, 1975.

power behind throne: Kealalio, Rutledge.

"a quarter of a million": Miyagi; David Thompson. "It was a fiasco," said Thompson.

decided to launch: 4th LCON, Honolulu, September 23–26, 1959, p. 54.

not the paper Hall wanted: McElrath. Koji Ariyoshi said Hall and McElrath did not back the *Record.*

"caves of Yenan": an allusion to Ariyoshi's service in the U.S. Army during World War II. He served in China, where he lived for a time in caves in Yenan like Mao Tse-tung and Chou En-lai.

"We are pushing": 4th LCON, p. 56.

"exciting idea": Watson to Hall, memorandum, August 7, 1957.

would not fight the project: Miyagi.

"truly independent": letter dated January 7, 1960, included in minutes of LEB, January 11–13, 1960.

"don't think it any secret": LEB, August 21–23, 1959, p. 19.

hoped to reach twenty thousand: ibid.

sent Fujisaki out: LEB, December 12–14, 1959, Report of President.

Thompson and Ariyoshi on Kauai: LEB, July 14–16, 1960, Report of President.

solicited public sales: letter dated January 7, 1960.

"doesn't have orientation": Goldblatt to Hall, September 6, 1960.

public's identification: letter dated January 11, 1960, in minutes of LEB, January 11–13, 1960.

"defeat for the union": LEB, July 14–16, 1960, Report of President.

fired Friel: Hall to Roger, October 12, 1960.

"If Sexton can do a job": ibid.

served as "antidote": ibid.

"real people's government": *S-B,* August 1, 1960.

Miyagi denounced blockade: *Adv.,* October 24, 1962.

Hall supported Shiroma: Miyagi, Shiroma. Shiroma said: "Miyagi thought it was a dark conspiracy."

"No problem, Maui": Miyagi.

"You're pretty good": Miyagi.

good relationship with McElrath: Goldblatt.

smart, capable; indecisive, lazy: Yoshiko Hall.

took abuse of employers: Babbitt, Rinehart, Maxwell, Miller.

"work up a hate": Goldblatt to Hall, February 4, 1957.

Bridges asked: Goldblatt to Hall, January 21, 1957.

"toning down": Hall to Goldblatt, January 24, 1957.

program was "pau": Hall to Goldblatt, January 5, 1959.

"No cloak and dagger": Hall to Goldblatt, December 4, 1958.

"fallen out of favor": *Adv.,* April 30, 1959.

improved his attitude: Hall to Robertson, January 19, 1959.

CHAPTER 75: THE "FAIR-HAIRED BOY"

talking to Tangen: The date stuck in his mind. It was the day President Kennedy was assassinated.

some said glib: Maxwell, Rutledge.

"need the sophistication": Hall to Goldblatt, January 16, 1964.

hard to explain: ibid.

"I promised those guys": Bridges.

"I made up my mind": *Adv.,* February 6, 1964.

meeting at Hall's home: Tangen.

"A lot of unions": *Adv.,* September 6, 1965.

"This little egg": Tangen to Lincoln Fairley, December 3, 1965.

"think it's unusual": *Adv.,* June 30, 1966.

filling in Salt Lake: *Adv.,* July 10, 1966.

badgered city council: Tangen to Herman G. P. Lemke, council chairman, June 22, 1966.

"architectural jungle": *Adv.,* September 25, 1965.

"While it appears": *S-B,* September 6, 1966.

"You may wonder": *Adv.,* September 25, 1965.

"just as much a paradise": ibid.

"found it necessary": 7th LCON, Honolulu, September 22–25, 1965, Policy Statement 9.

"papers played it up": Tangen to Fairley, December 3, 1965.

"fair-haired boy": ibid.

"added a new dimension": *Adv.,* October 12, 1966.

"The News found itself": *Maui News,* October 2, 1965.

[footnote] "didn't know a thing": Tangen to Fairley, December 3, 1965.

"We need a person": Goldblatt to Mumford, Amenia, N.Y., December 9, 1965.

former student: Tangen.

paid him $2000: Hall to Goldblatt, February 1, 1967.

"We're going to be": *Adv.,* June 30, 1966.

"good planning makes": Temko to Hall, December 19, 1966.

"What is this mad concept": *Adv.,* June 30, 1966.

"we love you": *Adv.,* February 2, 1968.

his "wider view": Hoshijo to Zalburg, November 27, 1978.

"no eviction" policy: ibid.

"union sat down": ibid.

Hall was moving force: ibid.; and Palk.

[footnote] program continued: Hoshijo to Zalburg, November 27, 1978.

inspected low-rent: Palk.

"project is catching": Hall to Goldblatt, August 3, 1966. Hall conceived the idea of the Housing Council. (Palk; and *Voice of the ILWU,* July 1974)

interested in Kukui Gardens: Hall to Marshall Kaplan of Kaplan Gans Associates, San Francisco, October 12, 1966.

sources of financing: ibid.

HCHA bid "far superior": Hall to Senators Hiram Fong and Daniel Inouye and to Representatives Spark Matsunaga and Patsy Mink, February 13, 1967.

"I would hope": ibid.

"What I would like": Bridges to Miyagi, October 20, 1966.

"letter is kind of long": Hall to Bridges, November 7, 1966.

"*Nobody* is going to make a buck": ibid.

did not accomplish as much: Tangen.

went back to mid-1950s: Hall to Sam Gilbert, Bell, Calif., September 27, 1956, and October 1, 1956.

impressed with Blackfield: Hall to Gilbert, September 27, 1956.

[footnote] HCHA's record: The 1975–1976 "Annual Report of the HCHA" listed a "ten-year profile of HCHA accomplishments."

cost $9000 to $10,000: Goldblatt to Hall, May 7, 1956.

at cost plus ten percent: Hall to Herbert Jackson, Kahului Development Co., Kahului, Maui, undated.

could not arrange financing: Hall to Gilbert, September 27, 1956 and October 1, 1956.

"never put it together": Hall impressed Blackfield. "He would have been a great man in private enterprise," said Blackfield.

"especially our children": Hall to ILWU members, July 5, 1966.

"doing everything possible": Hall to workers in concrete industy, November 19, 1966.

"New joints organized": Hall to Bob Kraschmer, Beverly Hills, Calif., May 24, 1965.

"opening like a rose": Hall to Mrs. John L. Burton, San Francisco, March 16, l966.

host to a million: Hall to ILWU members, July 5, 1966.

concentrated on Neighbor Islands: Hall to Robertson, June 1, 1966.

"Minus the 5,000 jobs": Damaso, Samson, and Miyagi to Robertson, December 14, 1966. Also 8th LCON, Honolulu, September 27–30, 1967, Local Officers Report, p. 3.

subscribe two dollars each: Hall to ILWU members, July 5, 1966.

"not charity": ibid.

CHAPTER 76: POLITICIANS AND OTHERS

"There are two things": *S-B,* February 1, 1965.

met at Wagon Wheel: Yagi, Cravalho.

Cravalho wanted to leave: *Adv.,* December 29, 1961; *S-B,* November 24, 1961.

"you put me in a spot": Yagi said the incident taught him a lesson. "You do what's good for the union and not what's good for the individual."

didn't use his muscle: McClung. Quinn said Hall was probably "the most powerful guy around. When you look at how much that union established itself in the power center. . . . My golly, you couldn't name an important post that they didn't have at least one representative [on]. . . ." (Quinn interview) As of November 24, 1975, as an example, a total of twenty-nine ILWU members were serving on fifty boards and commissions.

"exert raw power": McClung.

a small bite: Hall in a talk to the Pacific Club, Honolulu, April 27, 1964, p. 2.

"continuing millions": ibid.

"narrow and selfish": McClung to Hall, February 28, 1963.

"so long as we have taxes": Hall to McClung, February 28, 1963.

raised by $34.2 million: Advisory Committee on Taxation and Finance to Governor Burns, December 14, 1964.

called idea "vicious": *Adv.,* December 18, 1964.

"bosses a well-run outfit": *S-B,* December 19, 1964.

legislative investigation: 1st Legislature, General Session, 1961, House Resolution No. 45, House Draft 2, "relating to alleged violations concerning the expenditure of public funds by public officials of the County of Maui. . . ."

four hearings: Report of Select Committee of Representatives, No. 17, Honolulu, May 8, 1961, Re H.R. No. 45, H.D. 2, p. 1.

meeting at Iao Needle: ibid., p. 3.

"According to the ILWU": ibid.

"Chairman Tam states": ibid., p. 4.

Hall wanted contract deferred: ibid., p. 5.

"influence of the ILWU": ibid., p. 7.

"The hearings pointed out": ibid.

called Gill "brash": *S-B,* September 3, 1966. Gill's opinion of Hall was best expressed in a story which Gill confirmed as accurate. Gill was quoted as saying: "Hall, who is a very brilliant, gutsy guy, suffers from one great disappointment. He can't get elected to office so he satisfies himself by manipulating those who he can. If he can't manipulate an office holder, that person is likely to be on the dump list." (Gardiner B. Jones, *Adv.,* January 19, 1968) "not frighten those people": *S-B,* September 3, 1966.

One out of four: in answer to a questionnaire sent to 39,918 ILWU members and pensioners, 25.9 percent said they voted for Gill. (*Adv.,* June 1, 1967)

"We are disappointed": *Hawaii Hochi,* October 4, 1966. Burns defeated Randolph Crossley in the general election by only four thousand votes. Hall said the vote was close because the Democrats failed to put up a candidate for lieutenant governor who was acceptable to independent voters. "It's quite apparent that the ILWU vote was held together, as usual," said Hall. (*Adv.,* November 10, 1966)

"Neither political party": Hall's Labor Day speech, Hilo, September 3, 1962, p. 7.

"That's our job": Hall in talk to Industrial Relations Assn., April 27, 1964, p. 1.

"Who are Democrats?": *New York Times,* November 18, 1961.

"more interested in themselves": *Adv.,* December 17, 1961.

"never 'fixed' a ticket": Hall to Manipon, November 3, 1959.

McLaughlin appealed to Miyagi: Hall to Goldblatt, January 18, 1961.

lacked judicial temperament: *Adv.,* September 6, 1959.

"a lost soul": Hall to Goldblatt, January 18, 1961.

"better guy for us": ibid. Goldblatt agreed. He said perhaps the ILWU could help McLaughlin. "We do have several people [in Washington] to whom we might be able to pass the word along. . . ." (Goldblatt to Hall, January 20, 1961)

had not liked Bouslog: Yoshiko Hall.

"Remember when she said": Hall to Goldblatt, November 20, 1960.

[footnote] Pioneer's rocky land: Goldblatt, Moir.

CHAPTER 77: "LIVE AND LET LIVE"

"It was much easier": *Adv.,* January 14, 1969.

"I want his future": ibid.

"once I wanted socialism": ibid.

reaction embarrassed him: Hall to George Chaplin, *Advertiser* editor, June 18, 1969.

sound "more mellow": *Voice of the ILWU,* January 1968; also *Adv.,* January 17, 1968.

"Certainly in my lifetime": ibid.

"insignificant minor exceptions": from Hall's Labor Day speech, Honolulu, September 4, 1967, p. 5.

[footnote] Hall taught the guild: Roy Cummings to Zalburg (undated).

[footnote] called Murphy "ruthless": *Adv.,* July 10, 1965.

[footnote] "harder than nails": Hall to S. G. Bergman, Wilmington, Calif., August 30, 1965.

[footnote] "most strike-happy": *Adv.,* July 10, 1965.

[footnote] longest pineapple strike: Pineapple Companies of Hawaii, Release No. 7, April 9, 1968. The industry said 59,800 tons of fruit spoiled in the fields —that is, six percent of the crop, with a sales value of $7,350,000.

with most influence: McElrath, Steele, Maxwell.

"with a silver spoon": Kobayashi.

"I hope we can prevent": *S-B,* August 8, 1967.

"vastly better for us": *S-B,* February 1, 1965.

three to five hundred dollars: Kagel.

charged $2500: Kagel to Hall and to Allen C. Wilcox, Jr., Employers Council president, January 29, 1962.

"rip-snorting": Glazier to Hall, February 5, 1962.

"You should know": Hall to Kagel, February 6, 1962.

"A little weak": Bridges wrote his comment in pen on his copy of Hall's letter to Kagel.

CHAPTER 78: FEIG THE FEARLESS

Feig background: Feig.

earned high school diploma: *S-B,* September 28, 1964. The article said the ILWU conceded that Feig was a bright man, "but somewhat of a troublemaker."

own locks and seals: Feig.

"This guy usurped": LEB, May 7–8, 1964, p. 5.

"Throw this man out": *Adv.,* October 7, 1966.

King was assigned: LEB, May 7–8, 1964, p. 5.

"we will probably": ibid., p. 9.

"doesn't trust anybody": ibid., p. 10.

"I thought inasmuch": ibid., p. 5.

pickets marched: *S-B,* June 8, 1964.

voted to expel: LEB, September 8–9, 1964, p. 5.

circulated petitions: ibid.

378 to 33: *S-B,* September 22, 1964.

"I'm sure this guy": ibid.

by a slim margin: Damaso reporting, LEB, December 10–11, 1964, p. 5.

solicited donations: ibid., p. 5.

sold sausage: Feig.

filed suit: *Adv.,* February 20, 1965.

sent his application: LEB, February 11–12, 1965, p. 5.

it was premature: ibid. In December 1965, when Feig submitted his application, the court case was still pending. (LEB, December 9–10, 1965, p. 4)

settled out of court: *Adv.,* October 7, 1966.

fully paid-up member: LEB, December 2–3, 1966, p. 3.

letter reinstating him: Miyagi to Feig, October 4, 1966.

ran for business agent: ILWU report, November 20, 1967.

[footnote] election tally: ibid.

CHAPTER 79: LEAVING

"plough horse": 18th ICON, Los Angeles, April 7–12, 1969, p. 366.

"raring to go": Tangen to Wayne Newman, ILWU Local 9, Seattle, April 21, 1969.

"lots of ideas": *Adv.,* April 29, 1969.

"a real giant": 18th ICON, p. 416.

"My ears are burning": ibid., p. 420.

"trade unionist of century": ibid.

"by acclamation": Hall to Mrs. John A. Larson, Klamath Falls, Ore., April 17, 1969.

endorsement of every caucus: *Adv.,* April 29, 1969.

"My campaign fund": Hall to William Lawrence, Jamesville, Calif., March 10, 1969.

"I can guarantee": Tangen to Jack Puljan, Aberdeen, Wash., April 18, 1969.

"Even though we'll suffer": Tangen to Eugene R. Bailey, North Bend, Ore., April 18, 1969.

asked Chester: Hall to Chester and Piercy, May 5, 1969.

"led the ticket": *San Francisco Chronicle,* January 4, 1971.

Five names mentioned: Yagi.

"Compromise": Bridges. Robertson said: "The local people recognized [McElrath's] ability and wanted to cash in on it because they didn't have that [ability]. . . . They wanted a McElrath there who had the brains and the know-how, with all his shortcomings." (Robertson interview)

how they voted: Yagi, McElrath.

"proven ability": Hall's press release, September 3, 1969.

"awful big shoes": *Adv.,* September 7, 1969.

"Whenever they need me": *Adv.,* April 29, 1969.

"for major political problems": Hall to Fong, April 17, 1969.

[footnote] Hall's career: "A Short Biography of Jack W. Hall," ILWU files (undated).

"Tell your fat friend": Rutledge.

"Moving after fifteen years": Hall to Mrs. Larson, April 17, 1969.

more than a thousand guests: *S-B,* June 21, 1969.

"So many nice things": *Adv.,* June 7, 1969.

"it does not exaggerate": *Adv.,* June 6, 1969. The press was kind to Hall during his last years in Hawaii. He admitted the union enjoyed "favorable press coverage." (Hall to Joe Ibarra, ILWU Local 26, Los Angeles, April 22, 1969)

"I wondered what": Hall to Chaplin, June 24, 1969; published in *Adv.,* June 28.

"Mahalo to friend and foe": ibid.

Hall had Parkinson's disease: Butler.

CHAPTER 80: AILING

bought a house: Hall to Butler, November 26, 1969.

"We are finally set": Hall to Leo Lycurgus, November 4, 1969.

"recapturing of work": IEB, San Francisco, June 30–July 1, 1969, p. 13.

"basic longshore muscle": Hall memorandum, August 10, 1969.

out of town twenty-five days: Hall to Priscilla Shishido, December 26, 1969.

"It's not Puuwaawaa": ibid.

"not as honest": *S-B,* April 28, 1970.

"thing I really miss": Hall to Nick Lycurgus, November 4, 1969.

"Dear Sammy": Hall to Samson, August 19, 1969.

underwent multiphase: Hall to Butler, November 26, 1969.

"Except for being tired": ibid.

"on right track": Hall to Butler, July 10, 1970.

"We shall see": Hall to Priscilla Shishido, July 15, 1970.

undergo brain operation: Hall to Butler, July 10, 1970.

"Only the left side": ibid.

"not a death sentence": Hall to Priscilla Shishido, July 15, 1970.

by initials "P. D.": Hall to Priscilla Shishido, August 5, 1970.

"a little confining": ibid.

ordered to Mt. Zion: Hall to Butler, October 8, 1970.

"There is no trembling": ibid.

diabetes under control: ibid.

took part in "mobilization": Hall to Butler, November 26, 1969.

marched down Kalakaua: LEB, December 4–5, 1969, p. 8.

"a lot more comfortable": Hall to Butler, November 26, 1969.

[footnote] "not broad enough": David Thompson.

"jobs coming out": 7th LCON, Honolulu, September 22–25, 1965, p. 11.

Thompson asked Hall: Thompson to Hall, January 21, 1970.

"waste of time": memo attached to Hall to Thompson, January 26, 1970.

"Where is the ILWU?": Hall to Priscilla Shishido, Thompson, and McElrath, undated memorandum, enclosed in an envelope postmarked October 14, 1969.

ridiculed Hall's ideas: Sidney Roger. He was editor of the *ILWU Dispatcher.* Bridges fired him.

seemed "demonic": Barry Silverman. Silverman was ILWU director of research.

didn't disguise his contempt: Yoshiko Hall.

"Things are confused": Hall to Priscilla Shishido, March 24, 1970.

"wheeling and dealing": Hall to Priscilla Shishido, August 5, 1970.

welcome for "coast *haole*": 9th LCON, Honolulu, September 8–13, 1969, p. 14.

cities rotting: ibid., p. 15.

"criticism of Burns": ibid., p. 18.

"may have to crawl": ibid.

"will go down the tube": Hall to Bridges, April 6, 1970.

CHAPTER 81: DYING

"everyone wants to keep living": Hall to Joyce Lea Walker, West LaFayette, Ind., January 5, 1966.

it was a struggle: Yoshiko Hall, Butler, McElrath, Roger, Nagaue. Also Hall's letters to Priscilla Shishido and to Butler and Yoshiko Hall's letters to Priscilla Shishido.

"How are you?": Roger.

went anyway: Yoshiko Hall.

Oreste's bar: Roger.

favorite drink: Roger.

"Someone has to do it": Yoshiko Hall.

To get into a car: McElrath.

couldn't handle the spoon: McElrath.

picked him up: Butler.

"I'm dying, Kats": Nagaue.

lost the will: Priscilla Shishido to Mrs. John A. Larson, Feburary 26, 1971.

assigned Kelley: McElrath

"more helpful than Kelly Girl": Hall to Priscilla Shishido, October 13, 1970. Hall also told Butler that without Kelley he "would not have made it." (Hall to Butler, October 8, 1970)

fell out of bed: McElrath.

put on his socks: McElrath.

stuck in rest room: Kelley, Butler.

union meeting: Hall to Priscilla Shishido, October 13, 1970.

"making like a Moiseyev": ibid.

"brain scan, x-rays": ibid.

"like morning sickness": ibid.

pleaded with him: Yoshiko Hall.

"nothing I could do": Yoshiko Hall to Priscilla Shishido, December 17, 1970.

lucid reports: IEB, Vancouver, B.C., December 2–4, 1970, p. 23.

"had a political alliance": ibid.

"special breed of cats": ibid., p. 25.

"if it were not for": ibid., p. 27.

"isn't worth fiddling": ibid.

"in very bad shape": Yoshiko Hall to Priscilla Shishido, December 17, 1970.

on a dark day: Yoshiko Hall.

protested "about Jack": Yoshiko Hall to Priscilla Shishido, December 17, 1970.

"top guy at Kaiser": ibid.

might be away: Bridges to all locals, December 11, 1970.

came home at six: Yoshiko Hall to Priscilla Shishido, December 17, 1970.

to seventy pounds: Yoshiko Hall.

in hospital ten days: Frank Heydman, director, Medical Records, Kaiser Foundation Hospitals, San Francisco, to Zalburg, July 12, 1977.

a severe setback: Yoshiko Hall to Priscilla Shishido, December 17, 1970.

"a dream of a daughter": ibid.

pictures of him laughing: John Hall, Yoshiko Hall.

had not eaten breakfast: Yoshiko Hall.

"a particularly pretty one": Yoshiko Hall.

"For a guy who likes": Yoshiko Hall.

suffered a massive stroke: Yoshiko Hall. Mrs. Hall said her husband had had two "little strokes" previously but didn't tell anyone about it.

pale but conscious: Arena.

Arena called ambulance: Arena.

briefed the doctor: Yoshiko Hall.

"Don't let them": Yoshiko Hall.

knew her husband was dead: Yoshiko Hall.

died late at night: Yoshiko Hall. Hall's death certificate (State of California, Department of Public Health, Certificate of Death No. 3801) says that Hall died at 1:50 PM on January 2, 1971. The time is incorrect. It should be 1:50 AM, according to Mrs. Hall.

The causes of death were listed as follows: immediate cause, cerebral thrombosis; due to cerebral vascular insufficiency, due to cerebral arteriosclerosis, which, according to the death certificate, Hall had suffered from for at least five years. Other significant conditions contributing to his death, according to the death certificate, were diabetes mellitus and gout.

screamed at him: Yoshiko Hall.

CHAPTER 82: MOURNING

Comments by Kaneda, Copess, Goldblatt, Rutledge, Grunsky, and Trevedi are part of a Hall obituary folder in the ILWU Anne Rand Research Library in San Francisco. Bridges' statement about Hall appeared in the *San Francisco Examiner,* January 4, 1971. *The Nation*'s editorial was published in the February 15, 1971, issue.

41,000 government workers: from *The Public Employee,* an HGEA publication, January 13, 1971.

closed their ports: *ILWU Dispatcher,* January 22, 1971.

"Jack had brains": "Stop-Work Tribute to Jack Hall," an ILWU leaflet, January 5, 1971.

A thousand people: *Adv.,* January 8, 1971.

Michele had written: Bridges.

McElrath phoned: Roger.

felt it was insulting: Bridges.

Eric Hall Fund: "Stop-Work" leaflet.

wrote obituary: Roger.

"didn't invent it": Roger.

"Thompson wrote it": Roger. Bridges' criticism of the obituary on Hall aroused considerable resentment. Priscilla Shishido said Roger did a good job "in spite of harassment and vendetta. Can you imagine!" (Priscilla Shishido to Michele Hall Burton, February 11, 1971)

Mrs. Shishido said Hall's severance pay from Local 142 amounted to $14,000. Mrs. Hall got a $150-a-month pension from the ILWU; a few years later it was raised by $30 a month.

one of those splendid days: *Voice of the ILWU,* February 1971.

"Sailor Remembered": the ILWU provided a copy.

in honor of Altgeld: Altgeld pardoned three defendants in the Chicago Haymarket Massacre case (1886) after they had served seven years and that ended Altgeld's political career.

started to read: *Voice of the ILWU,* February 1971.

cast the ashes: John Hall.

two red carnation leis: *Voice of the ILWU,* February 1971.

poured into the ocean: ibid.

broke the tension: Priscilla Shishido to Mrs. Burton, February 8, 1971.

INDEX

⅄ Production Notes

This book was designed by Roger Eggers and typeset on the Unified Composing System by the design and production staff of The University Press of Hawaii.

The text and display typeface is Compugraphic Times Roman.

Offset presswork and binding were done by Halliday Lithograph. Text paper is Glatfelter P & S Offset Vellum, basis 55.